D0871130

TCHAIKOVSKY

TCHAIKOVSKY

The Quest for the Inner Man

———•———

ALEXANDER POZNANSKY

SCHIRMER BOOKS
Simon & Schuster Macmillan
New York

Prentice Hall International
London   Mexico City   New Delhi   Singapore   Sydney   Toronto

Schirmer Books
Simon & Schuster Macmillan
866 Third Avenue, New York, N.Y. 10022

Library of Congress Catalog Card Number: 91-10095

PRINTED IN THE UNITED STATES OF AMERICA

printing number
2   3   4   5   6   7   8   9   10

Library of Congress Cataloging-in-Publication Data

Poznansky, Alexander.
     Tchaikovsky : the quest for the inner man / Alexander Poznansky.
        p.   cm.
     Includes index.
     ISBN 0-02-871885-2 (hc), 0-02-871886-0 (pb)
        1. Tchaikovsky, Peter Ilich, 1840–1893.   2. Composers—Soviet
Union—Biography.   I. Title.
ML410.C4P85   1991
780'.92—dc20
[B]   91-10095
                                                                              CIP
                                                                              MN

The paper used in this publication meets the minimum requirements of American National Standard for Information Sciences—Permanence of Paper for Printed Library Materials. ANSI Z39.48-1984. ∞"

Contents

Contents

Illustrations

These illustrations follow page 424

Note to the Paperback Edition

Working on this book during the last decade, I could hardly imagine that the days of the Soviet Union were numbered and that glasnost would actually bring more openness to Russia. But what I could not foresee at all was that one day I would find myself in Tchaikovsky's very house and would be able to fulfill my dream of holding in my own hands the original documents.

It was on 7 May 1992, precisely on the 152nd anniversary of the composer's birth, that I had the chance to work in Tchaikovsky's archive at Klin. There I was given access to the letters and diaries of the composer and his brother Modest and to various memoirs. It was the most gratifying experience of my life as a scholar. My years of research finally came fully to fruition: the conclusions in this book that were based on intuitive reconstruction of gaps in Tchaikovsky's intimate life were fully confirmed by inspecting materials that had been suppressed, distorted, and bowdlerized by Tchaikovsky's relatives and by Soviet censors, or that still remained unpublished. Even my textual conjectures in a number of cases amazed me by their closeness to the originals. I found definitive answers to prove my theories regarding Tchaikovsky's first manifestations of homosexuality at the School of Jurisprudence, his devastating marriage to Antonina Milyukova, his lifestyle and his accidental death from cholera—emphatically not by suicide.

I also discovered a lot of material not yet published that covers many other aspects of the composer's life, and realized that much work is still needed to document fully the true Tchaikovsky, not only for Western readers but also for the Russian people who have been kept ignorant of Tchaikovsky's private life.

The study of Tchaikovsky's private life has begun in earnest. I am sure that the near future will bring us new, valuable facts concerning Tchaikovsky, his environment and creativity. Meanwhile, I trust that my portrayal of "the inner man" as a spiritually healthy, even though flawed and idiosyncratic individual—a far cry from stereotyping him as mad Russian or tormented homosexual—is accepted by the reader as a decisive and convincing step in the right direction.

It is a great pleasure for me to express my gratitude for the warm welcome I received at the Tchaikovsky House-Museum at Klin, and I especially appreciate the invaluable help given me during my stay there by Galina Belonovich and Polina Vaidman.

Alexander Poznansky

Preface

This is not a study of Tchaikovsky's music. This is a study of the man who wrote the music. It could be called the story of a soul finding itself. The quest, naturally conditioned by the time and the culture in which Pyotr Ilyich Tchaikovsky lived, resulted in a life emotionally rich and creatively triumphant.

The very idea of an inner life so intimately linked to the dynamics of creativity resists scholarly definition. Inner life is something vaster than pure biography or pure psychology. Psychoanalysis or behavioral psychology may provide valuable insights when applied to a creative mind, but in the end, they inevitably simplify an unencompassable subject matter. The experience of passionate engagement, intellectual crisis, and intuitive illumination can elude any single conceptual framework, making what remains serve the interests of a clinician rather than those of a student of culture.

This is why, if one aims at a comprehensive view of the creative genius, an accurate description, based on solid evidence, of his relationship to the world and to himself may be preferable to an interplay of restrictive definitions or to fashionable modes of interpretation. The present book is therefore not another effort in psychohistory; although many constructive elements of the modern psychological inquiry are acknowledged and used in it, it does not cleave to a fixed orthodoxy. Rather, it seeks to depict a great man's interaction with his environment, in all the complexity of its affectional, sensuous, and sexual aspects. The abundant and varied documentation that survives on Tchaikovsky's life reveals in him a fascinating mixture of openness and reticence, of boldness and delicacy, of sensuality and self-discipline, that makes his "inner man" so rich a subject for close examination.

It is obvious that the mystery of art cannot be explicated merely by the study of the artist's environment. Fits of ecstasy or lonely creative labors do not yield to an explanation and, at best, allow only an attempt at imaginative reconstruction. Art seldom directly relates to fact; the discussion of art on its own merits is a perfectly legitimate enterprise, yet the impulse to balance one's life and one's art is commoner and perhaps nobler. What truly lives among us now are, of course, Tchaikovsky's perdurable works of music: the great operas, the symphonies, the piano and violin concertos, the ballets, the chamber music, the songs, and many other works that will continually be rediscovered and performed. The existing commentary on this legacy is musicologically sound and abundant.

Yet, however great Tchaikovsky's music, the life he led knew its own heights of sublimity and depths of despair. It was replete with faults and confusions, but at the same time, it offers frequent examples of virtuous and even heroic stands and constitutes a generous achievement worth examining for its own sake. While it is true that no amount of detailed knowledge about the composer's vicissitudes at various stages of his career, about his public engagements or his private anguish, about his domestic routine, about his friendships and enmities, will ever enable us to solve the riddle of the spell his music casts upon us, still we may learn from all this how to experience an even richer enjoyment of his work through sympathy or a sort of complicity, how to conjure up his very presence across the gap of a hundred years, and even how to penetrate on occasion the deeper recesses of his mind.

Leon Edel rightly asserts that "the passional life of a biographical subject is a distinct part of his or her total being."[1] In accord with that principle, the extensive discussion in this book of Tchaikovsky's private life has been motivated not by idle curiosity or a thirst for the sensational, but by a desire to discover through his mundane, affectional, and erotic experiences fresh ways toward an appreciation of the lasting oeuvre of a man who can be truly called a genius of emotion. Although Tchaikovsky himself once predicted, with sadness and even foreboding, that someday people "will try to penetrate the intimate world of my feelings and thoughts, everything that all my life I have so carefully hidden from the touch of the crowd,"[2] it is not my intention to tarnish the memory of my subject, but to treat him with both objectivity and compassion. Elsewhere Tchaikovsky wrote, "In my compositions I appear as God created me and as I have been made by education, circumstance, and the character of the age and the country in which I live and work. I have never once betrayed myself. As for whether I am good or bad, let others judge."[3] This book is devoted to the man as God created him, to his education, to his circumstances, to the character of the age and country in which he lived and worked and loved. It is with an eye to all this that I have designed this book not as a psychohistory but rather as a study in historical psychology, a discipline that seeks to distinguish between universal and culturally influenced components of human behavior.

Tchaikovsky's life and personality are in many ways emblematic of his times and his society. Among other things, his was a society permeated by a cult of emotion in which Romanticism found so fertile a soil that it continues, often imperceptibly, to affect the lives of ordinary Russians to the present day. The story of Tchaikovsky's life and career offers a means to explore a broad spectrum of patterns and attitudes in pre-Revolutionary Russia, including such aspects as the psychological workings of the class system, the politics of art, the educational system, the complex of sexual mores, and the sexual underground. In learning about the life of one individual, we begin also to learn something about the cultural and social history of the times in which he lived.

The lives of great men inevitably become encrusted with a mythology that they themselves, their relatives and friends, their contemporaries, or their posterity produces, inadvertently or intentionally. This fact is aggravated by the present paradoxical status of the biographical genre. On the one hand, its scholarly aspect has by now reached a high level. An enormous number of documented facts have been brought to light, in some cases covering virtually every day of the subject's waking life, and the methods of interpreting this material have become increasingly refined. On the other hand, the increased popular interest in biographical works may seem to condone an urge toward mythmaking and sensationalism, featuring a revelation of "secrets" where none really existed. As a consequence, even though such stories have been repeatedly repudiated by specialists, we continue to hear of Salieri having poisoned Mozart out of envy or of Nikolay Gogol having been buried alive.

This dilemma is most evident in cases of truly complex figures, those who clearly had psychological dimensions that are by no means obvious, and it is to that category that Pyotr Tchaikovsky belongs. Here both biographical elements, the scholarly and the anecdotal, may enter into extraordinary correlation. But it also happens that mythmakers and sensationalists may triumph over fact finders and that both, in their zeal to destroy one myth, may unwittingly give rise to yet another.

Thus, the conscientious biographer must penetrate a double set of obstacles: idiosyncrasies created by the subject's cultural environment, and our own projected fashions and habits of thought. Naturally, it is not possible to produce history or biography entirely devoid of myth, which constitutes a component of any creative, even scientific, imagination.

All these perplexities are reflected in the record and the present state of Tchaikovsky studies. Not only his music but also his personality has suffered ideological distortions—crudely created in the Soviet Union and more subtly in the West—which, in the final analysis, may still be keeping us from a full appreciation of his life and achievement. In no small part, this situation has arisen from ignorance of much in the composer's private life and from reluctance to face and illuminate the issues.

In the Soviet Union there existed for many decades a virtual ban on any inquiry into such matters as the sexual habits of individuals elevated to the status of national celebrities. Even in the present era of *glasnost* Soviet publications continue to insist upon the moral inadmissibility of any adverse disclosure regarding a biographical subject's intimate life. Consequently, Soviet popular and scholarly books represent Tchaikovsky as nothing less than a model member of the "progressive artistic intelligentsia"—a trivial concept that strips him of his true identity. Hardly any other figure in the history of Russian culture has been subjected by government-controlled scholarship to such a degree of biographical falsification.

With such restrictions upon the printed word in the Soviet Union, it is not surprising that much biographical information about famous people circulates by word of mouth. But the very nature of such information, inevitably altered by each of the innumerable carriers of rumor, becomes, through mere gossip, popular myth. This is the case with Tchaikovsky's alleged suicide, a baseless legend that has recently found supporters in the West and has even found its way into such monumental works as *The New Grove Dictionary of Music*.[4] There exist no less than a dozen such versions of what Nicolas Slonimsky has called "Gothic horror tales," most of them mutually exclusive.[5]

Despite its abundance, the primary evidence concerning Tchaikovsky's life presents difficulties. In the first place, the original documents have undergone tampering and censorship over the decades, starting even at the hands of Tchaikovsky's relatives. Partly documentary and partly memoiristic, the three-volume *Life of Pyotr Ilyich Tchaikovsky* composed at the turn of the century by his brother Modest (available in English only in an abridged edition by Rosa Newmarch, published in 1906) remains one of our major sources of information and still exercises a strong influence. Yet, the presentation of the composer's personality by this first biographer, though done with considerable literary skill, is nonetheless singularly biased. Modest spared no effort to display his brother in a light that would best appeal to his audience. Any potential source of embarrassment is avoided, one result of which is that very little is revealed of Tchaikovsky's personal life, to the point where at times his behavior—for instance, during the period of his short-lived marriage—seems merely unmotivated and enigmatic. For this reason, Modest's narrative must always be approached with a measure of caution, as even his direct quotations from his brother's letters are often adulterated.

Most of the existing memoirs about Tchaikovsky were written following the appearance of Modest's work and were thus powerfully influenced by it. Their authors wrote, as a rule, late in their lives, supporting their failing memories with material from Modest: the same stories, with the same authorial intonation, migrate from one memoirist to another. Some of the rarer and virtually unknown narratives preceding Modest's or otherwise independent of him are utilized for the first time in this book.

The safest way to delineate the true Tchaikovsky is to steep oneself in his own words and writings, primarily his letters and diaries, and in the testimony of reliable witnesses—of whom, contrary to widespread opinion, there are not all that many. The emphasis must be on the truly documentary texts, eloquent and fascinating in themselves, though on the whole little explored by scholars. Many sources, unfortunately, are not easily available or remain confined in the Tchaikovsky archives at Klin under very strict supervision, excluding both Soviet and foreign researchers. Necessarily, one must rely on the published texts, their insufficiencies and varying degrees of accessibility notwithstanding.

Soviet censorship of biographical material on Tchaikovsky has been both rigorous and erratic, depending on the period and the editors involved. We are fortunate that their inconsistency allows occasional reconstruction of important lacunae by means of comparative textual analysis. The earliest Soviet publication, a 1923 edition of Tchaikovsky's surviving diaries (inadequately translated into English by Wladimir Lakond in 1945), went virtually uncensored.[6] Close scrutiny of the original Russian text necessitates penetrating the defenses of the equivocal, elusive, and at times coded language to reveal the true sense and workings of the composer's psyche.

Published in the Soviet Union in three volumes between 1934 and 1936 and translated into English only partially in a variety of publications, Tchaikovsky's correspondence with Nadezhda von Meck, his benefactress, provides a rich and nuanced, if occasionally contrived, self-portrait. Much of his personal life is clearly, if implicitly, reflected in their exchange and highlighted by the editorial commentary of Vladimir Zhdanov and Nikolay Zhegin, which is filled with quotations from unpublished material.

The first volume of the projected two-volume edition of Tchaikovsky's *Letters to Relatives* remains one of the most valuable Soviet publications. Embracing the composer's correspondence with his family from 1850 to 1879, the volume appeared in 1940, toward the end of a surprisingly relaxed period of Soviet censorship. The backlash, however, was swift. The edition was suppressed almost immediately; its editor, Vladimir Zhdanov, for a time demoted; and the planned second volume, aborted.[7] Now a bibliographical rarity, the first volume of this collection is mined extensively in the present study. The volume reveals Tchaikovsky's intimate preferences and preoccupations, which he was accustomed to confess frankly to his brothers. For whatever reasons, the censorship was not effective enough to obscure the meaning of many such confessions, so that, properly handled, these texts yield a wealth of information concerning all facets of Tchaikovsky's life.

The same is also true, though to a lesser extent, of the first volume of Tchaikovsky's candid correspondence with his friend and publisher Pyotr Jurgenson, which appeared in 1938, two years before *Letters to Relatives*, and also went relatively unabridged. However, a subsequent volume of the correspondence with Jurgenson, along with a selection entitled *Letters to His Family*, both published in the mid-1950s, underwent thorough manipulation by Zhdanov.[8] (Ironically enough, the mutilated *Letters to His Family* has found its way into an English translation by Galina von Meck, which appeared in 1981.)[9]

In 1959 all of Tchaikovsky's known letters began to be compiled and published in the Soviet Union as part of his *Complete Works*. Completed in 1981, this collection comprises fifteen volumes and over five thousand letters. The censorship is severe and at times even absurd, but the cuts can frequently be restored on the basis of earlier publications. In any event, we now possess an uninterrupted context within which the personal and emotional life of the composer may be discussed.

While the advantage of organizing this book around the words of Tchaikovsky himself is clear, this alone is insufficient to the ultimate purpose of illuminating the dynamics of his psyche. The man cannot be fully comprehended by merely compiling a selection of his writings or a documented chronicle of his life. (The production of this last constitutes, incidentally, one enduring and uncontroversial achievement of Soviet Tchaikovsky scholarship.)[10] The composer's acute and unrelenting self-consciousness, particularly in regard to his modes of literary (as opposed to musical) expression, prompted him to write in his diary on 27 June 1888:

> It seems to me that letters are never entirely sincere. I judge at least by my own example. To whomever and for whatever purpose I write, I am always concerned with what impression my letter may make, and not on the recipient only, but on any chance reader as well. Consequently, I pose. Sometimes *I try to make* the tone of the letter simple and sincere, that is, I try to make it seem so. But apart from letters written in moments of *passion,* I am never myself in a letter. But then this last sort of letter is always a source of repentance and regret, sometimes quite agonizingly so.[11]

This self-observation is accurate: Tchaikovsky was on the whole a master of introspection. When his letters (often several on a single day to various correspondents) and his diaries are placed side by side, it is not difficult to see the extent to which the figure emerging from the diary entries differs from that depicted in his letters. This is perhaps nowhere more relevant than in regard to his correspondence with Mrs. von Meck and the extraordinarily delicate relationship that developed between them.

For the biographer, then, those passages written by Tchaikovsky "in moments of passion," to use his own phrase, become all the more precious. There are more than a few of these passages, found most notably in his letters to his brothers. Yet, the confession from his diary that I have just quoted strongly suggests that the need for self-censorship was part of the very fiber of Tchaikovsky's psychological makeup. In addition, it should be remembered that Tchaikovsky was, in many respects, a child of his time. Despite a sizable measure of free thought and feeling in matters of personal and social relations, his sensibilities and self-expression inevitably reflected the accepted societal conventions and prejudices of the latter half of the nineteenth century in Russia and the rest of Europe. As we listen to Tchaikovsky's own voice, we must be alert to its tone and timbre. In this way, we may examine the depths and secrets of his inner life within the context of his own views and motives as well as from the perspective of contemporary psychology. Of course, at times this examination will hinge on conjecture and hypothesis, as must any historical reconstruction. Supposition must serve when concrete evidence is lacking, provided it plausibly explains the available facts, interpreting them in accordance with the logic of circumstances and of the characters of those involved. It is hoped, above all, that these ideas may in the future be confirmed or refuted when all documents that relate to Tchaikovsky become available in unexpurgated texts.

The recent controversy over Tchaikovsky's death has revealed how little, in fact, we know of his inner life, despite the considerable literature about him, and the extent to which his personality, on the surface so easy and outgoing, remains enigmatic. Yet, only a few out of the multitude of books published on Tchaikovsky in the West call for special comment, the earliest (1936) being Nina Berberova's novelization of his life, executed with sympathy and tact, but more of literary than scholarly value.[12] Herbert Weinstock's book (1943) is a solid study, but outdated in regard to factual evidence, and it suffers from a strong psychoanalytical bias.[13] Vladimir Volkoff's impressionistic portrayal (1975) is again the work of a writer, not a scholar, and though it demolishes some of the mythology surrounding Tchaikovsky, it replaces it with the author's own favorite myths.[14] Any other book-length biographical efforts are thus far overshadowed by David Brown's four-volume treatment (1978–).[15] This is an ambitious and in many respects admirable project, but it centers on the creative development of the composer and on an analysis of his music, offering little insight into his personality and private life. Regrettably, Brown succumbed to the extraordinary and undemonstrable view of Tchaikovsky's death as a suicide forced upon him by a conspiracy of his former classmates.[16] None of these authors fully utilizes the available documentary evidence, and none of them, with the exception of Berberova, has proved to have a real grasp of the social and cultural realities of nineteenth-century Russia.

It has taken almost ten years to complete this book, and without the help of several individuals, it could not have been done. My particular gratitude must go to Vasily Rudich, who offered invaluable constructive criticisms and comments along with his unstinting and generous assistance at every stage of the work-in-progress; to Ralph Burr, Jr., who provided the poetry translations and whose editorial skills, perceptive suggestions, and sheer hard work have helped to make the book readable in English; and to Lowry Nelson, Jr., whose thoughts, criticisms, and patient encouragement have proved of immeasurable value. I am extremely grateful to Steven Oyler for a fine performance of Tchaikovsky's op. 21 and for his expertise in musicological matters. Also I want to express my thanks to Alex Hvatsky, Vincent Giroud, and Edith Lounès for their interest and enthusiastic support, and to Tchaikovsky's grandniece Ksenya Davydova for her helpful information. Thanks are also due my tireless editor, Robert Axelrod.

Most of all, however, I owe the completion of this book to my wife, Elena, whose love and patience never ceased to provide me with confidence and inspiration.

To work with the friendly and unfailingly helpful staff of the Yale University Library has been a particular joy. I am especially grateful to Maureen Malone Jones of Yale's Interlibrary Loan Department, who did everything possible to find much-needed books anywhere in the world. In addition, this study would have been impossible without access to the collections of the Saltykov-Shchedrin Public Library in Leningrad, the Helsinki University Library, and various archives in the Soviet Union.

Special thanks go to my friends and acquaintances in the Soviet Union who provided photographs from their own collections. Without their contribution this book would be incomplete.

Dates in the book are given according to the Julian calendar, which remained in effect in Russia until 1918 and which in the nineteenth century lagged twelve days behind the Western Gregorian calendar; for references to Tchaikovsky or others while abroad, both the Old and New Styles are given.

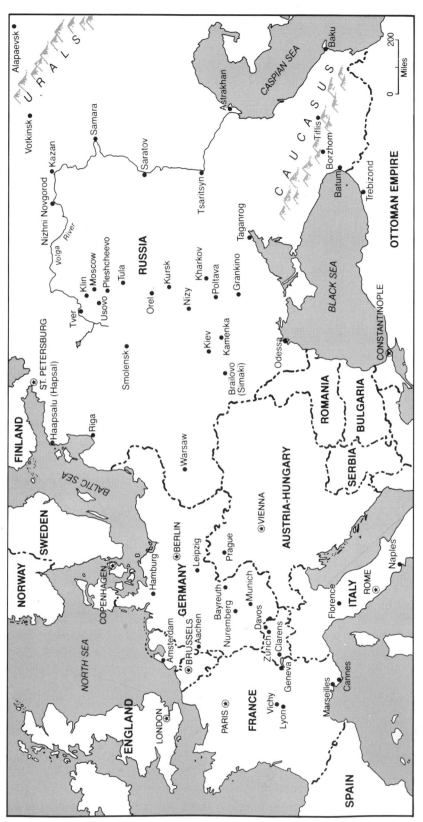

Russia and Europe During Tchaikovsky's Lifetime

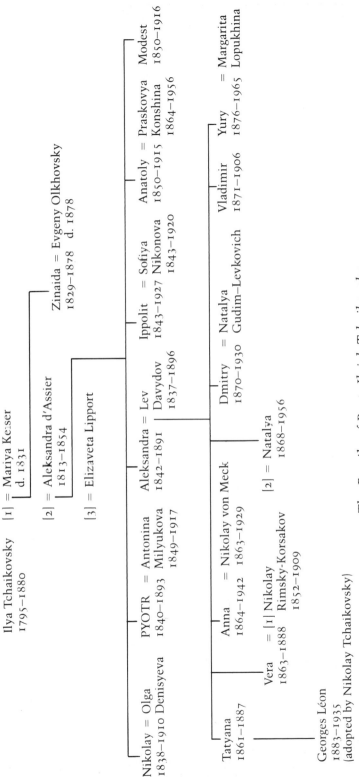

The Family of Pyotr Ilyich Tchaikovsky

TCHAIKOVSKY

Part One

PREPARATION
1840-1865

CHAPTER ONE

Early Anguish

Ilya Petrovich Tchaikovsky, the composer's father and by the late 1830s manager of the ironworks at Votkinsk in the Ural Mountains, was a man of unremarkable intellect. Yet, it is clear that the emotional side of Ilya Tchaikovsky's character and, in particular, what might frankly be called his sentimentality were developed in him to an exceptional degree. Modest Tchaikovsky describes his father thus: "Kindness, or rather an abundance of love, was one of the main traits of his character. In youth, in maturity, and in old age he invariably believed in people and loved them. Neither the hard knocks of life nor bitter disappointments nor gray hair could ever quell his ability to see in every person he met an embodiment of all virtue and merit."[1]

The few published extracts from Ilya Tchaikovsky's letters fully support this description, even suggesting that this "abundance of love" might become at times, especially with members of his family, a surfeit. Though colored by rhetorical conventions of the period, the overflow of amorous language in his letters to his second wife, Aleksandra, the composer's mother, was exceptional and often bordered on the hysterical. "What is the meaning of [your] tears?" Ilya, then thirty-eight, wrote in one letter to his twenty-year-old bride before their marriage in 1833. "Please tell me, tell me candidly. I did not think to see them, but since I saw them, must I not assume that it was I who caused them? My dearest, my adored one! . . . From the moment when you uttered the fateful word *yes*, when the fire ran through my veins, when I counted myself on the peak of heavenly happiness, when everything

3

else turned dim before my eyes and I saw only you, I have suffered increasingly from the thought that you may regret that quick response, that most blessed word said to me. . . . I could not close my eyes for three nights in a row."[2] Ten years later his letters to her had undergone no change: "My angel, parting with you yesterday I was restrained from open crying only by the fear of looking fainthearted in the eyes of those who were present: still, huge tears began to flow from my eyes unwillingly, and I had to shut them."[3]

Understandable in his adoration of his infant second son, Pyotr, born 25 April 1840, these effusions would seem excessive when, years later, the senior Tchaikovsky might close a letter to his then twenty-five-year-old son by kissing "your dear eyes and all of you from your feet to your head."[4] To such gushing may be traced the acutely emotional tone of young Pyotr's letters to his parents. And it is no surprise to learn from Modest that the theater-loving Ilya was, when in his eighties, "almost every time moved to tears by a performance, even when the play offered nothing particularly touching."[5]

There is reason to believe that there may have been a distinctly erotic aspect to the senior Tchaikovsky's overflowing affection. From the available evidence he appears to have been quite a ladies' man, though never straying beyond the bounds of propriety or law. In her memoirs, Fanny Dürbach, the Tchaikovsky children's governess, recalls that on her initial arrival at the home of her new employers "Mr. Tchaikovsky came up to me and, without a word, embraced me and kissed me like a daughter,"[6] she being, of course, a young woman whom he had never before met. He seemed able to create about him an erotic aura indefinable and innocent and yet attractive to women, a quality passed on to his son. Thrice married, the third time at age seventy, and the father of seven children, Ilya Tchaikovsky also felt a nearly fanatical attachment to family life. In letters from the period of his own marriage, Tchaikovsky insisted that his father's ardent wish to see him married was one of the major reasons he made that fateful decision. Certainly the father's reactions to the matrimonial plans of his son tended to be ecstatic. "Désirée, that is, the desired, must undoubtedly be beautiful in all respects," Ilya Tchaikovsky wrote in 1868 concerning the news of his son's engagement, later broken, to Désirée Artôt, "because my son Pyotr has fallen in love with her, and my son Pyotr is a man of taste, a man of intelligence, a man of talent, and judging by his character would have to choose for himself a wife with the same qualities."[7] Nine years later, in response to Tchaikovsky's announcement of his impending marriage to Antonina Milyukova, the father exulted anew: "My darling, dear, and most excellent son Pyotr!

Tolya [Anatoly, the composer's younger brother] has given me your letter, in which you ask my blessing on your marriage. It made me so
very happy and delighted that I crossed myself and even jumped for joy.
Praise God! May the Lord bless you!!!"[8]

It is reasonable to assume that his father's character and his views
on the proper relations between the sexes exerted a strong influence
on Tchaikovsky's psychological development, even though this influence was, in effect, ambiguous. On the one hand, Ilya Tchaikovsky's
emotional behavior stimulated his son's already heightened excitability and contributed to the emergence of what might be called a "familial erotic" sensibility in the latter. On the other hand, his father's
reputation as a lover of women may also have provoked in the boy,
possibly at a subconscious level, a reverse reaction—if only by virtue
of a child's rebellion against paternal authority and example. It may
also have induced in Pyotr some aversion for women, engendering a
conflict between duty and desire that would long torment him, a conflict resolved only in the experience of his tragicomic marriage.

In telling of the relatives on his mother's side, Modest lets drop the
curious observation that his maternal grandfather, Andrey d'Assier, a
French émigré, suffered from nervous attacks very similar to epilepsy,
which were inherited by his eldest son, Mikhail. Further on, in the
spirit of the positivistic thought of the time, Modest notes that "Pyotr
Ilyich's only legacy from his ancestors was probably his extraordinary
nervousness, which in his youth could result in fits and in later years
was expressed in frequent hysterics, and which, most likely, he inherited from grandfather Assier."[9] Neither Tchaikovsky's father nor his
mother, however, appears to have been notably neurotic. Regarding the
character of his mother, her husband's second wife and eighteen years
his junior, Modest writes, "In contrast to her husband, Aleksandra Andreevna, in family life, seldom expressed any warm feelings and was
sparing in her show of affection. She was very kind, but her kindness,
in comparison with her husband's constant affability toward all and
sundry, was austere, and was displayed more in actions than in
words."[10] Set against his father's emotional expansiveness, his mother's reserve can only have further sharpened young Pyotr's acute sensibility. But for all her undemonstrativeness, Aleksandra clearly doted
on her second child. Another son, Nikolay, had been born two years
before, but it was Pyotr, or Petya, who would be her "treasure," the
"gold of the family."[11] As for Pyotr, he worshiped the very ground his
mother walked on.

While the family was living in Votkinsk, in the Ural Mountains,
Pyotr would often spend part of each summer alone with his mother.

When he was five, the two visited the nearby Sergiev Spa, of which Modest writes that "later the stay at the spa itself, where he did not share the affection and attention of his idolized mother with anyone else . . . left him with the brightest and most gratifying memory of his childhood."[12] Elsewhere Modest tells of the return in late 1846 of their parents from St. Petersburg, where they had traveled to fetch from school Zinaida, Ilya Tchaikovsky's daughter from his first marriage. Pyotr "remembered also the heavenly bliss he felt as he pressed himself against his mother's breast after the three or four months of separation" and, Modest adds, "for a very, very long time, even as an adult, he could not speak about his mother without tears, to the point where those around him would avoid bringing her up in conversation."[13] Tchaikovsky himself much later remarked of his mother that "she was a magnificent, intelligent woman who loved her children passionately."[14]

We know about young Pyotr's exceptional susceptibility and sensitivity not only from Modest, who, ten years younger than his famous brother, could have obtained this information only at second hand, but also from a direct and keen observer. When the French governess Fanny Dürbach arrived in the Tchaikovsky household in November 1844, the family's "common pet," then four and a half, became immediately her own favorite as well. According to Modest, Fanny "for fifty years kept as sacred relics even the briefest of his notes, any scrap of paper scribbled on by his childish hand."[15] Fanny found evidence of the child's exceptional charm "in nothing in particular and in absolutely everything that he did. In class no one could have been more diligent and quick, at recreation time no one invented more amusing games; when we read for entertainment no one listened more attentively, and at twilight on the eve of a holiday, when I would gather my charges about me and have them each by turns tell some story, no one was more charmingly imaginative. . . . His sensitivity was extreme, and so one had to treat him very carefully. Any trifle could hurt or offend him. He was a child 'of glass.'"[16]

Citing examples of this extraordinary sensitivity, the governess touches on the earliest of the boy's friendships known to us. Venedikt Alekseev, the son of a factory worker, was Pyotr's own age; he had lost his mother and the Tchaikovskys had taken him in to be tutored along with their own children. Fanny recalls that after one particular prank in which Venedikt had been especially mischievous, for which reason she had intended to punish him more severely, Pyotr interceded, insisting that all the children—himself, though innocent, included—be punished alike.[17]

The child's sensitivity, constantly sprouting into sentimentality, was directed toward everything around him. One is especially struck by its intensity in reading his childish verses, written mainly in French, which are quite awkward but manage nonetheless to create an impression of odd sincerity. "In them we hear of orphans, dead children, maternal love, and poor animals," Modest comments, and among the titles of the seven-year-old's poetic output we find the likes of "Death of the Infant Paul" and "A Mother and Her Child Whom She Loves."[18] In connection with this same heightened sensitivity, Modest elsewhere observes: "A love for unfortunates also manifested itself in his unusual sympathy for Louis XVII. According to Fanny, he never tired of asking for all the details of the death suffered by the innocent martyr. As an adult he continued to be interested in the unfortunate prince; in 1868 he acquired in Paris an engraving depicting him in the Temple and had it set in a frame. Together with a portrait of Anton Rubinstein, these were the first, and for a very long time the only, adornments of his lodgings."[19]

A further instance of young Pyotr's sensitivity was directly related to music. While not a flashy child prodigy, as a boy Tchaikovsky showed an uncanny susceptibility to music. Modest relates an episode recalled by Fanny. Once the Tchaikovskys had guests, and the whole evening was spent in musical entertainment. Pyotr "was at first very lively and merry," writes Modest, "but toward the end of the evening he became so tired that he went upstairs earlier than usual. When Fanny some time later went into the nursery, he was not yet asleep but was crying agitatedly with glistening eyes. When asked what was the matter, he answered: 'Oh, this music, this music!' But there was no music to be heard at that moment. 'Save me from it! It's here, here,' said the boy, sobbing and pointing to his head, 'it never leaves me in peace.' "[20] The episode clearly shows the tendency of Tchaikovsky's excitability to cross over into a morbidly high-strung state verging on hysteria. In the first chapters of Modest's biography of his brother, we often find Pyotr in tears. He sobs as he speaks of his love for his father, as he saves a kitten, and as he plays the piano.

Music was a part of life within the Tchaikovsky household. Ilya Tchaikovsky was fond of the orchestrina; melodies from Rossini, Bellini, and Donizetti being played on the orchestrina filled Tchaikovsky's early childhood, while strains of *Don Giovanni* set the tone for his later love of Mozart. His mother had a fine singing voice and in her younger years also played the harp. Memories of her singing Aleksandr Alyabyev's "The Nightingale" made that song one of Tchaikovsky's favorite pieces. It was very likely his mother who first placed young

Pyotr at the keyboard of a piano. Almost from the start, the boy showed perfect pitch and a remarkable musical memory that allowed him to reproduce tunes with striking ease. In August 1844, Ilya Tchaikovsky wrote to his wife, who had traveled to the capital, that Pyotr and his nineteen-month-old sister, Aleksandra, or Sasha, were singing a song entitled "Our Mama in Petersburg." Written by the four-year-old Pyotr, it is Tchaikovsky's earliest recorded musical composition.

Fanny Dürbach later recalled that after long improvising at the piano, her charge would often come back to her "in a state of nervous distress."[21] Eventually she even decided to restrain his intense fascination with music. Her efforts, however, had little effect. One day, the boy became so engaged in some rhythm, rapping with his fingers on a windowpane while "displaying his best inventions," that he managed to break the glass, cutting his hand.[22] The incident finally moved his parents, over the objections of his governess, to engage a music tutor for their young son.

In 1843 a third son, Ippolit, had been born. The Tchaikovskys belonged to the lower ranks of the hereditary gentry, and by this time the family, comfortably well-off if not actually wealthy, enjoyed a position of relative social prominence in the provincial mining town of Votkinsk. But, in February 1848, Ilya Tchaikovsky resigned his post at the ironworks and in September of that year moved his family to Moscow, where he had hopes of a new appointment. The eldest children, Nikolay and Pyotr, were enrolled in school, and with the family's future still uncertain, Fanny left to take up a post in another household. Parting with his beloved governess and with the home and surroundings he had known all his childhood was for the young Tchaikovsky the first truly poignant trauma of his life. On 30 October, Tchaikovsky wrote to Fanny, "We have been in Moscow more than three weeks now, and every day all the members of our family think of you; we are so sad. . . . I mustn't recall that life in Votkinsk; I want very much to cry when I think of it."[23]

The family remained in Moscow less than a month, for the appointment Ilya had sought fell through. By November he had moved his family to St. Petersburg, thinking he might have better luck arranging a position in the capital. In St. Petersburg, Nikolay and Pyotr were enrolled in the private Schmelling School, where "instead of their former companions, . . . they encountered a crowd of urchins who met them, as newcomers, with the usual bullying and drubbing."[24] Having missed part of the curriculum because of the family's recent moves, the Tchaikovsky boys were forced to study that much harder to catch up. They left for school in the early morning and did not return home until five in the afternoon, and spent the rest of the evening buried in homework.

The departure from the familiar surroundings of Votkinsk, from Fanny and Venedikt and others close to him there, and now the grim stay at Schmelling School—these apparently trivial events aggravated young Pyotr's already strained emotional state. His crying and erratic behavior increased markedly. Finally, an attack of the measles "brought his nervous disorder to a head."[25] He began to suffer violent attacks, and the doctors diagnosed a disease of the spinal cord. As Modest himself admits, no further details about this illness are known. One plausible view, however, has it that Tchaikovsky was at this time already suffering from what was then called neurasthenia and that his problems were not physical but psychological in nature. Not surprisingly, his behavior and disposition somewhat lost their earlier mildness. Writing to Fanny in February 1850, Aleksandra Tchaikovskaya complained about her son's changed character: "He has become impatient, and at every word spoken to him that is not to his liking— there are tears in his eyes and a ready retort."[26]

Short though it would be, the St. Petersburg stay did further contribute to Tchaikovsky's musical development. His parents arranged for him to take piano lessons with a professional teacher, and while the lessons, interrupted by his illness, were few, their impact was significant. Years later, when asked when he had started composing, Tchaikovsky would often respond that he had done so ever since he had come to know music. "And he had truly come to know [music]," adds Modest, "during his first stay in Petersburg."[27]

But that stay was soon over. In May 1849, Ilya Tchaikovsky was appointed manager of a metallurgical plant in Alapaevsk, and the family, with the exception of Nikolay, who remained in boarding school in the capital to pursue his studies, moved back to the Urals. Alapaevsk turned out to be a small town populated primarily by working-class people and boasting little cultivated society. In this bleak outpost Pyotr continued to pine for their life in Votkinsk. To his former governess he wrote, "The whole evening was merry for the adults, but for me, just think Mlle F[anny], my brother, my friend, and my kind, excellent tutor whom I so loved in Votkinsk were all missing. Oh! I should love to spend some time with her or at least with Venichka [Venedikt] and Kolya [Nikolay]."[28]

It is not merely by chance that Nikolay, by this time studying at the St. Petersburg Mining College, is mentioned here. Tchaikovsky's elder brother played an important role in his emotional life from his earliest childhood through the beginning of adolescence. Modest testifies that Nikolay was "the most brilliant in appearance" among the children, adding, "Adroit, handsome, refined, a passionate lover of physical exercise, he was in relation to Pyotr Ilyich exactly what Volodya in Lev Tolstoy's *Childhood* and *Boyhood* was to Kolya [the novels' child-hero]."[29] In addition to being an excellent student, Nikolay was a fine pianist, and at the Mining College he was making "such great progress in music that he has surpassed all his classmates," wrote Pyotr to Fanny in March 1850.[30] It is not impossible that the example of his elder brother may have had some influence on the musical studies of Tchaikovsky himself.

In Alapaevsk the nine-year-old Pyotr was cared for mainly by his half-sister, Zinaida, and a cousin, Lidiya, neither of whom had any great understanding of child psychology. He was continually chastised for his laziness and lack of interest in learning, and only his music studies seemed to progress. "[Pyotr] plays piano very nicely," Lidiya informed Fanny. "One might think he were an adult; one cannot compare his present skill with what he had in Votkinsk."[31] This was echoed by Pyotr himself, who wrote, "I . . . never leave the piano, which makes me happy when I feel sad."[32]

His parents, however, had rather cooled toward their son's musical passion. They had decided to make a civil servant or military officer out of him. Despite some moderate success, the family still felt inferior to its origins. With luck, Pyotr's graduation from one of the elite aristocratic schools might lead to an influential career in government service. In fact, the prestigious School of Jurisprudence in St. Petersburg, where it was finally decided to send the boy, had been created partly with a view to helping members of the lesser nobility improve their status. Moreover, the strict discipline for which the school was famous would, his parents believed, have a beneficial influence on their son's moral education. On the other hand, in Russia at that time little, if any, social prestige was associated with the profession of a musician, nor did there exist any professional musical institutions for young boys. Thus, at the end of 1849 a new governess, Anastasiya Petrova, recently graduated from the Nikolaevsky Teaching Institute in St. Petersburg, was engaged to ready Pyotr for enrollment in the preparatory class of the School of Jurisprudence and to help him take the step that would ultimately cost Tchaikovsky thirteen years of doubt and hesitation as to his true vocation.

On 1 May 1850, Aleksandra Tchaikovskaya gave birth to fraternal twin boys, Anatoly and Modest. Despite his early and short-lived intimacy with Nikolay, it would be the twins and his sister, Sasha, to whom Tchaikovsky was to grow most attached during the course of his life. But the birth of his two brothers and the celebration of his father's name day later that summer were for the boy the last happy events experienced in Alapaevsk. In August, accompanied by his mother, Zinaida, and Sasha, he set off for St. Petersburg to be enrolled in the School of Jurisprudence. In the capital he had a respite before taking up his new studies in those strange and rather forbidding surroundings. On 22 August his mother took him to see Mikhail Glinka's *A Life for the Tsar*, the first great Russian opera on a national theme. Although much may have been beyond the grasp of a boy of ten, the production made a profound and lasting impression on Tchaikovsky. A year later, he would point out in a letter to his mother the anniversary of that experience,[33] and Glinka's sister recalled that in his mature years Tchaikovsky admitted that the opera was especially dear to him, "since he heard it in the happy years of his youth."[34] In mid-October, Tchaikovsky would also see what was probably his first ballet performance, Adolphe Adam's *Giselle*, featuring the Italian ballerina Carlotta Grisi. A letter to his parents of 21 October unfortunately contains no description of his reaction to the performance, but it would hardly be wrong to suggest that this early impression contributed to his later passion for ballet.[35]

Aleksandra stayed in St. Petersburg until the end of September, visiting her son in the preparatory class and taking him off on holidays. But all too soon it was time for her to return to Alapaevsk. Ilya Tchaikovsky had already foreseen the pain that this parting would cause their son when on 16 September he wrote to his wife, "Darling Petya is accustomed to the caresses of his father and mother, but now will be a long time without this happiness—and as he is sensitive and finds it difficult to part with people, you must naturally instill in him *courage*."[36] On the morning of their departure, Tchaikovsky drove with his mother and sisters to the central turnpike, where those leaving along the Moscow road quit St. Petersburg. Modest, in his biography, describes the scene:

During the drive, Petya shed some tears, but the end of the journey seemed far off and, treasuring every moment of his mother's presence, he appeared relatively calm. But, arriving at the place of separation, he lost all self-control. He pressed himself against his mother and could not tear himself away from her. No caresses, no assurances, no promises of a speedy return could have any effect. He heard nothing, saw nothing, and he seemed to merge as one with his venerated mother. It was necessary to resort to force, and the poor child had to be torn away from Aleksandra Andreevna. He clutched at anything he could, unwilling to let her go. At last they succeeded. She took her seat with her daughters in the carriage. The horses started off, and then, gathering the last of his strength, the boy broke away from [Ilya] Keiser [an accompanying relative] and darted off after the carriage with a mad cry of despair, trying to seize the footboard, the splashboards, anything, in the vain hope of stopping it. . . . Never in his life could Pyotr Ilyich speak of this moment without a shudder of horror.[37]

Tchaikovsky wrote later that this was one of the most terrible days of his life.[38] Even after thirty years he would confess that he could not "calmly pass by this way without experiencing anew that mad despair that possessed me when the carriage carrying away everything most dear to me disappeared from sight."[39] According to Modest,

> even though later in life he would know incomparably greater and more terrible sorrows and losses, experience far more grievous and painful privations and calamities, and endure disappointments and sufferings alongside which this temporary separation was only a small unpleasant detail of existence, still, so true is it that it is not the event that is important but its impact on us, that until his dying day, having tolerated all his adversities and forgotten all the pain from the past, he could never tolerate, could never forget the burning feeling of resentment and despair that he had felt while running after the carriage that was tearing his mother away from him.[40]

During his two years in the school's preparatory class, Pyotr wrote his parents constantly. These childish letters are remarkable for their profusion of tender diminutives, breathless endearments, and emotional outpourings of longing coupled with incessant and often futile wishes and even prayers to see again his "dear wonderful and beautiful Mama and Papa" as soon as possible. "I kiss your little hands, your little feet, and all of you warmly, my darlings," he wrote in one letter. "I kiss your hands a million times and ask for your blessing." In another letter, he wrote that he longed "to cover you both together with kisses" and that he had "tried to be good all the year so that I might kiss both my angels together." In August 1851 he promised that when they came to St. Petersburg, he and his brother Nikolay "shall cover you with kisses so that you will not go back anymore to nasty Alapaikha [Alapaevsk], but stay here to live forever. However, maybe Papa has again changed his mind and again will not wish to come see his chicks." In March 1852 he wrote, "You write us, beautiful angels, that you will come in May, which means that we shall not even see the passing of March or April, or the coming of this most happy month of the year. How happy we shall be when we can cover you with kisses, my beautiful ones; I shall jump to the ceiling for joy." A few weeks later, he rejoiced that "very soon now I shall not be writing you letters, but shall be speaking with my angels in person. Oh, how nice it will be for the first time in my life to come home from the school, see you, and cover you with kisses; it seems that this will be the greatest happiness I have known."[41]

These are but a few examples of his peculiar vocabulary and intonation. When one considers that in most of these letters such expressions occur several times over, the general effect becomes more singular still. The multiplicity and manner of these outpourings seem hardly explicable merely by the spirit of the times (though the influence of the family environment and, in particular, of his father's lexicon does make itself felt) or by the tender age of their author. It is useful to turn again to Modest's testimony. "The first thing one notices is the striking abundance of love in the correspondent," he remarks.

> Out of all the thirty-nine letters there is not one in which he speaks of anyone disapprovingly, not one person for whom he has anything but praise. All those around him are kind to him, affectionate, attentive, and he looks on everyone with love and gratitude. . . . Moreover, the sincerity and straightforwardness of these letters are especially characteristic. . . . This also stands out clearly in a comparison of the letters of the two brothers. Nikolay, by nature less sensitive, . . . addresses his parents in such a way that at every step is felt a formality that conceals—despite the unquestionable presence of a strong affection for his parents—some coldness of attitude at the actual moment of writing the letter. . . . There is nothing like this in the letters of his younger brother. He does not stint on tender expressions and favorable opinions; on the contrary, far more often he resorts to them, but always in such a way that involuntarily you believe him to be sincere—you see that the letter is dictated not only by his mind, but also by his heart.[42]

Modest's comments here are important, not as a panegyric of an adored brother already possessed of every virtue from early adolescence, but as an affirmation that even in his childish correspondence,

with all its naïveté and profusion of clichés, certain features of Tchaikovsky's mature personality are already apparent: a capacity for passionate attachment and a tendency toward emotional excess. These
qualities might be called, depending on one's temperament, either romantic or sentimental, and accordingly praised or condemned. It is important, however, following Modest's lead, to stress their naturalness.
In all his childhood, as later in his adult, letters there is no trace of
false intonation, despite his diary confession that he "posed" in his
letters. This suggests that at least while actually composing a letter,
whatever his attitude afterward, Tchaikovsky experienced precisely
what he was writing about and that if he wished to cry or if he was
overcome by erotic desire, he could tell of this to his intimate correspondents with charming ease. This quality is obviously responsible
for the disarming frankness in his later letters not only to relatives in
whom he confided fully, especially Anatoly and Modest, but to a certain degree also to Mrs. von Meck, with whom, despite the extreme
delicacy and tact demanded by their curious relationship, he would
feel a strong spiritual affinity. More than once in the following chapters
we shall come across this candid self-expression, which has so discomfited Soviet censors.

Despite the number of letters surviving from the period, little is
known about Pyotr's attachments while in the preparatory class of the
School of Jurisprudence. Initially the Tchaikovsky boys were under the
supervision and essentially the guardianship of a friend of their father,
Modest Vakar, and later of his brother Platon, himself a graduate of the
School of Jurisprudence. It may indeed have been on the recommendation of Platon Vakar that the boy was first sent to the school.[43] With
the Vakar family was connected another early trauma, when during a
scarlet fever epidemic young Pyotr, though himself not taken ill,
brought the disease into the Vakar home, which the eldest son, Kolya,
then five years old and "his parents' pride and joy," contracted. Pyotr
adored the child. "Kolya Vakar is simply an Angel; I love him very
much," he declared in a letter to his parents of 21 October 1850.[44] Four
weeks later, little Kolya Vakar was dead. "It is necessary," writes Modest, "to be aware of how Pyotr Ilyich reacted to the death not only of
relatives and acquaintances but even of perfect strangers, especially if
they were young, in order to imagine what a terrible effect this event
must have had on him then."[45]

Only two names from among Tchaikovsky's classmates of the time
are known to us, and the only mention of them in letters is found in
yet another sentimental context. "On Wednesday, 25 April, I celebrated my birthday and cried a lot," he wrote his parents in 1851, "re-

membering the happy time I spent in Alapaikha [Alapaevsk], but I had
two friends with me, Belyavsky and Dokhturov, who comforted me.
Mama, you saw Belyavsky when I entered the prep[aratory] cl[ass], and
I told you that he was my friend."[46]

It would be wrong, however, to think that Tchaikovsky was constantly in a sad or sentimental mood during his years in the preparatory class. Like most children his age, he was well disposed to having
fun and even playing pranks. In one letter to his parents, he described
how he played a humorous polka on the piano while the other pupils
danced, making such a noise that they drew the displeasure of an instructor who had forbidden dancing at this time. At his appearance
everyone fled in all directions; but Pyotr alone was not quick enough,
and when asked who had been dancing, he replied that there had been
so many that he could not remember. The instructor, Joseph Berrard,
who taught both literature and French language, was Pyotr's favorite
and for long afterward he felt remorse at having lied to him. In Tchaikovsky's words, the elderly Berrard possessed a "purely angelic kindness,"[47] and it was partly through his influence that the ten-year-old
Tchaikovsky began composing French verses again, as he had before
with Fanny. One of his poems from this period, naive but sincere, has
survived:

> Quand je prie de tout mon coeur
> Dieu exauce ma prière.
> La prière est une soeur
> Oui elle est comme une lumière
> Qui éclaire notre âme.[48]

(When I pray with all my heart, God harkens to my prayer. Prayer is a
sister; yes, it is like a light that illuminates our soul.)

With his fellow pupils young Pyotr attended a ball at the Assembly
of Nobles, where for the first time he saw Tsar Nicholas I. There, too,
he danced and took part in a raffle, in which he won a toy soldier in a
three-cornered hat and an eraser set in ivory. In June 1851 he was the
guest at the country house of acquaintances, but the main theme of
his letters to his parents continued to be his longing for them to come
to St. Petersburg. Finally, in September, his father arrived in the capital
for a short time on personal business. Conditions in Alapaevsk were
proving unpleasant, and now, in addition, there was the education of
both Sasha and Ippolit to think of. The Tchaikovskys had therefore
decided to look for some way to resettle the family in St. Petersburg.

For the few weeks of his stay in the city, Nikolay and Pyotr lived with their father, to Pyotr's great comfort and delight. But with Ilya's departure Pyotr's longing resumed and he began to count the weeks and days until his family's arrival in the capital. Although Ilya soon left his post as director of the ironworks in Alapaevsk, he was slow in moving the family back to St. Petersburg. They had still not come in January 1852, when Pyotr wrote to his parents that not long before, while playing the piano at the school, he had begun playing Alyabyev's "The Nightingale" and suddenly remembered how he used to play this piece before. "I was overcome by a terrible sadness," he told them, "since I recalled how I used to play it in Alapaevsk in the evening with you listening, or four years ago in St. Petersburg with my teacher Filippov, and I recalled how you used to sing this piece together with me. In short, I recalled that it had always been your favorite piece. But soon a new hope appeared in my heart: 'I believe that on such-and-such a day or on such-and-such a night you will come again and I shall again be in my own home.'"[49]

In May, Pyotr successfully passed the entrance examination into the School of Jurisprudence proper and was enrolled in the junior course. At the same time, his most fervent prayers were finally answered, for he was at last reunited with both his parents when the entire family arrived in St. Petersburg that spring. It was the first St. Petersburg summer that Tchaikovsky had spent with his family. His father rented a country house on the Black River north of the city and invited his two young nieces, Lidiya and Anna, to stay with them. Though ten years older than Pyotr, Anna and her young cousin became fast friends and would remain close until the end of their lives. Many years later, Anna (whose married name was Merkling) remembered Tchaikovsky as having been "a thin, nervous, extremely sensitive boy . . . notable for his affectionate sensibility, in particular toward his mother."[50]

Pyotr's letters virtually ceased upon reunion with his family. "The only things he recalled from this time," writes Modest, were his mother's "visits to the school, his delight at this, and later, how he managed to catch sight of her sometimes and to blow her kisses from the corner dormitory of the fourth form when she visited her sister . . . who was living directly across from the School of Jurisprudence."[51]

In light of so ardent an attachment to his mother, whom, in his own words, he "loved with a kind of morbidly passionate love,"[52] her sudden death of cholera on 13 June 1854 could only strike him as an unspeakable tragedy and shock. Twenty-five years later, on the anniversary of her death, Tchaikovsky would confess in a letter to Mrs. von Meck that "this was the first powerful grief I experienced. This death had an enormous influence on my own fate and that of my whole family. . . . Every minute of that horrible day is etched in my memory as if it were yesterday."[53] Ippolit later recalled that during their mother's illness the children were taken to the home of their aunt. When it was clear that death was approaching, Pyotr and Sasha were allowed to go to her to receive her final blessing. The younger children remained behind. But Ippolit managed to slip away and ran back to the apartment alone. "I reached the gates of our house," he writes, "just as Petya . . . and Sasha were coming out, and they told me that it was all over."[54] It was not until more than two years after the event, in 1856, that Pyotr felt able to write about his mother's death to his beloved Fanny Dürbach. "Finally, I must tell you of a terrible misfortune that occurred two and a half years ago," he wrote. "Four months after Zina's [Zinaida's] departure, Mama fell ill with cholera. The danger was great, but thanks to the redoubled efforts of the doctors the patient almost recovered, but not for long, because after three or four days of convalescence she died without having had time to bid farewell to those around her. Although she had not the strength to utter a word, it was understood that she wanted to receive last communion and the priest arrived with the Holy Sacraments just in time, for, having taken communion, she gave up her soul to God."[55]

The sense of misery that had run through his early years at the School of Jurisprudence culminated in the death of his mother. This was an encounter with harsh reality that he long refused to accept. Much later, on 23 November 1877, Tchaikovsky wrote in a letter to Mrs. von Meck, "Despite the all-conquering force of my convictions, I shall never reconcile myself to the fact that my mother, whom I loved so much and who was such a beautiful person, is gone forever and that I shall never have the chance to tell her that after twenty-three years of separation I still love her as much as ever."[56]

It is very likely that the shattering experience of his mother's death was one of the sources of the deep existential melancholy that was to become one of the constituents of Tchaikovsky's psychological makeup and was often to find poignant expression in his music. It was perhaps inevitable that the early years spent with his mother in Votkinsk would acquire in his boyish imagination the aura of an Eden. The loss of this golden time had left him with sad memories of an irretrievable happiness, memories that would haunt him to the end of his days, while the loss of his mother created a void that no one could ever fill and an indelible scar on his psyche. Whatever else St. Petersburg might come to signify in his life, from this moment the city of white nights would, for him, be forever shrouded by the remembrance of childhood despair.

CHAPTER TWO

In the School of Jurisprudence

The Imperial School of Jurisprudence, its vaulted windows overlooking St. Petersburg's Summer Garden from across the Fontanka River, had been founded in 1835 by Prince Pyotr of Oldenburg for the purpose of educating competent officers for the civil service, to be recruited mainly from the lower and middle strata of the nobility. Until this time, juridical activity had remained a privilege of the *raznochintsy*, the "classless" intellectuals. The enterprise was successful, and the new institution soon acquired a prestigious reputation, though one not unclouded at first by an air of rebellious liberalism, later suppressed by the reigning autocracy. The public came to see in the cocked hat of a student of the School of Jurisprudence the same symbol of high society as the red collar of a student of the Lyceum or the casque of an imperial page.[1]

The School of Jurisprudence provided a unique combination of secondary and higher education, with an emphasis on vocational training in the law, while graduation from the school secured for its students a privileged position in the ranks of the civil service. Preparation of this bureaucratic elite normally took seven years of study. Upon completing the two-year preparatory class and passing the entrance examination to the school proper, Tchaikovsky was admitted to the so-called junior course, forms seven through four. In these first four years, the students covered a general secondary curriculum, including physics, natural history, mathematics, geography, languages, and literature. From the fourth form a student would move up to the senior course, forms three through one, where he would concentrate on special jur-idical subjects, such as Roman law, state law, financial and police law, forensic medicine, comparative legal practice, and practical law.[2]

Within the strictly supervised boarding school, the junior and se-nior groups lived their own separate lives, each with its own dormi-tories and its own great hall that led directly into the classrooms. The halls were separated by massive doors. Juniors and seniors were kept carefully apart from one another, despite common use of the dining hall and yard. The seniors would be scheduled for everything—break-fast, dinner, recreation—an hour earlier than the juniors. In the words of one graduate of the school, "the juniors never penetrated into the territory of the seniors, and rarely would a senior pass through the hall of the junior course."[3]

Presiding over the school was a director endowed with virtually unlimited power. Each entering class was entrusted to one of the twelve tutors, who would lead it through to its final year. The guiding principle of the administration was, as one official put it, "not only to educate the rising generation but to instruct it in the spirit of Christ, of love and devotion to the Tsar and the Fatherland, of honor and duty, and to train it for orderly and systematic work."[4] It was not accidental that the school's motto was *Respice Finem* (Never forget the final pur-pose), adjuring an aspiration to excellence and an aversion to compro-mise.

By the time Tchaikovsky entered the school, the ideal and obliga-tion of disciplined service was impressed through an almost military regimen. Only a few years earlier, however, the school's students had enjoyed a far less rigid environment than that of other imperial schools. According to Vladimir Stasov, the famous music critic and supporter of the Mighty Five, who graduated from the school sixteen years prior to Tchaikovsky, the school in that early period had known "something recalling the family and home life."[5] Prince Pyotr often invited students to his palace and treated them like members of his own family, even throwing open his palace for parties. The first direc-tor of the school, Semyon Poschman, an authoritarian but good-hearted man, also held gatherings at his home, to which the students came for conversation and dancing, often with their parents and rela-tives. This warm atmosphere prevailed at the School of Jurisprudence until 1849, when Nicholas I introduced a strict military discipline throughout the imperial school system as a reaction against the revo-lutionary ideas then coming from Europe. Although the situation eased somewhat following the tsar's death in 1855, the earlier relaxed spirit was never completely restored.

Certainly it was difficult, especially at the beginning, for the young Tchaikovsky to accustom himself to the rigid daily schedule set for the students. With seven hours of classes six days a week, plus two to three hours of course preparation and another two to three hours devoted to meals and religious services, students were allowed little time for relaxation and nonacademic pursuits. Only Sundays and holidays brought relief from this regimented existence. The detailed regulations on student conduct stressed such commandments as honesty, honor, respect for authority, maintenance of order, attentiveness in class, correct dress and appearance, fulfillment of obligations, and avoidance of "immoral behavior."

Konstantin Arsenyev, four classes above Tchaikovsky, notes in his recollections of the school that "the main means of influencing the students were threats, verbal abuse and yelling."[6] As a rule, only students of the junior course were ever actually flogged at the School of Jurisprudence. Public flogging was regarded as an extreme measure and was sometimes carried out in the presence of both junior and senior students. For the seniors, however, flogging was not allowed. Vladimir Stasov has left an impressive description of one public flogging from his school years in the early 1840s. "The director shouted and threatened so much that he threw himself into an authoritarian hysteria from which he could not retreat," Stasov recollected. As a result, he decided to whip everyone in the class. The boys were lined up, and two soldiers seized the boy at the end, Vladimir Spassky,

> who resisted and fought back desperately; they stripped him naked, laid him on a bench and began to whip him. The director, his hands behind his back, walked to and fro about the room with uneven steps. The tutors kept official silence, buttoned up in their uniforms. . . . They flogged S[pass]ky first, then V[etlit]sky, . . . a fine troublemaker, but in this affair quite blameless. As he [Vetlitsky] was being whipped, he kept shouting in a heartrending voice that he was innocent. All my insides were trembling. Finally, the director shouted for them to stop and went away without saying a word or looking back. We dispersed and went to our rooms, but our indignation, our spite and loathing would not subside for the longest time. I have not forgotten that loathsome experience even forty years later. That picture is even now before my eyes.[7]

Such spectacles became more frequent in the 1850s with the appointment of Major General Aleksandr Yazykov as director, a former police commissioner for the city of Riga in Latvia who believed public floggings to be useful for disciplining the younger students. It was under Yazykov's directorship that marching exercises were introduced at the school and the position created of an "inspector of students," whose function, as seen by the boys, was to "go about the school observing, apprehending, punishing, and whipping."[8] Vladimir Taneev, the elder brother of the better-known composer Sergey Taneev and two classes below Tchaikovsky, provides a detailed, if highly subjective, description of life at the school in his later memoirs. But while Taneev, a zealously radical writer with an extreme intolerance for both autocracy and the contemporary system of education, recalls that "solitary confinement, birchings and expulsions from the school were *à l'ordre du jour en permanence*" and that the authorities "flogged without measure or shame,"[9] such punishment never dominated school discipline as it did in England.[10] Still, Modest informs us that his brother was forced on at least one occasion to witness "the public punishment of one of his comrades."[11] It is not difficult to imagine what a painful experience this must have been for the sensitive and impressionable adolescent.

Taneev describes the event that Modest probably had in mind. "A year before we entered the school, there was a pupil, Trepilsky, in the sixth form," he recalls. Trepilsky had remained in the sixth form a second year and, at seventeen, was much older than his classmates. "As a grown young man," writes Taneev, "he smoked." Smoking in the younger class was strictly forbidden. "Sinitsyn [a tutor] caught him with a cigarette and ran off at once to the director. The director gave his orders. The terrible [Colonel Aleksandr] Rutenberg [the first appointed inspector of students] appeared and began to flog Trepilsky in front of the whole form. He was given sixty-five strokes. One of his classmates, little Maslov, could not bear it and burst into sobs. Rutenberg shouted at him that he would lay him out right then and there and thrash him as well. The sobbing ceased. The boy made an unnatural effort to bring himself under control."[12]

In all likelihood this Trepilsky was indeed the classmate with whom, according to Modest, the thirteen-year-old Tchaikovsky so greatly sympathized. It cannot be ruled out that such incidents—characteristic, in fact, of most boarding schools of the period—may have left an indelible impression on his young consciousness and that this may have been to some extent responsible for such later peculiarities as his phobias, his suspiciousness, and his extreme vulnerability. His brother Ippolit, brought up in the same family environment, confessed that "when I had to watch and hear the squeal of the huge supple birches, brandished in three movements by robust soldiers striving one after another to strike a firm blow across the boy's scourged body, my legs grew weak, my head swam, and, closing my eyes, I would very nearly lose consciousness."[13] Tchaikovsky himself, however, was never whipped. His classmate Ivan Turchaninov writes that "there was undoubtedly something special about Tchaikovsky ·that separated him from the crowd of other boys and made our hearts go out to him. Kindness, gentleness, responsiveness, and a sort of insouciance with respect to himself were from early on distinctive features of his character. Even the stern and savage Rutenberg showed a special sympathy for him."[14]

In 1855 the "savage" Rutenberg died and was succeeded by Ivan Alopeus, a former artillery captain described as the kindest and gentlest of the tutors. Before his appointment as inspector of students, Alopeus had been the tutor for Tchaikovsky's class and had developed a fondness for the engaging and musically inclined adolescent. He called him by pet names, as he did his other favorites. "Alopeus had much more vocation for his profession than Yazykov or Rutenberg," writes Modest, "and revealed this in his ability to reconcile exactingness with gentleness . . . [and] to make himself not only feared but also loved."[15] After Alopeus's promotion to inspectorship, Baron Edouard Prosper Gaillard de Baccarat took over the duties of tutor for Tchaikovsky's class. His moral influence on the young men entrusted to him was minimal at best, and he did not inspire the slightest fear. Baccarat taught French, but he treated the students "with negligence and contempt" and the level of his teaching was low. "Gradually we forgot all the French we had learned at home," writes Taneev. "But the exams were no problem. Baccarat enjoyed the trust and regard of the administration. It never occurred to anyone to expose this deception."[16]

Taneev also describes in detail how examinations were effectively faked through the collusion of teacher and students. Indeed, as described by Taneev, the conduct of Baccarat was characteristic of the atmosphere of the school as a whole, reflecting the entrenched hypocrisy typically plaguing institutions of this sort. The gap between pretense and reality was often wide, touching even the minutiae of everyday routine, and behind the school's splendid facade of order and discipline lurked moral and behavioral chaos, at times verging on anarchy, which the administration never managed to suppress and often preferred to ignore. As Konstantin Arsenyev recalled in later years, "the inner life of the students . . . remained beyond any direct influence on the part of the administration. . . . The authorities were concerned only with the implementation of certain external rules and the observance of a certain external order."[17]

To a large extent, then, the students were left to their own devices and relationships. Often these relationships were harsh, modeled in part on those between them and their teachers and inspectors. "The strong treated the weak with the same violence as the authorities behaved toward the students," Taneev writes. "The seniors would harass the new boys, teasing and beating them. . . . [They] looked upon the juniors with arrogance, while the juniors regarded the seniors with awe."[18] Such a state of affairs was typical of boys' boarding schools of the time. The treatment of juniors almost as slaves, a pattern of relations not unlike British "fagging," was well established at the School of Jurisprudence. Taneev, in his vivid memoirs, recalls one classmate, Brailko, who "would carry a whip or a knout and chase the [younger students] running [around the yard], at times lashing them quite painfully." In winter this same Brailko would ride about the yard in a "troika . . . harnessed with students. Every student saw it as an honor to be on the troika team. . . . When the 'horses' grew tired, they were replaced by new ones."[19]

But even in such an atmosphere, Tchaikovsky's class, according to Taneev, managed to acquire an unusual and dubious reputation in the annals of the school:

> In that class everybody behaved till the day of graduation like a stupid schoolboy. They called harassment the "chase." . . . They had a special society of the "chase" which had its own regulations and was made up of a "Chief Master of the Hunt" and several "Huntsmasters" who took turns being "on duty." They "chased" mainly two of their schoolmates, Kablukov and Snarsky, who were called the "boars." Each morning the "duty-master" woke the "boars," informed them that he had been assigned to them for that day, and then threw his boot at them. The "chase" consisted of constant mockery, insulting nicknames, pushing, pinching, punching, etc. The poor young men—they were twenty-one when they graduated from the course—did not possess sufficient energy to arm themselves against their persecutors. To kill any of their persecutors would have been too weak a revenge for what they suffered at their hands. They were in a constant state of nervous tension. Clearly, they must have been psychologically maimed for the rest of their lives.[20]

Tchaikovsky's comrades harassed not only their schoolmates but also some of their instructors. Fyodor Maslov, a friend of Tchaikovsky's,

organized the "cohorts," who would accompany the instructors along
the corridors and down the stairs with squeals, shouts, and insults.[21]

It may well be that Taneev exaggerates in ascribing all these outrages to Tchaikovsky's class alone. Nevertheless, this kind of behavior
is certainly characteristic of the conduct of groups of adolescent males
in close surroundings. In any event, we can no doubt assume in the
sensitive Tchaikovsky an element of compassion for the harassed students and of disgust with their persecutors. Given this, his later antipathy to Vladimir Taneev would seem more understandable. According
to his own memoirs, Taneev, who tended to regard all around him as
idle drones, took part in a variety of pranks, and his friend Bulanin
ridiculed a friend of Tchaikovsky's "in the most unbearable manner."[22]
Even in later years, Tchaikovsky obviously disliked Taneev. An entry
from Tchaikovsky's diary for 13 February 1886 reads, "Heat was unbearable and the insufferable V. I. Taneev topped off all the discomfort."[23] It may well be that the antipathy was mutual. This would explain the curious fact that the composer's name is virtually absent
from Taneev's memoirs, being mentioned only once, while several of
Tchaikovsky's classmates figure there more or less prominently.

A more invidious evil at the school, from the administration's
point of view, was smoking. This was strictly forbidden to the juniors,
but somewhat tolerated within the senior course. Konstantin Arsenyev observes that if the first and fundamental requirement of the
school was obedience to the superiors without objection or argument,
the next in importance was the prohibition on smoking. He emphasizes that "most of the class 'scandals' were the direct result of smoking, and nonetheless it continued on the same scale." Students
"smoked in classrooms, in bedrooms, on the staircases, in the 'rooms
of free debates' [lavatories]; not only the reckless souls but also many
of the well-behaved students smoked. It seemed that the strictness of
the prohibition only inflamed the desire to violate it."[24]

Taneev reveals several curious details related to the modes of
smoking practiced by the students in the school's halls. Those wishing
to smoke would gather around the stove vent and hide the smoker,
who would lie down on the floor and smoke into the vent. It is notable
that "the smokers in each class constituted a special group united by
their common interest. A strict order was observed in the process of
smoking based on the seniority of these groups. The members of the
first—that is, final—form would begin, followed by those of the second
and lastly of the third." The greatest temptation, fraught with the risk
of demerits or punishment, was clandestine smoking near the stove in
the common hall. Each participant's turn was known as a "horn," this
also being the term for the cigarette used in such circumstances.

"Whoever had the first horn would lie on the floor and begin smoking the cigarette. He normally did not finish it, and his place and the same cigarette would be taken by whoever had the second horn, then the third, and so on. When someone finished the cigarette, the next would light up a new one."[25]

Quite probably it was under such circumstances that Tchaikovsky first contracted the unhealthy addiction to smoking that remained with him to the end of his life. Many years later he would write that in his school years he had found pleasure in this clandestine smoking precisely because of the risk and anxiety associated with it.

Drinking flourished as well, and again this was a vice typical not so much of this particular institution as generally of adolescence, and is explicable in terms of the necessity of self-assertion and imitation of adults. The extent of its popularity is revealed in an episode recounted by Taneev, in which two senior students from the school, visiting the fashionable Palkin restaurant, happened upon two "very young boys" from the junior course totally drunk. One of the boys, a close friend of Taneev's, had reportedly begun drinking, sometimes to the point of delirium, at the age of fifteen and barely managed to graduate.[26] But while the high-minded Taneev strongly disapproved of drunkenness, Tchaikovsky's frank and revealing confession in a diary entry from 11 July 1886 displays a markedly different attitude. "It is said that to abuse oneself with alcoholic drink is harmful," he wrote. "I readily agree with that. But nevertheless," he added self-mockingly,

I, that is, a sick person full of *neuroses,* absolutely cannot do without the alcoholic *poison* against which Mr. *Miklukho-Maklay* [a Russian ethnographer and a strong advocate of sobriety] protests. A person with such a strange name is extremely happy that he does not know the delights of vodka and other alcoholic drinks. But how unjust it is to judge others by yourself and to forbid others what you yourself do not like! Now I, for example, am drunk every night, and cannot do without it. . . . In the first stage of drunkenness, I feel complete happiness and *understand* in such a condition infinitely more than I do when I am without the *Miklukho-Maklay* poison!!!! Also, I have not noticed that my health suffers particularly from it. But then: *Quid licet Jovi non licet bovi* [What is allowable for Jove is not allowable for the ox]. As yet, God knows who is more right: myself or Maklay.[27]

As is evident from Tchaikovsky's letters and diaries, alcohol played a significant role in his life until the very end. It had been for him a

means of dealing with nervous and psychological tension, and in time
turned into a habit, though never an obsession. He never became an
alcoholic in the true sense of the word.

Theater was quite a different passion of the students of the school,
particularly St. Petersburg's fashionable Mikhailovsky Theater, with
its French troupe and a repertory consisting mainly of popular drawing-
room comedies. Since the time of Catherine the Great, French had
been the language of the Russian aristocracy, and virtually all the students at the School of Jurisprudence had grown up immersed in French
culture. Often it might happen that just about every seat in the upper
circle of the Mikhailovsky was occupied by a young man in the
school's green uniform, excitedly following the action of some French
farce. For many of these youths, French theater constituted not merely
an entertainment, but a school of frivolous attitudes toward life and
love. Tchaikovsky himself would never cease to enjoy French theater,
but his response to it was primarily aesthetic. He appreciated its peculiar artistry and elegance, and later in life, during his numerous visits to Paris, he never missed a single worthwhile production.

Students of the school also frequented the Italian opera. Various
Italian companies were constantly appearing in St. Petersburg, their
productions customarily richer and more luxurious than those of any
Russian troupe. The Italians brought with them their finest operas:
Rossini's *Otello* and *Barbiere di Siviglia*, Bellini's *Sonnambula* and
Norma, Verdi's *Traviata* and *Rigoletto*. They also presented works by
Mozart, Meyerbeer, and others, sung in Italian. The superb voices and
star appearances of such internationally renowned singers as Pauline
Viardot lent the Italian performances an irresistible brilliance and
charm. No wonder, then, that Tchaikovsky, like many of his comrades,
became enamored of their art and came to know their repertory well.
It was during these hours spent outside the school, in visits to the
theater and occasional concerts, that the future composer came into
contact with the world that best responded to his own secret strivings,
as yet not fully formed or realized.

Within the walls of the school, however, Tchaikovsky's musical
activities were exhibited only minimally. During the school's first decade of existence, musical activity had flourished at the school, and its
founder, Prince Pyotr, a noted music lover, actively encouraged the
musical pursuits of the students. Professional musicians, some of
them quite famous, such as Clara Schumann, were invited to perform
in concerts at the school or at the prince's own palace, in which the
students themselves occasionally took part. But in later years, as one
former student observed, music as such became "no more than a 'nook'

in the life of the School of Jurisprudence into which most students never entered at all."[28] Very little evidence exists about the role of music during Yazykov's administration. Tchaikovsky seems to have studied with Franz Becker, the school's music teacher, but we find no mention of this in the reminiscences. He did sing, however, in the school chorus under the direction of Gavriil Lomakin, and in a letter to Mrs. von Meck more than twenty-five years later, Tchaikovsky remembered his experience with obvious pleasure. "When I was a boy I had a splendid voice, a treble," he wrote, "and for several years in a row I sang the top part in the trio which in the bishop's service was sung by three boys at the altar at the beginning and the end of the service. The liturgy, particularly in the bishop's service, made on me then (and in part even now) the most profound poetic impression. . . . How proud I was then that with my singing I was taking part in the service! How happy I was when the metropolitan thanked and blessed us for this singing!"[29]

Outside the school, Tchaikovsky took music lessons on Sundays from the pianist Rudolph Kündinger. But these lessons were irregular and did not continue for very long (1855–1858), and as may happen with great artists, the teacher discovered in his pupil no particular talent. Most likely nobody, with the exception of a few close friends, foresaw in the young Tchaikovsky what he would later become. His classmate Vladimir Gerard, for instance, recalled that "after choral rehearsals in the White Hall . . . Pyotr Ilyich would sit at the harmonium and improvise on the themes that we had been given (for the most part, of course, from fashionable operas). We were amused, but were not imbued with any expectations of his future glory."[30] Fyodor Maslov wrote that "with respect to music Tchaikovsky, of course, occupied the primary position, but he did not find any serious sympathy for his vocation among his comrades. They were amused merely by the musical tricks he would demonstrate, such as guessing keys and playing the piano with the keyboard covered by a towel."[31] We even learn that with respect to music Tchaikovsky "not only found no encouragement on the part of the administration, but even did not enjoy any special attention on the part of his comrades."[32] Far greater attention was enjoyed, for example, by Avgust Gerke, a classmate of Vladimir Taneev and the son of a pianist well known in Russia at the time.[33]

Throughout his life Tchaikovsky would have divided feelings about his former school. On the one hand, he was capable of nostalgic reminiscences of his years there and obviously considered it appropriate that his younger brothers and nephews follow in his footsteps and attend the school in their turn. On the other hand, various events and individuals associated with the school would forever cause in him re-

sentment and irritation to the point of hostility. His ambivalent attitude can be traced in his correspondence. After one of his visits there,
Tchaikovsky wrote to Modest on 6 September 1879, "I was at the
school. How I had dreamt of this moment—but I was greatly disappointed."[34] And when, in July 1887, Tchaikovsky ran into another of
the school's graduates, Baron Vasily Wrangel, on a train in Germany,
he was much displeased and "bolted" at the first opportunity.[35]

Two years before this, in 1885, on the occasion of the school's fiftieth anniversary, Tchaikovsky composed a chorus, "Song of the Students of the School of Jurisprudence" (the music has not been found),
and "The Jurists' March" in D major. In a letter to Mrs. von Meck dated
27 September 1885, he noted that he had not written a cantata for the
school's jubilee, although this had been commissioned by the organizers of the festivities, "but simply a chorus which the students are to
perform at the celebration. I had also to write the text of this chorus
myself."[36] A month later, he again wrote to Mrs. von Meck in irritation, "Now, when there remains but a month before the jubilee, they
ask me to write something else for the orchestra. On the one hand, to
write these pieces is extremely boring and unpleasant, but on the other
hand, to refuse would be embarrassing. So today, having sat over my
music paper quite some time, [I composed] the themes for the march
that I have nonetheless decided to write and arrange."[37] In a letter to
his sister-in-law of 4 November he complained even more openly. "To
refuse is impossible," he wrote, "and despite my extreme disgust I have
already been sitting in the same spot for several days plugging away at
this march."[38]

Tchaikovsky dedicated his "Song of the Students" to the school's
founder, Prince Pyotr of Oldenburg. The verses he wrote for this "can-
ticle" are filled with the rhetoric of a loyal subject of the crown, which
in Tchaikovsky's case was quite sincere, for if nothing else, the school
had succeeded in making of him a staunch monarchist:

> The pure flame of radiant truth
> Burned to the end in the soul
> Of the man by whom was laid
> The first stone of our school.
>
> In his tender concern for us
> He spared neither trouble nor strength,
> He made of us trustworthy sons
> For our fatherland.
>
> Student of the School! Like him,
> Hold high the flame of truth,

Deeply devoted to honor be,
The enemy be of any lie,

And, striving boldly for good,
Remember the maxim of your schooldays,
That firmly for the cause of truth
The student of the School must stand.[39]

Tchaikovsky flatly declined an invitation to attend the festivities, using the performance of his works as an excuse not to be there. He mentioned this to Vladimir Stasov in a letter of 27 November, in which he
confided that "it would be uncomfortable for me to be in Petersburg at
the present moment, because the celebrations in honor of the school
are going on there now and I have no wish to be present at these festivities, if only because I wrote at the request of the organizers a march
that is to be performed and that it would be torture for me to hear."[40]
Both works were presented in their author's absence on 5 December
1885. Modest, who attended the anniversary celebration, wrote his
brother the following day, "Your chorus, which everyone persists in
calling a cantata, was performed rather poorly, but was nevertheless an
enormous success. . . . The march, performed in the Assembly of Nobility during dinner, was also greeted very loudly."[41]

In the last years of his life, Tchaikovsky visited the school on only
a few occasions, once in connection with the affairs of his nephews
and once to conduct an orchestra made up of students of the school.
Alina Bryullova, the mother of Modest's later pupil Kolya Konradi, recalled that Tchaikovsky felt little fondness or commitment to his alma
mater, and particularly to its graduates. "He had another little eccentricity—his reluctance to meet with his former schoolmates from the
School of Jurisprudence, where he had felt very lonely and abandoned,"
she recollected. "I had two acquaintances, former schoolmates of his,
charming men and utterly antimusical, which ought to have constituted in Tchaikovsky's eyes an additional attraction: not having to talk
about music with laymen. They dined with me frequently. Pyotr Ilyich
would always look at me beseechingly: 'Do not invite D. and Sh. when
I visit you.' Of course, I granted his request unquestioningly. The only
exception Tchaikovsky made was for [Aleksey] Apukhtin and [Prince
Vladimir] Meshchersky. Why he was friendly with the latter is a mystery."[42]

One curious document has been preserved from the jubilee year: a
letter to Tchaikovsky from his classmate the poet Aleksey Apukhtin
cleverly stylized in eighteenth-century epistolary language. In it Apukhtin, under the joking pretense of thanking Tchaikovsky for having

written the chorus and thus having absolved him of such a burden, bitingly and hilariously ridicules the coming anniversary and their alma mater in general. The students of the school are referred to as "castrati" and the school itself branded as having been "created for sneaks and philanderers."[43] The letter obviously suggests that the same feelings of contempt and mockery were shared by author and addressee. Still, as was characteristic for their milieu, this attitude toward the school and its graduates did not prevent Apukhtin from writing a poem—and a fine one at that—for the anniversary, "Our celebration, friends, is both bright and sad," recited at the jubilee by Vladimir Gerard in Apukhtin's name.[44]

The years of adolescence shape the major constituents of the individual psyche. No experience undergone in this period is ever entirely lost. It is important to explore the origin of the ambiguities manifest in Tchaikovsky's attitude toward the School of Jurisprudence. What led him to accept a commission to celebrate his alma mater with a hymn while declining all official invitations to visit it or to shun most of his former schoolmates, with the exceptions of Apukhtin and Prince Meshchersky? What so linked the composer with these two that he felt comfortable in their presence but not in that of anyone else from the school? The answer almost certainly lies in Tchaikovsky's emotional entanglements during his seven years at the School of Jurisprudence, for it was this aspect of his experience there, more than any teachers or lectures, that was to leave the deepest and most lasting mark upon him.

CHAPTER THREE

Special Friendships

By all accounts, the same effortless charm that had made Tchaikovsky the "universal pet" within his own family circle quickly ensured his popularity at the School of Jurisprudence. His classmate Fyodor Maslov stresses that "Tchaikovsky was a favorite not only of his fellow students but also of the administration," adding that "no one else enjoyed such widespread affection and liking."[1] Another classmate, Vladimir Gerard, confirms this view: "His gentleness and tact in his relationships with all his fellow students made Pyotr Ilyich everybody's darling. I do not remember him ever having any serious quarrel or enmity with anyone."[2]

Similar testimony comes to us from other schoolmates as well. Even Vladimir Taneev told Modest personally that "Tchaikovsky had been everybody's pet," while in Taneev's memoirs the sole mention of Tchaikovsky is the assertion that the future composer was considered one of the handsomest students in the senior course.[3] Aleksandr Mikhailov, who was four classes below the composer at the school, has left us an engaging portrait of Tchaikovsky the student: "Always pensive, preoccupied with something or other, with a slight but charming smile and girlishly pretty, he would appear among us in his little jacket with the sleeves rolled up and spend hours on end at the piano in the music room."[4]

It is no secret that adolescence is a period fraught with erotic and emotional confusion. It is a time when patterns of future sexual behavior are developed, or possibly imposed, through the singular and

31

often nebulous interaction of external circumstance and internal experience. Such essentially ungovernable factors as a sexually permissive or a sexually prohibitive environment, or the intensity—and the degree of reciprocity—of an adolescent fixation on a particular male or female acquaintance, can be instrumental in determining individual modes of sexual behavior. Tchaikovsky's lifelong homosexuality is a matter of record. It was acknowledged in print as early as 1934 by Soviet scholars with access to the Tchaikovsky archives at Klin.[5] To what extent Tchaikovsky's experiences at the School of Jurisprudence determined his homosexuality or fostered an already existing and perhaps inborn proclivity cannot, of course, be ascertained with any real accuracy. That his school years did, however, significantly influence his sexuality can hardly be doubted.

Both the fact of its being an all-male institution and the transitional age of its students contributed to the homoerotically charged atmosphere at the School of Jurisprudence. The rigid institutional structure, with its strong emphasis on discipline, conspired with the educational ideas of the time, which held that boys and girls should generally be discouraged from one another's company before reaching marriageable age. On the whole, society actively hampered early harmonization of physical and passional love in the adolescent mind. The ideal image of a woman that boys at the School of Jurisprudence, as at any boarding school, tended to bring with them from home was soon transformed into a precocious and ostentatious cynicism. In the company of one's peers, any manifestation of intense emotion with respect to a woman was most often regarded as weak and unmanly, provoking jeers and mockery.

This atmosphere was only intensified by those few seniors who had already experienced sexual relations during visits to prostitutes or "summer adventures" on their estates. All kinds of stories on the subject, often spiced with obscene details, were told to the juniors, who accepted them on faith, regardless of their (usually dubious) veracity. This is reflected, for instance, in a confession by Vladimir Taneev: "I did not understand at all what sexual relations consisted in, but everything that I heard in conversation with my fellow students about relations between the sexes was so dirty, cynical, revolting and ugly that I would have considered merely touching a woman the greatest of sins. With horror I drove any such thought out of my mind."[6] At the age of nineteen, Taneev accompanied a few of his bolder classmates to a bordello, but once there, he would have nothing to do with any of the women. In explaining his behavior, he refers to his youthful idealism;

to Christian views on carnal love, "which amount to a repudiation of women"; to his lack of experience; and, characteristically, to his fear of venereal disease.[7] Such attitudes were, for all the boasting of the seniors, largely typical of most students at the school. For various reasons of age, religion, personality, aesthetics, or hygiene, heterosexual affairs were usually postponed by all but the most daring and reckless of seniors until some indeterminate time after graduation.

For the most part, the blend of sensuality and sensitivity so acute during adolescence, combined with the marked absence of any female element within the walls of the school, led the boys instead to engage in sexual experimentation among themselves. Here, too, the common social behavior of sexually segregated groups came into play, with such patterns as real or symbolic initiations, mutual or unilateral attraction, love-hate relationships, and direct physical contact, from blows to embraces.[8] Moreover, under the conditions of communal life and lack of privacy at the school, masturbation inevitably turned from a "solitary vice" into mutual manipulation, and thus into a literally homosexual activity.

Other aspects of life at the school added to the homoerotic atmosphere. In the dancing lessons held once a week, the young men were naturally obliged to dance with each other, one taking the role of the gentleman and the other that of the lady.[9] The common bath gave the adolescents an opportunity to study attentively all the physical changes going on in their own bodies and those of their schoolmates and to note the difference in one another's physical development—another potential source of erotic concentration on each other.[10] And whatever the fear and disgust provoked by flogging, that practice could only stimulate the students' interest in, and perhaps morbid fixation on, the male buttocks. Psychologists have long pointed to the psychoerotic and even psychosexual impact of punishment by whipping a naked body. For all the participants in that act—the punishers, the punished, and those who witness the punishment—both the deep motivation and the ultimate consequences of the act may lead to sadomasochistic or homosexual gratification.[11]

On top of everything, there was the example of the seniors, who were already accustomed to finding a source of sexual gratification in relations with one another or by abusing the juniors. All in all, the environment at the school proved eminently favorable to a pervasive kind of "situational" homosexuality—that is, one in which the partners feel moved to commit a homosexual act by circumstances that seem beyond their individual control. With his universally attested

physical attractiveness, the young Tchaikovsky must have been particularly vulnerable to this kind of pressured homosexuality at the
school.

In many instances, of course, the homoerotic impulse extended no
further than one boy's vaguely amorous crush on another. Thus, for
example, one Russian contemporary of Tchaikovsky offers a surprisingly candid account of his infatuation with a fellow student:

> I have never experienced true homosexual sensations. But I re-
> call that between the ages of twelve and thirteen the appear-
> ance of one of my classmates of the same age as I used to cause
> me a mild sexual excitement. He had very delicate skin and
> hair that, though cut naturally, was like that of a girl. Undoubt-
> edly for this reason his presence would please me: I liked to
> pinch his neck lightly, to embrace his waist. I never thought
> about his sex or about the possibility of physical relations with
> him, and I did not even dream to see him naked, but nonethe-
> less his image often appeared in my erotic dreams: I would
> dream of some part of his body naked (not his genitals, but, for
> instance, his arm or shoulders), of embracing him and kissing
> his cheeks, all of which would lead to a nocturnal emission.
> This is the only recollection related to homosexuality from my
> entire existence. Still, we never exchanged a tender word or
> any manifestation of "special friendship." I believe that the
> only reason for my erotic emotions was the delicacy of this
> boy's skin.[12]

But relations between the students ran the full gamut of expression, from such barely acknowledged infatuation to outright debauchery. This was true not only of the School of Jurisprudence but also of
other, comparable institutions throughout Europe. Similar adolescent
attachments in British boarding schools have long been familiar. "One
thing at Harrow very soon arrested my attention," writes another contemporary of Tchaikovsky, the British writer, poet, and art historian
John Addington Symonds, in a candid autobiographical passage. "It
was the moral state of the school. Every boy of good looks had a female
name, and was recognized either as a public prostitute or as some big-
ger fellow's 'bitch.' Bitch was the word in common usage to indicate a
boy who yielded his person as a lover. The talk in the dormitories and
the studies was incredibly obscene. Here and there one could not avoid
seeing acts of onanism, mutual masturbation, the sports of naked boys

in bed together. There was no refinement, no sentiment, no passion; nothing but animal lust in these occurrences."[13]

In Russia, as in Britain, complaints about homosexuality were not unique to any single school. Of St. Petersburg's various military academies for sons of the nobility, the Page Corps was flatly called by one writer "a school of debauchery,"[14] and a (fictional) student of the Corps was made the hero of an obscenely explicit homosexual poem entitled "Adventures of a Page."[15] The Junker School was likewise undistinguished in its morals, as the youthful and little-known pornographic (and strongly homoerotic) poems of one of Russia's greatest poets, Mikhail Lermontov, bear witness.[16] And the Cadet Corps was described by one of its alumni as "a sort of special world, part barracks and part monastery, where the vices of both are combined. There is no sensual depravity . . . that has not occurred there. Its door is wide open to all vices, while not a single measure is taken to suppress them."[17] According to one story, the War Minister, Prince Chernyshev, once summoned the Inspector of Military Schools, Yakov Rostovtsev, and relayed to him the tsar's order that homosexuality be dealt with more firmly in the military academies. "After all," the minister added, "it has a harmful effect on the boys' health." "I beg to differ, Your Excellency," replied Rostovtsev. "To be frank, when I was in the Page Corps, many of us engaged in this; I myself was involved with Traskin [later a prominent general], and our health was not affected in the least!" Prince Chernyshev roared with laughter.[18]

The administration of the School of Jurisprudence, against its own strictest prohibitions, seems by the time of Tchaikovsky's arrival to have regarded the sexual play of its students as inevitable and accordingly dismissed it as a cause of concern unless public scandal threatened. Such scandals were rare at the school, although we hear of one curious episode concerning an "unspecified sickness"—most likely masturbation—that caused the expulsion of a student in the early 1840s as a lesson to the others. The motive for the expulsion was supplied by alarmed relatives of the boy, who themselves became aware of the "vice" in their ward and asked the director to "take measures." The action prompted a storm of indignation from the rest of the students. "What if the whole world were to take it into its head to act in this way?" the former student Vladimir Stasov later wrote with feeling and understanding. "Why, most likely half of Russia would have to be expelled from some place or other, from schools, universities, regiments, monasteries, anywhere you like, all in the name of the most pure and perfect morality."[19]

A more significant episode, illustrating the relaxed and tolerant attitude of the students at the School of Jurisprudence toward the homosexual behavior of their fellows, is reported at length by Taneev.[20] In 1860, a year after Tchaikovsky's graduation from the school, a student of the third form, Vladimir Zubov, waylaid and raped a younger student in the park at Pavlovsk, outside St. Petersburg. Though word of the incident spread swiftly among the students of the school, the administration, being either unaware of what had happened (in which case one can only marvel at the students' unanimity in forestalling any complaint) or unwilling to take action (in which case the attitude of the administration is far from trivial), did nothing. Taneev, therefore, took matters into his own hands, calling a meeting of the entire senior course to try Zubov for the rape.

In the parody of a trial that followed, Taneev himself played the role of prosecutor. Not one but several students came forward to act as counsels for the defense, the gist of their argument being that Zubov's action was a private matter and public intervention was therefore unwarranted—an odd finding for students of the law. Student sentiment ran clearly in favor of Zubov, and Taneev admits to resorting to a bit of verbal sleight of hand in order to win a conviction, asking not whether Zubov should or should not be expelled from school but whether he should be ostracized by the students or denounced for his crime to the administration. By a "vast majority," the student assembly voted to ostracize Zubov. It is obvious that they condemned Zubov not out of indignation at the outrage he had committed but in order to prevent disclosure of the episode to the administration, which would have been forced to take disciplinary action when the incident became public. In essence, then, the students acted in the interest of Zubov.

The episode underscores the evident indifference of the students of the school to any moral principle regarding homosexuality. It was, after all, not a question simply of a secret vice, of two people caught in the act, but of an older boy who had forcibly raped a younger boy. This point in particular should be borne in mind when discussing the speculations that Tchaikovsky himself might have died as the victim of a "court of honor" imposed upon him by his former classmates from the School of Jurisprudence. As can be seen in Zubov's case, these students were singularly disinclined to persecute anyone on such grounds. In fact, their attitude is expressed pointedly in a ribald school anthem glorifying the pleasures of homosexuality that is preserved in an uncensored foreign edition of Russian pornographic poetry.[21] This cheerfully obscene text, similar to those penned by the young Lermontov, circulated clandestinely among the students of the School of Jurisprudence and was almost certainly known to Tchaikovsky and his peers. It and similar compositions were at that time the very stuff of the folklore of boarding schools for boys.

All this pertains to the physical and situational phenomena of adolescent homosexuality, paralleled in other sexually segregated communities, such as prisons or the army. The urge for sexual release tends to make such practices common. Indeed, it took strong will or commitment to abstain from participating in them. As his life and letters amply demonstrate, Tchaikovsky possessed neither. Though highly conscious of ethical standards and strictly observing them in society, he never extended moral judgments into the realm of sexuality. He experienced constant difficulty in resisting the temptations of gambling and alcohol, and it would go against the logic of his pliant character—incapable as he was of withstanding peer pressure, not to mention his adolescent sexual urges—to deny a very high probability of his actual involvement in erotic games or sexual play with his companions at the school. The fact of the composer's youthful "sexual singularities" has been reluctantly admitted even by those Soviet scholars who have full access to documents that unfortunately remain beyond our reach.[22]

It should be stressed, of course, that such youthful homosexual practices, situationally abetted by an all-male environment and often simply confined to casual physical contact, do not affect the great majority of participants in their later acceptance of heterosexuality.[23] Thus, when confronted with a case, like Tchaikovsky's, of a lifelong homosexual orientation, the biographer must consider additional factors that may have induced or perpetuated the orientation. One such factor not infrequently responsible for what may be called "intentional," as distinct from "situational," homosexuality is a male adolescent's intense emotional fixation on a friend, ranging from hero worship to what have been called "special friendships," which have often been considered gravely sinful in many ecclesiastical establishments. At times, passionate involvement of one boy with another, even if not consummated sexually, may prove powerful enough to leave an indelible mark in the memory and to influence subsequent sexual preferences. This pattern of youthful romanticism in the relations of two adolescents is poignantly portrayed, for example, in Thomas Mann's novella *Tonio Kröger*, which is revealed by the recent publication of Mann's diaries to have been directly based on the experience of Mann's own youth.

Aleksandr Herzen, the nineteenth-century Russian memoirist and political activist, experienced in his youth the whole spectrum of adolescent "special friendship" with the future poet and revolutionary Nikolay Ogarev. Herzen describes this candidly in his splendid memoir *My Past and Thoughts.* "I do not know why a kind of monopoly is given to the memory of first love over the memory of youthful friendship," he muses. "The reason first love is so fragrant is that it forgets the difference of the sexes, that it is passionate friendship. For its part, friendship between youths has all the ardor of love and all its character: the same shy fear of touching on its feelings with a word, the same mistrust of oneself, the unconditional devotion, the same excruciating anguish at separation and the same jealous desire for exclusivity. For a long time I loved Nick, and loved him passionately, but could never resolve to call him my friend." Still, adds Herzen, "since 1827 we had been inseparable. In every memory of that time, specific and general, he is there in the foreground with his boyish features and his love for me."[24]

Even in the recollections of Vladimir Taneev, who elsewhere shows himself to be fundamentally homophobic, one can detect various nuances of similar experience. The most pronounced instance occurred as Taneev reached the senior course. Unable to withstand the tense homoerotic atmosphere at the school, Taneev gave in to a strong infatuation with a student from Tchaikovsky's class, the Fyodor Maslov mentioned earlier in connection with the whipping episode.

According to his memoirs, Taneev had already noticed Maslov in the preparatory class, where the latter had been "smaller than anyone else, thin and pale, and whose ears someone was always pulling." In 1858 both youths stayed at the school during Christmas vacation and became closer friends. Taneev's tone in describing Maslov comes very close to amorous passion. "The little boy had grown up," he writes. "He was the same age as I, but already graduating from the course. Pale, with large pensive eyes, thin and shapely, he seemed to me extraordinarily beautiful." In order to conquer Maslov, the rationalist Taneev took an unprecedented step: "I decided, whatever the cost, to win the sympathy and friendship of this youth to whom I was drawn. . . . I almost never talked to students from the other classes. Even to my own classmates I talked seldom. Never before had I gone up to anyone to start a particularly friendly or polite conversation. Maslov was totally unknown to me. I made an effort. . . . We became close very quickly. We spent all of Christmas at the school together."[25] Once while in the senior course Taneev organized an amateur performance in which Tchaikovsky, Maslov, and other seniors participated. With fond indulgence he comments on his friend's failure as an actor, "Only my dear Maslov, whom I considered a paragon of beauty and elegance, . . . made the worst possible mess of his role."[26]

Their friendship came under attack from all sides, chiefly because of Taneev's difficult character and his contempt for the other students, but still the two managed to remain friends to the end of their lives. It is conceivable that Taneev's intimacy with Maslov may have contributed to the antipathy between Taneev and Tchaikovsky, for Fyodor Maslov was also a close friend of Tchaikovsky's, especially at the start of the junior course. Later Maslov recalled, "When we entered the seventh form, Pyotr Ilyich was particularly friendly with Belyavsky, but I soon replaced the latter. During the second semester of the seventh form and the first semester of the sixth we were almost inseparable."[27]

It is quite likely that the majority of Tchaikovsky's friendships at the school were erotically innocent, though several were still close in the "special" sense. One friend who was very close both spiritually and emotionally was Vladimir Adamov, though he was only in the same class with Tchaikovsky a few months before he was promoted. The two shared a passionate love of music and a fond dream, never realized, of traveling together through Italy and Switzerland on foot. Modest tells us that Adamov became his brother's "true and intimate confidant" and that "their friendship was unbroken until the death of Vladimir Stepanovich [Adamov] in 1877; this event shook Pyotr Ilyich very deeply."[28] An early death unexpectedly cut short the brilliant career of this friend, of whom, in regard to work, Tchaikovsky had made for himself "a model that he sought in vain to imitate."[29]

Another early friend, Ivan Turchaninov, later recalled that he first met Tchaikovsky in the preparatory class and that they became closer when, from 1856 on, they both began to spend their holidays on Vasilyevsky Island, at the farther end of St. Petersburg, and therefore would make the trips there and back together. Still later, in the senior course, they took turns staying at one another's home while preparing for examinations, so that Turchaninov soon became a familiar figure in the Tchaikovsky household. After graduation, however, their ways parted and the two saw each other rarely.[30]

A shared aversion to mathematics apparently gave rise to Tchaikovsky's friendship with Lev Shadursky. In the fifth form, in 1854, the two were so "carried away and overjoyed when for the first time in their lives they succeeded, without any outside help or explanation, in solving an algebraic problem" that in their surprise and delight "they began to embrace one another."[31] In Shadursky, who was "by nature an aesthetician," Tchaikovsky found a kindred spirit as woefully unsuited to his role as a future bureaucrat as Tchaikovsky was himself.

Also among Tchaikovsky's intimate friends at the school was Vladimir Gerard, the future lawyer and public activist, with whom he became particularly close only in the last year of the senior course. The available evidence for an "erotic" element in their relations is slim, though Tchaikovsky's closeness to Gerard is attested by a photograph of the two of them together that was taken the year they graduated from the school and was hung near the composer's writing table at his last home in Klin, near Moscow.[32] Still, some scholars have insisted—with reference to unpublished documents—that the *Romeo and Juliet* Fantasy-Overture, though composed ten years later in 1869, arose out of Tchaikovsky's "agonizing and unrequited" love for Gerard.[33] Such a view would make suspect those parts of Gerard's memoirs where he somewhat ostentatiously implies Tchaikovsky's interest in the opposite sex.[34] On the other hand, it is also possible that this interest was in some part feigned for the purpose of reassuring both Gerard and himself that their affection was in no way out of the ordinary and that their friendship in fact conformed to the standards accepted by society.

Of course, from early childhood Tchaikovsky had been predisposed to close, though hardly erotic, friendships with women. Among his most lasting attachments was his friendship with his cousin Anna Merkling, some ten years his senior, to whom he would later dedicate his *Menuetto scherzoso*, op. 51, no. 3. According to Modest, they were bound together both by a mutual sympathy and by their love of mischief and practical jokes. His intimacy with the young and charming Annette suited perfectly the adolescent Tchaikovsky's delicate psychological disposition. The style of relationships among most of his male peers was tense and competitive, contrasting with the sense of ease and relaxation he felt in her company. "It was not enough for them to be together inseparably on holidays," writes Modest. "They would write to one another during the week and, interested in the slightest details of each other's lives, they would exchange the intimate secrets of their hearts."[35] The ambiguity of this somewhat amorous preoccupation seems reflected in the young Tchaikovsky's tendency toward slips of the tongue, faithfully reported by Modest, who of course had no idea of the Freudian theory of *lapsus linguae:* "Being absentminded, Pyotr Ilyich would at school call his friends 'Annette' and at home would call her . . . 'Lyolya.'"[34]

As Modest notes, "Lyolya" (a nickname properly derived from the female name Elena) was Aleksey Apukhtin.[37] Of all Tchaikovsky's friendships at the School of Jurisprudence, that with the poet Apukhtin stands out prominently. There is no doubt that it was the chief influence on Tchaikovsky's development and, above all, on the passional and erotic aspects of his maturation.

As an artist, Aleksey Apukhtin was one of the tragic figures of his time. His natural talent, according to the unanimous opinion of his contemporaries, was extraordinary, and at the outset of his literary career he was considered a prodigy by both his peers and his teachers. He entered the school's preparatory class in 1852 at age eleven. In the spring of the following year, he performed brilliantly on the entrance examination for the seventh form, and in the autumn he took another examination and moved up to the sixth form, where Tchaikovsky was then studying. According to Modest, even at this time Apukhtin possessed "an aura of 'future renown.'" Witty and elegant, the boy must have appeared uncommonly mature, and he so succeeded in impressing the authorities of the school that the "august founder" himself, Prince Pyotr of Oldenburg, singled him out for personal talks and even honored him with "letters written in his own hand." The school's director, Aleksandr Yazykov, followed suit, housing the budding celebrity in his own home when classes were not in session and working to get the young poet's verses into print. Even more notably, Apukhtin's work was encouraged by such luminaries as the novelist Ivan Turgenev and the foremost poet of the time, Afanasy Fet.[38]

Without question, Apukhtin holds a place as a prominent and popular figure in Russian lyric poetry of the second half of the nineteenth century. Nevertheless, his poetic output never measured up to the expectations of friends and acquaintances who saw in the boy genius a second Pushkin. Ultimately, his was a failure of ambition and accomplishment, explicable in part by his later poor health, suffering as he did from obesity and severe shortness of breath; in part by the inertia or sluggishness so common among the Russian nobility (for which Ivan Goncharov coined the term "oblomovism," after the passive hero of his famous novel *Oblomov*); and in part, not inconceivably, by his perpetual erotic and emotional turmoil.

Apukhtin's entrance into Tchaikovsky's life was dramatic, and it led to Tchaikovsky's break with his earlier intimate friend, Fyodor Maslov. Maslov recalls that in late 1853, when he emerged from the infirmary after an illness, he was shocked to see that his deskmate was no longer Tchaikovsky. "He was sitting with his new friend Apukhtin," writes Maslov. "A quarrel ensued. The former friends ceased to speak with one another." Although they later made up and were friendly for the rest of their lives, their "original intimacy was never restored," and Maslov was "never again friends with Apukhtin."[39] Maslov's account is most curious. The boys were only thirteen years old then. At this age, they would hardly have been able to see any erotic meaning in their relations. Intuitively Maslov might have sensed the difference in the attraction between his two friends and understood that mere friendship was not enough for them, but in this struggle for love he lost to an intellectually seductive rival.

It is clear that Tchaikovsky's relationship with Apukhtin constituted a crucial juncture in his adolescent experience. Modest writes that "from this time until their graduation from the school, he [Apukhtin] played an enormous role in Pyotr Ilyich's life."[40] Tchaikovsky was more attractive and better-looking than Apukhtin. According to the recollections of former students of the school, Apukhtin was at that time "a small, thin, blond youth with light-blue eyes."[41] Modest writes in his autobiography of recalling "a pale and skinny little student" whom he personally "found displeasing, but since he [Tchaikovsky] liked him, one had to like him."[42] Elsewhere he mentions that Apukhtin was "sickly, physically weak, and homely" and that "he was often ill and always went about with his cheek tied up."[43] This evidence suggests that the erotic initiative, whatever form it may have taken, must have originated with Apukhtin. At the same time, it is not hard to imagine the fascination the impressionable Tchaikovsky must have felt toward his brilliant new companion, who had cast a spell over many experienced and important adults. In Apukhtin, Tchaikovsky encountered something notably absent in his earlier environment: an individual of both intellectual power and emotional authority.

"I remember as if it were yesterday," their schoolmate Prince Vladimir Meshchersky recalled later, "our hall at the School of Jurisprudence and, strolling to and fro about it every evening, the two friends Apukhtin and Tchaikovsky."[44] Three poems by Apukhtin dedicated to the future composer have survived from the School of Jurisprudence period. The earliest of these, from 1855, is a parody of the poetic experiments of Tchaikovsky himself. Another, written the following year, is called "On the Way." In it Apukhtin recalls an outing with his friend in St. Petersburg. The theme of joyful bliss at the presence of his friend is heard distinctly in such lines as these, describing a boat ride along the Neva River:

> Everything fell silent. Unstirring is
> The sleepy wave—
> The heart breathes deep its freedom,
> And comfort fills the breast,
>
> And to the measured rocking
> Of the scintillating boat
> We keep silence, and hold our breath
> In sweet oblivion.[45]

The third poem, dated 5 July 1857, was a comic epistle from Apukhtin, who was spending the summer on his estate at Pavlodar, southwest of

Moscow, in central Russia. It was designed as a reply to a letter from
Tchaikovsky sent with no return address.[46]

Something about the style of their relationship seems implicit in
one of Apukhtin's finest poems, which he addressed to Tchaikovsky
twenty years later:

> You remember how, hiding in the music room,
>   Forgetting school and the world,
> We would dream of an ideal glory—
>   Art was our idol,
> And life for us was fanned by dreams.
> Alas, the years have passed, and with terror in our breast
>   We see that everything's behind us now
>   And the cold of death lies ahead.
> Your dreams came true. Scorning the beaten way,
> You obstinately struck a new path for yourself,
>   You took fame by storm and drank deep
>   Of this cup of poison.
> Oh, I know, I know how ruthlessly and long
> A harsh fate for this wreaked vengeance upon you
>   And how many prickly thorns
>   Are twined into your laurel wreath.
> But the clouds dispersed. Obedient to your soul,
>   The songs of bygone days revived,
>   And spite's craven babble
>   Before them faded and fell silent.
> While I, finishing the course an unrecognized poet,
> Take pride that I guessed the spark of divinity
>   In you, then scarcely glimmering,
> Now burning with so powerful a light.[47]

Although written with the advantage of hindsight, the poem appears
to contain a basic emotional truth, which seems confirmed by the
poem's effect on Tchaikovsky himself, who wrote to his brother Anatoly from San Remo on 21 December 1877/2 January 1878, "I received
a letter today from Lyolya with a wonderful poem that made me shed
many tears."[48]

After 1853 the attraction between Tchaikovsky and Apukhtin continued to grow in strength. But their friendship was rather less smooth
than Apukhtin's romantic verses might lead us to assume. The precocious young poet possessed a difficult—and, in the view of many, ob-
noxious—character. Spoiled by family and teachers alike, he was "especially despotic with those whom he loved."[49] Even though, as

Modest claims, Tchaikovsky "was unusually complaisant concerning anything that did not touch the depths of his mind and heart,"[50] the friends had frequent fallings-out, which sometimes lasted quite some time, but were always followed by reconciliation.

Matters were further complicated by Apukhtin's awareness, even at that time, of his own unambiguous homosexual inclinations. His sexual preference was common knowledge during his life and is often referred to in the memoirs, diaries, and correspondence of his contemporaries. Apukhtin himself, in beautiful lines written when he was seventeen and still a student at the School of Jurisprudence, recalls a passionate love for (as is clear from the context) a male companion that drove him to thoughts of suicide:

> I shall tell you how, in unexpected melancholy,
>   Seeking the boundary of desires,
> I once fell in love—a love so strange
>   That long I did not dare believe it.
> God knows whether pent emotions burst importunately
>   To pour forth suddenly on anyone at all,
> Or imagination was seething with idle force,
>   Or my breast was breathing sensuality,—
> I only know that in a life of loneliness
>   Those were the best years,
> And that I so ardently, honestly and deeply
>   Shall never love again.
> And what then? Unrecognized, ridiculed, broken,
>   At the feet of commonplace vanity
> My fervent dreams, with sudden darkness covered,
>   Have fallen all about.[51]

The poem is striking for its conscious articulation of the uncommon nature of his passion. We know of several crushes Apukhtin had on other schoolmates during these years—among them, Boris Karataev, Nikolay Martynov, Vladimir Yuferov, and Vladimir Adamov, to whom, as to Tchaikovsky, verses of his are dedicated. Eventually, to all appearances, he came to take his sexual orientation as a matter of course. Vladimir Taneev, with characteristically sharp disapproval, notes Apukhtin's early and open involvement with men. "On leaving school . . . owing to his unfortunate vice, he lowered and abased himself, and perished," Taneev writes. "He spent his time in the most evil and despicable society, made up of everything that was the very worst of societies—the Russian aristocracy and the guards."[52]

One can only conjecture about how, or how much, Apukhtin's sexual orientation might have influenced Tchaikovsky's own attitudes and conduct. In view of the poet's forceful personality and the future composer's impressionable sensitivity, it is not unlikely that with Apukhtin, Tchaikovsky first experienced the union of physical and passional eroticism and began to realize the direction of his own sexuality. Certainly Apukhtin, cultivated and erudite as he was, would have been precisely the one to supply his friend with wide-ranging arguments justifying homosexuality—historical precedents from antiquity to the Renaissance, sociological data, and common experience. For many years to come, in fact, Tchaikovsky would be a regular frequenter of Apukhtin's circle of homosexual friends and lovers. This is not to say that during his school years Tchaikovsky already conceived of himself as exclusively homosexual. In most respects, his amorous experiences probably did not differ radically from the homosexual play of the rest of his fellow students, for whom it was a transient phase and mattered little more than as a pleasurable and convenient release of sexual energy. In fact, right up to the time of his marriage, Tchaikovsky would continue to believe himself capable of experiencing a "normal" attraction to the opposite sex, despite his contemporaneous homosexual activities.

One must not overlook, even in this early period, the creative dimension of Tchaikovsky's relationship with Apukhtin. A former student recalled that "art within the walls of the school found a refuge only in the intimate circles that gathered around the most talented personalities and found expression only in the collective reading and recitation of literary works, in the amateur performance of musical pieces, in group visits to the theater, and in heated debates about art."[53] Very likely the circle around Apukhtin, so much in favor with the administration, was just such a focal point for a chosen few, Tchaikovsky among them. From their school years, there existed between the classmates Apukhtin and Tchaikovsky—on a playful level, of course— a "poetic" rivalry. Tchaikovsky actively contributed to the poetry section of the *School Herald*, a journal that Apukhtin, already making a name for himself as a poet in the capital and beyond, had founded. The clumsy verse compositions of the young Tchaikovsky, "which appeared in almost every issue of the school journal, would always of course elicit the friendly laughter of his fellow students and . . . Apukhtin would hasten to respond immediately to every appearance in print of his unlucky pen-fellow."[54] He poked good-natured fun, for example, at Tchaikovsky's versifying efforts in the jocular epistle "The Poet's Genius," written in 1855:

Marvelous genius! Into the darkness of the abyss
The colossus has thrown his verse—
Twisting the neck of Pegasus,
Roping his muse with a lasso,
Charging headlong, heeling back toward Parnassus,
The powerful giant gallops along.[55]

Tchaikovsky, however, did not take offense. Nor did he stop writing verses. We have not only his playful poetic improvisations but also texts written by him for his own songs, choruses, and opera arias. Later, the poet and the composer would collaborate on a number of projects.

In 1859, their last year at the School of Jurisprudence, Apukhtin's mother died unexpectedly. Having lost his own mother five years before, Tchaikovsky would have understood his friend's grief as no one else could. No doubt he sought to help Apukhtin through this difficult period. Sharing this sad experience—which must have brought back keenly the pain of Tchaikovsky's own loss—would not only have brought the two friends still closer but may also have contributed, consciously or otherwise, to the creation of an adolescent myth of an ideal woman, like their mothers, whom they would never find in their own lives.

When discussing the possible homosexual influences on Tchaikovsky during his School of Jurisprudence period, one other individual must be taken into account—Prince Vladimir Meshchersky. Destined to play a prominent role in Russia's political history at the turn of the century, becoming a leading reactionary journalist and the adviser and confidant of the last two tsars, Alexander III and Nicholas II, Meshchersky grew into a striking though mostly detested public figure. His career and social status were marked by a high degree of ambiguity and by repeated scandals, owing both to his strong political views and to his unconcealed homosexual activities, which were seen by many as outrageous. "Prince of Sodom and citizen of Gomorrah" he was called by the philosopher Vladimir Solovyov in a biting epigram.[56]

Soviet biographers have striven to avoid placing any emphasis on Tchaikovsky's friendship with Meshchersky, despite the fact that the sources make it patently clear that for a long time the two enjoyed a close relationship. Even though Meshchersky was two classes ahead of Tchaikovsky at the School of Jurisprudence, there is evidence that they became friendly while still at school, continuing their relations after Tchaikovsky's graduation. In a letter to his sister written on 10 March 1861, Tchaikovsky described Meshchersky as a "warm, likable person."[57] It seems that the sympathy was mutual. For many years Meshchersky's name continued to surface in Tchaikovsky's correspondence in reference to various favors the prince granted to him and to his brothers. In addition, Meshchersky was to serve as an important link between the composer and the court.

In Modest's biography, Meshchersky's name is mentioned only in a short footnote on the complete break between the two friends in the last years of Tchaikovsky's life. This may be explained by the fact that the prince, still alive when Modest's work was published, was universally hated and despised by both liberal and not so liberal circles. This would also account for Modest's omission of Meshchersky's name in his discussion of Tchaikovsky's friends at the School of Jurisprudence.

Modest's only other omission in the list of his brother's friends from that period is no less telling. This is his concealment of Tchaikovsky's relationship with Sergey Kireev, who graduated from the School of Jurisprudence in 1865. Vladimir Zhdanov in his commentary to *Letters to His Relatives* notes frankly that Kireev and Tchaikovsky "were bound by a 'special friendship' during their years at the School of Jurisprudence."[58] That Tchaikovsky's attachment to the youth was indeed very strong is also attested by two photographs of Kireev that hung on the wall by the composer's writing table at his home in Klin.[59] It may be that Modest was worried by the fact that Kireev was only thirteen years old when he met Tchaikovsky, who was then a senior. Only once does Modest inadvertently admit the existence of their relationship. He relates his brother's own recollection from his last school years of how once, while walking at study time through the *dormitory* of the junior course with one of his friends ("Unfortunately I do not recall his name," interjects Modest), he ventured to express his certainty that he would become a famous composer. "Having said this, he grew frightened by the madness of his words, but to his surprise his listener did not laugh at him, and not only did he not contradict him, he even supported him in this self-conceit, which touched the unrecognized musician to the depths of his soul."[60] Of all Tchaikovsky's school friends, only Sergey Kireev would at this time have been in the junior course. According to the school regulations, the seniors were discouraged from visiting even the classrooms of the juniors, much less their dormitories. It would seem that the young Tchaikovsky had his own special reasons for disregarding these prohibitions.

In congratulating Modest on his graduation from the school in 1870, Tchaikovsky wrote to him on 26 March, "Vividly I recall what I myself experienced eleven years ago, and I wish that your joy may not be mixed with the bitterness I felt then . . ."[61] This statement is immediately followed by a cut, which in all Soviet editions of Tchaikov-sky's letters is inevitably connected, as close scrutiny proves, with some homosexual context. It is quite possible that the end of the sentence omitted here (by Modest or by the Soviet censors) could have read, "because of my separation from Sergey Kireev." They appear to have continued to see each other for several years following Tchaikovsky's graduation. A letter of 10 March 1861 to his sister, Aleksandra, with whom Tchaikovsky was particularly cautious in his correspondence, alluded indirectly to these "special relations." "My heart is in the same state," he wrote. "The *holy family* [the Kireevs] has so captured it that it allows no one else within the distance of a cannon shot. Seryozha [Sergey] has been ill for three months already, but is now recovering."[62] It is suggestive that he wrote first about his friend's health and only then, as if out of necessity, mentioned Sergey's sister Sofya, even though he wanted—consciously or instinctively—Aleksandra to believe that it was in fact with this Sofya Kireeva that he had fallen in love: "Sophie came for a short while from Saratov, and I had the good fortune to see her at the theater. She has grown terribly pretty."[63]

One of Tchaikovsky's early songs, "My genius, my angel, my friend," composed in the late 1850s, may have been dedicated to Sergey Kireev. The date of composition coincides with the peak of their relationship, and the thirteen dots indicating the letters of the unspelled dedication match the number of letters in the Russian dative case of Kireev's first and last names.[64]

It is difficult to say much about the later development of Tchaikovsky's relationship with Kireev. In 1867, when he was already in Moscow, the composer met him at the theater, as he described to his brother Anatoly in a letter of 31 October: "The other day I met Kireev at the opera, and today he visited me; you can guess how pleased I was. How sweet he is, though not so handsome as formerly." In the same letter, he noted that "yesterday I spent the entire day with Kireev, dined with him, and later went with him to the gypsies [that is, to a restaurant with a gypsy chorus, a favorite diversion of the Russian aristocracy], whom he likes very much."[65] The detail is interesting: at twenty-two Kireev, though "sweet," is "not so handsome as formerly," which is to say, during their time at the School of Jurisprudence—an evident indication of Kireev's weakened erotic appeal for Tchaikovsky by this time. Little is known of Kireev's subsequent life, save that he became justice of the peace at Kaluga, near Moscow, and died in 1888.[66]

There is much else that may come to light. A group photograph of the twentieth graduating class of the School of Jurisprudence has been preserved. In the first row, there is an attractive adolescent whose neighbor has pressed up against him, tenderly holding his hand. The attractive adolescent is Tchaikovsky. The name of the classmate cannot be established, for lack of documentation, which is unfortunate, since of the thiry-two young men in the photograph, only Tchaikovsky and his friend constitute a couple in such obvious and close physical contact with one another.

CHAPTER FOUR

Man About Town

On 12 May 1859, Tchaikovsky left the School of Jurisprudence and two weeks later began his civil service career in the first administrative division of the Department of Justice in St. Petersburg. His duties were not particularly burdensome, and he set about meticulously and industriously preparing documents of various sorts. Tchaikovsky himself would write in one of his letters that he made "a poor civil servant," but the archival evidence quite contradicts his modest self-assessment.[1]

This St. Petersburg period of Tchaikovsky's life—beginning with his entry into civil service at the Ministry of Justice and ending with his studies at the St. Petersburg Conservatory—is the least satisfactorily explored by his biographers. This is unfortunate. It was during these years that Tchaikovsky experienced the inscrutable accumulation of creative energies that burst forth shortly afterward. He entered this period of his life an average young man, scarcely distinguishable from the host of his peers and contemporaries. He emerged from it a musician of promise, already noticed by the luminaries of the day. It seems to have been a confusing and unsettling time in Tchaikovsky's life and, despite the appearance of frivolity and high living, not at all an easy one, especially at first. It was marked by strong conflicts between his inborn timidity and a striving for social self-assertion, between a sense of responsibility toward work and family and the appeal of sensual pleasures, between the temptation of idleness and the vague but growing demands, only gradually realized by himself and others, of his creative instinct.

That Tchaikovsky's biographers, beginning with Modest, tend to bypass the particulars of these conflicts, hastening instead to concentrate on the subsequent outburst of his creativity, may be, at least in part, a deliberate strategy aimed at concealing the circumstances of his private life. During this "society interlude," Tchaikovsky evidently found numerous opportunities to engage in fleeting homosexual affairs with members of his own class. His available correspondence contains unmistakable hints of such activities, though little can be established with certainty, owing to the multiple layers of censorship to which the published texts have been subjected.

To appreciate properly the diverse facets of Tchaikovsky's intimate life and social behavior, it is necessary to set them against the background of sexual mores within Russia as a whole in the latter half of the nineteenth century and within the diverse milieus in which Tchaikovsky found himself during his life. Russian culture has historically exhibited a peculiar mixture of a theoretical and superficial prudery and an extraordinary moral laxity in everyday life. Neither the severe injunctions of ecclesiastical authorities nor the no less severe prescriptions of the *Domostroy*, the medieval code of family conduct, could prevent the Russian populace—in particular, its male component—from indulging in any sexual practice or vice it may have fancied. For all its influence, the Orthodox church never fully succeeded in suppressing a powerful pagan heritage and was at times forced even to accommodate the ancient orgiastic fertility cults.

Within the upper classes, sexual licentiousness had been a norm of life during many centuries of serfdom and, indeed, had long since ceased to be regarded as corrupt in any true sense. Never having undergone the chivalric experience of European knighthood, the Russian nobility possessed neither an ideal of courtly love nor an elaborate code of honor. It had likewise known no consistent moral education, since the government did not conceive of itself as the guardian of public morality. As a consequence, the concept of personal integrity inevitably suffered. Then, beginning in the late eighteenth century, the educated classes were exposed to a flood of Western, mostly French, literature of libertinage, which, even if not officially allowed, was easily available in the underground. Such exposure contributed to the development of a willfully frivolous mode of life within fashionable society and the upper strata of the intelligentsia, reflected in such masterworks of the Romantic period of Russian literature as Aleksandr Push-

kin's *Eugene Onegin* and Mikhail Lermontov's *A Hero of Our Time,*
which discuss at length the art of seduction, among other fashionable
matters.

By the middle of the nineteenth century, much of the earlier sentimental romanticism regarding amorous relationships had died out,
and a substantial portion of the gentry and intelligentsia—precisely the
strata, in fact, to which Tchaikovsky belonged—had largely lost the
religious or economic grounds for observing strictures on sexual indulgence. Furthermore, sexual license had become one of the many individual responses to political despotism. It is thus not surprising that
some of Tchaikovsky's contemporaries found Italy, traditionally considered the country of sexual freedom, incomparably more restrictive
in this regard than Russia, "where under the despotic regime the mores
are so liberal."[2] Even so conservative a figure as the literary critic Nikolay Strakhov would say, with a mixture of grief and admiration, to
the cultural historian Vasily Rozanov, a great expert in sexual matters,
that "the Europeans, seeing in their countries the multitudes of Russian tourists, are struck by their talents and their refinement in debauchery."[3]

This relaxed atmosphere in the Russia of his time proved intoxicating to the young Tchaikovsky, fresh from the rigid confines (for all
its secret dissipation) of the School of Jurisprudence and suddenly free
to indulge fully his whims and desires without restriction. "In the first
years after his graduation from the school," writes Modest of his
brother, "he remained the former adolescent schoolboy. The same insatiable thirst for merriment, the same continual pursuit of pleasure
at all cost, the same superficial view of the serious aspects of life, all
remained as much a part of him in his liberty as they had been at
school."[4]

In his mature years Tchaikovsky developed a genuine phobia about
large crowds of people and reacted to any crowded gathering with extreme discomfort. The mere thought of public meetings or private parties where there would be many people whom he knew hardly or not
at all could drive him to desperation, and in the year he died, he was
even prepared to turn back halfway to Cambridge University, where he
was headed to receive an honorary doctorate.[5] Yet, nothing of this sort
can be seen in Tchaikovsky's behavior during most of the period from
1859 to 1865. He gave himself up to high living and the social whirl.
At the same time, his strenuous efforts to establish himself in St. Petersburg society ran directly counter to his natural timidity, and the
young man went through agonies. Several years later, he would confess
in a letter to his brother Anatoly, "I find it funny to recall, for example,

how I agonized over not being able to enter high society and be a fashionable man! Nobody knows how much I suffered on account of this and how much I struggled to overcome my incredible shyness, which at one time even reached the point where I couldn't sleep or eat for two days in anticipation of a dinner at the Davydovs'!!!"[6]

But he persevered, and in company this shyness seems to have been hardly evident, and when feeling relaxed, he could be thoroughly charming. One friend of those and later years, the music critic Hermann Laroche, insists that "the Tchaikovsky of the 1860s and the Tchaikovsky of the 1880s were two different persons." In his early twenties the future composer cut, according to Laroche, the classic figure of "a young man about town, clean-shaven in spite of the then already universal fashion and dressed somewhat carelessly in clothes from an expensive tailor but not quite new, with charmingly simple and, as I thought at the time, rather cold manners; he had countless acquaintances, and when we strolled together along Nevsky [Prospect, or Avenue] there was no end to the greetings and bows." Laroche goes on to stress that it was by and large "the elegant people" who greeted his friend.[7]

In a characteristic succession of moods, Tchaikovsky expressed himself in a letter to his sister, Aleksandra, of 23 October 1861:

I confess that I feel a great weakness for the Russian capital. What can one do? I have become too accustomed to it! Everything that is dear to my heart is in Petersburg, and a life outside it is for me utterly impossible. Besides, when one's pocket is not too empty, one's soul is merry. . . . Do you know my weakness? When I have money in my pocket I always squander it on pleasures. This is base and foolish, I know; strictly speaking, I can have no money at all for pleasures: there are enormous debts demanding payment, there are necessities of the very first order, but I (again because of my weakness) disregard all this and enjoy myself. Such is my character. How shall I end? What does the future hold? It is frightening to think about this. I know that sooner or later (but more likely sooner) I shall no longer have the strength to struggle with the difficult side of life and shall smash myself to pieces, but until then I enjoy life as I can and sacrifice everything for this enjoyment. But here it is, two weeks already of troubles from every quarter: at work things are going extremely badly, my rubles have long since melted away and I am unhappy in love; but all this is nonsense—the time will come again for having fun. Some-

times I'll even cry for a bit, but then I'll take a stroll on foot
along Nevsky, on foot return home—and my mood is already
better.[8]

These thoughts and sentiments, even if fashionably stylized to fit the
stereotype of a young dandy, nonetheless seem to reflect Tchaikovsky's
genuine concerns—concerns no different from those of an average
youth of his class on the threshold of maturity. His extraordinary spiritual potentialities were yet to be discovered, and his "libido"—in the
broad, energetic sense of the word—turned naturally to hedonistic pursuits, which at his age are all but inseparable from the erotic.

Through his friendship and close companionship with Apukhtin,
Tchaikovsky was inevitably introduced into homosexual circles. His
letters leave no doubt that at this time his affection for the poet was
strong and tender. "I see Apukhtin every day," he wrote to Aleksandra
on 10 March 1861. "In my court he continues to hold the position of
best jester and in my heart that of best friend."[9] Modest tells us that
during this period Apukhtin's "inventive humor and inexhaustible delight in boyish pranks enthralled his group of rakes like himself, and
Pyotr Ilyich, when he wished, was always a glad and welcome guest
among them."[10]

After graduating from the School of Jurisprudence, Apukhtin pur-
sued his amusements openly and with no attempt to conceal his homosexual proclivities. "Wholeheartedly he mingled with the gilded
youth of Petersburg," recalled one contemporary, "and shared the passions of their 'frenzied nights.' . . . One fine summer evening Petersburg's high society, while [promenading] on the point of Elagin Island
[and] observing the setting sun, caught sight of a most eccentric amazon in a fantastic costume surrounded by brilliant young cavalrymen.
The cavalcade galloped past twice, and many of his acquaintances finally and not without surprise recognized the mysterious amazon to
be Apukhtin."[11] Another memoir writer noted that the walls of Apukhtin's apartment were covered with photographs of pages and guards-
men.[12]

The poet's biographers suggest that Apukhtin was spoiled by his
success, that he was vain and weak-willed and had a penchant for frivolous entertainments. There were endless banquets, picnics, parties,
rides, and shows. Naturally, in the atmosphere of the society salons,
Apukhtin, acknowledged as a brilliant wit, would eclipse the shy
Tchaikovsky. Apukhtin's epigrams, puns, and jokes were on everyone's
lips, and such influential society hostesses as Ekaterina Sushkova-
Khvostova, Mikhail Lermontov's onetime companion, copied out his
verses into their guest albums.

But, as a musician, Tchaikovsky soon distinguished himself from the swarm of society amateurs by singing fashionable arias and songs or playing the piano with improvisatory skill. Few others could perform on the spot an operatic tune heard for the first time just the night before or satirical ballads from some musical comedy. In addition, Tchaikovsky could compose uncomplicated arrangements for a family production, write a waltz or a musical joke, and even sing an Italian coloratura aria. He wrote of such pastimes in one letter to his sister: "I went with Apukhtin to say good-bye [to one of their female society acquaintances]. Apukhtin presented her with some verses and was so moved that he started sobbing. I cannot stand such vulgarities. I promised to write her a song, but I was lying. She is a lovely person."[13] Though himself very sentimental by nature, Tchaikovsky disliked any public demonstration of sentimentality.

Just being in Apukhtin's circle might well have led Tchaikovsky to homosexual relationships—not necessarily the casual street contacts that would come later, once he had decided to exile himself from high society and concentrate on his creative work, but more likely flings with members of his own class, which, in that milieu, could be kept fairly decorous, brief, and superficial. It was a sort of comedy of manners, perhaps best characterized as "gay" in the original sense of "carefree" or "lighthearted." It was also during this period in his early manhood that Tchaikovsky, through Apukhtin and Meshchersky, made the acquaintance of the diplomat Prince Aleksey Golitsyn, a central figure in yet another homosexual circle, who would later live openly with his lover Nikolay Masalitinov. Golitsyn, while genuinely interested in culture, was not an easy person to get along with, being both possessive and unduly inquisitive. Yet, despite their occasional fallings-out, Golitsyn eventually became one of Tchaikovsky's intimate friends.

In sum, this demimonde existence gave Tchaikovsky full opportunity to satisfy his secret desires, and he took it as the path of least resistance. It seems unlikely that at this time he perceived his homosexual inclinations as uncontrollable or irreversible. Still, the milieu in which he found himself allowed the young Tchaikovsky to experience occasional sensual pleasures with little thought or pain—a milieu that Modest fails to describe in any significant detail. Yet, looking beyond Modest's equivocal language, it is difficult not to see an occasional allusion to his brother's amorous pursuits. "In the elegant salons, at the theater, in restaurants, and on strolls along Nevsky Prospect and in the Summer Garden at fashionables times of the day, in everything, everywhere, he sought and found the flowers of life's joys," Modest writes at one point. "The field of these flowers appeared boundless to him and there seemed to be enough of them for him to pick for his entire life, and nothing else did he know or wish to know."[14]

In the autumn of 1858, Tchaikovsky's father had been appointed director of the Technological Institute in St. Petersburg. Some time before, Ilya Tchaikovsky had entrusted his fortune to an engineer's widow of his acquaintance. That spring, in a disastrous business dealing, the widow had lost both Ilya's money and her own. At age sixty-two, Ilya found himself suddenly bankrupt. Despite a lengthy legal battle, the money was never recovered, and Ilya was forced to seek new employment. The directorship of the institute finally eased the family's financial situation and brought with it a spacious apartment. During the school year the new director's home became a favorite gathering place for students of the institute, and in the summer a country house outside the capital was rented by Ilya and thrown open to those poorer students who could not afford to go home for summer vacations. According to Modest, "the large Tchaikovsky family seemed to grow larger still by half a hundred young men." Students and family members alike joined in the summertime diversions and entertainments, and Pyotr, "as always and everywhere, was also popular here and became close friends with many of the technological students."[15]

On the threshold of his maturity, as during his adolescence, Tchaikovsky possessed a great personal charm that entranced all those around him. It is possible that his exceptional allure owed something to an unconscious erotic radiance. "It was impossible not to love him," recollects his society friend Konstantin de Lazari. "Everything, starting with his youthful appearance and his marvelous, intense gaze, made him irresistibly attractive. Most of all, it was his striking . . . modesty and his touching kindness. No other person could treat everyone so cordially, no one else possessed such a childlike, pure, and bright view of people. Everyone felt, in talking with him, a special warmth and caress in the sound of his voice, in his words, and in his glance."[16]

No less tellingly, the descriptions of Tchaikovsky's physical appearance and his mannerisms during his school years and later suggest that he frequented homosexual milieus. He is repeatedly called "girlishly pretty." The erotically charged atmosphere of these circles in which he moved during his "society interlude" most likely encouraged a nonchalant affectation in his manner and behavior at this time. Rarely in later years would he allow himself to display decidedly feminine mannerisms so openly in public. As Modest recalls, "he knew how to make the unacceptable permissible," his captivating charm forestalling criticism even of his passionate love of impersonating female dancers. Modest somewhat ruefully notes that he too "loved to do this, but those around me, both adults and peers, made fun of me and called it an affectation." His brother, however, "would do this openly and . . . would give full-scale performances that everyone applauded and no one saw as unsuitable for a boy, and his peers in fact took part in them with pleasure."[17]

Modest here seems still to be referring to his brother's school years. But in his own autobiography Modest speaks already of his brother's civil service period, when Tchaikovsky would take pains to explain to him "the difference between the positions of [individual] female performers" and, "dancing himself," would demonstrate what he considered proper ballet form, calling Modest "Savrenskaya (a third-rate female dancer of the Russian opera) and himself [Amalia] Ferraris [an Italian prima ballerina]—because of the fluidity and classicism of his movements."[18] Hermann Laroche and other critics would later casually suggest that even Tchaikovsky's music bore the imprint of his "feminine" nature.[19] This was a description the composer himself strongly disliked.[20]

Despite his outwardly relaxed behavior, Tchaikovsky in early manhood still remained in many ways an impressionable and timorous adolescent. Laroche writes that "he enjoyed excellent health, but was extraordinarily fearful of death, fearful even of anything that so much as hinted at death."[21] The thought that one of his relatives had died would haunt him "constantly and steadily," as he wrote in a letter of 1 December 1866.[22] His great fear of death may well have derived from his early experiences of the loss of his mother and the tragic death from scarlet fever of his boyhood friend Kolya Vakar. Certainly, this fear may have contributed to his emotional hypersensitivity, which, even by the standards of a highly sentimental age, was at times truly excessive.

At the Department of Justice, Tchaikovsky's attention was drawn to the sixteen-year-old clerk Efim Volkov, later a painter, "in the expression of whose eyes something special was to be felt."[23] He helped the young man in every way possible and even did what he could to pull strings for him. One can only guess what the "something special" may have been that Tchaikovsky discovered in Volkov's eyes, but the inclination to favor and support attractive young men remained with him until the end of his life.

During this same period he became friendly with Ivan Klimenko, an "attractive dark-haired young man with a flat Tatar face and small eyes."[24] An architect by training who eventually went to work for the Moscow-Kursk Railroad, Klimenko was also a passionate music lover. Though he never developed his own musical abilities and remained all his life only a dilettante, he was nonetheless able to recognize what he liked in music and why. According to Modest, Klimenko "attached himself [to Tchaikovsky] with all his soul and was one of the first who foretold to him his significance in Russian music." At the same time, since Klimenko possessed a great inborn sense of humor and power of observation, the relations between the two friends took on, as Modest puts it, "a particularly jocular tone that covered the warmest mutual affection."[25] Klimenko himself, later recalling their first encounter, confessed that Tchaikovsky immediately "captivated" him: "[Tchaikovsky was] very young, extraordinarily affable, well-mannered, infinitely modest, and somehow peculiarly handsome. . . . From that memorable evening we took a liking to one another, which increased with each new meeting and eventually grew into a most sincere attachment."[26] Their friendship lasted for many years and, to judge from their letters, was not without a playful erotic element.

The reverse side of Tchaikovsky's society life was the necessity of a certain measure of conformity. Like any other young man about town, he was expected to court young ladies, with an eye to choosing a bride. And even though it was very likely during this St. Petersburg period that Tchaikovsky's homosexuality grew to become the emotional and erotic axis of his personality and thus an irreversible trait, it does not mean that he himself necessarily realized this with any degree of clarity or certainty. Rather the contrary, for the young man seems to have interpreted his inclinations as a carryover from his school years and to have nourished the illusion that he had only to wish it or to fall truly in love, in order to reorient himself toward women without any difficulty. Thus, he may have had at this time a twofold motivation for courting young ladies: a desire to mask his true amorous yearnings; and a genuine curiosity and interest regarding the opposite sex, based on self-inducement and a hope that he could eventually be like everybody else.

Thus, we should not be surprised by, for example, a letter to his sister, Aleksandra, of 9 June 1861. "Sophie Adamova told me that last year both Varenkas had been seriously in love with me and that many tears had been shed!" Tchaikovsky wrote. "This story did wonders for my self-esteem. . . . Not long ago I made the acquaintance of a certain Mme Gerngross and fell a little bit in love with her elder daughter. Imagine how strange! For she is named SOPHIE. Sophie Kireeva, Sophie Lapinskaya, Sophie Boborykina, Sophie Gerngross—all of them Sofyas! There's something to ponder."[27]

One must not forget, of course, that this letter is addressed to his sister, for whom Tchaikovsky often dissembled out of a desire to conceal an actual situation. Obviously, he could not share with her his experiences with his occasional male lovers. Despite his great devotion to Aleksandra, societal conventions, his own self-delusions, and his prudent need to dissimulate resulted in a certain amount of artificiality and insincerity in his letters to her. It was indeed quite convenient that Aleksandra had very soon left St. Petersburg. On 6 November 1860 she married Lev Davydov, a well-to-do landowner and the son of a participant in the 1825 Decembrist rebellion against Tsar Nicholas I, and the couple went to live on his family's estate of Kamenka in the Ukraine.

In the summer of 1861, Tchaikovsky traveled abroad for the first time, accompanying an acquaintance of his father's, the engineer Vasily Pisarev, for whom he performed the function of "something like a secretary, interpreter, or dragoman."[28] During his weeks abroad he visited Berlin, Hamburg, Antwerp, Brussels, London, and Paris, but of all the cities he saw on his travels, only Paris managed to impress him favorably. Moreover, his relationship with the uncouth Pisarev eventually turned uneasy and Tchaikovsky left him. In Hamburg, however, he happened to meet two former acquaintances from the School of Jurisprudence, "very nice young men," and later in Paris he met another friend from the school, Vladimir Yuferov, and the two took an apartment together. "In general, life in Paris is extremely pleasant," he wrote to his father on 12/24 August. "Here you can do anything you like, and the only thing you can't do is be bored. You have only to go out onto the boulevards and already you feel cheerful. . . . When we're at home we sometimes play on a very decent piano that we've rented for 15 francs a month. . . . We have a great deal of fun, and quite cheaply, but," he added dutifully, "we have not neglected to visit the juridical sites as well."[29]

After his return to Russia he received news that Aleksandra had given birth to her first child, a girl, named Tatyana. The delighted Tchaikovsky even composed a poem dedicated to his infant niece, who was the first of four daughters born in succession to the Davydovs. Two years later, Vera would be born, followed by Anna in 1864 and Natalya four years after that.

Tchaikovsky decided to spend the summer of 1862 in St. Petersburg. "I hope to be promoted soon to the position of clerk of special commissions at the ministry," he had written to his sister some months earlier, in December 1861. "It means a raise of twenty rubles and less work. God grant that it works out."[30] According to Modest, never did he work so industriously and zealously at the ministry as during these summer months. After working all day at his office on Malaya Sadovaya Street, he would bring work home and write reports at night. He even moved with one of his new acquaintances, Vladimir Tevyashev, to an apartment on Mokhovaya Street, not far from his work. Only on holidays did he allow himself the luxury of visiting the country house outside St. Petersburg taken for students of the Technological Institute. "This has been my sole consolation," he wrote to his sister on 10 September 1862. "I'm sure you have not forgotten my weakness for [that] country house; this weakness has not grown any less." There was also at least one other consolation: sixteen-year-old Aleksey Davydov, the younger brother of his sister's husband, who had "become so good-looking in his lyceum uniform that rarely will a woman pass by him without falling in love." In the same letter to Aleksandra, Tchaikovsky wrote ingenuously that Aleksey often visited his apartment, usually with Anatoly and Modest, and that "he sleeps beside me; we recite verses to one another and laugh constantly."[31]

All his efforts at the ministry, however, were of no avail: he was passed over in the list of appointments, and someone else filled the vacancy. His disappointment was great, and Modest suggests that the loss of this promotion was instrumental in his brother's decision to forsake the civil service and embark on a musical career.[32] The decision was not as abrupt as Modest implies. Tchaikovsky was still unsure of the step he was about to take, and in the letter to Aleksandra of 10 September he had written judiciously, "I shall not of course give up my job altogether until I am altogether certain that I am an artist and not a bureaucrat."[33] But his failure to win the new appointment seems to have freed him from the misguided notion that by seeking to make his way up the bureaucratic ladder, he was somehow fulfilling his obligations to his family.

Though only now about to germinate, the seeds of his musical vocation had been sown long before. It is likely that the young man first began to recognize where his true future lay through the influence of his curious friendship, dating back to his days at the School of Jurisprudence, with the Italian musician Luigi Piccioli, a voice instructor in the capital and later a professor at the St. Petersburg Conservatory. By all accounts, this Piccioli was an odd character. He refused to admit his age, which he carefully tried to conceal with hair dye and makeup. Modest judges him to have been around fifty at this time, though "evil tongues said that he was nearly seventy and that besides cosmetics he wore a small device at the back of his head to pull the skin of his face tight and smooth away wrinkles."[34] The friendship between the young Tchaikovsky and this man "old enough to be a grandfather to his new acquaintance" is said to have developed "on absolutely equal terms,"[35] in itself a remarkable fact. But Piccioli's chief influence on his young friend and pupil appears to have been the instilling in Tchaikovsky of his ardent enthusiasm for Italian opera. Years later, in 1891, Tchaikovsky himself recollected in an interview with an American newspaper, "I was seventeen years of age when I made the acquaintance of my singing master, Piccioli, and his influence over me was enormous. To this very day, it is with tears in my eyes that I hear the melodies of Bellini."[36] At the same time, this patriotic infatuation with the Italians made Piccioli reject all other national music, from Beethoven to Glinka, and for a long while the impressionable Tchaikovsky, revering the views of his older friend, remained exclusively captivated by Italian opera and paid little attention to symphonic music.

According to Modest, his brother's change of heart in regard to his career was already evident in 1861, and the first indication of it seems to be in a letter to his sister from 10 March of that year. "At dinner my musical talent was discussed," he told her. "Papa insists that it is not too late for me to become an artist. If only that were so. But the fact is that even if I do have some talent, it is probably already impossible to develop it. They have made a clerk out of me, and a poor one at that: I try to improve as much as I can, to take my work more seriously— and now to study thoroughbass at the same time!"[37]

Tchaikovsky's metamorphosis took longer than may appear from Modest's memoir. A taste for *la dolce vita* was working against such a change and would not soon be satiated. The first sign of a real transition came with an increasing sense that music was his calling and his destiny. This may have been partly the result of an accident. Nikolay Kashkin, a music critic and professor at the Moscow Conservatory, recalls that Tchaikovsky had a cousin, a young officer in the Horse Grenadiers, who also loved music very much and studied it zealously. The young men met frequently in society and, to a certain degree, vied with one another musically. "Once we met somewhere and began to talk about music, and he said in passing that he could make the transition from one key to any other in no more than three chords," Tchaikovsky reportedly told Kashkin. "This caught my interest, and, to my amazement, whatever complicated transitions I could invent he performed instantaneously. I considered myself more talented than he musically, but at the same time I was quite unable to do such a thing. When I asked where he had learned this, I found out that the Russian Musical Society offered classes in music theory where one could learn all these clever tricks; I went immediately to those classes and signed up to audit one taught by Nikolay Zaremba." Kashkin concludes by noting that "such an apparently insignificant circumstance may have served as the turning point in Pyotr Ilyich's whole life."[38]

Despite some oversimplification and exaggeration (the letters draw a rather more complex picture), Modest seems to be essentially correct when he insists that by the autumn of 1862 music had come to consume his brother, displacing his former society acquaintances and diversions. "People teased him for letting his hair grow long, were bewildered and reproving, and sighed at his resolution. . . . He was tender with Papa, stayed at home, began increasingly to neglect his appearance, labored assiduously, . . . and cared about such things as formerly had been incompatible with the image of a brilliant rake."[39]

Perhaps not entirely by chance, Tchaikovsky's serious interest in music coincided with a crucial moment in Russian musical life. In 1857 the Russian Musical Society was formed, and it soon brought classical music out of the salons of the aristocracy and made it accessible to everyone. The goal of the society was "the development of musical education and of a taste for music in Russians and the encouragement of native talent." By the mid-1860s, in the space of just a few seasons, the concerts of the Russian Musical Society had introduced the general public not only to all the symphonies of Beethoven but also to all his overtures and piano concertos. The public also heard the oratorios of Handel, the cantatas of Bach, the operas of Gluck, and the works of Schumann and Schubert. Russian music was also performed, and the operas of Glinka, Dargomyzhsky, Anton Rubinstein, and other composers were presented. Most important, however, were the music classes offered by the society, first in St. Petersburg and later in Moscow. These classes were open to all and eventually gave rise to professorial education. Before this, music had been taught in Russia only in the homes of the aristocracy and in private schools. As a result, native Russian musicians and performers were very rare. Classical concerts were usually performed by foreign musicians, most often from Germany. In addition to the classes of the Musical Society, the Free Music School, which emphasized choral singing, was also formed. The classes and the school quickly became popular, surprising many by the number and diversity of those who wished to take part, among whom could be found bureaucrats, merchants, tradesmen, and university students, as well as many young women who lacked the means to study privately.

On 8 September 1862 the St. Petersburg Conservatory was opened. The first institution of its kind in Russia, it had grown out of the musical classes offered by the Russian Musical Society. Tchaikovsky was among its first students. If in the classes offered by the Musical Society he had studied "haphazardly, like a mere amateur,"[40] at the conservatory he began to devote himself to his studies in earnest. As Hermann

Laroche recalls, the spur came from a conversation with Nikolay Zaremba, a professor of composition at the conservatory: "One time after class, Zaremba called Tchaikovsky aside and began to exhort him to apply himself more seriously, telling him, among other things, that he had unquestionable talent and in general displaying an unexpected warmth toward him. Deeply moved, Pyotr Ilyich decided from that moment to cast aside his laziness and began to work with a zeal that never left him during his whole time at the conservatory."[41]

From its very founding, the St. Petersburg Conservatory established a curriculum designed to provide a vigorous professional education. Each student at the conservatory had to study certain general, required subjects as well as courses in his particular area of specialization. Tchaikovsky had chosen to specialize in music theory and composition, which required classes in piano, an orchestral instrument, and conducting. By autumn 1863 he had successfully completed classes in both harmony and counterpoint under Nikolay Zaremba and had begun studying orchestration with Anton Rubinstein, the director of the conservatory and one of the foremost figures of the Russian musical scene at the time. In addition, he was taking a complementary class in organ music with Heinrich Stiehl, as well as flute lessons with Cesare Ciardi and piano with Anton Gerke.

Nikolay Zaremba, a musician of the German school, in which he had been trained, was not a composer in the true sense. He in fact composed very little and published almost nothing. It is known only that he wrote at least one symphony, a quartet in the manner of Haydn, and an oratorio entitled *John the Baptist*. This was a modest output for a conservatory professor and was ultimately responsible for the undistinguished opinion held of Zaremba—an opinion that came to be shared by Tchaikovsky, on whom Zaremba's teaching made little impression, even in his early studies.

By contrast, Anton Rubinstein's powerful artistic personality impressed the young man deeply. Rubinstein's methodology combined practical work in composition with instrumentation, and as his student, Tchaikovsky produced scores of exercises for various instruments that he would find very useful. In later years Tchaikovsky's enthusiasm for Rubinstein was to cool perceptibly for both personal and professional reasons. He began increasingly to resent the man's despotism, his intolerance of the opinions of others, and his narrow musical outlook, which was largely limited to Chopin, Schumann, and Mendelssohn. But writing to the German critic Eugen Zabel in 1892, Tchaikovsky recalled that in those early years he had adored his professor, "not only as a great pianist and a great composer but also as a man of rare nobility, sincere, honest, magnanimous, alien to any baseness or vulgarity, with a clear, straightforward mind and infinite kindness—in short, a man superior to all other mortals. As a teacher, he was incomparable. He got down to business without bombast or lengthy perorations, but always with a very serious attitude toward the business at hand."[42]

According to his classmates and to Rubinstein himself, Tchaikovsky's own industriousness in his conservatory years was remarkable. A most conscientious student, he showed himself capable of sustaining the whole weight of knowledge and skill required of him. It was in these years that the groundwork for the strong musical self-discipline so characteristic of him in his later life and for his highly professional attitude toward the technical aspects of his craft was formed.

The most important friendship Tchaikovsky forged during his years at the St. Petersburg Conservatory was that with Hermann Laroche, who later went on to become a prominent music critic. At this time, Laroche, according to Ivan Klimenko, looked like "a boy, with a face that resembled . . . a bust of Schiller, straight Liszt-like hair, and such a leanness in his face . . . that he had no front—only a profile."[43] Klimenko also recalls that the two friends "made an amazing four-hand couple" and that they "felt each other so deeply that they could quite freely improvise four-hand duets."[44] Music, indeed, seems to have formed the major bond between the two men. Though their interests developed in different directions and their early intimacy gradually dissolved, they preserved until the end of their lives an intense intellectual friendship. Even at that young age, Hermann Laroche was immensely knowledgeable about music and held strong opinions. Under his influence, Tchaikovsky realized how terribly ignorant he himself was in this regard and hastened to start filling the many gaps in his musical learning. In Laroche's company he sat late in the conservatory's library studying works of Schumann and Beethoven adapted for four hands and the new Russian music, in particular Glinka. Together they attended the evening concerts at City Hall, sponsored at this period by the Russian Musical Society, as well as all the rehearsals and recitals of conservatory students. One of their chief passions was the now all but forgotten composer Henri Litolff, whose two concert overtures *Robespierre* and *Die Girondisten* sparked in Tchaikovsky a lasting interest in program music.

With his entry into the conservatory, Tchaikovsky began to experience a conflict between the desire for physical pleasure, which demanded that he continue to live in the style of the past few years, and the necessity for persistent labor, which took an enormous amount of time and energy. His energetic libido was sublimated from the material world to the realm of the spirit. Sex, or rather the behavior related to it, and the study of music came into sharp and ever-increasing conflict with one another. This conflict persisted in the composer his entire life and at times would even grow stronger with age. Even at the very beginning of his creative period, Tchaikovsky strove to avoid his society friends and to seek solitude.

Yet, despite the enormous commitment demanded by his musical studies, Tchaikovsky's erotic desires were not entirely suppressed. Even at the conservatory he encountered bright and attractive young men to whom he responded with sensually colored interest. One such seems to have been a very handsome boy of sixteen whom he and his friends accepted into their circle "with open arms." Half German and half English, Joseph Ledger was the son of an interpreter at the admiralty and spoke fluent English, German, and French, and only slightly less fluent Russian. He is described by Laroche as having been "small, very thin, blond, and pale, with the madly ecstatic blue eyes quite often found among the English." Despite his evident talent and initial enthusiasm, a disease in the muscles of his arms hampered his progress, and, "now lazy, now sickly," he graduated only many years later. Ledger subsequently wandered in and out of a variety of occupations in Russia and abroad, and finally perished in 1889 in Paris while attempting to perform a bizarre stunt atop a fast-moving carriage.[45]

Laroche's lengthy digression on Ledger in his memoirs about Tchaikovsky can scarcely be accidental. In fact, Laroche devotes no less space to Joseph Ledger than, for example, to Nikolay Hubert, who is known to have been one of Tchaikovsky's closest musical friends. Such an excursus leads one to surmise that, at least during the conservatory period, Tchaikovsky and Ledger entertained quite intimate relations, even though the name of the latter does not figure in any published correspondence. It is, however, found in Tchaikovsky's diary, in a somewhat ambiguous context. In an entry from the summer of 1886, when the composer was visiting Paris, he wrote, "Ledger (mysterious and enigmatic personality)."[46] Words such as "mysterious" and "enigmatic" belong to the set of euphemisms that the composer consistently employed to denote things or phenomena related to homosexuality.

On 11 April 1863, Tchaikovsky submitted his letter of resignation to the Ministry of Justice, "owing to domestic circumstances." On 1 May he was released from his post, though he was still considered to be attached to the ministry in a sort of unsalaried reserve position. The timing of this step proved rather poor. That same spring, Ilya Tchaikovsky had retired from the directorship of the Technological Institute and the financial situation of the Tchaikovsky family again became very strained. The young conservatory student was forced to spend much time earning his living by giving music lessons and accompanying singers on the piano.

His inner conflict between sensuality and creativity was still far from resolved. Despite the inner drive he felt with regard to his studies, Tchaikovsky continued to meet regularly with Apukhtin and his circle, and even spent the summer of 1863 at the poet's estate at Pavlodar. It may have been on this occasion that Apukhtin wrote his poem "Fate: On Beethoven's Fifth Symphony," which was dedicated to Tchaikovsky. Both this dedication and the poem itself have been preserved in Modest's diary, though in the Soviet edition of Apukhtin's works the dedication is omitted. The main motif of the poem is that of an amorous meeting, into which is woven a persistent refrain of fate and destiny. When the personal predilections of these two former students of the School of Jurisprudence are taken into consideration, the following lines in particular acquire a special meaning:

> And then she [Fate] comes, and in an instant
> Love, anxiety, expectation,
> Bliss—all flow together for them
> In one mad kiss![47]

Besides Apukhtin, Tchaikovsky also saw much of the homosexual Prince Golitsyn and, the following year, accepted an invitation from the prince to spend the entire summer as his guest at the Golitsyn family estate at Trostinets, near Kharkov, in the Ukraine. Despite Tchaikovsky's having turned away from amusement to the study of music, Golitsyn had displayed an even greater affection for the poor conservatory student and music tutor, helping him to find pupils and inviting him to sumptuous feasts at his home in St. Petersburg. Modest's explanation that his brother accepted the prince's invitation to visit that summer primarily for financial reasons seems not entirely persuasive. Had he wanted to, he could easily have declined, for he had received several other invitations for that same summer—from his sister, Aleksandra, and her husband, for example, and again from Apukhtin.

Tchaikovsky was to recall his stay at Trostinets that summer as, in Modest's words, "something out of a fairy tale." Surrounded by luxury and magnificence such as he had never before known, he enjoyed complete freedom to spend his days in the two pursuits that were fast becoming his favorite activities—composing and solitary strolls. Only at dinnertime and in the evening would he join his host and the other guests. On Tchaikovsky's name day, 29 June, the prince organized a festival in honor of his friend. A ceremonious breakfast was followed later that evening by a carriage ride through the forest, "where the whole road had been flanked with flaming pitch barrels, while in a pavilion in the midst of the woods a feast for the peasants had been set up as well as a sumptuous supper in honor of the cause of the celebration [Tchaikovsky]."[48]

"I make no secret," Tchaikovsky wrote to his sister with some pleasure on 28 July 1864, "that I feel very well here."[49] Eventually he decided to extend his stay by a few weeks and wrote to the conservatory that he was suffering from a toothache and fever.[50] It was at Golitsyn's estate that Tchaikovsky met for the first time Nikolay Kondratyev, with whom he later became good friends.

While at Trostinets, Tchaikovsky, as a vacation exercise, wrote his overture to Aleksandr Ostrovsky's play *The Storm*. Anton Rubinstein disapproved of the piece, which in Laroche's opinion represented "a museum of antimusical curiosities." This suggests that despite having had such favorable conditions for creative work, the young composer was not yet up to his own standards. It may well be that Golitsyn's companionship was not entirely conducive to his guest's creativity. He was eight years Tchaikovsky's senior, and his character and life-style already tended to irritate the younger man even at this early stage of their acquaintance. Yet, the conservatory student's continuing relations with the prince and his circle were typical of the concessions Tchaikovsky was prepared to make to the temptations of society life and to pleasures that were not to be as easily rejected as he may have thought.

CHAPTER FIVE

His Brothers' Keeper

From the start, Tchaikovsky's classes with Anton Rubinstein in orchestration and composition became the centerpiece of his entire course of studies at the St. Petersburg Conservatory. In striking contrast to the competently systematic but pedantic lectures of Nikolay Zaremba, Rubinstein's teaching was improvisational and more than a little slapdash. But he was energetic and exacting, and he both pushed and stimulated his students. Where Zaremba would merely point out the technical errors in a student's work, Rubinstein would stride about the auditorium with the student's exercise in hand, brilliantly explaining and offering corrections with illustrations from the work of famous composers. Then he might stop suddenly at the piano to improvise inspirationally, commenting on the form or content of the original. Above all, he relentlessly pushed his students to overcome their technical timidity, which he saw as destructive, and to give free rein to their musical imagination. To this end, he would, for example, at the start of a class in composition, recite a poem to which the students had immediately to sketch a vocal setting, turning in the completed work by the following day.[1]

Rubinstein recognized Tchaikovsky's talent very early and worked to prod and encourage his pupil. On one occasion he burst into Zaremba's class and all but literally dragged Zaremba and his students off to hear an exercise Tchaikovsky had written, a musical setting of Vasily Zhukovsky's poetic ballad "Nocturnal Parade." Mikhail Glinka had already written a song with Zhukovsky's poem as text, but Tchai-

kovsky presented in his own intricate arrangement a strikingly different interpretation that owed nothing to Glinka's earlier composition.
The episode is one of the earliest known instances of public approba-
tion of Tchaikovsky's work at the conservatory.[2]

Later, Rubinstein arranged for Tchaikovsky to assist in teaching
the harmony class, which brought the struggling student a small but
welcome salary, and in 1865 he secured for him a commission for a
Russian translation of François Gevaert's *Traité général d'instrumentation*, which had appeared in 1863. Tchaikovsky worked on the translation during summer vacation. He spent the vacation at the Davydovs' estate at Kamenka, near Kiev. It was his first visit to his sister's
home and the place that was to be his summer refuge for many years
to come. Prominent in Russian history as a frequent meeting place of
the conspirators in the Decembrist Revolt of 1825 and as an occasional
retreat of, among others, the poet Aleksandr Pushkin, Kamenka was a
beautiful village boasting a beet-sugar refinery and was populated
largely by Ukrainians and Jews. The legal owner of the estate was Lev
Davydov's elder brother, Nikolay, a retired officer and a gentleman of
considerable learning and culture. Nikolay Davydov still lived at Kamenka with his brother and his brother's growing family, but he had
handed over the management of the estate to his more capable brother,
Lev, some years before.

Tchaikovsky's memories of that first summer at Kamenka were
very happy ones. "I have never spent such a pleasant summer," he
wrote to Aleksandra shortly afterward. "I cannot reproach myself for
idleness, and at the same time, I have so many sweet recollections."[3]
Besides his sister and her family, he took particular pleasure in the
presence of the twins, Anatoly and Modest, who also came to Kamenka that summer.

In the delicate matter of Tchaikovsky's relations with his younger
twin brothers—as in the whole of his inner life—our chief source of information remains the composer's correspondence, at present available
only in censored form. Close and careful comparison of the various
editions of this correspondence reveals that the cuts made by Soviet
editors in these letters occur almost exclusively in passages that appear
to deal with homosexuality. But, beyond this external censorship, we
have also to sift through the often circumlocutory conventions of self-
expression common in the Russia of Tchaikovsky's time. Even in private correspondence, nineteenth-century Russian practice differed radically from the outspokenness on every issue from politics to sexuality
in present-day Europe and America. A long history of official control
over intellectual matters had forced nineteenth-century Russians to

learn to speak and write in an allusive, Aesopian language, or verbal code, on subjects and opinions frowned upon by the authorities or the public. Particular words and phrases would acquire additional weighted meanings readily comprehensible to like-minded contemporaries or, in the case of the sexual or political underground, to select initiates. A well-known example from the realm of politics was the apparently innocuous word *stikhiinyi* (elemental), used in the sense of "spontaneous." Its usage in print was officially banned by the government censors, as it was believed to connote "revolutionary" in the mind of the reading public.

The impact of such conditions on the mentality of the time went beyond a mere surface dissimulation as a rational means of self-protection. It penetrated into the deeper recesses of consciousness and even into the subconscious, becoming a habit and a reflex and resulting in a continual, though not always fully recognized, form of self-censorship. Often such coded language formed the only available method of referring to subjects or ideas generally considered unspeakable. To this category belonged virtually all aspects of sexuality. A vast discrepancy existed between the official prohibitive attitude and the sexual permissiveness that in fact prevailed at all levels of society. From the official standpoint, sex was barely acknowledged to exist—a view subscribed to well into the twentieth century by a Soviet educational system that until very recently taught, even at the university level, that sexual problems were the exclusive domain of the decadent bourgeoisie. A hundred years ago, as today, a literate sexual vocabulary was largely lacking, and the subject was discussed only in juridical or medical jargon. Even the mechanics of human sexuality, to say nothing of homosexuality, were often misrepresented or misconceived. This was perhaps most notoriously attested by the (quite serious) pronouncement of Nicholas I in the case of a young noblewoman who had been secretly married against her family's wishes. "The marriage," decreed the tsar, "shall be dissolved and the wife henceforth considered a virgin."

Even those contemporaries of Tchaikovsky's who were rather better educated in such matters than the tsar often preferred to resort to paraphrase, euphemism, or circumlocution when referring in conversation or correspondence to the taboo themes of sexuality. Nor was Tchaikovsky himself completely free of such self-restrictions. It is true that on occasion he was unusually candid in his letters to his brothers, particularly Modest. Still, in addition to the not unnatural pressure to conform to prevailing patterns of self-expression, it is possible that somewhere at the back of his mind lurked the thought that his letters might eventually reach the public domain—to say nothing of the more immediate and very real possibility that (as seems to have been the case when his brothers were studying at the School of Jurisprudence and again, years later, when his servant Alyosha was in the army) his letters might be opened and inspected by the authorities. Consequently, he quite often yielded to convention and resorted, when relating his amorous experiences, to hints and allusions that largely concealed sexual innuendo beneath the guise of emotional outburst. This he practiced even more rigorously in the extant portions of his diary, where he went so far as to invent coded abbreviations. All such passages, many of them further distorted by the Soviet censor's cuts, require reconstruction. In some cases this reconstruction is irrefutable; in others it is conjectural to a degree.

All of this must be taken into account when dealing with Tchaikovsky's relations with his brothers Modest and Anatoly. Close reading of their correspondence cannot but lead to the conviction that their relations contained for all three of them a dimension beyond that of ordinary fraternal affection. The ambiguously phrased passages, the nuances of which are sometimes lost in the English rendering, accumulate to the point of corroboration. Gradually one learns to distinguish, in the frequent emotional outbursts, between the language of affection and the language of passion. Short of allowing the presumption that all three brothers were involved in homosexual incest, the evidence seems sufficient to indicate that there did exist between them a strong erotic tension, extravagant and even incomprehensible if considered solely within the bounds of familial love. It may well have owed something to the sensual aura surrounding their overtly sentimental father, Ilya Tchaikovsky. What other expression, beyond that found in the letters, this erotic tension may have taken is anyone's guess. Given the physical closeness between the family members, an inherent feature of Russian life (so that, for example, it was a matter of no consequence that the brothers, despite the difference in their ages, slept in the same bed), it is not inconceivable—though by no means provable—that, drawn as he was to adolescent males, Tchaikovsky, himself still psychologically immature in these early years, may on occasion have engaged with the twins in less innocuous activities that extended beyond platonic caresses into more tangible sexual play.

The death of Tchaikovsky's mother had left the family in a difficult situation. Ilya was a loving parent, but his character was hardly suited to the task of rearing children, whereas it was precisely someone to rear them properly that was needed by the younger children—and especially the twins, Anatoly and Modest. In the beginning, it was their sister, Aleksandra, eight years older than the twins, who presided over their upbringing, a fact that doubtless contributed to the exceptional devotion that Pyotr, Anatoly, and Modest displayed toward Aleksandra almost until the end of her life. After Aleksandra married and left for Kamenka, however, the twins, whom Tchaikovsky even in his childhood letters to his parents used to call "the little angels," became wholly his responsibility. Tchaikovsky now had to take the place not only of the twins' mother and, to a certain degree, their father but also of their sister, while remaining both their brother and their nurse. Of the three oldest brothers, Nikolay was already off pursuing his career as a mining engineer, while the duties of a naval cadet kept Ippolit similarly occupied. Neither Nikolay nor Ippolit was to share in the close relationship of their four siblings and in general they remained only on the periphery of Tchaikovsky's familial interests and commitments.

A passage from Modest's recollections referring to the period before their sister's marriage gives some idea of how the young twins perceived their brother at what Modest calls that "prehistoric" stage of their lives: "When he agreed to 'torture' [that is, play with] us, he did not condescend, but actually had fun himself, and this made his participation in the game so entertaining for us. He would improvise and create things and thus amused himself as well. His games were unlike anything else, and everything proceeded from his strange and magically enchanting nature."[4] For as long as they could remember, Modest and Anatoly had looked up to their brother as "a creature not like the rest," one whose "every word seemed sacred."[5]

With the departure of their sister, the two ten-year-old boys and the young man of twenty grew dramatically closer. Tchaikovsky's new and multifaceted role in the lives of the twins formed the basis of an exceptional depth and stability in their relations that throughout their lives would verge continuously on a sort of mutual adoration. Modest recalls the particular episode that signaled the start of this new intimacy. "On one of those bleak evenings when we were ready just to repeat the word 'boring, boring' and wait impatiently for when we would be sent to bed, Anatoly and I were sitting on the windowsill in the hall, dangling our legs and having not the least idea what to do with ourselves," he writes. "Just then Petya came along. . . . Simply knowing that he was home and seeing him cheered us, but how great was our joy and our delight when he did not pass by as usual but stopped and asked, 'Are you bored? Do you want to spend the evening with me?' And to this day my brother Anatoly and I preserve in our memory the slightest detail of this evening that marked a new era in our existence, because with it began our triple union, to be broken only by death."

From that time on, Modest tells us, neither "the wisest and most experienced teacher" nor even "the most loving and tender mother" could have taken the place of their brother—who was, in addition, both playmate and trusted friend. "Everything in our hearts and our minds we could confide in him without the least doubt that it would interest him: we joked and romped with him as with an equal and at the same time trembled as before the strictest judge and punisher." Tchaikovsky's influence on the twins was such that "a frowning face and a sort of castigating glance" were discipline enough. Perceptively, Modest implies that a pervasive sense of loneliness drew his brother to them, noting that "he was always at ease and relaxed in our company." The three brothers formed, as Modest puts it, "a family within a family": "For us he was brother, mother, friend, tutor—everything on earth. We in turn became his favorite concern in life and gave it meaning."[6]

This somewhat idyllic picture is largely supported by Tchaikovsky's own correspondence. On 10 September 1862 he wrote to his sister, "My attachment to these two little fellows—and in particular (this is in confidence) to the first [that is, Anatoly]—increases with every passing day. Inwardly I am terribly proud of, and value, this best feeling of my heart. In life's sad moments, I need only remember them and life becomes dear to me." In the same letter he noted, in words echoed by Modest many decades later, that he tried "as far as possible to make my love a substitute for the caresses and attentions of a mother, which they, unfortunately, cannot know or remember, and it seems to me that I am succeeding."[7] Several years later, in a letter to Mrs. von Meck, Tchaikovsky wrote that he had "wished to be for them what a mother is for her children, because I knew from experience what an indelible mark is left in a child's soul by motherly tenderness and motherly affection."[8] It is quite likely that the reverse was also true and that, just as Tchaikovsky tried to be a mother to the twins, so the twins became for Tchaikovsky a substitute for his mother's love and affection.

From the autumn of 1863, when Tchaikovsky had to move in with his father, the greatest intimacy with his younger brothers began. During this period, Tchaikovsky took great pleasure in simply having Modest and Anatoly physically near him. For a young man of Tchaikovsky's age and way of life, dividing his time between his studies and his society friends, it was at least unusual to demand, as he did, the almost constant companionship, day and night, of his two adolescent broth-

ers. Most people in such circumstances would have found it both desirable and expedient to arrange for the twins to live elsewhere, with
relatives or friends.

It is important to emphasize that while the twins were studying at
the School of Jurisprudence and for some years thereafter, Tchaikovsky's relationship with each of them developed rather differently. As
he confided frankly in his letter to his sister, Tchaikovsky felt a
marked preference for the young Anatoly. His relations with Modest
at this time were noticeably tense and contradictory. There was much
that worried him in the boy—not least Modest's efforts to imitate his
beloved elder brother in everything. To Modest, Tchaikovsky would
complain in a letter of 12 March 1875 that his brother was "not free of
a single one" of his own shortcomings. "You are too much like me,"
he wrote, "and when I am angry with you, I am actually angry at myself, for you are ever playing the role of a mirror in which I see the
reflection of all my weaknesses."[9] To a degree, Tchaikovsky seems to
have regarded Modest in these early years as his "shadow," in the Jung-
ian sense—a collection of qualities he disliked in himself leading a sort
of independent existence. Even many years later, people were struck
by the uncanny resemblance between the two brothers. "Modest Ilyich
seemed almost to be Pyotr Ilyich's double," the actor Yury Yuryev observes in his recollections, "so like his elder brother was he in practi-
cally everything. I am convinced that they conceived, sensed, and experienced life absolutely alike. Even their voices and manner of speech
were similar."[10]

At the School of Jurisprudence, Modest fared far less successfully
than his twin. Having had to repeat the fifth form, he graduated a year
later than Anatoly. Writing to Lev Davydov on 23 April 1870, just before Modest's graduation, Tchaikovsky confessed his fear that his
brother would be a failure—"though not an uninteresting one."[11] A
year earlier, Tchaikovsky had warned his brother, somewhat less than
charitably, of the same possible fate. "You have had the misfortune to
be born with the soul of an artist," he wrote in a letter dated 1 February
1869, "and you will be constantly drawn into this world of the highest
artistic values, but since you are not endowed with any talent to go
with the sensitivity of an artistic nature, for God's sake, beware of
yielding to your inclinations." After such a categorical pronouncement, the next lines must have seemed to the young addressee as a
halfhearted attempt to soften the blow, coupled with some plainly
moralistic lecturing: "Remember that, on the other hand, you possess
all the necessary capacities to be a notable figure in the very field [that
is, the civil service] for which you are being prepared by the school. . . .

If, having resolved to be a disappointed and melancholy youth, you stop studying or do not take seriously your future professional obligations, then you will make yourself, and therefore all of us, miserable."[12]

These expostulations from his brother can have given the young man little pleasure. What is more, Tchaikovsky, in a letter of November 1868, even commented critically, but as if in passing, on Modest's appearance. It is not clear whether this was done deliberately or out of a lack of sensitivity to the pain such a comment would inflict on the self-esteem of a youth already in the process of homoerotic self-definition. "Your photograph," Tchaikovsky wrote, "made me think with sadness that in real life you are not at all so charmingly good-looking as in your portrait."[13]

Most striking, however, and more than a little surprising, is a passage on masturbation found in a letter Tchaikovsky wrote to Modest in early or mid-February of 1866, a passage somehow overlooked by the Soviet censors in early editions of Tchaikovsky's correspondence. "As for Tolya's [Anatoly's] nagging you to stop indulging in masturbation, it is I who encourage him in this," Tchaikovsky told his brother. "Only by constant surveillance and even actual pestering can you be cured of this shamefulness. . . . In general, masturbation should be seen as an abominable habit that can become very deep-rooted, and therefore, it is better to offend at times your self-esteem and to cause some slight annoyance than to allow your ruin. You know that even if Anatoly really does get on your nerves sometimes with his governessing, he does it in fact out of love and a wish to do you good. Likewise, you should also watch his unbearable habit of grimacing and drive him crazy until he is cured of it."[14]

This singular text shows the unusual openness with which the Tchaikovsky brothers dealt with matters more or less unspeakable in well-mannered society at that time and more appropriately the subject of a confession to one's priest than of an epistolary harangue. Masturbation is, of course, one of the most intimate and anxious experiences of one's coming of age, but in this case it seems evident that Modest himself requested his elder brother's opinion on the subject, as well as his intervention against Anatoly's nagging, for the passage appears in the letter under the heading "The answers to your questions are the following." It would seem, then, that Anatoly did not indulge in masturbation, which in itself is curious, but his spying on his brother was approved as both praiseworthy and reasonable. The possibility was even entertained of involving a third party in the control of Modest's masturbatory habit: Tchaikovsky informed his brother that he had "even thought to write to Tolstoy [a classmate of Modest] so that he might keep an eye on you and shame you in case you were caught." According to the standards of the time, which in this matter were no different from those of Victorian England, the entire situation was quite out of the ordinary.

Tchaikovsky's judgment of the actual "vice" was severe in the extreme and conformed fully to the prevailing medical and religious views of the time. "Shamefulness," "abominable habit" and "ruin" were the words he used to refer to it. But at the same time, perhaps trying to soften the blow to Modest, he equated it in seeming seriousness with Anatoly's "habit of grimacing"—that is, a sexual sin condemned by the church and bad manners in society. In any event, the letter obviously shows the presence of something unusual uniting the three brothers on a profound psychological level. How much of this may have been conscious and how much unconscious cannot be ascertained, but some element of special intensity does appear to be evident.

Particularly odd is the fact that this letter was written at a time when Tchaikovsky must already have at least suspected or, what is even more likely, known for a fact that his brother Modest was "too much like him" in his sexual preference as well. It is uncertain to what degree his own behavior may have contributed to Modest's sexual development. The possibility cannot be excluded that without so intending, he did exercise a certain influence in that direction. In Modest's autobiography, for instance, we find the following interesting confession: "Calling me over to him, he would make me say [in a play on the diminutive of 'Pyotr']: 'Pita, Pita-pitatura, Pita, Pito . . . Pite . . . Petu . . . Petrusha!'—and after this would let me kiss him, and nothing seemed so witty and charming as this."[15] One should note the sexual ambiguity of the Russian word *petu[shok]* (cock[erel]), which, like its English equivalent, can also connote the penis.

It is difficult to claim with assurance that Modest's homosexuality was reinforced in part by his fanatical desire to imitate his elder brother in all things. Yet, such cases are not unknown to psychologists, and if one bears in mind the degree of Modest's adoration of "Petenka," the possibility cannot be altogether dismissed.

Certainly the most revealing passage with respect to Modest's homosexuality must be one from his brother's letter to him of 13 January 1870. This letter, however, has not only been severely censored by Soviet editors, but also seems to have been tampered with by various individuals, among them undoubtedly Modest himself, who had access to the archives before the revolution. In the letter, Tchaikovsky wrote, "If there is the slightest possibility, try to be [deleted in the original, most probably the word was 'normal']. This is very sad. At your age one can still force oneself to love [also deleted in the original, most probably 'a woman']; try at least once, maybe it will work out."[16]

This passage, coupled with the earlier diatribe on masturbation, gives the impression that Tchaikovsky had accepted his responsibility as guardian of the twins' morals and seems to imply a negative attitude toward homosexuality on his part. In reality, the matter was far more complex in both these respects. At the very least, Tchaikovsky's censure of Modest was inconsistent with the general tenor of their relationship. During this same period and throughout their lives, while tending to be rather patronizing toward his younger brother's homosexual acquaintances, Tchaikovsky remained clearly indulgent and amused. A telling example is a humorous note he sent to Modest on 16 October 1865. Betraying Tchaikovsky's playful penchant for turning masculine names into feminine ones, the note reads, "A dinner on Saturday, 16 October, is ceremoniously ordered by the Queen of the Netherlands Elizaveta Andreevna [Schobert-Litke, their aunt]. Gentlemen are to be in full-dress uniform, ladies in Russian costume. To the Grand Duchess Modestina the Princess Lenina has been appointed lady in waiting. Be there not later than half past four. Peter IV."[17] Similar passages from his correspondence make it clear that this sort of wordplay always served to indicate Tchaikovsky's involvement in some predicament that he at least perceived to have a distinctly homoerotic coloring. Nikolay Lenin, the "Princess Lenina" of the invitation, was a classmate of Modest with—as is clear from this and several other contexts—the same tastes. Three years older than Modest, Lenin (whom the Soviet editors in their ideological zeal deliberately misname Lepin in the published texts in order not to compromise the leader of the world proletariate) was eighteen when this note was written.[18]

In later life, Tchaikovsky never exhibited any moral remorse in regard to his homosexual pursuits. On the contrary, with the exception of very rare moments of a particular hypochondria, mainly stemming from an acute realization that the instability of his way of life often hampered his creativity, he perceived them as a natural source of pleasure. His anxiety, and indeed psychological torment, resulted from his knowledge of the views held by other people on the subject; despite his many declarations to the contrary, he remained all his life highly sensitive to public opinion. The same dichotomy can be seen in the passages cited above, which show, on the one hand, a sort of playfulness (with names, for example) and, on the other, apprehension or inhibition (the advice to Modest to be "normal"). Ultimately, however, the sexually indulgent, if not sexually provocative, attitude he often displayed toward the twins was justified in his eyes as relating, first, to a pleasure he himself preferred and, second, to his long-held belief that homosexual urges yielded to in youth did not prevent the eventual establishment of orthodox relations with women.

In any event, it seems indisputable that the relationship of the three Tchaikovsky brothers was saturated with eroticism, including its physical manifestations, to an extraordinary degree. "Soon I shall send a very large sum of money for Tolya, whom I commission you to smother with kisses," he wrote Modest on 1 February 1869, adding, "And are you pleased at this opportunity to spoon a bit with your brother?"[19] The passage was by no means exceptional. The direct physical imagery contained in such outpourings clearly went beyond Tchaikovsky's customary effusive sentimentality and would have embarrassed even the most practiced and gushing letter writers of the time.

Most of this material suggests that in terms of emotional tension the relationship between Modest and Pyotr was unequal. The former's stance is unequivocal: absolute adoration. Tchaikovsky himself was perfectly well aware of this, and it is not without a sort of malicious coquetry that he would sign a letter to Modest of 3 March 1870, "Yours, adored by you."[20] Indeed, their early relationship shows hints of a certain sadomasochistic element, as seems to surface in some of the emphatic passages addressed to Modest and stressing his lack of talent and good looks or sharply criticizing his masturbatory habit and the like. But an equilibrium was maintained, and their relationship later became one of the great examples of brotherly cooperation and mutual love.

Modest Tchaikovsky, for all his problems, was nevertheless endowed with certain gifts and would not pass on without making some mark on Russian culture: he wrote several plays as well as, first and foremost, his monumental biography of his brother, the prose style of which is often quite exquisite. In great contrast, his twin, Anatoly, was to all appearances an entirely average person. His main virtues were kindness, moral decency, and a commitment to his elder brother almost as self-absorbing as that of Modest. There is no doubt, however, that for a long time Tchaikovsky clearly preferred Anatoly to his twin. Their nephew Yury Davydov recalls, "The second twin, Anatoly Ilyich, possessed a very nervous and effusive character. These traits . . . made his life quite complicated. . . . He loved his brother Pyotr selflessly and, like Modest Ilyich, was willing to make any sacrifice for his sake. This affection was mutual, and Pyotr Ilyich loved him probably more than all the rest of his brothers."[21]

Moreover, Tchaikovsky's letters to Anatoly create an impression of

passion verging on the amorous—a trait largely absent from the correspondence with Modest. Again, the vocabulary is striking and extravagant, displaying a pathos and ecstasy not fully explicable by a mere
reference to the emotionalism generally characteristic of Tchaikovsky's literary style. In the letters to Anatoly, we find repeated expressions such as "I kiss you passionately every place!"[22] or "My little
dove!"[23]—the latter a rather bizarre address, in the feminine gender in
Russian, to a sixteen-year-old male. Anatoly Tchaikovsky was heterosexual, yet the context of their relationship would suggest perhaps that
he may have "allowed himself to be loved" by his adored and adoring
elder brother.

It is interesting that Tchaikovsky harbored no illusions that his
favorite had any special gifts or abilities. As early as 1866, when the
twins were still at the School of Jurisprudence, Tchaikovsky was already preparing Anatoly for a solid but undistinguished career. Although the gist of his advice differed little from that given to Modest
three years later, this letter from 6 February 1866 was far gentler in
tone. "As for the thoughts that haunt you about being a useless nothing, I advise you to cast aside these ridiculous fantasies," Tchaikovsky
wrote. "This is extremely out-of-date; in our day such self-pity was
fashionable, it was the general trend, which only testifies to the fact
that our education was conducted with great neglect. Young men of
sixteen should not waste time pondering their future activity. You
should only seek to make the present attractive and such that you are
satisfied with yourself (that is, with the sixteen-year-old Tolya). . . . But
the most important thing of all is not to think too much of yourself
and to prepare yourself for the lot of an average mortal."[24]

Here, as elsewhere in his letters to the twins, Tchaikovsky's assured manner in dealing with even the most intimate physical, spiritual, and emotional problems of his brothers supports the contention
that Modest and Anatoly indeed kept little secret from their elder
brother. This air of deep mutual trust was to remain with them always.
Moreover, the "familial erotic" complex in Tchaikovsky's emotional
makeup that formed during these early years with his brothers accompanied the composer to the end of his life, finding repeated expression
in his amorous concentration on various of his young male relatives.

The three brothers left Kamenka at the end of August 1865. Tchaikovsky was pleased with his work that summer. Besides his translation of Gevaert's treatise, Tchaikovsky had completed the sketch of his
Overture in C Minor and had also set down the theme of the Ukrainian
folk song that he would later use in his *Scherzo à la russe*, op. 1, no.
1, for piano. But the journey back to St. Petersburg was unpleasant and

at times even harrowing. At one point, the brothers found themselves clinging to one another in terror as the horses bolted and pulled their carriage headlong down the mountainside to the very brink of a precipice, miraculously turning aside at the very last minute and coming out on the bridge. To make matters worse, they were hungry, for the Grand Duke Nikolay and his enormous retinue, traveling through the region at the same time, had all but exhausted local supplies along their way. Modest recalls that for some two days he and his brothers lived on nothing but bread and water.

St. Petersburg met them with rain. But the discomforts of the journey and the gloom of their welcome were quickly forgotten when Tchaikovsky learned that the day before their arrival Johann Strauss the younger had conducted at Pavlovsk the first public performance of Tchaikovsky's *Characteristic Dances* for orchestra, later incorporated into his opera *The Voyevode* as "Dances of the Chambermaids." It was, indeed, the first public performance of any of his works, and an auspicious debut for the young man, who would not graduate from the conservatory until December of that year. The premiere appears, oddly enough, to have taken Tchaikovsky quite by surprise, and it is unclear just how it came about, though most likely it was Anton Rubinstein who arranged to bring the work of the unknown composer to the Waltz King's attention.

During the last several weeks of 1865, Tchaikovsky lived in Aleksey Apukhtin's apartment, moving in when Apukhtin left for a visit to the country. Earlier in the year, Ilya Tchaikovsky had married his third wife, Elizaveta Lipport, but his continuing financial troubles had prompted him to leave the capital that spring to stay for a year with Tchaikovsky's half sister, Zinaida, and her family in the Urals. His stepmother, with whom Zinaida was not on good terms, had remained in St. Petersburg and was living with her own relatives. For a short while after his return from Kamenka, Tchaikovsky moved in with his aunt, Elizaveta Schobert, but her home was noisy and damp. In Apukhtin's apartment he finally found again the tranquillity required for study and composition.

To be sure, his own financial position was still dismal. An apartment and a servant of his own would require money, and already debts were piling up. That autumn, things had reached the point where Tchaikovsky even flirted for a time with the idea of returning to the civil service, while some of his friends advised him to accept the vacant post of meat inspector at one of St. Petersburg's markets. But Tchaikovsky's years at the conservatory had seen his commitment to music become irrevocable. "I begin to consider the future," he wrote to his sister on 8 September 1865, "that is, what I am to do upon graduating from the conservatory in December, and I am becoming more and more convinced that there is now already no other path for me except music. I have lost touch with civil service work. . . . I am unable to live anywhere but Petersburg and Moscow. It is very likely that I shall leave for Moscow."[25]

His father did not altogether agree with these plans. On 3 December 1865 he wrote to his son on the subject, "Your passion for music is praiseworthy, but, my friend, this is a slippery road: the reward for the labor of genius comes much much later. . . . Devote yourself to the civil service."[26]

But the resolution to devote his life to music came as the result of an inner maturation, and the young man was experiencing this critical moment of his life with secret and jealous self-confidence. Outward circumstances toward the end of this year appeared favorable. Besides the performance of the *Characteristic Dances* conducted by Strauss in August, Tchaikovsky was already the author of the String Quartet Movement in B flat and the Overture in F, both of which were performed that autumn in student concerts at the conservatory. Then, with his graduation still several weeks away, the young composer received an invitation from Anton Rubinstein's brother Nikolay to come to Moscow in January to teach at the newly founded Moscow Conservatory. Thus, it was with justifiable pride that Tchaikovsky wrote to his sister in early October, "In general, despite a few troubles, my disposition is rosy, mainly it would seem because of the fact that my self-esteem, which gnaws at me continuously (this is my chief shortcoming), has been flattered lately by several musical successes, and I foresee others ahead."[27]

Tchaikovsky's bright prediction failed to come true in the next several months. This and his own anxieties led him into depression. Gripped by a sudden fear of the public examination preceding the performance of his cantata on the text of Schiller's ode "An die Freude" (an ambitious idea, given Beethoven's famous treatment of the same text in his Ninth Symphony), the young man simply did not show up at the graduation concert on 29 December. Anton Rubinstein was so furious at him that there was even talk of depriving him of his diploma. Moreover, reaction to the work was almost uniformly unfavorable. The composer Aleksandr Serov, who attended the concert, was disappointed, commenting, "No, the cantata is not any good. I expected much more from Tchaikovsky."[28] Also at the concert was the composer and music critic César Cui, who published in the *Petersburg Register* a sarcastic review in which he asserted that "the composer

Mr. Tchaikovsky is utterly weak . . . and if he had had any talent, then somewhere at least it would have broken the chains of the conservatory."[29] Cui's remarks set the tone for the relationship between the two men, which remained cold throughout Tchaikovsky's life.

When Tchaikovsky asked Anton Rubinstein for his opinion of the piece, it was clear that the conservatory director liked it no better, and he reluctantly agreed to include the cantata in an upcoming concert of the Russian Musical Society only on condition that Tchaikovsky make "substantial changes" in the work, which he eventually refused to do.

Some weeks later, on 15 January 1866, Tchaikovsky wrote to his sister. But in a characteristic move, later to be employed frequently in his letters, he did not inform his relatives of the creative failure that had caused his depression. Instead, he embellished the event, though at the same time he did not hide from them his depressed mood: "I was writing my cantata, which those who were to pronounce judgment on it much admired. But in general I was suffering from an unbelievable depression and hatred of humanity. At present, this disease of the spirit . . . has far from ceased."[30] This strong reluctance to associate depressive moods and creative failures, combined with a questioning of his own psychological and spiritual health, would in time become a prominent feature of Tchaikovsky's self-appraisal.

Only his friend Hermann Laroche supported the discouraged young composer. In a letter of 11 January 1866, Laroche called the cantata "the greatest musical event in Russia" in recent times and Tchaikovsky "the only hope for our musical future." At the very close of his letter, Laroche declared, "I am so deeply fond of you, not for what you have done up to now, but for what you may write in the future, bearing in mind the power and vitality of your genius. The samples you have offered until now are only solemn promises to surpass all your contemporaries."[31]

Part Two

CREATION

1866-1876

CHAPTER SIX

The Lovable Misanthrope

Tchaikovsky arrived in Moscow on 6 January 1866, determined now to devote his life to music. In social terms, such a decision could not have been easy. The overwhelming majority of the Russian aristocracy still considered music to be, at best, merely a hobby for a gifted dilettante; at worst, musical professionalism was associated with one's social inferiors—the "music servant" or a tutor. Thus, when a person of upper-class or even upper-middle-class origin became a musician, this was usually interpreted as the result of unfortunate circumstances. Only many years later did the musical profession begin to become fashionable in society-at-large.

Both the St. Petersburg Conservatory and the Moscow Conservatory, which officially opened in September 1866, mirrored this societal attitude. Most of the students in these early years came from poor families and, as such, lacked the refined upbringing afforded in wealthier homes. A generally bohemian atmosphere prevailed among the students and was furthered by the fact that the members of the faculty were for the most part artists rather than teachers and were thus very relaxed in their methods.[1]

The guiding genius behind the Moscow Conservatory was its director, Nikolay Rubinstein. Rubinstein was a complex and remarkable man, a great pianist and conductor and an individual of rare spiritual and charismatic strength. Extremely thrifty in dispensing public funds, he was generous to the point of recklessness with his own money. He was equally popular among students and influential members of the upper-class English Club, and his inherently democratic manners made him almost as well known to street musicians, cabdrivers, and choristers as he was to the famous artists and noble patrons of the arts whom he met both as a professional musician and as a socialite. Though not very tall, Nikolay Rubinstein was solidly built, with broad shoulders, strong arms, and "thick, large fingers like iron" that could "produce sounds of terrible force" at the keyboard. Pianos that were not solid enough are said to have broken apart "like so much kindling" under his assault, and a spare instrument was essential at his concerts. His voice was loud and domineering, his expression and manner stern and imposing, and the long habit of continually curbing his unruly students and establishing order in the orchestra made his bearing all the more imperious.[2]

Rubinstein's treatment of his students was, to say the least, eccentric. For a bad performance he slapped one clarinetist repeatedly in the face until he broke down and cried. One student who was late to class was ordered by him to strip to the skin and get dressed again within five minutes. The female students seem to have been a particular bane of Rubinstein's existence. Many of the young ladies at the conservatory enrolled not with any serious desire to pursue an artistic career but simply to obtain a general musical education. Some, we are told, "behaved as though they were quite mad," and in class they would "shout, grimace, be obstinate, mince, swoon, even run out of the classroom, and altogether exasperate the professors." But Rubinstein reacted to such antics with equanimity. If a girl swooned, he would say, "Take her away!" or, more effectively, "Pour a glass of water over her head!"[3]

All the same, it was considered a great good fortune to get into Rubinstein's class, for which he chose the students himself. Despite his arrogance and willfulness, Nikolay Rubinstein was not only a great teacher and musician but also a kind and generous man. Virtually his entire salary went to support the poorer students, and there were always several students living in his apartment.

It is not surprising, then, that the first response of the director to Tchaikovsky's arrival was his support and a genuine desire to help him in any way possible. He invited him to share an apartment and helped him get settled in his new life. The older man developed a true fatherly affection for the young musician. On 23 January 1866, Tchaikovsky wrote to his brothers, "[Rubinstein] looks after me like a nanny and is determined to go on playing this role. Today he presented me forcibly with six shirts. . . . On the whole, he is an amazingly charming man!"[4] Their subsequent relationship, though at times stormy, was marked by genuine depth and mutual commitment, despite their quarrels and disagreements. Nine years later, Tchaikovsky would remark of his friendship with this man of wistful and unpredictable character that "when he has been drinking, Rubinstein likes to say that he feels a tender passion for me, but when he is sober, he can annoy me to the point of tears and insomnia."[5]

Almost at once Tchaikovsky began finding friends among Moscow musicians and his colleagues at the conservatory. The new arrival was widely liked and quickly appreciated. Tchaikovsky, together with Rubinstein and Prince Vladimir Odoevsky, a prominent literary figure, was a speaker at the conservatory's official inauguration in September of that year, and it was Tchaikovsky again who represented the conservatory during Hector Berlioz's stay in Moscow in late December 1867 and served as the distinguished visitor's guide. Berlioz conducted two concerts in Moscow and enjoyed a most enthusiastic reception. At a ceremonial banquet in Berlioz's honor, Tchaikovsky delivered "a beautiful speech in French, in which he appraised with his characteristic enthusiasm [Berlioz's] high merits."[6]

Of his initial circle of musical friends in Moscow, there were three with whom Tchaikovsky would enjoy particularly close professional ties during his Moscow period: Kashkin, Albrecht, and Hubert. Nikolay Kashkin was the first professor at the conservatory whom Tchaikovsky met after his introduction to Rubinstein. During the many years of their subsequent friendship, Kashkin often acted as a first critic, intelligent and benevolent, of Tchaikovsky's compositions. Along with their professional interests, the two men also shared a taste for cards and carousing. For Karl Albrecht, inspector at the conservatory, Tchaikovsky became virtually a member of the family. He dined regularly with the Albrechts at their home, greatly enjoying their company. Also, Tchaikovsky appreciated very highly Albrecht's musical abilities and regretted that he chose not to compose. Nikolay Hubert arrived at the conservatory from St. Petersburg somewhat later, in the early 1870s. He taught music theory, and while he enjoyed Tchaikovsky's great affection, this would not prevent Tchaikovsky from later noting that his friend, though a kind and intelligent man, was utterly lacking in any true independence of mind.[7]

Meanwhile, his old friend Hermann Laroche, who graduated from the St. Petersburg Conservatory a year after Tchaikovsky, also moved to Moscow to take up teaching. Thus did an intimate circle of friendly and congenial minds take shape around Tchaikovsky, adding pleasure not only to his professional routine but also to his leisure. It was also in these first years that Tchaikovsky and Pyotr Jurgenson struck up an acquaintance that was destined to develop into close business and personal ties. In 1861, Jurgenson had founded a music publishing house in Moscow, and he would later propose that Tchaikovsky publish his work with his firm. Tchaikovsky would readily have agreed, but by then he had an arrangement with the publisher Vasily Bessel in St. Petersburg, which it would take him some time to end.

Although the Moscow Conservatory would not open officially until September 1866, music courses were already being given when Tchaikovsky arrived, and he was shortly to begin teaching classes himself. Many of his students, as it turned out, were young women. "My lessons have not started yet," wrote Tchaikovsky, then twenty-five, to his stepmother, Elizaveta, on 15 January 1866, "but yesterday I had to give an examination to everyone who had entered the course. I confess I was terrified at the sight of such an enormous number of crinolines, chignons, etc. But I still hope that I shall manage to captivate these fays, since in general the local ladies are awfully passionate. Rubinstein has no idea how to rid himself of the whole army of ladies who offer him their . . . charms."[8] Ilya Tchaikovsky reacted to his son's predicament in his own inimitable style in a letter of 5 February: "I imagine you sitting at the rostrum; you are surrounded by rosy, white, blue, round, thin, chubby, white-faced, round-cheeked maidens desperately in love with music, and you lecture to them like Apollo sitting on the hill with his harp or lyre while around him the Graces, just like your listeners only nude or draped in gauze, listen to his songs. I should be very curious to see you sitting there, blushing in confusion."[9]

But the playful tone in several of Tchaikovsky's letters of the time masked a growing sense of anxiety caused by the conflict between the exigencies of his creative work and the pedagogical pressures on his time and energy. Early in 1866 he began work on his Symphony no. 1 in G Minor, which he was to entitle *Winter Dreams* (or in a more correct translation of the Russian, *Winter Daydreams*). Increasingly, his immersion in serious creativity, with the requisite psychological commitment, was leading him to a painful nervous reaction against external demands. The difficult struggle to establish a rigorous working routine is reflected in his letters of the period, with their frequent complaints about his health and his mood.

Such complaints were to become a recurrent feature of his correspondence, so much so that many scholars have even questioned his mental stability. This traditional view, familiar to Western readers, depicts Tchaikovsky as a suffering psychotic and more often than not links his condition to the issue of his homosexuality. Such a notion is, however, misconceived, for it is based on a superficial reading of his writings and an uncritical acceptance of the claims of certain memoirs.

That Tchaikovsky suffered at times from hypersensitivity and nervous tension is beyond doubt. But these are conditions quite common in creative intellects. If our concept of "normality," in its usual sense, is to be based on an evaluation of Tchaikovsky's outward conduct and not on his often morbid self-evaluation, it must be recognized that in his behavior Tchaikovsky met every social requirement, despite the hardship and discomfort that, as we know from his letters and diaries, he often endured.

A characteristic blend of complaints about creative difficulties, social pressures, and what Tchaikovsky considered problems of his health is seen in a letter to Anatoly of 25 April 1866,[10] wherein Tchaikovsky described for his brother the daily routine he had managed to establish by this time. It was a routine that was not to change significantly for the rest of his life. After waking between nine and ten, he would take his tea and then, at eleven, either give a lesson or work on his symphony until half past two, followed by a stroll and then dinner at four o'clock either at friends' or at a pub and, after dinner, another stroll or more work. Evenings were usually spent with friends or at a club, and it seems that about this time he acquired the habit of playing cards, to which he later became quite addicted. Returning home around midnight, he would compose again for a while or write letters and then read for a long time in bed before going to sleep.

But, he told his brother, for some while he had been suffering from insomnia, which, under his pen, took on the proportions of a physical illness. "Lately I have been sleeping abominably," he wrote. "My little apoplectic fits recur with greater force than earlier, and by now I can always tell, when I am going to bed, whether I shall have them or not, and if so, I try not to sleep; thus, for instance, two days ago I did not sleep almost the entire night. My nerves are again utterly shot." Tchaikovsky found some outlet for his external and internal pressures in caffeine and alcohol, which presumably stimulated his nightly work but also no doubt contributed to depression and insomnia. He himself seems to have recognized this, and surely it was not by chance that in the same letter he wrote, "Starting yesterday I have stopped drinking vodka, wine, and strong tea."

Tchaikovsky's own explanation for his nervous condition mingled several elements: the sluggish progress on his symphony; the relentless teasing of Rubinstein and other friends who, having observed his timorousness, had taken to startling him at every turn; and, most suggestive, "the thought pursuing me constantly that I shall soon die and shall not even have time to complete my symphony successfully." All this confusion and tension led him to a sudden outburst of misanthropy. "In general, I hate the human race," he claimed, "and should gladly withdraw into the desert, with only the smallest retinue."

It would be wrong to take this and similar statements at face value. Repeatedly the evidence of Tchaikovsky's life and work belies the hatred of mankind he vented in darker moments. But this one letter alone, with its intertwining complaints of both a material and a spiritual nature (and much more such evidence is found within the body of his correspondence), seems to offer sufficient basis for the belief that in Tchaikovsky's case the themes of physical health and psychological health constitute two facets of a single subject that cannot be discussed in its entirety from only one particular angle. We encounter here, as in almost everything related to the composer, various levels of apparent contradiction or exaggeration.

Even during the summer of 1866, spent with relatives outside St. Petersburg, when Tchaikovsky himself asserted that his health was in a "desirable state," he was troubled by "little fits" that would interfere with his work. Modest gives a dramatic description of that summer's tribulations. His brother's nerves were becoming more and more upset. The abnormal labor was killing his sleep, and the sleepless nights were sapping his energy and paralyzing his creative powers. "At the end of July," recalls Modest, "all this broke out in attacks of a terrible nervous disorder such as was never again repeated in his life. The doctor . . . summoned to treat him found that he was 'one step away from madness' and during the first days considered his condition to be almost desperate. The main and most dreadful symptoms of this disease were that the patient was tormented by hallucinations, overcome by a terrifying fear of something, and that all his extremities were completely numb."[11]

At least one of Tchaikovsky's ancestors on his mother's side suffered from epilepsy. The possibility cannot be altogether dismissed that Tchaikovsky may have displayed, albeit in a lesser form, certain secondary manifestations of this disorder. It may be tempting to seek a hereditary source of the "little apoplectic fits" that Tchaikovsky experienced from time to time throughout his life, but it seems no less plausible to see them as simply one of the most palpable somatic manifestations of his hypersensitive constitution. Tchaikovsky's personal physician, Vasily Bertenson, unequivocally embraced the latter view. "In his childhood Pyotr Ilyich would very often awake in the middle of the night in hysterical fits," the doctor recollected. "In later years this nervousness manifested itself in insomnia and in phenomena that he called 'little fits,' that is, a sudden awakening from some sort of jolt, with a sensation of insurmountable terror. These 'little fits,' at times recurring nearly every night, drove him to a hatred of going to bed that sometimes lasted for months, and during this time, he would fall asleep only in his robe, now sitting in his armchair, now stretched out on the sofa."[12]

That Tchaikovsky's neurosis often manifested itself psychosomatically, binding his psychological condition and physical well-being inextricably, helps to explain both his drastic shifts in mood, with an attendant impetuosity, and his commitment to the iron discipline required by his work. Tchaikovsky himself was well aware of the interrelation of his physiological and psychological problems, speculating on them sometimes to inadvertent comic effect, as when he wrote in a letter to Modest of 9 September 1877, "These past days I have even suffered from diarrhea caused by that particular sensation of terror characteristic of nervous persons with respect to strong and unpleasant sensations."[13]

The conflict between his creative needs and external pressures was to develop into a major part of Tchaikovsky's psychological experience and may account for many of his later idiosyncrasies. During the months he worked on his First Symphony, one of the offshoots of this conflict was a change in Tchaikovsky's attitude toward his former companions and acquaintances from St. Petersburg's homosexual circles—the more so as some of them had not supported his resolute choice of a musical career. His recognition of the new period opening in his life not only made Tchaikovsky abandon the earlier, somewhat dissolute ways of a young socialite but also led to his disappointment in, and disapproval of, those who encouraged a mode of existence he now considered meaningless. On 16 April 1866, for example, Tchaikovsky wrote bitterly to his brothers of a recent visit from Prince Golitsyn. "I dined with [Golitsyn] at Dussot's restaurant," he told them. "I cannot say that I was especially glad to see him; he is not at all one of my closest friends; besides which, I have begun to be particularly struck lately by the emptiness and insignificance of these people!"[14] Nonetheless, this new outlook would not prevent him making the journey four years later from Switzerland to Munich in order to spend a day with Golitsyn, who was serving in the Russian embassy there.

Somewhat similar sentiments must have been reflected in a letter to Apukhtin that has not been preserved but to which the poet responded at length in May 1866. Its lighthearted tone notwithstanding, Apukhtin's response illuminates the very different attitudes and opinions of the two men, which eventually contributed to a growing coolness in their relationship, and it raises some important issues that seem to have concerned Tchaikovsky at the time. "You seem to have become carried away there in Moscow by historical reminiscences and to have taken as your model Andrey Kurbsky," wrote Apukhtin, referring to the sixteenth-century Russian general who defected to Poland, whence he carried on a correspondence with Ivan the Terrible sharply critical of the tsar.

> You've run away somewhere and now hurl abusive letters at me from there. You have definitely gone mad, calling me a "court rhymester to G[olitsy]n," etc. On reading your letter, I of course became furious and began casting my eyes about for Vasily Shibanov in order to run him through with something like a pike [a reference to a ballad by A. K. Tolstoy, in which Shibanov (Kurbsky's servant) is tortured by Ivan for delivering one of Kurbsky's letters], but instead of your faithful servant I saw a postman, unspeared and asking for three k[opecks] which I didn't have. As for the content of your letter, I can only wonder at the strange contradiction: expressing your disappointment in Golitsyn and Co., preaching your proudly contemptuous and perfectly justified view of people, you at the same time continue to believe, like a naive schoolgirl, in *labor* and *struggle*. Strange that you've not mentioned *progress* as well. Why should we labor? With whom should we struggle? My dear pepinyerka [a female student at a fashionable boarding school], be convinced once and for all that labor is sometimes a bitter necessity and always the greatest punishment allotted to man, that an occupation chosen according to one's taste and inclination is not labor, and that musical composition is for you the same sort of labor as conversations with Mitya are for Mrs. Nilus [two Moscow acquaintances of Tchaikovsky's] or buying a new tie for [Golitsyn's lover] Masalitinov. And can it be that my admiring the beauty of X is also to be regarded as labor? Don't be . . . stingy with your letters and answer at once. You are among the few people whom I endure.[15]

Apukhtin's letter juxtaposes two archetypal views of art and life: the idealistically inclined soul and the hedonistic and cynical individualist; or, in historical terms, Romanticism and the reaction against it. The letter also leaves no doubt that the two of them were still informed about one another's amorous life: we notice the condescendingly ironic epithet "pepinyerka" (feminine in Russian, from the French *pépinière*), while the undecoded "X" whose beauty the poet admires is scarcely likely to have been female. At times, such a tone may well have struck Tchaikovsky as offensive. In any case, outside the realm of eroticism Apukhtin was quite unsuccessful in his role as tempter. Tchaikovsky never surrendered to moral relativism or general cynicism, and to a great extent, he preserved until the end of his life the youthful idealism (equally characteristic of his father) that made his personality so attractive.

Quite possibly, this conflict of values was the underlying cause of Tchaikovsky's ultimate nonacceptance of Apukhtin. Nonacceptance, however, is not rejection, and Tchaikovsky's letters leave little doubt of his strong attachment to Apukhtin, despite their periodic quarrels and disagreements. He even encouraged his brothers' visits to Apukhtin (as well as to Golitsyn), apparently not in the least disturbed by the matter of homosexuality.[16] But on one occasion at least, Apukhtin, for whatever reason, seems by some intrigue to have aroused discord between Tchaikovsky and his brother Anatoly. The latter complained in a letter to Tchaikovsky of 30 January 1866, "Apukhtin has been assuring me that you wrote him that I allegedly behave very badly toward you. At first, of course, I did not believe him, but then he spoke so persuasively that I started to believe him a bit."[17] Tchaikovsky's reaction to this was indignation; nevertheless, he allowed Anatoly to turn to Apukhtin for some financial assistance.[18]

The correspondence of these years suggests that the aspiring composer continued in spirit to be very much with his brothers in St. Petersburg. He followed anxiously the routine of their lives and was informed in detail of every development. Indeed, by the end of March 1866, Tchaikovsky could no longer bear the separation and went to St. Petersburg on two weeks' vacation to be with his brothers.

It was this same spring that Tchaikovsky made the acquaintance of the "exceptionally daring and brazen" actor and baritone Konstantin de Lazari, well known to Muscovites by his stage name of Konstantinov. In his memoirs, de Lazari offers a picturesque and humorous description of their first meeting. He had once stayed the night, he tells us, at Nikolay Rubinstein's apartment, and in the morning he asked the servant Agafon to bring him a cup of tea. A moment later, he heard another voice, "tender and resembling a contralto," demand the same. Putting on his dressing gown, de Lazari went into the next room and there surprised a young man "of charming appearance and magically expressive eyes" still in bed, who cried out that he was not yet dressed and embarrassedly covered his naked chest with the blanket. De Lazari, remarking that his new acquaintance behaved like a frightened maiden, told him not to be afraid and asked his name.

"I am a professor at the conservatory here, and my name is Tchaikovsky."

"You're a professor?" exclaimed de Lazari. "You're joking! What kind of professor can you be! You must be a student!"

"As you wish," answered Tchaikovsky irritably.[19]

A companionable socialite, de Lazari knew everyone in Moscow theatrical circles and introduced his new friend to, among others, the prominent actor Prov Sadovsky, who took an instant and intense liking to the young composer, whose "modesty, magic face, pleasant laughter, and, in general, some kind of particular fascination charmed everyone."[20] The elderly Sadovsky, upon Tchaikovsky's entrance into a room, "would always dissolve into a blissful smile, then, having shaken his hand, would pull him close, kiss him, and make him sit for a few minutes beside him on the sofa; then, fixing, as it were, a greedy look on Petya, Sadovsky would quickly grab his shoulders, draw him near, and kiss the nape of his neck with a smack, and, pushing him away, would exclaim, 'Who are you?' and again would draw him close, kiss his neck and push him away; one could not watch this amusing scene without laughing."[21]

It was also de Lazari who one time brought Tchaikovsky to the country home of Vladimir Begichev, the repertory director of the Moscow state theaters. Here Tchaikovsky was introduced to Begichev's wife, Mariya Shilovskaya, and to her two sons from her first marriage, Konstantin and Vladimir. Although he became friendly with the elder brother, Konstantin, it was his acquaintance with the younger brother, Vladimir, that was to become one of Tchaikovsky's most intimate and significant friendships of the coming years. It was Vladimir Shilovsky whom de Lazari had in mind when he told Tchaikovsky, before taking him to the Begichev home, that there was "an extremely talented boy in that family who will probably need music lessons, to be paid for handsomely."[22]

The Begichev household was far from ordinary. Mariya Shilovskaya was an amateur actress and singer who managed to gather about her all musical and literary Moscow. She was both willful and capricious, and according to some accounts, her personal life before her marriage to Begichev had been quite stormy. This appears to have been also the case with Begichev himself, who enjoyed the reputation of a philanderer and had wild success among the ladies of high society. It is understandable, then, that the marriage was also a stormy one, marked by numerous scandals, breakups, and mutual recriminations. Harassed by her stepmother, Begichev's daughter by his first marriage has left some colorful recollections of her father and her stepmother, "who played a fateful role in his life."[23]

Both of Mariya Shilovskaya's sons showed artistic and creative promise and a passionate love of art, Vladimir in particular. Konstantin wrote good poetry and stories, painted and sang well, and also composed gypsy songs that for a time made him famous throughout Moscow. But in his private life Konstantin was a man of many enthusiasms and extreme disorderliness, whose interest would shift suddenly from alchemy to black magic, from the everyday life of ancient Egypt to the customs of pre-Petrine Russia. A lifelong theater lover, he constantly took part in amateur productions, and later, when the Shilovsky fortune was lost, he even joined the Maly Theater as an actor.[24] Such dilettantism—or, as Modest puts it, "a superficial upper-class attitude toward work"—ultimately prevented both Konstantin and his apparently more-gifted younger brother from developing into serious artists. Vladimir Shilovsky spent his life stubbornly trying to compose, but he was no less passionate in collecting precious stones, being especially fascinated by diamonds.

But in 1866 the adolescent Vladimir gave the impression of being a child prodigy. "He was then a fourteen-year-old boy," Modest tells us, "weak, sickly, with, as a result, a neglected education, but endowed, as it seemed then, with phenomenal capacities for music. In addition, his appearance was unusually attractive, his manners most spontaneously charming, and his mind, despite his poor education, sharp and observant." Modest notes that "Pyotr Ilyich was bound to his pupil not only by the boy's talent, likeable character, and a pity for his sickliness, but also in great measure by that love verging on adoration which he instilled in the boy."[25] This last observation is important: though Tchaikovsky's profound attachment to Shilovsky cannot be doubted, the emotional initiative would almost always proceed in the opposite direction, namely, from pupil to teacher.

During the many years of their acquaintance their relationship was psychologically turbulent and from time to time fraught with ruptures and hysterics. The main fault seems to have been that of Shilovsky, who had inherited his mother's unruly character. But at first Tchaikovsky was utterly delighted with his new acquisition. Even a year later, in October 1867, he would write to his aunt Ekaterina Alekseeva in Baden-Baden, where Shilovsky had also gone to take the cure, "I can imagine how fond you have become of my Volodka [Vladimir]: this little gentleman seems to have been created to captivate and charm one and all. God grant that he may later shine also with his talent as he does now with his other qualities. For his talent is most remarkable."[26]

It was not only the exigencies of old and new friendships that weighed on Tchaikovsky in the course of his first season in Moscow. Again and again, in public and in private, he had to confront the matter of his attitudes toward, and relations with, the female sex. On the one hand, he still felt continuing pressure from his aging father, who passionately wished to see his son wed, and on the other hand, in closest proximity, there was the powerful and domineering Rubinstein, with his aggressive heterosexuality, and the provocative behavior of his many female students. Not only male but also female students were invited by Rubinstein to spend the night in his apartment, and Rubinstein would in turn often visit these young ladies in their hotels or apartments.[27] Meanwhile, the reputedly unruly contingent of young and often flirtatious women at the Moscow Conservatory inevitably contributed to a peculiar, erotically charged atmosphere within its walls. In essence, everything in Tchaikovsky's new environment impelled him to follow the rules of the game and initiate the courtship of a suitable young woman, with the eventual purpose of marriage.

Despite his distinct preferences and his earlier homosexual infatuations at the School of Jurisprudence and during his St. Petersburg period, Tchaikovsky seems still at this time to have believed that he could somehow conform to heterosexual standards of conduct without any great difficulty. Not only did the prevailing view hold that sexual games between boys were merely transitional and a matter of course, by no means excluding heterosexuality, but the constant presence of women had been, after all, a conspicuous circumstance of Tchaikovsky's childhood and adolescence. His mother; his governess, Fanny Dürbach; his sister, Aleksandra; and his cousin Anna Merkling were among the people he loved most in his life. This love can in no way have been erotic in character: even in the case of Fanny Dürbach and Anna Merkling it began too early. Yet, it is very possible that just such an intimate friendship with his sister or cousin may have contributed to Tchaikovsky's conviction that to love a woman would not constitute a problem for him, psychologically or otherwise. The physical aspect of sexuality was relegated in nineteenth-century Russia, as in Victorian England, to the margin of ordinary consciousness. This must certainly have been the case with Tchaikovsky as well. It is likely that he did not give much thought to any possible inadequacy, especially as dozens of young ladies were falling in love with him.

As testified universally by the memoirists writing about this period in his life, the young Tchaikovsky was very good-looking and presumably sexually attractive. "How I remember his appearance then," recalls one of his former students at the time of his Moscow Conservatory professorship. "[He was] young, with nice-looking, almost beautiful features, a deep expressive gaze in his beautiful dark eyes, fluffy, carelessly combed hair, and a marvelous blond beard."[28]

It was almost immediately upon his arrival in Moscow that a young woman appeared on his horizon. She was the niece of Rubinstein's neighbor Tarnovsky, Elizaveta Dmitrieva, nicknamed Mufka by her family. The two were brought together by Rubinstein, who had had a brief affair with Mufka some time before. Tchaikovsky wrote to Modest in February 1866, "I am rather often at the home of our neighbors the Tarnovskys. There is one niece who is more charming than anything I've seen. To tell the truth, I am quite preoccupied by her, which gives Rubinstein occasion to pester me in the most awful manner. No sooner do we arrive at the Tarnovskys' than they start to tease her and me and push us together. She is called Mufka at home, and at present my chief thought is how I, too, might gain the right to call her by that name; for this, one has only to be more intimately acquainted with her."[29]

Ilya Tchaikovsky, who followed the amorous life of his favorite son with the greatest attention, was delighted with the description of Mufka in a letter (now lost) from Tchaikovsky to which he replied on 14 March 1866: "I shall tell you frankly: in your letter I liked best of all the niece. She must be most pretty, most lovely, and certainly quite clever. I have so fallen in love with her that I wish to see her without fail. Please afford me this opportunity when I come to Moscow."[30] But the old man's joy was premature. A letter to Anatoly of 6 March already revealed the change in Tchaikovsky's attitude toward Mufka: "I continue to visit the Tarnovskys constantly, and, though I am not (for certain reasons) in love with Mufka, I still find pleasure in chatting with her."[31] And to both his brothers he wrote on 16 April, "I have utterly cooled toward Mufka. . . . In general, I am very much disappointed in her."[32] Tchaikovsky declined to elaborate the reasons for his disappointment. But, in fact, the young man remained rather cool toward women in general, and if he did occasionally become inflamed, it was for a brief time only. Women, on the contrary, fell in love with him far more passionately and lastingly, and would continue to do so for many years to come.

The young conservatory professor's music was beginning to be heard more and more often in public concerts. On 1 May 1866, Anton Rubinstein conducted Tchaikovsky's Overture in F at the Mikhailov

Palace in St. Petersburg. In his letter quoted earlier, Apukhtin wrote, "I attended a popular concert (and made this sacrifice solely for the sake of your overture, since the very name of the concert, 'popular,' filled me with rage). I applauded your overture madly and was very pleased with it."[33]

Tchaikovsky spent the summer of 1866 at a country house near St. Petersburg rented by Aleksandra's mother-in-law. He had for company his brother Modest, then sixteen, while the other twin, Anatoly, for financial reasons, stayed with their sister and her husband at Kamenka. In early June, Tchaikovsky wrote to Anatoly that he thought of him "every minute" while Modest slept nearby "disturbing the night's peace with his heavy snoring." But, commenting on Modest's good behavior, he pointed out that "he has much improved with respect to his touchiness . . . [and] all day long he sings or dances in the most harmless and inoffensive manner. His constant gaiety and equanimity even have a very pleasing effect on me."[34] That same summer, Tchaikovsky and Apukhtin made a brief journey to the shores of Lake Ladoga, north of St. Petersburg, and visited the ancient monastery on Valaam Island. Dating from the tenth century, the monastery is surrounded by numerous hermitages scattered about the many smaller islands of the lake. The bleak beauty of the landscape, with its crisp, dense forests, and wide expanse of lake, made an unforgettable impression on both Tchaikovsky and Apukhtin, and was later described in Apukhtin's poem "A Year in a Monastery."[35]

Throughout the summer months Tchaikovsky continued to work regularly at night on his symphony *Winter Dreams*, which, having completed the sketches in early May, he began scoring in June. But physical exhaustion and nervousness brought on by working at night prevented Tchaikovsky from finishing the symphony, and he would not complete the score until his return to Moscow. Nevertheless, while still in St. Petersburg, he decided to show the unfinished work to his former professors Anton Rubinstein and Nikolay Zaremba. To his dismay, both men expressed dislike of the symphony, greatly offending Tchaikovsky, who found few of their criticisms acceptable. The event laid the foundation for the cooling of his relationship with Anton Rubinstein.

The "Moscow Rubinstein," Nikolay, on the other hand, very much liked the symphony and in December played the scherzo from it at a concert of the Russian Musical Society. The full work would not be performed until more than a year later on 3 February 1868, with Nikolay Rubinstein again conducting. In spite of Zaremba and Anton Rubinstein's opinion, the performance was a resounding success and the young composer was called back repeatedly. Together with those of Rimsky-Korsakov and Borodin, Tchaikovsky's *Winter Dreams* was one of the first symphonies written by a Russian composer. Filled with a distinctive blend of anguish and youthful expectation, and clearly much influenced by Russian folk motifs and melody, the work, it can be argued, already possessed the imprint of the young composer's individual style. It was also his first real triumph, but it made him no less self-critical. Aware of a number of weaknesses in the work, he decided to rewrite portions of it, though he would carry out these revisions only some six years later, in 1874.

In November 1866, Tchaikovsky received an official commission to create an overture on the theme of the Danish national anthem to be performed on the arrival in Moscow of the Russian heir apparent, the future Alexander III, with his Danish bride. In the end, the festivities were postponed until April 1867, and Tchaikovsky's overture (op. 15) was not performed owing to an overloaded schedule. For his efforts, though, the composer was awarded a pair of gold cufflinks—the first gesture of appreciation and favor on the part of a man who, as tsar, would become one of his most ardent admirers. The overture received its premiere, under Rubinstein's direction, on 29 January 1867 and was greeted most favorably. Tchaikovsky himself genuinely liked it and much later wrote that "in its musical quality it is far better than the *1812* [Overture]," even though the latter work, written in 1880, became far more famous.

During the winter of 1866–1867 Tchaikovsky often attended meetings of the so-called Artistic Circle, founded by Nikolay Rubinstein and the renowned Russian playwright Aleksandr Ostrovsky in October 1865. In the course of his many evenings spent there, Tchaikovsky's interest in card playing deepened and turned into a passion. Two of his frequent partners in the game were his devoted admirer Prov Sadovsky and another prominent actor, Vasily Zhivokini. Konstantin de Lazari recalls the peculiarities of Tchaikovsky's conduct at cards. "He was awfully infatuated with the game itself," he notes, "and became angry when he was losing, but when luck was on his side, he seemed even more upset. . . . There was no end to his apologies for every lapse, yet he was never cross with a partner for making an error, but on the contrary, tried to intercede on his behalf if the others attacked him."[36]

It was also at this time that Tchaikovsky struck up a friendship with Ostrovsky and eventually asked him to write a libretto for an opera he was contemplating based on the playwright's classic *The Storm*. Two years earlier, at the St. Petersburg Conservatory, Tchaikovsky had composed an overture on the same subject. But to his disappointment, he learned that the same opera project had already been undertaken by another young composer. To compensate, Ostrovsky agreed to produce for his new friend, without a fee, a libretto based on another of his plays that he felt would work well as an opera, *A Dream on the Volga.* In early March 1867, Tchaikovsky received from the playwright the text of the first act and immediately sat down to work on this, his first opera, which he retitled *The Voyevode.* Tchaikovsky composed with great speed and enthusiasm, but in his inexperience he made a number of scenographic errors. He would later admit that the opera had been written too hurriedly and in a form unsuitable for performance: "I merely wrote music to a given text, without a view to the immense difference between symphony and opera in terms of style."[37]

In an attempt to speed his work along, Tchaikovsky copied various portions of the text in shorthand, noting only the initial words of the individual vocal parts. It is hardly surprising, then, that he was devastated when he happened to lose Ostrovsky's original libretto at the end of April. His work was brought to a temporary halt. "I have suffered depression all week long," he wrote to Anatoly on 2 May 1867, "of which the following circumstances are the causes: (1) bad weather, (2) lack of money, (3) the abandonment of any hope of recovering the lost libretto."[38] He attempted to produce a few sketches of the vocal parts, but could do nothing without the text. Ostrovsky promised to recreate the libretto, but by the middle of June, only the text of the first act had been completed and another pause in their collaboration ensued. Tchaikovsky would not return to his opera until autumn, writing the remaining portions of the libretto himself and not completing the full opera until July of the following year.

As the summer of 1867 began, Tchaikovsky found himself in obvious financial straits. He had planned at first to spend the summer with Anatoly in Finland, but within a week his money had run out and the two were forced to return to St. Petersburg. Tchaikovsky then decided that they should join Aleksandra's in-laws, the Davydovs, this year vacationing in Haapsalu (Hapsal), Estonia, where Modest had been since the start of the summer. But conditions in Haapsalu left much to be desired. The Davydovs were less than hospitable, and the three brothers found themselves having to dine apart from their in-laws. Owing to their lack of money, Tchaikovsky would order for the three of them a meal for only two, a state of affairs of which the Davydovs, according to Modest, were well aware. In addition, with his growing dislike of crowds, especially when he was trying to compose, Tchaikovsky was soon irritated by the myriad new acquaintances inevitable in such a resort and welcomed into the Davydov circle. He longed to work quietly on his opera and wished for no other company than that of the twins. Though "separately very pleasant," the new acquaintances, writes Modest, were "en masse burdensome and little suited to his favorite way of life."[39]

Being surrounded by his sister's in-laws, Tchaikovsky, in his correspondence with Aleksandra, naturally could not express the full extent of his annoyance. Still, some of his disappointment was plain. "From the moment our small circle was broken open," he wrote in one letter, "and whole heaps of acquaintances poured in on 'ours' [that is, the Davydovs] and thereby in part on us, I began to frown and have made an inner vow never again to spend the summer in such places where people dance virtually every day and pay visits to one another every minute. . . . But here's the nasty part: I have had continual opportunity at Haapsalu to become convinced that I harbor within me the disease called 'misanthropy.' I am overcome here by terrible fits of hatred toward mankind."[40]

These final sentences are very characteristic of Tchaikovsky's epistolary practice: circumstantial nuisances and a bad mood resulting in the immediate exaggeration of labeling himself a "misanthrope." It is important to stress that such pronouncements should be taken not literally but rather as the momentary judgment of a foul mood. Tchaikovsky's physician, Vasily Bertenson, would later touch upon this matter. "They say that Pyotr Ilyich was a *misanthrope*," he wrote. "Was this so? True, he used to avoid people and felt most comfortable in his solitude, and this to such a degree that even people so close to his heart as his sister and brothers could be a burden to him, and at certain periods he was sometimes happy when there was no one except the servants about him. . . . Yet, all this in no way stemmed from a dislike of people but, on the contrary, from an excess of love for them. . . . He wished everything and everyone well and was only truly happy when he had succeeded in making someone else happy, or helping someone, or supporting something beautiful."[41]

Tchaikovsky himself was not unaware of the greater complexities in his attitude, and in his more sober moments, he waved off any claims of true misanthropy. "I am a misanthrope not in the sense of hating people but in that of finding contact with their *society* irksome," he would confess to Mrs. von Meck in a letter of 15 October 1879.[42] He further recognized the fundamental contradiction between his fear of solitude and his almost equal fear of people's company. While noting at one point that he had "become intolerably depressed as a result of a strong nervous disorder" and that he longed "to go away somewhere and hide in some lonely backwoods,"[43] he elsewhere confessed that he was "really disturbed by this unbearable state of mind, which overcomes me every time I am abroad alone! There is something morbid in this!"[44] He also freely acknowledged how difficult he would be to live with: "My strange irritable character *à la longue* must be burdensome and difficult for any continuous cohabitation."[45]

Misanthrope or not, his capacity for inspiring love and devotion never ceased, a fact that at Haapsalu further aggravated the situation for Tchaikovsky, who was quite unprepared for any serious feelings toward a woman. Staying at Haapsalu was Vera Davydova, the younger sister of Tchaikovsky's brother-in-law, Lev Davydov. That the young lady experienced quite deep feelings for the aspiring musician had been more or less common talk among his relatives at least as far back as October 1865, when Tchaikovsky had written to his sister, "As regards what you wrote me concerning memories left at Kamenka, I refuse to believe it, this never entered my head, and if it were true, that is, serious, then it would affect me in the most unpleasant way."[46]

Now, when Aleksandra wrote asking him why he had decided to go to Haapsalu knowing that Vera was there, Tchaikovsky, in his defense, attempted to transfer the whole issue to another plane altogether. "It seems to me that if what you assume does in fact exist, then my absence is probably more harmful to her than my presence," he wrote to his sister from Haapsalu on 8 August 1867. "When I am not around, my person can perhaps be imagined worthy of love, but when a woman who loves me confronts daily my far from poetic qualities, for example, my untidiness, irritability, cowardice, pettiness, vanity, secretiveness, and so on, believe me the halo surrounding me when I am far distant vanishes very quickly. Perhaps I am blind and foolish, but I swear to you that aside from the most simple friendliness I have noticed nothing." He begged his sister not to think that he would "deliberately inflame a tender heart so as then to strike it down with still colder indifference. I am completely incapable of such great villainy."[47]

Yet, despite the clear lack of any feelings of attraction on his part, it was in Haapsalu that the tension between Vera Davydova and Tchaikovsky reached its peak, even though Tchaikovsky intransigently refused to acknowledge it. "Either I am completely stupid or Vera Vasilyevna is such an actress as has not been seen for ages," Tchaikovsky, justifying himself against the continued reproaches of his sister, wrote to her on 11 October. "If earlier I may still have feared what you consider to be established fact, this summer I became convinced once and for all that apart from the most routine, so to say, ordinary, albeit strong, friendship on her part, there is nothing else. . . . As regards your supposition that I stir up her feelings because of my empty vanity, I hope you have already abandoned this idea. . . . I swear to you to behave henceforth as you find fit, and if you command it, I shall refrain from any trips to Petersburg, since to be in Petersburg and not visit them [Aleksandra's in-laws] is impossible."[48]

For all his protestations, it was precisely at this time that Tchaikovsky wrote his *Souvenir de Hapsal*, op. 2, which he dedicated to Vera. The manuscript of these piano pieces she adoringly kept in a special folder all her life. In dedicating them to her, either Tchaikovsky was somehow deluding himself for the moment as to his true feelings or—which seems more likely—not wishing to offend her, he was attempting to humor to some degree her amorous mood. In any event, by the following spring things had reached the point where at least one party could envision the prospect of marriage. "The one thing that torments and worries me is Vera," Tchaikovsky wrote in a letter to Aleksandra of 16 April 1868.

> Teach and guide me: what am I to do and how am I to behave toward her? I am well aware of how all this should have ended, but what would you have me do if I feel that I would have come to hate her if the question of culminating our relations in marriage had become serious? I know that she out of pride, and others out of ignorance or extraneous considerations, do not imagine this at all, but I also know that despite any obstacles, I should have taken on myself the initiative in this matter and considered a favorable resolution to it the greatest happiness for myself, since there are no creatures anywhere so wonderful as she. But I am so base and ungrateful that I cannot act as I ought to, and, for God's sake, tear up this letter.[49]

Finally, in a rather convoluted letter to Aleksandra written on 24 September 1868, Tchaikovsky attempted to explain his position conclusively, though still with extreme caution.[50] The prevailing tone of this letter, which reflects a recurrent pattern in his attitude toward women, was one of misery and discomfort. "It is unquestionable and inevitable," he wrote, "that I shall always suffer somewhat from my powerlessness to make her [Vera] happy, to provide an outlet for the emotion that, as she puts it, has absorbed her whole existence. The matter here is one of the happiness of an entire life, and it would be strange were I to be utterly indifferent to her love for me. It is precisely because I love her and am grateful to her with all my heart that I must feel some torment. Of this, then, please assure her, if (which surprises me) she can still have doubts that I have long responded to her in my heart with the warmest friendship and gratitude."

The thrust of his argument to his sister was the sharp distinction between passion and sympathy, love and friendship. It was the latter alone that he felt for Vera, and implicit in the argument was his demand that a woman who felt for him a whole spectrum of emotions, erotic love included, limit herself solely to spiritual companionship: "As regards my coldness, which so distresses her, it stems from numerous causes, of which the chief is that I love her as a sister, but our relations (owing to the pressure of various social conventions) cannot be sincere, and this places between us a sort of wall through which we cannot relate to one another directly." His words betray a certain homoerotic subtext, of which Aleksandra would obviously not have been aware. This can be divined, for instance, in the reference to "the pressure of various social conventions" that prevent their relations from being sincere, that is, from acquiring a character desired by many homosexuals who wish to have a woman as a close friend, the equivalent of a sister or a mother, thoroughly devoid of any erotic dimension, and who believe that this can be achieved through frank confession and subsequent mutual understanding—a goal Tchaikovsky sought for some time.

A "myriad of psychological subtleties" that "perhaps a Tolstoy or a Thackeray might be able to analyze" further prevented their prolonged closeness. "In the first place," he continued, "we both constantly lie to one another; she (fearing, in her words, to bore me with a sanctimonious mien) feigns indifference, and I pretend not to understand anything or know anything. But meanwhile, we both understand and know one another—and thus in our conversations there resounds a certain dissonance. This irritates me, I begin to grow angry and feel that I cannot hide it; she is distressed, I feel this; she feels that I feel this; I feel that she feels that I feel this, and so on ad infinitum." The unspoken inference suggested itself: only if they were apart could their relationship be true and meaningful.

Tchaikovsky suspected that the root of Vera's love for him was her belief in his musical genius, which irritated him all the more when he himself was very often tortured by self-doubts. If at such a moment she began to admire his compositions or asked him to play, he was "gripped by a terrible anger" both at himself and at her. When, on the contrary, he was "filled with confidence in my abilities," as was the case, he noted, in Haapsalu, her high opinion of him flattered and pleased him, and "owing to this invisible cause, relations between us become more affectionate." The human response, he told his sister, was unpredictable. "Some valve in the heart will suddenly close, and however you force yourself, you remain cold; then, also for no particular reason, the valve will open and you are moved by the tenderest of brotherly feelings; but repentance appears, malice overcomes you, and the valve has closed again."

It is not impossible that Tchaikovsky's own homoerotic experience (with Kireev, for instance) was ultimately responsible for his closing comment on the tortuous interaction between the lover and the beloved, an archetype recognized from Plato's time. "I'll tell you," wrote Tchaikovsky, "that there is an inexplicable law of fate, whereby a person who is strongly loved, no matter how kind and gentle he may be at heart, cannot but tyrannize and torment a little the one who loves. I have frequently felt myself yield to this force, and if I inflict harm on a person so kind and loving and by me beloved, I do so not of my own will."

Many of these same moral and psychological points were to re-emerge in far more refined fashion in Tchaikovsky's later relations with Nadezhda von Meck—of whom, in this particular sense, Vera Davydova can be seen as a forerunner.

Despite the mounting pressure from his family to marry Vera, Tchaikovsky eventually managed to reshape the budding affair along the lines of a noncommittal yet lasting friendship. "Time alone," he told Aleksandra in the same letter, "can heal our wounds, eliminate misunderstandings, and make our relations as simple and sincere as we both wish them to be." In the end, especially after her own marriage, Vera succeeded in fulfilling this expectation and Tchaikovsky's unexpressed demand that her relationship with him relinquish passionate love and abide in the friendship of spirit and intellect.

Tchaikovsky's prudent and sensitive handling of this potentially embarrassing situation showed again a solid common sense incompatible with the popular view of the composer as a living illustration for a textbook on psychopathology. Despite the sharp shifts of mood and emotional excesses often reflected in his correspondence, in the main Tchaikovsky was endowed with both mental and spiritual good health, if this is understood as a sense of measure in outward conduct and a capacity for sober introspection. It is true that Tchaikovsky's inward image as it emerges from his own writings and from the recollections of those closest to him, though hardly psychopathic, is unquestionably neurotic. Yet, his phobias and foibles, while numerous, were of a secondary nature. It is naive and ultimately misguided to attach exaggerated significance to his homosexuality, blaming it and it alone for his fits of depression and nervous tension, instead of placing the whole complex matter in proper perspective. Though by no means a trivial factor, Tchaikovsky's homosexuality was only one of many conscious and subconscious conflicts affecting his creativity. His rich and complex inner life cannot be reduced to its erotic content, however sublimated. There still remains a personality of diverse and sophisticated psychological and spiritual vitality.

The image he presented to most of his acquaintances was one of perfect normality, which no doubt fostered the universal affection he continued to enjoy. "Before my eyes," writes Konstantin de Lazari, "Tchaikovsky's popularity grew not daily but hourly. Everyone who joined his circle fell immediately under his spell. By the beginning of the 1868–1869 season, he was already numbered among Moscow's greatest favorites, not only as a composer but also as a person."[51] Contemporary testimony abounds to counterbalance the all too common emphasis on the composer's misanthropy, bouts of hypochondria, and other idiosyncrasies. Hermann Laroche, for instance, noted that "the number of people who had made a favorable impression on him, whom he liked, whose kindness, charm, and so on he praised in their absence in intimate conversation, sometimes simply astonished me."[52] When venturing into social life, Tchaikovsky was full of energy, though somewhat less so with age; possessed a well-developed sense of humor and self-irony; and loved merriment and jests. De Lazari flatly insists that he never met anyone able to enjoy himself "so genuinely and infectiously" as Tchaikovsky and that there was "something childishly sweet in his joy and infinitely attractive."[53]

Ivan Klimenko, whose memoirs were not influenced by Modest's biography, offers a series of amusing episodes illustrating Tchaikovsky's unconventional sense of humor and his "amazing self-control in the most comical situations, which he himself created." In one, Tchaikovsky was traveling on a train in the company of Nikolay Rubinstein, Pyotr Jurgenson, Nikolay Kashkin, Nikolay Hubert, and Klimenko:

> Petya started playing about and imitating ballet recitatives (he did this marvelously), striking various ballet poses, and suddenly proposed to us: "Gentlemen, would you like me to dance the mazurka before the ladies [who were traveling in the next compartment]?" And without waiting for a reply, he began to sing passionately the mazurka air from *A Life for the Tsar* and dashed courageously and with an inspired face into the next compartment, dancing the mazurka, and then, saying "pardon" to the ladies, turned round before them and with the same ma-

zurka step returned to us maintaining a completely serious expression on his face. Then, of course, he joined in our friendly laughter.[54]

Such anecdotes as this—and they are not few—attest to his sense of play and improvisation, the necessary kernel of any creativity, which in Tchaikovsky was expressed in his eccentricity, affectation, mischievousness, and what is customarily regarded as youthful high spirits— endearing traits he retained throughout his life.

To be sure, there were moments when Tchaikovsky experienced a painful sense of the abyss that made him fear the approach of madness. His heightened sensitivity, forged by a child's feeling of paradise lost, honed by the experience of his mother's death, and tested by a whole series of emotional crises—coupled with a high degree of intellectual honesty—at times made his life all but unbearable. Yet, at the last, as Hermann Laroche would rightly point out, Tchaikovsky was "one of those happy few whose life organizes itself in complete accordance with the demands of their consciousness and their inner nature."[55] Just as the slightest intrusion on his music and his work could plunge him into fits of despair and "misanthropy," so could his creative drive draw him out of despondency. Righting the balance was for him a necessary way of living.

CHAPTER SEVEN

Desires and Flames

On 26 May 1868, Tchaikovsky departed on an extended European vacation in the company of his favorite pupil, Vladimir Shilovsky; Shilovsky's stepfather, Vladimir Begichev; and their mutual friend Konstantin de Lazari. Shilovsky had not only invited Tchaikovsky to join them but was also paying all his travel expenses. "I live with very wealthy people who are nice besides and very fond of me," Tchaikovsky wrote to his sister on 20 July/1 August from Paris.[1]

But despite the material comfort, the journey presented Tchaikovsky with a psychological dilemma that was destined to become a recurrent pattern in the years to come: when in Russia, he would dream of traveling to Europe, and when abroad, he would inevitably experience a growing nostalgia for home. "I long terribly for my homeland," he told Aleksandra, "where so many persons dear to me live with whom I can only live during the summer." Also gnawing at him was the thought of being maintained by a wealthy admirer. Even in later years, with a benefactress of such exceptional generosity and tact as Mrs. von Meck, this position would chafe his pride and cause him periodic anxiety. "It somewhat maddens me to think that out of all the people who would have been glad to spend these three free months with me, I have chosen, not those whom I love most, but those who are richer," he confessed in his letter to his sister.[2]

Moreover, the European excursion with Shilovsky was far from an unqualified success. In his vivid recollections of their holiday abroad, de Lazari notes that he was particularly struck by an incident at the

Zoological Garden in Berlin. When workers at the zoo asked the Russian party whether they wished to watch the huge boa eat, Begichev readily agreed and a rabbit was placed in the boa's cage. In a flash, the rabbit disappeared into the serpent's maw. At the same moment, Tchaikovsky let out a terrible cry. "He burst into sobs and became completely hysterical," recalls de Lazari, "and we had to take him back to the hotel at once. It was a long time before we were able to calm him down. Until evening he remained feverish, and he could not eat anything."[3] In his letter to his sister, Tchaikovsky complained that after their week in Berlin they had now been stuck for five weeks in Paris, detained there by Shilovsky's ill health. Their dreams of "visiting the most picturesque spots in Europe" would have to be abandoned.[4] In Paris, while Shilovsky rested at the hotel, Tchaikovsky, Begichev, and de Lazari spent many of their evenings at the Opéra Comique, where one time they saw the French composer Daniel François Auber. Tchaikovsky, recalls de Lazari, was beside himself, constantly glancing over at Auber and whispering, "He's so charming!"[5]

Returning to St. Petersburg in early August, Tchaikovsky went to visit his brothers, who were staying with the Davydovs, this time at Sillomäkki, near Narva, in Estonia. At the end of the month, he departed for Moscow, where classes were to start at the beginning of September. In the course of the summer, he had got out of the habit of teaching. "At my first lesson," he told Anatoly on 10 September, "I became so confused that I had to leave for about ten minutes in order not to faint."[6]

The end of 1868 coincided with an altogether new amorous development—his "affair" with the well-known French singer Désirée Artôt. If the situation with Vera Davydova in some respect anticipated the later arrangement with Nadezhda von Meck, the adventure with Artôt, which while ultimately and predictably unsuccessful, nonetheless proceeded to the point of betrothal, can be seen to resemble in certain essential features Tchaikovsky's later failed attempt at marriage to Antonina Milyukova. In both cases, music and fame played a significant role in the attraction of one partner to the other: in the former, Tchaikovsky's to Artôt, and in the latter, Milyukova's to Tchaikovsky. The major difference, however, lay in the composer's actual choices. Artôt was a formidable personality, a prominent singer and a woman of intelligence, whereas Antonina Milyukova was a virtual nonentity.

Désirée Artôt was the professional name of Marguerite Joséphine Montagney, a French soprano (and, later, mezzo-soprano) of Belgian origin. Having studied under Pauline Viardot, she began singing with the

Paris Opéra in 1858. It is impossible to overestimate the significance for Tchaikovsky of the fact that Artôt belonged wholly to the world of art and music. This fact indeed seems to have formed the psychological basis of his infatuation. Not without reason does Hermann Laroche emphasize that to Tchaikovsky, Artôt appeared "as the virtual personification of dramatic singing, a goddess of opera uniting within herself alone gifts usually scattered among various contrasting natures."[7] One is inclined to imagine that he fell in love not so much with her as with her voice and her performance, the more so as she was neither very young, being five years Tchaikovsky's senior, nor exceptionally beautiful. She is described by Laroche as "a thirty-year-old spinster with a plain and passionate face who was just beginning to grow stout."[8] De Lazari concurs, noting that "her nose was broad and her lips somewhat too thick." Her style and talent, however, made up for everything, and above all there was her voice, "tender, passionate, and soul-stirring."[9] At a supper in Artôt's honor given by Mariya Begicheva when the singer first performed in Moscow in the spring of 1868, the entire gathering fell in love with her on the spot. The delighted hostess even knelt before Artôt in front of everyone and kissed her hand.

It was at the home of the Begichevs that Artôt and Tchaikovsky met briefly for the first time, but her name does not begin to appear in his letters until her autumn tour during that same year. We find the first mention of her in his letter to Anatoly of 10 September: "Artôt sang charmingly."[10] Two weeks later, he wrote of her again, this time more intimately. "Artôt is a splendid person," he told his brother, "she and I have become friends."[11] A month after that, he claimed that "I am now on very friendly terms with Artôt and enjoy her very noticeable favor; rarely have I met a woman so lovely, intelligent, and kind."[12] In November, a similar effusion, but one of an artistic rather than an erotic nature, appeared in a letter to Modest: "Ah! . . . if you knew what a singer and actress is Artôt! Never yet have I been under so strong a spell of an artist as this time. And it is such a pity that you cannot hear or see her. How you would admire her gestures and the grace of her movements and poses!"[13] The two brothers, of course, paid much attention to the cultivation of posture and gesture and even imitated female dancers.

By December, Tchaikovsky's infatuation with Artôt had grown obvious to everyone. Many spoke of it. De Lazari later recalled clearly "the faces of Artôt and Tchaikovsky as they gazed at one another, their mutual embarrassment when they talked, and the beaming delight in their eyes."[14] Even Prince Vladimir Odoevsky, the eminent writer and

philosopher and a man at the fringe of Tchaikovsky's circle of acquaintances, noted in his diary for 22 November, after a concert in which
Artôt had participated and at which Tchaikovsky had been present,
that "Tchaikovsky seems to be paying great court to Artôt."[15] And Anatoly wrote from St. Petersburg on 3 December, "I have heard that in
Moscow all anyone talks about is your marriage to Artôt."[16]

All this clarifies the opening of a letter to Modest from mid-
December: "I have not written to you in a long while, . . . but there
have been a great many circumstances depriving me of the opportunity
to write letters, since all my free time I have been devoting to one
person, of whom you, of course, have heard and whom I love very, very
much. By the way, tell Papa not to be angry at me for not writing him
about what everyone is saying. The fact is, nothing at all has happened
yet, and when the time comes and everything is resolved one way or
another, he will be the first to whom I shall write."[17]

The promised detailed and solemn letter to his father was finally
written on 26 December. This lengthy account of his involvement
with Artôt displayed little of the flaming passion that his sentimental
and romantic father would no doubt have preferred to find in his beloved son, still regrettably a bachelor. Rather, Tchaikovsky's recital
was crisp and matter-of-fact. "I became acquainted with Artôt last
spring," he told his father, "but visited her only once, at a supper after
her benefit performance. When she returned this autumn, I did not
visit her at all for a month. We met accidentally at a musical party;
she expressed her surprise that I had not called on her; I promised to
do so, but should not have fulfilled this promise (owing to my characteristic reluctance to make acquaintances) had not Anton Rubinstein,
who was passing through Moscow, dragged me to see her. From then
on, I began to receive invitations from her nearly every day, and little
by little I grew accustomed to visiting her each evening."

As to the matter of what Tchaikovsky termed "lawful wedlock,"
there remained a series of obstacles to be overcome, chiefly the opposition of Artôt's mother, who found Tchaikovsky too young for her
daughter, and the disapproval of his friends, especially Nikolay Rubinstein, who regarded the whole project as ill-advised. "They say that
if I become the husband of a famous singer, I shall play the highly
pathetic role of my wife's husband," he wrote, "that is, I shall travel
with her to every corner of Europe, live on her earnings, grow unused
to work and have no opportunity for it; in a word, when my love for
her will have cooled off slightly there will remain only broken pride,
despair, and ruin." Artôt, meanwhile, despite her professed love for
Tchaikovsky, was by no means prepared to abandon the stage, "to

which she is accustomed and which brings her fame and money," and to remain unemployed and unoccupied with her prospective husband in Russia. For the moment, Tchaikovsky informed his father, Artôt had already left to sing in Warsaw, and they planned to meet that summer at her estate near Paris, "and there must our fate be decided." Although neither she nor he was willing to sacrifice career and future for the other, Tchaikovsky insisted that he was bound to his fiancée "by all the powers of my soul" and that he could scarcely imagine living the rest of his life without her. Still, "cool reason"—which by definition bears little relation to the ardor he claimed to possess—forced him, as he put it, "to consider seriously the possibility of those misfortunes that my friends have drawn for me."[18]

To this exposition, presented for his judgment and advice, the elderly Ilya Tchaikovsky quickly responded in his own inimitable manner and his unconquerable optimism. He strongly disagreed with the suggestion of Rubinstein and others that Tchaikovsky might lose his talent with the important change. "If for the sake of your talent you abandoned service to the crown, then certainly you will not cease to be an artist, even when at first you are not happy," he wrote to his son. "It is so with nearly all musicians. . . . A good friend will manage to spark your inspiration—you'll scarcely have time to write everything down. With such a person as your 'Desired' [Désirée] you will rather perfect than lose your talent." She should not leave the theater, Ilya advised his son, nor should he abandon his vocation as an artist. "Why assume that you will be deprived of the opportunity to proceed along your own path if you follow her blindly?" he asked. "Does this mean that you do not possess your own character, but would be a mere hanger-on, carrying her train and then slipping off into the crowd like a simple servant? No, my friend, be a servant, only an independent servant: when she sings your aria so that the applause belongs to you both—why then follow blindly? . . . Have you tested yourselves? . . . Test yourselves once more and then decide."[19]

A few days before his father's letter, Anatoly remarked from St. Petersburg that "there's no need to mention what a stir the rumors of your marriage have caused here, for you yourself know to what extent those who know you [probably Apukhtin and his circle] might have expected such a trick from you."[20]

The reaction of his sister, Aleksandra, was more anxious. "It has already been three days since I received your letter, dear Petrusha," she wrote, "and still I cannot calm down, my heart beats, I feel feverish and cannot sleep, all because my joy is mixed with anxiety; I think this is how mothers must feel when giving a sixteen-year-old daughter in marriage."[21] It was the woman's heart and the friends' perspicacity, not the father's equanimity, that in the end proved correct.

There exist several eyewitness accounts of the development of the affair—by Modest, Laroche, and Kashkin—but the most interesting is the lesser-known recollection by Tchaikovsky's acquaintance Konstantin de Lazari. According to de Lazari, a crucial role in the eventual rupture was played by another of Artôt's many admirers, an Armenian designated only as "X"—"a small, round, vivacious and energetic man with black hair and narrow, shrewd little eyes, who inevitably sat in the front row at every performance in which Artôt appeared." He had fallen madly in love with the singer and showered her with costly gifts. What is more, he undertook a vigorous campaign to win the support of Artôt's mother, who, according to Tchaikovsky, exercised considerable influence over her daughter. The shrewd Armenian took every opportunity to regale the old woman with lavish tales of his own riches, all the while vilifying his rival. "He used to tell her fictions about Tchaikovsky being the son of Sadyk-Pasha [the pseudonym of a Polish writer and mercenary whose real name was Czajkowski; the composer Modest Mussorgsky, who disliked Tchaikovsky, nicknamed him Sadyk-Pasha], a bankrupt gambler, utterly in debt, and other nonsense that the foreign lady believed all the more easily as she was utterly unfamiliar with the conditions of Russian life," recalls de Lazari. "The result was that Artôt's mother became terribly stirred up against Pyotr Ilyich."

One day in December 1868, de Lazari went to see the composer and found him depressed and upset. "I visited her yesterday," Tchaikovsky told his friend. "At first, she was sweet to me as always, but then I noticed that she was not herself, that she was worried about something. I asked what it was. At this moment her mother came through and barely greeted me. It was then that I guessed that someone had been slandering me to her. 'My mother is set against you,' Artôt told me, 'but whatever they may tell me, however they may try to separate us, please know that I shall always be true to you and shall never belong to anyone but you, but please understand too that it still pains me to see how Mama has yielded to the aspersions that are cast upon you.'" Try as Tchaikovsky might to find out what had been said about him and by whom, Artôt refused to tell him and, assuring him of her love, asked him to leave so that she could talk with her mother alone and try to calm her down.[22]

Probably by the beginning of 1869 the rumors had already reached Tchaikovsky that all was not well with his fiancée. He wrote to Anatoly, "Concerning the love affair that you know happened to me in the

early winter, let me tell you that it is very doubtful whether my entry
into the bounds of Hymen will take place; this affair is beginning to
fall apart somewhat: it is still too early to speak now of particulars;
when we see each other, perhaps I shall tell you." In a postscript, he
added, "What nonsense you two [that is, the twins] write, saying that
I shall cease to love you because of Artôt. Even if a dozen such as she
were to appear, I should still love you as before."[23]

As Tchaikovsky had written to his father, the company to which
Artôt belonged had moved on to Warsaw. And it was there that she
suddenly and unexpectedly married a baritone from the same company, Mariano Padilla y Ramos. De Lazari reports that it was Nikolay
Rubinstein, one of the most resolute opponents of the composer's marriage plans, who jubilantly broke the news to Tchaikovsky. "Lord, how
glad I am!" Rubinstein cried in triumph as he showed Tchaikovsky the
letter he had just received. "Thank God, thank God! Artôt has got married! And do you know to whom? Padilla! Well, wasn't I right when I
told you that it was not you she needed for a husband?! Here's a real
match for her, whereas you are needed by us, understand, by us, by
Russia, and not as the servant of a famous foreigner." Tchaikovsky, we
are told, turned pale and left the room without a word.[24]

Several days later, however, de Lazari recalls that Tchaikovsky was
"again content, calm, and wholly engrossed in his work." Indeed, his
behavior following the rupture suggests that Tchaikovsky was not so
much suffering the pain of a lost love as smarting from a sense of humiliation and betrayal. Particularly curious were his comments in a
letter to Modest of February 1869. "The business with Artôt has resolved itself in the most amusing manner," he wrote. "In Warsaw she
fell in love with the baritone Padilla, who here had been the object of
her ridicule—and she marries him! What sort of lady is that? One must
know the details of her and my relations in order to have an idea of the
degree to which this denouement is ludicrous."[25]

From the tone of his words it is difficult to ignore the feeling that
Tchaikovsky's homosexuality must have been somehow related to
what happened. Little else can be stated with any confidence or certainty. We can only speculate. Could the singer have believed the Armenian and, being of a delicate nature and, moreover, genuinely sympathizing with her fiancé, decided to make the break as painlessly as
possible? Or did she indeed fall quite unexpectedly in love with Padilla? Certainly, if this were the case, it seems strange that she did not
inform Tchaikovsky of it herself as the social conventions of the time
would have demanded. Indeed, Artôt's conduct could easily have been
interpreted even by her well-wishers as scandalous. Might Tchaikov-

sky have deceived himself? Until further documentary evidence from Soviet archives comes to light, such questions must remain unresolved.

Ilya Tchaikovsky, responding on 23 March 1869 to the news, was predictably encouraging: "Mme Artôt's action pleases me. Thank God, it means she had not entirely captivated you; an *intrigante*, a passionate and false woman—that's what she is. Therefore she is no match for you—and good luck to her!"[26]

Tchaikovsky's wounded self-esteem had still not healed by the autumn of that year. But when, in the latter part of October, Artôt was scheduled to appear in St. Petersburg, he advised Modest to see her, "and when you look at her, think that I nearly bound myself to her with the ties of Hymen."[27] Having attended her concert, Modest wrote back to his brother that Artôt "drove me to indescribable ecstasy. . . . And, in general, as a woman she impressed me greatly with her manners and face, perhaps because I was thinking all the while of the feeling she had aroused in you."[28] Even in this, Modest continued to imitate his brother.

Artôt's tour took her inevitably to Moscow, and on 30 October, Tchaikovsky wrote to Anatoly of his ambivalent anticipation of her arrival: "Soon I shall have to meet Artôt. She will be here in a few days, and most likely, I shall have to meet her, since immediately after her arrival the rehearsals begin for [Auber's opera] *Le Domino noir* with my choruses and recitatives, and it is essential that I attend these rehearsals. This woman has done me much harm, and when we see one another, I shall tell you in what manner; but nevertheless an inexplicable sympathy draws me to her to such a degree that I begin to await her arrival with feverish impatience. But, alas!" he concluded, "this, all the same, is not love."[29]

Nikolay Kashkin describes Tchaikovsky's reaction to Artôt's performance in Moscow: "I happened to be sitting in the stalls near Tchaikovsky, who became very anxious. When the singer appeared on stage, he covered his face with his opera glasses and did not remove them from his eyes until the end of the act, though he could scarcely have seen much since tears were streaming down from behind the glasses, yet he seemed not to notice them."[30] In fact, Tchaikovsky is known to have often wept when listening to music. Knowing his sentimentality and even oversensitivity regarding everything related to art, one wonders whether these tears reported by Kashkin may have been caused less by the memory of their affair than by the sheer power of her performance on stage. This might largely explain the spell she continued to cast on him even after the collapse of their affair.

Their next encounter took place six years later, in 1875, when the singer was again appearing in Moscow, this time in Meyerbeer's *Les Huguenots*. On one of Kashkin's visits to Moscow he and Tchaikovsky went together to Nikolay Rubinstein's office, where they were told that "a foreign lady" was already in there with him. The two waited outside the office, and when the visitor came out, Tchaikovsky "suddenly jumped from his seat and turned completely pale." The lady turned out to be Artôt, who "in her turn gave a small cry and became so flustered that she started looking for the exit in the solid wall and then, having spotted the door, went out quickly into the lobby." After a short pause, Tchaikovsky burst out laughing. "And I thought I was in love with her!" he exclaimed.[31]

In a letter to Anatoly of 11 December 1875, shortly after this encounter, Tchaikovsky spoke very coolly and even callously of his former fiancée. "Yesterday Artôt premiered here," he reported. "She has grown fat to the point of ugliness and has nearly lost her voice, but her talent could still be felt."[32] Some thirteen years would pass before the two saw each other again, in Berlin in 1888. This time they could meet as old friends, chatting amiably as if nothing had ever happened between them. In November 1868, at the peak of their abortive affair, Tchaikovsky had dedicated to Artôt his *Romance* in F Minor, op. 5, for piano. Twenty years later, in 1888, he would dedicate a second composition to her, his Six French Songs, op 65.

In the autumn of 1868, Tchaikovsky had completed his symphonic poem *Fatum* [later given opus number 77], an enigmatic work that both Kashkin and Klimenko have claimed to contain "something autobiographical" and "pertaining to [Tchaikovsky] alone."[33] The music had already been composed before a program text—Konstantin Batyushkov's verses on the futility of human life—was chosen at the last moment by Tchaikovsky for the performance. The choice of the lines had in fact been not the composer's own idea but the suggestion of his friend Sergey Rachinsky, a professor of botany at Moscow University and a great music lover. With its majestic introduction, lyrical and dancelike allegro, and cheerful finale, the music seems to bear little relation to the text or even to the title, and at its premiere on 15 February 1869 the audience was predictably baffled by the discrepancy between music and title. Still, the work was well received, and Tchaikovsky himself appeared satisfied in a letter to Anatoly that same night: "My fantasy *Fatum* was performed for the first time. It seems to be the best thing I have written so far; at least that is what people are saying (a considerable success)."[34] More hostile, however, was the response of the critics, who charged the work with artistic unevenness.

Soon Tchaikovsky, once the initial euphoria had passed, began to regard it as a failure, and eventually he destroyed the score.

Later that winter, on 30 January 1869, the premiere of Tchaikovsky's first opera, *The Voyevode*, took place, and again the audience responded warmly, giving the composer fifteen curtain calls and presenting him with a laurel wreath, while the critics were less impressed. The enormous potential of the young composer was recognized by all, but the opera was criticized for showing various foreign influences, chiefly German and Italian. Curiously, this dichotomy between the responses of the general public and professional critics established a pattern of sorts that would be repeated often in the coming years. By this time, Hermann Laroche had abandoned his ambition of becoming a composer and devoted himself entirely to music criticism. In an article on *The Voyevode* he accused his friend of an insufficient knowledge of Russian folklore and of repeated failings in technique. So offended and resentful was Tchaikovsky that he resolved to have nothing more to do with him, and when the friendship was restored several years later, it no longer had its former intimacy. Yet, after only the fifth performance of the opera Tchaikovsky withdrew the score from the theater and destroyed it, as he had that of *Fatum*. Both the symphonic poem and the opera were reconstructed from the surviving orchestral parts only after his death, *Fatum* in 1896 and *The Voyevode* in 1933.

Clearly, Tchaikovsky was still in quest of a form and style closely linked to his choices of subject matter. His work on *The Voyevode* seems to indicate an attempt to create a national opera in the same vein as Mikhail Glinka's earlier *A Life for the Tsar* (1836) and *Ruslan and Lyudmila* (1842). *The Voyevode* having proved unsuccessful, Tchaikovsky turned to a non-Russian topic for his new opera project. This opera, however, was to suffer an even worse fate than *The Voyevode*. From early February through the middle of April 1869, Tchaikovsky worked on *Undine*, based on the fantasy by the German Romantic writer Friedrich de la Motte-Fouqué, which had been translated into Russian by Vasily Zhukovsky. Well liked by Tchaikovsky's friends, the score was rejected by the Mariinsky Theater in St. Petersburg for the "ultramodern direction of its music, slipshod orchestration, and unmelodiousness."[35] The enraged composer eventually set a torch to this work as well, and while portions were later reused in *Swan Lake*, the Second Symphony, and the incidental music for Ostrovsky's play *The Snow Maiden*, at present only three original fragments from *Undine* are known to exist: the introduction, Undine's aria from Act 1, and the chorus, duet, and finale from the same act, all performed at a concert in March 1870.

Meanwhile, various social engagements continued to interfere with his work. In early March 1869, Tchaikovsky attended a masked ball for Moscow's artistic circles dressed in a splendid domino, or hooded robe and mask, causing a considerable stir. Two versions of the episode have survived. According to one, Tchaikovsky had been persuaded by the Begichevs and the Shilovskys to appear at the masquerade in the guise of a witch, broomstick and all. Yet, through a complex series of misunderstandings, it was Mariya Begicheva who ended up donning the witch costume, leaving Tchaikovsky to put on her own exceptionally elegant domino of black lace set off by diamonds and an ostrich-feather fan. When the pair arrived at the ball, Mariya's husband, Vladimir Begichev, had been flirting with a young actress. Discomfited by the appearance of his wife, whom he assumed to be wearing her domino, Begichev confided his annoyance to the witch, whom he believed to be Tchaikovsky but who was in fact his wife. The ensuing scandal is said to have been hushed up only with considerable difficulty.[36]

The second version of the story claims that Nikolay Kashkin and Tchaikovsky made a bet whereby each had to come up with a costume for the event so effective as to render him utterly unrecognizable. Tchaikovsky's solution was the domino, which he borrowed from a society lady of his acquaintance.[37] In either event, the domino episode itself was hardly invented. During this period of his life, Tchaikovsky's fondness for mischief and practical jokes was often evident, while his penchants for imitating female dancers and for using feminine names in reference to himself or other male homosexuals were quite pronounced. The idea of appearing in female dress at a masked ball must have held for him the allure of a novel but safe adventure. Demanding a certain amount of daring, it was still within the bounds of convention, stretched as they were by the carnival-like nature of the event. And it is tempting to see the younger and notoriously reckless Vladimir Shilovsky as the actual mastermind behind the escapade—and also very possibly the wearer of the witch costume.

Through much of the spring and summer of 1869, Tchaikovsky's attention was diverted to various family and practical matters. In May, Anatoly graduated from the School of Jurisprudence and received a position in the Court Office in Kiev, Tchaikovsky having pulled numerous strings in influential circles on behalf of his brother. June and July he spent in the Ukraine with his sister's family at Kamenka, and by early August he had returned to Moscow and to Nikolay Rubinstein's apartment. Living with Rubinstein was an arrangement not without its inconveniences for Tchaikovsky, but so wholly was he under the spell of Rubinstein's authoritarian personality that he dared not even allude to his desire to take an apartment of his own for fear of angering or offending his protector. Instead, he continued to follow him in his moves from apartment to apartment, one of his sole consolations being the services of Rubinstein's servants, Agafon and his wife, who looked after the young musician and prepared his meals.

On his return to Moscow, Tchaikovsky met Mili Balakirev. It is unclear precisely when Tchaikovsky first became acquainted with the founder of the so-called Mighty Five, the emerging nationalistic group of composers and theoreticians that also included Nikolay Rimsky-Korsakov, Modest Mussorgsky, Aleksandr Borodin, and César Cui. While Tchaikovsky's dealings with the other members of the Five were often strained, his relationship with the group's leader had grown quite friendly, and for a time Balakirev was to exert a considerable influence on him. It was Balakirev who that summer proposed to Tchaikovsky the subject for what was to become one of his best and most famous works, the *Romeo and Juliet* Fantasy-Overture. Tchaikovsky worked on the overture from early October through the second half of November. Its first performance, conducted by Nikolay Rubinstein on 7 March of the following year, would go virtually unnoticed, and the next summer, Tchaikovsky revised the work in response to Balakirev's criticisms. Ten years later, in 1880, he would give the piece a third and final revision.

Tchaikovsky himself persistently held a very high opinion of his *Romeo and Juliet*, referring to it at one point as "the best work I have ever done."[38] There is no doubt that he wrote the overture with extraordinary enthusiasm. Here, for the first time, he voiced the main emotional themes of all his subsequent oeuvre—the psychological drama of unfulfilled and frustrated love and of impossible youthful passion consumed by omnipresent death. Rimsky-Korsakov, in discussing Tchaikovsky's *Romeo and Juliet*, would contend that its main melody "does not yield to elaboration, as is the case, in general, with all genuine long and distinctively exclusive melodies." But, he continued, "how very inspirational it is! What ineffable beauty, what burning passion! It is one of the finest themes in all of Russian music![39]

Considerable caution is always required when relating a musical composition directly to biographical tribulation, for a work of art nearly always obscures and transcends the experience that gives impetus to its composition. Still, from the point of view of creative psychology, the two realms must necessarily be connected, however mysteriously or unpredictably. In the case of Tchaikovsky's *Romeo and Juliet*, an intimate link can be seen between this fervent piece of music and an obscure drama unfolding in the composer's life at the time of its composition: his infatuation with a young man by the name of Eduard Zak.

Tantalizingly little is known about Eduard Zak. At the time of composition of *Romeo and Juliet*, he was only fifteen. This was the age that Tchaikovsky always considered to be the peak of male adolescent beauty, and the "tenderness and sweetness of love"[40] revealed in the music of the overture is well in tune with the theme of youthful passion. From Soviet commentary we learn only that Zak had been, strictly speaking, not Tchaikovsky's pupil but the cousin of his Moscow Conservatory student Rudolph Köber, about whom we know virtually nothing. Zak is mentioned only three times in Tchaikovsky's published writings and not at all in Modest's biography. It is a significant loss, for there is reason to believe that he was one of the great passions of Tchaikovsky's life.

The first mention of the young man occurs in a letter of 28 November 1871 to one of Tchaikovsky's rare correspondents, his elder brother Nikolay, who was then living in the provinces, where he worked for the railroad. Apparently Zak had been hired by Nikolay, most probably on his brother's recommendation, for a job that involved some exhausting labor and travel. The conditions in which his young protégé was working worried Tchaikovsky deeply. "Since you (to my extreme pleasure) want to save Zak from business trips during the winter," he wrote to his brother, "would you not consider it possible and to his benefit to give him in the near future a brief vacation in Moscow? I feel that he needs this, that he might feel refreshed in a milieu somewhat superior to that which surrounds him. I am afraid lest he should grow coarse and his instinct toward intellectual refinement die out." Pleading his case, Tchaikovsky begged his brother "to allow and even order [Zak] to take a trip to Moscow; in doing this you will also give me great pleasure. I have missed him terribly and fear for his future: I fear lest physical activity should kill in him his loftier strivings. I shall tell you frankly that if I observe in him any moral or intellectual decline, I shall take measures to find him other work." And he added, in a exceptional show of anxiety with regard to the then seventeen-year-old Zak: "Be that as it may, it is absolutely essential for me to see him. For God's sake, work it out."[41]

At some point a couple of years later, Zak turned up in Moscow, and on 16 May 1873, Tchaikovsky sent a note to Karl Albrecht asking him to permit Zak to enroll in an acting class at the conservatory.[42] Eventually the young man seems to have found his way into Shilovsky's circle, so that Tchaikovsky inquired briefly in a letter to Shilovsky from Kamenka of 18 June 1873, "And what of Zak? Was it successful or not?"[43] There is no way to clarify the meaning of this inquiry or to ascertain to what it might refer.

Then, unexpectedly, tragedy struck. On 2 November 1873, Eduard Zak, at the age of nineteen, took his own life.[44] Though Zak's name is never mentioned, his suicide is alluded to in Tchaikovsky's letter to his St. Petersburg publisher, Vasily Bessel, three days later. "I now find myself under the impress of a tragic catastrophe that has occurred to someone close to me, and my nerves are terribly shaken," he told Bessel. "I am unable to do anything. Therefore I ask you not to rush me with the piano pieces."[45] The Soviet commentator's simplistic and sociological explanation of Zak's suicide is clearly untenable: "On the basis of R. Köber's letters to Tchaikovsky, it may be concluded that E. Zak perished because of the incompatibility of his intellectual needs with the living conditions in which he had been placed."[46] On the contrary, this young man with his intellectual needs would have had an inspiring and influential protector in the person of Tchaikovsky. As for Köber's letters referred to here, they remain unpublished.

Finally, there are two tortuous diary entries made by Tchaikovsky some fourteen years after the young man's death—a span of years that in its very length testifies to the intensity of Tchaikovsky's feeling. On 4 September 1887 he wrote, "Before going to sleep, thought much and long of Eduard. Wept much. Can it be that *he* is truly gone??? Don't believe it."[47] On the following day, he made another entry, even more significant: "Again thought of and recalled Zak. How amazingly clearly I remember him: the sound of his voice, his movements, but especially the extraordinarily wonderful expression on his face at times. I cannot conceive that he should be no more. *His* death, that is, complete nonexistence, is beyond my comprehension. It seems to me that I have never loved anyone so strongly as him. My God! no matter what they told me then and how I try to console myself, my guilt before him is terrible! And at the same time I loved him, that is, not loved, but love him still, and his memory is sacred to me!"[48] This last entry (which, it may be noted in passing, is the lengthiest entry in the entire diary devoted to a single individual) is remarkable in many respects. Taking into consideration the entry's truly striking emotional force ("I have never loved anyone so strongly as him") and the suspicious and no doubt deliberate omission of Zak's name throughout the various memoirs and testimonies, one begins to sense the presence of some complex and intense psychodrama almost entirely hidden from view, one in which Tchaikovsky, probably without actual guilt, felt himself guilty. Yet, at present, there is no way to ascertain further facts in order to comprehend precisely what he might have had in mind when speaking of his guilt and his futile self-consolation.

The Six Pieces on One Theme, op. 21, mentioned by Tchaikovsky in his letter to Bessel, were completed by the end of November 1873. This cycle for piano, dedicated to Anton Rubinstein, bears the imprint of tragic events. Among the pieces is a Funeral March, and all but the final Scherzo are written in a minor key. Two years later, César Cui, arguably the most severe of Tchaikovsky's critics, wrote in his review of the work that the pieces were "highly remarkable and must be numbered among Tchaikovsky's finest compositions."[49]

In the end, it seems reasonable to suggest that it may have been Eduard Zak, and not Vladimir Gerard, as some have proposed, who served as the source of inspiration for *Romeo and Juliet*. By 1869 ten years had passed since Tchaikovsky's graduation from the School of Jurisprudence and his alleged infatuation with his heterosexual classmate Gerard, while the context of the letter to his brother Nikolay gives grounds to assume that by 1871 Zak and Tchaikovsky had already known each other for some time. If, as is claimed, Modest does refer to Gerard in this connection, it may well have been a deliberate ruse on his part.[50] Zak, after all, had taken his own life, and the brother-biographer, for whatever reasons, evidently considered the young man's name unmentionable. Balakirev, to whom the fantasy-overture was actually dedicated, would later comment enigmatically that "there is little of the inner love of the soul in the love theme of *Romeo and Juliet*, but only a fantastic and passionate anguish."[51]

The beginning of the year 1870 was marked for Tchaikovsky by the visit of Balakirev and Rimsky-Korsakov to Moscow. Balakirev's affection for Tchaikovsky had grown rapidly, so much so that Tchaikovsky could confess to Modest in a letter of 13 January that he "begins so to adore me that after all I do not know how to thank him for all this love."[52] Rimsky-Korsakov, meanwhile, dedicated to his Moscow colleague "a very pretty song" entitled "Where are you, my thought?"[53] Throughout the winter months Tchaikovsky was composing steadily. After completing the initial version of *Romeo and Juliet* he had written his Six Songs, op.6. The cycle includes one of the composer's most popular songs, to Goethe's text, "No, only he who has known," widely known in English by the title "None but the lonely heart."

In 1870, Tchaikovsky also set to music a verse written by Aleksey Apukhtin, "So soon forgotten," one of six songs that he was to compose to lines written by his poet-friend. In these years Tchaikovsky and Apukhtin still met each other often, in either St. Petersburg or Moscow, and corresponded regularly. Tchaikovsky would worry openly about the poet's emotional state, as when he asked Anatoly, "Yesterday I received a desperate letter in French from Lyolya [Apukhtin]. What is the cause of his dark melancholy?"[54] The two continued to offend, and to forgive, one another. Modest, in a letter to his brother, would note after visiting Apukhtin that "he was very courteous and asked to tell you that considering your genuine repentance, he forgives you."[55] Or Tchaikovsky himself would tell Anatoly about meeting Apukhtin at the theater: "At first he did not wish even to recognize me, so angry was he, but after lengthy explanations was finally mollified. The next day, we dined together at the English Club, and there after dinner he began to feel unwell, so that I became terribly frightened, but not losing my head, I grabbed him and dragged him with great difficulty into the garden, where he soon recovered."[56] A few days later he reported that "Apukhtin . . . charmed everyone here and left yesterday to my great sadness."[57]

An interesting sketch of Apukhtin's character and conduct during these years can be found in the reminiscences of the physician Vasily Bertenson. Unfailingly courteous and polite in the company of women, in male company Apukhtin was utterly transformed into a fascinating storyteller who with the most innocent face delighted in scandalizing his audience with "all manner of *horreurs* in verse and prose." Despite his apparent cynicism, Apukhtin's conversation "was imbued with such wit and clothed in such attractive form that for the sake of this alone one forgot the frivolity of the contents."[58]

Apukhtin's sexual tastes were discussed openly in the salons of high society and ridiculed in the press. One particularly caustic epigram appearing in the St. Petersburg satirical journal *Spark* remarked pointedly that the poet was "famous for that for which Vigel is famous," referring to the Russian statesman Filipp Vigel, a notorious homosexual of the early nineteenth century.[59] Apukhtin responded to this with perfect equanimity. Typical was an amusing episode also recounted by Bertenson: "Once I visited Apukhtin on a medical call. I found with him a very respectable lady. Later, two more appeared to take the place of the first. When all the guests had finally left and I could commence my examination of the patient, I observed with a smile, knowing that women were not one of Apukhtin's weaknesses, 'So the ladies love and pamper you all the same?!' 'Yes,' Apukhtin replied modestly, 'though I personally have nothing to do with it.'"[60]

This is not to say that Apukhtin did not suffer. Yet, his suffering stemmed not from his considering his tastes to be a vice or a sickness, but rather from unrequited love. The following first draft of a poem written by Apukhtin in 1869 was addressed to the twenty-year-old Aleksey Valuev, a classmate of Modest at the School of Jurisprudence:

> The dry, infrequent, accidental encounters,
> The empty cold conversations,
> Your deliberately evasive talk

And your intentionally stern and heavy gaze—
Everything says that we must part,
That happiness was—but now has passed.

And it's as bitter for me to admit this
As it is difficult to give up life.
As before, everywhere irresistibly
The fateful question troubles me:
What is in your heart? Does peace reign there,
Or is it plagued by melancholy,
And where are you now, and who now is with you?

As before, I hate that day
When I shall no longer tell you my anguish,
Shall no longer see your welcoming smile
And no longer shake your hand.[61]

In a letter to Modest of 17 September 1870 Tchaikovsky remarked that
"Apukhtin is utterly delirious about your Valuev."[62]

Often Apukhtin himself would send his verses to Tchaikovsky,
asking him to set them to music. About one of these, his poem that
begins "In the cold of the world, shivering and exhausted, I thought
there was no love in my tired heart," he asked Tchaikovsky in a letter
of 25 October 1877, "If you are able, write some music for it and send
it to me. It was written in a happy moment and I had a passionate
desire to *sing* it. I tried to write a song myself, but had no success."[63]

Tchaikovsky did not always respond to these requests. Including
"So soon forgotten," he probably wrote six songs to texts by his friend:
"Who goes?" (no opus, 1860); "He loved me so much," op. 28, no. 4
(1875); "No response, or word, or greeting," op. 28, no. 5 (1875);
"Whether the day reigns," op. 47, no. 6 (1880); and "Frenzied nights,"
op. 60, no. 6 (1886). Probably because the question of Apukhtin's authorship of the texts for "So soon forgotten" and "He loved me so
much" is a matter of some dispute, neither verse is to be found anywhere within either the manuscript or the published legacy of the poet.
We have the testimony of the singer Aleksandra Panaeva-Kartsova that
some of Apukhtin's verses were so altered by Tchaikovsky as to arouse
the poet's displeasure.[64] Apukhtin is known not to have worried about
the publication of his poems and to have made gifts of them readily to
friends and acquaintances. The originals of these two poems might
well have become lost while in Tchaikovsky's possession, and these
songs may represent the only surviving text of the verses. Tchaikovsky
even confessed in one letter to Modest, "I lost my notebook with Apu-

khtin's poems and sketches, and for the past several days I've been searching for it in vain."[65]

Their open sincerity of lyric expression made Tchaikovsky's songs very popular in Russia. Save for the unfortunately lost setting of Apukhtin's "Who goes?" all the rest are highly accomplished. Tchaikovsky knew how to hear in the commonplace and sometimes even the hackneyed those vivid motifs that could move the listener. Thus, "So soon forgotten" is significant in its development of the main theme, both poetic and musical, creating an aural image born of the intonation of emotional discourse, with a dramatic ending that has prompted some musicologists to refer to the song as a "minisymphony." "Frenzied nights" is a passionate monologue-reminiscence and, as certain critics have noted with irony, "has meaning, but according to one's own taste, since in it definite concepts are replaced by symbols."[66] The song "Whether the day reigns," dedicated to Panaeva-Kartsova, is one of Tchaikovsky's finest achievements, an aria with, like "So soon forgotten," an almost symphonic development. Meanwhile, the verses for "He loved me so much" and "No response, or word, or greeting," so brilliantly and passionately written, inevitably prompt the question of the identity of the young admirer to whom the poet might have addressed these rather ambivalent-sounding lines. In putting them to music, Tchaikovsky undoubtedly would have known his identity, and it may well be that this increased his creative ardor. This may also be the reason why Soviet commentators have called into question the coauthorship of these richly emotional works by two men with unorthodox erotic tastes.

Another of Tchaikovsky's homosexual friends from the School of Jurisprudence, Prince Vladimir Meshchersky, busy with his political and journalistic career, is frequently mentioned in the composer's letters of the time. For Tchaikovsky, companionship never excluded criticism, and it seems that Meshchersky, a man of willful character, could at times become a burden. "What is the tyrant Meshchersky doing?" he asked in one letter.[67] "I shall only mention," he grumbled in another, "the heavy pressure from Meshchersky, on the one hand, and from Balakirev on the other, so that you might understand what is was like for me between the two fires."[68] In yet another he wrote, "I spent a week in Petersburg and lived in absolute dependence on Meshchersky, who would not allow me to be anywhere but with him."[69] At the same time, he did not stint his praise: "But in all fairness I must say that he is exceptionally courteous."[70]

During the period when these letters were written (1869–1870), Tchaikovsky seems to have made an attempt to exploit Meshchersky's influence to launch the careers of Anatoly and then Modest. "I have had quite detailed news about you from Meshchersky," Tchaikovsky told Anatoly on 30 October 1869, "but still this is not enough for me. Naturally, we see each other every day and have already had two or three serious conversations. . . . I am pleased that he likes you so much. By the way, in Petersburg he will do everything possible for you."[71] A few weeks later, on 18 November, he reported that "Meshchersky, when leaving here, gave me his word to petition zealously for you in the ministry, and I do not doubt that your wish to receive the investigator's position will be fulfilled."[72] And on 7 December he sent his brother "Meshchersky's letter for your information and the carrying out of his advice."[73] Similarly, Tchaikovsky would inform Modest in a letter of 1 November 1870, "Perhaps your cherished dream to live in Petersburg will work out if Meshchersky petitions for you energetically."[74] The prince's willingness to pull strings for Anatoly and Modest suggests at least the possibility that Meshchersky may have taken an erotic interest in the two promising young men. While it cannot be ruled out that he consented to these efforts simply as a favor to an old friend, Meshchersky was renowned for his egotism and for promoting the careers of young men he hoped to seduce. Ultimately, whatever efforts he may have made proved of little help. Anatoly's career moved sluggishly at best, and Modest's stint in the civil service was to be an outright disaster.

One of Tchaikovsky's closest companions of the period in Moscow was Vladimir Bibikov, who worked in the Office of Petitions to His Imperial Majesty. The homosexual element of Tchaikovsky's friendship with Bibikov is suggested by the frequent censorial cuts accompanying references to Bibikov in Tchaikovsky's letters to Modest, as well as by the fact that several of these references crop up in the context of thinly disguised homosexual gossip and in the same breath as references to other known homosexuals, such as Vladimir Shilovsky. It is not surprising that Bibikov is mentioned most frequently in letters to Modest. By this time, the nineteen-year-old Modest was already much involved in homosexual activities, to which Tchaikovsky seemed to refer when he noted in a letter to Anatoly of 10 September 1869 (in a passage later expunged in the *Complete Works*) that "it was unpleasant to find that he is the same type of person as I am."[75]

Even though preoccupied with his work during these months, Tchaikovsky still found time to go out almost every evening, "mostly with Bibikov, who comes to pick me up." This sentence in his letter to Modest of 12 October 1869 is followed by a cut, telling in itself, while the close of the letter offers further evidence of the familiarity of relations between the three young men, for Tchaikovsky writes his brother that "Bibikov kisses you."[76] In a letter of 18 November, Tchaikovsky told his brother that he still saw Bibikov regularly, followed at once by a mention of Meshchersky whose tastes, of course, were an open secret.[77] Tchaikovsky's intimacy with Bibikov continued for some years, and they were still seeing each other quite often in early autumn 1870.[78] But, by later that same year, their meetings had already grown less frequent, an evident sign of their mutual cooling.[79] The last mention of Bibikov's name appeared two years after that in a letter to Modest of 2 November 1872 in which Tchaikovsky noted that his "relations with Bibikov are strained."[80]

In February 1870, Tchaikovsky embarked on his third opera, *The Oprichnik*, adapted from the tragedy by the historical novelist Ivan Lazhechnikov and set during the reign of Ivan the Terrible in the sixteenth century. But having composed several scenes, Tchaikovsky began to feel that his resourcefulness was exhausted. Depression set in, and by 1 May he was outlining for Ivan Klimenko the tribulations of the year thus far: "(1) Illness, I grow exceedingly fat, my nerves are strained to the utmost; (2) my financial affairs are a mess; (3) I am sick to death of the conservatory and I grow increasingly convinced of my inability to teach the theory of composition."[81]

In addition to everything else, he was also looking forward with trepidation to a coming journey abroad to visit the ailing Vladimir Shilovsky. Tchaikovsky's charming pupil had continued to move erratically into and out of his tutor's life. The destructive elements in Shilovsky's nature that would repeatedly lead him to hysteria and scandalous behavior were by now revealing themselves insistently. His situation at home was in part to blame: "Volodya is in good health, but such dramas are now being played out in their family that I fear he will go mad."[82] The young man's nervous fits and collapses seem ultimately to have been the cause of Tchaikovsky's periodic coolness toward him. In the previous autumn, Tchaikovsky had flatly refused Shilovsky's persistent urging to abandon the conservatory and travel with him again through Europe, fearing the antagonism that material dependence on his pupil would inevitably bring.[83] Shilovsky's poor health continually led him to seek relief at various spas and resorts abroad. This time he intended to be away some two years.

Though Tchaikovsky refused to go with him, he could not turn down Shilovsky's request to accompany him at least as far as St. Petersburg. He had hoped to stay in the capital incognito, but in this he was unsuccessful. His relatives, having learned of his presence in the city and his failure to visit them, felt offended and insulted, and in a letter to Aleksandra of 15 September 1869, Tchaikovsky begged his sister to mediate. "Since this poor boy is going abroad for two full years and is very sad at having to part with me, I decided to go to Petersburg for two days but not to show myself anywhere," he wrote. "In the meantime, everyone learned of my arrival. . . . For God's sake, Sanya [Aleksandra], if [the Petersburg Davydovs] write to you, explain to them that I did not see them in order to avoid visiting our aunts and other relatives, which would have taken all of my time when I had actually come for Shilovsky and stayed with him."[84]

Once Shilovsky was abroad, he renewed his appeals to Tchaikovsky, now returned to Moscow, writing that he was ill and longed to see his tutor. For some time, Tchaikovsky hesitated, having received upsetting news of the young man's behavior. In a letter to Modest of 26 March 1870, he described a visit from Shilovsky's new guardian, Ryumin, who, arriving from Switzerland, "told me many things about Volodya, who has been making more of a fool of himself this winter than ever before. He has spent about sixteen thousand silver rubles and upset his health to the point where he faints four times a day." But, he told his brother, he misses me very much and I gave him my word to come in the summer, at least for a month."[85] A few weeks later, he made up his mind. "In the middle of May, I shall probably go abroad," he informed Anatoly on 23 April. "I am partly glad and partly distressed; glad, because Europe has always held a fascination for me; distressed, [because] I fear that Shilovsky will poison my pleasure with his crazy escapades, though in his letters he swears up and down that he will cherish and pamper me in every way possible."[86]

For all his apprehension, Tchaikovsky, by his very nature, could perhaps have done nothing other than respond to his pupil's appeal. Time and again during his life, despite his own intense and irrational fear of everything related to sickness and dying, Tchaikovsky would rush to be with a friend who was seriously ill or lying on his deathbed. He left for St. Petersburg on 17 May and from there traveled through Germany to Paris, where he spent several days before going to Soden, near Frankfurt am Main, where Shilovsky eagerly awaited him. He arrived on 1 June. "I feared to find Shilovsky dying, but although he is very weak, I had expected worse," he wrote to Anatoly later that same day. "His joy at seeing me was indescribable. . . . I was very frightened by Volodya's fainting fit, but everything turned out well. . . . I take very seriously my obligation to look after Volodya. He hangs by a thread, and the doctor said that the slightest imprudence could lead to consumption, but that if he keeps up his treatment properly he may be saved. His love for me and gratitude for my arrival are so touching that I accept with pleasure the obligation of being his Argus, that is, the savior of his life."[87]

There were respites from the sickbed and the generally idle life in Soden. Spending two days in nearby Mannheim, Tchaikovsky was present at the music festival commemorating the centenary of Beethoven's birth. He found the program for the festival "most interesting" and the quality of the various performances of the great composer's music "marvelous," and he was especially struck by the *Missa Solemnis*, which he, hearing it for the first time, described as "a musical composition of the greatest genius."[88] After visiting the vacationing Nikolay Rubinstein in Wiesbaden, Tchaikovsky, on 5/17 July, accompanied Shilovsky to Switzerland, where they spent the greater part of July and August. For Tchaikovsky, however, these weeks in Interlaken were something less than idyllic. In a letter to Modest written a few days after his return home, he complained that his charge had "so far abased himself morally" and become "so disgustingly vulgar and empty" that for the most part Tchaikovsky found himself compelled to leave him to his own devices. "Although I walked about Switzerland and saw such splendors that must be seen to be imagined," he wrote, "still the constant cohabitation with such a trifling, petty tyrant as Shilovsky has now become would get on anyone's nerves."[89]

After six weeks in Switzerland, Tchaikovsky headed for home, stopping in Munich to see Prince Golitsyn. Arriving in Russia on 24 August, he received the news that he was an uncle again, Aleksandra having given birth two weeks before to her first son, Dmitry. From 1 September he resumed his duties at the Moscow Conservatory, where he was now to teach the class in orchestration. Hampered as always by his teaching responsibilities, his own work proceeded sluggishly. He attempted to continue with *The Oprichnik*, but interrupted his work on the opera to reshape the score of *Romeo and Juliet*. In October an idea for a ballet based on the tale of Cinderella had to be abandoned for lack of inspiration. During the winter he spent much time attending concerts.

In February 1871, Rubinstein asked Tchaikovsky to prepare a program of his own music for a concert at the Assembly of Nobles. Inviting a large symphonic orchestra for the occasion was deemed too costly, and Rubinstein suggested that Tchaikovsky instead write a string quartet. The idea caught Tchaikovsky's interest, and before the month was out, the String Quartet no. 1 in D Major, op. 11, had been composed and fully scored. Held 16 March 1871, the concert was a great success and included in its program the Three Pieces, op. 9, performed by Rubinstein; a duet from *The Voyevode*; the Six Songs, op. 6; and a new vocal trio entitled *Nature and Love*.

But it was the quartet, and in particular the second movement, *Andante cantabile*, that made the greatest impression on the audience in the Lesser Hall of the Assembly of Nobles. A year later, the work went on to produce no less a sensation in St. Petersburg, and by the end of the century would take first place in popularity and number of performances within Russia. Later critics have agreed that in many aspects the First Quartet clearly presaged the salient characteristics of the mature Tchaikovsky's musical style. Even Hermann Laroche, who at the time tended to be critical of Tchaikovsky's work, praised in his review of the concert the quartet's "lush melodies, beautifully and intriguingly harmonized."[90]

Certainly the rapidity and intensity of Tchaikovsky's creative development during his early years in Moscow had been remarkable. In the five years from 1866 to 1871 he had produced some thirty compositions, among them two operas, one symphony, two symphonic fantasies, an overture, a quartet, twelve pieces for piano, a collection of fifty arrangements of Russian folk songs, numerous transcriptions, and various music for dramatic productions. This would have been a considerable achievement for anyone, but in the First Symphony, the *Romeo and Juliet* Fantasy-Overture, and the First String Quartet could already be sensed the hand of a mature master.

CHAPTER EIGHT

The Petrolina Letters

In the spring of 1871, Tchaikovsky resumed work on *The Oprichnik* in earnest and was soon devoting all available time to the opera. He continued to compose at Kamenka, where he arrived with Anatoly in early June, and by the end of his visit several weeks later, the first act of the opera was completed. From Kamenka he traveled to Nizy, in nearby Kharkov province, to visit his friend Nikolay Kondratyev. At Nizy he briefly diverted his attention from his opera to work on a textbook on harmony to be used by students at the conservatory, which he managed to finish at Vladimir Shilovsky's estate at Usovo, near Kiev, before setting out for Moscow on 29 August.

After his arrival in Moscow in September, Tchaikovsky finally moved out of Rubinstein's home and found an apartment of his own. Nikolay Kashkin later described the new apartment as "very tiny," consisting of two rooms and a kitchen. In the kitchen lived Tchaikovsky's servant, "a village lad," whose duties included preparing his master's dinner, "which invariably, it seems, consisted of buckwheat kasha and cabbage soup, since he was unable to cook anything else."[1] Kashkin noted that "these household inconveniences were not a great burden to Pyotr Ilyich, but he could not confine himself to the lad's company and even took into his home a male sponger in the person of a certain Bochechkarov, whose good-naturedly complacent narrow-mindedness occasionally, but by no means always, amused him"[2]

The village lad whom Tchaikovsky had hired almost immediately after moving into his own apartment was Mikhail Sofronov, a twenty-three-year-old peasant from the Moscow region who had previously been in the service of Fyodor Laub, another conservatory professor. Tchaikovsky found Mikhail spoiled by service to other masters and, more important, already past the age that he would always consider attractive. At the first opportunity, therefore, he took on, in addition to Mikhail, the young man's twelve-year-old brother, Aleksey—despite the boy's utter lack of experience in this occupation—and the older youth was eventually dismissed altogether.

Mikhail Sofronov seems, though, to have been sufficiently attractive to elicit the erotic interest of Modest. In one of Tchaikovsky's most sexually suggestive letters to his brother, written on 2 December 1872, he spoke of "Mikhailo—the object of your love" and, alluding to the factotum in Mozart's *Don Giovanni*, went on to observe that "this Leporello has grown remarkably comical of late. But I am very pleased with him and even more so with his brother."[3] There is some evidence that Modest was also interested in the young Aleksey, known as Alyosha, sufficiently at least for Tchaikovsky to confide to him in a letter of 14 September 1875 that "Aleksey Ivanovich Sofronov, who right now is standing behind me scratching my head, asks to convey to you his deepest regards. He is as charming as he was, but has grown up a bit!"[4] This head-scratching became a favorite form of caress that the servant might give to his master. Even much later, Tchaikovsky would never fail to mention it regularly in his diary.

With his unsettled bachelor ways, his perpetual moving about from place to place, and his incapacity for dealing with everyday life, it is little wonder that Tchaikovsky grew so thoroughly attached to Alyosha Sofronov. By virtue of the situation alone, Alyosha, particularly after the dismissal of his brother, was the one person required to be with Tchaikovsky nearly all the time, and he was destined to take on a far greater significance for Tchaikovsky, one that would continue to grow throughout the course of their lives. Tchaikovsky's pleasure from Alyosha's services gradually and imperceptibly developed into a steady emotional commitment. "The very thought of Alyosha causes a painful longing in me," he would write to Modest from Florence on 27 April/9 May 1874.[5] And in the summer of 1875 he informed both servants from Usovo that "I sleep in the same room and am quite heartsick that my dear Lyonya [Alyosha], of whom I think constantly, is not with me as he was last year."[6] And from Kamenka on 7 June 1876, he wrote, "My dear Lyonya! I have missed you terribly" (this followed by a suspicious cut).[7]

For Tchaikovsky, Alyosha was many things at once: servant and traveling companion, housekeeper and nurse, friend, pupil, and, in a sense, even son. He was also, without doubt, his master's lover. Even Soviet commentators, who have had unlimited access to the composer's archive in Klin, do not dispute this fact.[8] While it is not clear at what point the intimacy between Tchaikovsky and Alyosha took a sexual turn, certainly it had done so by December 1877, when Tchaikovsky, going through one of the darkest periods in his life, wrote to Anatoly of the solace he had found with his young servant: "He [Alyosha] has understood exceptionally well what I need from him right now, and he more than satisfies all my demands."[9] The sexual overtones are clear, and the passage was deleted by Soviet censors in all later editions of Tchaikovsky's correspondence.

Tchaikovsky himself sensed the abnormality in the closeness of their relations. For all his force of feeling and progressive views, he remained a child of his age, and class prejudices revealed themselves time and again. In a letter to Anatoly from January 1879, Tchaikovsky remarked irritably, "It is a surprising thing how nice he [Alyosha] can be when you keep him in the position of a lackey, . . . and how he immediately becomes spoiled when . . . you live with him not as a servant but as a comrade."[10] Much later, in a diary entry from 22 May 1886, he wrote, "I must confess that with his mania for arguing always and about everything he does become *à la longue* insufferable in terms of pleasant companionship. . . . In general, I value and love Alyosha fully only in the countryside, where everything is all right and there's nothing to argue about."[11] Yet, even though Tchaikovsky was frequently annoyed by those dearest to him, it is striking that in the whole huge corpus of his letters and diaries triflingly little that is negative is said about Alyosha Sofronov. Between the two poles of passionate emotion for a lover and son and irritation with an inferior, the strange affair between gentleman and servant steadily grew and developed. In September 1876, when Alyosha was seventeen, Tchaikovsky wrote to Modest that Alyosha "has grown up and become inexpressibly less good-looking, but for my heart he has remained as dear as ever. Whatever happens, I shall never part with him."[12]

As for the other person mentioned by Kashkin from among Tchaikovsky's immediate Moscow entourage, this "certain Bochechkarov," not a servant but a parasite, was indeed a colorful and individual figure. That he managed to establish himself so firmly within Tchaikovsky's little household says as much about the composer as about this odd old man. Tchaikovsky probably became acquainted with Nikolay Lvovich Bochechkarov through Vladimir Shilovsky. Rather stout and sporting a small mustache *à la Régence*, Bochechkarov, according to Modest's curious description, possessed "the venerable appearance of an important out-of-touch dignitary living in retirement in the former capital [Moscow] and the manners of old-fashioned aristocrats, with their habits of speech abounding in gallicisms and in words borrowed from their old nurses."[13] But, notes Modest, as with "ladies in the deep province," no sooner was it necessary to say something coherent in French than Bochechkarov would become quite flustered, since in fact he did not know the language at all.

The emphasis Modest places on Bochechkarov's feminine characteristics seems not to be accidental. He writes that Bochechkarov "would cross himself as do important ladies—with a tiny, tiny sign on his breast" and that while he doubts that Bochechkarov ever in his life read a single one of the Gospels, "his religiosity, like that of a Moscow goodwife, had no need of this."[14] To a great degree, Bochechkarov's mannerisms call to mind the popular image of the elderly homosexual who cultivates effeminate behavior. Certainly Bochechkarov's chief occupation seems to have been another activity associated in the popular imagination with middle-aged, middle-class women—gossiping. "He was known by a good half of so-called 'society' in Moscow, and he knew everything that went on there. Everywhere he was received with pleasure, because with his lively and very cheerful air he was liked by all; then, too, he always brought with him heaps of the most interesting news, both what he had heard the day before and what he had learned from the police gazette."[15]

Apart from this, we are told, Bochechkarov "did absolutely nothing, not only in his old age but apparently as far back as he could remember." Always wearing "a mask of satisfaction with life and of well-being," he was, in fact, a pauper and lived exclusively on handouts. He was supported throughout his life by various friends and acquaintances, and despite his carefree manner, he would not hesitate to give a "thorough dressing-down" to anyone imprudent enough to ridicule him. "As a result," remarks Modest, "he was even rather feared."[16]

Modest is obviously at pains to provide a reasonable explanation of why this somewhat clownish figure could have attracted such a refined soul as Tchaikovsky to such a degree that, when the latter "with joy realized that he could support him," he then "took upon himself, for as long as Bochechkarov was alive, all of that man's monetary concerns."[17] In particular, Modest suggests that his brother saw in Bochechkarov, with his old-fashioned customs and eccentricities, a "fragment of the past." "To study the habits of this old man, to listen to his discourses, and to learn his prejudices—this became his favorite way of spending his free time."[18] Even when Bochechkarov intruded on Tchaikovsky while he was working, he "had only to utter some word

that smacked of Moscow before the French invasion and [Tchaikov-
sky's] anger would melt away and be replaced by laughter, the work
would be set aside, and the friendship restored."[19]

Tchaikovsky's own letters and diaries, however, make it clear that
there was more to Bochechkarov's role than being a source of entertainment for Tchaikovsky, be it in the capacity of an eccentric, a jester,
or a parasite. Bochechkarov served also as a kind of link between the
composer and the Moscow homosexual underground. Tchaikovsky's
newly acquired freedom in his living accomodations also enabled him
to keep his movements independent of Rubinstein or anyone else. This
led to an increased interest in the life of those who shared his own
proclivities—an interest that could now be exercised with a greater
sense of security. Now, for the first time, this homosexual underground, the peculiar world of the *tyotki*, or "aunties" (contemptuous
slang for passive homosexuals, modeled on the French *tantes*), entered
his correspondence, and it was Nikolay Bochechkarov who would be
his chief informant concerning the happenings, scandals, and gossip of
this world.

By the second half of the nineteenth century, homosexuality had
acquired a complex and partly paradoxical status in Europe. The situation differed, of course, from country to country, but there were also
certain common aspects and trends. Scholars have noted the existence
of a distinct homosexual subculture throughout the major urban communities of western Europe. The causes for this phenomenon were
several and the process of the subculture's emergence very gradual, but
two things clearly served as catalysts: the social and political upheaval
in the wake of the French Revolution and the decline in influence of
both the Catholic and Protestant churches. In Romanic countries the
Napoleonic Code had done away with penalties for homosexual acts
between consenting adults, and the impact of this was felt in certain
other nations of continental Europe. In Germany, for instance, a movement had already emerged calling for repeal of the antihomosexual
paragraph of the Imperial Code. Not many years later, the measure was
being debated on the floor of the Reichstag and, but for the outbreak
of World War I, would very likely have been passed.

A relaxation of tensions was aided by the proliferation of medical
and clinical research. Leading contemporary authorities in the field
from Richard von Krafft-Ebing to Havelock Ellis had asserted that so-
called sexual aberrations could not be regarded as crimes, since they
represented various forms of psychic disorders for which their carriers
could not be held responsible. As a consequence, homosexuality began
to be treated punitively by the state solely in instances of violations of

public decency or brash scandal, and the punitive measures actually taken fell far short of not only the severe penalties of earlier times but even the penalties prescribed by existing laws. In effect, these laws went unenforced or were enforced very selectively and for unsavory purposes, such as personal and clandestine official vendettas.

Many people, particularly among the privileged, the educated, and the bohemian element, had ceased making any effort to conceal their unorthodox sexual tastes. Even the sexual mores of the lower classes were treated by the authorities with indifference unless the public order or public health appeared threatened. Only the middle class remained in any real danger—not from criminal prosecution but from social ostracism. These were people for whom favorable public opinion formed the cornerstone of material or hierarchical success: businessmen, civil servants, certain categories of the intelligentsia (doctors, teachers, lawyers), and those aspiring to a political or military career. Here was the greatest potential for blackmail on the part of both the authorities and one's enemies.

These conditions—with the decrease in the threat of punishment, on the one hand, and, on the other, the continuing need among various members of the middle class for maximum secrecy—created in Europe a situation in which only particular circles of people became aware of the various ways, places, agents, and possibilities for fulfilling their sexual desires. They knew in which street and squares in each city the sexual outsiders gathered, in which restaurants, hotels, or bathhouses male prostitutes, through some connivance or oversight of the police, could still be found. Individual homosexuals held differing views of this shadowy subculture, depending on their particular predilections or psychological constitutions. Some took on mannerisms and peculiarities of conduct that differed subtly or radically from accepted proprieties. Others, on the contrary, attempted to mask an idiosyncrasy that they often scarcely dared acknowledge even to themselves. But in either case, the ability to recognize others like them almost at a glance inevitably sharpened.

Much the same process could be seen in Russia. As prevailing European medical and juridical theories began to make their way into Russian legal circles, existing punitive law became increasingly neglected or only selectively applied. From memoirs and diaries of the period it is clear that one hardly had need of court pronouncements or juridical proofs to be aware of the sexual preference of this or that prominent individual. Within society circles such matters were common knowledge. Rumors circulated, epigrams (not necessarily malicious) were composed, people talked. But those discussed, epigrammatized, or gossiped about were never stigmatized or excluded from the salons. Quite the contrary, the notoriety often lent them an added glitter, while many were simply too powerful to be seriously attacked without woeful consequences for the attackers.

Throughout the nineteenth century in Russia persons recognized as homosexual by consensus of their contemporaries occupied numerous and responsible public offices and played substantial roles in the political and cultural life of the nation. The butt of several well-known Pushkin epigrams lampooning his sexual tastes, Prince Aleksandr Golitsyn had remained one of the most powerful men in the realm under Alexander I and as chief of the Ministry of Spiritual Affairs had spurred the tsar's own interest in the mystical quest. A central figure under Nicholas I was Count Sergey Uvarov, the Minister of Education and originator of the formula "autocracy, orthodoxy, ethnicity," which defined the ideological face of the reign. To the position of vice-president of the Academy of Sciences, Uvarov appointed his favorite, Prince Mikhail Dondukov-Korsakov. The homosexuality of both men was no secret to their peers, as evidenced again by the epigrams and diaries of Pushkin. Meanwhile, one of the most noted religious writers of the period and another contributor to official doctrine, Andrey Muravyov, was a constant object of both epigrammatic humor and veiled attacks by the liberal press.

Those were just some of the more notorious examples. Reactionary views or difficult personalities had won such men as Uvarov and Muravyov more than a few enemies ready to stop at little to bring about their downfall. Yet, not one of them was to fall victim to a charge of homosexuality, nor was recourse to existing legislation likely to have entered the mind of even one of their enemies. Insinuation designed to discredit them in public opinion was the farthest anyone went.

The outward manifestation of homosexuality and the unsensational attitude toward it in Russian society are reflected in a scene from Tolstoy's *Anna Karenina* in which Vronsky, composing himself before a horse race, has his solitude interrupted by the appearance of two officers. "One was quite young, with a thin, delicate face, and had recently joined their regiment from the Page Corps; the other was a pudgy old officer with a bracelet on his wrist and tiny bloated eyes." The two attempt to strike up a conversation, the younger officer "casting a timid look sideways at Vronsky and trying to catch with his fingers his scarcely visible mustache," but Vronsky pointedly ignores the pair and they soon go out. At that point, "the tall and stately Captain Yashvin" enters the room and, "nodding condescendingly and scornfully at the two officers," goes over to Vronsky. "'There go the inseparables,' said Yashvin, glancing mockingly at the two officers as they left the room."[20]

Similar attitudes are apparent in the memoirs of various men and women of the time, most especially those from the gentrified and urbanized intelligentsia to which, both socially and psychologically, Tchaikovsky himself belonged.[21] Though it might elicit either bewilderment or embarrassment, rarely did homosexuality evoke outright rejection or condemnation.

Tchaikovsky's letters and diaries make it clear that his own feelings regarding the homosexual underground were always divided. The exotic subculture and the various individuals who belonged to it simultaneously repelled and attracted him, and he never completely resolved the ambiguity of his attitude. Without doubt, he very much resisted any outright identification with this subculture and spurned most of the mannerisms associated with it. But, at the same time, something within him responded positively to certain striking aspects of the behavior of the aunties—to their appearing in drag at a masked ball, for instance, or to their habit of calling one another by female names. Most typical of his relations with Modest, this playful element of Tchaikovsky's personality was also vividly evident in his correspondence with Ivan Klimenko, who, like Bochechkarov, was one of the first guests in Tchaikovsky's new apartment.

Ivan Klimenko remained for the most part outside the world of the aunties. Indeed, he would eventually marry and raise a family, to all appearances quite happily. Yet, despite his apparent heterosexuality, Klimenko's memoirs and, even more so, Tchaikovsky's letters to him suggest that their friendship was colored by distinct homoerotic and even sexual overtones. The particular playfulness of Tchaikovsky's vocabulary in his letters to Klimenko, and most notably his persistent feminization of Klimenko's name, could reach the point of undisguised flirtation. "Forgive me, dear soul, for taking so long to respond," he wrote in one letter, "but better late then never my darling Klimenochka! . . . I end this letter with a prayer: do come, I crave you irrepressibly."[22] Except when writing to Modest, Tchaikovsky never allowed himself the degree of verbal unruliness he used in his correspondence with Klimenko. His letters were saturated with sexual symbols, implications, and double entendres. During the course of this friendship, with its endless mischief and pranks, Tchaikovsky also addressed several humorous verses to his friend, some of them ambiguous and even obscene in their content.[23] All this was jocularly exaggerated and indeed at times very witty—the two were obviously enjoying their game. But every joke contains a grain of truth. Close reading of several of the letters leads to the suspicion that not only may this humorous play have served on occasion as an appropriate outlet for the release of erotic tension but even moments of sexual intimacy may have existed between the two men.

Perhaps most revealing is a letter from Tchaikovsky to Klimenko written on 12 September 1871, shortly after moving into his new apartment. The following passage from this letter, wherein the addressee is amusingly treated as a concubine in a sultan's harem, is absent from all editions of the composer's correspondence and is found only in Klimenko's memoirs:

> But can you, the most beloved of the concubines of my harem, you, the beautiful and at the same time young Klimcna, doubt for even a single moment my love for you? No, my silence can be explained merely by the laziness of your voluptuous Sultan; ever postponing a pleasant moment of conversation with you, in the end he has brought this almost, I think, to the point of a rendezvous with you. Strictly speaking, it would not even have been worthwhile writing you, since we shall soon see each other; but I took pen in hand at the relentless request of my divan, which, having been reupholstered with new fabric on the occasion of my move to the new apartment, is drooping out of longing for you and prays, on your arrival in Moscow, to soothe your tired limbs on its resilient shoulders newly furnished with fresh springs. To its request I add my own as well. If you wish to give us both considerable pleasure, stay at my place and live with us as long as you like. I hope you will not force me, that is, the Sultan, and my Divan, that is, my government, to turn our requests into commands, disobedience of which entails the penalty of death by impalement.... So I await you! Truly, it grows dull without Klimena.[24]

After quoting this letter in full, Klimenko comments, "I yielded to the lovely invitation and lived for some time with Pyotr Ilyich."[25]

The abuse of the feminized form of Klimenko's name; the pun on the word "divan" (in its two meanings, in Russian as in English, of both a sofa and a Turkish council of state), which is prepared to "soothe his tired limbs"; and the "threat" of the "voluptuous Sultan" to punish the "beloved concubine of his harem" with "impalement" are suggestive in the extreme. In literature the sofa often figures in an erotic context, as is clear from Edward Gorey's recent satire of older pornography, *The Curious Sofa*. An eminent example is *Le Sopha* by the eighteenth-century French author Claude Prosper Crébillon. In Crébillon's novel, which was widely read in the French-speaking high society of Moscow and St. Petersburg, the animated sofa becomes indeed the main character, serving as witness to an endless succession of amorous couples who make love upon it. It goes without saying that the "threat" of "impalement" was meant as a quite explicitly sexual (that is, homosexual) joke.

Whatever the truth of Tchaikovsky's friendship with Klimenko, chance was soon to separate them. In May 1872, Klimenko left Moscow in search of employment and, though long wanting to return, remained stuck in the provinces.

But if Klimenko seems to have stood apart from the circles of the aunties, Modest was clearly well acquainted with them. Along with the ambiguous wordplay and flagrant feminization reminiscent of his correspondence with Klimenko, gossip from this underground filled Tchaikovsky's letters to Modest. Two letters from the end of 1872 are especially notable. Supplying curious information about not only the world of the aunties but also Tchaikovsky's relation to it, they arguably reflected the peak of his interest in the matter. Both letters were signed "Petrolina" and the first even added, "your devoted and loving sister." Modest himself was addressed in the first letter as "young Tchaichikha" and in the second as "amiable Modestina" and "dear sister."

In the first of these letters, dated 2 November 1872, Tchaikovsky wrote:

From the news let me tell you the following: (1) Kondratyev spent a week and a half in Moscow, then went abroad, abducting the unforgettable Alyosha Kiselev [Kondratyev's male servant and lover]. . . . In Moscow he was more amusing than ever. (2) Volodya [Shilovsky] has settled in Moscow and bought himself a charming little manor house into which he will soon move. (3) Old Lvovna loafs about as before and has become for me as essential [a cut in the text; my conjecture: "as toilet paper"] and music paper for orchestration of a symphony. She often recalls the Bessarabian girl from Cherkassy [that is, Modest, who at the that time was serving as an investigator in the town of Cherkassy, near Kiev]. (4) I made the acquaintance of a friend of yours (as he claims to be): Nikolay Burnashev. He reminds me very much of Masalitinov [Prince Golitsyn's male lover] and in general I do not like him in the least. . . . (8) [Sergey] Donaurov wrote me a very touching letter from Petersburg on the eve of his departure abroad, where it seems he is going for a very long while. On what money?—I don't know. (9) Relations with Bibikov are strained.[26]

In the second letter, dated 2 December, Tchaikovsky wrote:

> I find Burnashev (who continues to call you his tender friend) offensive in the extreme, but still he visits me. Here in the world of the *aunties* an abominable incident took place between [Mikhail Bek-] Bulatov and [Nikolay] Glebov, about which I shall tell you when we see each other.[27]

The context of these letters makes it clear that the characters who figure in them all belonged to the homosexual milieu. "Old Lvovna" from the first letter was obviously Bochechkarov, Lvovna being the feminine form of his patronymic. The tone if far from respectful. It is notable that Modest, quoting the letter in his book, found it necessary to change the feminine Lvovna back to the masculine Lvovich.[28] In a letter to Modest a year later, Tchaikovsky would mention, rather bafflingly given his circumstances, the apparent appearance of a lady: "Sofya Lvovna represents a great resource for me, but more as a material attribute of my surroundings than a serious friendship."[29] Nowhere in the memoirs or correspondence do we encounter any woman by this name, and it comes as no surprise when Modest alters this text to read "Bochechkarov represents a great resource for me."[30] It is also worth noting that in the letters Bochechkarov is referred to in the same breath as socially more exalted homosexual figures, such as Shilovsky or Golitsyn, and far inferior ones, such as Pyotr Okoneshnikov.[31]

  Bochechkarov served repeatedly as a source of scandalous information: "Nikolay Lvovich [Bochechkarov] appears periodically with a supply of gossip about Bulatov, [Vladimir] Benediktov, and *tutti quanti!*"[32] (These two names, like certain others, crop up in the correspondence with Modest primarily in candid, homosexually related passages.) He also mediated the various squabbles so frequent in this sort of underground. "Some five days ago [Shilovsky], drunk, burst into Bulatov's apartment at four in the morning, hurling a whole series of insults at the latter," Tchaikovsky wrote Modest at one point. "It goes without saying that Nik[olay] Lv[ovich] was the intermediary and, my God, how much argument, weighing of every word, and profound debate there was concerning this!"[33] No doubt it was also Bochechkarov who informed Tchaikovsky of another "abominable incident," whatever its nature, between this same Bulatov and Nikolay Glebov, mentioned in the second of the Petrolina letters.

Besides his role as an entertainer and a supplier of dubious or scandalous information, Bochechkarov also rendered Tchaikovsky various small services in practical affairs, though not always with complete honesty. "I understand," Tchaikovsky wrote to Modest in one letter, "that you have come to pity the old man. But, all the same, he has cheated me terribly, and in addition, he neither asks forgiveness nor sends his account."[34] At times, the old man could show his claws, and on one occasion, he sent to Modest a letter "of basest nature."[35] The tone of the references to him in the letters can be complex, a mixture of sarcasm and sympathy, annoyance and pity. With the old man's growing decrepitude, it was pity that gradually supplanted all else. One is almost amazed at the perfect degree to which Bochechkarov embodied the stock character of the parasite in ancient Roman comedy—a witty and unprincipled figure of secondary importance, but without whom the more exalted dramatis personae cannot succeed in furthering their intrigues and satisfying their desires.

In the same sense that Bochechkarov represented the world of the aunties, the far loftier level of the homosexual subculture, the real demimonde, was in many respects remarkably embodied in the person of another of Tchaikovsky's close companions, Nikolay Kondratyev. It was in this context that his name came up in the first of the Petrolina letters. Socially, while not belonging to the upper aristocracy, Kondratyev was a prominent figure. He was also a graduate of the School of Jurisprudence, though, as Modest note, he "left the school before Pyotr Ilyich entered it, so that it was not as schoolfellows that they became close."[36] Kondratyev chose not to go into the civil service but to embark upon the idle life of a landowner and playboy. He was marshal of the nobility for the Sumsky district of Kharkov province in the Ukraine and "carelessly ran through the vast fortune of his ancestors."[37] The photographs that survive show a broad-shouldered, solidly built man with a square face and heavy chin.

In the early 1870s, Tchaikovsky was spending a great deal of time at Kondratyev's estate of Nizy, in Kharkov province. It is interesting that Modest himself draws attention to the strangeness of this friendship: "At first glance, there was nothing in common between the modest conservatory professor absorbed by his interest in his art, who was neither fashionable nor sociable, working from morning to night, and this arch-elegant dandy with his refined and aristocratic ways of behavior, a society chatterbox slavishly following the latest word in fashion." Nonetheless, "in actuality they became not simply close acquaintances but friends bound by an almost brotherly love."[38] As in the case of Bochechkarov, Modest claims that the fundamental cause of Tchaikovsky's attraction to Kondratyev was the latter's unceasing joie de vivre.[39] "For such an incorrigible optimist as Pyotr Ilyich," writes Modest, "for such a sensitive responsiveness to the sufferings of his neighbor as he possessed, to have before his eyes the constant confirmation that life is beautiful, to feel that he was in the company of those who were happy and contented, and as far as possible to be the cause of their contentment and happiness—this constituted what was needed for the peace and perfect equilibrium whereby he himself could only be happy and content."[40]

From the letters and diaries, however, emerges a different and far more complex relationship. In general, they draw a rather stormy picture of the relations between the two men, leaving little doubt that Kondratyev was a capricious, selfish, and willful person and extremely difficult to get on with, especially for so sensitive and delicate a companion as Tchaikovsky. And yet, despite the categorical assertions quite often found in his writings, Tchaikovsky continued to take pleasure in Kondratyev's company. Years later, in 1887, he would even write in a letter addressed to Modest that "fate has turned out thus that for you and me Nik[olay] Dm[itrievich Kondratyev] has been more than a friend and, as it were, the closest of relatives."[41] This last, rather odd phrase may in fact contain a hint at the essential circumstance that in many respects determined their friendship and to which Modest, the cautious biographer, never alludes—namely, the sameness of the sexual preferences of all three men, the landowner, the composer, and the composer's brother.

Kondratyev was married and had one daughter, but his marriage was a constant drama and fraught with scandals. Occasional references in Tchaikovsky's letters to his friend's family life indicate that the chief source of trouble between husband and wife was the sybaritic Kondratyev's sexual relations with his male servants. This situation was one which in Russia at that time was not at all uncommon. Three and a half centuries of serfdom had deeply ingrained patterns of social behavior that the 1861 abolition of serfdom had in fact done little to eradicate. Though now legally free, the lower classes remained subservient to the upper classes in every respect, and for the average youth or young woman of peasant origin to yield to the sexual advances of the *barin*, the gentleman or master, could still seem natural enough and could often lead to tangible benefits. Far from being the exception, sexual exploitation of peasants by their former master continued to be widely regarded as the norm even several decades after emancipation. Indeed, a similar relationship with his servant Alyosha was becoming an important constituent of Tchaikovsky's own private life.

Certainly it is no accident that one of the chief themes of classical Russian literature is that of the heartless seduction of humble peasant girls by wealthy and cynical scoundrels. Nostalgia for these past ways of country life has been powerfully expressed even in the twentieth century in the stories of Ivan Bunin. One of Tchaikovsky's own contemporaries, writing of a time well after the abolition of serfdom, describes his family summers spent in the country when—in an allusion to the hedonistic philosophical school of ancient Greece—he would indulge in "truly Cyrenaic" pleasures: "I lost no time in developing relations with these girls. My cousin taught me the art of seduction and making these muscled amazons yield; it was enough to offer them some trifling gift like a packet of pins, a cheap ribbon, candies, a pie, even a bit of sugar."[42] The same mentality was at work in the homosexual milieu as well, and especially in Kondratyev's relations with his male servants.

Among these servant-lovers the most scandalous figure was certainly Aleksey Kiselev, who appears occasionally in Tchaikovsky's letters and diaries. In a letter to Anatoly, the composer described the quite abnormal state of affairs between masters and servants at Nizy: "His servants are so undisciplined that they behave like the real masters and treat their own masters and their masters' guests as if they were their servants. The resulting disorder, lack of care, and unpleasantness daily exasperated me to the depths of my heart."[43] The main troublemaker was hinted at in the first of the Petrolina letters, with its reference to Kondratyev's departure abroad with "the unforgettable Alyosha Kiselev," whom he has "abducted."

The servant's boldness and arrogance, aggravated by his heavy drinking, often made relations with him all but unbearable. Yet, despite the periodic rifts he would cause not only within his master's family but also between his master and Tchaikovsky, Kiselev was to remain many years in Kondratyev's service. And for all their quarrels, Tchaikovsky would continue to single Kondratyev out of the crowd of his acquaintances: "I have many friends, but no one at all with whom you can pour out your soul like Kondratyev."[44]

Appearing frequently in the same circle as Kondratyev during this period was Shilovsky. At one point, Tchaikovsky would write of having arrived in Moscow with his sometime pupil and having had "a very jolly time, especially as N[ikolay] D[mitrievich] Kondratyev had also turned up here."[45] Bonds of greater intimacy seem to have been restored between the two men, at least for a time. Tchaikovsky became a frequent guest at Shilovsky's estate at Usovo and accomplished a great deal of work there. But the course of their friendship was never smooth for long. "I very often dine at Shilovsky's," Tchaikovsky would tell Modest on 28 November 1873, "but I find his company extremely trying; he becomes more unbalanced and burdensome with every passing day."[46] On the whole, the weight of emotions between Tchaikovsky and Shilovsky remained decidedly unequal throughout the period leading up to Shilovsky's betrothal in 1874. A passionate and capricious attachment to his teacher is attested on the young man's part, and no doubt to his amazement, Tchaikovsky found himself in the rather unusual position for him of the "beloved." Tchaikovsky, however, was in most cases inclined to yield to such pressure, particularly when exerted by someone as physically attractive as Shilovsky. The situation was in fact an archetypal example of a pupil's amorous infatuation with a teacher who in turn, not without pleasure, allows himself to be loved.

But then, quite unexpectedly, the twenty-four-year-old Shilovsky decided to marry. Very quickly the tone of Tchaikovsky's references to the younger man was to turn to one of pure resentment, untempered by either sympathy or compassion. It was with open annoyance that Tchaikovsky appears to have alluded in a letter to Anatoly of 26 January 1874 to his pupil's sexual practices before his engagement. "[Shilovsky] is planning to commit a terrible absurdity, that is to get married," he wrote. "This will be his undoing, especially as he is marrying a rich and very young girl who will be very surprised to discover [there follows a cut, for which it is easy to conjecture 'a homosexual']."[47] But some three years were to pass between the announcement of the engagement and Shilovsky's wedding day. All this time the young man apparently continued to indulge his old habits, and his relations with Tchaikovsky developed predictably. In one typical outburst, Tchaikovsky wrote to Modest, "God willing, may [Shilovsky] not get on your nerves as he does on mine. When I see him, it is as if someone has hung a weight around my neck. I've not the energy to tolerate his disorder and capriciousness."[48]

Their relations were further aggravated by Tchaikovsky's recurring financial problems. He was well aware of the opportunity he might seize upon to be supported by his pupil: "I could exploit Shilovsky with little effort, but this would mean burdening myself with a feeling of gratitude and putting myself into relations of an obligatory nature with him."[49] Such a relationship would supposedly have included, as his later association with Mrs. von Meck did not, an element of erotic intimacy, which Tchaikovsky, valuing his freedom above all else, wished to avoid, especially as his "pupil" continued to subject him from time to time to "nasty and dramatic scene[s] of jealousy, unappreciated love, and so on."[50]

It is clear from the texts that Shilovsky was more in touch than Tchaikovsky with the world of the aunties, of which Bochechkarov was so representative. As in the first of the Petrolina letters, the two names often figure in the same passage, together with those of other individuals involved in various homosexual intrigues and homosexually based scandals. Certain of these passages have been so severely tampered with by different censors that restoring the original meaning can be quite a puzzle, as is the case with a letter of 29 April 1876: "Shilovsky is in love, acts like a madman, and has moved out on [stricken from the original], [who(?)] was jealous and making scenes [both verb endings here are masculine in the Russian]. The object of his love is a tavern [stricken from the original; 'whore'?] living [feminine participle ending in the Russian] in a separate apartment maintained by her lover."[51]

The temptation to see in this mangled passage a description of some heterosexual affair of Shilovsky's should probably be avoided. The main aspect of the censorship exercised by Tchaikovsky's family over his letters, was precisely the concealment of any male names in unambiguously homosexual contexts. The logic of the first sentence goes also against a heterosexual interpretation. The customs of the times would have demanded in the case of a rupture between a man and his mistress that he throw her out, not that he move out on her. This first sentence would seem in fact to refer to a homosexual man (very possibly Bulatov, implicated in another of Shilovsky's scandals) whose live-in lover Shilovsky was at the time and who "was jealous and making scenes" after the latter fell in love with a "tavern [whore]" and eventually moved out. The masculine past imperfect forms of the Russian verbs "to be jealous" and "to make," which, given the tenses of the other verbs in the sentence, could only rather awkwardly refer back to Shilovsky but rather more plausibly could refer to the stricken name, still further strengthen this probability.

Tchaikovsky's familiar habit of turning masculine names to feminine would account for the Russian gender endings of the second sentence. It is indeed very likely that the "tavern [whore]" may have been a typically effeminate figure from a lower stratum of the homosexual subculture who appears fleetingly in various letters under the name Boriseta, a feminization of the male name Boris, which has no legitimate feminine counterpart. Shilovsky's brother Konstantin noted in one letter to Tchaikovsky that Boriseta is "such a sweet lady" and was not embarrassed to call "her" "him" in the same sentence.[52] The homeless Boriseta evidently spent most of the winter under Konstantin's roof, and understandably so, since in view of his betrothal Vladimir Shilovsky could scarcely have had so compromising a companion stay with him.

In addition to Bochechkarov, Kondratyev, Shilovsky, and Golitsyn (alluded to in the first of the Petrolina letters through the reference to his lover Masalitinov), all men who played notable and varyingly influential roles in Tchaikovsky's life, there were a number of chance acquaintances of little real significance in his life who belonged to various strata of the homosexual subculture. Some were acceptable in their behavior, and some, considerably less so. At least two such names figure in the Petrolina letters.

The poet Sergey Donaurov was one of the more curious figures among Tchaikovsky's circle of acquaintances during his Moscow period, having ties both to the musical world and to the homosexually colored demimonde. A graduate of the Page Corps, Donaurov attained considerable fame in his time as the composer of numerous popular songs dealing primarily with urban themes. Modest mentions that his brother's acquaintance with Donaurov, whom he met through Kondratyev in 1870, did not come about through music, as Donaurov was not a real musician and never considered himself to be one. While still an attaché with the Ministry of Foreign Affairs and a fashionable socialite, he began to compose songs for amusement. After abandoning the civil service, which Modest suggests he found financially disadvantageous, he made this activity a very profitable source of income. At the time the two met, Donaurov was at the height of his popularity, receiving four times as much for each one of his songs as Tchaikovsky.

Donaurov's homosexuality can be inferred from his mention in the first of the Petrolina letters, where no less than seven other homosexuals are mentioned, and from the cuts in other published letters dealing with him. Tchaikovsky's attitude toward him deteriorated over the years from sympathy to antipathy. In the mid-1870s he still thought his letters to be "very interesting" and found Donaurov himself, despite his "insatiable amorous appetites and . . . somewhat difficult disposition," to be, "*en somme*, a kind of nice fellow."[53] But meeting with him in Kiev in August 1880, he realized that he "never liked Donaurov" and that "seeing him was disagreeable. . . . [He] lies an awful lot and boasts of his conquests [a suspicious cut follows]."[54] It may well be that Tchaikovsky extended to Donaurov the ambivalent attitude that he felt toward the entire milieu to which the latter belonged to some degree.

Nikolay Burnashev was apparently the least socially acceptable of these lesser acquaintances of Tchaikovsky during this period, despite his having been also a graduate of the School of Jurisprudence. He has the peculiar distinction of figuring in *both* Petrolina letters, and in both instances in a negative context. Tchaikovsky appears to have considered the man an imposter who, using his casual acquaintance with Modest, was pretending to be the latter's "most tender friend" so as to insinuate himself into their circle. Tchaikovsky disliked him thoroughly, comparing him unfavorably with Golitsyn's lover Masalitinov. His attitude here was again typical: though finding Burnashev "offensive in the extreme," he continued the acquaintance. Years later, Burnashev would surface again, at which time Tchaikovsky could still consider it appropriate to lend him money, although his motivation in this cannot be truly established owing to further cuts in the text.[55]

While Tchaikovsky possessed a taste for amorous adventures of various sorts that would draw him into these underground circles, he seems to have largely disapproved of the ostentatious behavior of the aunties and the moral relativism often present in their attitudes. Although he considered his own homosexuality natural and no doubt deplored the social stigma it carried, he never related it in his mind to the rest of the ethical standards of the culture to which he belonged. His personality was at bottom very traditional, and the rigorous moral education he had received from his parents was only enhanced by his highly idealistic view of art and the artist and by his habitual religious reverence. Many years later, Tchaikovsky would state categorically in his diary that "Russian 'aunties' are loathsome."[56] The way of life of the homosexual underground, with its tendency to undermine socially accepted standards of public conduct, was ultimately unacceptable to him. But, by dint of habit or curiosity, as well as for more pragmatic reasons of sexual gratification, he continued to share the company of the aunties—a sign less, perhaps, of hypocrisy than of an inability to reconcile an intellectual position with instinctual demands.

With the growth of his popularity, Tchaikovsky was becoming an increasingly noticeable figure in salons and, more generally, in the musical and cultural worlds of both Moscow and St. Petersburg. He and his music were spoken of and written about in newspapers and journals, his opinion was sought after, and he was liked and admired. "Everyone loves me terribly," he remarked to Modest at one point, "and I don't know how to show them my gratitude for this."[57] But popularity and nascent fame had adverse effects as well. Now that Tchaikovsky suddenly found himself in the limelight, he inevitably became the subject of various rumors and speculations. Although most of the time he was blissfully unaware of this fact, now and then some such gossip happened to reach his ears and pain him deeply.

It is natural that his associations with Shilovsky, Bochechkarov, and the world of the aunties could not pass completely unnoticed. Indeed, the homosexual milieu was notable for its continual gossiping, scandals, and intrigues. Nikolay Bochechkarov was well known throughout Moscow as a notorious rumormonger, a role he played with gusto. It is hardly difficult to suppose that anyone who cared to might easily learn from Bochechkarov the details of life in the composer's apartment, where this inquisitive old man stayed so often and so long. Logically, therefore, there was no way for Tchaikovsky's homosexuality to remain a secret. Wide circles of society would eventually have come to be privy to this knowledge, with the degree of publicity no more than a matter of its definition.

Tchaikovsky, ostrichlike, could believe—or pretend to believe—that all this talk had nothing to do with him. But he can hardly have been altogether blind to the possibility that sooner or later the situation could well come to be of more immediate concern and that the slanderers might attack him directly. This, indeed, may shed more light on his fear of crowds and public appearances. From the 1870s on, the composer found himself the object of continuous and ever-intensifying public scrutiny, which at times drove him to panic. The disgust mixed with fear that he felt regarding this invasion would steadily develop into a consistently hostile attitude toward publicity that was later expressed unequivocally in one of his letters to Mrs. von Meck:

> I am a person who has a supreme and insurmountable aversion for publicity in general and newspaper publicity in particular. For me there is nothing more terrible, more dreadful, than to be the object of public attention. Having chosen an artistic career, I have naturally had always to be prepared to encounter my name in the paper and, however difficult it may be for me, still I am unable to prevent my music being discussed in print. Unfortunately, the papers do not limit themselves to a man's artistic activities—they like to delve further, into the private life of the man, and deal with the intimate aspects of his life. Whether this is done sympathetically or with an obvious intent to do harm, I find it equally unpleasant to be the object of attention.[58]

Perhaps inevitably, his way of dealing with this predicament had an indirect effect on Tchaikovsky's creative life. It may well have sharpened his sense of privacy and of the gulf between the ideal realm of art and the aggressive world of society. It may also have helped him control the claims of personal vanity, to the advantage of heroic self-discipline, and cleared a mental space for introspection and the musical creativity that was his real genius.

CHAPTER NINE

Becoming the Composer

Increasingly during the 1870s, Tchaikovsky came to feel the burden of his responsibilities at the Moscow Conservatory. He was now teaching harmony, orchestration, and a special class in composition. At times, he found himself spending close to thirty hours a week in the class-room. Well recognizing this waste of precious time that might other-wise be devoted to creative labors, he grew frustrated and dispirited. Writing to Anatoly on 2 December 1871, he even suggested that he would be privately pleased were the Moscow Conservatory to go bank-rupt, however much he might deplore the blow such an event would be to the world of culture. "I have grown so sick of my classes," he complained, "I am so weary and upset that I should be glad of any change, and of course I shall not starve to death."[1]

Even the furnishings there irritated him—the school desks and the dilapidated, untuned piano, with its yellowing keyboard. One former student recalled, "Standing at the blackboard, Tchaikovsky would have to write for us problems and examples; I remember the squeamish ges-ture with which, having thrown away the chalk and gray dustcloth, he would wipe his fingers on his handkerchief."[2]

More vexing still was his continual shortage of money. Tchaikovsky belonged to a category of people who seem to be thoroughly inept at handling financial matters. Certainly his genius did not extend to math-ematical calculation, and throughout his life money was to slip away at an alarming rate. At this time, in addition to meeting his own ex-penses, he was subsidizing not only his twin brothers but also Nikolay

Bochechkarov, and the old gossip was, it seems, a veritable sponge. For all this, his modest professor's salary was clearly inadequate. Even the large sums that came at regular intervals from his former pupil Vladimir Shilovsky would vanish almost immediately, and Tchaikovsky's debts to moneylenders during this period were considerable.

It was at this time that Tchaikovsky started his journalistic activities. For five years, beginning in 1871, he wrote regular reviews of musical life in Moscow, first for the journal *Contemporary Chronicle*, where he replaced Hermann Laroche, who had left for St. Petersburg, and later for the *Russian Register*. Besides being an additional source of much-needed income, this occupation had the further advantage of keeping Tchaikovsky in the swim of the major musical events of Moscow. Covering everything from the Italian opera to Russian folk choruses, Tchaikovsky argued with equal passion against the preponderance of the one and the extremes of the other, in a continuing effort to educate the musical taste of his readership. Indisputably an ardent patriot and a devotee of the Russian cultural tradition, Tchaikovsky was nevertheless closer in temperament to the musical sensibilities of western Europe, and this often placed him in an uncomfortable position between the camps of the Slavophiles and the westernizers. His outspoken views on Russian opera and his criticisms of performances of Russian folk songs at times evoked hostile reactions from strongly Slavophilic circles, which all too often passed from purely musical debates to outright personal attacks. This may have accounted for his never completing an ambitious essay on Beethoven, the first part of which appeared in Prince Meshchersky's periodical *The Citizen* in February 1873. Tchaikovsky's fear and hatred of such attacks on him were to be major factors in his ultimate decision to give up his duties as a critic in December 1875.

Work on his own Russian opera, meanwhile, continued to proceed sluggishly. Though Tchaikovsky himself had completed the libretto for *The Oprichnik*, he found the basic plot of the opera less than inspiring. On 23 April 1871 he had written to Modest, telling him how much more congenial he had found the story of his previous, failed effort, *Undine*. In fact, given the nationalistic trend of the time, Russian subject matter was virtually a requirement for any opera to enjoy success and public recognition. But for Tchaikovsky this, at the moment, proved to be an alien imposition. Seduced by the colorful theatricality of Lazhechnikov's long-running play, with its story of the guardsman (oprichnik) Andrey and his doomed love for the Princess Natalya, set amid the intrigues of the court of Ivan the Terrible, Tchaikovsky drew from it a libretto that attempted to combine the Russian national tradition of Glinka with the Romantic methods and principles of Meyerbeer. From the very beginning of his work on *The Oprichnik*, he sensed the contradictory character of this conflation and the incompatibility of the whole project with the nature of his own creative strengths. A new operatic vision, at once Russian and European, embodied in such masterpieces as *Eugene Onegin* and *The Queen of Spades*, was as yet several years away.

Tchaikovsky completed *The Oprichnik* in the spring of 1872. Following the failure of *The Voyevode* at the Bolshoy, he had lost any desire to have his new creation mounted in Moscow and decided to send the opera to the Mariinsky Theater in St. Petersburg instead. The production was not approved until late December 1872, only after Tchaikovsky had gone in person to St. Petersburg and played the opera through in order to convince the theater's managers.

But, for all his financial and creative troubles, Tchaikovsky, at scarcely more than thirty years of age, was still young and exuberant, and that was clearly what mattered. He strove to hide his concerns from colleagues and friends, who for the most part remember him in this period as a charming, cheerful, and even mischievous young man. Ivan Klimenko, for instance, recalls how he once suggested that for fun the two of them greet passing strangers as old acquaintances, upon which Tchaikovsky immediately leapt from their carriage and waved warmly to a gentleman riding toward them, to that gentleman's utter confusion.[3] It was this whimsical facet of his personality that was reflected most often in Tchaikovsky's letters of the period to his brothers, his sister, and Klimenko himself. Full of humor and wit, they might be written now in Church Slavonic, now in fractured English, and sometimes even in verse.

On 28 November 1871, Tchaikovsky's sister, Aleksandra, gave birth to her second son, Tchaikovsky's second nephew. She wrote to her brother, "After many anxieties and worries, and then great suffering, God gave me a son Vladimir; as he still lay there, having barely appeared in the world, . . . I rose slightly to look at him and my first words were: 'He looks like my brother Petya—God grant that he become just such a man!' Truly Volya [Vladimir] looks like you, and that pleases me very much."[4] Tchaikovsky could not then have realized the full significance of this event, for his nephew Vladimir, known as Bob, was destined to become the center of his emotional life during his later years. In responding to his sister's letter on 9 December, he noted that he had received her news "with rejoicing in my heart."[5]

A week later, after much hesitation, Tchaikovsky yielded to Shilovsky's appeal to accompany him once again on a journey abroad. He had written to his brother Anatoly of their coming departure and his desire that it remain secret: "At Shilovsky's importunate request I am going abroad with him around 15 December for one month, but since this should not be known even in Moscow, everyone (except Rubinstein) must believe that I am going to see Sasha [Aleksandra, in Kamenka]."[6] After visiting Prince Meshchersky briefly in St. Petersburg, the two then left for Nice. There Tchaikovsky spent three weeks and found it "extraordinarily bizarre to be transported from the deep Russian winter into a place where you cannot go out wearing more than just a frockcoat, where oranges, roses, and lilacs grow and trees are covered with bright green leaves." He walked a great deal and delighted in the sea, especially in the morning, when he would sit alone "beneath the rays of the burning, but not excruciating, sun."[7]

By this time, yearly trips to Europe were becoming a recurrent feature of Tchaikovsky's life. In many ways, as his letters indicate, they tended to be monotonous, though Tchaikovsky was nonetheless capable of keen enjoyment of a beautiful foreign city and its artistic treasures. Much depended on his mood of the moment. But through it all ran a greater conflict that he was never able to resolve. Feelings of homesickness and depression had already become almost inevitable adjuncts to Tchaikovsky's journeys abroad, his passionate desire to leave Russia for Europe and escape the pressure of social and professional obligations being matched by a scarcely less passionate desire, once there, to return at once to his homeland.

During that winter of 1871–1872, having left behind his creative tasks, Tchaikovsky found himself being drawn into the idle social whirl in which the wealthy vacationers passed their days. His mood grew steadily worse, and melancholy turned into burning homesickness. In mid-January, Shilovsky suggested that they visit Genoa and Venice, returning to Russia by way of Vienna. "However pleasant this whole journey," Tchaikovsky confessed to his father after his return, "in the end the idleness began to weigh heavily on me and I was glad to return to Moscow."[8] Nevertheless, his stay in the south of France had proved not entirely uncreative, and while there, he produced the Two Pieces, op. 10, for piano (one of which was his popular Humoresque), which he dedicated to Shilovsky.

In early February, *Romeo and Juliet* was performed at a concert of the Russian Musical Society in St. Petersburg. Even César Cui, a staunch opponent of Tchaikovsky's music, was forced to admit the excellence of the overture and described it as "an extraordinarily gifted work."[9] Later that spring, Tchaikovsky completed not only *The Oprichnik* but also a cantata for the inauguration of the Polytechnic Exhibition in Moscow commemorating the bicentenary of Peter the Great, for which he received the handsome sum of seven hundred and fifty rubles. The cantata was performed on 1 June at an open-air concert on the Troitsky Bridge. Classes at the conservatory had already ended, and later that same day, Tchaikovsky left Moscow to visit his sister in Kamenka.

The Davydov estate was already the composer's preferred vacation refuge, and he stayed until early July when he interrupted his orderly routine there to travel with Sergey Donaurov to Kiev. There they met Modest, who was living at the time near Kiev, and shortly all three proceeded to Nikolay Kondratyev's estate at Nizy. After staying ten days at Nizy, Tchaikovsky then set off for Usovo to visit Shilovsky. At one of the coach stops on the way, Tchaikovsky, just as a joke and because he wished to be served more expeditiously, declared himself to be Gentleman of the Bedchamber Prince Volkonsky. Amazingly, the ruse worked, and with the first horses available, he was sped on his way. At the next coach stop, he discovered to his horror that he had left his wallet with five hundred rubles and all his documents in it at the previous station. Cursing himself for his imposture, which might now be so easily exposed, he managed with great luck to retrieve the wallet with no unpleasant consequences.[10]

After a month at Usovo as Shilovsky's guest, Tchaikovsky returned to Moscow in mid-August. There Tchaikovsky, with his two male servants and a dog named Bishka that he had picked up on a Moscow street, moved to another apartment. As before, he invited Klimenko, now living in Odessa, to visit him in his new lodgings. Writing to him, he described the unchanging routine of his life in Moscow: "In the same way we go to the conservatory, in the same way we sometimes get together for drinks, with Jurgenson distinguishing himself as usual, and on the whole we are depressed. . . . In general, depression eats away at us, and this can be explained by the fact that we are growing older, for I cannot hide from you that every passing moment brings us closer to the grave. As for me personally, to tell the truth I have only one interest in life: my success as a composer."[11]

These last words were not written idly. Despite the peregrinations of the summer months, Tchaikovsky, somewhat to his own surprise, had managed to begin and virtually complete work on his Symphony no. 2 in C Minor, op. 17, known as the *Little-Russian*. Consumed by the new composition, he worked furiously at it after his return to Moscow, and by the beginning of November, he was able to write to Modest that "this work of genius (as Nik[olay] Dm[itrievich] Kondratyev calls my new symphony) is close to completion and will be performed as soon as it is scored." And he added, "I think this is my best work with respect to perfection of form, a quality in which I have not shined before now."[12]

Not unlike *The Oprichnik*, the Second Symphony, more than any other of Tchaikovsky's symphonic compositions, felt the influence of Russian musical folklore. Indeed, it consists almost entirely of variations on themes and melodies from popular folk songs. It was not by chance, then, that the work found favor with the Mighty Five. While in St. Petersburg that December to negotiate the production of *The Oprichnik*, Tchaikovsky attended a party at the home of Rimsky-Korsakov, where he was asked to perform something from his new symphony. When he had finished playing the finale, "the entire company," he would later tell Modest, "almost tore me to pieces in their enthusiasm."[13] The first public performance of the Second Symphony, originally scheduled for 11 January 1873, was postponed until the twenty-sixth because of the death of the Grand Duchess Elena Pavlovna, the patroness of the Russian Musical Society. In the audience was Hermann Laroche, who had made the journey from St. Petersburg expressly for the concert. In his review of the symphony in the *Moscow Register* on 1 February, Laroche wrote, "Not in a long time have I come across a work with such a powerful thematic development of ideas and with contrasts that are so well motivated and artistically thought out."[14]

Tchaikovsky described the success of the concert in a letter to his father of 5 February, noting that he "was called back several times and there were several curtain calls. The success was so great," he added, "that the symphony will be played again at the [Musical Society's] tenth concert, and a collection is now under way to present me with a gift on that day. In addition, the Musical Society has given me three hundred silver rubles as an honorarium for the performance of the symphony."[15] Eight days later, buoyed by his triumph and with tongue perhaps not entirely in cheek, he went on to boast ambitiously to Modest that "in general, the time is drawing near when Kolya, Tolya, Ippolit, and Modya will no longer be the Tchaikovskys, but merely the brother of *the Tchaikovsky*. I shall make no secret of the fact that this is the desired end of all my efforts. To grind into the dust everything around one by one's own greatness—is not this supreme pleasure?! So tremble, for soon my fame will crush you."[16]

In March 1873, Tchaikovsky hastily set about composing incidental music for Aleksandr Ostrovsky's play *The Snow Maiden*, based on the beloved Russian fairy tale of a girl carved out of snow who comes to life and then melts under the spring sun. Though at the time the play itself, which opened in early May, was given a poor reception, Tchaikovsky's music was noted favorably. With the money he had received for the music to *The Snow Maiden* Tchaikovsky decided to travel abroad, stopping first to visit Kondratyev at Nizy and, predictably, his sister's family at Kamenka. At Nizy he saw Apukhtin, but then caught a severe cold while taking a swim in a stream and was forced to spend several weeks convalescing at Kamenka under his sister's care.

As a result of this delay, he did not leave for Europe until 26 June. By 1 July he was in Dresden, where he found Pyotr Jurgenson. Together they made an excursion into the nearby mountains, saw a production of Mozart's opera *The Magic Flute*, and visited the famous Dresden picture gallery. From Dresden, Tchaikovsky traveled on alone to Switzerland, where he visited Zurich, Lucerne, and Geneva, stopping in Vevey at his sister's request to find out about possible future accommodations. He then passed down to Italy, harboring ambitious intentions of covering the length and breadth of that country, but the heat he encountered as early as Milan was too much to bear and he shortly turned north again and headed for Paris, which was "fine in any season." From there he wrote to his father on 23 July/4 August, "There is no way to describe how comfortable and pleasant life in Paris can be and how agreeably someone set on enjoying himself can spend his time here."[17]

His letters suggest that this was one of Tchaikovsky's few truly enjoyable European journeys and that it helped set his mood for embarking upon a new project suggested some months before by the music critic Vladimir Stasov—a musical fantasy on the theme of Shakespeare's *The Tempest*. Rested and relaxed, Tchaikovsky returned to Russia in early August and headed at once for Usovo. While spending two "blissful" weeks alone on Shilovsky's estate, he plunged into work on *The Tempest*, op. 18, with heady enthusiasm. Five years later, Tchaikovsky would recall this time eloquently in a letter to Mrs. von Meck: "I found myself in an exalted and blissful frame of mind, wandering alone about the woods by day and across the immeasurable steppe as evening fell, and sitting at night by an open window and listening to the solemn silence of that remote place, broken now and then by sounds I could not name. During those two weeks, without any effort, as if moved by some supernatural force, I completed a rough draft of the entire *Tempest*." But Shilovsky's return from Moscow broke the spell. "At once, all the charms of my direct communion with nature

in all its ineffable majesty and magnificence fell away. The corner of
paradise was transformed into a prosaic country estate. Staying on a
tedious two or three days more, I left for Moscow."[18]

In early October, Tchaikovsky again fell ill and did not teach, although during this time he managed to compose the Six Pieces, op. 19,
for piano, of which he dedicated the first to Kondratyev and the last to
Laroche. He also completed scoring *The Tempest* and wrote the Six
Pieces, op. 21, for piano, commissioned by the publisher Bessel. He saw
much of Kondratyev during these weeks and dined often at the home
of Shilovsky, but with Kondratyev's departure to Kharkov for the provincial elections there, he began to feel more keenly the tedious burden
of friendship with his young pupil. He found some relief from this tedium in the person of Bochechkarov, to whom his attachment had
steadily increased. To Tchaikovsky, as to many other Muscovites, the
amusing old man took the place of a local gossip rag.

The Tempest was given its premiere in Moscow on 7 December at
a concert of the Musical Society. Conducted by Nikolay Rubinstein in
a performance with which composer and musicians alike were well
pleased, the symphonic fantasy enjoyed a respectable, though less than
resounding, success, and Tchaikovsky received from the society a fee
of two hundred rubles for the work. A year later, the piece was performed in St. Petersburg, where it scored another success, winning
high praise from several members of the Five. But Tchaikovsky's own
opinion of his work would later waver, and at a performance of *The
Tempest* at the Châtelet in Paris in February 1879, he was very disappointed by the music of what he had once considered a splendid piece.

At the same time, in St. Petersburg *The Oprichnik* was being
readied for production, and in the latter part of January 1874, Tchaikovsky made the journey to the capital for discussions with the chief
conductor of the Mariinsky Theater, Eduard Nápravník. A composer
himself, Nápravník brought to Tchaikovsky's music an acute musical
comprehension. Despite Nápravník's reputation for pedantry and coldness, Tchaikovsky would eventually strike up a rewarding and lasting
friendship with him and, five years later, dedicate to him his opera *The
Maid of Orléans*.

Throughout December 1873 and the better part of January 1874,
Tchaikovsky's chief concern was with a new composition, his String
Quartet no. 2 in F Major, op. 22. Completed by 18 January, the new
work was given its first informal hearing in early February 1874 in the
apartment of Nikolay Rubinstein. Present also, and unfortunately so,
was Rubinstein's brother Anton. Kashkin recalls, "All the while that
the music continued Anton Grigoryevich listened with a dark, dissat-

isfied air, and as soon as it was over, he said, with his usual ruthless candor, that this was not at all in the chamber style, that he did not understand the composition at all, and so on. All the other listeners were, on the contrary, in ecstasy."[19] Not surprisingly, Tchaikovsky took great offense at such sharp words. From this point on he began to harbor an unmistakable ill will toward Anton Rubinstein that would only grow with the years. Some days after the incident, he wrote to Vasily Bessel that he found himself "in a darker mood than ever before."[20] Yet, in spite of his newborn rancor, Tchaikovsky had generosity enough to praise highly in print a concert appearance of Anton Rubinstein that he had attended on 5 March. "Rubinstein played much, long, and so well as only a virtuoso who possesses both the talent of genius and the inimitable mastery of long experience can play," Tchaikovsky wrote in his review published in the *Russian Register*.[21]

Rehearsals for *The Oprichnik* took Tchaikovsky back to St. Petersburg in late March, and for the premiere on 12 April, the entire Moscow Conservatory faculty, led by Nikolay Rubinstein, arrived in the capital. The performance, according to Bessel, was a "veritable triumph for Tchaikovsky,"[22] and at a celebratory supper afterward, Tchaikovsky was awarded a Young Composer's Prize, worth three hundred rubles, for his new opera. He stayed one more day in St. Petersburg, and on the fourteenth left for Italy, where he planned to attend a production of Glinka's *A Life for the Tsar* in Milan in his capacity as music critic for the *Russian Register*. Departing Russia under the impression that his opera had been an undoubted success, attested by the festive atmosphere of the premiere, he would learn some time later of the sharp criticism of César Cui, who devastatingly attacked the music of *The Oprichnik* as being "barren of ideas" and "without a single outstanding passage or a single happy inspiration."[23]

It is curious that—as had happened before and would happen again—Tchaikovsky himself came to echo the views of his hostile critics. From Florence, scarcely two weeks after his departure, he confessed to his cousin Anna Merkling in a letter of 25 April/7 May that "my opera, to tell the truth, is a terribly weak composition; I am very dissatisfied with it."[24] And complaining of his low spirits, he wrote to Modest two days later, "In fact, Petersburg is the cause of my melancholy. *The Oprichnik* torments me. This opera is so poor that at all the rehearsals . . . I ran away so as not to hear a single note, while at the performance I wanted to sink into the earth."[25] This interesting passage reveals not only Tchaikovsky's capacity for a sober and critical view of his work following the euphoria of popular success but also the deep-rooted uncertainty that in him, as in so many other artistic geniuses, went hand in hand with his confidence in the eventual achievement of greatness.

Learning that the Italians were introducing various changes into Glinka's opera to make it more to the taste of an Italian audience and that the production was for this reason to be pushed back to the middle of May, Tchaikovsky decided not to go to Milan, but simply enjoy Italy. On 17/29 April he arrived in Venice on his first visit to that fabled city, where his immediate impression was altogether somber. "Venice is such a city that were I forced to live here a whole week, I should hang myself out of despair on the fifth day," he wrote to Modest the day of his arrival. "Everything is concentrated on the Piazza San Marco. Beyond this, no matter where you go, you wind up in a labyrinth of stinking passageways leading nowhere, and until you sit in some gondola and order yourself taken about, you'll have no idea where you are." Floating along the Grand Canal was, he decided, "not bad, as there are palaces, palaces, and palaces, all in marble and each better than the last, though at the same time each is dirtier and more neglected than the last. . . . But the Doges' Palace is the height of beauty and interest, with its romantic aura of the Council of Ten, the Inquisition, tortures, oubliettes, and other such delights. Still, I ran through it thoroughly once again and, to clear my conscience, visited two or three other churches with a whole sea of paintings by Titian and Tintoretto, statues by Canova, and all sorts of aesthetic jewels." But, he repeated, "the city is gloomy, as though it were deserted. Not only are there no horses, I have not even seen a single dog."[26]

The next day, he fled Venice for Rome, where he spent his time touring the sights of the ancient city and strolling along the Via del Corso. He began to feel homesick in Naples, was impressed by Pompeii, and found that he very much liked Florence, though he stopped there only for one day. By early May he was back in Moscow, but only long enough to help conduct examinations at the conservatory before leaving for Nizy on 1 June.

His desire to write an opera had by no means cooled with his disappointment over the *The Oprichnik*, and now once again he had chosen, almost obstinately and probably under the influence of his Moscow friends, a strongly Russian theme. The libretto for his new work, based on Nikolay Gogol's comic fantasy *Christmas Eve*, was written by the noted poet Yakov Polonsky. This libretto was in fact the object of a competition offered by the Russian Musical Society. Winning the competition would secure his opera's production at the Mariinsky Theater in St. Petersburg, an honor Tchaikovsky coveted more than a monetary prize, "although money is also a good thing." Staying some six weeks at Nizy, Tchaikovsky found conditions at Kondratyev's estate admirably favorable to composition. He worked every day from noon until three and in his remaining time swam, played cards, or spent time with his host, as the mood struck him. Accompanying him this time was his adolescent servant, Alyosha, who was already in his master's estimation "the dearest and most obliging creature."[27]

From Nizy, Tchaikovsky traveled to Usovo, where by 21 August he managed to complete the scoring of his new opera, which he had titled *Vakula the Smith*. Happy to have the work completed before the beginning of the new term, he sent it off at once, submitting it anonymously, as required, with the motto *Ars longa vita brevis est* in place of his name. Only several weeks later did he discover, to his dismay, that the deadline for the competition was not January 1875, as he had thought, but the following August. He would have to wait anxiously for more than a year before the outcome of the competition was announced. "All my thoughts are now intent upon my beloved child, darling *Vakula the Smith*," Tchaikovsky wrote to Anatoly on 12 May 1875. "You would not imagine how I love him! It seems to me that I will positively go mad if I don't succeed with him."[28]

Returning to Moscow at the end of August, Tchaikovsky shortly changed lodgings yet another time, though this time simply moving to another apartment on the same street. He had found his previous apartment too small and inconvenient for composing and living together with two servants. Apukhtin, who seemed to be growing fatter and fatter, visited in September, but through most of the autumn Tchaikovsky found himself busy with classes. His Second Quartet was given its first performance in St. Petersburg on 24 October, with *The Tempest* following on 16 November. Both performances met with great success, and even Cui had to recognize the merits of the two works. Laroche, however, disliked *The Tempest*, and in his review he accused its author of imitating Schumann, Glinka, and Berlioz. This criticism deeply offended Tchaikovsky and must have contributed to his low spirits during the course of his labors on his Piano Concerto no. 1 in B-flat Minor, op. 21. The concerto was completed on 21 December. Eager to show his new work to Nikolay Rubinstein and learn his opinion of it, Tchaikovsky fully anticipated that the celebrated pianist would perform the piece at one of his next concerts.

He was thus stunned when Rubinstein subjected his composition to a devastating and pungent critique. Even three years later, describing the episode to Mrs. von Meck in a letter of 21 January/2 February 1878 from San Remo, he still could not speak of it without a bitterness that betrayed the extent of his hurt. Not being a professional pianist himself, he had needed "a stern but at the same time amiably disposed critic" to point out any purely technical flaws in the work, but he confessed in his lengthy letter to Mrs. von Meck that "some inner voice protested against the choice of Rubinstein as this judge of the mechanical side of my composition. I knew that he would not refrain from taking advantage of the opportunity for a bit of *petty tyranny.*"

When Tchaikovsky met Rubinstein and another friend and colleague, Nikolay Hubert, at the Moscow Conservatory on Christmas Eve, he proceeded to play the first movement of the concerto. Neither Rubinstein nor Hubert said a word. "If only you knew," he told Mrs. von Meck, "what a foolish and unbearable situation it is to offer a friend a dish one has cooked oneself and to have that friend eat and say nothing! Say something at least, curse me as a friend, but for God's sake, give me at least one sympathetic word, even if it's not one of praise." But Rubinstein, in Tchaikovsky's words, "was preparing his thunderbolts." The rather indecisive Hubert, meanwhile, was waiting "for the situation to be made clear and for there to be a pretext for him to join one side or the other." Steeling himself, Tchaikovsky played through to the end. Again there was silence. Finally, Tchaikovsky stood up and asked, "Well then?" And from Rubinstein's lips "the flood of oratory started to flow, quietly at first, then taking on more and more the tone of Jove the Thunderer." Rubinstein criticized every aspect of the concerto, saying "that it was impossible to play, that the passages were hackneyed, clumsy, and so awkward that there was no way even to correct them, that as a composition it was bad, vulgar." He even accused the composer of stealing this or that passage and ended by declaring that only "two or three pages" were salvageable and that the rest had to be redone entirely. "I cannot convey to you the chief thing, that is, the *tone* in which all this was said," Tchaikovsky wrote to Mrs. von Meck. "Well, in short, a stranger who happened to be in that room might have thought me a maniac, a talentless and thick-witted scribbler who had come to this famous musician to harass him with my nonsense."

Taking Rubinstein's tirade as a personal insult, Tchaikovsky left the room in silence. "It was wholesale, absolute condemnation," he recalled, "expressed in such terms and in such a form that I was stung to the quick. . . . In my agitation and anger I could say nothing." When Rubinstein later that same evening repeated his view that the concerto was impossible and pointed out numerous passages that he felt needed to be radically changed, further proposing that if the concerto were reworked according to his suggestions, he would reconsider performing the piece, Tchaikovsky answered, "I will not change a single note and will publish it exactly as it is now!"[29]

This entire episode is made even more puzzling by the fact that several years later Rubinstein was to reverse his position dramatically and indeed become one of the concerto's most prominent exponents. Very probably Tchaikovsky was right in diagnosing Rubinstein's initial response as a display of "petty tyranny." It may be that some unconscious jealousy or the accumulation of resentments unavoidably caused by the daily routine of working closely together at the conservatory also played a role. Whatever the case, Tchaikovsky's disappointment was as keen as the obvious blow to his self-esteem.

It was undoubtedly this incident that not only prompted but also colored the whole mood of his letter to Anatoly of 9 January 1875. In this letter, Tchaikovsky told his brother that he had fallen into a "great depression" over the holidays. "Besides that fact that there is no one here [in Moscow] whom I might call a *friend* in the true sense of the word . . . , I still found myself under the strong impression of a blow that had been dealt to my composer's pride, and by none other than Rubinstein," he wrote. Rubinstein and Hubert could not "get out of the habit of seeing me as a beginner in need of their advice, severe comments, and decisive judgments. . . . If you take into consideration that they are regarded as my friends and that in the whole of Moscow there is no one who might treat my work with love and attention, you will understand that this was very hard on me. . . . I am very, very lonely here, and if it were not for working constantly, I should simply give myself over to melancholy."

It was with this sense of creative frustration and betrayal by a friend and mentor that Tchaikovsky went on to indulge in an effusion that has often been misguidedly cited as proof of his supposed lifelong self-torment on account of his homosexuality. The forbidden theme is hinted at by the censorial cut. "It is also true," he wrote, "that . . . [the omitted phrase can probably be restored as 'my aberration' or possibly 'homosexuality'] creates an unbridgeable chasm between me and most people. It imparts to my character an estrangement, a fear of people, immoderate timidity, mistrustfulness, in short, a thousand qualities whereby I am growing more and more unsociable. Just imagine, lately I often dwell at length on the idea of a monastery or something of the sort."[30]

The context of the letter, however, makes it clear that the source of torment in this particular case had more to do with his composition of music than with psychosexuality. The lack of approval of his recent work exacerbated his sense of isolation. His mood of the moment was, in fact, a heightened example of what he called his "misanthropy," a neurotic mixture of a fear of people and a resentment at being alone. It had nothing to do with sexual frustration and everything to do with the incident of the First Piano Concerto. This incident not only wounded Tchaikovsky's pride but also provoked a pervasive depression on a scale disproportionate to its immediate cause. Perhaps in view of Tchaikovsky's extreme sensitivity to anything relating to his music, especially at this early stage, such a morbid reaction was to be expected. Indeed, it comes as no surprise that the disapproval of an older and venerated master could plunge him into self-doubt and self-pity, prompting him even to question aspects of his character that he did not otherwise doubt. But such wounded questioning and self-laceration, proceeding from a distorted perspective, were short-lived. In the letter to Anatoly the implicit link between what Tchaikovsky considered his "misanthropy" and his "aberration" was of the moment only, as is proved by his markedly different attitude in many other letters and writings in which he took his sexual tastes as quite natural for his individual constitution and as a source of enjoyment. Throughout his life Tchaikovsky would from time to time withdraw into isolation, or dream passionately of so doing, yet this would invariably be related not to his sexual pursuits but to his need for optimal working conditions.

A feature of a neurotic disposition is the periodicity of depressive fits. Tchaikovsky was becoming aware of this, and winter was obviously the most difficult season for him: "All winter, to a greater or lesser extent I have been constantly depressed, sometimes even to an extremity of disgust with life and a yearning for death. Now, with spring drawing near, these attacks of melancholy have altogether ceased, but since I know that with every year, or rather with every winter, they will return with the utmost force, I have decided to be absent from Moscow all next year. . . . I *must* have a change of place and surroundings."[31] It would be wrong to be misled by this "yearning for death." A belated adherent of Russian Romanticism, Tchaikovsky often used morbid imagery in a strictly figurative sense to connote low spirits and feelings of depression.

His persistent desire at that time to leave Moscow is, however, another matter. Beginning in this year, 1875, this desire would become obsessive, revealing an inner drive to break away from the conservatory and its environment—an environment that, particularly after the concerto incident, he increasingly felt as alien. Just as a few years before he had gradually come to view St. Petersburg social circles as an obstacle to his full immersion in creative work, so now he began to consider his social and professional obligations, and especially his teaching duties, to be burdensome and even destructive to his composing. In both cases, it was Tchaikovsky's growing sense of his artistic vocation that led to his desire to distance himself from his immediate milieu. In both cases, however, the break, when it came, was never absolute. Relations continued, but they acquired a new character that did not allow them to interfere significantly with the composer's concentration on his art.

Recovering with no small effort from the crushing critique of the First Piano Concerto, Tchaikovsky continued his conservatory routine. At a party at Rubinstein's home he made the acquaintance of the Hungarian violinist Leopold Auer, to whom he shortly dedicated his *Sérénade mélancholique*, op. 26, completed in February, following the scoring of the piano concerto. By mid-April he had produced the Six Songs, op. 28, and in early May *The Oprichnik* had its Moscow premiere at the Bolshoy. During rehearsals, Tchaikovsky "endured with stoic fortitude the systematic disfigurement of an already ugly and ill-starred opera,"[32] but the public greeted the production as enthusiastically as St. Petersburg audiences had the year before.

Examinations at the conservatory took on a special meaning for Tchaikovsky this spring, as he watched the graduation of his favorite and most promising student, the nineteen-year-old Sergey Taneev. He had first met and befriended the younger brother of Vladimir Taneev, the acerbic chronicler of life at the School of Jurisprudence, in his class on composition the previous year, and this same spring he had attended the young musician's first public concert, a virtuoso performance of the First Piano Concerto by Brahms. Sergey Taneev, who was to develop into a composer and musical figure of some note, and his former teacher would maintain their close, though chiefly professional, friendship for more than twenty-five years.

Immediately following the examinations, Tchaikovsky left Moscow and largely recapitulated the progress of the previous summer, immersing himself in work on his Symphony no. 3 in D Major, op. 29, known as the *Polish*, during three weeks at Usovo and then going on to finish the draft and complete the scoring of the symphony at Nizy in early July. With skill had also come increased speed in his work. The composer's archives, which preserve the starting and ending dates for the composition of each movement of the Third Symphony, testify that despite his traveling that summer, Tchaikovsky managed to complete the sketches for the symphony in less than two months. The rest of July and the first part of August saw him at Verbovka, the small village adjoining the Davydov's estate at Kamenka, and by the end of the month, he was again visiting Shilovsky at Usovo. It was to Shilovsky, on whose estate he had spent so many fruitful hours, that Tchaikovsky dedicated his latest symphony, which had a successful premiere on 7 November of that year under the direction of Nikolay Rubinstein.

When he returned to Moscow in September, Tchaikovsky was surprised to discover that Sergey Taneev had been practicing the First Piano Concerto and was playing it splendidly. Later that autumn, Taneev performed the "impossible" work at a concert of the Russian Musical Society on 21 November. Conducted by Nikolay Rubinstein, the concert was a great success, with which no one can have been more pleased than Tchaikovsky himself, who just three weeks before in St. Petersburg had heard his composition reduced to an "atrocious cacophony" by the pianist Gustav Kross.[33] He was even moved to dedicate the concerto to Taneev, though later he chose to rededicate the work to the noted German pianist and conductor Hans von Bülow, who on 13 October of that year had directed the world premiere of the concerto in Boston, where it was a resounding success.

In late November the Musical Society welcomed Camille Saint-Saëns to Moscow. Almost immediately the witty and charming French composer, with his "dash of originality, which Pyotr Ilyich always liked in people," had exercised his appeal on Tchaikovsky.[34] He possessed, according to Modest, "a certain ability to become intimate at once," and the two musicians were soon fast friends, which might have been facilitated by their recognition of their shared homosexuality.[35] They also discovered a shared fondness for imitating female dancers. In exhibiting this skill, the two men went so far at one point as to perform, on the stage of the conservatory concert hall and in the sole presence of Nikolay Rubinstein, a short ballet entitled *Galatea and Pygmalion,* in which "the forty-year-old Saint-Saëns was Galatea, playing the role of the statue with unusual conscientiousness, while the thirty-five-year-old Pyotr Ilyich undertook to play Pygmalion."[36] Sending his photograph to Saint-Saëns in January 1876, Tchaikovsky would remind him of this escapade in particular.[37]

In the midst of this jollity with Saint-Saëns came word that *Vakula the Smith* had been awarded first prize in the opera competition and would be produced on the stage of the Mariinsky the following season. So it was in high spirits that Tchaikovsky in late December left Russia for Europe, accompanied this time by his brother Modest.

Disappointed and tired of living and working in the provinces, Modest had lately begun looking for any job he might find in either St.

Petersburg or Moscow, and that autumn he had been considering an unusual offer, which in early December he finally accepted, with far-reaching consequences for the course of his life. He had been invited to become the tutor to the eight-year-old Nikolay Konradi, the deaf-mute son of Hermann Konradi, an agronomist and landowner, and his wife, Alina. Tchaikovsky strongly supported his brother's desire to accept this position. Unexpectedly, Modest would reveal impressive gifts as a pedagogue, forging a remarkable bond with his young charge and remaining with him for more than a decade. As a condition of his agreement with the boy's parents, Modest was to leave at once for Lyon to spend a year there learning the latest methods of teaching deaf-mutes at the private school of the well-known specialist Jacques Gugentobler. Only upon completion of this training were the Konradis prepared to conclude a legal agreement, which in fact was not made until November 1877.

To lend moral support and to visit their sister in Geneva, where she was living with the children while her husband, Lev, had a new and more spacious home built for his family at Kamenka, Tchaikovsky decided to accompany his brother as far as Paris. They left Russia in late December and headed first for Berlin, arriving in Geneva just before the New Year. There they found Aleksandra pregnant again, and in a letter to Anatoly of 31 December 1875/12 January 1876, Tchaikovsky wrote that "Sasha's belly has grown large, but she is very lively and healthy. The children are as sweet as they were in Verbovka. Tanya [who was now fourteen] has here lost her air of an idle young missy and, for this reason, makes a very pleasant impression. Baby [Bob, now four] has grown; he tyrannizes me and Modest cruelly, and we of course carry out his orders in bliss."[38]

After a week in Geneva the brothers proceeded to Paris, where Tchaikovsky on 8/20 January heard Bizet's *Carmen* and found it wonderful. Indeed, years later Tchaikovsky wrote of his feelings about *Carmen* in a letter to Mrs. von Meck: "This music has no pretensions to profundity, but it is so charming in its simplicity, so vigorous, not contrived but instead sincere, that I learned all of it from beginning to end almost by heart."[39] The stay in Paris was brief, and two days later it was time to part, Modest to Lyon and Tchaikovsky back to Russia. It was a separation that Tchaikovsky suddenly found acutely painful. "If only you knew how much I miss you!!" he wrote to Modest the next day from Berlin. "Yesterday I wept all evening, and today my heart aches constantly at the memory of you and my eyes fill with tears."[40] Their few weeks spent traveling together seem to have been, in some sense at least, a turning point in the relations between the brothers.

From now on, it would fall increasingly to Modest, not Anatoly, to play the role of Tchaikovsky's most intimate confidant.

As the twins graduated from the School of Jurisprudence and embarked on their own lives, Tchaikovsky's open affection for them had in no way diminished. During these years he had tended, however, to grow increasingly absorbed in his work, and of the twins it was, interestingly, the favorite, Anatoly, who seemed most often prone to take offense at the infrequency of his brother's letters, interpreting this as a lack of attention. Time and again, Tchaikovsky found himself having to pacify his touchy sibling. Just a few weeks before his departure abroad, he had assured him that "the less I write you, the more I love you, my dearest and best of all deputy prosecutors!"[41] And in his letter from Geneva he had written, almost in exasperation as he defended himself against his brother's paranoid suspicions: "How foolish you are, Tolya! How could you think for even a single second that I might hide from you in Petersburg? I cannot imagine ever in my life not being pleased to see you."[42]

Along with the protestations came the endless stream of endearments. "At least for my part silence cannot be explained by lack of love," he wrote in one letter. "My heart is aflame for you as always."[43] The amorous vocabulary of his letters appeared, if anything, to grow even more extravagant as the twins entered young manhood—but especially so in Anatoly's case: "Tolya, I kiss your little hands warmly. . . . I smother you with kisses." "I kiss both your little cheeks and the wart on your ear." "I look forward to seeing you with impatience, for I shan't hide that I shall be terribly happy to kiss you. Farewell, you fickle, weak-willed but very lovable scamp." "I kiss you everywhere [followed by a mysterious cut, not by the Soviet censors but by someone tampering with the original document]."[44] Somewhat ironically, at the very moment of this last declaration of all-over kissing, written in the winter of 1872, Anatoly was suffering from syphilis, which caused his brother no small anxiety when he learned of it. The illness lasted some time, at least three months. Tchaikovsky repeatedly urged his ailing brother, then living in Kiev, to visit Moscow. "I want to entreat you," he wrote on 31 January 1872, "to take a vacation and come to Moscow for a month. Though you are likely to be somewhat bored here, still there are splendid doctors here who will quickly have you back on your feet. Meanwhile, it will be more comfortable for you and extremely pleasant for me. Your illness and your being so far away from me have caused me much worry, and you would simply be doing me a service if you decided to come."[45]

By contrast, Tchaikovsky's manner with the other twin remained for the most part either didactic or jocular, even as their relationship developed less smoothly. Upon graduating from the School of Jurisprudence, Modest, rather overplaying, as was his habit, a version of his brother's life-style during his brief society interlude in St. Petersburg, had plunged into preoccupations typical of the "gilded youth," to which he did not belong in either position or means. In the spring of 1870 he had willfully accompanied his former classmate and close friend Aleksey Valuev—who was at one time Apukhtin's lover and of whom Tchaikovsky strongly disapproved—to Simbirsk, thereby riling his elder brother. "I am extremely displeased with Modest," Tchaikovsky confided to Anatoly. "Having wheedled some five hundred rubles out of Papa, he has squandered it all. . . . He has gone off to Simbirsk to live with that drunkard Valuev and to play billiards with him from morning to night."[46]

Tchaikovsky's habitual address to Modest during these years stood out clearly in a letter of 30 August 1870 that began in threats and ended in increasing affection. "You infuriate me," he scolded. "Were you not ashamed to waste money so thoughtlessly? Villain! I implore you to embark on your service energetically; by the word 'energetically' I mean the following: do what you are ordered to do, conscientiously; in the face of your superiors pretend deference; if need be, court your superiors' wives—in a word, do not neglect any means of attracting attention to yourself. . . . I kiss you tenderly. . . . Once again I embrace you, not without tenderness. Your adored brother Pyotr."[47] The closing to the letter is itself worthy of notice: evidently Tchaikovsky had no fear that his adoring brother might rebel, and in this he was right. Also of interest are the tactics that he suggested his brother employ for the sake of his career, which only serve to strengthen the idea that Tchaikovsky's own earlier flirtation with Elizaveta Dmitrieva in 1866 may have been undertaken with an eye to impressing Nikolay Rubinstein.

This mixture of tenderness and annoyance toward Modest is also found elsewhere. At one point, he charged Anatoly to "give Modka five cuffs on the face and eight [a cut follows here, probably of 'kicks in the ass']; let him not be angry at my sharp words about his drinking spree. I love him and fear for him."[48] But even in these earlier years we begin to catch glimpses in their correspondence of a far deeper and more significant aspect of their relationship, which served as a powerful unifying force between the two brothers: their shared preference in love. These glimpses are infrequent but unmistakable, and are nowhere to be found in the letters to Anatoly, to whom Tchaikovsky was prepared to pour out his soul. This was in fact a crucial though deeply hidden nuance of his attitude toward his two brothers thus far. Anatoly was the beloved, and Tchaikovsky knew that there was no need, up to a point, to dissimulate the erotic nature of that love for him. But Anatoly was also heterosexual, and while aware of his brother's homosexual involvements with others, he would scarcely have been interested, and would probably have been annoyed, to learn the details. Modest, though perhaps loved less passionately at first, began to be increasingly valued as an emotional accomplice, sharing the composer's own sexual interests. It is not surprising to find that in his letters to Modest the composer seems especially relaxed, and it is to Modest, of course, that the revealing Tchaichikha and Petrolina letters are addressed.

Now, with the letter from Berlin of 11/12 January 1876, the tone and vocabulary of Tchaikovsky's letters to Modest acquire a different flavor, one of almost amorous longing, which had earlier been the exclusive trait of his letters to Anatoly. The new depth of his feeling is felt in a seeming generalization that was obviously a result of recent experience. "Separation from a person whom one loves," he told Modest, "is only good in that it provides an excellent opportunity for measuring the strength of that love."[49] An unusual passage on Modest's religious beliefs in the same letter is also curious in the new context of their relationship. In earlier years Tchaikovsky had often implicitly questioned various aspects of Modest's moral character. Now he felt nothing but admiration: "I am very happy that you are religious. Theoretically, I do not agree with you in anything, but if my theories had shaken you in your faith, I should have been angry with you. I am as ardently prepared to debate with you the issues of faith as I ardently wish that you stick by your own religious beliefs. Religion of the sort that manifests itself in you testifies to the high quality of the metal from which you are cast."[50]

The last line of this letter emphasizes their spiritual and emotional intimacy: "In general bear in mind that I love you very, very, very much!"[51] It is tempting to see this as an indirect assurance that in Tchaikovsky's affections Modest would henceforth enjoy equal status with Anatoly. Certainly, it is clear that the company of his brother helped Tchaikovsky considerably in healing the final traces of the depression he had suffered in Moscow. After his return to Russia on 19 January 1876, he even endeavored to work out an arrangement that might allow him to return abroad on the pretext of some official business and rejoin Modest. He went so far as to discuss such a project with Mikhail Azanchevsky, the director of the St. Petersburg Conservatory. But, in the end, he remained hesitant and ambivalent.

"I find it both desirable and frightening," he wrote, "for after all I love Holy Russia terribly and fear I shall miss her."[52]

CHAPTER TEN

Tensions, Temptations, Melancholy

Once Tchaikovsky was back among family and friends in St. Petersburg, the pain of parting with Modest soon eased. Performances of the Second Quartet and the Third Symphony were scheduled for late in January 1876, and Tchaikovsky decided to stay in the capital some few weeks. His days were quickly filled to overflowing as Anatoly and the Davydovs, Laroche and Apukhtin, Kondratyev and Meshchersky all clamored for his attention. When he was not busy making the social rounds, he was invariably seeing to business obligations, while most evenings found him at the theater. He attended productions of Wagner's *Tannhäuser* and of Aleksandr Serov's opera *Rogneda* (written in 1865 to a libretto taken from Russian chronicles). He also attended the premiere of César Cui's *Angelo,* and though Cui's new opera was little to his liking, he was curious to note that its author, so sharply critical of him in print, now "showered compliments" on him in person.[1]

The St. Petersburg premiere of his own Third Symphony took place on 24 January, with Eduard Nápravník conducting. Tchaikovsky was pleased with the performance and wrote to Modest four days later, "The symphony went very well and was a considerable success. The public called my name and roundly applauded."[2] The response of the critics to both the Third Symphony and the Second Quartet, performed on 28 January, was more mixed, though for the most part favorable. "In the force and significance of its content, the versatile richness of its form, the nobility of its style, . . . and the rare perfection of its technique, Mr. Tchaikovsky's symphony," wrote Laroche, "is one of the

171

most important phenomena in the music of the last ten years, not only in our own country, of course, but in all of Europe." And of the Second Quartet he wrote that it was "perhaps of all the composer's works . . . the most distinctive and original."³

Cui, however benevolent in the person, was far more restrained in his review, and, while recognizing that the symphony was "indeed of serious interest," he noted also that "the first three movements are better than the rest, the fourth movement is of merely sonorous interest, almost without musical content, while the fifth movement, a sort of polonaise, is the weakest."⁴ Even such mild criticism rankled Tchaikovsky, who remarked in a letter to Modest of 11 February, seeming to ignore Laroche's favorable comments, that "the press treated my symphony rather coldly, Laroche included. Everyone agreed that there is nothing new in it and that I begin to repeat myself. Is that really so?"⁵

But, at the end of January, word came from the German conductor Hans von Bülow of the success of the First Quartet in Boston. The American audience had become increasingly enthusiastic about Tchaikovsky's music ever since the premiere in Boston the previous October of the First Piano Concerto. The news stimulated Tchaikovsky's creative energy. To supplement his income, he was already writing in his spare time the pieces for piano entitled *The Seasons*, op. 37b, which from the start of the year the periodical *Nouvelliste* had begun publishing in a monthly musical supplement. He now finished in short order his Third String Quartet in E-flat Minor, op. 30, begun recently in Paris, and settled down to completing the work on his first ballet, *Swan Lake*, op. 20.

The commission to write the music for a ballet had come from the directorship of the imperial theaters the summer before, and, although Tchaikovsky himself acknowledged that he did it "partly for the money,"⁶ it was no doubt his love for the genre, evident from his early youth, and a desire to test himself in this new and unfamiliar endeavor that prompted him to accept the commission. The story line for *Swan Lake* had been developed by Shilovsky's stepfather, Vladimir Begichev, together with the dancer Vasily Heltser, and at Verbovka the previous August, Tchaikovsky had sketched out the first two acts of the ballet. But only now did he seriously set about working on it. Within a few weeks the ballet was finished. The ballet, with its melancholy, emotional nuances, and tragic denouement (in the first version of the ballet Siegfried and Odette perish), inhabits the same inner landscape that Tchaikovsky's imagination had explored during the first period of his musical creativity in such works as *The Tempest, The Oprichnik*, and *Romeo and Juliet*. The most striking quality of its music is a painful longing for an ideal never satisfied. This impulse, heard later both in the opera *Eugene Onegin* and in the Sixth Symphony, became the driving force of *Swan Lake.*

In Lyon, Modest was already immersed in the studies required for his future position, having been joined in Paris by his young charge and the boy's governess, Sofya Ershova. Some doubts and hesitation about whether he was right to accept the Konradis' offer, about whether he would be able to manage the task of educating Kolya, continued to haunt him, and Tchaikovsky, in his letters, counseled caution. "Always bear in mind that you have not yet bound yourself to the Konradis' service," he wrote on 28 January. "You must carefully consider the whole situation now that you are in Lyon; weigh all the pros and cons, and if on mature reflection the labor appears to be beyond your abilities, then decline it. I have seen the Konradis several times, and they seem to me to be good people. In the worst case, I shall take upon myself any money that you have spent and pay it without much difficulty out of the royalties for *Vakula.*"[7]

But, as his new surroundings and the methods he was learning at Gugentobler's school became familiar, Modest fast regained both his good spirits and his confidence. Jokingly Tchaikovsky noted in his letter of 11 February that "at least your stay in Lyon should be very beneficial to you, if only in terms of the French language, which you must speak perfectly upon your return—or else I won't want to know you."[8] In the meantime, after his return to Moscow in late January, he kept his brother informed of the city's news and gossip, writing in detail of the "dramatic scenes" made by Shilovsky, the "heap of rumors" brought round regularly by Bochechkarov, and the continuing troubles within the Kondratyev household over the unruly behavior of Kondratyev's servant-lover Aleksey Kiselev. Kondratyev, who had been visiting St. Petersburg, accompanied Tchaikovsky on the train to Moscow and on his return home found that "some unimaginable scandals had taken place in his absence. Mariya Sergeevna [Kondratyev's wife, called by the anglicized nickname Mary] dismissed Alyoshka [Kiselev], and now they are playing out quite a drama. Alyoshka weeps and swears that it's the last time; Nikolay Dmitrievich wants to keep him; she says that she'll leave if that happens—in short, the devil only knows what."[9] In the end, Tchaikovsky was moved to intervene in the squabble and eventually prevailed upon his friend to send the offending favorite, at least for a time, back to the country.

Modest, in his turn, and to his brother's delight, filled his letters with descriptions of life in Lyon. "You wouldn't believe," exclaimed Tchaikovsky on 3 March, "how the details of your existence in Lyon interest me. I was simply beside myself with pleasure reading your account of the seminarists' procession to the cathedral, and how well I understand your feelings [this is followed by a cut, very probably removing some comment of an erotic nature]. Finally, your description of [Gugentobler] and his wife is a little literary chef d'oeuvre."[10]

Modest had, indeed, pronounced literary ambitions, but the presence of Kolya Konradi, coupled with the dominating personality of his brother, proved an indisputable obstacle to their realization. Still, "little by little" he began writing, first a novel that was never published and later several plays that had varying degrees of success. Tchaikovsky had a high opinion of his brother's literary abilities. "Modest has a serious, positive talent," he declared to Anatoly at one point. "If that endurance, patience, and perseverance in labor of which I may boast were added to this, he would long since have written several remarkable things."[11] He later urged the aspiring author, "For God's sake, write your story. Only labor, and specifically artistic labor, can divert your thoughts from the *misères de la vie humaine*. . . . Write, write, write."[12]

In one of his letters, Modest informed his brother that he had met Saint-Saëns in Lyon and had asked him when Tchaikovsky's *Romeo and Juliet* was scheduled to be performed in Paris. "He was very courteous, remarking that he had received your letter with the photograph, and said that he did not know exactly when the performance of *Romeo* was to be, but that he would make inquiries and write to you. The whole time he called you 'ce cher Tchaikovsky.'"[13] His brother was less than thrilled by this initiative. "He [Saint-Saëns] may imagine that I am dying of desire to be performed in Paris," he replied querulously on 24 March, adding, "Granted, this in fact is very nearly the case, but Saint-Saëns must not by any means know it."[14] Later that year, Tchaikovsky would ask Taneev during a stay in Paris to begin negotiations with the conductor Edouard Colonne and his orchestra about performing a concert of his works in the French capital. Expenses, however, for such a concert were to prove so high that in the end he would be forced to abandon the project.

On 2 March the Third Quartet was performed privately for the first time at the home of Nikolay Rubinstein. Provoking none of the dissension or bluster of the tryout of the First Piano Concerto, the new work was praised by all present, Tchaikovsky alone having mixed feelings about his composition. By the end of the month, the quartet had been given three more performances—once at the conservatory on the occasion of a visit by Grand Duke Konstantin Nikolaevich and twice in public. "Everyone likes it very much," Tchaikovsky wrote Modest on 24 March. "During the andante (*Andante funebre e doloroso*) many people (so they say) were weeping. If this is true, then it is a great triumph. But," he added, "a restored *Oprichnik* is being performed here [at the Bolshoy] in a most shameful and, for me, embarrassing production."[15]

By the second half of March, Tchaikovsky was busy scoring *Swan Lake*, even as rehearsals for the ballet's first act got under way at the Theatrical School. The preparations amused Tchaikovsky, who told Modest, "If only you knew how comical it was to watch the ballet master [Julius Reisinger] creating dances with a most serious and inspired air to the sound of one little violin. At the same time, it made one envious to watch the ballerinas and danseurs casting smiles at an imaginary audience and reveling in the easy opportunity for leaping and whirling about, thereby fulfilling their sacred duty. Everyone at the theater raves about my music."[16] Pressed to finish the full score of the ballet as quickly as possible, Tchaikovsky retreated to Konstantin Shilovsky's estate at Glebovo in late March, and on 10 April, the score completed, he returned to Moscow.

Tchaikovsky was destined never to see on the stage a worthy realization of his first ballet. When *Swan Lake* had its premiere a year later, on 20 February 1877, the production was, by all accounts, pitiful. Tchaikovsky himself came away with a low opinion of his work, though later this opinion was to change and in 1888 he would even experience "a moment of absolute happiness" from a performance of the ballet's second act in Prague.[17]

Having caught cold during a hunt at Glebovo, Tchaikovsky remained ill the rest of the spring. Freedom from the conservatory was still more than a month away, and Tchaikovsky's increasing irritation with, and exhaustion from, teaching were making themselves felt to his crowded classes more strongly every day. Very few of his students, in fact, were able to penetrate the professional arcana of his lectures, and it is not surprising that Tchaikovsky had come to concentrate more and more openly on only the more-talented among them. It was a situation that inevitably led to resentment among the others, along with accusations of favoritism.

There was a certain truth in these accusations for a somewhat different reason as well, in that the educational process is implicitly charged with eroticism. Just as a heterosexual teacher inevitably reacts, consciously or not, to the physical attractiveness of students of the opposite sex, so Tchaikovsky was attracted to the male adolescent charms he valued so highly. The fact has duly been noted by the memoirists. One graduate of the conservatory observes that Tchaikovsky treated his male students with far greater understanding and leniency than the female ones. With the young men "Pyotr Ilyich was wonderfully gentle, considerate and patient; with some of the senior students he had close, purely amicable relations."[18] The violinist Samuil Litvinov recollected that at the age of thirteen he was singled out by Tchaikovsky, who not only praised his performance but took advantage of any opportunity to pay attention to him. When for lack of finances Litvinov's parents decided to remove him from the conservatory and prepare him for a different career, Tchaikovsky unexpectedly intervened and offered to pay for the boy's further musical education himself.[19] Unfortunately, nothing else is known of their relationship.

Another of Tchaikovsky's conservatory students, though primarily heterosexual, also played an important part in the composer's emotional attachments. Iosif Kotek, who was graduating this year, studied composition with Tchaikovsky and violin with Ivan Hřímalý. In time, he would develop into a modestly renowned violinist. Modest stresses not only the young man's great musical sense and virtuoso talent but also his good nature and his extraordinary attractiveness. From his first day in class, Kotek caught Tchaikovsky's attention and soon became his favorite pupil. "Contributing not a little to this," remarks Modest, "were the young man's ecstatic response to Pyotr Ilyich's works and his display of deep attachment to him personally."[20] In a letter to Modest of 2 January 1877, Tchaikovsky would note that their common acquaintance Kotek, whom "I love to distraction, . . . visits me quite often."[21] Not surprisingly, the two men eventually became lovers. Indeed, Tchaikovsky would later decide against dedicating his Violin Concerto to Kotek precisely because of his concern about the gossip this might cause concerning his relationship with the young violinist—gossip for which, as even the Soviet commentators admit, there was "ample foundation."[22]

Tchaikovsky's predilection for young men—so much in contrast to his colleagues' pursuit of young women among the conservatory students—would only have confirmed the various rumors that may have reached the place. There is little doubt that many of his colleagues, and certainly those closest to him, knew or guessed the true nature of his sexual preferences, a fact of which Tchaikovsky himself was well aware. A few years later, feeling pique at Nikolay Rubinstein but also already pondering his decision to leave the conservatory, Tchaikovsky would unjustly write to Anatoly, "He [Rubinstein] continues to think that I am maintained by his benefactions alone. Do you know what I see at the root of all this? Still the same thing. Blackmail! He's saying that with my shameful reputation I should thank my lucky stars that he still keeps me on. Upon my word, it is so!"[23] Although full of indignation, his tone is clearly still not panicky. Meanwhile, Kashkin in his recollections is as candid as the standards of the time allowed: "Of the fact that Pyotr Ilyich . . . was an abnormal man, at least with respect to [matrimony], I have no doubt."[24]

Classes finally dragged to a close, the last senior examination in harmony was completed, and, on 26 May, Tchaikovsky left Moscow. He had received an official invitation to the first Bayreuth Festival, which was to be held in August and which he had arranged to report on for the *Russian Register*. Before heading abroad, he decided to stop at Nizy, where he found "a very pleasant company" that included, besides Kondratyev and his wife, Kondratyev's brother Evgeny and Sergey Donaurov. But within three days he stormed off his friend's estate in a rage, and it was from Kiev that he wrote to Anatoly on 2 June. The banished servant Kiselev had not, it seems remained in disgrace for very long. "Everything would have been fine," Tchaikovsky explained to his brother, "but that the lackey Aleksey every night organizes drinking bouts with his servant friends, as a result of which it is impossible to get any sleep. One night, quite fed up, I came out of the cottage in which I was staying and made an awful scene. I woke the master of the house and flatly announced that if Aleksey were not thrown out the next day, I would leave. Aleksey was not thrown out, and consequently, I am now in Kiev, whence I shall depart early tomorrow morning."[25]

Two days later, he was in Kamenka, and two weeks after that, having spent the full two weeks recovering from yet another cold, which he caught in Kiev while swimming in the Dnieper, he was on his way to Vienna. There he had promised to Lev to meet Aleksandra on her way back from Switzerland with the children, who now, following the birth of Yury in Geneva just months before, numbered seven.

In Vienna, Tchaikovsky waited for his sister almost a week. On 23 June/5 July he wrote to Modest, who was awaiting his brother's arrival in Lyon, that "I do not like Vienna and to spend several days here alone seemed to me the height of tedium. . . ."[26] The censorial cut at this point, appearing to break Tchaikovsky off in mid thought, is more than a little suspicious. Judging by the tone, one would expect there to follow a description of some event that had made his stay in Vienna more interesting. Such would seem to be confirmed by his decision to prolong his stay there by several days after Aleksandra's departure, before proceeding to Lyon. The announcement of this intention in the same letter to Modest is interspersed with still more cuts: "Sasha will arrive tomorrow [24 June/6 July] and I shall spend the whole day with her.

But this letter is being written with the following aim. Please know that Sasha leaves on Friday, but that I, alas, am not leaving then, and therefore, do not look for me earlier than next week. Thus, from here I leave [a cut follows] on Monday evening; [another cut] only on Wednesday [30 June/12 July] will I depart from Munich directly to Lyon, where I look forward to folding you in my arms." This letter, first published only in 1961, appears to shed some additional light, however faint, on Tchaikovsky's obscure and chance erotic adventures abroad, which only begin to be evident starting this year. Before this, by his own admission in a letter to Modest of 28 January 1876, he had restrained himself from such contact, even while recognizing the absurdity of his restraint: "There is nothing more foolish than to travel avoiding any acquaintance with the locals, as I usually do."[27]

In any event, Tchaikovsky clearly freed himself sooner than he expected, and by Monday evening, 28 June/10 July, he was already in Lyon ringing the bell at 3, place Perrache, and being let in by a surprised Modest. In a letter to Anatoly of 3/15 July, Tchaikovsky shared his first impressions of their brother's life in Lyon. "I cannot describe to you how pleasant it was for me to see Modest and his family," he wrote. "I caught them in the evening as they were putting Kolya to bed. From the first moment, I found myself completely and forever enchanted by Kolya." Each morning during Tchaikovsky's short visit, Modest and Kolya would stop at the hotel to see him on their way to Gugentobler's and then return at noon to spend the rest of the day together. "My love for Kolya, based, first, on his wonderful gentle disposition and intelligence and, second, on a deep compassion for him, grew in geometrical progression with every passing minute," Tchaikovsky told Anatoly, "and now he is one of the creatures dearest to my heart in all the world." He was, moreover, amazed at the intelligence, tact, conscientiousness, and skill that Modest was bringing to his new occupation. "If I have always loved Modest very much, I now also respect him deeply," he confessed. "The attachment that unites teacher and pupil is extraordinarily moving, and in the course of these three days, there were many moments that brought tears of emotion to my eyes."[28]

Modest and Kolya's stay in Lyon had two main goals: to acquaint Modest with methods of educating and rearing deaf-mute children and to teach Kolya to pronounce sounds correctly. A half hour each morning and evening was devoted to phraseology, a half hour to pronunciation, and the same to arithmetic and penmanship. The remainder of the day's five hours of lessons was used variously for oral conversation, dictation, and reading. From the start everything had proceeded well.

Kolya had quickly made friends with his schoolmates and had taken a ready interest in his studies, though getting him to stay still in one spot for any length of time was no mean feat. He was unpredictable in his behavior and very active, yet "he studies extremely well, despite being overloaded with work," wrote Modest to Kolya's mother on 30 May/11 June.[29] Kolya's inquisitiveness was extraordinary. "Everything interests this boy, and his capacities are truly amazing," Tchaikovsky would later write to Mrs. von Meck. "As a result, my brother ends up having to teach him not only in class but during the whole rest of the day, during walks and at table and always."[30]

Pleased by what he saw in Lyon, Tchaikovsky traveled on to Vichy to take the waters. But all too soon he was complaining miserably to Anatoly that "everything has conspired here to make my stay unbearable."[31] He hated rising at five in the morning, he hated taking the baths, he hated the crush for every glass of mineral water and the idle bustle of the resort town, and he even hated the landscape. But worst of all was the loneliness that poisoned every waking moment. Unable to endure the full course of treatment, Tchaikovsky invented a story for his doctor to the effect that family circumstances prevented him from staying in Vichy more than ten days, and on 12/24 July he returned to Lyon.

The rest of July was spent together as the foursome (including the governess) traveled by steamer along the Rhône to Avignon, and from there by train to Montpellier, in the south of France, and the little resort town of Palavas-les Flots, on the shores of the Mediterranean. The journey was "a success, full of interesting and charming things," as Modest later recalled.[32] Less pleasant was the journey's end, where the local water made all the travelers, including Kolya, ill from the very first day. Writing to Modest later that summer after his return to Russia, Tchaikovsky shuddered to remember their stay in Palavas: "I could have forgiven that detestable village the scorching heat, and the absence of vegetation, and its generally depressing appearance—but what I will never forgive is that it made us all . . . tirelessly, day in and day out, [run to the toilet]. . . . If only Kolya had been healthy all this time, I might have forgotten the rest, but he, too, [suffered], the little dear. Modya, kiss this divine boy's little hand, his little foot, but especially his wonderful sweet little eyes! You don't know how much I adore him. Not a minute goes by that I don't think of him."[33]

Tchaikovsky always loved children. It reflected, above all, the sentimental cult peculiar to the entire Tchaikovsky family and Tchaikovsky's own acute and unconventional attachment to his twin brothers after the death of their mother. With them, he had played the roles of both mother and father, and thereby filled a need in his own emotional life. At the same time, several of those passages displaying Tchaikovsky's unconditional and impassioned worship of the boy Kolya reveal also an unmistakable erotic element. "I adore him passionately and think of him every second"—this was his constant cry during the first few years of their threefold relations.[34] But perhaps most extravagant of all was the close of a letter to the boy himself: "I kiss you warmly 1,000,000,000 times. Petya."[35] So informal a signature in a letter from an adult man to a boy of eight would even today be considered strangely inappropriate in Russian society, where one would expect something along the lines of "Pyotr Ilyich" or at least "Uncle Petya."

Filled with his thoughts about Kolya, Modest, and the fate that had brought them all together, Tchaikovsky quitted the unpleasantness of Palavas with some regret and proceeded alone toward Bayreuth. He went by way of Paris, where he bought clothes for himself and presents for his friends and for his servants, Mikhail and Alyosha. From there, he wrote to Modest in an elevated mood, "In general, I have lost all reason and throw money about with almost a voluptuousness. What the hell, having fun's the main thing. Unfortunately, despite all my love for Paris, I still miss you very, very much, though not nearly so much as after our separation last winter. This is understandable. Now I no longer worry about you. . . . Besides which, I have developed such an adoration for Kolya that I should now feel simply terrible were he to be left in anyone else's hands."[36] One image in particular remained with Tchaikovsky long after taking leave of his brother and his young charge and heading north: Modest in a blue frock coat and shoes of woven leather, with a book under his arm, an umbrella, and, hand in his, Kolya trailing after him along the sandy beach of Palavas.[37]

Arriving in Bayreuth on 31 July/12 August, Tchaikovsky was met by his colleague Karl Klindworth, a violinist and professor at the Moscow Conservatory, who, along with Laroche, Cui, Nikolay Rubinstein, and many others, had made the journey from Russia for the event. The opening of the Bayreuth Festival, with the first complete performance of *Der Ring des Nibelungen*, had drawn a flood of several thousand visitors to the tiny Bavarian town, and the crowds and the bustle were all but guaranteed to drive Tchaikovsky to distraction. The presence of his fellow Russians was small comfort, with Laroche drunk from morning until night and continually quarreling with Cui. He did manage to make the acquaintance of Franz Liszt and to visit Wagner's home, though Wagner himself was not there to receive him. It was quickly evident that both Tchaikovsky's name and his work were well known in Germany, and his days in Bayreuth were busy with other professional meetings and conversations.

The cycle began with *Das Rheingold* on 1/13 August. Tchaikovsky was struck by the production as a theatrical spectacle first and foremost. As for the music, his first impression of Wagner's opera was of "an incredible chaos through which are caught occasional fleeting glimpses of extraordinarily beautiful and striking particulars."[38] From Vienna a week later, he would confess candidly to Modest that while the *Ring* might indeed be a great work, he had found it tedious, drawn-out, and long-winded. "The conglomeration of the most complex and refined harmonies, the colorlessness of everything being sung onstage, the endlessly long dialogues, the pitch-darkness in the theater, the lack of any interest or poetry in the story—all this is exhausting to the nerves in the extreme," he wrote. "And so this is what Wagner's reform seeks to achieve! Before, music strove to delight people—now they are tormented and exhausted."[39] His remarks were telling. In Tchaikovsky's view, although art may often be a source of torment and exhaustion to its creator, it must not cause this same effect in its audience. Herein lay one important difference between the Romantic and the early modernist mentality.

Thus exhausted and in gloomy spirits, Tchaikovsky left Bayreuth on 6/18 August. He stopped for a day in "charming" Nuremberg, where he wrote a less than enthusiastic account of the festival to be published in the *Russian Register*, and five days later he was in Kamenka. He stayed in the house at nearby Verbovka, arriving there, in his own words, "in a dreadful emotional state and with horribly shattered nerves."[40]

The Wagner Festival had strained his nerves, but his depression was not a mere aftereffect of his trying stay in Bayreuth. Tchaikovsky had been pondering hard the ethical and psychological questions posed by his homosexual brother's association with the deaf-mute boy entrusted to his care. They were questions made all the more pressing by his own sudden emotional entanglement with this restless, nervous child for whom the simple act of communication was a painful struggle. His own heart had gone out to Kolya in a rush of love. He was moved by the clear devotion between the boy and his tutor. But where might it lead unchecked? Did not the very combination of Modest, with his inclinations, side by side with the governess, Sofya Ershova, who must logically have taken the place of the sickly child's absent mother, make glaringly clear the full falsity and artificiality of the situation? Tchaikovsky genuinely admired his brother's pedagogical gifts and abilities, but nobody could vouch that as the boy grew older Modest might not influence, even inadvertently, his charge's sexual preference, and with unpredictable results. In the weeks since leaving Palavas, with the experience of living closely with his brother and his brother's young pupil fresh in his mind, such were the rather unexpected and disturbing conclusions that Tchaikovsky had begun to draw. Now, in Verbovka in August 1876, his musings rapidly crystallized into a moral dilemma of far-reaching consequences in his own life.

The first sign of the crisis came with a long letter to Modest written from Verbovka on 19 August. Filled with various local tidbits and trivialities, the letter ended suddenly with the following: "I am now experiencing a very critical moment in my life. When I have the chance, I shall write to you of this in greater detail, but for the time being, I shall say one thing: *I have decided to marry.* It is inevitable. I must do this, and not only for myself, but also for you and for Tolya and for Sasha and for all whom I love. For *you* in particular! But you also, Modya, need to think seriously about this. [a cut in the original, most likely something along the lines of 'a homosexual and a pedagogue'] cannot live in harmony with one another."[41]

Without waiting for Modest's reply to this bombshell, Tchaikovsky sought to explain further his motives from Moscow on 10 September. Since leaving Palavas, he told his brother, he had done a great deal of thinking about himself and about Modest and about their future. "The result of all this pondering is that from today I seriously intend to enter into lawful matrimony with anyone at all," he wrote. "I find that our *inclinations* are for both of us the greatest and most insurmountable obstacle to happiness, and we must fight our nature with all our strength. I love you very much, I love *Kolya* very much, and for the good of you both I dearly hope that you never part, but a condition of the durability of your relations is that you no longer be *that* which you have been up until now. This is necessary not for the sake of *qu'en dira-t-on* [that is, public opinion], but for you yourself, for your own peace of mind." A cut follows at this point, and then: "You will say that at your age it is difficult to conquer passions; to this I shall answer that at your age it is easier to turn your tastes in a different direction. Here your religiousness should, I think, be a firm support to you. As for me, I shall do everything possible to marry this very year, but if I should lack the courage for this, I am in any event abandoning forever my habits and shall strive to be counted no longer among the company of [homosexuals]." And again at the end of the letter: "I think exclusively of the eradication of pernicious passions from myself."[42]

Tchaikovsky clearly found the emotional atmosphere surrounding his brother's relationship with his charge unhealthy and deeply troubling—at least potentially, if not in reality. Modest, after all, was a responsible and by now mature young man, while Kolya Konradi was at this time still of a more than tender age. But Tchaikovsky's imagination was rich and fertile, and it was made even more so by his own erotic attraction to the boy. He could envision all too easily where an innocent caress might lead and the possible consequences of this predicament only a few years hence. Increasingly he felt the horror of an unfolding immorality fraught with the threat of monstrous scandal.

A similar horror could easily extend to Tchaikovsky's own future: he, after all, had to deal with young pupils all the time. The full moral instability of his existence, perched on the edge of disgrace, must have been revealed to him with extreme clarity. Until then he had treated his homosexuality as morally indifferent. Now it seemed suddenly imperative to suppress his homosexuality and, what is more, to advise his brother to do the same. Indeed, his traditional relationship with his brother demanded that Tchaikovsky set an example of behavior to be imitated, an example that might save Modest from the danger of falling but without having to abandon his pupil, by now so deeply loved by both brothers. That he himself would have to make a certain sacrifice in this regard must no doubt have flattered the self-esteem of the composer, who may well have seen in the decision he had taken an almost heroic gesture.

There is every reason to believe, bearing in mind his affair with Désirée Artôt, that until the middle of the 1870s Tchaikovsky did not take his homosexuality too seriously and, as frequently happens, did not allow himself to think that his preferences might be irreversible or insurmountable. Most probably he thought that he could act on his inclinations for as long as possible, but that when it became absolutely necessary, he would simply abandon these habits.

But, almost from the start, his determination to marry proved less resolute than he had originally planned. Only a week later, he was writing to Modest in a rather more judicious frame of mind, "I cannot express to you that sensation of sweet tranquillity and *almost* happiness that I feel in my small, cozy, quiet apartment when I come home in the evening and pick up a book. At such moments, I probably hate no less than you do that beautiful unknown woman who will force me to change my way of life and my entourage. Do not be afraid for me. I do not intend to be hasty in this matter, and rest assured that if indeed I bind myself to a woman, I shall do so with great circumspection."[43] A letter to Anatoly of 20 September was even more definitive. "I felt I was *lying* when I told you that I had *firmly* resolved to make the drastic *change* in my way of life about which you know," Tchaikovsky wrote. "In fact, I have still by no means resolved to do this. I am only considering it seriously and waiting for something to force me to act. . . . I say again, I seriously mean *to become a new man*, only I wish to prepare for this gradually."[44]

His decision caused a great deal of anxiety among his relatives—not only Modest, who had his own reasons to be anxious, but also his sensitive sister, Aleksandra. Troubled by his "preconceived decision," she sought to mitigate the consequences of a rash marriage by suggesting as a suitable bride Lev Davydov's young niece Sonya Peresleni, "who after all is a relative, someone known to me."[45] Tchaikovsky's response was tender and familiarly pacifying in tone: "Please, my angel, do not worry on account of my proposed marriage. . . . Rest assured that I shall not throw myself carelessly into the whirlpool of a bad matrimonial union."[46] But he rejected categorically the young lady mentioned by his sister, whom, it seems, others in the family had also attempted to press on him. "Sonya Peresleni (who, by the way, would scarcely marry me anyway) has definitely been struck from the list of candidates," he wrote. "I have had occasion to convince myself of the exceptional heartlessness of that girl."[47]

In this way, considering the candidates and then discarding them, Tchaikovsky seemed to approach the matter methodically and seriously, notwithstanding what he would call in one letter to Mrs. von Meck his "inborn antipathy to marriage."[48] But, however vigorous in intent, this "preparation" for marriage did not proceed without setbacks, at times severe. In another letter to Modest, written on 28 September, following a passionate affirmation of the necessity of marriage that stressed the feelings of their family, he wrote, "In any event, do not be frightened for me, dear Modya. The realization of my plans is not at all as close as you think. I am so set in my habits and tastes that it is not possible to cast them aside all at once like an old glove. And besides, I am far from possessing a will of iron, and after my letters to you I have already surrendered some three times to the force of my natural tendencies."[49]

In the course, then, of less than a month, and despite all his determination and bravado, Tchaikovsky apparently had had three homosexual contacts. He was, in fact, forced to admit to his brother that "whatever vows one may make, it is impossible to resist one's weaknesses." Moreover, the expression "natural tendencies" demonstrates that Tchaikovsky never considered his "inclinations" (the word he used consistently in his letters) to be abnormal. Indeed, nowhere in any of his written texts known to us is there the slightest hint that he thought of himself as sexually pathological. This attitude, however self-delusive, underlay Tchaikovsky's crucial statement at the end of his letter to Modest: "I shall not enter into any lawful or illicit union with a woman without having fully ensured my own peace and my own freedom." The "freedom" that Tchaikovsky intended to ensure obviously referred to the freedom to indulge in those "weaknesses" which could not be resisted, "whatever vows one may make."

This brings up a curious implausibility in the argument of the letter. Determined to secure for himself sexual freedom even in marriage, Tchaikovsky at the same time regarded with contempt the married homosexuals among his acquaintances. "I remember that you have predicted for me the fate of Kondratyev, Bulatov, and *tutti quanti*," he noted in the same letter. "You may be certain that if ever my projects are realized, I shall by no means follow in the steps of these gentlemen."[50] In effect, he implied his intention to practice marital fidelity. This obvious contradiction, together with the fact that Tchaikovsky appears not to have been aware of it, reveals the depth of his divided feelings on the subject. On another level, of course, it reflects the divided feelings of a society that tacitly accepted homosexuality as long as it was not spoken about, yet condemned it when publicly exposed.

But, while the predicament of Modest and his deaf-mute charge was the immediate cause of Tchaikovsky's train of thought, it was not the only one. It is clear that family pressure—not always overt, but now given new force by Tchaikovsky's private misgivings concerning Modest and Kolya—was another major motivation for his decision. Especially burdensome in this regard was his father, Ilya, who fanatically and fantastically dreamed of a devoted wife for his favorite son. Later, Tchaikovsky would admit frankly to Mrs. von Meck, "You know, I wed partly to fulfill his long-standing desire to see me married."[51] This paternal prodding had been going on persistently and in diverse forms for several years. Loving his father and seeking to reassure him, Tchaikovsky would find various pretexts to evade the question. "Sometimes it crosses my own mind to get myself a little missus," he told his father in 1872, "as plump and kind as your dumpling [Elizaveta, Tchaikovsky's stepmother]—only I fear lest I should repent later. Although my income is quite sufficient (around three thousand a year), still through my negligence I am forever in bad straits. Being alone, it doesn't matter, but what would it be with a wife and small children!"[52]

To make matters more ticklish, Tchaikovsky's visit to Verbovka in August 1876 coincided with Ilya's own stay there. It was the first time in many years that the father and son had found themselves living in such close proximity. It is not difficult to imagine the old man hounding his son with questions about when he was finally going to marry and the effect this face-to-face prodding must have had on Tchaikovsky. We know Ilya Tchaikovsky's ecstatic response on finally hearing of his son's decision to marry the following year, which prompted the octogenarian father literally to leap for joy.

Coupled with the pressure of his relatives to marry was Tchaikovsky's fear that his homosexuality, if exposed, could bring shame and scandal to those he loved. In the same letter to Modest in which he confessed his new homosexual encounters, Tchaikovsky, responding to the "antimatrimonial" arguments of his brother (made in a letter still unavailable and probably lost), writes:

> You say that one should spit on *qu'en dira-t-on.* This is true only to a certain degree. There are people who cannot despise me for my vices only because they came to love me when they did not yet suspect that I am in essence a man with a lost reputation. *Sasha,* for instance, is one of these! I know that she guesses *everything* and *forgives* everything. Thus I am treated by very many people whom I love or respect. Do you really think that I am not oppressed by this awareness *that they pity and forgive me,* when in fact I am guilty of nothing! And is it really not dreadful to think that people who love me can ever *be ashamed* of me! But, you see, this has happened a hundred times before and will happen a hundred times again. In a word, I should like by my marriage or, in general, an open affair with a woman to shut the mouths of various contemptible creatures whose opinion I do not value in the least but who can cause pain to the people close to me.[53]

Even if unexposed, Tchaikovsky's homosexuality created suspense both for his relatives and for him. It made the people he loved "pity and forgive" him, which he resented because he was, in his own words, "guilty of nothing." That in the very same letter he should claim his innocence and acknowledge several sexual transgressions as he yielded to the "force of my natural tendencies" need not be seen as contradictory or surprising. His line of reasoning was based on the assumption that he was innocent because he was born a homosexual and that his tendencies were therefore natural. This same attitude was later echoed in the correspondence with Mrs. von Meck, to whom Tchaikovsky wrote, "With my hand on my heart I can say that my conscience is clear and that I have nothing to be ashamed of."[54]

The real contradiction in the passage from the letter to Modest arises more from social than sexual ambivalence. Believing himself "guilty of nothing," Tchaikovsky nonetheless called his inclinations "vices." In fact, he no doubt did so because in that period such was their customary designation: Tchaikovsky used the word for lack of any other. But for Russian society its literal meaning held true. However prepared, in practice, to tolerate and even condone closet homosexuals up to the very highest levels of government, the educated classes of the period remained unwilling to abandon altogether the traditional perception of homosexuality as a moral evil. It is not accidental that Tchaikovsky blamed his putative ruined reputation, and not the "vices" themselves, for causing pain and a sense of shame to those who loved him.

This matter of a "lost reputation" is more complex than it may seem. Significantly, "public opinion" is qualified as the opinion of "various contemptible creatures" undeserving of attention. In part, of course, this was the pose of a moment. Tchaikovsky abhorred even the most innocent gossip about himself. As for rumors about his homosexuality, Tchaikovsky himself threw further light on this particular issue in a letter to his publisher Pyotr Jurgenson written in January 1879 in response to newspaper attacks on Nikolay Rubinstein. "You are familiar with the tactics of these reptiles," he wrote, referring to newspaper reporters. "They spread rumors and blast their opponent with *insinuation*, and you know how vulnerable, unfortunately, I am in this respect. Experience has proved that any lousy scribbler can force me to keep silent with an allusion to a certain circumstance. And if for *my own sake* I should gladly spit on such allusions, for the sake of those people near and dear to me who bear my name I am compelled to fear this more than anything else in the world."[55] Contemptuous though he was of public opinion, Tchaikovsky found that he could not ignore it. He was never by nature a fighter, and in the end, he had no choice but to yield. In this, he was motivated primarily by an emotion more altruistic than selfish—a desire to ensure the peace of mind of his relatives and to retain a full and mutual understanding with them without the need for any reticence or deception.

Nikolay Kashkin also points out a certain sentimental factor in Tchaikovsky's decision: his need for a home and domestic comfort, for a woman not as a servant but as a comrade "capable of sharing his creative aspirations and being a trusty companion in life, while freeing him, incidentally, from any everyday concerns."[56] This longing is occasionally glimpsed in his letters. "I feel a strong desire," he wrote in a letter to his sister as early as 5 February 1870, "to hear the cries of children, to take part in various little domestic chores; in a word, I desire a family atmosphere."[57] A feeling of emptiness haunted him, and writing to his sister on 8 November 1876 he confessed, "I live the egotistical life of a bachelor. I work for myself, look after myself, and strive only for my own well-being. This is, of course, very calm, but at the same time it is dry, dead, and narrow."[58]

Such a sentimental outburst is still far from supporting the argument that Tchaikovsky wished to marry solely out of a desire for family comfort. In fact, he customarily extolled his bachelor's existence far more than he deplored it. Without pressure from his relatives and complex introspection related to his own and Modest's homosexuality, no sentimentalism, however strong, would have led him into a woman's embrace.

What is more, Tchaikovsky's remarks to Modest about the "freedom" he planned to ensure in any union with a woman and the impossibility of resisting his "weaknesses" betray his ultimate expectation that any wife of his must learn to tolerate submissively his homosexual adventures while providing the cover and comfort of legitimate Christian matrimony. Such hidden hopes were also implicit in a letter to Anatoly a year later in which Tchaikovsky, already engaged, saw the chief virtue of his future wife, Antonina Milyukova, in her being enamored of him "like a cat."[59] The dubious simile indicates the extent of his confidence in her infatuation with him, an infatuation he foolishly believed great enough, or perhaps blind enough, to allow him to continue to lead his customary—that is, homosexual—way of life without the risk of causing a family scandal. In this, Tchaikovsky was to make a serious psychological miscalculation. Always so sensitive in comprehending people of his own class and upbringing, he failed miserably to understand or sympathize with the unsophisticated and vacuous Milyukova. It was a failure that would lead to catastrophe for them both.

Before returning to Moscow in early September, Tchaikovsky, once again in desperate need of money, turned to Vladimir Shilovsky for a loan of some two thousand rubles. He despised himself for doing it. Since 1869 the composer, with his penchant for living in grand style, had periodically borrowed money from his wealthy former pupil. Such dependence weighed upon him and caused him much remorse, and financial problems had begun gradually to dominate the dealings between the two men. "All my relations with Shilovsky," he would write to Modest the following spring, "are in essence exploitation, and rather unseemly and humiliating for me. True, he has thrust money at me, but I could have simply not taken it."[60]

But he did take it, and in the end, this fact was to lead to the irrevocable deterioration of their once intimate friendship. Three years later, Shilovsky would start spreading rumors unfavorable to Tchaikovsky concerning their financial affairs. Learning of these rumors,

Tchaikovsky was incensed, yet he would manage to maintain an admirable, if icy, dignity in the face of his embarrassment. "From trustworthy sources it has reached me that you have been complaining of my ingratitude to all who'll listen," he would write to Shilovsky on 10 May 1879, "saying moreover that I have received from you twenty-eight thousand rubles!!!" Terming Shilovsky's unpleasant rumors of their financial dealings "a fitting punishment" for his own lack of discretion in procuring money over the years and for "that share of self-interest that I revealed in my relations with you," Tchaikovsky noted pointedly that their relationship evidently did not belong to those "rare cases where between friends similar monetary services by the wealthier of the two on behalf of the poorer of the two occur with impunity for the beholden, and do not lead afterward to bitter reproaches and misunderstandings."

Tchaikovsky blamed himself not for having taken the money, in which he saw "nothing dishonorable or shameful," but for having taken it from someone "who I always knew perfectly well would sooner or later tell people about it." By his own calculation, he had received some 7,550 silver rubles from Shilovsky during the ten years of their acquaintance—a considerable sum, though little more than a quarter of the amount allegedly claimed by Shilovsky. "This is both much and little," Tchaikovsky wrote. "Much, in terms of the absolute value of money. Little, if one takes into account all the innumerable moral torments that this money cost me; little, if one remembers that you are a rich Maecenas and I a poor artist; very little, if one recalls your endless assurances of your love for me and of your willingness to perform any sacrifice; and finally, absolutely nothing in comparison to what you so often promised me!" But even in his embarrassment at having the tale of Shilovsky's monetary gifts to him recounted by Shilovsky "at every opportunity," Tchaikovsky nonetheless acknowledged the sincerity of his former pupil's wish to help him. "God knows I am as grateful to you for this now as then," he confessed in his letter.[61] Like it or not, Shilovsky's generosity had rescued him from a number of tight spots over the years, and it did so again now in the summer of 1876.

Traveling by way of Usovo to get the two thousand rubles from Shilovsky, Tchaikovsky arrived back in Moscow in early September. There he returned wearily to his duties at the conservatory and waited for news from St. Petersburg about rehearsals there for *Vakula the Smith*. A week's visit by Anatoly somewhat lifted his spirits, but on the whole, the early autumn found him depressed and troubled as he continued to waver over his resolve for a radical but, as he tried to

convince himself, necessary change in his way of life. Fits of "misanthropy" plagued him periodically, and when he learned that Anton
Rubinstein's opera *The Maccabees* might precede his own *Vakula* on
the stage, he suddenly lashed out in a scathing and scarcely justifiable
invective against the man. "Lord, how deeply have I hated this man for
some time!" he ranted in a letter to Anatoly of 20 September. "He has
never ever treated me otherwise than with condescending neglect. No
one has ever so insulted my feeling of self-respect, my deserved pride . . .
in my abilities, as this Peterhof householder. And now, in addition, he
comes up with his miserable operas so as to hinder me. Is the fame he
has abroad really not enough for this most foolish and puffed-up of
men? . . . Were it not for the criminal code, . . . I should go to Peterhof
and gladly set fire to his filthy country house."[62]

Gradually his creative projects took over. In late September, as
Russian volunteers marched off to Serbia to fight in the war against
the Turks, he completed the patriotic *March Slav*, op. 31. He then immediately and with great enthusiasm began work on the symphonic
fantasy *Francesca da Rimini*, op. 32. A libretto for an opera based on
the famous episode from Dante's *Inferno* had been sent to Tchaikovsky
earlier that year by Laroche, but his work on *Swan Lake* and then his
travels abroad had prevented him from following through on the idea.
Later, Modest had suggested the same story of the doomed love of Paolo and Francesca as one of several possible subjects for an orchestral
work, and in the end, the opera project was abandoned. A full sketch
of the fantasy was completed by 14 October. That same day, Tchaikovsky sent a letter to Modest, telling him that "I wrote it with love and
that love, it seems, has come out quite well. As for the whirlwind,
something might have been written to better correspond to [Gustave]
Doré's illustration [of the Paolo and Francesca episode in his 1861 edition of Dante], but it did not turn out as I had wished. However, a true
judgment on this piece is unthinkable until it has been orchestrated
and performed."[63]

That autumn, Tchaikovsky still saw a great deal of Nikolay Kondratyev in his spare time, despite their row earlier that summer over
the behavior of the servant Kiselev. But their friendship had cooled
considerably, and Tchaikovsky noted in the same letter to Modest that
"Nikolay Dmitrievich calls me not Petya, as before, but Tchaikovsky."
He added that "Aleksey [Kiselev] turned up [in Moscow], and Nikolay
Dmitrievich claims that he has never behaved so well as now"—thus
giving his brother to understand that the affair between Kondratyev
and his servant continued.[64] That same month, another old friend,
Meshchersky, passed through Moscow on his way back from the Ser-

bian front. His reports on the war with Turkey in his periodical, *The Citizen*, were soon to cause a stir throughout Russia.

In late October, Tchaikovsky traveled to St. Petersburg for rehearsals of *Vakula* and then returned a month later for the premiere on 24 November. Nikolay Rubinstein was also present for the opening, along with several other friends from the Moscow Conservatory. Directed by Nápravník, the production "failed solemnly," as Tchaikovsky put it in a letter of 2 December to Sergey Taneev, then in Paris. The first two acts were played out amid a "deathly silence," and even though after the third and fourth acts the composer was called for many times, "this was accompanied by loud hissing from a significant portion of the audience." The opera's failure was made all the more painful by the fact that at the dress rehearsal everyone, including Cui, had predicted a great success. "Worst of all," confessed Tchaikovsky, "is that I cannot complain of either the performance or the staging. Everything was done meticulously, intelligently, and even sumptuously. . . . In short, I alone am to blame for the opera's failure. It is too overloaded with details, too densely orchestrated, too barren of vocal effects. . . . The style of *Vakula* is not at all operatic: it has no breadth or sweep"[65]

Interestingly, Cui's published opinion of the opera echoed the private one of Tchaikovsky himself. Cui found the opera to have "two fundamental shortcomings: first, the style of *Vakula* is not operatic but symphonic; and second, there is no correspondence between the music and what is taking place on stage." But, he added, "the music of *Vakula* is almost without exception noble and beautiful with respect to both theme and harmony."[66]

In the middle of December, Nikolay Rubinstein organized a small concert for Lev Tolstoy, who was visiting Moscow from his estate at Yasnaya Polyana. In the round hall of the conservatory a performance was given of Tchaikovsky's First Quartet. "Perhaps never in my life . . . has my composer's pride been so flattered and moved," he recalled ten years later, "as when L[ev] Tolstoy, sitting beside me and listening to the *Andante* of my first quartet, burst into tears."[67] During that month, the writer and the composer met again several times, and twice Tolstoy spent the evening at Tchaikovsky's apartment in friendly conversation. In a letter to Tchaikovsky he remarked frankly that he had enjoyed himself and had "never received so precious a reward for my literary labors as this marvelous evening."[68] Yet, the budding friendship would never reach fruition. For the next few years, Tolstoy would scarcely set foot outside Yasnaya Polyana, while Tchaikovsky was to abandon Moscow the following year, breaking for a long while all ties of friendship there.

But in these same last weeks of 1876, Tchaikovsky let pass virtually unnoticed another event, one that heralded the start of an association destined to transform the very shape of his life for a decade and a half to come. In December, while working on his *Variations on a Rococo Theme*, op. 33, for cello and orchestra, dedicated to the cellist Vasily Fitzenhagen, he received several handsomely paid commissions from a wealthy patroness of the arts, Nadezhda von Meck. Most likely, the commissions were arranged through the agency of Iosif Kotek, who at the time was employed as a resident musician in Mrs. von Meck's household.

Two weeks before the New Year, which he had decided to celebrate in Moscow, Tchaikovsky received his first letter (or, at any rate, the first that has survived) from his recent benefactress, whom he had never met and never was to meet in person. She thanked him for his speedy fulfillment of her request and expressed her extreme admiration of his music. "To tell you," she wrote, "to what raptures your compositions send me, I consider inappropriate, for you are accustomed to praises of a different sort and the admiration of such a nonentity in music as myself may appear to you merely ridiculous, whereas my delight is so dear to me that I do not want it laughed at; therefore, I shall say only, and ask you to believe literally, that with your music my life is made easier and more pleasant."[69]

"I am sincerely grateful to you for all the lovely and flattering things that you were so kind to write to me," Tchaikovsky replied. "For my part, let me say that for a musician, amid failures and all manner of obstacles, it is a consolation to think that there is a small minority of people, to which you belong, who so warmly and genuinely love our art. Faithfully and respectfully yours, P. Tchaikovsky."[70]

Part Three

ENCOUNTER
WITH FATE
1877-1878

CHAPTER ELEVEN

Two Women

"Sometimes it seems to me that Providence, so blind and unjust in the choice of its protégés, has deigned to care for me," Tchaikovsky confessed to his brother Modest in May 1877. "Really, I begin at times to perceive in certain coincidences of circumstances not *mere chance.*"[1]

For Tchaikovsky's relationship with women, the year 1877 proved indeed fateful. As he wrote these lines to Modest, he had already entered into what would be his most destructive and his most beneficial involvements with women. Before the year was out, his marriage to Antonina Milyukova was to bring him to the very brink of emotional ruin. By fate or by chance, salvation was to come in the form of his extraordinary, indeed unique, "epistolary friendship" with Nadezhda von Meck, which began at almost the same time.

The politely formal tone of Tchaikovsky's initial exchange of letters with Mrs. von Meck gives scant indication of the dimension this acquaintanceship was to acquire in both their lives. Modest was one of the first to stress the importance and the uniqueness of the friendship with Mrs. von Meck and the deep originality of this woman, who, with the exception of his mother, played a far more substantial role in the life of the composer than any other member of her sex. Their friendship, wrote Modest, had an unparalleled effect "on the whole of his subsequent fate," in that it "so thoroughly changed the basis of his material existence and, in consequence of this, so strikingly affected his artistic career, while at the same time it was of such a highly poetic

nature and so unlike anything that occurs in the everyday life of contemporary society."[2] For Mrs. von Meck, their correspondence remained for those many years the center of her spiritual and emotional
life.

The person whom Modest calls his brother's "guardian angel"[3] was
an exceptional woman. On the whole, women in nineteenth-century
Russia fared little better socially than did their sisters in Victorian England. Women of the upper classes led a largely parasitic existence, their
lives and conduct under the tight control of their husbands, while
those of the lower classes were mindlessly exploited. Yet, owing both
to circumstances and to the force of her own determined personality,
Nadezhda Filaretovna von Meck had managed to break out of these
confines to become a formidable businesswoman and an influential, if
highly eccentric, patroness of the arts. The daughter of landowner and
music lover Filaret Frolovsky (or, as some archival evidence suggests,
Fralovsky), Nadezhda was just sixteen when she married Karl von
Meck, a Baltic German engineer of then quite meager means. By her
own admission, the early years of their marriage were spent in virtual
poverty, a circumstance that made her responsive in later life to the
needs and plights of others. The dizzying financial success of her husband, who became a railroad tycoon, made them multimillionaires.
The couple had eighteen children, of whom eleven survived. After Karl
von Meck's death in 1876, the children became the subject of unending
concern for his widow, who in addition presided, in accordance with
her husband's will, over his financial empire.

With her great wealth and her passionate love of music, Mrs. von
Meck became a force to be reckoned with in the Moscow musical
world. She maintained a complex and thorny acquaintance with Nikolay Rubinstein, often quarreling with him even as she respected his
talents and energy. Already during her husband's lifetime Mrs. von
Meck was an active promoter and supporter of young musicians, of
whom several were continually in her employ, living in her household
and giving her pleasure by performing her favorite works. One such
artist in residence in 1876 was Tchaikovsky's friend and former pupil
the violinist Iosif Kotek. Although it is not known under what circumstances and at what moment Mrs. von Meck's interest in Tchaikovsky's music was sparked, it was no doubt Kotek who supplied her with
essential information about the composer, and for a while he was to
serve as intermediary between the two.

Nine years older than Tchaikovsky, Nadezhda von Meck was a
woman of considerable learning. Besides her knowledge of music,
which she had studied quite seriously in her youth, her letters to

Tchaikovsky reveal her wide familiarity with literature and history, her mastery of foreign languages (including Polish), and her capacity for appreciating the visual arts. She read such philosophers as Arthur Schopenhauer and the nineteenth-century Russian idealist Vladimir Solovyov and often entered into by no means trivial philosophical discussions, and she could make clear and perceptive judgments on matters of politics.

This is not to say that Mrs. von Meck was a paragon of lofty intellectualism. She attained such a level only infrequently and her arguments could betray naïveté and even banality. Yet, a general impression of their correspondence makes it possible to marvel at the ethical, spiritual, and mental compatibility of the two correspondents. In Tchaikovsky's letters there is never the slightest hint of condescension. When he argued with his "best friend"—and on matters of art he argued with her frequently and with passion—he did so naturally and on equal terms, which would have been impossible if he had not sincerely regarded her as his friendly equal: in the realm of art and creativity, which constituted the very heart of his spiritual existence and the entire meaning of his life, he was quite incapable of dissimulation. On the other hand, her letters do not reveal the least trace of the social snobbery of a wealthy patroness of the arts or the morbid pride of an arrogant dilettante accustomed to twisting artists' destinies as she chose and expecting gratitude as a reward.

Mrs. von Meck's own description of herself is revealing: "I am very unsympathetic in my personal relations because I do not possess any femininity whatever; second, I do not know how to be tender, and this characteristic has passed on to my entire family. All of us are afraid to be affected or sentimental, and therefore the general nature of our family relationships is comradely, or masculine, so to speak."[4]

Whether Mrs. von Meck had been happy with her husband, who died only a few months before her first letter to Tchaikovsky, we do not know. Not a word about this is found in even her most open and intimate letters. It would appear that the couple's tremendous fortune and eleven surviving children must have bound them closely to one another. One of her initial commissions to Tchaikovsky was for a funeral march, which suggests the depth of her mourning. After the death of her husband she ceased all social life and withdrew into total seclusion, even to the point of refusing to meet the relatives of those to whom she gave her children in marriage. Imperious by nature, she, by all accounts, presided over the members of her household with a certain despotism, holding them to principles of strict morality in amorous matters, as in others.

In curious contrast to her moralistic views on affairs of the heart, Mrs. von Meck delivered in her letters to Tchaikovsky repeated and passionate invectives against marriage as a social institution and confessed her hatred of it. "You may think, my dear Pyotr Ilyich," she wrote in a letter of 31 March 1878, "that I am a great admirer of marriages, but in order that you not be mistaken in anything referring to myself, I shall tell you that I am, on the contrary, an irreconcilable enemy of marriages, yet when I discuss another person's situation, I consider it necessary to do so from his point of view."[5] Elsewhere, in a more general way, but no less unequivocally, she declared, "The distribution of rights and obligations as determined by societal laws I find speculative and immoral."[6]

It is not easy to reconcile so militant an attitude with a commitment and devotion to the family. One suspects that her own matrimonial experience may have forced her to recognize and enjoy the benefits of having a family, while rejecting any real enjoyment of the sexual union between man and woman. Not without reason does she reveal at one point the sad thought that "I ceased to dream at the age of seventeen, that is, at the time I married my husband."[7] Matrimony, then, appears to be but an unfortunate prerequisite for creating a family. Perhaps for that reason also, she strove to get all of her children married as quickly as possible so as to ensure their social stability in the event of her death. But as for sexual relations between man and woman, for her they amounted to mutual exploitation. This was an attitude not far removed from the arguments of such contemporary Russian radical thinkers as Nikolay Chernyshevsky and Dmitry Pisarev, who considered matrimony a pillar of bourgeois society and advocated its abolition. Pisarev's work, in particular, was held in respect by Mrs. von Meck, who approved of nineteenth-century positivism as a matter of principle.

To a woman of her views, even Tchaikovsky's seeming misogyny and his professed aversion to marriage may have appeared attractive, while any rumors of his homosexuality (which at any rate must have sounded like so much gibberish to a woman of "Victorian" upbringing) would not necessarily have led to any explosion of indignation. Such an attitude allowed her to interpret passionate love between two men as an understandable sentimental excess, a platonic union that simply excluded undignified coitus with a woman. A sexual act between men was so impossible to imagine that the physiological component in any such union could be ignored altogether. Even if Mrs. von Meck was at some point informed of the erotic predilections of her "beloved friend," it by no means follows that this unprejudiced, unreligious, and independently thinking woman would have been prompted to repudiate him. Indeed, in one of her earliest letters she emphasized her utter contempt for public opinion: "But a person who lives as ascetically as I do logically reaches the point where all that which people call social relations, rules of fashionable society, proprieties, etc., become for him only sounds with no meaning."[8] And five years later, she would continue to insist, "I never trouble about public opinion."[9]

Such sentiments must have held a particular appeal for Tchaikovsky, who longed to be as dismissive of what other people might think and say about him. At the same time, he may have been somewhat dismayed to learn that in her zeal to find out more about him, his admirer gave ear even to that public opinion she professed to despise. Even at the beginning of their friendship Mrs. von Meck was insatiably curious about everything related to the man who had sparked her sudden and impassioned interest. "And this is why," she wrote in that same early letter of 3 March 1877, "as soon as I had recovered from the first impression of your composition, I at once wished to know what sort of man had created such a piece. I began to seek out opportunities to learn as much about you as possible, passing up no chance to hear something, listening to public opinion, to individual judgments, to every remark." But whatever she learned about him, good or bad, served only to fuel her admiration. "I shall tell you in this regard that often what others censured in you would lead me to ecstasy," she wrote. "I am so interested in knowing everything about you that at almost any time I can say where you are and to some extent what you are doing. From everything that I myself have observed in you and have heard from other sympathetic and unsympathetic sources, I have conceived the most cordial, kindly, and enthusiastic feelings for you."[10]

It was probably from Kotek that Mrs. von Meck learned of Tchaikovsky's financial difficulties. Here, for the first time, she displayed the extraordinary tact characteristic of her in her relationship with Tchaikovsky. She decided to help him by commissioning several simple works and recompensing him with uncommon generosity. Tchaikovsky, however, with his usual acumen very soon caught on to her design. This he made clear as early as May 1877. "It had already occurred to me at the time of your earlier musical commissions that you were motivated by two considerations in this," he wrote in response to Mrs. von Meck's recent request for another composition, with its implication of another extravagant reward. "On the one hand, you truly wished to have in some form or other one or another of my compositions; on the other hand, having heard of my perpetual financial difficulties, you were coming to my aid. I am compelled to think this by the excessively generous fee with which you have rewarded my insignificant labor."[11]

The financial aspect of their friendship inevitably created a certain emotional discomfiture and underlying tension. Tchaikovsky noted frankly to Mrs. von Meck that "in my relations with you there is the ticklish circumstance that every time we write to one another, money appears on the scene." Though they both learned to handle this awkwardness with admirable delicacy, Tchaikovsky could not help feeling vaguely uncomfortable about the shower of favors from the wealthy widow. At times, he even chafed at the unintentional imposition her requests put on him, and in the same letter he found himself turning down her latest commission. "I have no wish," he told her, "for there ever to be in our relations that falseness, that lie that would inevitably manifest itself if, disregarding my inner voice and unimbued with the mood you demand, I should hurriedly work something up, send this 'something' off to you and receive from you an unseemly reward."[12]

In a certain sense, it is legitimate to claim that on a spiritual and psychological plane the friendship with Nadezhda von Meck became in the life of Tchaikovsky a phenomenon commensurate with his future attachment to his nephew Bob Davydov. This sort of association with a woman is, in fact, often characteristic of a spiritually and artistically attuned homosexual male. According to Plato, the wise Diotima was Socrates' adviser in affairs of the heart, though Socrates was most certainly homoerotic, as the early dialogues show. Another instance, an even closer parallel to Tchaikovsky's friendship with Mrs. von Meck, is the platonic affair between Michelangelo and Vittoria Colonna, marchesa di Pescara (like Mrs. von Meck, a mature widow), who withdrew into a convent and from there exchanged passionate sonnets with the artist.

It was this recognition of a kindred spirit in Mrs. von Meck that allowed Tchaikovsky, beset by the perpetual financial disorder in his affairs, to pass with scarcely a pause from his gentle rebuke of her secret designs for aiding him financially to an open request for a loan of three thousand rubles. He managed this transition with perfect naturalness. "I have made up my mind to seek this help from you," he wrote. "You are the only person in the world whom I am not ashamed to ask for money. In the first place, you are very kind and generous; in the second, you are rich. I should like to unite all my debts in the hands of one magnanimous creditor and thereby free myself from the clutches of moneylenders." At the end of the letter, as if in passing, he mentioned that "now . . . I . . . am engrossed in a symphony that I began writing in the winter and that I want very much to dedicate to

Aleksandra Andreevna Tchaikovskaya, the composer's mother. MINIATURE BY LUDWIG BRAMSON, 1829.

Ilya Petrovich Tchaikovsky, the composer's father. MINIATURE BY AN UNKNOWN ARTIST.

The Tchaikovsky family in 1848. From left, Pyotr, Aleksandra Andreevna, Zinaida, Aleksandra, Nikolay, Ippolit, and Ilya Petrovich.

The building of the former Imperial School of Jurisprudence on the Fontanka River.

The twentieth graduating class of the School of Jurisprudence, 1859. Tchaikovsky is in front of the gentleman wearing the bow tie.

Tchaikovsky as a graduate of the School of Jurisprudence, 1859.

Aleksey Apukhtin in his school uniform, 1859.

Tchaikovsky's song "My genius, my angel, my friend" (c. 1855–1860), dedicated to Sergey Kireev. (The thirteen dots in the dedication correspond to the number of letters in the Russian for "To Sergey Kireev.")

Tchaikovsky, c. 1860.

Aleksey Apukhtin, c. 1860.

Lev and Aleksandra Davydov after their marriage, 1860.

Tchaikovsky as a clerk in the Ministry of Justice, 1862.

Tchaikovsky (standing far left) and Apukhtin (standing far right) among St. Petersburg beau monde friends, 1862.

Tchaikovsky, c. 1860.

*Tchaikovsky as a student at
the St. Petersburg
Conservatory, 1863.*

*Hermann Laroche, the
composer's friend from the St.
Petersburg Conservatory,
1864.*

*Tchaikovsky as a young
teacher at the Moscow
Conservatory, c. 1866.*

*Nikolay Kashkin, a professor
at the Moscow Conservatory.*

Pyotr Jurgenson, the composer's music publisher.

Group of Tchaikovsky's students at the Moscow Conservatory. From left, Anatoly Brandukov, Iosif Kotek, Stanislaw Barcewicz, and Andrey Arends.

Tchaikovsky, c. 1868.

Désirée Artôt.

Alyosha Sofronov, the composer's servant, c. 1873.

Tchaikovsky, 1875.

Modest Tchaikovsky, Nikolay Kondratyev, Anatoly Tchaikovsky, and the composer, c. 1875.

Aleksandra Davydova, the composer's sister.

Tchaikovsky; Modest;
Modest's deaf-mute pupil,
Kolya Konradi; and Kolya's
governess, Sofya Ershova, at
Montpellier, France, summer
1876.

Tchaikovsky and Kotek in
Moscow, c. May 1877.

Tchaikovsky and his wife, c.
July 1877.

Nadezhda von Meck, the
composer's benefactress.

Anatoly Tchaikovsky.

Modest Tchaikovsky.

you, since I believe you will discover in it echoes of your innermost feelings and thoughts."[13] He hesitated to send this letter, but having sent it, received from Mrs. von Meck a most cordial response written the next day: "I thank you sincerely, from the bottom of my heart, dear Pyotr Ilyich, for the trust and friendship that you have shown me by your appeal in the present instance. In particular, I very much appreciate that you have done this by addressing me directly, and I ask you sincerely always to address me as your close friend, who loves you sincerely and deeply. As for the means of repayment, I ask you, Pyotr Ilyich, not to think of this or to trouble yourself."[14]

This exchange of letters was in fact their first business deal. But it was preceded by several letters from Mrs. von Meck that are noteworthy because of their eloquence. On 15 February she had written (in a letter that, strikingly, still began with the words "Gracious sir"), "I should like to take this opportunity to tell you many, many things about my fantastic attitude toward you, but I fear to take up your time, of which you have so little free. Let me say only that this attitude, however abstract, is dear to me as the very best, the very highest of all feelings possible in human nature. Therefore, Pyotr Ilyich, call me a dreamer if you wish, or even a madcap, but do not laugh, because this would all be ludicrous were it not so sincere, and so fundamental."[15]

In her next letter, written on 7 March, she asked for his photograph, although confessing that she possessed two such already, and then went on directly to describe her "ideal of a human being," to which, as is clear from the context, her correspondent thoroughly conformed. This ideal was "necessarily a musician, but his human qualities must be equal to his talent. Only then does he produce a profound and complete impression," she wrote, adding, "I regard the musician-human as the supreme creation of nature." In her view, she told Tchaikovsky, "it is not relations alone that draw people together but, even more so, a similarity of views, equal capacities of feeling, and identity of sympathies, so that they can be close while far from one another." She was happy, she declared, "that in you the musician and the human being are united so beautifully, so harmoniously, that one can give oneself up entirely to the charm of the sounds of your music, because in these sounds there is noble, unfeigned meaning; they are written not for other people but for the expression of your own feelings, thoughts, and mood. I am happy that my idea is realizable, that I need not reject my ideal but, on the contrary, find it becoming even dearer to me, even lovelier. If only you knew what I feel with your music and how grateful I am to you for these feelings!"[16]

In Mrs. von Meck, Tchaikovsky, with his own almost irrepressible sentimentality, had found an eager and sensitive associate. Time and again they would speak in their letters of the likenesses of their natures and of their strong affinity. In his response to her letter on 16 March, Tchaikovsky gently warned her that he did not conform to the ideal she envisaged, yet he readily acknowledged the spiritual bond between them:

> You are quite right, Nadezhda Filaretovna, in assuming that I am able to understand fully the peculiarities of your spiritual being. I dare to think that you are not mistaken in considering me to be someone close to yourself. Just as you have sought to lend an ear to the judgments of public opinion concerning me, so I for my part have missed no opportunity to learn details about you and your way of life. I have always been interested in you as a person in whose moral constitution are many features in common with my own nature. The very fact that you and I both suffer from one and the same sickness draws us together. This sickness is misanthropy, but misanthropy of a special sort, which has at its base no hatred or contempt for people. Those who suffer from this sickness do not fear the harm that may ensue from the machinations of someone close to them, but rather the disappointment, the yearning for the ideal, that every intimate acquaintance entails.[17]

As these lines indicate, Tchaikovsky had also found in Mrs. von Meck someone whose unsociability and passion for seclusion not only matched but even exceeded his own. In her letter Mrs. von Meck had hinted, somewhat nebulously, at the form she would like their relations to take: "There was a time when I very much wanted to make your acquaintance. But now, the more fascinated I am by you, the more I fear acquaintance; I feel that I should be unable to speak to you, although if somewhere, unexpectedly, we were to meet up close, I should not be able to treat you as a stranger, and should stretch out my hand to you, but only to shake yours, and not to say a word." She preferred to think about him "in the distance," to hear him in his music and "to feel as one with you in it."[18]

Tchaikovsky thought he understood her fear of meeting him. "It does not surprise me in the least that, having come to love my music, you do not seek an acquaintance with its author," he told her. "You are afraid not to find in me those qualities which your idealizingly inclined imagination has attributed to me. And you are absolutely right. I feel that on closer acquaintance with me you would not discover that correspondence, that complete harmony of musician and human being, of which you dream."[19]

Her reply two days later was a lovingly indignant reproof in which she flatly denied any fear of not finding in him her cherished union of human being and musician. "I have already found that in you," she insisted, "this is no longer a question for me. In the sense that you have in mind, I may have been afraid earlier, before I became convinced that you in fact possess all that I impart to my ideal, that you embody it, that you make up for my disappointment, mistakes, and yearning; yes, if I had happiness in my hands I should give it to you. But now I fear acquaintance with you for quite a different reason and because of a different feeling."[20]

She did not elaborate further, but her meaning can be deduced. Despite an almost erotic passion felt in many of her letters to Tchaikovsky, she would remain quite content with their implicit mutual agreement never to meet face-to-face. In this, no doubt, not only did her apprehensions about her unprepossessing appearance and her more advanced age play some role. Far more fundamental was her conception of eroticism in sentimental rather than physical terms. The same narrowly pragmatic and even squeamish approach to sexuality evident in her negative views of marriage most likely gave rise to the incandescence of the platonic passion that characterized her attitude toward Tchaikovsky. The situation that developed satisfied her own deepest needs, allowing her to give free rein to her emotions while excluding, by definition, what she believed were the unpleasant, vulgar, shameful, and humiliating aspects of sexual love.

Mrs. von Meck would preserve until the very end her exalted image of her "beloved friend," at least as expressed on paper. Through the years, their letters revealed the numerous personal shortcomings of the two correspondents. Both possessed neurotic natures and were prone to depression, which they both called "misanthropy." Both were capricious and eccentric. The composer could at times be almost transparently disingenuous, while his benefactress was often obtrusive and inconsistent. Yet, each transcended these petty traits to make this long friendship perhaps the most attractive chapter in Tchaikovsky's life. Despite their final mysterious and unfounded estrangement, their mutual devotion can be seen, in its highest manifestations, as a model of the relations between two spiritually complex individuals. Mrs. von Meck gave Tchaikovsky more than thirteen years of liberated and fully realized creative life. Tchaikovsky, in turn, bestowed upon her not only his Symphony no. 4 in F Minor, op. 36, dedicated to his "best friend," and the happiness of his confidence, replete with tenderness and gratitude, which became for her a source of consolation and pleasure, "a fate," as she once wrote, "against which I am powerless,"[21] but also, of course, her own immortality in historical memory.

By May 1877, Tchaikovsky's detestation of Moscow and of his conservatory obligations had reached its peak. He felt increasingly repelled by his environment and especially by the world of the aunties and all their petty troubles. Even the thought of impending vacations did nothing to please him. "The examinations are ending," he wrote on 23 May to Modest—by this time already back in Russia and spending the summer at the Konradi estate at Grankino, near Poltava—"and my departure draws nearer, but I do not feel so lighthearted as I have in the past. The thought that I shall again have to endure the same tedious monotony, again the classes, again Nikolay Lvovich [Bochechkarov], again the various squabbles—all this upsets me and poisons the idea of three free months. I am growing old."[22]

Adding to his gloomy spirits was the sudden marriage in late April of his pupil Vladimir Shilovsky to the wealthy young countess to whom he had become betrothed a few years before. Writing to Modest on 4 May, Tchaikovsky had been rather snide in his reaction to the event, while the excisions made by the Soviet censors are eloquent in themselves. "Shilovsky's marriage has taken place," he wrote. "Before this solemnity he drank heavily without stopping [a cut follows]. Now he is utterly happy and content [another cut] and spends all day long paying visits to aristocrats. I dined at his home yesterday. His wife is terribly plain and seems quite foolish, but very *comme il faut*."[23] In fact, the countess turned out to possess a considerably strong character and exerted an unexpected power over her husband. A year later, on 10 March 1878, Shilovsky's brother Konstantin would write to Tchaikovsky, "I never expected that he might be capable of falling under his wife's influence to such an impossible degree. Just imagine, she has managed to distance him from all his acquaintances whose influence she feared for her own sake. Only Golitsyn and Benediktov enjoy her favor. Boriseta, for instance, has been flatly denied entrance."[24]

His pupil's marriage would appear to have been the final spur to Tchaikovsky's own resolution to marry. But what Tchaikovsky regrettably failed to take fully into account was the fact that at thirty-seven years of age he could no longer take the step so blindly or so lightly as a young man of twenty-four could.

The pathetic story of Tchaikovsky's marriage is convoluted and at times obscure. On 3 July, Tchaikovsky would recall in a letter to Mrs. von Meck how one of his students, Antonina Milyukova, had written him a confession of love. "From her letter I learned that she had already bestowed her love on me some time before. The letter had been written so genuinely, so warmly, that I decided to answer it, something I had carefully avoided in similar cases before. And although my reply did not offer the young lady any hope of reciprocity, a correspondence began."[25]

The recollections of the composer's widow, written in 1893, published in 1894, and reprinted in 1913, have never been made widely known.[26] This is an uncanny consequence of Modest's shrewd strategy, supported by other memoirists sympathetic to him or already under his influence, to exonerate his brother's memory in every conceivable way, a strategy that inevitably led him to place the burden of blame for the matrimonial fiasco and its repercussions on the composer's unfortunate wife. There can be little doubt that Modest must have hated her—because of the sufferings she caused his adored brother, because of the danger she always represented of potential exposure, because of Tchaikovsky's having concealed (from Modest in particular) his intention to marry her until the very last moment, and because of pure jealousy. Hence his claim that she was already mentally unbalanced at the time of the composer's proposal to her.[27]

In fact, Milyukova's recollections do not impress one as the work of a madwoman. They contain no traces of abnormality, but instead reveal a devotion to her husband's memory, an appreciation of his greatness, and the vague feeling of an enormous misunderstanding having taken place between them. The author is naive and superficial and not very intelligent, yet her mind, as reflected in her narrative, is quite coherent. Likewise, nothing in the reminiscences gives any grounds for suspecting them of being a forgery. On the contrary, the genuineness of the intonation, the idiosyncratic style, and the wealth of detail all attest its authenticity.

According to her own account, Antonina Milyukova met Tchaikovsky for the first time (probably in 1865) in St. Petersburg at the home of her brother's sister-in-law, Anastasiya Khvostova, who was a well-known singer and a friend of Aleksey Apukhtin. Anastasiya's brother Nikolay had also been a classmate of Modest's at the School of Jurisprudence. In any event, Tchaikovsky seems to have paid no notice at all to the chance encounter, but it is very possible that from the moment of this accidental meeting, Antonina, who in 1865 was only sixteen years old, began to feel an adolescent "crush" that would eventually develop into her amorous obsession with him.

Very little is known about Antonina Milyukova, apart from the fact that before entering the conservatory she worked as a professional seamstress. She might even appear enigmatic, were she not so emphatically deficient in character and personality. Indeed, she can be seen as an incarnation of the commonplace: her letters and memoirs rarely rise above the level of trivialities. Of her family we know only that they resided in the Moscow area and, although belonging to the local gentry, lived in poverty. In the same letter of July, Tchaikovsky described his choice to Mrs. von Meck: "She is twenty-eight years old. She is fairly pretty. Her reputation is immaculate. Out of love of independence she has been living by her own labor, although she has a very loving mother. She is utterly poor, educated not above an average level, ... apparently very kind and capable of permanent attachments."[28] It would almost appear that Tchaikovsky deliberately chose an average, unsophisticated woman to marry, in the hope that she would not be able to understand or to guess at his sexual orientation.

Milyukova had enrolled in the Moscow Conservatory in the early 1870s and, as she writes,

> I was extremely happy, meeting him [Tchaikovsky] constantly; he was always terribly affectionate to me. ... For more than four years I had loved him secretly. ... I knew perfectly well that he liked me, but he was shy and would never have made a proposal. I made a pledge to myself to go every day for six weeks to the chapel at the Spassky Gates to pray for him, no matter what the weather. ... After the six weeks I ordered a liturgy in the chapel and, having prayed some more at home, I up and mailed him a letter in which I poured out to him on the paper all my love that had accumulated over so many years. He answered me at once, and we started a correspondence that was not without interest.[29]

This account greatly compresses the long lapse of time. Milyukova omits her withdrawal from the conservatory about two years before her letter, presumably because of poor academic performance and lack of talent or perhaps money.[30] Inquiring of one of her former professors, Eduard Langer, what sort of student Antonina had been, Tchaikovsky received in reply a stream of "unprintable profanity," though admittedly it was a peculiarity of Langer always to speak ill of any student without talent.[31] By the time of her letter to the composer, she was already earning her own living, although we do not know the precise nature of her employment.

The peak of their "affair" came at the beginning of May. After the budding of his friendship with Mrs. von Meck (and thereby the sudden resolution of his financial problems) and after Shilovsky's marriage, the emergence of Antonina Milyukova, who effectually walked straight into his arms, was clearly the third in the string of coincidences that, as he wrote to Modest on 23 May, were "not mere chance." Tchaikovsky decided to take advantage of this turn of events.

In the Tchaikovsky archives are preserved three letters written to him by Antonina during this period. All of Tchaikovsky's early letters to her have been lost, as have Antonina's initial letter to him containing her confession of love and a probable second letter. In her first extant letter, dated 4 May, she wrote, "I already see that it's time for me to begin to restrain my feelings, which you yourself mentioned to me in your first letter. Now, though I can't see you, I console myself with the thought that you are in the same city with me, whereas in a month, or maybe even less, you will most likely leave, and God knows whether I shall ever see you again, because I, too, do not plan to stay in Moscow. But wherever I may be, I will never be able to forget you or stop loving you. . . . I do not want to look at any other man after you." Recounting how a week earlier she had had to listen to the confession of a man "who had loved me almost since his schooldays and had remained faithful for five years," she wrote that it had pained her to listen to him, adding, "I was thinking that it must be just as difficult for you to read my letters, having nothing pleasant to reply to me and, for all your good wishes, being unable to show me anything more than complete indifference."[32]

Sending this letter to Tchaikovsky by messenger, Antonina was surprised and dismayed to learn that he was not, after all, in the same city with her, having left Moscow to spend a few days at Konstantin Shilovsky's estate at Glebovo. The restraint promised only hours before was quickly forgotten as Antonina sat down at once to write another, more passionate letter. She begged him to meet with her. "Could you really stop our correspondence without seeing me even once? No, I am certain you will not be so cruel!" she wrote and then went on with ever-mounting emotion, "After your last letter I fell in love with you twice as much, and your shortcomings mean absolutely nothing to me. Perhaps if you were perfection, I might have remained quite cool toward you. I am dying with longing and burning with a desire to see you. . . . There is no shortcoming that would make me stop loving you. This is not a momentary infatuation, but a feeling that has developed over the course of a very long time, and I am quite unable now to blot it out, nor do I want to." She had been sitting home all day, she told him, wandering "up and down like a half-wit," thinking only about the moment when she would see him. "I shall be ready to throw my arms around your neck and smother you with kisses."

Here, as if suddenly coming to her senses, she hastened to reassure him of her good moral character. "Although I have confessed my feelings," she wrote, "I would be terribly distressed if you were to interpret this the wrong way. I can assure you that I am a respectable and honest girl in the full sense of the word, and I have nothing I might wish to conceal from you. My first kiss will be given to you and to no one else in the world." But the closing lines of the letter abandoned even this pretense at self-control, with an explicit threat to take her own life: "Good-bye, my dear. Do not try to make me disappointed in you any more, because you'll only be wasting your time. I cannot live without you, and that's why soon, perhaps, I shall kill myself. So let me look at you and kiss you so that I can remember this kiss in the next world. Good-bye. Eternally yours, A.M."

This second letter was not sent until two days later, on 6 May. In a last-minute postscript, Antonina passionately reiterated her appeal that he visit her, adding that she had to be away the following day, Thursday, but that on Friday she would be at home all day long waiting for him. She apologized for not being able to receive him "with the comfort that I should like, since I only have one room at my disposal, but I hope that I shall not fall in your eyes because of this."[33]

Such amorous outpourings—to say nothing of the threat of suicide—were not only extravagant but virtually inconceivable within the context of the period and the milieu, particularly since Tchaikovsky and Antonina seem scarcely to have known each other beyond the formal relationship of student and teacher. But the letters are filled with genuine anguish and longing. There is no doubt that the young woman was deeply in love with the composer, even if her passion was fanciful and misguided.

Finding Antonina's letters upon his return to Moscow, also on 6 May, Tchaikovsky began to reconsider his own attitude to her and to weigh the various prospects. To both Mrs. von Meck and Nikolay Kashkin he would later state that after receiving the letter of 4/6 May, he agreed to Antonina's request to visit her. Since Antonina had written that she would not be home on Thursday but would be waiting for him the following day, this visit very likely took place on Friday, 8 May. That same day, writing to his friend Ivan Klimenko (a man, as we have seen, of ambiguous bisexuality but with strong heterosexual inclinations), Tchaikovsky confessed that he had recently "changed a great deal both physically and, in particular, morally." Rather than suggesting any change in his fundamental view of homosexuality as morally neutral, his words in fact seem to imply his intention henceforth to conduct his existence more soberly and with a greater sense of responsibility. "Not a speck of merriment or desire to fool around is left," he wrote. "Life is dreadfully empty, dull, and vulgar. I am seriously thinking of marriage."[34]

Thus, he pondered and wavered until, by an irony of fate, a further coincidence came to play the role of catalyst in the unfolding drama. On 13 May, during an evening at the home of Elizaveta Lavrovskaya, a singer with the Bolshoy Theater, the conversation turned to possible ideas for an opera. Lavrovskaya suddenly suggested Aleksandr Pushkin's novel in verse, *Eugene Onegin*, an idea the composer at first thought absurd. But the more he thought about it, the more intrigued he became. "I rushed off to look for [a volume of] Pushkin," he wrote to Modest a few days later, "and finding one with difficulty, I went home, reread it enraptured, and spent an absolutely sleepless night, the result of which has been the scenario of a charming opera based on Pushkin's text."[35]

Another result of this night was the later notion that the composition of the opera *Eugene Onegin* was intimately related to Tchaikovsky's eventual decision to marry. This notion figures most prominently in the recollections of Nikolay Kashkin, who has provided us with the most detailed account of the composer's unfortunate marriage. According to Kashkin, Tchaikovsky, without the slightest prompting, quite suddenly revealed to him later his own version, in all its particulars, of the inward and outward events leading to his matrimonial catastrophe. Set down more than forty years after the events it describes and thus after the publication of Modest's biography, which could not but influence all subsequent writings on the subject, Kashkin's account, though at times persuasive, should be treated with extreme caution. The device Kashkin chose of narrating events in the first person—that is, in Tchaikovsky's own voice—is surprisingly effective and psychologically convincing. It should not, however, obscure for us certain implausibilities and partialities contained within it.[36]

In this version of events, Tchaikovsky confessed that at the time of his own real-life dilemma in 1877 he had been "captivated utterly and exclusively by the thought of *Eugene Onegin*" and, in particular, by the character of Tatyana, the innocent and deeply emotional heroine of Pushkin's novel in verse. Widely considered the supreme masterpiece of Russian literature, Pushkin's novel, completed in 1833, in fact contains little narrative action. Onegin, a dandy from the capital, unintentionally captures the heart of a young girl of the country gentry, Tatyana. Receiving her naively passionate letter in which she confesses her love, he courteously and yet condescendingly rejects her. In a foul mood, he begins to flirt with the girl's lightheaded sister, the fiancée of his friend the poet Lensky. This soon leads to a quarrel, a summons to a duel, and Lensky's death. When Onegin returns to the capital some years later, he encounters Tatyana, now a fine society lady married to an elderly general who adores her and to whom she is grateful, if little more. Onegin suddenly recognizes that she was the only true love of his life and belatedly he sends her a passionate declaration of love. But this time it is he who is met with refusal: though Tatyana has never stopped loving him, she follows her marital duty and remains faithful to her husband.

There is no doubt that the composition of the opera *Eugene Onegin* constituted Tchaikovsky's most profound creative involvement. "If ever music was written with sincere passion," he wrote to Sergey Taneev in January 1878, "with love for the story and the characters in it, it is the music for *Onegin*. I trembled and melted with inexpressible delight while writing it. If the listener feels even the smallest part of what I experienced when I was composing this opera, I shall be utterly content to ask for nothing more."[37]

Tatyana's famous letter to Onegin is the centerpiece both of Pushkin's original novel and of Tchaikovsky's opera. Tchaikovsky told Kashkin that, "yielding to an irresistible emotional need," he began to write the music for this letter before he had a libretto or even any general plan for the opera: "I had come to sympathize with the figure of Tatyana to such a degree that she began to seem alive to me, along with everything around her. I loved Tatyana and was terribly indignant with Onegin, who appeared to me a cold and heartless fop." It was Antonina's letter to him in which she threatened to take her own life that made him, we are told, suddenly recognize the similarity between Pushkin's story and his immediate predicament. In his mind, Antonina's passionate outpourings "merged with the notion of Tatyana, while I myself, it seemed to me, had behaved incomparably worse than Onegin, and I was genuinely angry at myself for my heartless treatment of a girl who had fallen in love with me." At once he made up his mind to go see Milyukova, "and thus began our acquaintance."[38]

This version would indeed seem to present the sort of integration of art and life that Tchaikovsky in a sense had striven for all along, were it not for the fact that the chronology clearly goes against certain particulars of the story. We know that the idea for this new opera was suggested to him no earlier than the middle of May, whereas, if Antonina was sending her letters by courier, Tchaikovsky would most likely have received the one in which she threatened to commit suicide no later than 7 May. His response to it, then, could not have been rooted in his contemplation of the Onegin-Tatyana relationship. Nor does his version mention the fact, clear from Antonina's letters with their references to two of Tchaikovsky's replies (the "first" and the "last"), that they were in fact already corresponding with one another. The impression created by the version Kashkin gives us is that Tchaikovsky, without ever having written a single line in response to Antonina's letters, simply went straight off to see her after receiving her threat of suicide.

Thus, instead of following blindly the traditional belief that Tchaikovsky's work on *Onegin* was partly responsible for his decision to marry, it might be fair to suggest that the process was actually the reverse and that his infatuation with Pushkin's story was, at least in part, one of the effects of his growing preoccupation with Antonina Milyukova. It seems evident, then, that Tchaikovsky, consciously or not, later falsified to some extent the course of events in order to fit them into a Pushkinian literary framework. Betraying the inherent romanticism of his mind, this wishful reversal reshaped events to accord more completely with artistic notions of coincidence and destiny. Fate, not his own folly, became for him the instrument of his undoing.

In describing these events several weeks later in his letter to Mrs. von Meck of 3 July, Tchaikovsky wrote that during his first meeting with Antonina he again explained to her that he felt for her nothing more than simple liking and gratitude for her love. Yet, as he told his benefactress, it seemed to him in retrospect "as if some power of fate drew me to this young woman," and he added, "If I did not love her, if I did not want to encourage her feelings, why then did I visit her and how would this all end?"[39]

Antonina's later account omits any reference to her own threats and entreaties, or even to this first meeting, but instead skips ahead several days to another meeting, which evidently took place on 20 May.[40] "One day," she writes, "I received a short letter: 'Tomorrow I shall visit you.' And he came. He always charmed all the young ladies, and then, in particular, his gaze was enchanting. Among other things he said: 'But I am nearly an old man! Perhaps you will be bored living with me?' 'I love you so,' I answered, 'that merely to sit by you, to talk with you, to have you always near me will fill me with bliss.' We sat together an hour. 'Let me think until tomorrow,' he said as he left."[41]

Under the impression of this meeting, Antonina wrote him yet another letter, sent either that same day or the next morning, 21 May. Receiving this letter, in which she most probably assured him of how idyllic life might be once they were married, Tchaikovsky, without further thought, decided to see her again that evening. He wrote to Mrs.

von Meck, "From her next letter I came to the conclusion that if, having gone thus far, I were suddenly to turn away from this girl, I should make her truly miserable and lead her to a tragic end. Thus, I was faced with a difficult alternative: either preserve my own freedom at the cost of this girl's ruin (and 'ruin' is not an empty word: she indeed loves me infinitely) or marry. I could but choose the latter."

Therefore, he continued, he went again to Antonina and told her frankly that he did not love her but would be, in any event, "her devoted and grateful friend." He described to her in detail his various shortcomings, his irritability and unevenness of temper, his unsociableness, and his financial circumstances. "After this," he wrote, "I asked her whether she wished to be my wife. The answer, of course, was positive."[42]

Antonina insists that this meeting took place that very next day and that Tchaikovsky had by this time already made up his mind: "Next day he said: 'I have thought everything through. Here is what I have to say. Never in my life have I loved a single woman, and I feel I am already too old for an ardent love. I shall never feel it for anyone. But you are the first woman whom I like very much. If you will be satisfied with a quiet, calm love, rather the love of a brother, then I make you my proposal.' Of course," claims Antonina, "I consented to all his conditions." For a while longer the two sat stiffly together. Then, as Tchaikovsky was leaving, he "somehow especially charmingly and graciously" turned to his fiancée, stretched out his arms, and said, "Well? . . ." "I flung my arms about his neck," recalled Antonina sixteen years later. "I shall never forget that kiss. Then he left at once."[43]

It is not necessary to believe all the details of this scene in order to recognize that for the most part Antonina's account corresponds with Tchaikovsky's own in his letter to Mrs. von Meck. He obviously made an effort to impress upon his future bride that their relations must be entirely platonic, and hence the emphasis on his age and on a brotherly love. But it did not occur to him that Antonina might misunderstand his set speech and see in it, not a renunciation of sexual relations, but merely an excuse for his lack of youthful passion, and attribute it to the difference in their ages.

In both accounts, of course, chronology is muddled. For Antonina, it was natural to believe so many years later that he had made his proposal as soon as possible. Yet, it appears to have been in Tchaikovsky's interest to prolong retrospectively the period of his hesitation in view of the romantic background he later supplied—that is, his involvement with *Onegin*. Thus, all chronological details are again avoided in his later version, recorded by Kashkin, where the crucial moment of his decision is firmly rooted in the Pushkinian literary framework, probably at least in part through retrojection. "To act like Onegin seemed to me heartless and simply inadmissible for my part," he reportedly told his friend. "I was in a sort of delirium." Apparently worst of all was the fact that "these vague hesitations" about the matter of Antonina hindered his composition: "I decided it best to have done with this question so as to free myself from it. . . . Having made my decision [to marry Antonina], I did not comprehend at all its importance or even realize its meaning and significance; it was essential for me to eliminate, for the immediate future at least, anything that prevented me from concentrating on this idea for an opera that had captivated my entire being, and it seemed to me most natural and simple to act as I did."[44]

In any event, it would appear that Tchaikovsky failed to tell Antonina the most important thing about himself—namely, that he preferred to have sex with young men, not with women. If so, he made a grave error, condemning both his life and hers to miseries that drove each to the edge of madness. Still, an alternative possibility presents itself: that Tchaikovsky did not avoid the forbidden topic, but in fact made an attempt to explain to her his predicament and failed in this because of a simple lack of verbal means. Conventions of the time demanded an allusive, euphemistic vocabulary in any discussion of sexual matters, to the degree that a naive and barely educated young woman like Antonina, in her confusion, might easily have failed to understand what he was talking about, blithely agreeing with anything he said. This would have led to an unwitting delusion on both sides: Tchaikovsky convincing himself that his bride had nothing at all against his sexual taste and would not mind marital abstinence, and Antonina entertaining no idea whatsoever that such tastes existed, much less in her bridegroom, and yet joyously anticipating something in their marriage bed, of which, being presumably still a virgin, she possessed only a vague notion.

In his letter to Mrs. von Meck, Tchaikovsky described his turbulent state of mind just after he had made his proposal. His words betray the painful complexity of his motivation and even hint at his reluctant resolve to seek a marriage of convenience in an effort to mask his homosexuality and avoid adverse public opinion. "I cannot convey to you in words the terrible feelings I went through the first days following that evening," he wrote. "To be drawn by force of circumstance into the position of a bridegroom, this without being in the least attracted to one's bride, is very difficult. It is necessary to change one's whole way of life, to strive for the well-being and tranquillity of another person linked with one's own fate—all of which is not so very easy for a bachelor hardened by egotism."

But he was determined to plunge bravely ahead, clutching almost desperately at the thought he had confided to Modest, that perhaps Providence had indeed condescended to care for him. "I have decided that one cannot avoid one's destiny," he continued to Mrs. von Meck, "and that in my encounter with this girl there is something fateful." He might well have added that there was something equally fateful in their own encounter. In many ways, the remarkable Nadezhda von Meck, who accepted him as he was and remained content to worship him intimately from a distance, was precisely what Tchaikovsky was looking for in a woman. But, for now, this kindred spirit, his "guardian angel," could do nothing but look on silently as he took as his wife a young woman who had no clue to understanding him and who would very nearly destroy him unawares.

More as if trying to convince himself rather than Mrs. von Meck, Tchaikovsky concluded, "Besides, I know from experience that in life very often that which frightens and terrifies sometimes turns out to be beneficial, and, on the contrary, disappointment may come from that which has been striven for in hope of bliss and happiness. What will be will be."[45]

CHAPTER TWELVE

Marriage

No more than three weeks were spent on the decision to marry Antonina. Then, laying the burden of the marriage preparations on his bride and concealing the fact of his betrothal from everyone around him, Tchaikovsky, his mind at ease, withdrew on 29 May, after the end of examinations at the conservatory, to Konstantin Shilovsky's estate at Glebovo, there to work on the libretto and music for his new opera. "A week later, he asked my permission to go to his friend's estate near Moscow," writes Antonina of that summer, "in order to write more quickly the opera that was already being composed in his head. This opera was *Eugene Onegin,* the best of all his operas. It is good because it is based on us. He himself is Onegin, and I am Tatyana. His operas written before and afterward are not warmed with love; they are cold and fragmentary. There is no wholeness in them. This is the only one that is good from beginning to end."[1]

At Glebovo, with its beautiful surroundings, Tchaikovsky found the very best of working conditions. On 9 June he wrote to Modest that he was wholly absorbed in the composition of his opera. "I have at my disposal an entire separate splendidly furnished house," he told his brother. "When I am occupied I see no one, not a single human soul except Alyosha [his servant Aleksey Sofronov]."[2] The composer would rise every morning at eight, bathe, drink his tea, and then work until breakfast. He had already developed a habit of taking long strolls, and at Glebovo he would go for a stroll after breakfast, work again until dinner, and then after dinner take another long stroll before evening.

215

So pleased was he with his stay there that somewhat later, in a letter to Shilovsky, he avowed, "My recollections of that month at Glebovo literally seem to me a *dream*, and a very sweet dream at that. . . . O, hundredfold wonderful, dear, quiet corner of the world, I shall never forget you!!!"[3]

Consumed by work in this "wonderful corner of the world," Tchaikovsky seems to have been all but oblivious of the proposal he had made to Antonina. It is remarkable that having resolved to proceed with so important a step as marriage, Tchaikovsky, in writing to his relatives (in his correspondence with whom he had used to be so intimate and frank), made not the slightest mention of his resolve. Until the very last minute there was no hint of the impending event. The tone of these letters in no way reflected the attitude of a man on the threshold of a new life, and the various plans he revealed for the immediate future left no room for the presence of a wife. Indeed, he seemed far more concerned with his former student Iosif Kotek than with his intended bride, Antonina. It was a photograph of him and Kotek that he sent to Modest on 23 May (with a suspicious cut in the published text of the letter following his mention of this photograph).[4] And on 9 June the young violinist's name cropped up again, as Tchaikovsky announced that he must "spend several days in Moscow with Kotek."[5] Nor did his domestic situation change. His beloved servant Alyosha, far from being sent off out of harm's way, remained constantly with him and is mentioned several times in his letters.[6] It is not inconceivable, in fact, that Tchaikovsky envisioned a future household not unlike the ménage of the married Kondratyev, with his wife tolerating—if only barely—a male servant in the role of her husband's lover.

Tchaikovsky, then, having made the solemn decision to marry, proceeded to take his marriage not in the least seriously. Not only did he try not to think about it, but his intimacy with Kotek suggests the true direction of his attachments. His sister had been correct in her anxiety, despite his assurances of prudence and circumspection. This marriage had burst forth unexpectedly, tempestlike, and his choice of a bride had been made hurriedly and, in fact, with little prudence or circumspection.

Tchaikovsky informed his father of his plans less than two weeks before the wedding in a letter of 23 June 1877:

Dear and beloved Papa! Your son Pyotr has decided to marry. Since he does not wish to proceed with the nuptials without your blessing, he asks that you bless him in his new life. I am

marrying a young woman named Antonina Ivanovna Milyukova. She is poor, but a good and honest girl who loves me very
much. My dear Papa, you know that at my age one does not
resolve to marry without quiet deliberation, so therefore do not
worry about me. I am sure that my future wife will do everything to make me calm and happy. I beg you not to speak of
this to anyone for the time being except Lizaveta Mikhailovna
[Tchaikovsky's stepmother]. I shall write Sasha and my brothers myself.[7]

Papa, of course, gave his blessing, literally leaping for joy at the news,
as he told his "most beautiful" son in his enthusiastic reply. "I do not
doubt that the person you have chosen is worthy of this same epithet
that you have merited from your father, an eighty-three-year-old man,
and from my whole family, and even, truth to tell, from all of mankind
that knows you," enthused Ilya Tchaikovsky. Then, addressing Antonina, on whom he had never set eyes, he added, "Is that not so, my dear
Antonina Ivanovna? As of yesterday I ask your permission to call you
my God-given daughter; love your chosen bridegroom and husband, he
is truly worthy of it, and you, my bridegroom, let me know the day
and time of your wedding. I shall come myself (let me know whether
you agree) to give you my blessing."[8]
    But his son did not agree to the idea of his father's attendance at
the wedding. Moreover, he was extremely hesitant to tell any of his
other relatives about his betrothal, betraying what must have been a
deep reluctance to go ahead with the plan. Tchaikovsky's sister and
brother-in-law are not informed until 5 July, that is, the exact eve of
the ceremony. "In announcing this news to you, I shall refrain for the
time being from describing the qualities of my bride, since besides the
fact that she is a quite decent girl and loves me very much, I as yet
know very little about her," he wrote frankly. "Only when we have
lived together for some while will the traits of her character be revealed to me with full clarity. . . . I can tell you one thing: I shall not
bring her to you in Kamenka until the thought that my nieces will call
her 'aunt' ceases to shock me. Right now, though I love my bride, still
it seems to me slightly impertinent on her part that she will become
an aunt to your children, whom I love more than any children in the
world."[9]
    Aleksandra, who had to have been shaken by this letter, responded
gamely on 12 July, after the wedding: "You are married, and this means
there is now another creature close to me, and consequently dear to
me, and so I shall not tell you everything I have been feeling these past

few days. May God give you happiness. If you wish to please me and set my mind at rest, bring your wife to me. I want to come to love consciously her to whose lot has fallen the happiness of being your companion."[10]

Also just on the very eve of the wedding, Tchaikovsky finally broke the news to Modest, thus ensuring that his impulsive younger brother would have no time to appear at the wedding, even if he should willfully decide to come anyway. "When you receive this letter, I shall already be married," Tchaikovsky told his brother. "This matter was decided at the end of May, but for the time being, I kept it secret so as not to torment you and everyone close to me with uncertainty and doubts until the deed was done. Proof that I undertake this quite calmly and rationally can be seen in the fact that in the face of my impending nuptials I lived an entire month quite tranquilly and happily at Glebovo, where I wrote two-thirds of my opera." He wrote that after the wedding, he planned to go with his wife ("how strange that sounds," he added) to St. Petersburg for several days and then would live with her until August, "and in August I shall do some traveling if there is enough money."[11] Not surprisingly, Modest took deep offense at such cavalier treatment from his adored brother. Tchaikovsky's motives are, however, understandable, apprehensive as he must have been of the exhausting and jealous argumentation that Modest would surely have launched, had he learned of his intentions earlier.

Of all his relatives, only Anatoly was invited to the ceremony. Steady and reliable, he was not likely to attempt to dissuade his brother from his clearly rash decision or to add further to his distress as the maternally anxious Aleksandra or the determinedly opposed Modest might well have done. Interestingly, Tchaikovsky, in notifying his brother Anatoly of his plans on 23 June, never made the slightest mention of his own feelings toward his bride:

> You have very rightly guessed that I am hiding something from you, but this something is not what you think. Here is what it is. At the end of May a certain circumstance occurred that I wanted for the moment to conceal from you and from all those near and dear to me, so that you would not worry in vain about what I am doing: who, why, is it the right thing, etc. I wanted first to finish the whole business and only then reveal it to all of you. I am getting married. . . . I have acted with much careful consideration and undertake this important step in my life quite calmly. . . . I am marrying a girl not particularly young but entirely respectable and who has one main virtue: she is in

love with me like a cat. She is utterly poor. . . . And so, I not only inform you of the coming wedding but also invite you to attend it. You, along with Kotek, will be the only witness of the ceremony to take place immediately after your arrival.[12]

It is evident from his words that Tchaikovsky had somehow convinced himself that Antonina's love for him must guarantee the success of their union. In assuming this, he had mistaken infatuation for unquestioning devotion, altogether brushing aside the sexual side of love. His error was to cost him dearly.

The calm tone of his letters to his family was for the most part deceptive. The extent of his anxiety and perplexity was evident, despite his professed optimism, in his letter to Mrs. von Meck written three days before the wedding. With her, who knew him far less intimately than his siblings, he did not feel the same need for self-control, and his letter to her, with its unprompted apologia of sorts, reveals his gnawing doubts and fears. "Do wish me not to lose heart in the face of that change in my life which now stands before me," he wrote. "God knows that I am, with regard to my life's companion, full of the very best intentions and that if she and I are unhappy, the fault will not be mine. My conscience is clear. . . . I have not lied, nor have I deceived her. I have told her what she can expect from me and what she should not count on."[13]

The wedding took place on 6 July in the Church of St. George on Malaya Nikitskaya Street in Moscow. The most detailed, if not always coherent, description of the wedding day is found in Antonina's recollections, though one inevitably wonders to what extent her account is a faithful reflection of what happened that day and to what extent it is colored by her knowledge of subsequent events. She begins with a bad omen: when she arrived at the church, it was discovered that the rose satin cloth for under the couple's feet had been forgotten. Someone was sent at once to fetch it, but it was brought only toward the end of the ceremony. "My best man placed his white silk handkerchief under P[yotr] I[lyich]'s feet and I just stood as I was," recalls Antonina.

After the ceremony Anatoly Ilyich went alone with P[yotr] I[lyich] back to his bachelor apartment. . . . Some time later, a carriage was sent for us and we went to the Hermitage Hotel. When we drove up, two footmen, as they say, handed me down from the carriage and led me in, one on each arm. At the foot of the staircase, Anatoly Ilyich met me and took my arm. The room where everything was prepared was large. It was decorated with bouquets. There were a great many dishes of every sort, but I barely touched anything. Even then I already had a presentiment of something bad. I simply felt cold from fear. Later, my cousin told me that it had been just like a funeral banquet, so cheerless was it. . . . After the dinner P[yotr] I[lyich] left again and went back to his bachelor apartment with his brother. . . . Toward seven o'clock in the evening, we took a train on the Nikolaev railroad, and I departed for Petersburg with my husband.[14]

On his wedding day Tchaikovsky sent a bravura letter to Vladimir Shilovsky informing him of the event.[15] But Tchaikovsky's actual feelings that day and the following night were in fact very far from any exultation. He revealed his real feelings in several versions, both in letters of the time and in later recollections. According to Nikolay Kashkin, Tchaikovsky later told him that he had been "in a sort of daze" throughout the ceremony, noting only the "characteristic artistic beauty" with which the priest, Dmitry Razumovsky, who was also a professor of the history of sacred music at the conservatory, performed the sacrament of marriage. "I remained a kind of outside figure, uninvolved," Kashkin reports Tchaikovsky telling him, "until Dmitry Vasilyevich [Razumovsky], at the close of the ceremony, made Antonina Ivanovna and me kiss each other; at this point, a pain struck my heart and such an anxiety gripped me that it seems I began to weep, but I made an effort to master myself quickly and assume a calm appearance; Anatoly, however, had noticed my condition, for he started to say something encouraging to me."[16]

In a long, candid letter to Anatoly on 8 July, Tchaikovsky described his inner turmoil in the aftermath of the wedding. Strikingly, his thoughts and affections seemed centered exclusively on his brother, and not at all on his new bride:

After such a terrible day as 6 July, after that endless moral torment, it is not possible to recover quickly. But all adversities have also their good side; I suffered unbearably, seeing how distressed you were about me, but at the same time, you are responsible for my struggling with my torments with such courage. Tell me, please, what meaning have all our ordeals, failures, adversities when compared with the force of my love for you and your love for me! Whatever may happen to me, I know that in your love I shall always find support and consolation. Even now you do not leave my mind for a second and

your dear image consoles, encourages, and supports me. The
hope of seeing you again soon will keep me from losing heart,
no matter what.

Tchaikovsky admitted to his brother that he was still by no means
accustomed to his new situation. When the train for St. Petersburg had
pulled out of the station, he had felt "ready to scream from the sobs
that were suffocating me." But he made an effort to engage his wife in
conversation at least as far as Klin "so as to earn the right to settle
down in my own seat in the darkness and be left alone," he confessed
frankly.

At the second stop, his old friend Prince Meshchersky suddenly
burst into the car. "Seeing him, I felt the sudden need for him to lead
me away somewhere as soon as possible," Tchaikovsky told his
brother. "Which he did. Before beginning any sort of conversation with
him, I had to give vent to a flood of tears. Meshchersky showed me
much tender sympathy and greatly raised my fallen spirits." It is noteworthy that it was the homosexual Meshchersky with whom Tchaikovsky could share his misery without embarrassment and who could
also manage to bring him back to a relatively calm state. "Upon returning to my wife after Klin," Tchaikovsky wrote, "I was much calmer." The prince arranged for the couple to be placed in a separate sleeping compartment. "And after this I slept like a log."

The rest of the journey passed without incident. But, again, Tchaikovsky's thoughts remained with his brother: "There was not a second
that I did not think of you. . . . The thought of you would bring tears
to me, but at the same time, it heartened and consoled me."[17] Upon
arriving in St. Petersburg, Tchaikovsky immediately telegraphed Kotek
to learn the emotional state of his beloved brother. As he told Anatoly,
"If I know that your mind is at ease and you are well, this will greatly
help me to attain a normal state of mind."[18]

To his relief, Antonina had remained oblivious to her husband's
poorly concealed anguish. "Even now she appears quite happy and content," Tchaikovsky told his brother. *"Elle n'est pas difficile.* She agrees
with everything and is content with everything."[19] On the evening of
their arrival the newlyweds took a carriage to the islands at the northern edge of St. Petersburg. The weather was foul and wet. They sat
through the first part of a concert program and then returned to their
suite at the Hotel Europa.

We do not know what actually happened that night. But part of an
extensive portion deleted from the text of Tchaikovsky's letter to Anatoly on 8 July published in the *Complete Works* is preserved in the

Letters to Relatives. There, following marks of deletion—and with Tchaikovsky's italics—we read:

> But we had conversations that further clarified our mutual relations. *She has agreed with absolutely everything and will never be displeased. She needs only to cherish and care for me.* I have reserved for myself complete freedom of action. After taking a good dose of valerian [a sedative] and prevailing upon my discomfited wife not to be discomfited, I again fell asleep like a log. Such sleep is a great benefactor. I feel the time is not far off when I shall calm down *completely.*[20]

What, then, did transpire? Despite the cut preceding this passage, these lines certainly make it clear that the marriage was not consummated. We might logically restore the preceding cut with some such phrase as "there was no marital intimacy," for otherwise it is difficult to account for the evident nervous state of both spouses. Quite probably, Antonina made some attempt to be seductive to her husband and, failing, became "discomfited." This would explain Tchaikovsky's comment in a letter to Anatoly a few days later that "in the physical respect, my wife has become *absolutely repulsive* to me"—which is again followed by a censorial cut.[21] Such an attempt alone may well have been sufficient to instill in Tchaikovsky a lifelong aversion to Antonina.

It is clear from Tchaikovsky's initial letter to Anatoly that at some point Antonina temporarily resigned herself to the situation. But why? Conceivably her husband may have attempted to discuss his own sexuality, only to be handicapped again by euphemistic and, to her, unintelligible language. He could, of course, have told her openly that in love he preferred young men to women, or he could have made some reference to some other cause, such as some inborn asceticism. It is less likely that he might have derogated his masculine pride at this point by claiming impotence, though that was another possible escape.

Quite possibly, Antonina regretted to the end of her days that by not displaying sufficient seductiveness she had botched the chance to give the great composer a normal sex life. Subsequent events show that Tchaikovsky's new bride was by no means persuaded by his arguments or simply failed to comprehend fully what he was telling her. She had, after all, noticed nothing wrong in her husband's conduct during the journey from Moscow. The apparent upshot of their discussions that first night in St. Petersburg was that Antonina decided that ultimately time was on her side, that patience and perseverance would make

everything all right, and so consented for now to her husband's abstinence, however strange it may have seemed to her in her virginal state.

The long letter to Anatoly ended on a note of calm. "And indeed,
why grieve?" Tchaikovsky wrote. "You and I are both very nervous,
and both capable of seeing things in a more somber hue than in fact
they are. I have so secured my freedom of action that as soon as my
wife and I have grown accustomed to each other, she will not constrain
me in anything. I must not deceive myself: she is very limited, but
that is even good. I should be afraid of an intelligent woman. But I
stand so far above this one, I dominate her to such a degree, that at
least I have no fear of her at all."[22]

From his earliest arguments to Modest on the need to marry, Tchaikovsky had stressed the importance of finding a woman who would
allow him complete freedom by tolerating, among other things, his
sexual predilections. For the moment, convinced by Antonina's seeming compliance, he believed he had achieved this purpose. Indeed, he
saw the cultural and intellectual gap between them as a way to aid
him in arranging his private life to his own satisfaction. A more sophisticated woman would, he believed, have been less pliant, more difficult to handle. Antonina, precisely because of her lack of sophistica-
tion, could be controlled, or so he tried to tell himself.

Tchaikovsky closed his letter to Anatoly with yet another passionate outburst to his brother, oddly comical from the pen of a man newly
married. "Tolya, if you were here, I would smother you right now in
my embrace," he wrote. "I do so in my fancy. You know, it's even a
good thing that such days as 6 July occur. Only on such days can the
love that binds me to you be measured in all its fullness."[23] His words
put an interesting twist on his decision to marry if, in large part, it was
to protect his family against scandal and adverse public opinion. It was
perhaps worth getting married to realize just how much he loved his
brother. A novel outlook on matrimony.

Naturally, Tchaikovsky could not write to Modest—who had vehemently opposed his experimenting with marriage—in the same vein
and with the same candid details as he could write to Anatoly. To reveal to him his miserable perturbations would have meant acknowledging that Modest had been right and he himself wrong. This consideration more than anything else explains the restrained tone of the
letter he sent to Modest that same day.

"I sense that you are worried about me and feel I must reassure
you," he wrote. "My wedding took place on 6 July. Tolya was present.
This day was, I'll admit, rather difficult for me if indeed only because

I had to endure the wedding ceremony, the long wedding banquet, the departure with everyone seeing us off, etc. I slept beautifully during the journey." But here again, following a description of their first evening in St. Petersburg and then a cut (arguably of a statement to the effect that there was no marital intimacy), he made his main point emphatically: "My wife has one enormous virtue: she obeys me blindly in everything." And he continued, "She is very accommodating; she is content with everything and wants nothing other than the happiness of being a support and consolation to me. I cannot yet say that I love her, but already I feel that I shall love her as soon as we grow accustomed to each other." This, of course, was wishful thinking. The letter ended with a profusion of fraternal love: "I kiss you tenderly, tenderly. . . . I love you, and among the petty upheavals I am going through now, I direct my thoughts on you with pleasure."[24]

Three days after their arrival in the capital, Tchaikovsky took Antonina to Pavlovsk to introduce her to his father and stepmother. It was an awkward visit. "Papa is enchanted with my wife, as is to be expected," Tchaikovsky wrote to Anatoly the next day. "Lizaveta Mikhailovna was very tender and attentive, but I noticed several times tears in her eyes. This perspicacious and kind stepmother probably guesses that I am going through a critical moment in my life. I confess that all this was very hard for me, that is, Papa's tenderness and endearments (so opposite to my own coldness to my wife) and the perspicacity of Lizaveta Mikhailovna."[25]

He painfully wanted to believe that "little by little" he was growing accustomed to his new situation. Yet, more than once in those first days in St. Petersburg he could not bring himself to tell the acquaintances he happened to meet that the lady with him was his wife.[26] He continued to delude himself about Antonina's true desires. The situation "would be utterly false and unbearable," he told Anatoly, "if I had deceived my wife in anything, but I have warned her that she can rely only on my brotherly love." This last phrase is followed by a cut—of precisely what we cannot guess, though it doubtless had something to do with homosexuality—and then by his remark that he now found his wife physically "repulsive."[27]

The peak of his desperation was revealed in another letter to his brother Anatoly, written on 13 July. "Tolichka, yesterday was perhaps the most difficult day of all since 6 July," he confided. "In the morning it seemed to me that my life is broken and I fell into a fit of despair." And following a cut: "Beginning today the terrible crisis has passed. I am recovering. But the crisis was *terrible, terrible, terrible;* were it not for my love for you and my other dear ones, which supported me in the midst of *unbearable mental torments*, it might have ended badly, that is, with illness or madness."[28]

Not until two weeks after the wedding did Tchaikovsky resolve to write his sister. His embarrassment at the turn his marriage had so quickly taken must have been particularly acute in regard to Aleksandra, with whom he could not begin to share the fundamental reasons for his agonizing predicament. Yet, even with her he did not attempt to conceal that he was far from happy. "I should be lying," he told her, "if I said I was swimming in an ocean of bliss." He admitted that Antonina "does everything possible to please me, is always content with everything, regrets nothing, and demonstrates to me in every way that I constitute the sole interest in her life." But already his dreams of a compliant and controllable wife were crumbling, something he could not entirely keep from his sister, writing that he was "too hardened in the bachelor life" and still could not "think without regret of the loss of my freedom." At times, he confessed, he could not refrain from being angry at Antonina when he recalled that "she, as it were, distances me from those closest to my heart." His final, somewhat feeble claim that he "already" loved his wife was all but swept away by a familiar refrain that must have done little to calm his sister's anxiety: "But how immeasurably far still is this love from that which I feel for you, for our brothers, for Lyova [Lev, his brother-in-law], and for your children!!!"[29]

The news of Tchaikovsky's betrothal had come as no less of a surprise to Mrs. von Meck than to anyone else and undoubtedly disconcerted her. She responded to the announcement, however, with good grace, even if certain intonations in her reply of 6 July bespeak the effort it cost her. "I am sure, my dear good friend," she wrote, "that neither in your new nor in any position will you ever forget that you have in me a friend who is deeply attached to you, and that you will deal with me *à part* all artificial, affected human opinions and will see in me only a person who is close to you and loves you. You will write all about yourself, very frankly, will you not, my dear Pyotr Ilyich? And you will not make me restrain myself in anything concerning you."[30]

In view of the financial perspectives of his new domestic situation, Tchaikovsky immediately upon his return to Moscow was compelled to turn to Mrs. von Meck once again with a request for a loan. His businesslike letter to her of 15 July, filled with details of the sorry state of his monetary affairs, concluded with the following apology: "Allow me, Nadezhda Filaretovna, to postpone an account of all that I have undergone of late until my next letter. In the first place, my nerves are so irritated now that I am unable to give a calm and detailed narrative, and in the second, I still do not know very well myself what is happening to me. I cannot yet decide whether I am happy or the reverse; I know only one thing: I am completely unable to work at present. This is a sign of a troubled, abnormal condition."[31]

Mrs. von Meck fulfilled Tchaikovsky's request with remarkable tact, nobly suppressing any jealousy at his marriage. "Upon receiving your letter, I, as always, rejoiced in it beyond words, but as I began to read, my heart was wrung with anguish and worry for you, my dear beloved friend," she wrote tenderly on 19 July. "But why are you so sad, so anxious? Such sorrow is easily assuaged, and there is no need to distress yourself: go somewhere to take a cure, enjoy nature, tranquillity, happiness, and think sometimes of me. I hope that your next letter will be longer, that it will tell me everything about you, everything, for this is such a joy for me, and I so eagerly await your letters." Only at the very end did she add this delicate note: "I am sending this letter separately from another package."[32] In his next letter (a short note) Tchaikovsky responded with a burst of emotion: "If I emerge triumphant from this devastating spiritual struggle, I shall have you to thank for it, you and only you. A few days more and, I swear to you, I should have gone mad."[33] Neither the first nor the second "loan" was ever paid back to the benefactress.

In the meantime, Tchaikovsky had made the acquaintance of his wife's family. His antipathy toward his new relatives was immediate and intense. "I like very little her family milieu," he wrote in his letter to Aleksandra of 20 July. "I spent three days in the country at her mother's and became convinced that everything I don't altogether like in my wife comes from her belonging to a very strange family, in which the mother was always at odds with the father and now, after his death, is not ashamed to malign him in every way possible, in which this same mother *hates!!!* some of her children, in which the sisters bicker with one another, in which the only son has fallen out with his mother and with all his sisters, etc. Lord, what an unpleasant family!" To Mrs. von Meck he would later confess that in the company of his in-laws, "all nearly at daggers drawn with one another," his "torments increased tenfold," adding, "I find it difficult to express . . . what a terrible degree my moral agonies were reaching."[35]

In Moscow the deadly life dragged on for several more days. Tchaikovsky began to take refuge in alcohol, glad of the "few moments of oblivion" it brought.[36] He dreamt of retreat and isolation. "I need to be alone," he wrote to Konstantin Shilovsky, "in order to look from a distance at my situation and decide finally whether I have acted rightly or wrongly. . . . I am trying to avoid, as far as possible, any encounters; until I become accustomed to married life, I do not wish to see anyone.

Nikolay Lvovich [Bochechkarov], however, does visit me. At heart he seems to be against my marriage, but he tries not to show it."[37] Tchaikovsky also continued to see a great deal of Kotek, who, as Tchaikovsky later told Mrs. von Meck, was the only person to know at this time the whole story of his misery: "I cannot tell you how much brotherly compassion he has shown me!"[38] Before departing for Kamenka in late July, the composer even left some of the money he had received from Mrs. von Meck with his publisher Pyotr Jurgenson to be sent to Kotek if he should need it, asking Jurgenson to keep the matter "between us."[39]

But from his colleagues at the conservatory Tchaikovsky tried to keep his marriage secret for as long as possible, avoiding many of them and showing the same embarrassment he had shown when running into acquaintances in St. Petersburg. Those closest to Tchaikovsky and more or less aware of his erotic preferences were particularly taken aback as word of the marriage finally got out. "The news was so unexpected and strange that at first I simply did not believe it, for it was not unusual for the most ridiculous rumors to spread through Moscow," Nikolay Kashkin later recalled. "However, in this case one soon had to believe, and the news came to me like a blast of cold air when [Karl] Albrecht confirmed the report, he himself sadly wondering about its meaning and significance. It was not the actual fact of Pyotr Ilyich's marriage that struck me unpleasantly, since of the possibility and even desirability of such a step he . . . himself had sometimes spoken with me. . . . [But] in the secrecy with which Pyotr Ilyich had surrounded his marriage I imagined I saw something threatening." Given the close relations that existed between Tchaikovsky and his nearest conservatory friends, such secretiveness seemed to Kashkin utterly inexplicable. Kashkin noted that "our circle was seriously worried about what consequences might result from the altered living situation of our friend, recognizing, however, that everything depended on who and what Pyotr Ilyich's chosen one, to us unknown, turned out to be."[40]

On 26 July, leaving Antonina in Moscow, Tchaikovsky departed alone for Kamenka. Two days later, he sent the promised detailed account to Mrs. von Meck, who was truly becoming his "best friend." Touching on the already familiar themes of his wish to fulfill his elderly father's "fondest dream" and the fateful "chain of circumstances" leading to his decision, the astonishingly frank letter to his benefactress also articulated a far stronger resentment toward his new wife than anything previously expressed in his letters to his brothers and sister. Moreover, his resentment was here linked for the first time to the fear that his marriage might spell his doom as a composer. "As soon as the ceremony had taken place," he wrote, "as soon as I found myself alone with my wife, with the realization that now our fate was to live together inseparably, I suddenly felt that not only does she not inspire in me even simple friendly feeling, but that she is hateful to me in the fullest sense of the word. It appeared to me that I, or at least the best, even the only good, part of myself, that is, my musical talent, had perished irretrievably. My future lot rose up before me as some pitiful vegetation and the most insufferable and pedestrian comedy."

Mrs. von Meck must have felt a growing chill as she read on and saw her friend sink further and further into morbid pessimism with every line. Tchaikovsky's mental crisis was all too frighteningly clear. "My wife is guilty of nothing toward me," the letter continued, "she does not solicit the bonds of marriage. Therefore, to let her feel that I do not love her, that I look upon her as an unbearable encumbrance, would be cruel and base. What remains is to pretend. But to pretend one's entire life is the greatest of tortures. How could I even think now of my work? I fell into deep despair, the more terrible in that there was no one to support and reassure me. I began passionately, eagerly to long for death." Fortunately, violent death was hardly a question, if only because of his deep attachment to relatives and dear friends "whose love and friendship bind me indissolubly to life."

Paradoxically, it was his music that turned him finally from thoughts of death. "I have the weakness (if it can be called a weakness) of loving life, of loving my work, of loving my future successes," he wrote Mrs. von Meck. "I have not yet said everything that I can and want to say before the time arrives to step over into eternity." His words reveal the essentially conventional nature of his desire for death. Tchaikovsky never showed any suicidal predisposition. Thoughts of death come quickly and naturally to anyone deeply distressed by adverse circumstance. The mere fact that Tchaikovsky wrote of this with remarkable candor to a great admirer of his work, who held his life to be one of the most precious things on earth, shows clearly that he cannot have meant his remarks to be taken with real seriousness. They seem obviously motivated by a simple desire for sympathy and compassion. Indeed, almost in the same breath with his insistence on the attractiveness of death in his present state, Tchaikovsky flatly refuted the intentions he professed to entertain. In referring to his relatives and friends whom he loved and to his love of life and his ambition, he showed a profoundly negative attitude toward suicide. In this crucial period of his life his chief motive was not so much his own interests as the welfare and peace of mind of those dear to him. Tchaikovsky made it clear to his benefactress that in the final analysis, madness seemed to him a far likelier fate than suicide: "I do not know how I have not lost my mind."

He concluded his long account to Mrs. von Meck in deep uncertainty about what the future held, but also with a hope that his stay in Kamenka, far from Antonina, might allow him to recover his equilibrium. "I do not know what will happen next," he confessed, "but right now I feel as if I have come to my senses after a dreadful, agonizing dream, or better yet, after a long and dreadful illness. Like a man convalescing after a fever, I am still very weak, it is difficult for me to collect my thoughts, . . . but then what a sensation of sweet tranquillity, what an intoxicating sensation of freedom and solitude!"[41]

That Tchaikovsky could unburden himself so completely to someone whom he had never met and with whom he had been in correspondence for only half a year in itself speaks eloquently of his emotional state and of his trust. His strength and his self-control had been stretched to the utmost. Tchaikovsky's inborn sentimentalism led him in this and subsequent letters to overdramatize the situation somewhat, but there is no doubt that despite his emotional and hypochondriacal nature, the experiences and feelings he recorded were quite sincere in their essence. Although he could not be as frank about the intimate details of his life as he could with Anatoly or Modest, he could nonetheless allow himself in his letters to Mrs. von Meck a freer hand in poignantly describing his miseries, forgoing the restraint he often used in his letters to his relatives so as not to worry them beyond measure. As for Mrs. von Meck, despite her own worries for him, she must also have been deeply gratified by such open confidence.

Tchaikovsky's departure for Kamenka concluded the first of the two brief periods of his living together with Antonina. Certainly, in no other sense than that of spatial cohabitation could their alliance be called conjugal. Thus, it is not surprising that Tchaikovsky should have been embarrassed when a year later Mrs. von Meck, with uncharacteristic importunity, sought to inquire into the delicate matter of their marital relations. "You know better," she wrote on 2 July 1878, "the nature of the individual in question and the quality of your relations with her while you lived together. But for me one aspect of them is shrouded in mystery, and this is the very subject that people (only not I—for me this attitude . . .")" At this point the published text of her letter ends abruptly.[42] Tchaikovsky, for obvious reasons, chose not to respond.

Despite what he had experienced during July 1877, Tchaikovsky wrote to Mrs. von Meck, perhaps believing it himself, that "if my knowledge of my own constitution does not deceive me, it is very likely that once I have rested and calmed my nerves, have returned to Moscow and fallen back into my usual routine, I shall look at my wife quite differently. In essence, she has many tendencies that might eventually constitute my happiness. She loves me sincerely and desires nothing other than that I should be calm and happy. I feel very sorry for her."[43]

As events would soon show, he had every reason to feel sorry for her and to fear for himself. His effort to change his social image even as he persisted in his sexual nature could lead only to catastrophe.

CHAPTER THIRTEEN

Escape Abroad

Weeks passed and Tchaikovsky lingered in Kamenka, putting off returning to Moscow and his wife. "Ah! how little I love Antonina Ivanovna Tchaikovskaya!" he declared to Anatoly in a letter of 2 September 1877. "What profound indifference this lady instills in me! How little does the prospect of seeing her please me!"[1] Finally, with classes at the Moscow Conservatory soon to resume, he could delay his departure no longer. Traveling through Kiev, where he tarried another three days, he finally arrived back in Moscow on 11 September, the day before the start of the new term.

For a time, Tchaikovsky tried to be optimistic about his marriage at least for the long run. Antonina met him at the station, and writing to Anatoly the next day, he described her tribulations in putting their apartment in order during his absence. "She has already replaced two cooks," he noted, "one of whom she brought before the justice of the peace, she has been robbed twice, and the past two days she has stayed at home, not trusting the apartment to the cook." He then touched on his own present mood: "You, of course, wish to know what I am feeling now. Tolya, let me not speak of that! It is hard for me: that is all I shall say. But this was inevitable after the complete happiness I experienced in Kamenka. I know that I must be patient a little while longer and imperceptibly tranquillity, contentment, and, who knows, perhaps happiness will appear."[2]

Hoping against hope that time and domestic routine would get him used to his new situation, Tchaikovsky affected an exaggeratedly relaxed and cheerful air. Despite his efforts to persuade himself and others that his marriage to Antonina would result in tranquillity and contentment, his friends noticed the artificiality. Tchaikovsky was a poor liar. He "never knew how to pretend, and the more he tried, the more obvious his pretense would become." Nikolay Kashkin wrote. "Noticing his nervous excitement, we all treated him most carefully, asking nothing, and waited for him to introduce us to his wife."[3]

When Antonina was finally presented to the conservatory circle at a party in the home of the publisher Pyotr Jurgenson shortly after Tchaikovsky's return, she made a generally agreeable impression, "both by her appearance and by her modest manner." Tchaikovsky himself scarcely left his wife's side. She "seemed either shy or to be having difficulty in finding the right words, and occasionally Pyotr Ilyich during her involuntary pauses would speak for her or supplement what she had said." His persistent intervention struck Kashkin as evidence of his fear that his wife might be incapable of carrying on a normal conversation with anyone. Among other things, Tchaikovsky must have been aware that he had made not only a social but also an intellectual misalliance, and indeed, his friends tended to find Antonina "rather colorless." Nikolay Rubinstein put it more strongly, commenting a few days after the party that "she is pretty and behaves nicely, but otherwise is not especially likable: as though she weren't real but just packaged goods." For most of those attending Jurgenson's party this would be both their first and last meeting with the new Mrs. Tchaikovskaya.[4]

Antonina herself describes their stay in Moscow during the autumn of 1877 in idyllic and sentimental tones and with endless dull details of their daily life. She was obviously still passionately in love with her husband. "Surreptitiously and unnoticed by him I was always admiring him, especially during morning tea; he just breathed freshness, always so handsome with his kind eyes that I was simply entranced by him. I would sit and think to myself while looking at him: 'Thank God he is mine and no one else's! Nobody can take him away from me because he is my husband!'"[5]

Thus, the wife rejoiced even as the husband sank into ever-deeper despair, as reflected with some candor in his letters to Mrs. von Meck. In them, the theme of death again became prominent. "A deep and interminable melancholy . . . resounds in perfect unison with the state of mind in which I have found myself since my departure from Kamenka," he wrote on 12 September, "and which today is inexpressibly, unspeakably, and infinitely heavy. In the end, death is truly the greatest of blessings, and I call to it with all the powers of my soul. That you may understand what I am feeling, suffice it to say that my one thought is to find an opportunity to escape somewhere. But how and where? It is impossible, impossible, impossible!"[6] As before, it would be quite mistaken to allow oneself to be misled, credulously, by this invocation of death, an habitual emotional eloquence spontaneously and ingenuously expressed by Tchaikovsky when in low spirits, even on retrospectively trivial occasions. What is important here is his urgent desire to "escape somewhere." The tenor of the letter makes it clear that whether consciously or not, he looked to Mrs. von Meck to provide the financial means to hide himself from the world. In his incantatory "impossible, impossible, impossible," one senses some hope of hearing his benefactress reply, "But it is possible, possible, possible, my dear and beloved friend!"

In such a state of mind, Tchaikovsky received a congratulatory letter from Kondratyev. This was the last straw. He wrote to Kondratyev, pouring out all his miseries in the childlike hope that his friend would leave everything and rush at once to save him. Of course, nothing of the sort occurred. Kondratyev's reply, which Tchaikovsky received only after he had fled abroad, suggested simply prayer and reliance on God's help.

It was at this time that Tchaikovsky was supposed to have made his desperate and, after the fact, almost tragicomic attempt to catch his death of cold by wading into the freezing waters of the Moskva River. We are told that years later, Tchaikovsky, in a fit of confession, gave his own dramatic account of this episode to his friend Nikolay Kashkin.[7] Of course, Kashkin's recollections cannot be entirely taken at face value. We already have seen that his account of what Tchaikovsky allegedly told him about the events surrounding his marriage suffers from much chronological confusion and retrospective dramatization. Moreover, Kashkin's story is not supported by any other evidence, direct or indirect, and since Kashkin never belonged to the circle of Tchaikovsky's most intimate friends, a strong doubt must remain that Tchaikovsky, generally reticent with those who were not very close to him, would indulge in this sort of revelation to Kashkin.

A more realistic echo of his torment can be sensed in Tchaikovsky's somewhat ironic letter to Karl Albrecht of 25 October/6 November 1877. Explaining his eventual escape abroad to resolve his matrimonial crisis, he wrote, "But what else could I do? In any event, it is better to be absent for a year than to disappear forever. Had I stayed but one more day in Moscow I should have lost my mind or drowned myself in the foul-smelling waves of the nonetheless dear Moskva River."[8] One can, however, discern a very different note here. In the letter, he speaks of drowning himself, not of literally catching his death of cold by wading into the freezing river. The idea of committing suicide by drowning remained firmly on the level of fantasy, even at the most desperate point in his crisis. The temperamentally suicidal urge that has at times been imputed to Tchaikovsky was, in fact, confined by him to his fictional characters, as when he later made Lisa in his opera *The Queen of Spades* throw herself into the river (in contrast to Pushkin's original story, where she ends up happily married).

Still, embellished though it may be, Kashkin's account of his impulsive late-night wading into the Moskva River reveals poignantly that Tchaikovsky's emotional state was rapidly approaching a breaking point. Beneath his superficial bravado, a sense of helplessness had been growing in him steadily. Recognition of his utter sexual and psychological incompatibility with his wife forced him to admit not only that he had failed in his plan to strengthen his social and personal stability, but that, on the contrary, he had further imperiled it and that the sham of his marriage might crumble at any moment and bring grief and scandal to his family. His marital predicament had led him to true despair, yet what he desired was not death but a return to his creative work and to a stable life.

Final crisis and even escape abroad brought to an unexpected close Tchaikovsky's second and last brief period of conjugality. The several accounts of the circumstances differ significantly, but the basic facts are clear. On 24 September, just two weeks after his return to Moscow, Tchaikovsky suddenly left for St. Petersburg, having received a telegram requesting his presence there in connection with a revival of his opera *Vakula the Smith* for the coming season. Immediately upon his arrival in the capital, he suffered a complete emotional collapse. A week later, apparently on the advice of his doctors, he went abroad. Accompanied only by his brother Anatoly, he reached Berlin on 4 October, spent there little more than a day, and then left for Geneva. They rented rooms at the Villa Richelieu in the nearby town of Clarens. There Tchaikovsky began his convalescence. It was from Switzerland that he wrote to Karl Albrecht on 25 October/6 November, "It is very difficult for me to speak of everything that has happened, so allow me to avoid this sad topic of conversation. Forgive me for not being able to follow your advice to endure for a year. Remember? I could not even endure for two weeks. No one knows all that I suffered during those two weeks!"[9]

There is one startling aspect of Tchaikovsky's subsequent behavior. All his references to Antonina from this time on would be filled, openly or implicitly, with fierce and passionate hatred. Even when he understood rationally and tried to persuade himself and others that she was little, if at all, to blame, and in a fit of repentance took the whole burden of guilt on himself—even then a mixture of hatred and revulsion can be felt in virtually every word. In his eyes, Miss Milyukova (for she was clearly still a virgin) became transformed into the most vile creation of nature imaginable, the basest human being on earth. He began to call her "the reptile" in his letters to his brothers, and with maniacal persistence he would continue to call her this and this alone, as though it were in fact her name given at birth.[10] In his correspondence with Mrs. von Meck, where rules of courtesy could, for all their frankness, not be broken, the unfortunate woman was almost consistently referred to by both parties (and this in itself is remarkable) as "the certain individual." Throughout the remainder of his life, any news whatsoever concerning his wife would drive Tchaikovsky to hysterics, to say nothing of letters she sent or accidental meetings with her. A single letter signed by her could upset his emotional balance for several days.

Deep reasons surely existed to provoke such reactions. By nature, Tchaikovsky was not prone to virulent hatred directed at any individual person, though he could rail at mindless mobs. It would seem likely that his nervous collapse was the result of some calculated change in Antonina's behavior toward her husband. By the time of his return to Moscow in mid-September, she had, no doubt, decided that the probation period had lasted long enough and that it was now time to demand fulfillment of her conjugal rights. Here, of course, lay her fateful blunder, which neither then nor later did she fully comprehend. Such a stand would alone have sufficed to drive Tchaikovsky to fits of despair. Tchaikovsky's masculine pride was severely wounded. When Antonina, her patience exhausted, finally requested directly that he have sexual relations with her—a request with which he could not comply—the inevitable result was mutual hysterics and his subsequent collapse. All the strain and tension of the summer came to a head, and it became clear to Tchaikovsky that he must flee from his worst troubles at once. Albrecht's advice to wait at least a year must now have seemed useless and hopeless.

In Tchaikovsky's eyes, Antonina had betrayed and deceived him when she violated the agreement to "brotherly love" that they seemed to have reached in July. Scarcely did it enter his head that he had deceived her even earlier by the very act of marrying her while fully aware of his sexual preference and that in her eyes it was he who continued to humiliate her by refusing to have sexual relations with her. Tchaikovsky's panicky view of the situation helps to explain why even

in his first letters from abroad Antonina was characterized with unprecedented vilification. It also elucidates his violent reaction to the
timid attempts of his relatives to express the hope that eventually he
and his wife might reconcile. For instance, on 17/29 October he wrote
to Modest:

> Whatever may happen, I shall never agree to spend even a sin-
> gle day with Antonina Ivanovna! I wish her every happiness,
> which does not prevent me from hating her deeply. I would
> sooner agree to any torment you like—so long as I never see
> her again. Therefore, it is a mistake for you to dream of altering
> her and making of her a suitable helpmate for me. In the first
> place, experience has proved that for me to live together with
> a wife is madness. In the second, even if it were possible, it
> could never be with Antonina Ivanovna. I have never met a
> more unpleasant human being. You are wrong to imagine that
> she is good-natured. You are simply deluding yourself. But I am
> not going to discuss her further. She is hateful to me, hateful
> to the point of insanity.[11]

These first letters from Switzerland present a pitiable mixture of
outrage at the "reptile," dread of the present and the future, and, understandably, excruciating self-flagellation. "How am I to have done
with Antonina Ivanovna?" he had openly asked Modest on 5/17 October. "How shall I venture to settle myself afterward? All this is
murky. I know only this: it is unthinkable for me to return to Russia
either now or in a few weeks. I must hide for a year."[12] A few days later,
on 9/12 October, he wrote, "Ah, what a fool I have been, and how much
harm I have done to myself! There is not even anyone at all on whom
to dump my misfortune; I alone am to blame for everything."[13] And in
the letter of 17/29 October just quoted: "I have become haunted by the
thought that everyone must despise and hate me. Contempt I deserve,
because only a perfect fool, a milksop, a madman, could commit such
a folly as I have done."[14]

The whole affair presented not only Tchaikovsky but also his
brothers and friends with much trouble in the telling of it. The full and
embarrassing truth of his matrimonial disaster had to be obscured to
avoid any scandal, and his flight abroad had to be justified. From Kashkin's recollections we learn two versions of what occurred. In his own
voice the memoirist writes, "In late September [Tchaikovsky] came to
the conservatory at the start of morning classes with such a painfully
tortured look on his face that even now I remember it clearly. Some-

how managing not to look at me, he held out to me a telegram and said that he needed to leave. The telegram was signed by [Eduard] Nápravník and requested his immediate presence in Petersburg. He told Nikolay Rubinstein that he was leaving by the mail train and did not know when he would be able to return."[15] But according to Kashkin's record of Tchaikovsky's own account of events, it was the composer himself who engineered the telegram from St. Petersburg. Realizing that he could not go on as he had, he wrote to Anatoly to telegraph him in Nápravník's name that he was urgently needed in St. Petersburg, and Anatoly did so at once. Of his stay in St. Petersburg, Tchaikovsky offered Kashkin only vague information and avoided any detail. He recalled "very little, and that by chance"—nervous fits, his physician Balinsky, his father and brothers.[16]

It would seem that the significance and magnitude of Tchaikovsky's nervous crisis was deliberately overplayed, first by Tchaikovsky himself and later by his brothers. A devastating psychological collapse, with hints as well of physiological repercussions, was put forth to replace in his biography what was hardly more than a protracted fit of hysteria. Modest, in recounting the departure from Moscow in his biography of his brother, wrote that around 20 September, Tchaikovsky "fell ill" and that when he left Moscow on 24 September "on the pretext" of the urgent summons from St. Petersburg, he was in a state bordering on madness. Nearly unrecognizable to Anatoly when he met him at the Nikolaevsky station, so much had his appearance changed in those few weeks, Tchaikovsky was no sooner brought to the nearby Dagmara Hotel than he suffered a "severe nervous attack" and fell into unconsciousness, allegedly remaining thus for "about two weeks." Once the danger had passed, Modest tells us, the doctors categorically prescribed a complete change of both surroundings and way of life as requisite not only for his recovery but for the very saving of his life.[17]

This account, clearly intended to be canonical, bears the imprint of Modest's brotherly bias. For him it was important to bring his narrative to a dramatic climax at this point by emphasizing the mortal danger in which his brother had been put by his nervous collapse and thus to obscure the actual state of affairs as well as to justify Tchaikovsky's escape from his wife. Obviously, it is difficult, indeed almost impossible, to imagine that even someone in a state of extreme psychic disorder might remain comatose for "about two weeks" following a nervous breakdown. Even if one allows (as an erratum for the biographical volume suggests) a misprint in the text to have substituted "weeks" for "days," the alleged period of unconsciousness is still inadmissibly long. What is more, there is something odd, if not downright suspicious, in the attitude of the reputable psychiatrist Ivan Balinsky, about which Kashkin himself expresses, albeit obliquely, some distrust. "I do not know in what manner Balinsky acquainted himself with the general state and living conditions of his patient," Kashkin writes, "but from the very outset he not only recognized the impossibility of [Tchaikovsky's] living together with his wife but emphatically insisted on the necessity of the couple's complete separation forever, and even on banning them from ever seeing each other in the future. Probably the patient in his delirium said something that led him to such a conclusion, because neither the brothers nor the father could have told him anything, as they themselves knew nothing."[18] Interestingly, too, the doctor prescribed for his patient's recovery an immediate departure abroad—just the escape for which Tchaikovsky had long been yearning.

While still in St. Petersburg, Tchaikovsky was quickly recovering. "I am finally coming to my senses and returning to life," he wrote as early as 1 October to Modest, who was then staying with his pupil Kolya at the Konradis' estate at Grankino in the Ukraine. "In those moments, the terrible moments I went through, I was supported by the thought of you and Tolya. . . . You two were the straw that I clutched at, and a straw in the shape of Tolya brought me to shore. I shall not elaborate much for now; I am still not calm enough to write a whole letter. I am very, very sorry that I cannot wait for you here. But I have no strength to wait anymore. I must leave as soon as possible and look round and think things through at a distance."[19]

Some idea of the complicated maneuvers undertaken by his relatives and friends to suppress the matter even within the family circle is provided by Iosif Kotek's postscript to this letter written at Tchaikovsky's unusual request. According to Kotek, the truth of what had happened was being carefully concealed from the elderly Ilya, and only Tchaikovsky's stepmother, Elizaveta, knew the fully story of his collapse. The version "agreed upon by all" was that Anatoly had gone to Moscow in order to travel abroad in company with both Tchaikovsky and Antonina, but that at the last moment Antonina was persuaded to stay in Moscow "because Petya, after all, is not quite used to her, is somewhat inhibited by her." The departure from Moscow "took place ostensibly in your presence," Kotek told Modest, adding that "everyone was happy, and all went quite well." The very fact of Tchaikovsky's presence in the capital was a closely guarded secret: "In Moscow it is being said that the couple went abroad from Petersburg, having joined each other here; in Petersburg, that this took place in Moscow."[20]

Kashkin recounts in some detail the negotiations with Antonina on her husband's behalf and, in particular, Nikolay Rubinstein's role in this interview, as related to him afterward by Anatoly. On learning that the purpose of Anatoly's arrival in Moscow was to inform Antonina of the "doctor-psychiatrist's verdict" and to work out a settlement for the couple's permanent separation, Rubinstein took it upon himself to intervene, fearing that the kindhearted Anatoly might not be sufficiently firm and clear in dealing with her. He resolved to handle the more delicate part of the interview himself. Together they called on Antonina, who welcomed them warmly and ordered tea prepared. Rubinstein launched directly into the matter at hand, telling Antonina "with unbending precision and determination" of her husband's condition and the psychiatrist Balinsky's conclusion that they must separate for good. Anatoly himself later told Kashkin that while listening to the "cruel precision of expression," he went "hot and cold all over." But as Rubinstein "sternly and resolutely" brought his harangue to a close, their hostess "heard him out with surprising calm, said that for the sake of 'Petya' she agreed to everything, and offered her guests the tea that had been brought in the meantime." Rubinstein, his mission accomplished, withdrew shortly thereafter to leave the in-laws to discuss family matters. Seeing him to the door, Antonina returned to the room "with a radiant face, saying to Anatoly, 'Well, I never expected that Rubinstein would be drinking tea at my home today!' "[21]

Her words astounded Anatoly. Far from showing distress at the news of her beloved husband's condition or at the prospect that they must forever part, Antonina seemed impressed solely by the fact that the great Rubinstein had come to call on her. Kashkin's "likely" explanation, discovered "many years later," was of course the idea that even at this time Antonina was not psychologically healthy. This theory conformed neatly to the "official" view, inspired by Modest, that the already oversensitive composer had fallen victim to a woman of unbalanced mind. But that is an unnecessary inference. Antonina's behavior is quite simply explained by her inability to grasp at the moment the full meaning of what she had been told, much less to digest it and venture anything more than a conventional and respectful response.

Despite indications that she eventually comprehended, at least in part, that there was something unusual in her husband's sexual habits, it seems likely that Antonina never fully recognized that it was his sexual orientation that in fact had led to the demise of their marriage. To the end of her days, she appears to have been convinced that she was the victim of some sort of intrigue on the part of Tchaikovsky's friends and relatives. Her own account of what in her opinion caused their separation is truly pathetic. She describes their last day together: "One day, he told me he needed to go away on business for three days. I accompanied him to the mail train; his eyes were wandering, he was nervous, but I was so far in my thoughts from any trouble already hanging over my head. Before the first bell he had a spasm in his throat and went alone with jerky irregular steps to the station to drink some water. Then we entered the car; he looked at me plaintively, without lowering his eyes. . . . He never came back to me."[22] That she actually insists on having accompanied Tchaikovsky to the Moscow station and having stayed with him until the very last moment is particularly interesting in light of her own attempt to explain the mystery of their failure as man and wife. "We were separated by constant whispering to Pyotr Ilyich that family life would kill his talent. At first, he paid no attention to this talk, but then he began somewhat to listen to it more and more attentively. . . . To lose his talent was for him the most dreadful thing of all. He began to believe their slanders and became dull and gloomy."[23] Thus, Tchaikovsky's collapse, according to Antonina, was caused by his heart being torn between her and his music.

Perhaps Tchaikovsky's most difficult task in the wake of his flight from his wife was to present the whole matter in the best light to Mrs. von Meck. His relations with Mrs. von Meck at this time required particular tact, the more so as he evidently expected that she would help him financially some way or other. He had to be circumspect in what he wrote to her, in order to avoid any indication of the real source of all the trouble, that is, his homosexuality. Not surprisingly, then, his earliest account to her, written on 11/23 October from Switzerland, was deliberately cursory and rather confused. Yet, despite his omissions and distortions, Tchaikovsky made little attempt to conceal the violent emotions he felt toward Antonina:

> I spent two weeks in Moscow with my wife. These two weeks were a series of unbearable moral torments. I felt at once that I could not love my wife, and that habit, on the force of which I had placed my hope, would never come. I fell into despair. I looked for death; this seemed to me the only way out. I began to be overcome by moments of madness, during which my soul was filled with such fierce hatred of my unfortunate wife that I wanted to strangle her. My work both at the conservatory and at home became impossible. I was at my wit's end. And all the while, I could blame no one but myself. My wife, whatever she may be, is not to be blamed for my having encouraged her, or for my having driven the situation to the point where marriage

became necessary. The blame for everything lies on my lack of character, my weakness, impracticality, childishness! At this point, I received a telegram from my brother that I was needed in Petersburg on account of the revival of *Vakula*. Beside myself at the joy of leaving, even for one day, the whirlpool of lies, falsity, and pretense into which I had fallen, I went to Petersburg. On seeing my brother, everything I had concealed in the depths of my heart during two endless weeks came to the surface. Something terrible happened to me that I do not remember. When I began to come to my senses, I learned that my brother had managed to go to Moscow, negotiate with my wife and Rubinstein, and arrange it so that he would take me abroad while my wife left for Odessa, but that no one would know of the latter. In order to avoid any scandal or gossip, my brother agreed with Rubinstein to spread the rumor that I was sick and was going abroad and that my wife was to follow me.[24]

But Tchaikovsky realized that a more satisfactory explanation was in order. This he sought to provide two weeks later. In this letter, written on 25 October/6 November, Tchaikovsky gave the lengthiest of his known descriptions of his wife, in an effort to persuade Mrs. von Meck—and perhaps himself—that the sole reason for their rupture had been psychological incompatibility and nothing more. The trial of painting a suitable portrait of Antonina was delicate, for he had to make it thoroughly negative and at the same time, being a proper gentleman, proclaim her innocence.

Several passages in this lengthy letter stand out. Tchaikovsky began by describing, not without a hint of sarcasm, Antonina's physical appearance: "Neither in the expression of her face nor in her movements is there that elusive charm which is a reflection of inner spiritual beauty and which cannot be acquired: it comes from nature. The desire to be liked is constantly, always, visible in my wife; this artificiality does her much harm. Nevertheless, she belongs to the category of pretty women, that is, those on whom men, when meeting them, direct their attention." Proceeding to an exploration of her "moral and intellectual side," Tchaikovsky confessed that here he was faced with "an insurmountable difficulty." "In her head as well as in her heart there is an absolute vacuum," he bluntly wrote. "Therefore, I am unable to characterize either the one or the other. I can only assure you in all honesty that not a single time in my presence did she express a single thought or a single heartfelt impulse. She was affectionate toward me, that is true. But it was a special sort of affection, consisting of perpetual embraces, perpetual caresses, even at those moments when I was unable to hide from her my probably unmerited antipathy, which was growing with every passing hour." It is not difficult to recognize the sexual subtext in this "affection" displayed by the young woman. "Not once did she reveal the slightest desire to learn what I did, what my work consisted of, what plans I had, what I read, what I love in the intellectual and artistic sphere," Tchaikovsky continued. Then he added, "Incidentally, the following circumstance surprised me most of all. She told me that she had been in love with me for four years; at the same time, she is quite a decent musician. Just imagine, that despite these two conditions, she did not know a single note of my compositions. . . . This fact utterly baffled me."

How, too, this must have shocked Mrs. von Meck, rapturously infatuated with his music above all, and must have dispelled any possible doubts that Antonina was indeed a gross marital mismatch. "You will ask, of course: but how did we spend the time when she and I were alone together? She is very talkative, but all her talk comes down to the following two subjects. Hourly she would repeat to me innumerable stories about innumerable men who had felt tender feelings toward her. For the most part, these were generals, nephews of prominent bankers, well-known artists, even members of the imperial family." It is questionable whether this last was a statement of truth or simply a rhetorical exaggeration for his benefactress's benefit. "Next, she would no less frequently, and with a sort of inexplicable passion, describe to me the vices, the cruel and base actions and detestable behavior of all her relatives, with every one of whom, it turned out, she is in enmity. Her mother would especially catch it in this. . . . The third topic of her tireless chatter was her stories of her life at boarding school. There was no end to them."

Tchaikovsky then offered a shrewd and quite genuine illustration of what to him appeared Antonina's insensitivity. "Desiring to know what maternal instincts she had, I asked her once whether she liked children. I received in reply: 'Yes, when they are clever.'" This, along with the description of Antonina's vilifications of her family and of her mother in particular, was, in its effect, a subtle and perhaps calculated appeal to Mrs. von Meck, the mother of eleven children and a fanatical proponent of the family as the sole justification of marriage. At the same time, Tchaikovsky implied that the idea of having children, a posterity, was not alien to him, but that his wife's incredible stupidity prevented any such realization. "She accepted my flight and the news of my illness, brought to her by my brother, with thoroughly incomprehensible indifference and immediately, then and there, recounted to him several stories of men who had been in love with her, then asked him what he liked to eat and ran off to the kitchen to fuss over dinner."

Having proceeded thus far with his invective, Tchaikovsky came up with the qualifications that were required by any code of gentlemanly conduct. "Justice demands that I add the following: she strove to please me in every way, she simply fawned on me; not once did she question any of my wishes, any of my thoughts, even if they touched on our everyday domestic life. She genuinely wished to inspire love in me and lavished endearments on me to the point of excess." This was followed by an abortive attempt to understand and explain his own actions. "Reading all this, you are surely wondering how I could have resolved to join my life to such a strange companion? Even I now find it incomprehensible. Some kind of madness came over me. I fancied that I might inevitably be moved by her love for me, in which I then believed, and that I might inevitably, in my turn, fall in love with her. Now I have formed an overwhelming inner conviction: she never loved me at all."

Much in this discourse depended on the ambiguity of the word "love." His logic seemed to be that had Antonina really loved him, she would have left him in peace and respected the conditions of brotherly affection on which he had consented to marry her. However unremarkable his wife's abilities, such an attitude was ultimately indefensible, and Tchaikovsky knew this. At least in his letter to Mrs. von Meck, he made an effort to do Antonina justice. "But one must be fair," he wrote. "She behaved honestly and sincerely. She mistook her desire to marry me for love." He did not add that this was in fact what himself had mistaken.

But the more Antonina fussed at trying to bind him to her, he told Mrs. von Meck, the more she alienated him from her. "In vain I have struggled against my feeling of antipathy toward her, which, in essence, she does not deserve; but what am I to do with my intractable heart! This antipathy would grow not daily, not hourly, but by the minute, and little by little turned into such a formidable, ferocious hatred as I have never before experienced or expected of myself. In the end, I was no longer able to control myself."[25]

Tchaikovsky then went on to mention to Mrs. von Meck a letter from Antonina just then received by his brother Anatoly. From what he also told Modest of this letter, it appears that his wife alluded to his homosexuality, though it is unclear to what extent she could have understood what this meant. Rephrasing her allegations, Tchaikovsky wrote to Modest, "I am in fact a deceiver who married her in order to disguise myself, I insulted her daily, she suffered much from me, she is horrified by my shameful vice, etc., etc. What vileness—but the devil take her!"[26] Tchaikovsky appears to have been disgusted by her rather than fearful for himself, even though her talk of "disguise" and "shameful vice" may possibly have been intended as a first hint of blackmail. Her several later attempts to blackmail him, uncomprehending and unsuccessful though they may have been, would cause him far more anxiety and psychological havoc.

As a matter of course, in speaking of this same letter to Mrs. von Meck, Tchaikovsky skirted any scandalous sexual reference:

> In it [Antonina's letter] she presents herself in an entirely new light. From a gentle dove she had suddenly become a quite angry, very demanding, very false person. She makes numerous reproaches against me to the effect that I shamelessly deceived her. I answered her. I explained to her flatly that I did not intend to enter into any arguments with her, as this would lead nowhere. Any blame I took on myself. I begged her earnestly to forgive me any harm I might nonetheless have inflicted on her, and I bowed my head in advance before any decision she might make. But I would never live with her; all this I announced to her in the most declarative manner. Hereafter, of course, I took on myself every concern for her needs and asked her to accept from me the means to live. I shall await her reply. At present, I have already provided for her for some time. . . . Looking back at our brief cohabitation, I come to the conclusion that *le beau rôle* belongs wholly to her and not to me. I cannot but repeat that she acted honestly, sincerely, and consistently. With her love she deceived not me but herself. She was, it seems, convinced that she did indeed love me. Whereas I, though explaining to her quite precisely that I felt no love for her, still promised to do everything possible to come to love her. And since I achieved completely the opposite, I have therefore deceived her. In any event, she deserves compassion. Judging by yesterday's letter, it is clear that an offended pride has awakened in her and begun to speak in loud tones.[27]

On the surface it might seem that in this final passage Tchaikovsky had at last reached the point of being able to recognize the measure of his own blame in all that was taking place. This impression, however, may be deceptive, by reason of the very formulation in the letter. The question was not his having deceived a woman by marrying her while fully aware of his own sexual tastes. Of this he could not of course write to Mrs. von Meck. His confession that he deceived Antonina because he had promised to love her but came to hate her was in fact no confession at all, but rather a self-justification. Justifying his actions both to Mrs. von Meck and to himself was indeed the aim of the whole letter. When Mrs. von Meck read the letter, it must have been clear to her that its author could not be accused of any wrongdoing. The portrayal here of the "certain individual" was so willfully devastating that even when Tchaikovsky was recognizing Antonina's virtues, he was in fact professing his own generosity.

As for his protestations of his wife's innocence, honesty, and sincerity, his letters to his brothers reveal his true, and quite opposite, opinion: the "reptile," as he continued to call her, was the meanest representative of the female sex in the world. In his letters to his sister he was, for understandable reasons, forced to refrain from writing of her in this vein and tended to express himself with exaggerated mildness. Mrs. von Meck, in this respect, occupied an intermediary position between enforced restraint and the full venting of his true feelings in his correspondence with his brothers. "When I imagine that you may be traveling with Antonina Ivanovna," he wrote to Anatoly on 5/17 December, after his brother's return to Russia, "the blood runs cold in my veins with horror! What can be more dreadful than to behold with one's own eyes this loathsome creation of nature! And why are such reptiles born! And why has this madness fallen on me, why has this whole vulgar tragicomedy occurred!"[28] Two months later, also to Anatoly, he raged that "one cannot trifle with this spawn of hell, generous feelings toward her are wasted,"[29] and in a letter the following day he wrote that "this creature is too contemptible to deal with politely."[30] Similar verbal abuse would continue throughout the course of the next thirteen years with inflexible and undiminished persistency.

But the conflict between the motive of marrying for the sake of his relatives and that of marrying to put order in his life and to mask his homosexual activities had to have left in Tchaikovsky a deep sense of guilt, despite his reluctance to confess all of this even to himself, save in moments of extreme depression. This guilt became the basis of an obsession equally grotesque and tragicomic. The arrival of one of her periodic letters was inevitably "a great misfortune," which would leave him for days afterward "literally unable to take pen to hand."[31] Any news of her, even the most innocuous, would cause him to lose sleep, his ability to work, and his appetite; to suffer diarrhea and hemorroids; to expect death; to write his will; and to endure every other discomfort. Two things, therefore, may define Tchaikovsky's hysteria: a sense of continuing guilt and a constant apprehension, not always conscious,

that his wife might fully recognize and broadcast his sexual preferences.

As early as his first letter to Mrs. von Meck from abroad, written
on 11/23 October, Tchaikovsky had plucked up his courage and asked
her for renewed assistance. Again he needed money, and again he could
turn to no one but her:

> It is terrible, it is painfully, tearfully difficult, but I must bring
> myself to do it, must resort to your inexhaustible kindness. Is
> it not strange that life brought me together with you just at the
> time when I, having committed a long string of lunacies, must
> for a third time turn to you with a request for help! . . . I feel
> that all must now despise me for my faintheartedness, weak-
> ness, and stupidity. I am mortally afraid that you, too, may ex-
> perience fleetingly a feeling close to contempt. But this is the
> result of morbid suspiciousness. In essence, I know that you
> will understand instinctively that I am a wretched but not a
> bad person. O my dear beloved friend! Amid my torments in
> Moscow, when it seemed to me that but for death there was
> no escape, when I had given myself up entirely to hopeless de-
> spair, the thought sometimes flashed through me that you
> might save me. When my brother, seeing that I had to be taken
> somewhere far away, took me abroad, I again thought that
> without your help I could not manage and that you would
> again appear as my deliverer from life's afflictions. And now, as
> I write this letter and am tormented by pangs of conscience
> toward you, still I feel that you are my true friend who can read
> my soul, despite the fact that we know each other only through
> our letters.[32]

When Tchaikovsky wrote these lines, he did not know that in a letter
of 29 September that had been sent to Moscow and that he had therefore not yet received, Mrs. von Meck, apparently worried by his prolonged silence and interpreting it as the result of financial problems,
had already offered whatever material assistance he might need.

"I am near the end of my life, and at any rate my life brings nothing
to the world, but you, my dear friend, you must be cared for," she
wrote. "You need, if not happiness, then at least tranquillity and
health. If all you need are certain material means in order to go somewhere to rest some more, do tell me so. For surely you know, Pyotr
Ilyich, what a loving friend you have in me and understand that I care
about you for my own sake. In you I cherish my best beliefs, convic-

tions, sympathies; your existence brings me infinite good. . . . I cherish you for the art that I worship, . . . for among its servants there is no one so captivating, so dear and precious as you, my kind friend." Consequently, her taking care of him, she told him, was "purely egoistic, and . . . I shall be grateful to you if you accept it from me."[33] Such an outpouring of love and devotion from this "instrument of Providence" was a balm to the tired and tormented man. "Your letter today eased my soul," Tchaikovsky wrote in his reply of 20 October/1 November. "I stood on the edge of an abyss. If I did not fall into it, I shall not hide from you that it is only because I trusted in you. To your friendship I shall owe my salvation."[34]

Mrs. von Meck, meanwhile, had responded to his initial request for financial assistance with her usual tact, bringing the matter up, as if in passing, halfway through her next letter. "My dear Pyotr Ilyich," she remonstrated, "why do you distress and hurt me thus by worrying so much about material matters? . . . By worrying this way, you mar for me the happiness of looking after you and seem to suggest that I am not someone close to you. Why do you do this? It pains me."[35] With this letter, apparently, was enclosed a note, the text of which has not survived, informing Tchaikovsky that he would henceforth be receiving a monthly subsidy. "Suddenly I have become, if not a rich man, then at least fully provided for over a long time," he wrote excitedly to Modest on 27 October/8 November. "An individual known to you has sent me three thousand francs and hereafter will be sending a thousand and a half monthly. All this has been offered with such wonderful delicacy, with such kindness, that I do not even feel particularly ashamed. My God, how kind, generous, and tactful is this woman! And at the same time how amazingly intelligent, because while rendering me such immeasurable service, she does it in such a way that never for a minute do I doubt that she does it with pleasure."[36]

The tone of his grateful letter to his "beloved friend" written the day before was thus predictable. "There are feelings for which there are no words," he wrote, "and if I were to try to find expressions capable of depicting what you inspire in me, I fear the result would be hollow phrases. But you read my heart, do you not? Let me say only this: until meeting you, I never knew that there might exist anyone with so unfathomably tender and sublime a soul. I am equally amazed both by what you do for me and by how you do it." He avowed that her letter contained so much warmth, so much friendship, that this alone was enough to make him love life again and endure steadfastly life's adversities. "I thank you for all this, my priceless friend!" he declared. "Every note that henceforth flows from my pen will be dedicated to you! To you I shall owe the love of labor returning to me with redoubled force, and never, not for a single second, shall I ever forget while working that you have given me the opportunity to carry on with my artistic vocation."[37]

It was perhaps inevitable that Mrs. von Meck would show unconditional approval of Tchaikovsky's conduct in the aftermath of his marriage, including what he considered the most shameful of his actions, his flight abroad. His marriage had disconcerted her and probably caused her great pain. She had already begun to feel strongly protective and even jealous of her "beloved friend," and she might easily have been pleased by the rupture with Antonina. What is more, with Tchaikovsky now deeply troubled, Mrs. von Meck found herself gratifyingly placed to succor him. "I am . . . glad that you have made that decisive step, which was necessary and which is the only right one in this situation," she wrote him. "Earlier I did not allow myself to express to you my true opinion, as it might have appeared to be advice, but now I believe I have the right, as someone close to you in my heart, to tell you my view of the accomplished fact, and let me say again that I rejoice that you have broken free from a position of pretense and deceit—a position uncharacteristic and unworthy of you." He need have no fear that her "inner attitude" toward him had changed. "My God, Pyotr Ilyich," she asked, "how can you think even for a minute that I would despise you when not only do I understand everything that happens to you but also feel, together with you, just as you do and should have acted as you have done, except that I would probably have taken earlier that step of separation which you have now taken, because I do not possess so great a quality of self-sacrifice as you have shown."[38]

Very soon Mrs. von Meck came to discuss Antonina's character with almost presumptuous confidence, as if she had known her for years. "It pains me greatly, Pyotr Ilyich" she wrote on 12 November, "that you accuse yourself so and worry yourself with compassion for your wife. . . . She is one of those happy natures, fully developed moreover by an appropriate upbringing, who cannot grieve strongly and lastingly because they are unable to feel anything deeply; they live an objective, even purely material, life, and you have undertaken to provide for this; consequently, the ideal of life for such natures—to eat well and to sleep even better—is being fulfilled by you for your wife, and you are entitled to naught but gratitude from her."[39]

Ultimately her consolation would, as it were, poetically expand the personal drama of Tchaikovsky's marital episode into the commonly accepted conflict between the gifted individual and an unresponsive society. Where she had painted Antonina as a shallow and unwittingly destructive force, Mrs. von Meck could well portray herself as offering the composer the spiritual companionship that befitted his art:

> How are those who are capable of feeling as deeply as you and I to be happy: for if life is called an ocean, then society, in any case, is a shallow stream in which only those who skim the surface come off well, but their name is legion! Yet, you and I, with our inability to treat anything whatsoever superficially, to amuse ourselves with trifles such as proprieties, public opinion, and programmed emotions—we, with our need for profound emotions, broad interests, must beat our breasts, our heads, and our hearts against the stony bottom of that stream and, grown weak in the unequal struggle of an entire life, must die without achieving that happiness which you know exists, which you see clearly before you, but which the shallow swimmers will not allow you to reach. They are not to blame, these flat-bottomed vessels, because they are fine as they are, but still how difficult it is for those who row deeply![40]

Such effusions, so like the reflections of a Chekhov character weary of present reality and eager to achieve a realm of pure spirit, were consonant with Tchaikovsky's own romanticized view of art and human relations. Certainly, his fears that his treatment of Antonina might harm his relationship with Mrs. von Meck, who, he was sure, might well have condemned him for weakness of character and pusillanimity, had proven quite groundless. The lady had no wish to acknowledge any shortcoming in her idol, and in fact, she transformed what he saw as his failings into virtues and thereby confirmed her own feelings. In her heart of hearts, she seems to have been content that his marriage had collapsed. Her sarcastic comments on Antonina betray her unexpressed joy. Offering Tchaikovsky a pure love in a realm of the spirit, she likely thought herself his only true match.

CHAPTER FOURTEEN

Consequences

Tchaikovsky's flight from Russia left a trail of complication and confusion in both family and society circles. Disoriented by what had happened and with no clear idea of the cause of it, his sister, Aleksandra, decided to play mediator and conciliator. She went straight off to Odessa to see Antonina and then invited her to stay at Kamenka with her and her family. Once there, according to Tchaikovsky in a letter to Mrs. von Meck of 23 November/5 December, she undertook with "incredible enthusiasm" to "reeducate" her, as he put it, all the while pestering him with letters in which she argued that Antonina in fact possessed many fine qualities and would in time make an excellent wife.

Tchaikovsky answered these letters as mildly as he could, acknowledging that the guilt was his, but asking his sister, "for the sake of God himself, never to mention the possibility of future cohabitation." His wife's name alone, he wrote, was enough to drive him mad. "The result of all this has been several letters from my wife. . . . In them, she was now lying and malicious, now humble and loving; she would accuse me of baseness and dishonesty, then beg and beseech me outright to return my love to her." As a consequence of Aleksandra's actions, he continued, "my wife, who on the way to Odessa had written to my brother [Anatoly] that she was having a gay time and that a colonel had fallen in love with her, has now, encouraged by my sister's affections, assumed the role of the unfortunate victim. And the main thing is that despite the fact that I have arranged for her financial security, she has no intention of leaving my sister, saying she has become attached to her and cannot live without her. . . . Of course, this cannot go on for long."[1]

Correspondence with his relatives at Kamenka while Antonina continued to live there inevitably caused Tchaikovsky much suffering. Every line of these letters is fraught with psychological tension. Writing to Mrs. von Meck, he formulated the essence of the predicament: "A most false situation has arisen.·The same woman who, unintentionally of course, has done me so much harm is living with my own sister in the home that I am accustomed to regard as a refuge from all troubles and my own warmest corner."[2] Especially painful must have been the fact that in these letters to his sister and her family he could not be as candid as in his letters to his brothers, could not let loose his anger and hatred, but on the contrary had to suppress and conceal his feelings as much as possible.

Still, he remained adamant that there was no hope of his ever returning to his wife. "For God's sake, let us abandon forever the question of our reconciliation," he wrote to Aleksandra on 26 October/7 November. "She and I are not at odds. She never intended to do me harm, and I do not blame her for anything. Even if you are right that she has a kind heart, even if I am entirely to blame that I could not appreciate her, even if it is true that she loves me, still I cannot, cannot, cannot live with her." This might very well be a sickness, he confessed, but it was an incurable sickness. "In a word," he insisted, "I do not love her in the full sense of the expression. Kindly inform her that I beseech her never again to enter into any explanations whatsoever with either myself or our brothers. . . . But above all, I beseech you on my knees— send her away from Kamenka. Do this for the sake of all that is holy in the world; it is essential for your peace of mind and mine."[3] In another letter, with barely concealed sarcasm and resentment, he wrote, "Allow me, my angel, to thank you with all my heart for everything that you are doing for me. I am not at all angry that you defend Antonina Ivanovna. I feel no malice toward her. Yet, I beg you, when you grieve over her sufferings, to recall that forty thousand of her moral sufferings would not compare with all that I have experienced this whole time!! . . . If I have unintentionally inflicted harm on her, then she has just as unintentionally inflicted a million times more harm on me."[4]

Inevitably, as he wrote to his sister of his present condition and future intentions, the question of divorce arose. If Antonina wished to divorce him in order to remarry, he was completely agreeable and would arrange it for her, but not now. "At the moment I cannot return to Russia. I am ill. I need to recover my strength. In my illness, that is, a powerfully shaken nervous system, there is nothing serious. But in my present condition I cannot deal with the fuss of a divorce."[5]

He began to receive letters from Antonina herself in which she asked time and again why he had treated her so ruthlessly and what she had done to deserve this. Tchaikovsky dreaded these letters bitterly. His most poignant plea to his sister, written on 12/24 November, was evidently prompted by the receipt of yet another of these unwelcome communications. Acknowledging his guilt with an almost exasperated "I am to blame, I am to blame, I am to blame!" Tchaikovsky touched on what he considered the deepest cause of what had happened: Antonina's intrusion in his life had threatened his very creativity and his art. "Look here, Sasha!" he wrote. "I must overcome my modesty and tell you the following: . . . I am an artist who can and must bring honor to his homeland. I feel in myself great artistic power. I have not yet done even a tenth of what I can do. And I want with all my heart to do it all. Meanwhile, I am now unable to work. . . . I am ill and, I swear to you, close to insanity." This high conception of himself as an artistic champion of his nation clashed violently with the nightmare Tchaikovsky saw embodied in his wife. "I implore her to give me the opportunity to calm down and begin to work properly. . . . She has now become the most ruthless butcher of my [a cut] all the enormity of that [another cut] you wish to do to me." The cuts suggest that Tchaikovsky referred here at least obliquely to his psychosexual dilemma, but he continued to insist that Antonina cease her attempts to discover the reasons for their rupture. "I myself know why and wherefore," he wrote.[6]

In early November, Tchaikovsky and Anatoly did some traveling. They went first to Paris, but the composer was in no mood to enjoy the city, and shortly they proceeded to Florence, Rome, Venice, and finally Vienna. But Tchaikovsky could not entirely escape reminders of his Moscow life. In Rome they ran into Prince Golitsyn's lover Masalitinov, who invited the reluctant Tchaikovsky to dinner. It was not as bad as he had feared. "He asked no questions," Tchaikovsky wrote Modest afterward, "treated me to a splendid dinner, took me for a drive to the Colosseum—in short, went out of his way to please me."[7]

In Vienna the brothers met up with a far more welcome and agreeable companion—Tchaikovsky's favorite pupil, Iosif Kotek, whose sympathetic role during the composer's matrimonial tribulations had greatly increased their mutual attachment. Since it was, moreover, Kotek who had helped fan Mrs. von Meck's original interest in the composer, it was only natural that Tchaikovsky celebrated Kotek's arrival in his letter to her of 23 November/5 December. "I have had many proofs of his most sincere friendship toward me, and last year we became very close. It seems to me there is a great deal of good in him, and he has a very, very kind heart. He was the first to teach me to love you, when I did not yet dream that someday I should call you my friend."[8] By this time, however, relations between Kotek and Mrs. von Meck had markedly cooled. To his credit, Tchaikovsky strove to repair the situation. "It would be very pleasant for me to expatiate in a letter to you sometime on this kind, lovely, and talented boy," he wrote Mrs. von Meck, "but I confess that I am restrained by the fear of touching upon a subject of conversation perhaps unpleasant to you. . . . As for his attitude toward you, suffice it to say that even before I made your acquaintance, I already felt the warmest sympathy toward you as a result of everything he had told me about you."[9]

The intercession was not successful. Mrs. von Meck did not even react to this part of his letter. The cause behind Kotek's fall from grace had been his amorous adventures at the "court" of his patroness. In the composer's correspondence, we find several references to the younger man's philandering, which at times irritated even Tchaikovsky, who tended to be quite tolerant in such matters: "He has become a desperate womanizer, and nothing but this subject interests him."[10] Such a rakish way of life could never have suited Mrs. von Meck, the mother of eleven children and surrounded, as she was, by a whole crowd of young women. Kotek, for all his charm, was also prone to nervous outbursts, something that would inevitably affect his relations with Tchaikovsky. Coming to the conclusion that Mrs. von Meck's coldness toward him came from his having contracted syphilis, he would even go so far as to accuse Tchaikovsky of telling tales about him to their mutual benefactress and thus bringing about his disgrace.[11]

Despite Kotek's aggressive heterosexuality, the flippant young man was clearly at some point Tchaikovsky's lover. Yet, in many ways their relations resembled far more those of father and son—from tenderness to irritability and clash of prides. In a characteristic passage from a letter to Anatoly of 8/20 January 1878, Tchaikovsky wrote, "You know what occurs to me? By living at another's expense, I am providing a bad example for Kotek. And he very naively voiced this in one of his last letters. . . . I really do not know whether he is right in deciding to remain abroad. I shall have to send for him and talk with him at length. It is so difficult now for me to give him advice. He asks me whether he should stay in Berlin to study with [Joseph] Joachim [the great Hungarian violinist]. Even if I felt that he should not, can I tell him so?

Surely he will answer that I say this to spare him the money."¹² For all
the frustration and irritation evident in Tchaikovsky's references to
encounters with his former pupil, in the general emotional balance of
their relationship sympathy and attachment clearly prevailed. "What
a lovely, naive, sincere, tender, kind creature!" the composer rhapsodized to Modest. "He is a charming creature in every sense of the
word!"¹³

In the end, Kotek decided to stay in Berlin and enter Joachim's
school. "He has made up his mind to write Mme Meck and ask her to
send him the hundred rubles she had granted his sisters, since they do
not need it now.... Judging by certain of Nadezhda Filaretovna's
hints, ... I have reason to believe that she will reluctantly grant his
request."¹⁴ Mrs. von Meck chose, however, to ignore Kotek's request,
and so he continued to suffer from a shortage of money during his studies in Berlin.

The period of Tchaikovsky's marriage and the events following it
led to an extraordinary intimacy between Tchaikovsky and his brothers, including a strengthening of its erotic component. Anatoly had
proved crucial during the time of his brother's nervous collapse and
abroad was inseparable from him for two months until the arrival of
Tchaikovsky's servant Alyosha Sofronov. Whether or not the intimacy
between the brothers went beyond the purely fraternal during this
time, the language and tone of Tchaikovsky's letters to Anatoly after
the latter's departure resemble in every respect the lamentations of a
forlorn lover. "When we came home and your room was empty, my
heart was wrung with pain, and this heartache continued *crescendo*
until evening," he wrote in a letter sent 1/13 December 1877, on the
heels of the just-departed Anatoly. "I ... at once, as was to be expected,
suffered a powerful hysterical fit.... I lost the power to control myself.... A few lines [in a telegram] from you could have calmed me
greatly." There were no words, he wrote his brother, to describe what
he felt: "My love [for you] is a bottomless pit." So great was his longing
for Anatoly that for a moment he nearly decided to return at once to
Russia rather than stay in Europe without him. "Farewell, my joy, my
dear," he added in a postscript. "It is terrible to think that I am writing
to you and not in your presence. It will take me a long time to get used
to it."¹⁵

Thanks to Soviet commentators, we possess a fragment of Anatoly's letter to his brother dated the same day: "When the train set off, I
did all I could to suppress my emotions so as not to burst out weeping,
and everything went all right. The German sitting with me was not a

witness to my shameful womanish lacrimosity. . . . The sole concern of my life from now on will be to make possible your return to Russia. . . . You cannot even imagine how I love you."[16]

The very next day, Tchaikovsky, having returned with his servant Alyosha to Venice, wrote again to his brother. "I wish you might answer me right now, this minute," he confessed. "My soul is filled with you. You can have no idea how I long for you. . . . Ah, how wretched, sad, and awful I feel! . . . At times, I would forget, and it seemed to me that you were nearby." In despair, he had downed two bottles of cognac on his arrival the evening before, had fallen sound asleep, and then had awakened and again had drunk to excess. Venice, where everything reminded him vividly of Anatoly and their recent stay there together, had become to him suddenly loathsome. On the journey from Austria he had traveled in the same car and the same compartment in which he and Anatoly had traveled. "This only doubled my torments. In my mind I followed you step by step, and when I wept, it seemed to me that at this moment you were also weeping for me, and this made me feel worse. . . . Farewell, my darling, my dear. I kiss you a million times. What would I not give to kiss you in actual fact!"[17]

On receiving word that Modest was coming to join him along with his young charge Kolya Konradi, Tchaikovsky's longing became somewhat subdued, and yet his tenderness for Anatoly did not diminish, becoming, if anything, even more sensual and poignant. "When I came home," he wrote on 21 December 1877/2 January 1878, "I lay on the bed and lolled about right up to dinner, pondering, thinking, dreaming, longing, covering you in my mind with kisses (ah, how I love you, Tolya!)."[18] A few days later, he confided that "sometimes my soul wants simply to leap out and fly to you. When shall I see you? I assure you, there is only one joy left to me now in life—two or three people whose presence on earth gladdens me and makes me love life. Everything else is hateful to me."[19] The months passed, but his passion remained strong. "I have come to the fourth page," he wrote on 27 April, "and now but for the fact that I love you passionately, I have absolutely no idea what to write to you. . . . I kiss you, my pet. . . . I kiss your neck. I kiss your eyes. I kiss your lips."[20]

Despite such outpourings, however, Tchaikovsky, as before, had no illusions of any special giftedness in his beloved younger brother, finding in him not so much intellectual as simply human excellence. In this spirit, he would counsel him from Florence in February 1878, "Please, my dear, take heart, do not fear being compared with anyone. Reconcile yourself that there are people more intelligent and talented than you, yet be imbued with the conviction that you possess a harmony . . . and this harmony places you infinitely higher than most people."[21]

Earlier, Tchaikovsky, on account of his marriage, had been forced to dismiss his servant Mikhail. But, in spite of the strained financial situation following the wedding and before the breakup of the marriage, he could not find it in himself to part with Mikhail's younger brother, Alyosha. Indeed, to the end of the composer's life, Alyosha Sofronov would continue to be among the people dearest in the world to Tchaikovsky. Almost immediately after his flight from Russia, in his very first letter to Modest from Berlin, written on 5/17 October 1877, Tchaikovsky had asked after Alyosha. "I am very worried about Alyosha! How shall I provide for him? How am I to live without him for so long? I am terribly accustomed to him and love him terribly."[22] This same anxiety was further elaborated in subsequent letters. He longed to send for his servant. "The thought of Alyosha simply torments me," he confessed to Modest from Clarens. "I feel that I cannot live without him. . . . You cannot imagine how much I love him."[23]

The day after his arrival in Clarens, Tchaikovsky had at last written to his servant personally: "My dear Lyonya! I received your letter and cannot tell you how pleased I was. Until then, I had had no news of you and was very worried. Thank God you are well. Please, my delight, take care of yourself and do not pine." He then went on to inform him, "In any event, I am not going to live anymore with Ant[onina] Iv[anovna] (only do not tell this to anyone)."[24] This last is followed by a suspicious cut, with another, no less suspicious, at the very end of the letter just before the signature, where most likely were found a variety of endearments that were considered shocking and inappropriate by the Soviet censors.

Finally, with Anatoly unable to put off his return to Russia any longer, Alyosha was summoned, and the beloved servant joined Tchaikovsky and his brother in Vienna on 28 November/10 December, the eve of Anatoly's unavoidable departure. Once united with his servant, Tchaikovsky never ceased to sing his praises in his letters to his brothers. "Alyosha is very sweet, affectionate, obliging," he reported at one point. "I should certainly be a hundred times worse off without him."[25] The young man was delighted with Venice and did everything he could to console and cheer his master.

However much he had missed his servant and dreamed of his arrival, it is interesting to note that in Tchaikovsky's letters to Mrs. von Meck he appears to have found it necessary to justify his decision to send for Alyosha. His apologetic tone was certainly due in part to financial considerations, Alyosha having, after all, to be supported at the expense of Mrs. von Meck herself, but also, perhaps, to a certain remorse—that by indulging this selfish, even amorous desire for Alyosha's company, he was not behaving with full propriety toward his benefactress. "At times, it occurs to me that it is not entirely prudent on my part to summon a servant from Russia," he wrote her. "But, on the other hand, what am I to do if I know that I cannot endure absolute solitude? Moreover, I know that my brothers will also feel better if I am not alone. Is it not true that you too advise me to safeguard myself against unconditional solitude?"[26]

Until his actual departure for western Europe, Tchaikovsky had evidently kept Modest uninformed of the truth of his matrimonial catastrophe. The motive is understandable: his marriage had been designed to teach Modest that he could in essence repress his homosexuality by doing the same, but this had failed. With this failure, the role of confidant, temporarily transferred to Anatoly, now returned to Modest. Still, some time was needed to heal the wounds. "Do not expect from me a description of all I have endured during the past month," he had written from Berlin. "I still cannot recall without burning pain the horrors I went through. Someday I shall tell you. . . . Farewell, my dear and beloved Modest. Oh, how I love you and how difficult it is for me to live without you for so long."[27]

Modest, who had sought to dissuade his elder brother from any matrimonial venture, had now triumphed unconditionally. In his next letter Tchaikovsky declared that if only he had "a million in capital" he would "gladly give eight hundred thousand" that Modest might join them.[28] Not long afterward, acknowledging his defeat in most apologetic tones, he told his brother in a letter of 17/29 October from Clarens, "It is only painful for me to think that all of you, that is, you, Tolya, Sasha, and Lyova [Lev], are at heart angry with me for jumping into marriage without consulting any of you and then hanging on your necks. I am ashamed to be causing you so many worries. Tell me that you are not at all angry and that you forgive me. . . . In a word, assure me that you love me indeed as before; I keep feeling that everything now has changed."[29]

Of course, this fear, the result of Tchaikovsky's depressed state, was quite unfounded. The loyal and ever-admiring Modest responded at once and almost ecstatically, with a lover's enthusiasm transcending even expected boundaries. "I love you more than anything in the world, never has anyone held a greater place in my heart, no one ever will," he wrote on 23 October. Since early childhood his elder brother had been for him "the embodiment of all perfections" and would always remain so. "I live for you," Modest wrote, "yes, positively for you, because all my life I have submitted and shall submit to your influence. One word, one movement from you has also been enough for me to divine your displeasure and to make myself over entirely to your fashion. If I have not become a good-for-nothing, it is thanks *to you*. In my youth especially I did not have my own criterion to follow and always lived and shall live to please you, because now I consciously regard you as the model of a human being."[30]

This far from trivial effusion touched Tchaikovsky deeply. "When you see Tolya, ask him what an impression your wonderful letter made on me," he wrote in reply, not without some embarrassment. "I was moved to the very depths of my soul. Thank you for your love. . . . I am in dreadful need now of the love of those whom I love more than anything on earth."[31]

After this, Tchaikovsky's letters to Modest became lighter in tone, acquiring again the easy candor of their earlier correspondence, and were filled with impressions of his travels and occasional intimate gossip about mutual friends such as Golitsyn and Masalitinov. Then suddenly it struck Tchaikovsky that Kolya Konradi's father might be able to arrange for Modest and Kolya to visit him in Clarens. This idea possessed him utterly. "It would be such bliss for me that I scarcely dare dream of it!" he wrote to Modest,[32] and then in his next letter, "I would truly be resurrected in spirit!"[33] Inflamed in his turn by the plan, Modest began to exert pressure on Hermann Konradi, to whom Tchaikovsky himself, ignoring the advice of Anatoly, addressed his own personal appeal. In explaining this move to Mrs. von Meck, he claimed depression and loneliness as his primary motives. The combined petitions proved successful. "So in two or three weeks I shall have the opportunity to live with my dear brother and his pupil, whom I love terribly," the letter to Mrs. von Meck continues. "You cannot imagine how sweet, intelligent, kind, and affectionate this poor child is. His attachment to my brother is beyond all measure. To see them together is moving. I am utterly happy."[34]

In his letters to Anatoly his degree of happiness was diplomatically subdued. His sister, Aleksandra, however, was told that "out of all the children existing in the world, after your own," he loved Kolya best, and they would get along "just like a family."[35] Finally to Modest, upon receiving word of their impending arrival, he wrote, "Not knowing how to give vent to my joy, I foolishly sent a telegram to Hermann Karlovich [Konradi] in which I expressed inadequately my gratitude. . . . What a wonderful man Hermann Karlovich is!"[36]

With the passing weeks and with the support and sympathetic

company of Anatoly and Kotek, then Alyosha, and, soon now, Modest and Kolya Konradi, Tchaikovsky's nerves had steadily improved. He was even working again, despite his continued complaints about being unable to do anything, and when Modest's telegram arrived telling of their arrival, he had been "sitting engrossed" in the orchestration of his Fourth Symphony. Meanwhile, another piece of good news had arrived from Kamenka: his sister, presumably with some intervention from Anatoly, had finally decided to oust Antonina.

A relieved Tchaikovsky shared the welcome news with Mrs. von Meck in a letter written on 4/16 December. Aleksandra, he told her, had "gradually come to the conclusion that, after all, anyone crazy enough to marry my wife would have no choice but to run away from her." Seeing at first in Antonina only an insulted and abandoned woman and roundly blaming her brother for destroying the life of his innocent and loving bride, she now understood that, as Tchaikovsky put it, "there was never any love—there was only the desire to find a husband." The various qualities and virtues she had imagined in her brother's wife proved on closer acquaintance not to exist at all. What she had found instead, wrote Tchaikovsky, in the response of a complex person to a lack of complexity, was no moral shortcoming, but rather "precisely that absence of any presence, which can be worse than any positive shortcoming."[37]

The denouement of the sad comedy being played out at Kamenka came just a few weeks later. "[Anatoly] finally turned my wife out of Kamenka," Tchaikovsky reported to Mrs. von Meck on 24 December/ 5 January. "Thank God, a great burden has been lifted from my mind." Apparently, Antonina had expressed a desire to become a nurse, which had very much pleased her in-laws, who supposed that she would eventually fall in love with some doctor or patient, wish to marry, and demand a divorce. Anatoly had even begun to make some efforts in this direction, but within a few days Antonina had changed her mind, declaring that she no longer wished to be a nurse. For the moment, she was living in Moscow. "I do not know her further plans," Tchaikovsky told Mrs. von Meck, "but I pray to God that she choose another place of residence by the next academic year. It would be very awkward and touchy to run into her."[38]

Mrs. von Meck was of the opinion that Tchaikovsky ought to return to Russia as soon as possible. He, however, was very reluctant to do so, and in a letter of 23 November/5 December had offered various explanations for this, both personal and social. "To Petersburg I neither can nor wish to go, because I cannot live there without seeing my father, but for me to see him now is impossible," he wrote. Ilya Tchai-

kovsky still knew nothing about the irrevocable collapse of his son's
marriage. He had been told only that his son's nerves were upset and
that he had gone abroad for a short time with Anatoly because Antonina, owing to her own affairs, was unable to leave, although she
planned to join them at the first opportunity. Even this much had
greatly upset the old man, and Tchaikovsky feared how the real story
about the couple's separation might affect him. "He may never learn
the actual truth," he told Mrs. von Meck. "It would be difficult for me
to lie to his face, and to his inquiries about my wife and why I live
without her (he liked her very much) I should be forced, finally, to tell
the truth, but to tell him the truth is terrifying."

Also, in St. Petersburg, as in Moscow, he would have to hide from
a great many acquaintances, relatives, and friends. "It is hard, but to
hide is essential," he confessed. "I am in such a state that I cannot meet
anyone other than those closest to me without terror and unbearable
anxiety." Indeed, the very thought of St. Petersburg struck him with
melancholy and despair. Of Moscow it was useless even to speak: to
go there now would be tantamount to condemning himself to madness. "It is difficult to convey to you, dear Nadezhda Filaretovna, the
awful agonies I endured there in September. I was a hairbreadth from
ruin. The wound is still too fresh." Only the routine of his work at the
conservatory had made life in Moscow truly tolerable, and for this he
was not yet ready. "I am still sick, I cannot endure it all."[39]

As for society in both cities, Tchaikovsky's precipitate departure,
first from Moscow and then from Russia, had indeed caused a stir, not
to mention speculation and gossip. Modest, attempting to play down
the repercussions, had described the climate in St. Petersburg with
forced cheer in a letter to his brother of 9 November:

> I am so happy, so pleased to receive [your letters] so frequently,
> with such pride report to all Petersburg the very latest news
> regarding you. When I say "all Petersburg" I do not exaggerate.
> [The subject of] your illness is terribly popular here and to-
> gether with news of the [Russo-Turkish] war serves as a topic
> of conversation from the drawing room of Grand Duke Kon-
> stantin Nikolaevich to the columns in the newspapers. . . . Al-
> most all the papers have published a refutation, I don't know
> by whom, of the rumor that you had gone mad, with even Clar-
> ens mentioned as your place of residence for the winter. People
> I scarcely know stop me on the street and at theaters to ask
> about you, and any of our good acquaintances whom I see in-
> quire after your address in order to write to you. I should have

hesitated to write you of this noise caused by your illness, knowing how you dislike being talked about outside your musical
activities, if in this universal interest in you I had not found in
most cases a good deal of sympathy and great concern.[40]

Anatoly's remarks a month later, following his own return to Russia,
were more sobering: "You would, of course, find it unpleasant in Moscow right now. There are so many rumors that God have mercy! All of
them, it is true, are in your favor, but what of it? I still understand that
it would be awkward and unpleasant for you here."[41]

Clearly, the brothers, despite the pain their cautious accounts
might have caused him, were preparing Tchaikovsky for the intense
public scrutiny he would have to confront on his return home. Thanks
to their efforts and those of other well-wishers, no real scandal broke
out, and in fact, public opinion tended to take the side of the runaway
husband. Still, Tchaikovsky was tormented by suspicions of intrigues
at every step and of public scorn. He had long since resigned himself
to the fact that some people around him were well aware of his homosexuality, but being the subject of public gossip was quite another
matter. Having his personal predilections known to a limited circle
was far different from having them shouted from the rooftops, bringing
shame and worse to his family. Abroad, in the first months especially,
he was consumed by the fear that everyone around him was longing to
discover the real reason for his separation from his wife. As a result,
his neurosis took a new twist, which he himself called "monomania"
and which amounted to a drive to isolate himself almost entirely. It
was in this vein that he wrote to Nikolay Rubinstein on 9/21 November, "For God's sake, do not summon me to Moscow before next September. . . . Despite all my attachment to all of you, I should perish at
the thought that I am being talked about, pointed at, etc. In a word,
my monomania has not passed."[42]

This same monomania was referred to in Tchaikovsky's later refusal to represent the Russian musical delegation to the Paris International Exposition of 1878. The project terrified him beyond measure.
"You know the cause of my monomania," he wrote almost hysterically
to Rùbinstein, the instigator of the idea, on 1/13 January 1878. "In
Paris, in every new acquaintance, of whom I would there be presented
with a multitude, I should begin to suspect people who know that
about me which I have sought so long and carefully to conceal. This
would utterly paralyze me. But in short, I am sick, I am mad, I cannot
live anywhere where it is necessary to be prominent, to thrust oneself
forth and call attention to myself."[43]

Tchaikovsky's close friends, recognizing his painfully morbid reaction to his failed marriage, tried to bolster his spirits as best they could. To their credit, they treated him with kind and affectionate indulgence. Rubinstein was among the first to write him in Clarens. "Try to calm down," he reassured him. "Look after your health and do not be afraid of anyone or anything; you are too well and highly placed as a musician for anything extraneous to compromise you."[44]

Aleksey Apukhtin, earlier offended by his friend's inattention during his visit to St. Petersburg with his wife, wrote to him on 25 October with understanding and compassion, probably having learned of his psychological state from either Kondratyev or Meshchersky. "Thousands of men get married, find out they can't go on with their wives, and separate. Generally speaking, dearest Petya, you attribute too great a significance to various rumors and gossip," he rightly pointed out. "For you, of whose name the land in which you were born will be proud, to bow your head before various Xs and Zs—this is incomprehensible and senseless! You must admit that it would be quite ridiculous for an eagle to be embarrassed before worms and reptiles. Well, fly away from them high in the air, to your creative height, whence they not only will no longer be visible to you, but where you must ignore their existence and cast from there a new *Tempest* or *Romeo:* let the weight of your fame crush these scoundrels!"

Anticipating the objection that an artist cannot live exclusively within himself, Apukhtin reminded Tchaikovsky that among his thousands of ardent admirers he had many true friends who, as the poet noted in transparently allusive language, "do not care what sauce you prefer on your asparagus: sour, sweet, or oily." He needed to cheer up, to raise his head and look everyone in the face "proudly and boldly," Apukhtin told him. "You have done nothing dishonest. The chief error in your life has been the concession to this base thing called public opinion! Take a look at the history of art: people such as you have never known happiness, but without them mankind would be bereft of its finest pleasures."[45] Touching with this last comment on Tchaikovsky's own innermost conviction, Apukhtin had gone to the very heart of the matter—the often tragic conflict between art and what we call reality.

Mrs. von Meck, although, unlike Apukhtin, unaware of the full truth behind what had happened, tried equally to be comforting in her letter of 18 November. She also counseled the composer to heed no one's judgment but his own and to arm himself "with firmness and equanimity" against all attacks and reproaches. "Do as I do, my dear friend," she wrote. "Not one, but hundreds of people criticize, condemn, and accuse me, personally and generally, according to their own views. I am not the least bit embarrassed or worried by this, nor do I attempt by a single word or action either to justify myself or to unde-ceive others; first, because perceptions vary and, second, so as not to deprive people of their pleasures. And I have not the slightest grudge against people, because in condemning me they are right from their point of view, and the difference is that we have different points of departure."[46] Faced with this distinctive dismissal of what others might think or say, Tchaikovsky had no choice but to profess his ad-miration: "I like your proud attitude toward public opinion. When I was in my normal condition, when I was not yet broken as I am now, I assure you that my contempt for *qu'en dira-t-on* was at least as strong as yours. Now, I confess, I seem to have grown more sensitive in this regard. But I am ill, that is, morally ill."[47]

It goes without saying that the correspondents were speaking here of two different things: she, most probably, of the intrigues against her in business circles, and he, most probably, of the increasing rumors of his homosexuality after the fiasco of his marriage. The expression "morally ill" seems here to connote his general state of disillusion-ment and disappointment with himself rather than his homosexuality, which he never conceived in moral terms. Nevertheless, it is true that this period immediately following his flight abroad was the one time during his long correspondence with Mrs. von Meck when Tchaikov-sky, his customary restraint weakened by his distraught state of mind, permitted himself to allude, however obliquely, to the subject of his homosexuality. Whether Mrs. von Meck could have known enough to read these allusions between the lines of Tchaikovsky's wandering pen remains conjectural. But it seems improbable that during the many years of their friendship, she could have remained entirely ignorant of Tchaikovsky's intimate life. He had his share of ill-wishers, while she, by her own admission, would eagerly snap up the least rumor about him. Most likely, as has already been suggested, she simply dismissed the whole matter from her thought, having either reconciled herself to it on her own independence of judgment or having refused to accept whatever rumors might reach her.

Only once in all his published letters and diaries did Tchaikovsky express any worry over the possibility that Mrs. von Meck might know his sexual secret. The absence of such concerns throughout the entire remainder of their acquaintance is remarkable. Not surprisingly, this one confession of uneasiness came just at the moment Tchaikovsky was most fearful of rumors about his flight from Russia. "I had already begun to imagine that she [Mrs. von Meck] had ceased to care for me, that she had learned about *that* and wanted to break off all relations," he wrote to Anatoly on 24 December 1877/5 January 1878, when his traveling and postal delays had left him for a time without word from his benefactress. "Until this morning I was even convinced of this." But, as with his family, his fears turned out to be groundless. "Just this morning I received a letter from her, so sweet, so affectionate, and with such sincere expressions of love. A lovely person, that Filaretovna!"[48]

On 27 December/8 January, Tchaikovsky was reunited with Modest and Kolya Konradi in Milan. "I felt indescribable pleasure at seeing my brother and his dear boy," he told Mrs. von Meck. "My heart at once grew light and warm. The entire evening passed in mutual interruptions and endless, merry, pleasant chatter."[49] But their joy was to be short-lived. When the party arrived in San Remo a few days later, it was discovered that Alyosha had contracted syphilis. Tchaikovsky was beside himself. "Tears, grief, despair," he summarized for Anatoly on 5/17 January.[50] He even went so far as to share the embarrassing news with Mrs. von Meck. As it turned out, there happened to be a Russian doctor in San Remo. He assured Tchaikovsky that there was no need to send the "culprit" away for treatment as he had feared, and Alyosha was put in the local hospital. There the patient convalesced successfully, and Tchaikovsky's anger and frustration gradually dissipated. Within a few weeks the servant was well enough to return to his master's household.

With the arrival of Modest, life fell into a routine that was reflected in Tchaikovsky's correspondence, interspersed with periodic panegyrics on Kolya Konradi. "What happiness to have such a child around!" he exclaimed in one letter to Anatoly. "How pleasant to caress and cherish him!"[51] The thought of eventually having to part with the boy was all but unbearable. "I cannot imagine how I shall live without him. I am so attached to him and love him probably more than either his mother or father does. . . . His chatter has become an essential part of my life."[52] Indeed, Kolya Konradi was included among those people—Anatoly, Modest, Mrs. von Meck—to whom "I most of all owe my recovery."[53]

When he wrote to Aleksandra in the same vein, the loving sister invited all three of them to Kamenka. "The closer I am to Modest and Kolya [that is, at Kamenka]," her brother then informed her, "the better."[54]

In his exchanges with Mrs. von Meck, which included similar effusions concerning his worship of the boy, he also described at some length the relations between pupil and teacher. "One cannot watch his behavior toward my brother without weeping. It is not love, it is some passionate cult. When he has done something wrong and my brother punishes him, it is torment to look at his face, so movingly does it express repentance, love, the begging of forgiveness. . . . The first day I saw him, I felt only pity for him, and his abnormality, that is, his deafness and muteness, the unnatural sounds he makes in place of words, all this instilled in me a feeling of insurmountable alienation. But this lasted only one day."[55] In a later letter, he wrote that Kolya "does not know, has absolutely no idea, what it means to lie or deceive," adding that "his face is very attractive, and in his eyes there is much intelligence and kindness."[56]

On the whole, Tchaikovsky's attraction to boys and young men tended to possess a strong aesthetic and artistic element beyond the physical or sexual. While in Florence he became infatuated with a young street singer named Vittorio, whom he had first noticed during his visit there with Anatoly the previous autumn. "My brother and I heard one evening singing in the street and saw a crowd, into which we made our way," he had told Mrs. von Meck in December. "It turned out to be a boy of about ten or eleven singing to the accompaniment of a guitar. He sang in a wonderful rich voice with a finish and warmth such as are rarely met even in genuine artists. Most curious of all was that he was singing a song with words of a most tragic nature, which sounded uncommonly sweet on the lips of a child."[57]

Two months later, finding himself once again in Florence with Modest and Kolya, Tchaikovsky thought again of the young singer and wrote to Anatoly, "In the evening I walked along the embankment in the vain hope of hearing somewhere a familiar wonderful voice. . . . To meet and once more to hear the singing of that divine boy has become my life's goal in Florence. . . . Suddenly I see in the distance a gathering, singing, my heart began to pound, I run, and, oh! what a disappointment! Some man with a mustache was singing, also well, but can one compare?"[58] A few days later he wrote, "After dinner I gadded about in the hope of meeting [the following name or word is cut], but without success. Yet, a different joy lay in store for me. On the Lungarno I came across some street singers and asked them directly whether they knew our boy. It turned out they did, and they gave their word that he would be on the Lungarno at nine o'clock."[59] The narrative was resumed in another letter to Anatoly a few days later:

> In the evening I had in store (1) a rendezvous and (2) a meeting with the boy singer. The hope of seeing the latter was so pleasant that it overcame the former. I got rid of the amorous rendezvous not without some difficulty and gave myself up en-

tirely to anticipation of the singing of our dear boy. Precisely at nine o'clock I approached the bridge. . . . First of all I noticed that he had grown a bit and that he was handsome, whereas before it had seemed to you and me that he was plain. . . . I expressed a doubt whether it was he. "You will hear when I start to sing that I was the one. That time you gave me a silver half franc!" All this was said in a wonderful voice and penetrated to the depths of my soul. But what happened to me when he sang? It is impossible to describe. I doubt that you take greater pleasure when you listen to the singing of [Aleksandra] Panaeva [a soprano with whom Anatoly had become hopelessly infatuated]! I wept, languished, melted with delight. Besides the song you know, he sang also two new ones, one of which, "Pimpinella," is charming. . . . Since that evening I have been utterly filled with one feeling [what follows has been cut].[60]

On 20 February/4 March the young singer visited Tchaikovsky's room in carnival costume and sang again for him. "He is positively beautiful with his inexpressibly attractive gaze and smile. . . . I wrote down all his songs. His photos will be ready after our departure; I'll send you one."[61] The song "Pimpinella" is set by the composer as the last of his Six Songs, op. 38.

Tchaikovsky also shared once more his impressions of Vittorio and his singing with Mrs. von Meck. The day of Vittorio's visit to his hotel, he wrote:

He again sang for me "Perché tradirmi, perché lasciarmi." I do not recall a simple folk song ever having such an effect on me. This time he acquainted me with a new local song, so charming that I intend to find him again and have him sing it several times so as to record the words and music. . . . How I pity this child! He is clearly being exploited by his father, his uncles, and various relatives. Now, on account of the carnival, he sings from morning to night and will go on singing until his voice vanishes irretrievably. Even now, in comparison with the first time, his voice is slightly cracked. This cracked quality adds a new charm to the phenomenally appealing voice, but it is not for long. Had he been born into a prosperous family, he might perhaps have eventually become a famous artist.[62]

Even if one disregards his clear infatuation with the young singer, the censorial cuts in Tchaikovsky's letters to Anatoly from Florence and, more strikingly, his unself-conscious mention of the "amorous rendezvous" he broke off in order to meet with Vittorio indicate that even so soon after the trauma of his marriage Tchaikovsky was again well enough to engage in the often anonymous homosexual encounters that were his practice when traveling both in Russia and abroad. By the end of 1877, his emotional agitation had diminished. He was now able to take a serious look at his situation and to appraise it soberly. "I now know from experience what it means for me to break myself and go against my nature, whatever that may be," he wrote candidly to Rubinstein on 23 December/4 January.[63] In early February 1878 he could, in a letter to Anatoly, sum up quite calmly and clearly his relations with Antonina. "I have ceased to look tragically upon Antonina Ivanovna and my indissoluble ties to her. As long as she leaves me and all those I love in peace, let her enjoy her life. . . . I suppose I must pay her everything she asks, yet not unconditionally, but rather demanding from her that she no longer trouble us. So let her give an absolute pledge to keep herself as far away as possible; otherwise, she will not receive [the rest is cut]."[64] Ultimately he could even claim, "I am not afraid of her slanders—they will run their course in any case."[65]

This was a major step toward recovery. Despite his several later relapses into temporary hysteria over the subject of Antonina, never again would he deteriorate into the abysmal condition he endured in the aftermath of his marriage, throughout the winter of 1877. He still hated, of course, any sort of gossip about himself, even the most innocuous, and often suffered from it painfully. Several months later, when back in Russia, he would chance to witness incognito a conversation among several strangers in a train compartment that caused him great distress. The talk was of various squabbles and rumors of the musical world, and at length they touched on Tchaikovsky himself. The strangers spoke, however, not of his music, but of his marriage and his supposed madness. "My God! How stunned I was by what I had to hear! . . . It was an entire ocean of nonsense, lies, absurdities." But most unbearable to him was not so much what was actually said as "the fact that they concern themselves with me, point me out, that I can be the subject not only of discussions of musical criticism but of plain gossip as well."[66]

Tchaikovsky understood perfectly well that in the circles in which he moved gossip about him, including inevitable rumors about his homosexuality, would circulate under any condition. This had been a fact of his life since his graduation from the School of Jurisprudence and one he had to accept. He knew that owing to the practical absence of prosecution for homosexuality in Russia, nothing serious could actually threaten him. Antonina, moreover, seemed to him so vacuous that he could not imagine anyone paying serious attention to her charges, and he concluded that she would be incapable of doing further harm to his reputation. He was learning to be reconciled both to his sexual orientation and to his environment. "The main thing," he wrote to Jurgenson on 17/29 January, in the somewhat coarse manner of their correspondence, "is that I want to spend the summer in the country and to be in Russia, as I am fed up, finally, with wanting to seem to be other than what I am, fed up with violating my own nature, however rotten it may be. In general, I have now come to this point: if you wish, then know, love, play, sing me, decorate me with laurels, crown me with roses, praise me to the skies; and if not—to hell with it! That is, this relates to the public, fame, and other such muck."[67]

Writing to Anatoly on 6/18 February, he would look back on the last "seven weeks spent here," that is, in Florence, and his newfound peace and clarity of mind. These weeks, he concluded, had done him tremendous good. "Thanks to the regularity of life, the sometimes dull but always inviolable tranquillity, and chiefly thanks to time, which heals all wounds, I have quite recovered from my madness," he wrote. "The man who in May decided to marry Antonina Ivanovna, in June, as if nothing had happened, wrote an entire opera, in July got married, in September fled from his wife, . . . etc. was not I, but another Pyotr Ilyich, of whom there now remains only his misanthropy, which, however, will probably never disappear."[68]

It is a paradoxical fact that Tchaikovsky's tragicomic marriage and his hysterical breakdown proved to be, in the final analysis, beneficial. It released an accumulated nervous tension and stirred his creative energies. His complaints of being unable to work often seem perfunctory and rhetorical. Only a month after falling ill on 24 September 1877, he informed Mrs. von Meck that he had resumed work on his Fourth Symphony. The symphony, dedicated to "my best friend," was completed and orchestrated during November and December and sent to Russia. Mrs. von Meck herself attended the work's premiere, under Nikolay Rubinstein's direction, on 10 February 1878 in Moscow. "The audience received it very well, in particular the *Scherzo*," she wrote the composer two days later. "There was much applause, and at the end the audience was calling for you and Rubinstein must have had to come out. I did not see because I was already on my way outside."[69]

In fact, the premiere was only moderately successful. The response of Tchaikovsky's friends and colleagues was contradictory. Nikolay Rubinstein, for instance, liked the finale, while Sergey Taneev, in a letter to Tchaikovsky, wrote of it with candid skepticism. It was not until a triumphal performance in St. Petersburg on 25 November 1878, under the direction of Eduard Nápravník, that the Fourth Symphony was recognized as a masterpiece. A critic for the *Petersburg Gazette* lauded the symphony as "the pure creation of an artful master possessing an entire palette of luxuriant musical colors."[70] This praise was echoed in the enthusiastic review of Hermann Laroche, who was particularly impressed by what he said was the expansion of the work beyond the traditional frame of the symphonic form.[71]

Outstanding in its mature complexity, the Fourth Symphony testifies to Tchaikovsky's steady progress toward the peak of his powers. That very complexity, however, makes it difficult to tie the work too directly to the painful experiences Tchaikovsky had recently undergone. In its chief characteristics, the symphony had been conceived and developed before the matrimonial catastrophe, though it was orchestrated and modified in its aftermath. Still, Tchaikovsky clearly considered the work a seminal achievement, embodying his emotional and creative anguish of the previous autumn and winter.

Responding to Mrs. von Meck's letter on 17 February/1 March, Tchaikovsky attempted to formulate the "program" of the symphony, the principal theme of which was the implacability of Fate—the very idea that had become his personal obsession during the preceding year. Man, he told Mrs. von Meck, was wholly governed by this "fateful force which impedes the impulse toward the happiness of reaching one's goal, which jealously ensures that prosperity and peace are never complete and cloudless, which hangs overhead like a sword of Damocles and steadily and continually poisons the soul. It is invincible, and you will never overpower it." Yet, regarding the fourth part of the symphony, he noted, "If you do not discover in yourself the motifs of joy, look at others. Go among the people. See how they are able to make merry, to give themselves up entirely to joyous feelings. . . . Blame yourself, and do not say that everything in the world is sad. Joys there are, simple but powerful. Delight in the merriment of others. Life is still possible."[72]

The last sentence sums up not only the symphony's apparent message but also the psychological and creative lesson derived from this most difficult period of Tchaikovsky's life. In the same letter, he admitted that the Fourth Symphony "serves as a faithful echo" of the severe depression he had been experiencing that winter. But he qualified this admission immediately by noting that it was "precisely an *echo*" and nothing more. "How to translate it into clear and definite sequences of words?—I cannot, I do not know," he wrote. "Much I have already forgotten too. General recollections have remained of the passion, the awesomeness of the sensations experienced."[73] Only a year and a half later, in a letter of 25 September 1879, would he proclaim to Mrs. von Meck in retrospect that the symphony was "a *memorial* to a time when, after a long-evolving spiritual illness and after a whole series of unbearable agonies of anguish and despair that had all but driven me to utter madness and ruin, there suddenly shone a dawn of rebirth and happiness in the person of her to whom the symphony is dedicated."[74]

The "best friend" was in raptures over the musical creation dedicated to her by her beloved composer. "How delighted I was to read your description of *our* symphony, my dear, priceless Pyotr Ilyich," she wrote on 27 February. By taking his personal anguish, the pain and baseness of the world, and transforming it into something sublime, Tchaikovsky had once again fulfilled the Romantic image of the artist she held so dear. "How happy I am," she added, "to have found in you the perfect corroboration of my ideal of a composer!"[75]

Thus, Tchaikovsky survived the trauma he had inflicted on himself. There were losses, but also gains. He had been able to resume both his creative work and his sexual habits—each, in its own way, a sign of recovery. His worst fear, the threat of social scandal, had been averted. This he had dreaded more than anything, not because of any shame or remorse for his homosexuality, but because of his deep concern for his family and friends and the suffering that any open scandal might cause them. It was precisely this family, these friends, who were crucial in his rescue and recovery: his two brothers, with their devotion; his servant, with his affectionate care; his benefactress, with her material and spiritual support.

One of the deepest gains was his insight into his own psychosexuality, which released him once and for all from further torment in that regard. An element of suffering naturally accompanied him, as in any great life, to the end of his days. But it is by no means evident that his homosexuality was the basic cause of this suffering. From now on, he regarded it as natural and felt no guilt for it. Belief in the possibility of full domestic relations with a woman had provided him with the hope of soothing his relatives and establishing general harmony. His brief married life with Antonina Milyukova had convinced him of the utter fallacy of that belief. After this, any illusions as to women were gone for good.

Throughout his continuing conflict with Antonina, Tchaikovsky's letters do occasionally reveal vague apprehensions over his homosexuality. It is indicative, however, that not once did he blame his "inclinations" for the catastrophe that had occurred. On the contrary, he bitterly criticized himself for having actually fought against them and for his attempts to suppress them. There can be no doubt that after his excruciating matrimonial experience Tchaikovsky never again felt any desire to learn to love a woman and enter into any "lawful or illicit union" with one. "Only now," he wrote conclusively to Anatoly on 13/25 February from Florence, "especially after the incident of my marriage, have I finally begun to understand that there is nothing more fruitless than wanting to be other than what I am by nature."[76]

Part Four

DOUBLE FUGITIVE
1878–1879

CHAPTER FIFTEEN

Elective Affinities

Tchaikovsky's friendship with Mrs. von Meck reached its intellectual and emotional peak during the next few years. Their relationship may best be described by the term used by Goethe as the title to his famous novel *Die Wahlverwandtschaften*—"elective affinities." For the upper classes in nineteenth-century Russia, life was charged with deep cultural influences. Literature served as a source not simply of entertainment but of instruction, giving eager readers models and modes of behavior. Both Tchaikovsky and Mrs. von Meck would have known and appreciated the title of Goethe's novel, which depicts a psychological drama played out by several complex characters who interact in rich and subtle ways, both amorously and spiritually. Certainly the notion, originally scientific, of elective affinities became one of the dominant themes of their correspondence. Both strove for an ideal relationship, and both, too, must have realized that any such ideal cannot be realized in this world. It is no accident that from its idyllic beginning, Goethe's novel proceeds, despite the best intentions of its characters, through irrevocable tension and conflict and ends in tragedy.

It was, however, the simple fact that Mrs. von Meck was a woman, and not a man, that was the intractable obstacle to the fulfillment of her spiritual union with the composer. Tchaikovsky remained devoted to his benefactress only up to the point where he began to sense what he perceived, not without reason, to be her amorous intentions toward him—intentions Mrs. von Meck was reluctant to acknowledge even to herself. As soon as he sensed any such designs or any threat to his freedom, he would shrink back and turn away her generous offers and invitations. It was an attitude not dissimilar, though milder in form, to his reactions to Antonina. But, bound to Mrs. von Meck by sincere fondness and gratitude, Tchaikovsky learned to handle this potential source of embarrassment with diplomatic skill.

Only one crucial matter was consistently given as little mention as possible by both the composer and his benefactress in their correspondence: their financial arrangements. Mrs. von Meck continued to send Tchaikovsky his regular subsidy, in installments diffidently called by both parties *lettres chargées*. The irregularities of the post caused occasional misunderstandings and at times great concern to Tchaikovsky, who was extravagant in his expenses and utterly helpless in financial matters. Of the fact that money slipped through his fingers, he was well aware. Especially in the earlier stages of their arrangement, he would now and then repent in writing or awkwardly, but not without charm, attempt to justify himself to his benefactress. "Nadezhda Filaretovna, forgive me that I have wasted so much money on my trip to Italy! I know that you forgive me, but I enjoy asking your forgiveness. By doing so, I lessen, at least somewhat, the overflowing cup of my anger and rage at myself. My God, how annoying and sad this all is!"[1]

Later, he got into the habit of asking her to send money for a few months in advance in case of special expenses, and as a rule, he would thus manage to cope with his financial loose ends. He made extreme efforts never to ask for additional sums unless needed for some unforeseen purpose. But occasionally Mrs. von Meck, as if intuiting his financial troubles, would send besides the subsidy some additional money on this or that pretext. "She, as usual, writes a thousand tender things and, lastly, sends a note for fifteen hundred francs over and above the monthly subsidy for publication of the [Fourth] symphony," Tchaikovsky wrote Anatoly on 9/21 January 1878. "I must tell you that my present financial situation is far from brilliant. My money has long since been spent. . . . These fifteen hundred francs are most timely. What an unfathomable woman! She guesses when and how to write just to console me."[2]

At times, Tchaikovsky felt remorse at his "exploitation of the amazing generosity of this woman,"[3] and he even forced himself to perform what he termed "feat[s] of uncommon civic courage" by refusing any additional money she might send. His feelings, however, were not always unmixed: "Along with a most affectionate letter, I returned twenty-two hundred francs to her and now (oh, shame and disgrace!) regret it."[4]

If Tchaikovsky supposed his friend's financial support would cease after his return to Russia, he was mistaken. Rejecting his suggestions that on returning to Moscow he would be prepared to cease accepting her subsidies, Mrs. von Meck wrote unequivocally in her letter of 12 February, "I do not set any term to my solicitude about all aspects of your life. It will last as long as the feelings that unite us exist, be it abroad, in Russia, in Moscow—everywhere it will be identical and in the very same forms as now."[5] In a dignified reaction to this extraordinary show of generosity, Tchaikovsky replied on 26 February/10 March that he was "not in the least ashamed" to accept from her the means to live. "My pride does not suffer a whit from this," he claimed. "I shall never feel heavy in my heart from the awareness that I owe everything to you. With respect to you, I have none of that conventionality that lies at the base of ordinary human relations. In my mind I have set you so high above the general human level that I cannot be embarrassed by the mere niceties of ordinary human relations. In accepting from you the means for a peaceful and happy life, I feel nothing but love, the most direct, spontaneous feeling of gratitude, and a burning desire to contribute whatever I can to your happiness."[6]

Yet, despite his carefully phrased claims, he was more embarrassed than he cared to admit. "Lord, how thankful I must be to this wonderful woman," he wrote to Anatoly the next day, "and how I fear getting into the habit of beginning to look at everything she does for me as something owed to me. I shall never ever be able to prove the sincerity of my gratitude. I have already now begun to find difficulty in writing to her. In essence, all my letters to her ought to be hymns of thanksgiving, but one cannot be forever devising new phrases for expressing gratitude."[7]

That he did not always remain true to his determination not to take the situation for granted should not be regarded as any personal shortcoming but rather as a simple weakness of human nature. However little he may have wished it consciously, with the passing years he did become somewhat spoiled. Not surprisingly, financial dependence created certain additional complications in Tchaikovsky's attitude toward Mrs. von Meck, and it is true that, as in the two passages just quoted, the tone of his letters to her differed sometimes quite noticeably from the tone of his references to her in letters to his brothers. Such discrepancies should not, however, be exaggerated, and to accuse Tchaikovsky of duplicity would be wrong. It must be recognized that he was a man of capricious and unstable temperament, dependent on the mood of the moment and tending to fits of irritation and anger even toward those of whom he was fondest. His letters bristle with expressions of this irritation, yet they are always quick to pass. Even the most scrupulous analysis could reveal no difference between the tone of these outbursts and the rare caustic remarks he expressed in regard to Mrs. von Meck.

All such unpleasant moments vanish in the great ocean of his expressions of gratitude, the sincerity of most of which can hardly be doubted. In that first year, such outpourings were particularly frequent, and not surprisingly so, for Mrs. von Meck had all but literally dragged him out of his madness. "I love you with all the strength of my soul," he wrote her in January 1878, "and every minute I bless the fate that brought me together with you."[8] He called her his "guardian angel"[9] and declared that "with each new letter I come to wonder anew at your astounding kindness."[10]

The same vocabulary and emotions are also to be found frequently in his letters to his brothers: "My God! What should I have done without Mme Meck! May this woman be blessed a thousand times over!"[11] And in a letter to Nikolay Rubinstein, who had clashed with her more than once, Tchaikovsky would defend her with chivalrous ardor. "Never have kindness, delicacy, generosity, and boundless magnanimity been combined in one person so completely as in her," he wrote. "I owe her not only my life but also the fact that I am able to continue working, and this for me is dearer than life. . . .She is decidedly not eccentric. For me she is simply an inexhaustible arm of Providence. One must know her as I do now not to doubt that there are still people so inconceivably kind and trusting."[12]

Clearly, the incandescence of emotions here is the equal of her attitude toward him, even if the intonation is somewhat less rhapsodic. Mrs. von Meck's fantastic infatuation with her invisible correspondent was undiluted in its expression. "You are the only person who affords me such profound, such sublime happiness," she would confess in one letter, "and for this I am boundlessly grateful to you and can only pray that what brings me this happiness never cease and never change, because such a loss would be most painful for me."[13] "It is impossible to describe what good these dear letters offer me," she wrote in another, "what a beneficent balm they are to my weary heart, possessed by uncontrollable longing. When I come out to my sitting room and find on the table an envelope with that so familiar, dear handwriting, I feel a sensation as from a whiff of ether that stops any pain."[14] And again, "My love for you is also fate, against which my will is powerless."[15]

Even allowing for conventional rhetorical flourishes and for the fact that they could never know each other as deeply as they would have in direct personal acquaintance, one can only appreciate the sublimity of feelings that they expressed to each other. But the crisis passed and Tchaikovsky's life returned to normal. Their relationship, by now well established, became more routine, and gradually and naturally the effusions of his letters became less frequent. Yet, it is significant that they did continue, and it would be no exaggeration to say that almost until the end of their correspondence there appeared from time to time flashes of the same emotional incandescence as at the beginning.

To be sure, Tchaikovsky repeatedly sought to reduce to human dimensions the idealized image of him venerated by his rhapsodic correspondent. "Your friendship is the greatest blessing for me," he wrote her on 28 August 1878, after returning to Russia. "Only one thing embarrasses me somewhat, and this I shall tell you without any false modesty in full awareness of the truth of my words. You have a far better opinion of me than I actually deserve. I write this to you not to receive in response new proofs of your high opinion of me as a person. For God's sake, do not reply to this at all. I assure you, my dear friend, that I have a very poor opinion of myself and that a complete abyss separates my ideal of a human being from my own person."[16] But his benefactress remained indifferent to such persuasions. "My God," she insisted, "how much brighter and warmer has my life become, how greatly has your consideration rewarded me, how much is redeemed by such a nature as yours!"[17] As always, her passion centered on his music: "I cannot convey to you what I feel when I listen to your compositions. I am prepared to give up my soul to you, you become deified for me; everything conceivable of that which is most generous, pure and sublime rises up from the depth of my soul."[18]

Elsewhere, however, she came close to violating the limits of intimacy that she herself had established. Among such passages belongs her attempt in a letter of 30 January 1878 to coax from Tchaikovsky whatever she might about his own amorous experience. "Pyotr Ilyich, have you ever loved?" she asked. "I think you have not. You love music too much ever to love a woman. I know of one episode of love in your life [most probably a reference to Désirée Artôt], but I find that so-called platonic love (although Plato did not love at all thus) is only a partial love, a love of the imagination and not the heart, not that feeling which enters the flesh and blood of a person and without which he cannot live."[19]

This is a most remarkable fragment, particularly in its reference to platonic love. We do not know whether Mrs. von Meck ever read the *Phaedrus* or the *Symposium* and, if she did, whether she was aware that the love in these dialogues, the "heavenly Aphrodite" over against the "earthly Aphrodite," mainly regards young men. Scholarly wisdom

of the time ignored any carnal aspect of Greek homosexuality and attributed to it a spiritual and pedagogical motive inherent in the ideal
of *paideia,* that is, the education of a young man by his teacher. But,
granting spirituality, any such view could hardly deny that in much of
Plato, love associates two individuals perhaps different in age yet both
male.

Mrs. von Meck's remark that "Plato did not love at all thus" seems
to counter the common idea that "platonic" refers to any loving relation between man and woman that stops short of physical sex. It may
possibly reveal her awareness of the homoerotic nature at the basis of
Plato's view of love. If so, it could well have been in such a "platon-
ized," and thus sanitized, sense that she may have interpreted any rumors about homosexuality that were especially observed in his close
relations with his young male students. In this way, she might have
allowed herself delicately to express her opinion of what she perhaps
thought some analogue to Platonic *paideia* as an exalted pedagogical
friendship between pupils and teachers. It would mean, too, that in
some form, however obscure or even distorted, Mrs. von Meck was
aware of the eccentricities of Tchaikovsky's erotic life from the very
beginning. Given her idealization of him, however, it may be surmised
that she would have banished all thoughts of any sodomitic act from
her mind.

By her own assertion, Mrs. von Meck was a person who placed
freedom and genuine feeling "above all else," even above ties of blood
and marriage. "I do not deny that blood ties, by their natural properties,
confer rights and impose obligations; still . . . I cannot but grant preference to another, no less natural, property of man: free feeling, personal choice, individual sympathies," she wrote in a letter of 12 February 1878. Marriage, she claimed, was a mere rite in which true
feelings of love and caring and compassion were too often lacking.
Laws that guaranteed binding rights and obligations to nonvolitional
ties of blood and presumptive ties of marriage were thus unjust and
plain wrong. "Yet, there is a third type of relations," she wrote, "vol-
untary and nonbinding, that is, not binding in the sense of a period of
time, but rendering the greatest rights and the greatest obligations. . . .
This third type of relations is that of various and sundry feelings, and
I myself acknowledge rights and obligations only on the basis of
these. . . . My love gives me a right to someone, his love imposes an
obligation on me, and so on, with no limit, as far as each person's nature allows."[20]

Ultimately, of course, these arguments on the ethics of human relations helped Mrs. von Meck to justify in intellectual terms her rela-

tionship with Tchaikovsky and, in particular, her commitment to caring unconditionally for "all aspects" of his life (a euphemism for financial support), "the more so," she continued with touching tact, "as I have grown convinced during the long years of my life that for a man of talent to move forward and receive inspiration, it is imperative for him to be well provided for in a material sense."[21]

Up to this point in her discourse about free individual choice, there is no mention of sex, nor is any sexual aspect presumed. Indeed, she speaks of her relationship with her children in the same context. Further on, though, the matter is brought up. For the person in love, she granted, the physical aspect plays a "great, irrefutable" role—but it must have a source. "It can only be the consequence of a love evoked purely by morality alone, with not the slightest admixture of appearance and physical impressions, and when a person has fallen in love in such a manner, physical relations then become a natural and essential requirement." Platonic love, she wrote, using the term here in its common meaning of love without physical expression, she could "neither comprehend nor recognize." "Only he loves who loves with his entire organism," she explained, "but with the genuine person the moral aspect everywhere and in everything must serve as the source."[22]

A logical extension of Mrs. von Meck's reflections was not only tolerance of some notion of *paideia* but also an implicit approval of spiritual and pedagogical intimacy between pupil and teacher as free choice mutually exercised in feeling and morality. This outlook could also sanction, for instance, Mrs. von Meck's continued encouragement of Tchaikovsky's unusual worries and concerns about Alyosha as expressed in his letters to her in a tone sometimes far exceeding the conventional relationship between benevolent master and beloved servant.

Of course, it is not difficult to note a contradiction in Mrs. von Meck's attitude toward "so-called platonic love" in the common sense of relations between man and woman short of physical intercourse. She professed "neither to comprehend nor recognize" this platonic love, and yet her own epistolary relations with Tchaikovsky, with their outpourings of highly charged emotion and the categorical decision never to meet face-to-face, corresponded to an extreme case of what she rejected. It was a reversal of any notion of courtly love. In terms very similar to those directed by Mrs. von Meck to Tchaikovsky, a Provençal troubadour might have addressed a distant lady whom he had never seen, knowing her only by hearsay.

But perhaps the contradictions in her views should not be treated too solemnly. Psychology defies logic, and the qualities we ourselves possess are often those we censure or question most hotly in others. Mrs. von Meck's letters to Tchaikovsky leave little doubt of the erotic element of her attraction to him, which was only aggravated by her worries about her unattractiveness, her age, and her motherhood. It was in part this intricate erotic mixture that made her speak of sublimity in the relations between the sexes while decrying merely "platonic" love between man and woman. This very erotic mixture alerted Tchaikovsky to a trouble to be avoided at all costs. If there was any eros in his attitude toward her, it was only that which is present in any creative inspiration. In this sense, Mrs. von Meck was undoubtedly Tchaikovsky's only muse of the female sex.

In the interval between her letter of 30 January asking whether he had "ever loved" and that of 12 February and its lengthy discourse on feelings, free choice, and a moral foundation, Mrs. von Meck received from Tchaikovsky a reply to her question—not direct but sincere for all its ambiguity, not complete but expressed with extreme dexterity. Written on 9/21 February, this reply is often cited by his biographers, both detractors and advocates:

> You ask me, my friend, whether I have known nonplatonic love. Yes and no. If this question is put somewhat differently, that is, ask whether I have experienced complete happiness in love, then I shall answer: no, no, and no!!! However, I believe the answer to this question is present in my music as well. But if you ask me whether I understand the full might, the full immeasurable force of this feeling, then I shall answer: yes, yes, and yes, and again I shall say that I have attempted with love to express the agony and also the bliss of love. Whether I have succeeded, I do not know or, rather, I leave it to others to judge.[23]

One could hardly better say everything and say nothing: agony and bliss together formed the very essence of Tchaikovsky's erotic life. But the passage is remarkable in its ambivalence and in the self-contradiction of the apparent claim that it is possible to understand the emotions of love without ever having experienced them and, moreover, to express the unexperienced emotion, be it agony or bliss, by means of art. In fact, the two correspondents were writing past each other, each meaning something quite different by the one ambiguous word "love": Mrs. von Meck, the love between a man and a woman, and Tchaikovsky, the love between two men. Yet, it follows from this same passage that in the realm of homosexual love the composer, though perhaps never having found the "complete happiness" that proves so often elusive, had known both agony and bliss, which he professes to have expressed in his music. It is important, despite whatever agony, not to overlook this positive mention of bliss. The combination of the two is indeed far from the facile notion of Tchaikovsky's having suffered self-torment and unending remorse to the point of suicide.

The understandable confusion of Mrs. von Meck's thoughts on erotic and perhaps homoerotic matters, coupled with the attitude of the time, which preferred to enclose the issue in silence, gradually allayed Tchaikovsky's fears that she might betray and abandon him if suddenly confronted with any revelation about his sexuality. In his letters to her he even ventured to allow some show of what could be construed as misogyny about the young women at the conservatory, apparently disregarding the thought that this might substantiate the rumors she may well have heard about his sexual habits. "But the female students!" he huffed in a letter of 14/26 March. "My God, what's the matter with them! . . . Sometimes I lose all patience with them, lose the ability to understand, and I fall into a fit of indescribable anger at them and especially at myself."[24]

But in Mrs. von Meck's eyes such behavior only constituted a virtue. "Of your antipathy toward the studies of young ladies at the conservatory I have heard previously and sympathize with it fully in the general sense," she replied, "and in you personally it pleases me tremendously because I see in this that in the matter of art you cannot be bought by anything, even young ladies, while at the same time I have heard that there are professors who make advances to them. What an abomination!"[25] Once again Mrs. von Meck misread Tchaikovsky. What was in fact a sign of his preference for young men—and subsequently of his resentment at the preponderance of young women at the conservatory—she took as the transcendence of everyday sexual (in her assumption, heterosexual) urges for the loftier and far worthier goal of art. The picture fit well her view of Tchaikovsky as model of an ideal Romantic artist and visionary. Even her further remark that morals at the Moscow Conservatory were such that she would "never send even a son there, much less a daughter," seems no allusion to homosexuality but rather a reflection of her view that moral corruption reigning at that institution affected the young men as well as the young women and led to general licentiousness.

Later, when passions had subsided, Mrs. von Meck asked Tchaikovsky directly about his separation from his wife—not, she claimed, out of mere curiosity but to avoid any misunderstanding. "I should like you to explain this for the simple reason that I do not like everyone

giving his own explanation for the causes of your rupture and a certain
individual acquiring an aura of undeserved matyrdom, whereas if
either of the two of you is a martyr, it is you," she wrote on 5 May.[26]
Whether or not something more specific was hinted at in Mrs. von
Meck's apparently innocent remark, Tchaikovsky reacted as though
there were. "As for any fears lest Rubinstein and others learn the real
reasons for my rupture with a certain individual, there is nothing to
worry about, my friend," he responded four days later. "First, they all
are well aware of these reasons. Second," he added, echoing his friend
Apukhtin's advice that, like an eagle, he allow the weight of his fame
to crush the slanderers and rumormongers from on high, "since recovering and becoming a person of normal mental faculties, I have
again stood on a height to which *les qu'en dira-t-on* do not reach."[27]
Again it appears that Mrs. von Meck failed to recognize in his reply
any hint of homosexuality.

Eroticism was by no means the only theme of the intimate and
spirited exchanges between composer and benefactress. The subjects
of their letters ranged over a broad spectrum, from personal confessions to theoretical discussions. She could tell him in detail of her difficult early years of poverty as the wife of a young unknown engineer
named Karl von Meck. He, in turn, could share with her even the most
delicate and painful recollections of his childhood and his mother.
"Yesterday I found at my sister's huge bunches of letters I had written
to my father and mother at some time from Petersburg when I was ten
or eleven and found myself entirely alone in a great alien city. It is hard
to convey what a moving impression was made on me by reading these
letters that carried me back almost thirty years and reminded me vividly of my childish sufferings out of longing for my mother. . . . The
result of this reading was a completely sleepless night. Now I feel an
indescribable exhaustion."[28]

Such outpourings indicate the depth of their mutual sympathy. In
dealing with psychological and spiritual matters (as opposed to matters
of money), Tchaikovsky was unconstrained and completely natural in
his letters to her. What is more, he never strove to embellish himself
in his letters, but rather the reverse, prone as he was to self-accusation.
He firmly knew and felt that his "best friend" accepted him as he was
(despite her ecstatic idealization) and would always find, he must have
believed deep in his heart, justification for his behavior. For this reason, his apologies and repentances, despite their sincerity, sometimes
sound artificial, like those of a man who knows he will be forgiven. As
for Mrs. von Meck, she seems to have been endowed with a rare ability
to combine idealization to the point of ecstasy with a practical view of

human nature. It is not easy to understand how she managed to do so, given her lack of any real saving sense of humor. She was apparently able, at certain times, to expel from her consciousness unpleasant truths forced on her by reason and to abandon herself to her feelings, but then to regain total sobriety. Not without justice did she write, at the very beginning of their correspondence, "Take my word for it, however much I may love someone, I am never blinded, yet I admire everything good with equal ardor, no matter whether in a stranger . . . or in someone close to me."[29]

Without exaggeration it is possible to say that, with the exception of his homosexuality, Tchaikovsky kept no real secrets from Mrs. von Meck. Indeed, several pages from his letters to her seem addressed more appropriately to a medical consultant than to a woman friend. But, for Tchaikovsky, complaints about his psychological condition were a natural extension of his emotional effusions and the description of his physical ailments was a natural extension of his nervous complaints. He opened himself up so candidly that he could even write to her about his abuse of alcohol, and moreover, he took her as inspiration for a vow of abstinence. "I give you my most solemn promise henceforth to turn to you in my thoughts when I need to struggle with temptation and to draw from your friendship the strength to stand firm against it."[30] Such matters turned up without the slightest prompting from the tactful Mrs. von Meck.

Tchaikovsky himself readily admitted the connection between his physical health and his psychological state. "In general," he wrote at one point, "I shall say that physically I am nevertheless a healthy person, though psychologically more sick than healthy, and though the one and the other are directly linked, about myself I can say that nonetheless my soul influences my body more than the reverse; that is, I have observed that when I am calm, I am also healthy."[31] Here it is clear that "psychological sickness" refers not to his sexuality but to his myriad phobias and what he called his "misanthropy," not to mention his hysterical disposition. "I have become extremely sensitive to all sorts of impressions," he confessed in another letter. "I have grown lachrymose, weeping constantly and without any need: because of a book, because of some music, or simply under the influence of the beauty of nature."[32]

Tchaikovsky's letters to Mrs. von Meck abound in detailed descriptions of various medical troubles. His characteristic conflation of physiological and psychological symptoms, along with ascribing his mental state to physical causes, was much in keeping with the medical views of his time. "I wish someone might explain to me the meaning and cause of these strange evening attacks of weakness, . . . which to a greater or lesser degree recur with me daily," he wrote in one letter. "The attacks themselves are very onerous and unpleasant, especially that indeterminate longing for something which seizes my entire soul with an unbelievable force and terminates in a quite definite striving for nonbeing, *soif du néant!* But most probably the causes of this phenomenon are quite prosaic; this is not at all an illness of the soul, but, as it seems to me, the consequence of poor digestion and the remnants of my stomach catarrh."[33]

Like his letters to his brothers, Tchaikovsky's letters to Mrs. von Meck served as an outlet for a range of accumulated frustration. There is little doubt that Mrs. von Meck represented for him not only a trusted friend and confidante but also a sort of mother figure and in this role, with time, came virtually to replace his sister, Aleksandra. More often than not, however, we encounter in this unexampled correspondence theoretical debates on subjects ranging far beyond personal matters. Tchaikovsky and Mrs. von Meck often argued on an equal footing with complete freedom and decorum. They argued about religion, he passionately opposing her atheistic utilitarianism. They argued about literature, he criticizing the populist civic-minded poet Nikolay Nekrasov and the utilitarian-positivistic critic Dmitry Pisarev, both of whom she adored, contrasting them with Pushkin, whom she would not even acknowledge. They even argued about music, where once again the composer expressed his opinions without the slightest arrogance, his tone not once colored by condescension or snobbery. For her part, while heeding with utmost reverence the judgments of his (for her) indisputable authority, she never yielded her position in matters of personal taste, though again without conceit or injured feelings. Thus, they were never able to agree about Mozart, whom Tchaikovsky idolized, but who for Mrs. von Meck represented the embodiment of everything superficial.

The essence of their difference is illustrated by two passages from a discussion on the nature of beauty, understood by Mrs. von Meck as outward appearance. Her comments of 29 November 1877 reveal a simply pragmatic viewpoint. "I am an enemy of all appearance, from beauty of the face up to, and including, respect for public opinion," she wrote. "Everything that fails in moral or essential meaning is antipathetic to me, but to such a degree that I think it degrading to human dignity to attach significance to its external aspect. . . . I link [appearance] with firmness of convictions, because people are in fact easily won over by many external appearances—beauty, surroundings, proprieties, pursuit of progress, liberalism, humanism, realism, materialism, nihilism, depending on what's fashionable, democratism, revolutionary fantasies."[34]

Tchaikovsky's response of 6/18 December claimed, quite erroneously, an essential agreement:

> Why do you say that we differ with each other on the subject of human beauty? Why do you think that I allot it a greater place in my estimation of a person? Yes, of course a person's beauty has an influence on me! But what is human beauty? This is a purely relative notion and has nothing in common with the absolute beauty revealing itself in art. The French have a vulgar yet very true definition of human beauty: *beau qui plaît*. But, indeed, an unattractive face can also *plaire*, and we are met with this fact every minute. Let me say more. Faces possessed of beauty in the classic sense rarely please. In a person's face, in his gait, manners, movements, glance, it is something elusive and indefinable that pleases. In essence this "something" is a reflection of spiritual beauty. In this sense, I of course yield readily to the charming effect of appearance. Consequently, as regards any view of human beauty, there exists a verbal misunderstanding. By a person's beauty is meant the external reflection of inner qualities, but no word exists for this external appearance.[35]

In fact, the difference in outlook is obvious and—in spite of the "elective affinities" the two correspondents possessed or claimed to possess—considerable. Tchaikovsky, as an artist, was affirming the primacy of art. Following Plato, he saw in beauty a reflection of a higher world. Mrs. von Meck, as a businesswoman, put ethics first, defining the beautiful in pragmatic and moral terms. Still, it is remarkable that even on such an abstract and elevated level these two so disparate people not only understood each other but also could truly empathize with each other, appreciating each other's views.

The one area in which Tchaikovsky and Mrs. von Meck had no disagreement was politics. Throughout his life Tchaikovsky remained a staunch supporter of the tsars, and his political views, like those of Mrs. von Meck, were of a pronounced conservative, even reactionary, character. Interestingly, in mid-April 1883 the composer and his benefactress briefly exchanged their own very disparaging views on the phenomenon of communism, a simplified version of the doctrines of French utopian socialists such as Charles Fourier and of Karl Marx, which advocated the abolition of all private property and which had been embraced by the Russian radicals known as Nihilists. Speaking out in passionate defense of private property and against the nihilistic tendencies of the times, Mrs. von Meck wrote on 14/26 April, "What a perversion of a common human quality is created by those people who worship [Pierre Joseph] Proudhon [the leading French anarcho-syndicalist] and have chosen as their motto the pompous phrase *la propriété c'est le vol.* What an absurdity! Every human being, whether educated or not, has nothing more valuable to him than his property; there is even a saying 'Everything of one's own is good.' Why, the entire doctrine (if Nihilism can be a doctrine) is built on this phrase, which is itself nothing but a soap bubble. What sorry times!"[36]

Tchaikovsky's response to this was unequivocal. "What you have said about communism is entirely true," he wrote. "It is impossible to imagine a more senseless utopia, something more discordant with the natural qualities of human nature. And how dull and unbearably colorless life will surely be when this equality of wealth reigns supreme (if ever it does). Indeed, life is the struggle for existence, and if it is permitted that this struggle not be—then neither will there be life, merely senseless perpetuity. But it seems to me that any serious implementation of these doctrines is still far off."[37] In this last opinion at least Tchaikovsky proved a poor prophet, for it was in fact to be less than thirty-five years later that the October Revolution would usher in the reign of communism in Russia and, with it, the "unbearably colorless life" that Tchaikovsky had predicted. But his music would survive, vibrant and vivid, full of movement and eloquence, and a memory of a life rich in color that once had been.

Mrs. von Meck kept a large staff, including personal physicians and musicians. Kotek had been for a brief time among the latter, as were many others who had come and gone before him. Yet, only one such young man would ever manage to ensconce himself in the von Meck family, a fact that alone tells of his exceptional opportunism, given that by all accounts the eccentric Mrs. von Meck was not an easy person to please. More significantly still, the young man was destined to play a crucial and ultimately quite sinister role in her relationship with Tchaikovsky.

The name of Kotek's successor was Wladyslaw Pachulski. He was of a poor Polish family and had been at one time a student of Tchaikovsky's at the Moscow Conservatory, and it was in the context of the conservatory that Pachulski was first mentioned, though not named, by Mrs. von Meck, in her letter of 4 January 1878: "I hear constantly from one of your former students that nothing is the same now, that no one can replace you. I should think so: it is you who gave the Moscow Conservatory its high status."[38] If this reflects what Pachulski actually said, then it was mere flattery, as Tchaikovsky must have realized. He well knew that as a professor he had in no way distinguished himself, considering his occupation merely a means of earning a living and hating it. On the other hand, this passage may signify a first indirect attempt on the part of Mrs. von Meck to implement a stratagem she must by that time have conceived—to interest her "priceless friend" in the musical gifts of the young man to whom she would later invariably refer as her "foster child" and "protégé." Although it is unlikely (but not altogether impossible) that she seriously expected Tchaikovsky to take Pachulski as a regular pupil, she almost certainly sought to induce the composer to guide the young man closely in his studies, and this she achieved. As it turned out, following her wish in this matter was in time to become a singularly painful burden to Tchaikovsky.

How does one explain the persistent and not unimpassioned interest of a woman known to have been a sober judge of character in this, to all appearances, unremarkable young man? The question is not a simple one and, given the present state of our sources, can hardly be answered with any certainty. Two aspects of it should in any case be singled out: her attitude toward Pachulski as a person and toward his potential musical future.

It is more difficult to form an idea of the young musician's estimation of himself, since only fragments of his own letters have been published. We can however, make educated guesses based on the correspondence between Tchaikovsky and Mrs. von Meck. There are two impressions that emerge. Pachulski clearly seems, on the one hand, to have considered himself extremely gifted, and even the most tactfully offered of Tchaikovsky's criticisms caused him great pain. On the other hand, he lacked confidence in himself as an artist, preferring to establish himself in the household of an imperious elderly lady to whom he would become in time both personal secretary and virtual factotum—duties that, not surprisingly, would often deprive him of the opportunity to do any creative work.

Pachulski's main achievement seems to have been his success in making himself irreplaceable in the von Meck household. In a letter many years later, when he was no longer her secretary, Mrs. von Meck acknowledged, "I shall never find another such as Wlad[yslaw] Alb[ertovich], for indeed he was educated by me and from me learned the whole system of traveling and foreign languages and financial knowledge, and since he is very clever at everything, understanding and mastering everything very quickly and thoroughly, he developed into such an exemplary secretary that he cannot possibly be re-placed."[39] Elsewhere she wrote that "he was my constant companion at billiards and croquet, for reading to me, for walks and such. He knew all my habits and tastes, was very attentive to me, and looked after me well."[40] From time to time, her references to him seem almost those of his owner or maker, and subconsciously she probably did to a certain extent regard her "foster child" as her property and her creation. And indeed, to some extent, and not without his own compliance, this was true. His capacity for adaptation and psychological dexterity may in part explain her high opinion of his character. "This man has revealed such a rare, unparalleled heart that despite his youth one cannot but respect him."[41]

On 6 March 1878, when Mrs. von Meck was first attempting to elicit Tchaikovsky's interest in her nursling, she wrote to him concerning the performance of "their" Fourth Symphony in Moscow on 10 February:

> I can tell you of the impression on one of your most intelligent, developed, and passionately music-loving pupils, Pachulski, whom I see often, and am quite able to judge the sincerity and profundity of his impressions. He is mad about your symphony. For several days he could neither speak nor think of anything but it. Every five minutes he would sit at the piano and play it. He has an excellent memory for music, and it is to him I owe a closer acquaintance with our symphony, since he now plays it to me constantly. This man has a most exalted passion for music. . . . In addition, he is endowed by nature with a most fertile musical imagination—if this is judged, of course, not by class exercises but by free expression of ideas. Of course, this is still merely raw material. If you were here, my dear friend, I should ask you to make some little investigation of his creative abilities. It seems to me that he possesses them, but then I am no competent judge in this matter, and I should be interested to know your opinion.[42]

Perceiving her inordinate concern about him, Tchaikovsky replied a week later, with an assurance ultimately rash and far-reaching, "Do not doubt that Pachulski will find in me every encouragement when I have become more closely acquainted with his musical sensibility."[43]

Mrs. von Meck would express most distinctly her motivation in her attitude toward Pachulski in a letter of 13 December of that year. "I take great care of him," she told Tchaikovsky, "first, because it is my nature, second, because I love music passionately, and, third, because I want to refute for myself, in every way possible, the charge that I ruin a musician [possibly a reference to the opinion of Nikolay Rubinstein, who disapproved of Mrs. von Meck's style as a patroness of the arts]. And since, in addition to all this, I consider him an exceptionally decent young man, I should like to arrange a good future for him, which in his case of course lies in music."[44]

Mrs. von Meck was of course not an artist but simply a dilettante, and so her exaggerated opinion on the merits of Pachulski's musical compositions may well be respectfully ignored. But Tchaikovsky was an exceptionally demanding artist. This fact alone would serve as basis for the subsequent inward, and sometimes outward, conflicts regarding Pachulski, who was to remain the one serious, though never acknowledged, source of unpleasantness between Tchaikovsky and his benefactress.

CHAPTER SIXTEEN

Freedom to Create

At the beginning of 1878 the emotional trauma of Tchaikovsky's entanglement with Antonina was already being displaced by practical worries. Financial arrangements between the two were complicated. In January, Tchaikovsky granted his wife a monthly pension. Originally set at one hundred rubles, the amount was to change repeatedly depending on her conduct. In the course of time, Tchaikovsky was also to make several attempts to reach some other sort of agreement with her, his particular hope being a final payment of a single sum in exchange for her signed renunciation of all further claims. Tchaikovsky tried, however, to distance himself from such details. Almost all dealings with his wife he conducted either through his brother Anatoly or through his publisher, Pyotr Jurgenson, both of whom he begged many times to trouble him about these matters as little as possible.

From the very first months of their separation, Tchaikovsky had sought to establish a style both authoritative and businesslike in his communications with Antonina. "I cannot help noticing that you have made too abrupt a transition from the role of a loving, abandoned, and betrayed woman to a role completely the opposite," he wrote in a letter to her of 8/20 January 1878. Responding to her demand for a written guarantee of a monthly pension of one hundred rubles, he told her that she would receive such a pension only as long as she gave him no reason to be displeased with her conduct and warned that the subsidy would cease immediately if ever she took any action "that is ill-disposed or tends to the disturbance of my tranquillity." In other words, she must live in such a way that he would never see or meet her. "You may say of me whatever you wish; if word reaches me that you have been speaking ill of me, I shall not be angry. In short, for my peace it is necessary that I keep away from you—and nothing else. So for this I am obliged to support you, but I shall give no written guarantee, since for my peace I also need freedom."[1]

Antonina did not, however, leave him in peace. On the contrary, she proceeded to write letters to Tchaikovsky's father, thus dealing her husband an especially painful blow. He confided this new trouble to Mrs. von Meck, noting that his wife was again playing the victim but that since she had "removed most flagrantly her vulgar mask" and had begun to press her various material demands, he no longer felt any remorse in regard to her. "I have been blameless before her ever since she revealed herself fully and ever since, in a material sense, she received far more than she could have expected," he wrote. Antonina's letters to her father-in-law never reached him, but instead were intercepted by Anatoly, who sent them back to her. This prompted her to start writing insulting letters to Anatoly.[2] Tchaikovsky, enraged, instructed Anatoly to write to the "spawn of hell," as he now called her, to inform her that she would receive nothing unless she gave a written undertaking to the effect that upon receiving a onetime sum of twenty-five hundred rubles and a renewed promise of a monthly subsidy of one hundred rubles, "she will consider herself to be fully content and satisfied and will never write anything either to me or to Papa or any of my relatives." Further in the same letter he flatly said, "She wants a divorce? So much the better."[3]

It was in this letter to Anatoly that Tchaikovsky in all earnestness first mentioned the possibility of divorce. And so began an onerous and complicated saga that would drag on for many years, ultimately being resolved to no one's satisfaction. Divorce in tsarist Russia was not a simple matter. The law provided very few grounds for dissolving a marriage: the sentencing of one or the other of the spouses to "the deprivation of all rights and status," the husband's inability to consummate the marriage (if this originated before the marriage was formally contracted), the "absence in place unknown" (for not less than five years) of one of the spouses, and certain other "valid reasons." Among the latter was "proven adultery," which constituted most fabricated grounds for divorce. But various bureaucratic obstacles further complicated the process. The fact of a spouse's infidelity had to be attested by witnesses (who, in the case of a fictive charge, were necessarily suborned), while the "guilty" party was commonly deprived of the right to marry again for several years. The divorce proceedings themselves, moreover, commonly dragged on for a year and a half or more. All of these factors conspired to make divorce an infrequent occurrence.

The attitude of both spouses to the prospect of divorce was at the outset ambivalent. Tchaikovsky, while longing to free himself forever from his wife, was fearful of the complications that could arise in the course of divorce proceedings. His dual position on the subject of his homosexuality—a rational awareness of his relative security and a frequent fear of scandal—kept him from taking a single tack and holding to it. Yet, Antonina had no intention of leaving him alone, and he found himself driven to occasional brief fits of wild panic and fury. In one such fit he confessed to Mrs. von Meck, in a letter of 3/15 February, that only now did he realize "that it is possible to feel in oneself a desire for the death of one's neighbor and to feel it passionately, furiously." Antonina had become a "terrible specter that will haunt me always to the grave." The very idea of her threw him "into a state of unbearable malice and rage."[4]

Antonina's attitude seemed to reflect a decidedly limited understanding of the situation. It is unclear whether she actually realized that their relationship had reached a deadlock. Although she was understandably angry and resentful at being abandoned, she nonetheless refused to make Tchaikovsky the guilty party in a charge of adultery. Such a step would legally exculpate her, releasing her from the socially awkward position of a husbandless wife while preserving her honor and allowing her the opportunity to remarry. Then again, remaining Tchaikovsky's wife also offered her certain advantages, not least of them financial. In the event of a divorce all her subsequent claims would become juridically invalid. Even if the court were to award her a large compensation, she would thereafter be unable to demand from Tchaikovsky so much as a kopek. The fact that Anatoly, despite all his efforts as a professional lawyer, was unable to resolve the matter satisfactorily testifies, however indirectly, to the complexity of the circumstances that produced it, in particular Tchaikovsky's homosexuality and the growing eccentricity in his wife's conduct.

Tchaikovsky first began seriously to contemplate divorce in mid-February, when Mrs. von Meck wrote to him offering to furnish the handsome sum of ten thousand rubles to be given to Antonina as support on condition that she agree to a divorce.[5] Tchaikovsky greeted this offer with enthusiasm, but specified that he could consent to it only in the event that Antonina should give her formal promise to divorce. "Otherwise," he wrote to Mrs. von Meck, "I find it more convenient to pay her a monthly subsidy and in this way to keep her dependent on me." He had in fact become convinced that Antonina would never leave him in peace unless restrained by the fear of losing her pension. "I shall grant her this pension conditionally," he continued, "that is, 'Behave yourself, pester neither me nor my relatives, . . . and then you will receive your pension. Otherwise do as you wish.' . . . One cannot mince words with her."[6] This steely attitude toward his wife, so striking in the inherently tenderhearted Tchaikovsky, would never after bend or soften.

On receiving Mrs. von Meck's offer, Tchaikovsky wrote to Anatoly and asked him to look into the details of going about getting a divorce. "As far as the consent of Antonina Ivanovna is concerned," he added, "I have no doubt about it, for one would have to be a complete idiot not to seize this offer with both hands."[7] Such optimism would prove premature. Told by his brother some days later of "difficulties in the matter of the divorce," Tchaikovsky reassured him that he knew that he would have to be "proven guilty of adultery" and that he was "quite prepared to commit adultery whenever you like."[8] More upsetting to him was the news that Antonina had somehow learned of his dealings with Mrs. von Meck, though for the moment this apparently had no consequence. In any event, further action was postponed until after his arrival in Kamenka.

Meanwhile, having returned with Modest, Kolya, and his servant Alyosha Sofronov to Clarens of 25 February/9 March, Tchaikovsky found his domestic tranquillity once again disturbed by Alyosha's antics. Barely recovered from his bout with syphilis, Alyosha had already set off on another amorous adventure. "While working, I heard Alyosha frolicking with Marie [the landlady's maid] in the next room," Tchaikovsky wrote to Anatoly. "Just imagine, this charming girl is in love with Alyoshka; every time [she gives him French lessons] she writes him declarations of love in French on his slate, and they have some mysterious intrigue going on. But I shall never allow [the rest is cut by a censor]."[9] Though not particularly given to jealousy by nature, Tchaikovsky was obviously annoyed and allowed that mood to color his attitude toward his servant, writing about him in unexpectedly harsh terms to Anatoly on 14/26 March. Gone were the panegyrics of just weeks earlier. He complained of Alyosha's "insufferable" behavior before and during his illness and suddenly accused him of "impudence, conceit, even rudeness." Characteristically, however, Tchaikovsky confessed that his own tenderness was to blame for everything. "I spoiled him too much," he admitted to Anatoly. "Because of my monstrous affection he fancied himself more intelligent and better than anyone else in the world. This was an enormous mistake on my part." Tchaikovsky questioned even his servant's devotion, declaring that he had "become convinced that in essence he loves me little." This minor episode reveals not only Tchaikovsky's sentimental temperament but also his intimate bond with Alyosha. "Henceforth," Tchaikovsky vowed to his brother, "he will be nothing else but a good servant. The former, oversalted affections will not return."[10]

But the resolution to treat Alyosha as no more than a servant was hasty and illconsidered. The "oversalted affections" would indeed return. Some months later, in fact, Tchaikovsky would undergo a change of heart, coming across, perhaps not entirely innocently, an unexpected explanation for his favorite servant's "bad behavior" of the previous winter. "While Alyosha was at church yesterday, I happened to need some paper and, looking for it in his chest of drawers, I came upon a very interesting manuscript," he wrote to Modest. "It was a diary that, it turns out, he kept in San Remo last year. I devoured it with great interest. It appears that he only pretended to be so insensitive, while in fact he suffered and grieved terribly. I was terribly moved by it. Now he has gone to town for stamps, and I shall take advantage of this to copy out several passages for you; they are of great interest."[11] These extracts have unfortunately been omitted by the Soviet editors, but this omission, together with the context of Tchaikovsky's letter, indicates that they were intimate in nature and that they quite probably reflected the relations between the two men. It is worth noting, too, that Tchaikovsky—in a tradition inherited from the days of serfdom—felt no scruple in going through, and even sharing, his servant's personal papers.

Another source of anxiety was Kotek, who joined Tchaikovsky's party later. Writing to Anatoly on 6/18 March, Tchaikovsky implicitly compared the young violinist's financial dependence on him and others to his own dependence on Mrs. von Meck. "In my heart of hearts I am not exactly angry at him, yet I find it somehow unpleasant that he is growing accustomed to living on other people's money," he wrote. "But I shall never dare articulate this to him." At the same time, Tchaikovsky found himself moved by Kotek's love for him and valued immensely "his kind heart, his simplicity and naïveté." The result was yet another little drama: conflicting feelings on Tchaikovsky's part, Kotek's realization that his teacher's affection is "no longer as before," and, in turn, Tchaikovsky's annoyance at them both. "I cannot tell him the whole truth," he explained to Anatoly, "nor do I wish to upset him. In short, there are moments when I am angry at myself and angry at him and the result of all this has been the sulks." In the next breath, however, he sought to reassure his brother, apparently with sincerity. "But do not pay attention to this, and do not think that he is a burden to me. In the first place, I enjoy making music with him; in the second, he is essential for my violin concerto; in the third, I love him very, very much. He has the kindest and most tender of hearts, and his character is extremely comforting and pleasant."[12]

Indeed, so relaxed and lighthearted had Tchaikovsky grown in the company of his brother and friends that one day, in a particularly good mood, he decided to "revive the past" as he had not done since his impromptu ballet with Saint-Saëns in 1875 and, as he wrote to Anatoly, "performed a grand *pas de deux* with Modest that was favored with loud approval of the spectators, that is, Kotek and Kolya."[13] Part of the reason for such high spirits was his immersion in a new composition, the Violin Concerto in D Major, op. 35. Tchaikovsky conceived the idea of a work for violin and orchestra shortly after Kotek's arrival in Clarens, and he was soon engrossed in the new project. In a little more than two weeks, he completed the sketches for the work, and by the end of the month, with Kotek's help, the entire concerto was orchestrated. Kotek was soon delighting Tchaikovsky and Modest with his playing of the new work, having busied himself "lovingly" with it. Tchaikovsky even considered dedicating the concerto to his young friend, but decided against it for fear that it might cause gossip.[14] In the end, he dedicated it to the Hungarian violinist Leopold Auer, whose fame he hoped would help promote the concerto.

Finally, in mid-April, Tchaikovsky returned to Russia, together with his brother, Kolya, and Alyosha, all having been invited to Kamenka. They traveled by way of Vienna, and there Tchaikovsky wrote to Mrs. von Meck, "Leaving foreign lands . . . as a completely healthy, normal person, full of fresh strength and energy, I must once again thank you, my priceless, kind friend, for everything I owe you and shall never, never forget."[15] He expected that on his immediate return to Russia he would experience a "strong and sweet sensation." In fact, nothing of the sort occurred. At the border they were met by a "rude and drunken" gendarme who refused for a long time to let them pass "as he could not at all comprehend whether the number of the many passports handed over was the same as the number of people to whom they belonged." Next, a customs official and a porter "plowed through" their trunks, while another official looked Tchaikovsky up and down suspiciously and examined him a long while before finally deciding to return his passport. All this, as Tchaikovsky wrote to Mrs. von Meck, together with the dirty cars on the train, "poisoned for me the pleasure of seeing my native and passionately beloved land."[16]

At Kamenka, where they arrived on 11 April, Tchaikovsky was given a completely separate little cottage, or "hut," across from the main house and with a beautiful view of the village. His youngest nephew, Yury Davydov, writes in his recollections that the composer was very pleased with the hut, which consisted of just two rooms with a kitchen. Lev Davydov had even found for him an upright piano so that he could work on his compositions in peace. "Here," notes Yury, "he was not disturbed by the crowd of people in his sister's house."[17] Until their departure in mid-May, Tchaikovsky shared the hut with Modest and Kolya and spent his time working on his Piano Sonata in G Major, op. 37, recently begun abroad; on piano pieces for the *Album for Children*, op. 39; and on the op. 40 set of twelve salon pieces.

Now, in a far more peaceful frame of mind, he was able to turn his thoughts back to the matter of divorce. Shortly after his arrival he wrote to Mrs. von Meck in a calmly businesslike and even optimistic tone, telling her that Anatoly had found out in great detail about the whole divorce procedure. It was quite uncomplicated, his brother had told him, but would required from three to four months' time. The main business would be conducted in St. Petersburg, and sometime in the middle of the summer it would be necessary for Tchaikovsky to travel to the capital in person for a couple of weeks. Meanwhile, Anatoly had already set things in motion by writing a letter to Antonina in which he offered her a divorce as a condition of a handsome lump settlement and asked her to have ready her reply by the time of his arrival in Moscow. That the money to pay Antonina was actually to come from Mrs. von Meck would, Tchaikovsky assured his benefactress, be known to no one apart from himself and Anatoly.[18]

Most important, it was Antonina herself who would have to take the formal initiative in the proceedings by applying to the Orthodox consistory requesting that the marriage be dissolved. Tchaikovsky had no doubt that she would agree. He was soon proved wrong. Anatoly's meeting in Moscow with Antonina failed utterly. She accused Tchaikovsky's relatives of being her enemies and Tchaikovsky himself of acting under the influence of their conniving. Not wanting to write to his brother directly lest the news upset him too much, Anatoly sent an account of the interview to their sister. But Tchaikovsky, upon learning of the failure to convince Antonina, claimed to be less distressed than might have been feared, and his reaction in fact seems to reveal his own ambivalence toward the issue of a divorce. "Indeed, what is there to be afraid of here?" he wrote Anatoly on 1 May. "In the first instance, I am almost certain that the divorce will take place, and in the second, even if it doesn't, what does it really matter? One can live without it. She, to be sure, will later repent, the bitch, but it will be too late."[19]

Nevertheless, keyed up by the news of Anatoly's failure and facing a sleepless night, he proceeded, after first "arming" himself with "sedative drops," to write his own letter to his wife. A rough copy of that letter has survived. Written in the dry businesslike style Tchaikovsky had adopted with Antonina, it began with a categorical attempt "to destroy utterly, once and for all, the sad illusion" his wife still harbored about the possibility of a reconciliation. "Never, under any circumstances, by any means or for anything in the world will I ever consent to live with you," he wrote, reiterating the terms of his offer of divorce: that she must initiate the proceedings through a lawyer, that he would accept the whole burden of guilt while she would retain the right to remarry, that he would take care of all expenses and, in addition, would pay her ten thousand rubles when the matter was finally settled. "I am offering you a deal that, it seems to me, is convenient and advantageous to us both," he noted in conclusion. "If you are agreeable, then let us get started directly without wasting time; if not, I shall have to take other measures to secure my freedom of action."[20]

Writing to Mrs. von Meck a few days later, Tchaikovsky expressed feelings similar to those in his letter to Anatoly. He was clearly worried, though not to the extent that his health might again suffer. As he noted, his conscience would "remain clear," even if his "desired goal" was not achieved. "I have now done everything to make up for my fault before a certain individual," he wrote. "I now have all too obvious proof of the extent to which she is bereft of the aggregate of those human qualities which are called the soul. She cannot, and never will, know moral suffering. In her, all that can suffer is the most pitiful pride of a creature of the female sex obsessed by a monomania that consists in the fact that all creatures of the male sex, myself included, appear to her to be in love with her. She is completely unable to admit that I, in fact, seek this rupture because of a moral aversion toward her."[21]

Antonina responded to her husband's letter on 15 May. Her answer was less than coherent, a fact evidenced in the very first line: "You ask for a divorce, but I do not understand why it is necessary to demand it in court." Predictably she accused him of egoism and complained of "the grief that you have made me endure since October, abandoning me mercilessly to the mockery and ridicule of all." Citing his contention that he cared nothing for public opinion, she claimed that the mere fact of a divorce suit would place upon her an "indelible stain." Actually, even in nineteenth-century Russia this was not entirely true: since Tchaikovsky was prepared to accept the blame of (fictitious) adultery, it was he, not she, who exposed himself to the public disapproval that a charge of adultery could entail. "Where is the man," Antonina then went on to exclaim pathetically, "whom I considered a sort of demigod and who in my eyes could have no faults!" She accepted the offer of ten thousand rubles, but demanded in addition that he still take care of her debt of another twenty-five hundred rubles. And finally she added, "Your remorse will be your greatest punishment. But let God [judge] which of us is right and which to blame."[22]

Interpreting Antonina's letter as a conclusive sign of her agreement, Tchaikovsky rushed to share his relief with Mrs. von Meck. "Among her phenomenally foolish and idiotic remarks there is nevertheless a formal consent to a divorce." he wrote. "Upon reading it, I went mad with joy and ran about the garden for an hour and a half to suppress with physical exhaustion the joyous excitement that it had caused me."[23]

Yet, even as he celebrated with Mrs. von Meck the hope of a happy ending to this whole drama, Tchaikovsky was already feeling some apprehension about a subtle change in his relationship with his benefactress. It was gradual but increasingly hard to ignore, especially after Mrs. von Meck's generous offer of assistance in the settlement for Antonina. For all the endless tact and delicacy that they showed each other, Tchaikovsky's financial dependence on Mrs. von Meck continued to cause him some embarrassment. Having grown more acutely conscious of the value of his work and of his musical talent, the composer was also growing more mature, and his dependency brought some displeasure, tinged with a sense of humiliation. Even his gratitude, which had originally poured out of him so naturally, became less and less easy to express. "Whether from a sense of shame," he told Anatoly, "or because it is difficult constantly to thank and thank again, it took me great pains to write [to Mrs. von Meck this time]."[24]

Now his indebtedness to her was becoming an ever more palpable constraint. "I know that N[adezhda] F[ilaretovna] will not fail me," he wrote to Modest in May. "I know there will be money—but when? how? how much? where?—I do not know any of this. In short, I must wait for a handout from my benefactress. Granted, the benefactress is so tactful, so generous, that her beneficence is no burden. But at such moments you feel all the same the abnormality, the artificiality of my relations with her."[25] His words betray his annoyance and frustration at what he perceived, not without reason, to be her increasing imposition on his life and his freedom. The passion always present in Mrs. von Meck's attitude toward Tchaikovsky prompted her to a generosity that he often could not help but feel stifling. Although resolved never to meet him face-to-face, Mrs. von Meck had taken it into her head to have Tchaikovsky near her as often as possible. To this end, she began pressing him to accept her hospitality both in Russia and abroad, inviting him to stay at her big house in Moscow or one of her estates or in apartments she rented for him in Florence or Paris during her stays there.

Although Mrs. von Meck seems to have tolerated (in her letters at least) his periodic rcfusals without hint of reproach or irritation, more often than not Tchaikovsky felt he could not say no to her, and he would grumble in letters to his brothers that her intervention had upset his plans or was hampering his freedom. Yet, almost always he fully enjoyed the luxury in which he was housed by his benefactress, feeling quite happy, despite any initial misgivings, and filled with a profound and genuine gratitude toward her. For her part, the mere awareness that the object of her affection was residing somewhere close by was sufficient to inspire in her ecstasy, and she took every opportunity to entreat him to live somewhere near her—though always without coming into personal contact.

In November 1877 she had already suggested that if he wished to return to Russia but still remain incommunicado, he was welcome to reside at her home on Rozhdestvensky Boulevard in Moscow while she herself was abroad. "Everything in my household is prepared," she had told him, "and between us there will be in common only the household and our friendship, which is so dear to me, in the same arrangement as now and not, of course, otherwise." She went on to note that under these conditions no one would even know of his presence in Moscow. "You know what a secluded life I myself lead, and all the servants are accustomed to living as if garrisoned in a fortress. Consequently, you would here be inaccessible."[26] Tchaikovsky had not taken advantage of the offer then, but a year later, in September 1878, did stay at the house on Rozhdestvensky Boulevard in her absence. His detailed account of his visit gave her, predictably, great delight.

But before this, almost immediately upon Tchaikovsky's arrival in Kamenka, Mrs. von Meck invited him to visit her estate at Brailovo, not far away. She would be in Moscow at the time, and Tchaikovsky accepted the invitation with pleasure, spending there the last two weeks of May. In a letter to his sister of 18 May, Tchaikovsky described the von Meck estate: "I am living in clover here. . . . I live in a palace in the literal sense of the word, the furnishings are luxurious, apart from polite and affectionately obliging servants I see no human figures and no one comes to make my acquaintance, the strolls are charming, and at my disposal I have carriages, horses, a library, several pianos, a harmonium, a mass of sheet music—in a word, what could be better."[27] Alyosha joined him shortly and fell into ingenuous raptures: "What a house, what a garden, what people, what food, and you can ride in the woods too, and it's peaceful and pleasant, etc." Observing how all the other servants treated Tchaikovsky, he also began to treat his master with more respect than usual, though, as Tchaikovsky wrote Modest, "on our walks together in the woods we still bicker about this or that."[28] During his stay Tchaikovsky wrote three violin-piano pieces, *Souvenir d'un lieu cher,* op. 42, which he offered as a gift to Mrs. von Meck in remembrance of his visit to Brailovo.

But even the splendid surroundings at Brailovo could not entirely erase the worries from his mind. Besides the divorce preliminaries, for which he would shortly have to travel to Moscow, Tchaikovsky found himself faced with another problem, smaller in scale yet threatening to have some impact on his life. A conflict long brewing between Modest and Kolya Konradi's parents, especially his mother, Alina, had now come to a head, with Modest insisting that he and his charge ought to live apart from them. Along with the purely human frailties of those involved in the conflict, there was apparently also a genuine psychological incompatibility between Modest and Alina Konradi. The problems with the Konradis had even come to strain the mutual love between tutor and charge, already fraught with emotional tension. In July, Tchaikovsky would write Anatoly that Modest had begun to express doubts about Kolya, complaining of "the dryness of his heart" and fearing that he might come to resemble his parents.[29] Tchaikovsky professed to share his brother's antipathy toward the boy's mother, telling Anatoly that "the mere tone of her letters to Modest is sufficient to understand his aversion to her." But at the same time he legitimately asked, "How can one separate Kolya from his parents?! Granted, they are not especially strongly attached to him. But surely self-respect will not allow them to part with their son. What will people say?"[30]

Among Modest's ideas on the subject was that of joining permanently with his already famous brother and living all three together, much as they had during their sojourn abroad. This plan Tchaikovsky, despite the idyllic picture of their travels together in his letters to Mrs. von Meck, rejected categorically—not least because of his continuing fears lest his own and Modest's sexual tastes be directed toward the growing young boy living so closely with them. His letter to Modest from Brailovo of 20 May 1878 implied as much, together with certain other considerations:

> It is not possible for you to live with me for a thousand reasons. (a) I do not love Kolya enough, after all, to change so radically my whole way of life for his sake. (b) I find it better that Kolya

contemplate the various shortcomings of his parents . . . than contemplate my vices and my shortcomings, which I have not the strength to rid myself of for his sake. (c) The responsibility that would lie on me from the moment I became *the head* of a family in which Kolya happened to be *is beyond my powers.* (d) [the entire item has been excised by the censors, an obviously revealing deletion]. (e) I am too irritable and value too much absolute calm to burden myself with the constant life with a child, especially one so difficult and morbidly restless as *Kolya.* (f) As a matter of principle, I am generally against cohabitation with anyone, even those people *nearest* and *dearest* to me.[31]

In the same letter Tchaikovsky suggested that Modest was being as blind in this matter as he himself had been in the matter of his marriage. But he insisted on his own "boundless" love for his brother, assuring him that under "normal circumstances" to live with him would give him the "greatest happiness." "I do not doubt your love for me for a minute," he went on, "and here is a sacrifice that I ask of you for my sake. . . . Abandon, forget your intention to leave the Konradis. I may rest easy concerning you only *while you and Kolya are in their home.*"[32] This and the reference to his own blindness regarding his marriage give reason to suppose that Modest's homosexuality remained for Tchaikovsky a source of apprehension. "I see your relations with Kolya as a *cross* that you bear with great Christian virtue," he wrote. "Why has all this happened? Perhaps it is for the better, perhaps not, but *I understand very well* the full burden of this cross. And nevertheless my heart senses much *misfortune* if you do not listen to me."[33]

For the moment he could do no more. On 30 May, Tchaikovsky left for Moscow in the hope of getting the business of divorce formally under way. In Moscow he found himself drawn at once into the unpleasant atmosphere of the Orthodox consistory and diocesan court. "The consistory is a still quite living remnant of ancient litigiousness," he described to Mrs. von Meck. "Everything is done for bribes; the tradition of bribes is even so strong in this little world that they are not in the least ashamed of setting flatly the sum required. Every step in this process has its own tax, and every bribe is at once divided among officials, clerks, and the priest mediator."[34]

From a secretary of the consistory, Tchaikovsky learned the complicated particulars of the divorce proceedings: first of all, his performance of a confession of supposed adultery; a letter from a witness to his wife with an account of the details of this confession; her applica-

tion to the archbishop for the dissolution of the marriage; receipt by
both spouses of an edict from the consistory; on the grounds of this
edict, the prerequisite admonition to the spouses by a parish priest;
receipt of permission from the synod to begin the actual proceedings;
summons of the two spouses and their witnesses to the consistory for
interrogation; another summons of the spouses for the reading of the
evidence and signing of the statements; and a final summons for the
pronouncing of the decision. The lapse of time between these various
stages—whether days or weeks—was for the most part unspecified and
unpredictable.[35]

But it was perhaps predictable that the behavior of Antonina would
prove less than manageable. She perceived herself a victim, forcibly
driven to agree to a divorce that she was actually against. Her presumed role in the proceedings had to be just the opposite, that of the
accuser desiring the dissolution of the marriage at all costs. And since,
as Tchaikovsky noted, she "has shown a totally inconceivable lack of
understanding, it is first of all necessary that someone undertake to
teach her precisely and in detail what she must say and how she must
conduct herself in every instance."[36]

Having no wish to spend the summer in Moscow, Tchaikovsky decided to postpone the matter of the divorce until autumn. He obviously could not be involved in his wife's behavioral indoctrination,
and so his publisher Jurgenson undertook to see to it. In the meantime,
however, Antonina had first to be found, since she seemed at the time
to have disappeared. "Whether she is hiding on purpose or this is by
chance I cannot decide," Tchaikovsky wrote Mrs. von Meck.[37] In any
event, leaving Jurgenson to look for Antonina, he departed Moscow on
3 June without awaiting further results, though still worried about her
unpredictable behavior. "The least instability in her role can compromise the whole affair," he told Modest on 9 June, "and given that wonderful woman's colossal intellect, there's no telling what mess she
might make if not properly and thoroughly drilled."[38]

On 16 June, Tchaikovsky received a long letter from Jurgenson de-
tailing his troubles in finding Antonina and then his eventual meeting
with her. The interview emerges as a seriocomical series of misunderstandings. "The conversation went literally round in circles, like a
squirrel on a wheel," the publisher reported, "and we kept finding ourselves again at the starting point." At first she decided that Jurgenson
was "one of the agents of the divorce proceeding" and declared that she
wanted to deal with no one but her husband. She then suggested that
Anatoly, Rubinstein, Aleksandra, and others had planned "all this . . .
even before the wedding," though for what conceivable purpose she

would not say. Finally she declared that she would "not lie [about her husband's fictitious adultery] for anything in the world" and, moreover, that she would "prove the opposite"—that is, his innocence from such a charge. Throughout she remained adamant that her husband come see her himself "and we shall manage without the circuit court."

Clearly, Antonina still failed to understand the point that Tchaikovsky and his relatives and friends had tried repeatedly to impress upon her: that there was no hope of turning things around or of any possible reconciliation with her husband. "At present," Tchaikovsky reported to Mrs. von Meck, after quoting for her several passages from Jurgenson's account, "she has become fixed on the idea that I am in fact in love with her . . . and that I must return and fall down at her feet." As the only conceivable response under the circumstances, he was forced to abandon for the moment the idea of pursuing divorce negotiations with her—reluctantly, but probably not without secret relief. He had convinced himself of the "phenomenal and total stupidity" of his wife. Divorce would only be possible, he concluded, if Antonina herself desired it so as to marry again or for some other reason. "Even if through pressure her consent were finally obtained to begin the business," he wrote Mrs. von Meck, "it is impossible to be sure she would not compromise it during the various delicate procedures that cannot be avoided."[39]

Shortly after this, Tchaikovsky received another letter from Antonina, which, apart from showing that she had only the vaguest notion of how divorce was handled, also showed unmistakable signs of mental instability. "It is clear that she has completely lost her mind," Tchaikovsky told Modest bluntly. "I am beginning to worry that she will never leave me alone." Her letter apparently expanded her original propositions: "She gives her consent to a divorce, but demands that it be carried out thus: I must come to her in Moscow, then she and I shall go to the people (sic!) and face their judgment and she will tell them fearlessly the whole truth of my base behavior and after this let the people, if they wish, divorce us—she is prepared to make this sacrifice." He answered "on a half-page" that she would receive her twenty-five hundred rubles to pay off her debt and would also receive her monthly pension "insofar as possible," but that her behavior had cost her the offer of ten thousand rubles, which he now withdrew, while her letters to him would from now on be returned to her unopened. "I have now rid myself of my first impression and begin to forget that all this ever happened. But God forbid in some evil moment I should happen to meet her in Moscow. I am afraid lest I give way to fury."[40]

Mrs. von Meck, however, continued to nourish the hope that di-

vorce might till be possible. Tchaikovsky had to reassure her repeatedly that that was not the case, it being obvious from everything she
had said and written that his wife "is losing her sanity, if she has not
lost it already."[41] Later, he elaborated both on her and on his own condition. "It is plainly clear that she intends to play the role of some
supreme arbiter of my fate. . . . If you had read her last letter to me,
you would have been horrified to see how far one can go in mad disregard for truth and facts, in insolence, stupidity, audacity," he wrote
on 6 July. "When I think of her, I am seized by such rage, such loathing,
such a desire to commit toward her a criminal offense, that I frighten
myself. It is a sickness for which there is only one remedy: not to see
her or meet her, and as far as possible avoid any confrontations. Even
now, as I write these lines to you, with the hateful image willy-nilly
before my eyes, I grow agitated, suffer, rage, and hate myself no less
than her."[42]

During his brief "business visit" to Moscow, Tchaikovsky had met
with colleagues from the conservatory, had dinner with the "aged but
very sweet" Bochechkarov, and found his brother Anatoly quite exhausted and sick from overwork and a rakish amorous life. In general,
Moscow this time filled Tchaikovsky with disgust, seeming "so dreadful" to him that he "barely endured these three days" and on his departure felt only "bliss and pleasure."[43] Together with Anatoly he set
off for Kamenka, deciding on the way to stop and visit Nikolay Kondratyev on his estate. At Nizy they discovered the household once
again in turmoil on account of the renewed outrages of Kondratyev's
servant and lover Aleksey Kiselev. Now married, Kiselev was carrying
on even more disgracefully than two years before when his riotous behavior had forced Tchaikovsky to leave in a rage. He lived on his master's estate "like a totally independent lord," Tchaikovsky informed
Modest, and he was again creating scandalous scenes of "general
drunkenness, shouts and noise all night long, vomiting, . . . in short,
such insolence that Tolya and I did not sleep all night and had our
nerves shattered by our fury." This time, however, a feeling of pity for
his old friend kept Tchaikovsky from making a fuss, and instead the
two had a long talk, the result of which was that Kondratyev "agreed
with me on all points and gave his word to depart abroad."[44] That the
insolent servant was not fired by the master and the master ended up
fleeing the servant is a telling comment on Kondratyev's curious me-
nage.

After a few days of this unpleasant atmosphere, Tchaikovsky and
his brother were more than happy to be on their way again, and after

another two days spent in Kiev, they finally arrived back at Kamenka. Tchaikovsky took up residence once again in the hut, although on at least one occasion he would write to Modest "not on my own paper, for Anatoly has again renewed his affair with Agafya [a peasant girl from Kamenka] and is at the present moment in our little house with this local girl."[45] Modest arrived in Kamenka from Grankino on 20 July, apparently having managed to patch up his relationship with Kolya Konradi's mother. On his way he had also seen Apukhtin at the estate of the poet's friends the Zhedrinskys. At the beginning of August, this time with Modest, Tchaikovsky again stopped in to visit Kondratyev at Nizy, and from there Modest returned to his pupil while Tchaikovsky, at Mrs. von Meck's renewed invitation, went on for another stay at Brailovo. Writing to his benefactress from her estate on 13 August, he confessed frankly, "I am one of those people who can very rarely say of themselves at a given moment: I am happy. Here I can say this. Yes, I am happy, *dans toute la force du terme.*"[46]

But as September drew nearer, and with it the return to Moscow to take up his teaching responsibilities once more, his mood grew steadily worse and he began feverishly searching for any pretext to abandon the job he had come to hate. Unexpectedly such a pretext presented itself. Traveling with his brother-in-law, Lev Davydov, to Kiev at the end of August, he picked up a copy of the newspaper *New Times* at one of the station stops. In it, he came upon a satirical article "dedicated to a dirty, base, vile, slander-filled philippic against the conservatory." He described the article in a letter to Modest written on 29 August:

> There is almost nothing there about me personally, and it is even mentioned that I am occupied only with music, taking no part in the intrigues and squabbles. But one part of the article talks about the amours of the professors with the girls and at the end is added: "There are at the conservatory also amours of a different kind, but about them, for a very obvious reason, I shall not speak" etc. It is clear what this is an allusion to. Thus, that sword of Damocles in the form of newspaper insinuation, which I fear most in the world, has again struck me in the neck. Granted, the insinuations have not touched me personally this time, but so much the worse. My [homosexual] reputation falls upon the whole conservatory, and for this I feel even more ashamed and more wretched. I endured this unexpected passage heroically and philosophically, continuing to

discuss black earth and such with Lyova [Lev] until Kiev, but inside I was sick at heart.

But later in the same letter he added, *"Après tout,* all is for the better, and right now I have calmed down with regard to any newspapers. At bottom, it's all one, when there are people whom you love as I do you and as you do me."[47]

This last is revealing. Tchaikovsky, so painfully sensitive to any adverse publicity, was by this time able nevertheless to endure "heroically and philosophically" the newspaper insinuation possibly directed at him. And not only to endure this blow but also to realize that it was "all one" so long as there were people who loved and valued him. What is more, Tchaikovsky had even decided to take advantage of the article in order to make his ultimate departure from the conservatory. With the newspaper in his hands, as he confided to Modest in the same letter, he resolved to abandon his professorship. He was even tempted to resign at once and not return to Moscow at all. "But the apartment is rented [and] they are counting on me at the conservatory," he explained to his brother. "Well, in short, I have made up my mind to endure until December, then leave for Kamenka for the holidays and from there to write that I am sick, having naturally informed Rubinstein secretly beforehand so that he might look for another professor."[48]

For obvious reasons, Mrs. von Meck's approval was crucial to this plan. In the event of Tchaikovsky's leaving the conservatory, she would have to agree to increase her financial support, as this subsidy would then become virtually his sole source of income. *"Vive la liberté et surtout vive* Nadezhda Filaretovna!" he wrote frankly to Modest. "There is no doubt that she will approve my decision and that consequently I can lead the delightful wandering life, now at Kamenka and Verbovka, now in Petersburg with you, now abroad."[49] For the time being at least, his desire for freedom from the conservatory outweighed his apprehension about the further impositions on his freedom that would come from increased dependence on Mrs. von Meck. Arriving in St. Petersburg on the first of September, Tchaikovsky wrote to her in Paris, where she was then staying, a long letter in which he emphasized his shock at reading the *New Times* article. "I cannot tell you the impression that this article made on me: you could have knocked me down with a feather!" he declared. "Many times before, I have had to suffer at the hands of invisible friends depicting me in print as someone worthy of every compassion or at the hands of invisible enemies slinging mud at my person by means of newspaper insinuation, but before, I was able to bear patiently these kind services and to accept without shuddering both the inappropriate expressions of sympathy toward my person and the poisonous attacks. Now, having spent an entire year far from the centers of our public life, I have become unbearably sensitive to such manifestations of publicity."[50]

As he had told Modest, the *New Times* article had contained no direct attacks on Tchaikovsky. On the contrary, he was declared to be one of the most decent people at the conservatory, and the allusion to "amours of a different kind" was made without mentioning any names.[51] But even though he was obviously using the article to convince Mrs. von Meck to increase his subsidy so that he might leave the conservatory, it is worth noting that by describing to her his strong or hysterical response to the newspaper piece he also risked drawing her attention to the real nature of his fear. Either this was a simple slip or Tchaikovsky had by this time been sufficiently convinced of the intimacy and mutual trust between them to be no longer troubled by the thought that his homosexuality might be "exposed" to her and work irreparable damage to their friendship.

After venting his indignation at the *New Times* piece, Tchaikovsky hastened to acknowledge that the basic idea of the article was "not without some truth." He condemned Rubinstein's "despotism" and confessed his wish to be no longer Rubinstein's "lackey" and the subject of common gossip. He had been seized, he wrote to his benefactress, by "an infinite, indescribable, invincible need to run away and hide, to leave all this" and by "an inexpressible dread and terror" in the face of his impending return to Moscow and the conservatory. He claimed even to have been overcome at times by a desire for "unconditional peace, that is, death." But, he assured her in a subtle turn of thought, "this would pass and there would appear again the thirst to live in order to finish my work, to say what has not yet been said." And he then asked rhetorically, "But how to reconcile the one and the other, that is, to protect myself from contact with people, to live apart from them, yet at the same time to work, to go further, to perfect myself?"[52]

The litany was familiar, theatrically tragic perhaps, with its appeal to death and dream of flight. But whereas the preceding autumn there may have been serious grounds for such frustration and despair, a year later this was no longer true. His letter to Modest written just a few days before was quite calm and ordinary in tone, as were all his letters to his brothers and family at the time. There is little doubt that this letter to Mrs. von Meck was to some extent expressly designed to appeal to her Romantic and idealistic sensibilities. With perhaps conscious calculation Tchaikovsky was bringing into play the same rhetorical clichés that had worked so well once before, in the hope and expectation that, like a fairy godmother, Mrs. von Meck would grant his heart's desire and release him from his pedagogical bondage.

That same evening, to ensure that Mrs. von Meck might understand him correctly, he wrote that a "fit of misanthropic depression" awaited him with his work at the conservatory. Then, after a lengthy discourse on his inability to live either in Moscow or in St. Petersburg, with mention of Antonina thrown in for good measure, he came finally to the point: "And so, my friend, what would you say if I were to leave the conservatory? I have by no means made up my mind yet to do so. I shall go to Moscow and make an attempt to get used to it. But I need absolutely to know how you view all this." Both rhetorically and psychologically, this clothing of his request in the guise of an appeal for counsel smoothed matters for both of them, allowing Mrs. von Meck to offer her help without his having to ask for it directly. "Not for anything in the world," he continued, "should I wish to act not in accordance with your advice and instruction. Please answer this question."[53]

Having sent this letter and certain of her positive response, Tchaikovsky proceeded with a light heart to enjoy his stay in St. Petersburg, and despite a few undesired encounters, he remained in high spirits throughout the visit. He entertained himself in the company of Apukhtin and the latter's young friends the Zhedrinsky brothers, Vladimir, Aleksandr and Dmitry—of whom he found the first "grown terribly unattractive, but still nice," the second "very likable," and the third "a most delightful creation of nature were it not for his hands."[54] Adolescent, almost infantile hands were objects of particular fascination for Tchaikovsky, nearly to the point of fetishism. He always remembered the hands of his mother, a woman "with a lovely gaze and exceptionally beautiful hands,"[55] and he paid constant attention, as in the case of Dmitry Zhedrinsky, to the hands of the young men he met, although the "feetlike" hands of a mature man he found extremely unpleasant.[56] As for the "very likable" Aleksandr Zhedrinsky, both Tchaikovsky's letters and his diaries are filled with mentions or descriptions of young men (as a rule, of more or less adolescent age) using this same Russian adjective *simpatichny*, or "likable," which in Tchaikovsky's vocabulary almost certainly connoted "sexually appealing." He would also indulge in more-expansive expressions of delight at male beauty, as in a diary entry that records "a heavenly vision in the third-class car, in a felt coat."[57] It is clear that in this and many other such instances Tchaikovsky was registering male attractiveness automatically, simply as a natural reflex. Nothing even remotely similar can be said of his appreciation of female attractiveness, and with the exception of a few occasional mentions, women seem not to have interested him physically at all.

The one disquieting note during his stay in the capital came from his meeting with his father. He found the elderly Ilya "healthy and cheerful," but as he mentioned in a letter to Modest, "for the first time in my life I experienced an awkward sensation from Papa's company. This is because of his silence about my catastrophes of last year and the recollection of how carried away he was by [Antonina]."[58]

He left for Moscow on 10 September without yet having received a reply from Mrs. von Meck. Two days later, he wrote her another long letter, in which he elaborated with even greater candor and insistence his need to leave the conservatory. In Moscow classes began, but Tchaikovsky felt out of place. His "misanthropy" mounted. "I find Moscow utterly disgusting," he told Anatoly. "I try to avoid any company and any meetings. Everyone I see, with the exception of Nikolay Lvovich [Bochechkarov], is intolerable to me, not excluding Kashkin or Albrecht or Jurgenson or Laroche. . . . In the conservatory I feel like a guest."[59] On Nikolay Rubinstein's return from Paris, where as part of the International Exposition he had directed a triumphant performance of Tchaikovsky's First Piano Concerto in the hall of the Trocadéro, Tchaikovsky spoke with him and told him of his desire to leave the conservatory in December, to which Rubinstein consented.

The delicate situation became rather tense and uncertain. There had been no letter from Mrs. von Meck for some time, and Tchaikovsky did not know how things would stand if he in fact went ahead with his ardent intention. Yet, in the end, he was not mistaken in his expectation of his benefactress's response. She wrote to him from Italy on 20 September. "Yesterday I received your letter, forwarded to me from Paris, my dear incomparable friend, and I hasten to reply to your question that I shall be extremely pleased if you leave the conservatory because I have long thought it supremely absurd that you, with your intellect, development, education, and talent, should be dependent on gross arbitrariness and despotism."[60]

Tchaikovsky was ecstatic. "My happiness knows no bounds whatsoever. . . . How I shall work, how I shall strive now to prove to myself that I am indeed worthy of what you are doing for me. Often, very often, the thought weighs on me that you give me too much happiness. . . . My God, what happiness freedom is!"[61] Even the latest tactics of his wife could do nothing to spoil his joy. Antonina had so "conscientiously fulfilled" his condition to stay out of his way that he had no idea even "whether she is here [in Moscow] or has moved somewhere else." But he seemed more amused than anything when he told Mrs.

von Meck that Antonina's mother "bombards me with letters with expressions of the tenderest love, invitations to call on her, and even a request to be a sponsor at the wedding of her younger daughter, saying that my blessing will bring her happiness."[62] If true, such gestures suggest that Antonina, in her delusion, continued to misrepresent even to her own mother the true state of affairs between herself and her husband.

"Ah, my God," Tchaikovsky added, "how good to be far away from all this!" Indeed, he had not the patience to stay in Moscow until December. On 2 October 1878 he announced his departure to Rubinstein, while in a letter to Mrs. von Meck he shared his immediate plans: he would spend October in St. Petersburg and at the beginning of November would return to his beloved Clarens in Switzerland. So began his years of wandering, with no fixed home in Russia or abroad.

CHAPTER SEVENTEEN

Invisibility Presumed

A new phase of development in the relationship between Tchaikovsky and Mrs. von Meck had opened earlier in the year 1878 with her suggestion that they switch from the formal Russian *vy*, or "you," to the more familiar *ty*, or "thou," in their correspondence. This was a bold gesture, being in the Russian language and in social custom a sign of intimate friendship that might be considered inappropriate between a man and a woman not related to each other. The suggestion was made, of course, with the utmost delicacy and reserve. "I need nothing more from you than what I now enjoy," she wrote, "save perhaps a slight change in form: I should like you to address me, as is usual between friends, with 'thou.' I think that in correspondence this would not be difficult, but if you find it improper, I shall have no pretensions, because I am happy as it is; may you be blessed for this happiness! At this moment I should like to say that I embrace you with all my heart, but I fear you may find this far too odd."[1]

She was not mistaken, and Tchaikovsky no doubt found her wish "far too odd" indeed, even though he denied it in words, admitting merely that such tendernesses embarrassed him, as he felt himself "little worthy" of them. But her suggestion of greater intimacy in their address he tactfully rejected, citing the awkwardness and unnaturalness he feared such a change might bring. "We absorb convention with our mother's milk," he explained, "and however far above it we may put ourselves, still the slightest violation of this convention gives rise to awkwardness, and awkwardness, in its turn, to falsity. Meanwhile,

I want always to be myself with you and value beyond all measure this unconditional genuineness."[2]

Competing with her beloved friend in diplomacy, Mrs. von Meck in her next letter hastened to apologize for her rash suggestion. When making it she had been, she now confessed, "in such an abnormal, distracted condition that I even forgot what planet I was on, I was feeling your music and its creator." The formal "you" had seemed to her in that moment a "refined invention . . . of proprieties and politeness, by which hatred, malice, and deceit are so often disguised." Yet, the very next day, having returned to "normality," she had already repented of what she had written and feared lest Tchaikovsky, to humor her, should consent to her request even though it might be difficult for him. "I thank you all the more, my priceless friend," she wrote, "that you have spared me the knowledge of having abused another's kindness, and furthermore, I thank you for that good opinion of me that you have expressed by your frankness."[3]

With that, the matter was laid to rest, never to be broached again. Their relationship, nonetheless, continued to grow in intimacy. Both the bright and shadowy aspects of their communion were sharply evident in an unexampled Florentine idyll—their two-month stay "together" in that city in November and December 1878, during which time they exchanged some fifty letters.

On 22 October 1878, as Tchaikovsky prepared to leave St. Petersburg and go once more abroad, Mrs. von Meck wrote to him, "How I should like, my dear, for you to change your route slightly, namely to come first to Florence for about a month and half and then go to Clarens. . . . If you decided to come to Florence now, I should prepare an apartment for you in the city so that during this month and a half you would not need to worry about a thing and might concentrate solely on what is dear to you and to me—music. . . . How I should like to tempt you with Florence!"[4]

He answered at once, telling her that no sooner had he received her letter than he had decided to change his plans. "That you desire me to live in Florence now, while you are also there, is sufficient for me to rush with all my heart to that city. Irrespective of this, I myself by no means wish to pass up an opportunity to be near you for a while."[5] Her response to his consent was euphoric. "What a wonderful person you are, what a matchless heart you have, my dear incomparable friend!" she wrote. "Every sincere, heartfelt appeal finds always an echo in your noble, tender heart. Your readiness to come to Florence moves me to the depths of my soul, but your own kindness and magnanimity, with which you are ready to give to another everything kind and good, prevents me from accepting it unconditionally. Therefore, I ask you in earnest, my priceless friend—I demand—that you not come to Florence if you have even the slightest wish not to. . . . Oh, how dear you are to me, how I love you, how grateful I am to you!"[6]

This was her strongest declaration yet of her love for him, and indeed, such an effusion seems almost excessive, however sincere. Rendering the composer a rare service, offering him a princely state for rest and work in one of the most beautiful cities in the world, she still saw in his consent a good deed that he had done for her. But it was, of course, a rhetorical strategem like the one Tchaikovsky had adopted to convince her that he should leave the conservatory, the argument constructed in such a way as to leave the other correspondent no room to disagree. It is not surprising that he answered her from Kamenka on 6 November with his repeated consent. "And please, my dear, do not think that for the sake of fulfilling your desire I undertake any sacrifice, although I am prepared for the latter at any moment of my life," he wrote. "If I were to listen to you and stay here, the thought that your desire had not been fulfilled would poison my existence."[7]

Staying in the immediate proximity of Mrs. von Meck did, however, worry him more than a little on the eve of his departure from Kamenka. "Nadezhda Filaretovna has already rented me an apartment," he wrote to Anatoly on 14 November, "and although, judging by the description, the apartment is in a lovely spot with a marvelous view of Florence, it is two steps from the villa where N[adezhda] F[ilaretovna] lives, and I fear that this will constrain me."[8] On the journey to Italy he continued to be troubled by the thought that Mrs. von Meck would be so close that they might too easily run into each other, and he even began to suspect that she planned to invite him to visit her. But on his arrival in Florence on 20 November/2 December a letter from her awaiting him in his rooms reassured him. "It can be very easily arranged," he wrote Anatoly the next day, "that there will be no meetings at all."[9]

His stay in Florence was orchestrated by Mrs. von Meck with a delicate care bordering on the unbelievable, right down to books, newspapers, and his favorite cigarettes. They corresponded almost uninterruptedly, and his letters represent an endless flow of delight, gratitude, and praise, surpassable only by the answering flow of her ecstatic letters. But the very perfection of the arrangement served also to feed Tchaikovsky's deeper embarrassment at this incessant shower of blessings to which he could not adequately respond materially or, he felt, emotionally. As he had predicted, he began to feel constrained, and in a letter to Modest a week after his arrival he complained that even though nothing prevented him from changing his residence and way of life whenever he wished, the nearness of Mrs. von Meck made his stay "somewhat lacking in freedom all the same." Furthermore, it seemed to him that Mrs. von Meck herself must sense "something abnormal" in the entire arrangement. "She, poor woman, considers it her duty to write me letters every day," he told Modest, "and it is obvious that sometimes she is hard put to come up with material for conversation. For my part, I do not always have something to write either, yet find myself also obligated to write every day."[10]

But the thought that haunted him most of all, he confessed to his brother, was whether she did not in fact want, as he put it, to "lure" him to her. It was an interesting choice of word, very probably derived, at least in part, from his recent matrimonial experience and a spontaneous fear of being once again "entrapped" by a woman. In his mind, the most innocent gesture threatened to acquire some weighty significance. "I keep thinking she wishes to meet me," he wrote to Anatoly two days later, on 29 November/11 December. "For instance, every morning I see her stop while passing by my villa and try to catch sight of me. How am I to act? Go to the window and bow? But, in that case, why not also shout from the window, 'Good morning'?" The result was an oscillation between apprehensiveness and reassurance. "However," he admitted, "in her long, sweet, intelligent, and wonderfully affectionate daily letters there is not a single hint of any desire to meet."[11]

If some of the comments and overtones in these letters to his brothers seem to contradict the emotions expressed in his letters to Mrs. von Meck, these are by no means sufficient grounds to accuse Tchaikovsky of insincerity. In fact, the letters to his brothers from this period, despite some discrepancies in tone with those to his benefactress, prove, rather than disprove, the depth of his actual emotional and thankful commitment to her.

This commitment was further solidified by the news of the successful St. Petersburg premiere in late November of his Fourth Symphony, dedicated to Mrs. von Meck. Modest wrote with delight that the symphony had created "a genuine furor."[12] By early December, bouyed by the success of "their" symphony, Tchaikovsky already felt his feeling of constraint being replaced by a pleasant sense of routine. "Nadezhda Fil[aretovna] has ceased to inhibit me," he reported to Anatoly on 5/17 December. "I have even grown used to the daily correspondence, though one must give credit to this not only wonderful but also most intelligent woman. She manages to arrange it so that I always have lots of material for correspondence. . . . We saw each other once at the theater, but there have not been the slightest hints of a desire to meet, so in this respect I am quite at ease."[13] It is not clear whether their both being at the theater was wholly accidental or arranged by Mrs. von Meck in order to see him, as seems not unlikely.

Throughout the "Florentine idyll" of 1878, Mrs. von Meck's new favorite, Wladyslaw Pachulski, proved to be an important topic of their correspondence. Having familiarized himself with the compositions of her young protégé, Tchaikovsky, on 22 November/4 December, wrote Mrs. von Meck a lengthy letter in which he confessed that he saw no talent in Pachulski's works, only musical abilities and those "unexceptional." He advised her to "do everything possible to encourage and help him to study" so that he might acquire the piano technique necessary for any composer.[14] This sober opinion, once stripped of the ornaments of epistolary courtesy, clearly contrasted with Mrs. von Meck's own exaggerated enthusiasm. Yet, she was grateful even for this and responded with her habitual poise. "You have treated my request about Pachulski so kindly and attentively that I already fear lest his visits disturb you," she wrote. "You have only just got free of the conservatory, and here again you have to discuss harmonic incongruities and melodic requirements. Please, my dear, kind, good Pyotr Ilyich, do not constrain yourself in the slightest. If this business bored you yesterday, drop it today; if it should bore you Saturday, then drop it Sunday."[15]

But Tchaikovsky replied no less gracefully, begging her not to worry on account of his lessons with Pachulski. "He is so much a musician that it is by no means tiresome for me to talk with him. Next time, I shall ask him to improvise."[16] It seems that by this time he had already decided that the supervising of the young man's studies was his duty, the least he could do for Mrs. von Meck in return for the beneficent flow of gifts for him since the start of their acquaintance. For the same reason he seems also to have understood that so long as he did not go against his own artistic conscience, his opinions of Pachulski, even if critical, should on the whole be as favorable as possible.

His benefactress was pleased. "Your judgment made me very happy," she wrote on 24 November/6 December, "and you know I take your word as gospel. . . . Your lessons with him, my incomparable friend, are such a boon to him and will have the most tremendous significance for his whole musical career."[17] Of course, it cannot be ruled out that at first Tchaikovsky may genuinely have seen something in his new pupil. A remark of 29 November/11 December, for instance, sounds quite sincere: "I was very very pleased today with the work Pachulski did for me. I confess I did not expect that he would be able to satisfy at once and so successfully all my demands."[18] And the following day he wrote, "I have now no doubt that Pachulski can compose. Whether he will bring something of his own to his work is another question, which cannot yet be answered at present. Time will tell."[19] With time, however, Mrs. von Meck came to realize that Tchaikovsky's efforts on behalf of Pachulski did not reflect any artistic interest in her protégé but rather a desire to please her. "I accept all this," she would write on 7/19 January 1879, "as an expression of your dear friendship for me."[20]

It was by no means only the increasing intricacies of his spiritual friendship with Mrs. von Meck that occupied Tchaikovsky in Florence; the more earthly dimension of his sexuality became evident there as well. Apparently, while in Florence the previous year, he had made the acquaintance, to judge from various hints and the censor's cuts, of a homosexual pimp by the name of Napoleone. This time he attempted to avoid Napoleone, but in vain, as he described to Modest, without hiding his ambivalent feelings, in his letter of 21 November/3 December: "But whose steps do I hear behind me? Who seizes me by the waist in a friendly manner and says to me, *Ah, birbante, io vi ritrovo!* [Ah, scalawag, I find you again!] I turn and see—*il signore* Napoleone, in his eternally gray coat and a hat set back on his head. He resembles the sun; that is, he forever makes one and the same circuit. I was both glad and not glad. He says he has quarreled with his brother, who cut him with a knife. He has a huge scar on his cheek that is barely healed. Can it be so? [A cut follows.]"[21] A few days later he wrote again, this time decisively: "I scarcely go into town. The reason for this is Napoleone. I cannot help meeting him, and this is especially irksome to me. [A cut.] He gave me two photos, taken for me and you, for which he received fourteen lire and a promise to meet one another. But there will be no meeting."[22] For the moment at least, he appears to have decided not to succumb to further temptation.

In early December, Mrs. von Meck, preparing to leave Florence for Vienna and clearly having enjoyed her stay so close to her idol, proposed a similar plan for Paris. She suggested that rather than proceed directly to Paris, as he had planned, Tchaikovsky instead go first to Clarens and then "join" her in the French capital in February: "Then we might again live together, even though of course in Paris we should feel farther from one another, as the city is huge and crowded; but for me this would still be a joy."[23] It was another princely offer, given that, just as in Florence, she proposed to pay all expenses, in addition to his monthly subsidy. But Tchaikovsky, writing to Modest on 6/18 December, was far from pleased by the idea, regarding it as an encroachment on his freedom. He was already disturbed by hints in her letters that "she would like things *always* to be as they are now and herself *always* to look after every aspect of my welfare." This new proposal made him quite angry, as he told his brother. "You will say that I am too well-off," he added. "This is true, but it is also true that however delicately, however tenderly, Nadezhda Filaretovna still hampers my freedom somewhat, and if it were possible, I would refuse her apartments with pleasure, since the money she gives me is quite sufficient for my well-being. Lord, forgive my sin! That *I* should complain of N[adezhda] F[ilaretovna]! This is terrible baseness!"[24]

He had also professional reasons for resenting the timetable she proposed, chief among them his wish to visit Paris sooner in order to collect material for his latest operatic project, *The Maid of Orléans.* The idea for an opera about Joan of Arc had first taken hold of him some weeks before at Kamenka, where he happened upon Vasily Zhukovsky's translation of Schiller's *Die Jungfrau von Orleans.* He had begun to compose music for the opera in Florence, but having as yet no libretto, he had broken off. In Paris he was eager to find a copy of the libretto for Auguste Mermet's 1876 opera *Jeanne d'Arc,* on which he planned to base his own work. Yet, once again, he felt he could hardly refuse his benefactress altogether, and his response to her, written on the same day as his letter to Modest, was quite different in tone. "I shall proceed as you advise me," he assured her, "only with the small difference that I shall still go to Clarens through Paris and shall stay there two or three days. . . . Then with great pleasure I am prepared to go to Clarens, work hard there for a while, and after that, toward February, come to Paris, which, of course, will be twice as lovely, dear, and pleasant for me because you will be there. After all, you desire it, and for me this is reason enough to desire sincerely the same."[25] Her reply was customarily ecstatic and apologetic: she had written without any expectation of his consent; he continued to spoil her; if he had the slightest hesitations, he should not do it; and so on.

It is curious and telling, given his perception of her presence as a constraint on his freedom, that Tchaikovsky plunged into depression as soon as Mrs. von Meck left Florence. No less striking than his earlier resentment and embarrassment at her nearness, the force of his attachment to her surprised even Tchaikovsky himself, and he admitted that the longing and emptiness he felt after her departure were "beyond expectation." In a letter to Modest of 15/27 December, he confessed that the sight of her deserted villa brought tears to his eyes and that the streets of the beautiful city had become gloomy and dull. "I have grown so used to communicating with her daily," he wrote, "to watching her pass by every morning with her whole entourage, and what at first constrained and embarrassed me now constitutes an object of the most genuine regret. But, Lord, what an amazing, wonderful woman! How touching were all her concerns for me, extending to the petty details but in general making my life here supremely enjoyable."[26]

Two years later, again in Florence, Mrs. von Meck recalled their autumn idyll there with no less nostalgia and emotion. "Here I am in Florence, in my spacious Villa Oppenheim," she wrote, "but, my God, how dreary, how sad that you are not here, my dear, incomparable friend." Almost immediately after her arrival, she took a drive to glance at the little house that she had rented for Tchaikovsky during their stay there and that had thus become "so dear to me and full of such precious recollections of when I felt you in it, saw unseen your dear image, heard the sounds flying from your fingers and was so happy." But now she felt only the same tearful longing Tchaikovsky had felt on passing her empty villa, and this grief was instantly replaced by bitterness at the thought that someone else was now living there. "This someone else appeared to me so nasty and offensive," she told him, "that I wanted to drive him out of there at once and rent this house so that no one might live in it, but," she added wryly, "I restrained myself, for I am already considered an eccentric as it is."[27]

Tchaikovsky left Florence for Paris on 16/28 December. He had been somewhat reticent in claiming to Mrs. von Meck that the only reason for stopping over in Paris on his way to Clarens was the need to collect material for his opera. Of no less importance was his desire to meet with Kotek, whom, as he confessed to Anatoly in a letter of 8/20 December from Florence, he had summoned to the French capital, "since Kotek has vacation at Christmas, since he is very upset that our meeting [in Berlin] did not take place, and since I want very much to see him and play [music] with him."[28] But in his letters to Mrs. von Meck, whose break with her former protégé had proved irreparable, Tchaikovsky kept prudently silent about this visit.

Kotek arrived in Paris on 19/31 December, but their reunion was a disappointment, even though the young man was not to blame. Tchaikovsky, short of money, had fallen into another gloomy mood, which "unfortunately reflects on my relations toward dear, kind Kotek. What a difference between the endearments I lavished on him in writing and my present passive affection. He had to come upon me just when I am angry at everything and everybody."[29] Owing to this irritability, Tchaikovsky found himself angered by everything about Kotek—his lack of manners, his poor sense of humor, and "especially . . . his unbelievable womanizing," on which "all of our conversations turn."[30] Once again the familiar mixture of resentment and repentance so characteristic of Tchaikovsky's "misanthropy" tainted any enjoyment at seeing his former pupil. On the one hand, he found "his company more unpleasant than pleasant," while, on the other, he felt "terribly ashamed [at having] complained about dear, kind, loving Kotek!"[31]

Much the same were his shifts of mood regarding Alyosha, though with his servant positive emotions on the whole prevailed. In Vienna on the eve of their departure to Florence they had visited the opera together. "Alyosha was beside himself with delight. I am very pleased with him. Only one thing irritates me—that on the road he always sleeps. From Vienna to Florence he slept nearly the whole time. But his spirits are good. He is affectionate to the point of tenderness."[32] He even mused that he failed to recognize in this "affectionate, kind, sweet, cheerful Lyonka" the "ill-tempered creature" of the year before.[33] But all was not rosy, and there were moments of disappointment and longing for others. To Modest he had confided while still in Vienna that Alyosha alone was not enough for him. "There ought also to be at least one of you two [that is, Modest or Anatoly]," he wrote, "and then it would be fine!"[34] And later from Paris, with the same irritability he showed with Kotek, he complained, "Today I am displeased with Alyosha. First, he belittles everything, as was to be expected; second, he stops in front of every store and says, 'That'd be nice to buy!' Granted, this is partly in jest, but I am a little annoyed with him all the same."[35]

The irritability and bad humor that plagued Tchaikovsky throughout his brief stay in Paris appear to have stemmed ultimately, and not surprisingly, from the reemergence of Antonina. "A dread specter," he proclaimed dramatically to Mrs. von Meck, "has once again appeared before me. . . . I am sad and depressed, and take very little pleasure in the Parisian gaiety."[36] In December, shortly before leaving Florence, Tchaikovsky learned that Modest had been approached by a certain Kolreif, a moneylender whom the brothers knew and who had offered his services to follow Antonina with the aim of exposing *her* as an adulteress. Tchaikovsky's violent reaction in a letter to his brother of 12/24 December was quite inconsistent with what prompted it. He upbraided Modest for not "spitting in Kolreif's mug" and rejecting the offer on the spot. "In such cases, you can be extremely light-headed and careless," he grumbled. "I beg and implore you, if you have not yet written [to Kolreif], then write at once that since I am not contemplating divorce at all, there is no need at all for his spying." Most of all he feared that Antonina—"who," he noted parenthetically, "despite her stupidity is very shrewd"—might learn that she was being followed and shout to everyone that he was setting spies on her. The whole

matter left him feeling "crazed and irritated in the extreme," he confessed to his brother. "The name of this creature simply causes me a
kind of physical pain."[37]

Two more things happened at the very end of the year to cause
Tchaikovsky sharp worry. One of these was a letter that Antonina
wrote to Pyotr Jurgenson, in which "without any cause she heaps upon
him a whole series of incomprehensible insults."[38] Having been sent
this letter by Jurgenson, Tchaikovsky told Anatoly that he experienced
"a feeling of disgust at the sight of her handwriting," and he begged his
brother, "If the reptile actually takes it into her head to appeal to Modest or to Sasha, for God's sake, ask them for me and tell them that I
implore them on my knees not to answer her."[39]

Almost simultaneously Tchaikovsky learned a more disturbing
piece of news, one that he interpreted as an attempt to blackmail him.
Anatoly had received a visit from an unknown gentleman by the name
of Simonov claiming to be Antonina's relative and close adviser. This
Simonov, though not endowed with power of attorney, informed the
composer's brother that Antonina had been to see a lawyer and was
now herself demanding a divorce and, to settle the matter "peaceably,"
wished to know her husband's conditions. Writing to Mrs. von Meck
"with heart contracted and with anguish and grief in my soul," Tchaikovsky summarized for her his response to Anatoly. Although he consented in principle to a divorce "at any moment," he refused to negotiate the matter with someone who had not received his wife's formal
power of attorney, "especially when this person, as Anatoly writes,
praises the virtues and intellect of a certain person." He was still prepared to take the expenses of the proceedings on himself, but as he had
warned her when she had backed out of the negotiations of the preceding summer, Antonina had forfeited his earlier offer of ten thousand
rubles. Moreover, the proceedings would begin "not when she wishes
it, but when I return to Russia, and my return I cannot make subject
to her caprices."[40]

Clearly, he had strong doubts about this most recent development
in "this muddle." "In essence, one should rejoice that the certain individual has finally come to her senses," he added to Mrs. von Meck.
"But there is no way to foresee and to know just how serious this is
and whether she is not up to some new trick." His anxiety was expressed more strongly in the letter to his brother, Tchaikovsky suggesting that Simonov seemed to him to be a swindler with unspecified
designs and declaring that "no secrecy and no interference on his part
is necessary." He then went on to ask, "What can she have in mind?
There is no need to coerce me into a divorce on grounds of, say, im-

potence, since I have agreed anyway to base proceedings even on that very pretext. And no one can force me to give her money as capital. So do not reply or write to Mr. Simonov, who seems extremely suspect to me." But in case Simonov did address him again, along with the conditions he had spelled out, he added that as far as any pretext was concerned, he was "agreeable to adultery, impotence, or whatever she likes."[41]

His subsequent letters suggest, however, that his initial panic, and especially his fear that the appearance of Simonov signaled an attempt at blackmail, had been greater than he had cared to show. "Tell Tolya that today, having slept quite well, I regarded the story of his visitor quite calmly," he wrote to Modest on 22 December/3 January. "Can I fear for a single minute her attempts to play dirty tricks on me? . . . She probably wouldn't mind blackmailing me. But one would have to be as nervously impressionable as Tolya and I to become frightened right away and talk seriously with some stranger about a peaceful settlement!"[42] To Anatoly he was more explicit, writing that he saw Simonov's visit as "a very rude and clumsy attempt at blackmail" and that Antonina "does not want to lose the ten thousand—that is all." After a censorial cut, the letter continues, "I cannot imagine any other causes for her initiative here, but blackmail is also impossible, even should she make up her mind to go ahead with it. My letters contain only arguments in my favor. I have been unconditionally honest toward her and have not once used a single expression that might compromise me."[43]

Tchaikovsky was confident that he had nothing to fear. He knew that to be convicted on a charge of homosexuality prosecutors needed material proof of the "crime." Such proof could be either the exposure of the accused in flagrante delicto or the testimony of at least two persons who had been victims or participants in the act. Moreover, this law was virtually never applied to individuals belonging to the privileged classes of society. Tchaikovsky, a jurist by education, would have known all this and would have recognized that Antonina's chances for successful blackmail were negligible. Hence his militant posture: "What have I to fear? I am not afraid of her gossip, and it will run its course in any case. She wants a divorce? So much the better. She wants to blackmail me by denouncing me to the secret police?—well this I do not fear at all."[44]

This, of course, was the attitude dictated by reason. But Tchaikovsky was often reluctant to acquiesce unfailingly in arguments of reason, and despite his own known immunity, he was plagued at times by panic and intimations. He himself wrote of this to Anatoly on 23

December/4 January: "Now, when I have begun to calm down a bit and return to normal, I must confess to you that your letter with the news about the visit of the strange gentleman made on me a crushing impression. Although my mind was telling me that it was all nonsense, still my entire being was stung by this reminder of the reptile. . . . Just seeing her handwriting was enough to make me feel at once miserable and make my spirits sink. Such is the nature of this serpent's poison. Your letter finished me."[45] But such nightmares quickly passed and, in a letter that followed three days later, were made the object of derision. His momentary belief that Antonina might actually be contemplating criminal proceedings against him on a charge of sodomy had conjured an awful fantasy in Tchaikovsky's mind. "I vividly imagined myself in the dock, crushing the prosecutor in my final speech, but still perishing under the weight of the shameful accusation," he revealed to Anatoly. "In my letters to you I put on a brave front, but in fact, I considered myself already ruined. Now this all seems like sheer lunacy to me."[46]

Of course, as he well realized, the possibility of blackmail was quite unlikely, but it was still conceivable that the homosexual issue might surface during a divorce action and cause trouble. It was essential to Tchaikovsky that Antonina stick to one particular version of events throughout the proceedings, without the slightest deviation, something he was not at all certain she would manage. For this reason, he would consult with Anatoly some months later as to whether he could provide her with a single large sum instead of a pension and thereby protect himself from future harassment on her part without resorting to a divorce "which she does not want and which I fear, if one takes into consideration that she could cause a scandal during the course of the proceedings."[47]

In his final verdict on the subject, in a letter to Mrs. von Meck of 13/25 January 1879 from Clarens, he came as close as he could to revealing the truth without spelling it out. "She continues to wish a divorce, but in a completely idiosyncratic manner," he wrote. "Meanwhile, a thoroughly conscientious attitude toward the matter from both parties is essential here; otherwise, a very dangerous and unpleasant story may be played out. Thus, I have now reached the point where, although in absolute terms a divorce would be a priceless blessing for me, in relative terms, considering the circumstances and the character of the dramatis personae, it frightens and terrifies me, and I shall only undertake it with extreme caution."[48]

Even before leaving Paris at the end of December, Tchaikovsky had begun to shake off the gloom cast by this latest appearance of his wife.

Despite his claim to Mrs. von Meck, he could not entirely resist the charms of the "Parisian gaiety" and particularly of the Parisian theaters. Twice he visited the Comédie Française, where he became infatuated with a handsome young actor name Boucher, whom he and Modest had first seen during their visit to Paris two years before. "[The actor Got] is a young and incredibly noble man who receives a slap in the face at the end of the play," he wrote in a letter to Modest from 26 December/7 January. "What I wouldn't give to have that same hand that insulted Got give me a hundred slaps in the face! This hand belongs to a divine creature whom you and I both admired in that memorable production in 1876. His name is Boucher. Do you remember him? What an enchanting person and what a marvelous actor he is!"[49] Besides its frank delight in the young man's beauty, this passage is striking in its evocation of Tchaikovsky's near-fetishistic obsession with male hands.

Tchaikovsky arrived back in Clarens four days later, on 30 December/11 January, taking up residence again at the Villa Richelieu, where his landlady, the hospitable Mme Mayor, surrounded him with care and attention. He had become "truly attached" to the family of his hostess and her boardinghouse and to the lovely landscape about Lake Geneva. The half-empty boardinghouse suited him perfectly for the composing, because he could sing and play but not worry about disturbing anyone. The day after his arrival, he plunged into work on *The Maid of Orléans*, writing music in the mornings and toiling over the libretto in the evenings. The Mermet libretto had turned out to be of little help, and Tchaikovsky had decided to fashion his own text from Zhukovsky's translation of *Die Jungfrau von Orleans*. Schiller's idealism cast a perennial spell on the composer, as it did on so many of his Russian contemporaries. One of them, Aleksandr Herzen, observed that Schiller could be disliked only by "bores or old men," while Dostoevsky placed him at the center of his "'sentimental' education." "In the end, I have come to the conclusion," Tchaikovsky explained to Mrs. von Meck, "that Schiller's tragedy, while not consistent with historical truth, still surpasses all other artistic representations of *Joan* in its depth of psychological truth."[50]

Between his work sessions Tchaikovsky took daily strolls, the nature of which is persistently excised in all published editions of his letters to his brothers, whether by Soviet censors or Modest in his own handling of the originals. Censorship speaks for itself. It is likely that these strolls entailed not only physical recreation but also encounters with young men.

He was also very pleased with the "tender affections" of Alyosha.

In his free time Tchaikovsky drilled him in French, and clearly bene-
fiting from these lessons, the young servant continued his amorous
advances toward Mme Mayor's charming maid Marie, for whom Tchaikovsky himself had come to feel "a great *penchant.*" In a letter to his
sister of 21 January/2 February, he confided, "I live in my snug little
corner and live pleasantly, though somewhat monotonously, but then
my work is in full swing. I see absolutely no one; my company consists
of Alyosha, Marie, . . . books and music. I have so much to do that I
do not even notice the day passing."[51] The closer it got to his departure,
the dearer the Villa Richelieu became to him. "I now feel thoroughly
at home here," he confessed to Modest, "and have begun to view Mme
Mayor as a close relative and Marie as a dear friend." He had also become quite close with the landlady's thirteen-year-old son Gustave
who, he found, had "blossomed and grown inexpressibly prettier."[52]

For all the comfort of Clarens, Tchaikovsky still longed for St. Petersburg and missed terribly his brothers, father, and other "dear people," including Modest's young charge, Kolya Konradi. He again showered the familiar repertory of endearments upon Kolya, imaginatively
applying all manner of kisses to "his little eyes, little lips, little
cheeks." He saw and kissed the boy in his dreams, wrote him separate
letters, and again covered his replies with kisses.[53] His letters also offer
scattered allusions to Modest's own amorous anguish. "How well I understand your situation," he wrote his brother in a letter of 2/14 January. "This has happened to me quite often. In fact, you are not in love
with any of the three young ladies, since being in love consists precisely in the fact that there exists nothing on earth more beautiful than
she."[54] Considering the clear sexual preferences of both brothers, it is
not difficult to infer the true gender of the young "ladies." The word (if
not impudently interpolated by Soviet censors) may well have been
used in fear that the letter might be seen by young Kolya or his parents.

Even before it began, Tchaikovsky and Mrs. von Meck's stay in
Paris "together" in February 1879 proved considerably less idyllic than
their Florentine experience. Financial circumstances were once again
the cause of embarrassment. Tchaikovsky had overspent in Clarens
and was expecting the arrival there of the "budgetary sum" (yet another euphemism for his monthly allowance), while Mrs. von Meck,
thinking he was to arrive in Paris on the first of the month, had been
impatiently awaiting their reunion there to have it delivered to him
directly. Upon realizing his predicament, she sent him at once a thousand francs ("because I have nothing smaller right now"), along with a
thousand apologies.[55]

Following his arrival on 6/18 February, there ensued a whole series of misunderstandings concerning his apartment. The one she had taken for him he found inordinately expensive, even though she was covering the full cost of the rent. He moved to a second one and regretted that he could not rent a third and even less expensive one. As a result, their correspondence became a flow of exaggerated mutual apologies. "How happy I am that you have finally arrived, my dear, priceless friend," Mrs. von Meck wrote, "but for God's sake, forgive my incompetence this time. I made you so many firm promises about the apartment and kept so few."[56] Tchaikovsky wrote in return, "I am indescribably grateful to you my dear friend, but I regret having committed a whole string of foolishness."[57] It seems likely that Tchaikovsky was in a peevish state from the moment he arrived. He had, after all, little desire to go to Paris solely at the insistence of his benefactress, as he had written Jurgenson quite explicitly from Clarens: "How and why [I am leaving for Paris] is a long story. But the whole point is that I must do it, although truthfully I would be quite happy to remain here."[58]

For Mrs. von Meck, of course, he projected just the opposite meaning on the situation. "Do you know, dear friend," he wrote, "that I blame myself somewhat for the fact that you are now in Paris, which, if I am not mistaken, is not at all suitable to the present demands of your health. For surely it is I who, with my rhapsodizing about Paris, gave you the idea to come here from Vienna?"[59] It is not difficult to draw from this passage the inference that the lady should blame herself for Tchaikovsky's having to come to Paris, which did not at all correspond to the present demands of his mood.

The entire style of their relations in Paris differed from what it had been in Florence. Mrs. von Meck found herself suffering from migraines and for this reason asked Tchaikovsky to slow down their correspondence to one letter a week. Ironically, Tchaikovsky straightaway interpreted this as a change in her attitude toward him: "In Florence it was just the opposite. She wrote me every day, and so did I. I believe she has simply got bored with conducting this correspondence. In any event, it appears very strange. What need had she for me to live in Paris at the same time as she? In Florence we saw each other and exchanged letters daily, but here, were it not for Pachulski, who comes to take lessons, we should have absolutely nothing in common. Unfortunately, it must be confessed that our relations are abnormal and that from time to time this abnormality shows."[60]

The slowing-down of that same correspondence that he had earlier regarded as a burden now almost offended Tchaikovsky, and in this, one sees clearly his habitual insecurity, even paranoia. There can be no doubt that Mrs. von Meck's headaches were by no means a pretext but in fact a source of real suffering. "My head is so upset that I cannot bend over the table to write to you," she explained at one point, "but write upright, holding the paper level with my head, and therefore in pencil."[61] Indeed, her attitude toward her friend had not changed in the least, as this admonition from her letter of 6/18 February, for example, makes clear: "In short, I ask you, my dear, to tell me quite frankly all your wishes concerning your lodgings, and I shall try to provide for you in full accordance with your wish, because I warn you, my dear friend, that not for anything shall I yield to you my legitimate right to provide you lodgings in Paris. I shall not interfere in any of your other expenses, but your lodgings must be my responsibility, and this I shall not yield to you, my precious friend, because you came for my sake, as my guest, and I want you to have such lodgings as I wish."[62] At any rate, their correspondence very soon returned to its previous pace, tone, and volume.

Throughout January and February, Tchaikovsky worked intensively on *The Maid of Orléans* and regularly reported on its progress in his letters to his brothers. Finally, on 22 February/6 March, he informed Modest that "yesterday was a very significant day for me. Quite to my own surprise, I have *entirely completed* my opera. . . . Say what you like, it's an exhausting business to squeeze music out of one's head at a certain time every day for nearly two and half months, sometimes with great ease but at other times laboriously. Still, how much rest I shall now have! The scoring is just brainwork! It's embroidery with a ready-made pattern."[63]

Tchaikovsky left Paris for Berlin six days later and from there returned to St. Petersburg. On 15 March he and his brothers traveled to Moscow to attend the dress rehearsal the following day and the first Moscow performance, on the seventeenth, of *Eugene Onegin*, performed by students of the conservatory at the Maly Theater. The performance was a resounding success. But on returning to St. Petersburg two days later, Tchaikovsky was met by a quite unexpected and tragicomic series of misadventures.

Antonina had not only surfaced but had come to the capital in search of her peregrinating husband. As he described the events to Mrs. von Meck in a letter of 24 March, apparently Antonina had for some time been watching the building in which Anatoly lived and in which the composer was now staying. Let into the building by the doorman, she was shown into Anatoly's study. Tchaikovsky, warned by the doorman, managed to prepared himself for the visit, but no sooner did he step into the study than Antonina threw her arms about his neck, repeating over and over that she could not live without him, that she would agree to any conditions if only he would come back to her. To this, Tchaikovsky answered that however much he was to blame in her regard, he would never agree to their living together. Antonina burst into sobs and again repeated her assurances of love. Desperate to put a stop to this scene, Tchaikovsky begged her to give him time to think things over, promising to write or see her personally in Moscow. Only then, somewhat appeased, did she agree to leave, though managing before she did to allude in passing to several instances of men who, she claimed, had recently professed their love to her.

Summing up this "shattering" scene in his letter to Mrs. von Meck, Tchaikovsky noted, "It proves to me that only abroad and in the countryside am I safe from the pestering of the certain individual. As far as divorce is concerned, it's no use even thinking about that. Apparently nothing in the world can eradicate her delusion that I am actually in love with her and sooner or later must live with her. She does not want even to hear about divorce, and as for that gentleman who during the winter came to my brother in her name with an offer of divorce, she swears that he is a base schemer who is in love with her and acted against her wishes."[64] This was, however, yet another instance of her increasingly erratic behavior.

As it turned out, Antonina did not return to Moscow as she had promised, but continued to lay siege to her husband, trying to catch him walking near the house where he was living and even renting an apartment there. Again confronted by her, Tchaikovsky told her that she was seeking to meet with him in vain, to which she responded that she was unable now to live far from him and would depart for Moscow together with him. In addition, on 28 March, he received a letter from her in which she declared again her undying love: "Come to me, my dearest, visit me. . . . No power on earth will make me stop loving you; treat me at least with compassion. I belong to you body and soul—do with me as you wish. After meeting with you, I cannot put my nerves in order and I start to weep several times a day. I am afraid now even to ask you about myself, but meanwhile, I am terrified that I shall again have to drag out such a life as I have done all this time."[65]

Tchaikovsky was outraged. However simpleminded, the letter must surely have expressed the genuine feelings and frustration of an abandoned woman for her intolerable circumstances—both with and without a husband at the same time, subject to gossip and condemnation. Yet, Tchaikovsky, who so often suffered along with those around him, proved utterly incapable of sympathizing with her. He simply never managed to recover from the consequences of the overwhelming shock of his apparently devastating experience during their brief second period of cohabitation. Out of this shock had come the myth of a vicious "reptile," which effectively replaced in both his conscious and unconscious imagination the living and suffering human being.

As for Antonina, these were her last futile efforts to recover that benevolence on his part that she remembered from the earliest time of their acquaintance. When Tchaikovsky left again for Moscow on his way to Kamenka, she followed in pursuit. By now, however, apparently having recognized her failure at reconciliation, she reverted understandably to her future welfare. On the eve of her husband's departure from Moscow a few days later, she unexpectedly burst in on him, this time with her sister. The two stayed some two hours, during which time Tchaikovsky barely managed to control himself. But when "instead of tears and hysterics" she suddenly turned to the question of money, he felt relief. Listening to her various allusions to Mrs. von Meck, of whom she had learned and whom she somehow fantasized to have made her a large offer, he bluntly asked her how much she needed. Her answer was fifteen thousand rubles, that she might forever quit Russia, "where everyone looks at her strangely and where for this reason she cannot work," and go abroad to give herself to music. Replying that he did not have such money but was receptive to her demands, Tchaikovsky "had the imprudence to say that, besides the pension, I would sometimes pay her extraordinary subsidies, and allow her to address me in cases of special need."[66] After dinner that same evening, coming home to find a note from her with a request for fifty rubles, he "had the weakness" to send her half that sum.

Writing to Mrs. von Meck of this episode, Tchaikovsky noted that "more than ever before, this unfathomably strange human being has revealed her predilection for filthy lucre." His written response to his wife, he told Mrs. von Meck, was that capitalization of the pension was impossible, "as there is no way without a formal divorce to put an end to her harassments once and for all," and that, since she either did not want a divorce or could not understand the formal procedure of obtaining one, everything therefore remained as before. "Generally speaking," he concluded to his benefactress, "I can live quite peacefully so long as I am not in Moscow and not in Petersburg. . . . In the event that I have to visit Petersburg or Moscow on musical business, it will be necessary simply to arrange things so that she cannot burst in on me unexpectedly as happened now."[67] This resolve he fulfilled, and Antonina became one of the major factors driving the composer away from both cities.

On 6 April, Tchaikovsky, together with Modest, Kolya, and their niece Anna Davydova, who was returning from school, traveled to Kamenka. All the way there he suffered from painful hives, apparently a neurotic and somatic consequence of his latest encounter with Antonina. Only as they approached their destination did he feel a sudden and complete relief. In one of his first accounts sent to Anatoly in St. Petersburg he wrote, "How magnificent are the mornings, how incredibly beautiful the sunsets and the moonlit nights with the nightingales, how the trees blossom, and what ecstasies come over me at times as a result of these delights! . . . I feel superb."[68]

But, even at Kamenka, Antonina continued to disturb his thoughts. The idea of a "legal separation" had taken hold of him after all, and he asked Anatoly to find out whether it might be possible to capitalize her pension and thereby gain his freedom without a divorce, obtaining from her an affidavit that all her claims had been satisfied.[69] The necessary money he expected to be able to get from Mrs. von Meck. But his wife did yet another about-face, writing to Anatoly that she was sick of insults, wanted a divorce, and would contact him through a lawyer. In a shrewd move, Tchaikovsky sent both this letter and her previous one to Mrs. von Meck so that the latter might "get a true idea of this unfathomable personality." In doing so, he noted, "I am ashamed to confess my faintheartedness, but I must tell you that I did not sleep all last night and today feel quite unglued because of seeing the handwriting of a certain individual!"[70]

Reading the letters must have dispelled any lingering doubts Mrs. von Meck might still have had about her friend's intolerable situation. On 5 May she counseled him to "do everything" to free himself from his wife completely. "Do not stop before the unpleasant aspects of divorce," she urged. "It is better to pass once through a dirty, stifling atmosphere and then find yourself in clean, fresh air than all your life to swallow periodically such miasmas. And if you do not get a divorce, you will never know peace, and eternal flight is intolerable. Do not stop either before the financial aspect; pay her ten or fifteen thousand—you know that I shall gladly provide it if only your tranquillity might be secured."[71] Thus, for the third time within a year, the prospect of divorce proceedings arose, and Tchaikovsky authorized Anatoly to recommence negotiations, again agreeing to play the guilty party on her choice of pretext—adultery or impotence—and to cover all expenses, provided she seriously wished a divorce.[72] He instructed his brother to offer her money, if necessary, but to claim that it would be provided by Lev Davydov: "If he [Antonina's lawyer] mentions the name of Mme Meck, then laugh and say that Mme Meck has sometimes made me commissions and paid me well, but that it does not follow from this that she could lend me several thousand."[73]

With this, he sought to put the matter from his mind and to relax in the familiar comfort of Kamenka. Here, amid his loved ones, he easily found diversion from his worries, and perhaps the most pleasant diversions of all were his adored nieces and nephews. In light of the closeness between Tchaikovsky and his sister, Aleksandra, it is not surprising that her children occupied an important place in his heart. Although a host of physical and psychological troubles would plague them as the years passed, nature had also endowed the seven Davydov children with a distinct physical beauty, immediately recognized by Mrs. von Meck upon receiving a family photograph. "It is so charming that one does not want to take one's eyes away," she declared. "Tatyana Lvovna is a beauty as always; Anna is lovely as an angel of God descended on earth; her sweet innocent expression is enchanting. Yury is a picture. What beauty! Mitya [Dmitry] and Bob [Vladimir] are the most charming schoolboys that nature ever created. It is remarkable what a handsome family it is; nature seems to have taken deliberate care with them, as if to show the world what miracles it is capable of producing—delightful!"[74]

While still in Paris, Tchaikovsky had written to his brother-in-law in a letter of 22 February/6 March of his impatience "to see the proudly elegant Tatyana, the fragrant violet Vera, the delectable fresh garden cucumber Tasya [Natasha], the martial and knightly Mitya, the poetic Bobik and, finally, the incomparable Uka [Yury], as well as the beautiful parents of this younger generation."[75]

All four of Tchaikovsky's nieces were rapidly approaching young womanhood. Tanya, the eldest of the Davydov children, was now eighteen. Even before her birth Aleksandra and Lev had dreamt of a fabulous future for their firstborn child, and she remained the indisputable favorite of the family. Growing up in an atmosphere of universal adoration, Tanya herself had long since come to believe in her extraordinary destiny. Her brother Yury later recalled that his sister began to distinguish herself early. "At age three and a half she was already reading and attempted to write her diary in French. Learning came easily to her. She read a great deal, especially history, and was noted for her artistic abilities—she loved music, played piano from childhood, studied at the conservatory in Geneva, sculptured not badly, was very fond of needlework." In addition, "by fourteen or fifteen Tatyana Lvovna looked a perfect beauty."[76] In early 1879, Aleksandra began bringing both Tanya and her second daughter, Vera, to St. Petersburg to introduce them to society. The lovely Tanya immediately attracted the attention of the capital, and she would do so again later that same year during a visit to her aunt Vera Butakova in Yalta, where she was soon besieged by suitors.

Of his three nephews, it was originally the youngest, Yury, who in his infancy elicited the loudest raptures from Tchaikovsky. "If only you knew what Yury is like!" he once gushed to Anatoly. "He is absolutely indescribable. It is such an original charm, such incredible humor! . . . In addition, he is uncommonly good-looking!"[77] To Mrs. von Meck he rhapsodized on Yury's "splendid childish beauty"[78] and elsewhere declared, "Ah, what an inexpressibly wonderful child! . . . His disposition is remarkable. He is an unusually gentle and obedient boy, always cheerful, affectionate, and sweet. He has an incredibly vivid imagination. . . . There is no way to convey in words and descriptions his charm, but we enjoy him endlessly."[79] Over the years, as the boy grew up, this ecstasy on his uncle's part gradually diminished, but the warm attachment between the two continued until the very end of Tchaikovsky's life.

There was no such warmth of emotion in his attitude toward his eldest nephew, Dmitry. Yury Davydov writes in his recollections that Tchaikovsky "loved his first nephew less than his younger brothers and sisters." One reason for this absence of sympathy was that Dmitry never showed any interest in music, preferring poetry, and lacked the patience to listen to a whole program of a symphonic concert or an entire opera. But, in addition to everything else, recalls Yury, "in his nephew's [Dmitry's] childhood years Pyotr Ilyich was somewhat irritated by his noisy, lively disposition. He did not approve of his very light-minded attitude to learning and to life in general."[80] Very likely, this description is deliberately softened. In Tchaikovsky's diary, for instance, one finds this harsh entry: "Bob fell from a horse because of that good-for-nothing Mitka's fooling around. . . . After dinner Mitya was killing dogs for pleasure. I began to hate the loathsome urchin at once and was so shocked and upset that I could hardly take part in a game of *bouts-rimés.*"[81]

It was the second nephew, Bob, who would eventually become the center of his uncle's emotional life. According to Yury, it was young Vladimir himself who, unable to pronounce the English "Baby," as his family used to call him, came out with "Bob" instead, and the nickname stuck. Modest, in his account, notes that when Bob was younger, Tchaikovsky would pamper him more than the other members of the family, but that his preference for the boy was not yet "of a serious character." But from the time Bob began to turn into a young man, his uncle's sympathy for him began to grow, and little by little he came to love the boy as he had loved Modest and Anatoly in their childhood. "Despite the difference in ages," remarks Modest with just barely implicit erotic overtones, "he never tired in the company of his favorite, felt anguish at their separation, confided his most intimate thoughts to him, and in the end made him his principal heir, entrusting him with the care of all those whose fate after his death worried him."[82]

Tchaikovsky himself acknowledged his love for Bob. "He is my favorite," he confessed to Mrs. von Meck. "However delightful his younger brother may be, Volodya [Vladimir, that is, Bob] still occupies the warmest corner of my heart."[83] Indeed, the language he used in reference to Bob was much the same ecstatic language he had used when addressing the beloved adolescent Anatoly years before. "I embrace all the children warmly," he wrote to Aleksandra in one letter. "Lord, what I would give at this moment to kiss Baby's little cheek."[84] And in another letter to his sister, he noted, "How happy I was to receive a letter from Bobik. The lines he inscribed were covered with kisses."[85]

With stubborn passion and a degree of wishful thinking, Tchaikovsky strove to discern the promise of artistic talent in his eight-year-old nephew. "Bobik is a little poet," he declared. "All day long he picks flowers, admiring the flowers, the sun, the birds."[86] To Mrs. von Meck he wrote that Bob was making progress in music and revealed remarkable abilities for drawing. "All his free time he devotes either to drawing or to music or to flowers, for which he has a passion."[87] A year later, also to Mrs. von Meck, he concluded, "My favorite, Volodya, will probably be an artist; he continually reveals signs of a very rich artistic imagination. He does not have any great talent for music particularly, although he makes progress in this as well. Probably he will become either a painter or a poet."[88]

His attachment to Bob later grew ever stronger: "Ah, what an adorable creation of nature; I fall in love with him more and more!"[89] In 1878, Tchaikovsky had made his first musical dedication to Bob, the piano pieces of his *Album for Children*. "Tell Bobik," he wrote movingly to his brother-in-law on 12/24 December, "that the music has been printed with pictures, that this music was composed by Uncle Petya, and that on it is written: Dedicated to Volodya Davydov. He, silly boy, will not even understand what 'dedicated' means! . . . To Bobik, if only for the sake of his inimitably charming little figure when he plays, looking at the music and counting, one could dedicate entire symphonies."[90] His words were prophetic. Completed on the eve of his own adventitious and entirely unforeseeable death, Tchaikovsky's last and most famous symphony, known as the *Pathétique*, is indeed dedicated to his beloved nephew.

CHAPTER EIGHTEEN

Fireworks at Simaki

It is human nature to create one's own mythology. Secret emotions and feelings are communicated to others in language and looks and gestures. The process is often unconscious in the individual: symbol or myth mediates between the need to express oneself and the impossibility or reluctance to do so openly.

In December 1878, while still in Florence after the departure of Mrs. von Meck, Tchaikovsky, to his own surprise, had composed a poem celebrating his favorite flower, the lily of the valley. "I am terribly proud of this poem," he noted to Modest in a letter of 15/27 December. "For the first time in my life I have managed to write a fairly good poem, which moreover is *deeply heartfelt.* I assure you that although is was very difficult, still I worked on it with the same pleasure as I do on music."[1]

Tchaikovsky's passion for lilies of the valley was endearingly deep. "You know what drives me mad?" he confided to Modest during one of his stays at Brailovo. "Here there are literally no lilies of the valley. I had not quite believed the assertions of the butler that in the entire district there is not a single lily of the valley, but yesterday in the woods, despite a most thorough search, I didn't find so much as a leaf."[2] And in one of his early letters to Mrs. von Meck, he had asked, "Do you like flowers? I feel a passionate love for them, especially those of the forests and the fields. I consider the king of flowers to be the lily of the valley; I have a sort of wild adoration for them."[3] Even for the

335

sentimental Tchaikovsky this is strong language. One may surmise
that this flower had for Tchaikovsky a deep and intimate meaning.

That Tchaikovsky would call the lily of the valley the "king" of
flowers is not accidental. In Russian the word *landysh*, or "lily of the
valley," is masculine, something that cannot be ignored when reading
his only serious poem. Every reference to the "yearning" that fills his
breast, to his "longing" for the flower's return, is unavoidably colored
by the fact that it is not a "she" but a "he" that, "like flowing wine,
warms and intoxicates me, like music, takes my breath away, and like
a flame of love, suffuses my burning cheeks." It is likely that Tchaikovsky saw the lovely flower as a symbol of a young man's fleeting
beauty. If so, the poem, entitled simply "Lilies of the Valley" and translated here in full for the first time, must be read in such a key:

When at the end of spring I pick for the last time
My favorite flowers—a yearning fills my breast,
And to the future I urgently appeal:
Let me but once again look upon the lilies of the valley.
Now they have faded. Like an arrow the summer has flown by,
The days have grown shorter. The feathered choir is still,
The sun more charily grants us its warmth and light,
And already the wood has laid its leafy carpet.
Then, when harsh winter comes
And the forests don their snowy cover,
Despondently I roam and wait with new yearning
For the skies to shine with the sun of spring.
I find no pleasure in books, or conversation,
Or swift-rushing sledges, or the ball's noisy glitter,
Or Patti, or the theater, or delicate cuisine,
Or the quiet crackling of smoldering logs on the fire.
I wait for spring. And now the enchantress appears,
The wood has cast off its shroud
And prepares for us shade,
And the rivers start to flow, and the grove is filled with
    sound,
And at last the long-looked-for day is here!
Quick, to the woods!—I race along the familiar path.
Can my dreams have come true, my longings be fulfilled?—
There he is! Bending to the earth, with trembling hand
I pluck the wondrous gift of the enchantress Spring.
O lily of the valley, why do you so please the eye?
Other flowers there are more sumptuous and grand,

With brighter colors and livelier patterns,
Yet they have not your mysterious fascination.
Where lies the secret of your charms? What do you prophesy
   to the soul?
With what do you attract me, with what gladden my heart?
Is it that you revive the ghost of former pleasures,
Or is it future bliss that you promise us?
I know not. But your balmy fragrance,
Like flowing wine, warms and intoxicates me,
Like music, it takes my breath away,
And like a flame of love, it suffuses my burning cheeks.
And I am happy while you bloom, modest lily of the valley,
The tedium of winter days has passed without a trace,
And oppressive thoughts are gone, and my heart in languid
   comfort
Welcomes, with you, forgetfulness of trouble and woe.
Yet now you fade. Again in monotonous succession
The days will begin to flow slowly, and stronger than before
Will I be tormented by importunate yearning,
By the agonizing dream of the happiness of days in May.

And then someday spring again will call
And raise the living world out of its fetters.
But the hour will strike. I shall be no more among the
   living,
I shall meet, like everyone, my fated turn.
And then what?—Where, at the winged hour of death,
Will my soul, heeding its command, soundlessly soar?
No answer! Be silent, my restless mind,
You cannot guess what eternity holds for us.
But like all of nature, drawn by our thirst to live,
We call to you and wait, beautiful Spring!
The joys of earth are so near to us, so familiar—
The yawning maw of the grave so dark![4]

"Lilies of the Valley" offers an allegorical description of a love too passionate to be directed at a mere flower, even a favorite one. Not without reason did Tchaikovsky call the poem, in his letter to Modest, "deeply heartfelt." The poem's amorous vocabulary and phraseology, for all its submission to poetical clichés, reveal a poignancy of emotion that cannot be explained away as but another instance of Tchaikovsky's emotional exultation. The tension running through the entire poem—strikingly evident in such phrases as "I urgently appeal," "dreams come true, longings fulfilled," "with trembling hand," "your mysterious fascination," "prophesy to the soul," "the ghost of former pleasures," "future bliss," "agonizing dream," and so on—transcends the framework of rather trivial and abstract philosophizing typical of Russian poetry at that low point in its history. Written in the form of a monologue, the poem is clearly divided into four stages of intonation and sense that correspond essentially to the cycle of nature: expectation (the farewell to spring and summer, winter, the waiting for spring), catharsis (the arrival of spring, the conversation with the flower, the joy of this intercourse), abatement (the departure of spring, the expectation of a new spring's arrival), and serene sorrow (the futility of worldly vanity and the joy of being and of meditation). But the poem yields also a more intimate reading, and veiled behind the abstract formal structure is a depiction of the dynamics of erotic attraction, from its beginning to its dying away, through langour, torment, hope, and expectation, and incorporating into this emotional spectrum sensations of the transience of youth and youthful beauty. It is, in fact, a dynamics echoing what many feel in much of Tchaikovsky's music, particularly in his symphonies, with their similar cyclical structures and similar correlation between personal experience and universal meaning.

It may well have been the intimate significance of the poem, and not modesty alone, that made Tchaikovsky so firmly set against publication of his quite successful effort. Although he did ask that it be shown to, among other people, Apukhtin, he declined Modest's offer to publish it. "Proud as I am of 'Lilies of the Valley,' nevertheless I do not find it suitable for publication," he explained. "My poem is outstanding with respect to myself, that is, someone who is not an expert. But what is it in comparison, for example, with the verses of Apukhtin? No. Spread my poetic fame, trumpet and roar, but don't commit it to print."[5] Still, having polished the poem, he sent it to Mrs. von Meck on New Year's Eve 1878 with the following apology: "My delight in the lily of the valley is celebrated somewhat exaggeratedly and not altogether accurately. For instance, it is quite untrue that 'neither books nor theater nor conversation give me any joy.' All this has its value. But with what will one not slander oneself for the sake of verse! For God's sake, forgive me for making you read my poetic experiments, but I wish so much to show you a work that has cost me such labor and filled me with such pride!"[6]

Considering the likely symbolism of the poem and its erotic significance, it is possible that by sending it to Mrs. von Meck, Tchaikovsky meant to convey some message to her, even a coded confession of his erotic preference. The emotional pressure Tchaikovsky felt in the wake of their stay in Florence, where he had been conscious every minute of her presence close by and bombarded by her daily notes and letters, was almost stultifying. The lily of the valley may have become a subtle way of communicating to his benefactress that his erotic nature was directed toward young men, not mature women.

But, if this was his implied or subconscious message, Mrs. von Meck either ignored it or misunderstood. Her response, while predictably appreciative, gave little hint of anything more. "I thank you very, very much, my dear friend, for your verses," she wrote. "They are charming and their story is very original. Well, how many multifaceted talents you do possess! If I did not fear for your music, I would advise you by all means to devote yourself to poetry, but I do love the former even more than the latter."[7] In fact, she very possibly interpreted Tchaikovsky's poetic outpouring in precisely the opposite way to that intended—as a declaration of his tender feelings for *her*. Since the convention of the time dictated that verses inspired by love be presented to the object of that love, it would have been easy to assume that this was the actual meaning of her beloved friend's gesture. In her eyes, the poem was clearly interpretable, if not as an outright declaration of love, then as something close to it. Thus encouraged, however mistakenly, Mrs. von Meck resolved very soon after her return to Russia in the spring of 1879 to have Tchaikovsky near her yet again.

The divorce negotiations were proceeding poorly. Antonina's intermediary, the same person who had visited Anatoly in the winter, had shown up, but he impressed Tchaikovsky's brother as almost as dense and confused as Antonina herself. As for Antonina, it was impossible, Tchaikovsky told Mrs. von Meck, to conduct business "with a woman who stubbornly refuses to understand what is said to her . . . and does not want today what she wanted yesterday."[8] Although a tentative agreement was finally reached that proceedings would begin in the autumn, Tchaikovsky remained skeptical and worried. To distract him, Mrs. von Meck invited Tchaikovsky again to visit Brailovo in her absence, and in early May he arrived for a stay of some ten days. But her cherished wish, as she revealed to him shortly afterward, was to arrange at Brailovo an interlude in proximity such as they had shared in Florence.

"I have near Brailovo a cottage, Simaki," she wrote. "[It] is very nice, lying in a shaded forest at the edge of which runs a river, and with nightingales singing in the garden. . . . This cottage is four versts [two and a half miles] from Brailovo. . . . I am sure you will like it." Extolling the poetic character of Simaki and the complete seclusion he would enjoy there, she proposed that he might come in mid-June and stay as late as mid-September. "For me, in part, the most delightful time of my life on Viale dei Colli [in Florence] would be repeated," she wrote. "Although, of course, at Brailovo I could not go strolling by your apartment every day, I would still feel every day that you were near, and this thought would make me just as happy, cheerful, calm, and bold; in the same way, I should feel that when you are near me, nothing bad can come to me. Think about it, my dear, good darling, . . . and let us live all summer together. . . . My dear, do come!"⁹

Tchaikovsky felt decidedly ambivalent about this new invitation. In the first moment, as he confessed to Modest on 9 May, he was quite angry. Besides being disturbed by the renewed constraint on his freedom and by the possibility that people might begin to look askance at their relations and "say devil knows what," he was also very much annoyed that she seemed not to take into account that he might want to spend some time with his relatives at Kamenka, as was his habit every summer. "Of course," he conceded, "she proposes this solely in order to afford me an opportunity to live alone in a charming spot."¹⁰ The mere physical proximity of Mrs. von Meck was what troubled Tchaikovsky most of all, even though he knew that no one was likely to disturb him at Simaki. He was accustomed to viewing Mrs. von Meck as "a sort of distant and unseen good angel." The knowledge that she would be living just a few miles away "like an ordinary mortal" did not appeal to him.¹¹

Naturally, the tone of his response to her was very different. "Your offer to stay at Simaki moved me indescribably, my dear friend!" he wrote. "On the one hand, such a life comprises the ideal of what I might wish, and I have not the strength to refuse it. But, on the other hand, before me rises a set of obstacles that embarrass me." These obstacles, he explained, included his fear of offending not only the Davydovs but also Anatoly, who wanted to spend his vacation with him, and Kondratyev, who had invited him to visit Nizy that summer, as well as the possibility of the start of divorce proceedings. "Perhaps if I had known earlier that such a scheme was possible, I might have managed to remove all these obstacles," he claimed. Nonetheless, he promised vaguely to try to find "at least one month" between 15 June and 15 September "that can be devoted to the fulfillment of my passionate wish to live near you, in a cozy cottage amid a shady garden, close to a forest, on the shore of a wonderful little river!" He even added, "My God! This is indeed the utter fulfillment of the most ideal of my dreams!"¹²

After his return to Kamenka on 14 May, the epistolary negotiations were resumed, and not without overtones of emotional anguish. "I am very, very sad that I cannot arrange your residence at Simaki right away," Mrs. von Meck wrote on 15 May. "Coming from Moscow, I was so dreaming of this, so delighting in the thought that it might take place and therefore I thank you with all my heart, my priceless one, for not depriving me of the hope of realizing such a splendid dream."[13] Two days later, Tchaikovsky reiterated his gratitude for her offer, but begged that she forgive him for still postponing a decisive answer. "I wish only for you to tell me that I am free regarding choice of time," he wrote, "and that in any event you will not be upset with me!"[14] As he no doubt expected, Mrs. von Meck hastened to assure him that it was he who should not be upset about anything in her regard, noting only that there was a possibility that she might go abroad at the beginning of August. "Therefore," she wrote, "if you agree to be my guest at Simaki I should, of course, like it to be for a sufficiently long period before my departure, that is, that it take place between 1 June and 1 August, though I repeat that the question of my going abroad is far from decided, and I actually prefer not to go."[15]

Feeling increasingly pressured and inconvenienced by her insistence, Tchaikovsky, on 8 June, confided to Modest, with obvious annoyance, "How can I not be angry at such a splendid, intelligent woman when she stubbornly refuses to understand that I do not want to live almost next door to her as a mysterious stranger? . . . How can she not understand that this is all uncomfortable and constraining?"[16] To make matters worse, the von Meck family was, as Tchaikovsky put it, already "in full assembly" at Brailovo, together with several people from the conservatory whom he would just as soon avoid. In the end, he sent Mrs. von Meck a long letter telling her that he could only come in early autumn, hoping, as he admitted to Modest, that since she was going abroad in the autumn, she would finally understand.[17]

But, to his dismay, the strategy backfired, and his hope that Mrs. von Meck might sense his predicament was betrayed. Rather than travel abroad, she preferred the opportunity to live for a while near her idol. "I see and recognize fully, my dear friend, that it is impossible for you to come to me either in June or in July," she wrote, "therefore I ask you, my good dear, to make me a present of the month of August, but, please, no less than a month."[18] She urged him to come no later than 1 August and to depart no earlier than she herself would leave Brailovo, about 10 September. Tchaikovsky had no choice but to surrender. "It goes without saying," he wrote on 12 June, in what seems little more than the putting of a brave face on a sorry business, "that I shall with the greatest pleasure spend August as your guest. . . . I shall look forward to August with impatience."[19]

Scarcely had he written this when an unexpected bit of news from an altogether different quarter arrived with a letter from Marie, the Swiss maid whom Tchaikovsky had found so charming at the Villa Richelieu in Clarens. Marie wrote that she was pregnant and that the father of the child was none other than his servant Alyosha. She accused Alyosha of nothing, confessing that it was she who had seduced him and that she was still in love with him. She did, however, hint that she expected the father to help her. Tchaikovsky's reaction to this development was quite extraordinary. "I have no grudge against either Alyosha or Marie," he wrote to Modest, "although I have a feeling this child will cause me worry in the future. I felt, first of all, compassion for poor Marie and, in the second place, a rush of strong paternal tenderness for the embryo in her womb. By this feeling I was able to measure the force of my deep-rooted love and attachment to Alyosha. His child! It seems to me as if it were mine as well!"[20]

His startling confession reveals not only Tchaikovsky's strong paternal sentiments, seen earlier in his relationship with the twins and later with his nephews, but also his regret that he would never have children of his own, though this is something he never expressed in his available letters or diaries. At the same time, he himself closely associated his feelings for the unborn child to the force of his love for Alyosha. Tellingly, prudent Soviet censors disapproved of this juxtaposition of Tchaikovsky's love for his servant and his affections for that servant's unborn child, and the entire passage was excised in the later edition of the composer's letters.

Alyosha himself responded to the news more predictably. First he paled, then suggested that the child was not his but somebody else's, finally declared that if it turned out to be a boy, he was prepared to recognize him and give him to his mother to bring up. The news did nothing however, to stop the servant's philandering at Kamenka. In a long and comforting letter to Marie, Tchaikovsky, while making no formal promise to assume responsibility for the fate of the child, told the girl that he would in any case come to her aid.[21]

Far more distressing was the news that came that summer from Kondratyev, who urgently summoned Tchaikovsky to Nizy, where Nikolay Bochechkarov was sick with dropsy. The composer spent the last two weeks of June at Kondratyev's estate, witnessing the agony of his dying friend. Aleksandra, who was skilled in nursing, sent advice by mail for treatment of the patient, but to little avail. Tchaikovsky left Nizy to return to Kamenka without any hope of seeing "the poor old man" alive again, and indeed, a few weeks later, on 13 August, he received the "killingly sad news" of his death two days earlier. In a letter to Modest describing Bochechkarov's final hours, he reflected on his long acquaintance with his friend. "I shall never reconcile myself to the fact that Nikolay Lvovich is no longer in this world," he wrote sadly. "Moscow has become hateful to me. The remembrance of the great part he played during the whole course of my Moscow life cuts into my heart like a knife. . . . He possessed an amazing faculty for reconciling one with life; his presence and his company were always an irreplaceable source of entertainment, calm, and consolation to me. What matter that he was a nonentity in terms of moral and intellectual power! He was pleasant always and to everyone, and this took the place in him of a great mind or great talents."[22]

A visit by Kotek to Kamenka helped lighten the mood. "I am very pleased at his arrival," Tchaikovsky told Modest.[23] The young man was as much a Don Juan as ever and obviously appealed to the female members of the Davydov family: "Sasha suspects that all [the young ladies] are in love with him."[24]

In early July, Mrs. von Meck asked Tchaikovsky whether he wished to go abroad in the coming winter. In his evasive reply he pleaded his worries about the coming months, especially in light of the prospect of divorce proceedings. If it seemed that this time a decisive outcome to the business could be expected, he explained, then he would have to remain in Moscow for an indefinite period. "But, if it turns out to be just renewed beating of the air," he added, "I shall go at once abroad or to Kamenka."[25]

In the meantime, he fulfilled his promise to spend at least a few weeks in Mrs. von Meck's cottage at Simaki, near Brailovo. He left for Simaki on 8 August, deciding to stay until the end of the month. The comfortable little cottage was set well apart from the rest of the estate. At the end of the dense, overgrown garden ran a river, and all around lay fields and copses where Tchaikovsky could take long walks without meeting a soul. No sooner had he arrived than he dashed off a note of effusive thanks to his benefactress, who was living with her family and other guests in the main house at Brailovo: "I feel a need to write you a few words immediately upon arriving to say that I am happy, that I am delighted, that one could not imagine anything better than the surroundings in which I find myself here!"[26] A letter to Anatoly dated the following day was equally full of praise, though with one substantial reservation. "But alas!" he complained, "there is never a barrel of honey without a spoonful of tar! The role of the tar is played by the closeness of N[adezhda] F[ilaretovna] with her family suite. Although I am completely convinced that no one will disturb me, this closeness somewhat bothers me all the same."[27]

Mrs. von Meck's reaction to the arrival of her precious guest was rather the reverse. "What happiness, rising each morning, to feel that you are near to me, my dear, priceless friend," she wrote to him, "to imagine you in a dwelling so familiar and dear to me, to think that perhaps at this very moment you are admiring from the balcony the same view of the village that I also love so, or perhaps are strolling along that shaded path that I always delight in; to feel that you are at my home, *que je vous possède* as the French say—all this is a pleasure that I enjoy at this moment and for which I am infinitely grateful to you, my incomparable, kind friend."[28]

Much to his dismay, Tchaikovsky found himself met on his arrival by Mrs. von Meck's favorite protégé, Pachulski, whom she continued to regard as a musician of promise. But Tchaikovsky's original antipathy toward him was quickly exacerbated when Pachulski not only escorted him to Simaki but then proceeded to stay the entire evening. Just as Pachulski was leaving, Tchaikovsky decided to take a resolute measure and told him bluntly that for seven days he wanted to remain completely alone. "In this way, I have protected myself for a rather long period," he told Anatoly.[29] But in his letters to his benefactress he remained unchangingly tactful, though cautious, on the subject of Pachulski's personal, if not musical, qualities. "The fullness of young life that runs through him and is reflected in his every word, as any manifestation of lively youth, has great charm," he wrote from Simaki, "but there is also a danger in this. It is most essential that he be enthusiastic not only in word but also in deed. I do not know why, but it seems to me that Pachulski has certain features of a Turgenevan hero, that is, a very capable man, who has an entirely genuine and ardent desire to fulfill the most wide-ranging plans, but. . . ."[30] There he broke off, leaving it for Mrs. von Meck to infer his doubts about her protégé's musical future.

Three noteworthy incidents marked Tchaikovsky's stay at Simaki. The most unsettling, for Tchaikovsky at least, was his only face-to-face encounter with Mrs. von Meck during the whole of their relationship. Describing this "most embarrassing occurrence" in a letter to Anatoly on 15 August, Tchaikovsky wrote that the day before he had driven to the forest around four o'clock in complete confidence that he would not meet Mrs. von Meck, who customarily dined at that time. As it happened, he had gone out somewhat earlier than usual, while she was late. "I met her nose-to-nose," he told his brother. "It was terribly awkward. We were face-to-face for only an instant, but all the same, I was dreadfully embarrassed, although I did tip my hat politely. She, it seemed to me, became utterly distracted and did not know what to do. And . . . behind her were two more carriages with her whole family."[31]

Tchaikovsky immediately interpreted their encounter as a terrible gaffe on his part. "Forgive me, for God's sake, Nadezhda Filaretovna, for having miscalculated the time," he hastened to apologize in a note written as soon as he returned to the cottage. "I landed right in your way. . . . It turned out I left not at four o'clock, but a little earlier."[32] But Mrs. von Meck, ecstatic, needed no apologies whatsoever. "I am delighted at this meeting," she wrote back, and went on with increasing ardor, "I cannot convey how sweet and wonderful it was when I realized that we had met you, when I, so to speak, felt the reality of your presence in Brailovo. I do not want any personal communications between us, but silently, passively to be near you, to be under the same roof with you, as in the theater at Florence, to meet you on the same road, . . . to feel you not as a myth but as a living person whom I love so and from whom I receive so much good, this gives me extraordinary pleasure; I regard such episodes as extraordinary happiness."[33] The contrast in their reactions to one another is uniquely touching and comical. It is also instructive: while she was increasingly obsessed by her idealized and even erotic passion, he remained apprehensive of any passion for him from her or any other woman.

Tchaikovsky responded very differently some days later to Mrs. von Meck's whimsical request that he visit the main house at Brailovo to see her new acquisitions of artwork and furniture one day while she and her family and guests were absent for several hours. "They all went to have dinner in the forest," he wrote Anatoly the following day, 26 August, "and it was for this time that she invited me. It was very pleasant. In general, I feel that despite certain circumstances which have prevented me from fully enjoying life here, my stay at Simaki will leave me with very poetic recollections."[34] As his words indicate, Tchaikovsky was well aware of his tendency to look back fondly at events that at the time may have seemed irritating intrusions in his quiet routine. Time and again (and not only in his relationship with Mrs. von Meck), he would agree only with great reluctance to something that would seem to promise pleasure, anticipating all manner of possible unpleasantness and continuing to complain unceasingly about sundry annoying trifles during the actual experience, and yet later recall the past episode with great nostalgia. Indeed, even as the month drew to a close, Tchaikovsky, somewhat to his own surprise, found himself relishing not only the solitude of Simaki but the whole atmosphere of his stay, which he had originally viewed as an onerous but unavoidable duty.

The evening following his visit to the main house, Mrs. von Meck arranged for Tchaikovsky to be present—unseen—at a display of fireworks in celebration of her son's name day. Quite possibly, it appealed to the element of childlike playfulness in Tchaikovsky's nature to hide in the dark and observe everything unobserved. Certainly, he seemed genuinely to enjoy himself, and the relaxed, natural, and even amused tone of his impressions in a letter to Mrs. von Meck written afterward differed markedly from the somewhat strained and artificial efforts in much of their Simaki correspondence. "I found it surprisingly pleasant to be so near to you and yours, to hear the voices and, as far as my eyesight allowed, to see you, my dear friend, and yours," he told her. "Twice you passed very close to me, especially the second time, after the fireworks. I was the whole time near the pavilion at the pool. But my pleasure was all the time mixed with a certain fear," he added. "I was afraid the watchmen might take me for a thief."[35]

Unremarkable though the adventure may seem, it had evidently worked some sort of catharsis in Tchaikovsky, relaxing a tension that had been growing between them and perhaps threatening their friendship. In the same letter, he suddenly wrote disarmingly and without the slightest hint of mere flattery, "The thought that I might outlive you is unbearable to me," whereupon he touchingly asked her to take care of Alyosha, should he happen to die before her.[36] His heartfelt sentiment filled her with joy and prompted yet another passionate declaration of the power and depth of her own love for him. "It is not only love; it is adoration, deification, worship," she wrote ecstatically. "However burdensome, bitter, or painful something might be for me, a few of your kind words make me forget and forgive everything. I feel then that I am not entirely alone in the world, that there is a heart that feels as I do, a person who understands me, sympathizes with me, looks so kindly, so humanely on me—my God, how grateful I am to you, and how dear you are to me! Ten times a day I read this sentence and involuntarily press the letter to my heart with overflowing gratitude."[37]

All the while, it was his music that sustained her passion. During his short stay at Simaki, Tchaikovsky took full advantage of the peaceful seclusion of the little cottage by the river, completing the orchestration of *The Maid of Orléans* and also finishing his Suite no. 1, op. 43, for orchestra. Begun the previous summer as a rest from symphonic music but later interrupted by work on the opera, the First Suite was unofficially dedicated by Tchaikovsky to his hostess in gratitude for her hospitality. He left Simaki on 31 August, and shortly thereafter, Mrs. von Meck obtained a copy of the recently published piano-duet version of the Fourth Symphony. Over and over again she played the symphony, which she continued to call "our" symphony. On 14 September she wrote that "these divine sounds embrace my whole being, excite my nerves, drive my brain to such an exalted state that I have spent these past two nights without sleep, in a sort of delirium, and from five o'clock in the morning cannot close my eyes at all, and once I rise in the morning, think only to sit and play again as soon as possible."

Mrs. von Meck felt more empathy for the Fourth Symphony than for any other work by Tchaikovsky. It was, after all, dedicated to "my best friend," to her, and its composition was linked to the time of her ascendancy in Tchaikovsky's life in the wake of the disaster of his marriage and his flight from Russia. He himself had revealed to her that Fate was the central theme of the symphony, and she had come to read in the work the triumphs and trials of her own life, her memories of the difficult early years, and her vision of a bright future in spiritual union with the symphony's creator. "My God, how were you able to depict the pain of despair, and the light of hope, and grief and suffering, and everything, everything of which I have experienced so much in my life and which makes this music dear to me not only as an expression of my life, my feelings," she went on in her letter. "Pyotr Ilyich, I am worthy of this symphony being mine: no one is able to sense in its sounds what I do, no one is able to appreciate it as I do; musicians can only appreciate it with their intellect, but I listen and feel and empathize with all my being. If I must die for listening to it, I shall die, but still I shall listen."

Carried away by the euphoria of the moment, Mrs. von Meck found herself confessing feelings that ordinarily she kept under tighter control. The vehemence of her unexpected exposure must have startled, even shocked, Tchaikovsky:

> I do not know whether you can understand the jealousy I feel for you, despite the absence of personal relations between us. Do you know that I am jealous of you in the most impermissible manner: as a woman of a man she loves? Do you know that when you married, I felt so terribly wretched, as though something had been torn from my heart? I found it painful, bitter, the thought of your intimacy with this woman was unbearable to me, and do you know what a loathsome person I am?—I rejoiced when you were unhappy with her; I reproached

myself for this feeling, and I seem to have done nothing to let you notice it, but nevertheless I could not destroy it—a person cannot command his own feelings. I hated this woman because you were unhappy with her, but I would have hated her a hundred times more if you had been happy with her. I felt that she had taken from me that which can only be mine, to which I alone have a right, because I love you as no one else does and value you above all else in the world. If it displeases you to learn all this, forgive me for this involuntary confession. I blurted it out—the reason for this is the symphony. But I think, and it is best that you know, that I am not only an ideal person as you believe me to be. And besides, this cannot change our relations in the slightest. I do not want any change in them; I indeed should like to feel secure that nothing will change until the end of my life, that no one—but this I have no right to say. Forgive me and forget everything I have said. My head is not right.[38]

In this emotional outpouring Mrs. von Meck reached the height of her passion for Tchaikovsky as it comes through in her letters. But if she hoped to prompt her beloved friend to a reciprocal confession, she was disappointed. It took Tchaikovsky eight days, from 17 to 25 September, to respond in a letter written in fragments in St. Petersburg and Moscow and at the Konradis' estate at Grankino. His reply was infused with profound gratitude, though even that slightly affected, and nothing more. "I tremble at the thought of what might have happened to me if fate had not brought us together," he wrote. "I owe you everything: my life, the opportunity to proceed toward a distant goal, my freedom, and such complete happiness as I earlier considered impossible."[39]

Tchaikovsky and Mrs. von Meck lived in Russia at a time when Romanticism in its heroic and revolutionary forms had long since declined as a cultural force or attitude. If Romanticism necessitated emotion, Positivism or Realism, which replaced it by the 1850s, emphasized the practical work of the mind, dismissing emotion as mere sentimentality. Judging from the sentiments expressed in her letters, Mrs. von Meck possessed a temperament better suited, perhaps, to some earlier, Romantic age. Yet, fate had also made her the ruler of a vast financial empire. Whether she would have actually chosen this role if circumstances had been different cannot be said, but the fact remains that she proved herself to be a supremely successful businesswoman, running her empire with sober efficiency. Necessities of business forced her to subdue and domesticate her Romantic nature, but in music or, more precisely, in her passionate communion with Tchaikovsky, Mrs. von Meck's Romanticism found an outlet. She subscribed to the definition of genius as identical with a supreme good, and that Tchaikovsky was a genius she never doubted. She worshiped the composer both as a creator of great art and as a possessor of great moral virtue: in this lay her persistent disregard of his human foibles and failings.

For his part, Tchaikovsky was temperamentally different from such Romantics as Byron and Beethoven. He lacked their grandness of ego and their heroic, passionate exuberance. His nature, owing in large part to his family upbringing, was more "sentimental" in Friedrich Schiller's sense, which was still widespread in music, literature, and the other arts all over Europe in the latter nineteenth century. It is no accident that Tchaikovsky's music found acceptance and popularity toward the end of the century. His work is far better suited to the *belle époque* than to the spirit exemplified in the music of Modest Mussorgsky or Nikolay Rimsky-Korsakov.

In response to Mrs. von Meck's effusions, Tchaikovsky could offer only self-doubt and self-pity, and reluctant skepticism with regard to others. Moreover, he must have found her passionate letter quite frightening, perceiving in it a declaration of love in some conventional sense and an unnerving reminder of the misery following his marriage to Antonina. It is perhaps in part because of this letter that he showed, with time, an increasing preference to evade, on various pretexts, her unending invitations to join him in this city or that. Though they later often made plans to meet somewhere abroad, these plans would usually for some reason or other fall through. Just two weeks before receiving her letter of 14 September, Tchaikovsky had gladly accepted her offer to come to Naples to be near her later that autumn. "My dear friend, I reply to your invitation: yes! with delight!" he wrote.[40] But after the arrival of her "confessional" letter, his enthusiasm for the idea quickly waned, and their Naples reunion did not take place.

However, Mrs. von Meck wrote on 19 September that "all my thoughts, strivings, expectations, and desires are directed toward Naples—where my resurrected heart will start beating again. . . . Oh, the life of the heart is the only life!" She repeated that she felt herself intoxicated by the Fourth Symphony "as though by opium." "The Fourth Symphony has captured all of me," she declared. "I hear those notes at night, and I cannot even look at them calmly with my eyes. The whole symphony is wonderful, but the first movement is . . . the last word in art, there is nowhere else to go, it is the limit of genius, the crowning triumph, the point of divinity; for its sake, one could give up one's soul or lose one's mind and there would be no repenting. . . . Now I am not in a condition to speak of anything else."[41]

Swept up in her enthusiasm, she soon conceived the idea of publicizing "their" symphony through the agency of one of the finest orchestras in Europe, that of Edouard Colonne. Tchaikovsky consenting to her plan, she empowered Pachulski on their arrival in Paris to undertake negotiations with Colonne personally. With the promise of significant remuneration by Mrs. von Meck, the French conductor proved readily agreeable, the more so as both he and his orchestra were already familiar with Tchaikovsky's music, having performed *The Tempest* in March. Tchaikovsky was grateful to both his benefactress and her negotiator, though he rather doubted that Colonne would actually include the symphony in one of his programs. There were, he thought, far too many native French composers already vying for that prestigious honor. No date had yet been set for a performance, and he was convinced in any event that the French public would respond negatively to the work. But Mrs. von Meck, stubbornly optimistic, was equally convinced that the symphony would be a great success both with the public and with the conductor, to whom a copy of the four-hand version had been immediately dispatched.

After leaving Simaki, Tchaikovsky spent September and October 1879 wandering. He went first to St. Petersburg, where he stayed with Anatoly. Negotiations with Antonina, it turned out, had again run aground. In August, Anatoly had received from her a letter that he had chosen not to send along to his brother at Simaki so as not to spoil his rest there, but that he called "a garland of nonsense and insanity." Antonina had once more disavowed her intermediary and refused to go forward with the divorce. "God knows how all this will end," Tchaikovsky had written to Mrs. von Meck on 27 August, "but the one thing that is clear is that a final solution is still far off and may never come about."[42]

Now in his brother's apartment he discovered and reread a whole pile of Antonina's letters, finding there, as he put it, "unquestionable proof of her insanity." He came to the conclusion that "stricter measures" needed to be taken against her: "I and all my relatives have been overly soft with her for too long."[43] He resolved to let pass one year, during which time he would neither take nor agree to any further action and his wife, at his urging, would think long and hard about what exactly it was that she wanted and where her real interests lay. Strangely enough, this new firmer policy eventually began to bear fruit. "Of a certain individual I have had . . . rather comforting news," he would inform Mrs. von Meck on 27 November. "She has finally understood that she can improve her material welfare, not through her phenomenally asinine pursuit of me, but through decent behavior. . . . I demand so little of her! Only that I should never meet her or see her handwriting—that is all I require."[44]

From St. Petersburg, Tchaikovsky passed through Moscow, where he spent three days of heavy drinking, caught up briefly in the already forgotten atmosphere of his earlier days in the city. Then it was on to Grankino, where Modest and Kolya were staying, and from there to Kamenka. With divorce proceedings no longer on the horizon, he was now able to go abroad freely and with a light heart, and after spending most of October at Kamenka, he made plans to leave Russia. Of his brief appearance back in the capital on his way to Germany, he instructed Anatoly to spread no word whatsoever. "This time I am definitely not going to visit anyplace or anyone except (1) Papa, (2) the Konradis, and (3) Lyolya [Apukhtin]," he warned.[45] He was particularly looking forward to seeing the last, along with Apukhtin's young lover, Aleksandr Zhedrinsky. Finally, on 9 November, Tchaikovsky left St. Petersburg for Berlin.

In Berlin he at once sought out Kotek, who was continuing his musical studies there: "This dear fellow expressed a wild joy when we met, and I was glad to see him. But having spent two hours with him and listened to an endless stream of all sorts of musical gossip and other stories, I was so tired that it is hard to describe, and when my poor Kotek went to a rehearsal for some concert, I was pleased!! A bewildering thing. The longer I live, the more unfit I become for living in society. There is no doubt that I am fond of Kot, but his chattering has an effect on me as of the most difficult physical labor."[46] This feeling, however, did not prevent, and probably even contributed to, his desire to offer his ever-strapped young friend some additional financial assistance.[47]

A few days later, on 13/25 November, Tchaikovsky arrived in Paris. Since their plans to vacation together in Naples had failed, Tchaikovsky evidently felt obliged to accept Mrs. von Meck's invitation to join her a second time in the French capital. Once again Pachulski was present. Mrs. von Meck had made a specific point of mentioning him when writing of the planned arrangements, but it seems that intuitively she had already begun to suspect Tchaikovsky's lack of sympathy toward her young protégé: "If you find it tedious, my friend, that Pachulski will be coming to meet you, I ask your indulgence. I suggested that perhaps he might not go to the station to meet you, but he answered me, 'My God, if I were two hours from death, even then I would go to meet Pyotr Ilyich!' After such an answer I felt it a pity to deprive him of such pleasure."[48]

Pachulski probably sensed the composer's dislike of him, and his apparent sycophantic insincerity could not have sat well with Tchaikovsky. Though hardly immune to flattery, he was quick to notice when it was exaggerated. Nevertheless, he remained a diplomat. "I enjoyed seeing him for his own sake," he wrote to Mrs. von Meck, "and also for the sake of Viale dei Colli [in Florence] and Simaki, of which he reminds me, and finally, most important, for the sake of the news he brought me about the relative well-being of your health."[49] Of course, the emphasis in his words was less on Pachulski than on Mrs. von Meck. Two weeks later, Tchaikovsky wrote to Anatoly from Paris, "N[adezhda] F[ilaretovna] has been detained here by the snows and frost, and God knows when she will leave. I am glad that she is near, but Pachulski—oh, how unappealing he is, and I have often to see him and work with him."[50]

In Paris, Mrs. von Meck had prepared for Tchaikovsky the same lodgings he had occupied the last time, in the Hôtel Meurice on the rue de Rivoli. He felt "completely at home" in Paris and wrote that his love for the city was as strong as ever.[51] The first day there, he visited Nikolay Kondratyev, who was in the city taking a cure for syphilis. Kondratyev was already greatly improved, and on the following day, 14/26 November, the two men and their servants all went to the circus together. But it appears that Mrs. von Meck found the great size of the city rather frustrating. The environment had none of the intimacy of Simaki or even Florence, and ultimately their stay in Paris differed little from their accidental contemporaneous stays in St. Petersburg or Moscow. Preferring some place smaller, she suggested that they move to the resort town of Arcachon, near Bordeaux. Tchaikovsky, however, was extremely reluctant, making various pretexts, and in the end, bad weather and Mrs. von Meck's renewed health problems intervened to keep her in Paris, where they corresponded virtually every day until her return to Russia on 4/16 December.

All in all, a uniform pattern can be seen in Tchaikovsky's conduct throughout this, the period of greatest intensity in their relationship. For most of the time, he enjoyed their eccentric friendship, provided it remained limited to writing letters and discussing any subject from abstract spiritual questions to intimate recollections of the past. But, at the first sign on her part of anything even remotely resembling an amorous impulse toward him, he would resume, often nearly in panic, the role of the fugitive, desiring to flee even when her presence nearby might mean his material and even psychological comfort. It was like the role he had played so dramatically in relation to Antonina. Indeed, it may very well be that the initial shock from his experience with Antonina was so powerful that it forever afterward prevented Tchaikovsky from enjoying fully even the geographical closeness of an admiring woman—no matter that she might be a remarkable woman friend to whom he felt deeply indebted and who, in rational terms, posed no conceivable sexual threat.

Part Five

TRANSIENT LODGINGS

1879–1888

CHAPTER NINETEEN

Patrons, Friends, and Protégés

Paris brought out the dandy in Tchaikovsky. "You'd really laugh if you could see me here," he confessed to Anatoly in one of his letters from the French capital. "I stroll the streets in a new gray overcoat and the most elegant of top hats, flaunting a silk plastron with a coral pin at my neck, and lilac gloves on my hands. Passing by the mirrored piers on the rue de la Paix or the boulevards, I'll invariably stop to admire myself, and I eye the reflection of my elegant person in all the shop windows. In general, I've been overcome at present (as has happened before) by a mania of coquetry. I've had a new suit of clothes made, and I've ordered a dozen shirts. The money flies, and in a few days I won't have single franc in my pocket."[1]

But even the glitter and charm of Paris tended to pale in due course. Restless to resume his nomadic wandering, Tchaikovsky was relieved when Mrs. von Meck finally left Paris in December 1879 and he could look forward to traveling on to Rome to join Modest and Kolya, who had arrived there in late November. Though Modest had written that he and his charge were greatly enjoying the city, Tchaikovsky was disturbed by news from Kondratyev that that "inseparable pair," their old homosexual acquaintances Prince Golitsyn and his lover Masalitinov, were also staying in the Italian capital. From Paris he wrote candidly to Modest, "You will not believe the *horror* that Golitsyn and Masalitinov instill in me. I like them both, but have grown terribly unused to them. For God's sake, prepare them for the thought that I am dreadfully depressed by my work, . . . that I lock myself in my room all day until dinner."[2]

Yet, arriving in Rome on 8/20 December 1879, he was pleasantly surprised. The warmth and sunny weather put him in good spirits, and even the prince and his lover proved tolerable, though little more. An ambivalent attitude stemming from his disenchantment with Moscow and the homosexual world of the aunties persisted. "My meeting with Golitsyn was extremely difficult," he told Anatoly. "I had to play a comedy, pretend to be glad, etc. Fortunately, I had sufficient fortitude to present myself in such a way that I shall be fairly free of them."[3] A few days later, he wrote, "How Golitsyn has changed in both body and spirit! He has become terribly malicious and does not have a good word to say about anyone. Masalitinov is the same as ever. *En somme*, they are quite unsuitable people, but they have ceased to frighten me."[4]

Tchaikovsky's few contacts with the pair introduced him to their local artistic and homosexual circle. At one point, with Golitsyn away at Naples for a week, he visited Masalitinov to hear a young singer of eighteen perform folk songs. And as the holidays approached, he and Modest planned a Christmas party. "It would have been very jolly and pleasant, if, because of Modya's carelessness, we had not had to invite Masalitinov, and because of that—Golitsyn, and because of that—the painter Giulio, who lives with them, and because of that—the young fellow Amici, who delighted me recently with his charming performance of folk songs, and because of that—Amici's brother, who accompanies him on the mandolin. Thus, an entire rout has been formed, the mere thought of which makes me tremble."[5] The tone of this passage, with its mixture of apprehension and anticipation, reflects, in addition to Tchaikovsky's habitual dislike of crowds, his divided feelings about the homosexual subculture and suggests that all of these persons were in various sexual relations with one another. Very likely, Amici and his friends represented the general promiscuity (and even prostitution) of the homosexual underground to be found in Italy at that time. Throughout the second half of the nineteenth century, that country was, in fact, widely considered an erotic paradise by European homosexuals.

Much to Tchaikovsky's relief, the Christmas "rout" did not take place: "Our Christmas party was charming, and it luckily happened that we were alone, even though we had been threatened with the invasion of Masalitinov and *tutti quanti*."[6] The expression *tutti quanti* was also used by Tchaikovsky earlier to refer to the homosexual aunties in Moscow. Throughout his stay in Rome, Tchaikovsky remained torn in his feelings toward Golitsyn and Masalitinov. His evident antipathy went hand in hand with an acknowledged interest and a fear of offending. It was, as he confessed to Anatoly, "impossible to be angry with Masalitinov, he is so kind, obliging, and affectionate,"[7] while in mentioning to his brother that he would be dining with the prince, lately returned from Naples, he noted with irony, but little malice, "He is a good and kind fellow, but why does he not prefer the climate of Naples to that of Rome? In that case, I might have dined at home."[8] Yet, such visits were rare, and Tchaikovsky found himself "constantly tormented" by the thought that Golitsyn was offended by his lack of attention.[9]

Shortly after the New Year, Kondratyev appeared in Rome, settling into the same hotel as the Tchaikovsky brothers to spend about a month before returning to Paris. With his arrival they began to see still more of Golitsyn and Masalitinov, and Tchaikovsky was soon almost grudgingly conceding, in a letter to Anatoly, that the pair had turned out to be less burdensome and demanding than he had originally feared.[10] As for his old friend Kondratyev, he had quickly become "a desperate debauchee and libertine here. Every day he has drinking bouts and amorous adventures. He swears that nowhere but in Rome can one live." Even so, Tchaikovsky was already growing tired of Rome. "Everyone lives well and freely here," he admitted to Anatoly. "I alone cannot develop a taste for Rome, and keep feeling drawn away from here to someplace else. I can say without exaggeration that my stay here has been a sacrifice offered on the altar of fraternal love. All the same, I am happy for Modest, who likes Rome very much, and for Kolya, for whom the Roman climate has proved extremely beneficial."[11] Going everywhere with Modest and Kolya, Tchaikovsky visited the Capitolium, the Palatine, and the Vatican. He was left cold by the athletic "muscles" of Michelangelo's frescoes in the Sistine Chapel that had Modest waxing rhapsodic. He preferred Raphael, "that Mozart of painting," but as for the plastic arts, he confessed to Mrs. von Meck that he felt he was "lacking by nature in sensitivity" to them. On the whole, he found museums frustrating. "They supply one with so much food that one cannot swallow it all in one gulp."[12]

On 8/20 January 1880, word came from Anatoly that their father, now eighty-four, lay seriously ill in St. Petersburg. Two days later, before Tchaikovsky had time to decide whether to return at once to Russia, a telegram arrived with news of Ilya's death the day before. Tchaikovsky, though deeply saddened, was not distraught. His father had lived an enviably long and emotionally fulfilled life. When Anatoly later wrote with details of their father's final illness and death, Tchaikovsky replied, "Your letter is infinitely sad, and at the same time it is infused with something ineffably radiant. . . . I think the soul of our dear departed was illuminating your thoughts when you wrote it."[13] Writing to Mrs. von Meck on the same day he received Anatoly's letter, Tchaikovsky told her that he had "wept a great deal" while reading the description of his father's end. "It seems to me that these tears, shed for the disappearance from this world of a pure man gifted with an angelic soul, have had a beneficial effect on me," he wrote. "I feel an enlightenment and a reconciliation in my heart."[14]

Tchaikovsky remained in Rome, deciding to make his way back to Russia later in February. Anatoly, who for some time had been searching unsuccessfully for a good position, had requested his brother's presence in St. Petersburg, hoping to use his society connections. But, in the meantime, he sent still more sad news. He wrote of the poor health of both their sister, Aleksandra, and her daughter Tanya. Three well-known specialists had been called in and had found Aleksandra to be suffering from a kidney ailment and from a general disorder of the nervous system. She was, in addition, thoroughly addicted to morphine, a widely used remedy at the time, which she had been using to deaden the often intolerable pain in her kidneys. The seventeen-year-old Tanya, diagnosed as having developed a stomach ulcer, was also, it seemed, pining over an unfortunate and unrequited love, from which not even a busy social life could distract her.

For some time Tchaikovsky had watched not only the health of his eldest niece but also her personality and behavior with growing concern. It is possible that he recognized in her character and her troubles some affinity with his own nature. Three months before, he had shared his worries in a letter to Mrs. von Meck. "I have to tell you that this girl, endowed with so many abilities, a marvelous heart, and extraordinary beauty, suffers from one rather unbearable fault—*she is constantly and always bored*," he confided. "Her nature is somewhat broken, fraught with agonizing doubts and lack of self-confidence, troublesome, filled with untimely disappointment. Seeing this continuous and, in the case of so young a girl, groundless depression is distressing for everyone and has a devastating effect on my sister, who recognizes her utter helplessness in remedying the situation."[15] At her wit's end, Aleksandra made a fatal move in attempting to alleviate her daughter's anxieties. It was evidently in this painful moment of Tanya's disappointment in love, compounded by her physical illness, that her mother first suggested that she try morphine as both a painkiller and a tranquilizer. For a time Tanya's condition would improve, but all too soon her uncle and her entire family were to watch in helpless horror as she, like her mother, became permanently addicted to the drug.

Amid these worries, happier news from Jurgenson came as a welcome relief. The publisher wrote of the growing popularity of Tchaikovsky's music at home and abroad. Performances of his music had been heard that autumn and winter in Berlin, New York, Budapest, and Paris, and in October, Nikolay Rubinstein had conducted the First Suite in Moscow to great acclaim. Meanwhile, after the sorrowful telegram with the news of his father's death came another, on 13/25 January, from the conductor Edouard Colonne, telling him that his Fourth Symphony had been warmly received at a performance at the Châtelet in Paris the same day.[16] Mrs. von Meck, having left Paris and returned to Moscow, was thrilled at the news, but Tchaikovsky's original suspicion that his music might be alien to the French audience was not entirely unwarranted. The Parisian papers responded to the performance with little enthusiasm, calling the symphony, in the words of the *Revue et gazette musicale de Paris*, a "dissolute and wild fantasia . . . of affectation and vulgarity."[17]

Tchaikovsky lingered in Rome until the end of February. When at last he departed for Russia by way of Paris and Berlin, he did so without Alyosha, whom he left behind to help Modest with Kolya. The parting with his servant grieved him, but already his thoughts were on a new composition. At the end of January, Tchaikovsky had witnessed the famous pre-Lenten Roman carnival. Struck by "the wild ravings of the crowd, the masquerade, the illuminations," he remarked in a letter to Mrs. von Meck that no matter what shape the merriment of the crowd took, it was always natural and spontaneous.[18] He had strolled through the festive streets and been inspired by the "charming themes" he heard in the melodies played and sung there. Transcribing some of what he heard and pouring also through several collections of folk songs and dances, he soon completed the first draft of the *Capriccio italien*, op. 45, in which he transformed into art the experiences and impressions of his three-month sojourn in Rome.

Tchaikovsky's ostensible reason for stopping first in Paris before continuing on to St. Petersburg was to see Kondratyev, who had returned there a week earlier. But an even greater attraction may well have been the company of Kondratyev's new and handsome young servant, Aleksandr Legoshin, whose praises Tchaikovsky had lately begun to sing. His extolling of the "adorable Sasha," or Aleksandr, would in fact continue for several years with never an unkind word, and his emotional involvement with the young man is plain. Tchaikovsky had probably begun paying his attentions to his friend's servant some time earlier, either in Paris in December or in Rome.[19] Arriving now in Paris early on the morning of 28 February/11 March 1880, Tchaikovsky checked into the same hotel at which Kondratyev was staying. As he confided in a letter to Modest later that day, even before he woke his friend at nine o'clock, "Aleksandr, with sleepy eyes, had already managed to visit mc." In the same letter, he wrote, with evident delight at young Legoshin, "When I asked Sasha what to tell you from him, he replied, 'Something very nice.' This was said in a very deep bass voice."[20] A few days later, he noted that "Sasha is very sweet, affectionate, and obliging."[21] His affair with his friend's servant had had, it appears, an auspicious beginning.

After the boisterous atmosphere of Rome, Tchaikovsky found Paris "prosaic and slightly banal."[22] But he enjoyed the theaters, his walks with Legoshin, and, to a certain extent, the company of Kondratyev, even though the latter often annoyed him. Late at night, as was his wont in most large cities, he would again "wander the boulevards" alone; and as always, any description of the particulars of these strolls is consistently censored by the Soviet editors in every edition of his letters. What hints remain are suggestive, for example: "I roamed all about [the city] senselessly and without pleasure until twelve midnight."[23]

If there was no pleasure, why did he not return earlier? In his sexual practices, Tchaikovsky was never monogamous. His upbringing, his usual timidity, and his deep commitment to his relatives prevented him from living openly with a male lover, as Golitsyn and Apukhtin both did. This forced him to search for sexual fulfillment through anonymous encounters. The writings of several sexologists and criminal authorities of the nineteenth century contain repeated references to particular areas in every large European capital where homosexual men would stroll and meet one another, so-called promenades, where "throwing but a single brief glance, they never erred and would meet men whom they had never seen before but whom they recognized [as fellow homosexuals] in a single second."[24] It was not necessary to be part of a specific circle in order to learn where these meeting places were in any large city. Even remaining on the fringes of the homosexual milieu, as Tchaikovsky certainly did, one inevitably heard rumors, and Tchaikovsky's letters and diaries show that he knew the spots where the aunties gathered in Paris and Berlin as well as in Moscow and St. Petersburg.

Before leaving Paris, Tchaikovsky, as often happened, quarreled with Kondratyev. Writing to Modest on 4/16 March, he insisted that he was determined never again to spend time with his friend other than in a large company. *"Tête-à-tête* with him is impossible," he declared. "His jokes have lost all their novelty for me. And then his boastfulness, unexpected shifts from one mood to another, narcissism, lack of truthfulness, petty conceit, pathetic though naive egotism, manifestations of the most abominable stinginess—in short, the whole Kondratyevan nature, which conceals beneath a thin attractive crust a rather rotten little soul—have become unbearable to me." In fact, though mentioned almost in passing, it was the "abominable stinginess" that was evidently crucial in this most recent falling-out between the two friends, which had been sparked by Kondratyev's unwillingness to lend Tchaikovsky "some money for the road" ("as if I had asked him to make me a present of it," he grumbled to Modest). So angry was Tchaikovsky that he almost left without saying good-bye, but he grudgingly thought better of it and the two "parted, it seems, as friends."[25]

Berlin struck Tchaikovsky as "vulgar and ridiculous" when compared to Italy and "pathetic and provincially shallow" when compared to Paris.[26] But he was now in no great hurry to return to St. Petersburg, Anatoly having informed him that he would be out of the city for a time—as would a mysterious individual whose name has been literally cut out of the original of Tchaikovsky's 4/16 March letter to Modest, possibly by the addressee himself. During his brief visit Tchaikovsky saw Wagner's *The Flying Dutchman* for the first time and found it boring and noisy. For a few more days he contented himself with resuming his promenades along the streets of Berlin, putting off his return to St. Petersburg until 7 March.

From the moment Tchaikovsky stepped off the train in St. Petersburg, he found the Russian capital "excruciatingly depressing and gloomy." The weather was awful—frost, snow, darkness. After three winters spent in warmer climes he was unaccustomed to the cold of a Russian winter. Anatoly, meeting him at the station, was upset and frustrated by continuing troubles in his own career. The two went directly from the station to the Chachor restaurant, where they were awaited by Apukhtin and his young lover Aleksandr Zhedrinsky, as well as Aleksandr's brother Vladimir. Also present, interestingly, was Aleksandr and Vladimir's father, who was the governor of Kursk in central Russia. The senior Zhedrinsky was almost certainly aware of the true nature of the poet's relations with his son. Apukhtin's homosexual reputation was a matter of common knowledge, and the two, moreover, spent much time together, not only in St. Petersburg but also at the Zhedrinsky family estate in Rybnitsa, in Orel province. The presence of Aleksandr's visiting father at this dinner suggests, if not his encouragement of this relationship, then at least his indifference to it, a tolerant attitude toward homosexuality often found among the Russian educated class at this time.

The mood of the dinner was as dismal as the weather. Aleksandr Zhedrinsky was soon to complete his studies at the Imperial Lyceum in Tsarskoe Selo, outside St. Petersburg, after which he was to leave the capital, and Apukhtin was in torment at the thought of this impending separation from his young lover. Beginning with his arrival, everything seemed to conspire to drive Tchaikovsky to melancholia. "Poor Russia," he wrote to Modest the next day, "and the poor people who are doomed to live here, poor Tolya [Anatoly] dragging out his unsettled life in this city gloomy as a grave. Somehow I pity everyone here."[27] That evening, he again saw Apukhtin, who "was very sad and . . . wept." When Tchaikovsky asked him why, the poet bowed his head. "Clearly, he dreads parting with Sasha [Zhedrinsky]," he told Modest. Tchaikovsky may have envied his friend such a reciprocated passion, so long lacking in his own life. "The firmness and strength of his attachment moves me deeply.[28]

The day after his arrival, Tchaikovsky made a brief visit to his stepmother, Elizaveta, still in mourning for his father's death, and the next day, he went together with her and Anatoly to visit for the first time the grave of his father at St. Petersburg's Smolensk Cemetery. It is unfortunate that Tchaikovsky left no account of his feelings on visiting his father's grave. Although the two men had had little real affinity, Ilya Tchaikovsky had for many years played a significant and fundamental role in his son's emotional life.

The following days were filled with the barrage of sundry business appointments and social engagements typical of Tchaikovsky's schedule whenever he visited St. Petersburg, and he found little occasion to feel bored. Depressed by the cold and the gray skies and by his brother's troubles, he very soon began to feel much as he usually did in the capital, frustrated and disoriented. His health remained good, and he was at least not plagued this time by the sleeplessness and other ailments that usually accompanied his bouts of anxiety and depression. But his efforts to get any work done were unsuccessful, and he found himself throughout his stay running about from morning until night on various matters related to the promotion of *The Maid of Orléans*. Moreover, his music was featured in three separate concerts held in the capital during his stay, one of which, an all-Tchaikovsky program, included *Romeo and Juliet*, the First Suite, and both Lensky's aria and the letter scene from *Eugene Onegin*. By the end of the month, Tchaikovsky was thoroughly exhausted and dreaming of his departure as of "some impossible happiness."

Adding to his worries was the crumbling domestic situation of Alina and Hermann Konradi, Kolya's parents. When Tchaikovsky arrived in St. Petersburg, not only was the couple in the midst of divorce proceedings but Alina was living with her lover, Vladimir Bryullov. Both Tchaikovsky and Modest were deeply troubled by the situation, especially by the effect his parents' impending rupture would have on Modest's young pupil. "Mme Konradi has never been a loving and tender mother for her son, and in this respect, Kolya loses nothing," Tchaikovsky had written bluntly to Mrs. von Meck from Rome. Nonetheless, he conceded, Kolya "*loves* his mother as the embodiment of everything beautiful and feels a sort of timid adoration for her, and it is terrible to think how this matter may affect him."[29]

In hope of mediating or at least easing the tension for Kolya's sake, Tchaikovsky met several times with the Konradis during his visit. But he quickly became convinced that both husband and wife were far too absorbed in their own quarrels to give any real thought to their son. Modest, he realized, would have to be, as indeed he long had been, "both father and mother" to the boy. These thoughts of Kolya, as always, put Tchaikovsky in a sentimental frame of mind, and he wrote to Modest who was still in Italy with his charge, "It is amazing how much I love him [Kolya]. Lord, what I would give to see from here his affectionate glance and the kiss he blows with his lips to the side—you know his smile, when he says, 'Dear Petya!'"[30] Kolya's parents were finally divorced later that spring. Kolya remained with his father. Though Modest took great pains to prepare the boy, now twelve, for the separation, still the news shook him deeply. Isolated from the world by his deafness and muteness, he could not understand why his mother had left home. Alina and Bryullov were married not long after the divorce.

The one pleasant recompense for the trying hours Tchaikovsky spent in the company of the Konradis during his stay was his acquaintance with the Konradis' servant boy Ivan, who had been specially hired by Modest. Taking a liking to the youth, Tchaikovsky indulged his penchant for playing benefactor to attractive young men and made him a present of some new clothes and even invited him to come visit him at Anatoly's apartment, where, as usual, he was staying while in the city.

Apart from this diversion and his meetings with Apukhtin, Tchaikovsky spent much of his free time during this visit with Prince Meshchersky. It was in fact during this time that Tchaikovsky resumed his old friendship with his former schoolmate. That Tchaikovsky continued to meet with both Meshchersky and Apukhtin, despite their homosexual reputation (and, in the case of Meshchersky, the public odium he inspired), suggests that he cared less and less what idle tongues might say of his companionships. As with Apukhtin, Meshchersky's homosexuality was a well-known fact in St. Petersburg salons. One finds a number of biting comments on the subject. "Meanwhile, his reputation was becoming ever more shameful," recalled Evgeny Feoktistov, head of the Chief Directorate for the Press. "Common opinion, not, it seems, without serious grounds, held him to belong to the ranks of the most heedless homosexuals. A scoundrel and a villain, a man without conscience or convictions, he pretended to be a zealous patriot—trenchant phrases about devotion to church and throne were ever on his lips."[31] The eminent statesman Count Sergey Witte complained in his memoirs about a more concrete issue: "All his life Meshchersky has always concerned himself only with his favorites: he has made of politics a trade in which he deals in the most unscrupulous fashion to his own benefit and that of his favorites. Thus, I can only say of Meshchersky that he is a most terrible man. This is known by almost everyone who has had dealings with him."[32]

The prince's remarkable career, which had taken shape quite unexpectedly, is striking evidence of how little weight the threats of scandal and exposure truly bore in the social and political life of nineteenth-century imperial Russia. A grandson of the famous historian Nikolay Karamzin, Vladimir Meshchersky, despite his title, did not belong to the highest ranks of the aristocracy. This had likely determined the choice of the School of Jurisprudence as a springboard to social advancement, as his way to the top. A gifted and presumably charismatic young man, he began his civil service as a "scrivener of police matters," but as early as 1859, at the age of just twenty, was appointed a civil court judge of the St. Petersburg region. But Meshchersky's character and temperament did not favor bureaucratic activities, and his resignation from civil service in 1876 was arguably the wisest move of his life. As a nonofficial, nonbureaucratic figure, he acquired a singular attractiveness in the eyes of the monarchs, avoiding the traditional fate of the minister-favorites for whom dismissal from office always signified a loss of imperial goodwill and thus political ruin.

In 1861, Meshchersky, through a female relative, made the acquaintance of the imperial family in the Crimea and favorably impressed Alexander II. After this, he became intimate with the eighteen-year-old heir apparent Grand Duke Nikolay Aleksandrovich and with his sixteen-year-old brother, Aleksandr Aleksandrovich, the future Alexander III. Meshchersky, who "knew how to please without crude flattery and to prove his own worth without boasting,"[33] moved firmly into the select circle around the young grand dukes, though certain tensions came and went. Grand Duke Nikolay once ironically termed Meshchersky's attitude toward him "the feeling of unhappy love for a woman who responds to it with indifference."[34] Nevertheless, he willingly met and corresponded with him.

After the sudden death of young Grand Duke Nikolay in 1865, the future Alexander III, who had adored his elder brother, treated the latter's friends with particular affection. He became much closer to Meshchersky than had the late heir apparent, who was a person of restrained and skeptical temperament. For a time, their friendship was even accompanied by a certain emotionalism, nightlong conversations and effusive assurances of mutual devotion. In the future tsar's first extant letter to Meshchersky, dated 14 January 1867, he wrote, "For all the torments and troubles you have suffered for my sake, I give you my friendship, because you have well deserved it. . . . Your friend Aleksandr."[35]

This friendship was not without its storms, in part because of Meshchersky's difficult character, in part because of external circumstances. In 1873 a rift occurred that would last for ten years. But beginning in 1872, Meshchersky published the government-subsidized newspaper The Citizen, which won scandalous fame both for the brilliant pen of its editor and for its reactionary positions. From this time until the end of his life, he remained one of the chief ideologues of the last two reigns. Meshchersky's concept of autocracy was simple in the extreme yet persuasive precisely by virtue of its coordination with the political sympathies and antipathies of both tsars. Its basic assumption was that the autocratic monarch was responsible for his deeds before God alone, that his thoughts and actions were inspired from above and therefore not to be judged by man. The sovereign was linked mystically to the people, and his will was the true will of the people, even if on the surface it might go against people's vicissitudinous and fleeting desires. For this reason, any restriction of the will of the monarch—not only through the introduction of a constitution but even through the personal influence of ministers upon the sovereign—was a distortion of the true will of God and the people and thus tantamount to blasphemy. Especially pernicious in this respect, Meshchersky held, was the impact of the St. Petersburg governmental bureaucracy.

During the fifty years he was politically and socially active in St.

Petersburg, from the 1870s until his death in 1914, Meshchersky, owing to his great gift for political intrigue, his excellent knowledge of all the secret connections of the political world, and chiefly his intimate ties with the two monarchs, gradually acquired the reputation of the man on whose word depended appointments, dismissals and awards, and sometimes even the direction of government policy. He gained innumerable enemies and grew to be hated and despised by many. Even so, he remained for a very long time (although with some lengthy interruptions) one of the closest advisers of both Alexander III and Nicholas II—no mean achievement for someone so little liked and so peculiarly temperamental.

No doubt one reason for Tchaikovsky's evident lack of concern for what people might say of his friendship with Meshchersky was his own growing fame as a composer and, with it, his increasingly unassailable position. His reputation had even attracted the attention of the imperial court. One evening during his stay in St. Petersburg in the spring of 1880, while he and Apukhtin were visiting in the home of his longtime friend Vera Davydova, Lev's sister, now married to Vice Admiral Ivan Butakov, Vera suddenly told him that Grand Duke Konstantin Konstantinovich, nephew of Alexander II, desired to meet him and had asked her to arrange it. Tchaikovsky was seized with "indescribable terror," and though Apukhtin suggested that Vera should invite the grand duke to come that very evening, he persuaded them with difficulty to put it off.[36] Six days later, on 19 March, Vera held a soirée to which both men were invited. Much embarrassed and dreading the meeting, Tchaikovsky, to his surprise, found the twenty-two-year-old grand duke to be a charming young man and a passionate lover of music. Grand Duke Konstantin was, in fact, an unusual figure in the imperial family. From childhood he had displayed marked inclinations toward literature and the arts and, in addition to his piano playing and musical composition, he had distinguished himself as a minor poet and even a religious dramatist under the pseudonym "K.R.," for Konstantin Romanov.

"Knowing my dislike of crowds and high society, he [the grand duke] requested that the evening be intimate, without white tie or tails," Tchaikovsky wrote in a letter to Mrs. von Meck the following day. "It was quite impossible to decline. But the young man proved to be extremely pleasant and very gifted in music. We sat from nine o'clock until two in the morning talking about music. He composes quite nicely, but unfortunately does not have the time to work at it persistently."[37]

A week later, Tchaikovsky spent an evening with the young man's father, Grand Duke Konstantin Nikolaevich, brother of the tsar and president of the Russian Musical Society, whom he found "very affectionate and pleasant."[38] He then saw the younger Konstantin once more, a few days before leaving the capital at the end of the month. Again the two talked long into the night. A special bond, suggesting a degree of elective affinity, was established between the two men, demonstrated after their second meeting by the grand duke's extraordinary proposal that Tchaikovsky accompany him on a planned voyage round the world. Loath to give up his freedom for the confinement of a cabin aboard ship for three years and uneasy about the inevitable strain of being continually in such august company, Tchaikovsky refused the tempting offer. But the mutual sympathy of composer and grand duke would grow and continue until the end of Tchaikovsky's life. "I am utterly charmed," he wrote Modest on 3 April, "by this uncommonly likable person."[39]

The evening following his arrival in Moscow on 2 April, Tchaikovsky quite unexpectedly found himself once again the guest of the senior Konstantin, having run into the grand duke, then by chance also in Moscow, earlier that day while out for a stroll and having felt compelled to accept the latter's invitation. But most of the following week he spent in the less-exalted company of friends and former colleagues from the conservatory before leaving for Kamenka on the eleventh. There, two weeks later, Modest, Kolya, and Alyosha Sofronov finally arrived from Italy, to Tchaikovsky's great joy. With Alyosha's return, peace, order, and good spirits returned to his master, upset only by worry over Modest, who immediately after his arrival fell ill with a stomach ailment, leaving Tchaikovsky to cope with Kolya. During the next several weeks Tchaikovsky busied himself correcting the proofs for *The Maid of Orléans,* and in late June he began composing the Six Duets, op. 46, dedicated to his niece Tanya, and the Seven Songs, op 47.

Not long before this, Tchaikovsky and Mrs. von Meck had begun to nurture one of her most cherished projects—to become relatives through a marriage between the von Meck and the Davydov families. Available candidates abounded on both sides. Little did the composer and his benefactress guess that far from confirming their friendship, the eventual realization of this idea would preserve their oddly close separateness.

From the very beginning, Mrs. von Meck had shown a keen interest in the lives of Tchaikovsky's relatives. She inquired about Modest's celibacy and expostulated on Anatoly's infatuations.[40] Their correspondence contains abundant information about the Davydov family and the inhabitants of Kamenka, and Mrs. von Meck's continuous questions seem to point to something more than merely polite interest. Possibly, the various business commissions she offered Lev Davydov through Tchaikovsky were made primarily to indulge her "priceless" friend. Tchaikovsky at one point even attempted, rather awkwardly, to press his brother-in-law upon her as manager of her estate at Brailovo. She declined delicately but firmly. But when later the estate was proving uneconomical and the threat of a sale loomed, she was prepared to consider such a possibility, in the evident hope that this able landlord might manage to save her property from ruin. She even suggested that he buy Brailovo outright. This time it was Davydov who declined, the first idea, on the pretext of his obligations at Kamenka, and the second, simply because he did not have enough money. Throughout these numerous negotiations Mrs. von Meck never personally met either Davydov or his wife, Tchaikovsky's sister.

Despite her disparaging views on matrimony (as she herself admitted at one point, she would have preferred humans to reproduce by mitosis like amoebas and avoid marriage altogether), Mrs. von Meck was very much concerned about getting her children settled down, even though she had in mind their social establishment rather than any personal happiness. For all her fulminations against it, she never offered any alternative to marriage. So long as a prospective spouse was socially acceptable and the young people expressed a corresponding desire, she, with her emphasis on freedom of personal expression, would grant her consent, secure the young couple financially, and thereafter consider them responsible for their own future. These marriages were by no means always successful. Although restrained on this topic, her letters betray occasional traces of irritation with various of her children's spouses. Her style was typically to agree to the marriage of one of her children while having scarcely met his or her intended and refusing, as as matter of principle, ever to meet their relatives. What did matter to her, in accordance with her matriarchal nature, were her in-laws' relations with the various members of the von Meck clan—in other words, the suppression of discord or quarrels in that large and growing family and the administration by the married couples of the property apportioned to them, again looking to the general family interests.

The only deviation from this policy, an instance of careful matrimonial preparation, was her orchestration of the domestic future of her son Nikolay. With patent indifference to the wishes and intentions of the young man himself, she resolved to marry him into the family of Lev and Aleksandra Davydov, in this way making herself a relative of her musical idol. All four of Tchaikovsky's young nieces were subjected to discussion in the correspondence between Tchaikovsky and Mrs. von Meck, though in response to her question as to which might be best suited to be a wife for Nikolay the composer diplomatically replied that he loved them all equally (yet each in her own way), and in the end, it was decided that the prospective bridegroom must meet them all personally, for which opportunities could eventually be arranged.

The initial discussion of these matrimonial plans coincided with yet another unwelcome reminder of Tchaikovsky's own marital woes. Because Antonina had not bothered him all winter, he had twice sent her additional sums of money as a "reward for good behavior," but by late spring the troubles began again. Antonina's mother, whom Tchaikovsky considered "as unbalanced as her daughter but even more wicked," visited his publisher Jurgenson in May, asking him to talk Tchaikovsky into a divorce. "As if I had ever been against it in principle," he huffed to Mrs. von Meck.[41] Still, he was determined to stick to the firm line he had established the previous autumn not to resume negotiations for at least a year, and then only if he were convinced that she had finally understood clearly her role and expected behavior during the divorce process.

Mrs. Milyukova then wrote to Tchaikovsky, suggesting that "in order to avoid the expenses of a scandalous divorce," he ought to provide capital to cover the alimony the court would otherwise impose on him and that he also approve a permanent passport for his wife. According to Russian law at the time, a married woman required the permission of her husband to obtain a passport allowing her to move or to leave the city for more than six months. Antonina would in turn leave Moscow forever and not remind him of herself in any way. "You are a genius," her mother asserted, her words veiling some trace of a threat. "Your good name must be valuable to you. Believe me, we will put no stain on it and will fulfill our honest promise as befits an honorable family."[42]

With the inconsistencies and changes in her daughter's mood, this idea never came to pass. Indeed, despite the repeated hints of both Antonina and her mother, the Milyukov family never resorted to blackmail, nor did Antonina ever officially demand a divorce on the ground of her husband's homosexuality. Their social status, that of impoverished petty gentry, relegated them to the middle class; Tchaikovsky, a well-known composer and beloved by the public, moved in privileged circles. It needed no great perspicacity to realize that public opinion in these circumstances would be directed against the Milyukovs and that any such attempts could bring them nothing. Partly for this reason, Antonina and her mother never dared anything more intimidating than making vague and impotent allusions.

On 25 June, Antonina's "good behavior" came to an abrupt end with a bizarre and characteristically incoherent letter, irrelevant to the divorce issue but upsetting beyond measure to her husband. "I do not want to be even nominally the wife of a man who so basely slanders a woman who has done him no harm," she wrote, and then, referring to unspecified rumors about her supposedly spread in St. Petersburg by Tchaikovsky and his family, "Why did you not start with yourself, and tell . . . of your own terrible vice, before judging me? After all this, you stress in your letters your kindness and generosity. But where are these qualities and how are they confirmed? Please do not trouble to answer me. . . . Everything is finished between us, and therefore I ask you, dear sir, not to indulge in any lengthy correspondence but to deal only with this matter." This was then followed by the most striking inconsistency of all: "But once again I repeat that I shall sign no filthy and untrue papers."[43]

While Antonina evidently recognized or admitted, at long last, the truth of her husband's sexual preference, his "terrible vice," she still failed to come fully to terms with what this had meant for their marriage. Claiming not to want to be "even nominally" his wife, she stubbornly refused to take the steps necessary for initiating divorce proceedings and freeing herself from a position that she herself described as untenable. As was to be expected, the letter unleashed a virulent reaction. "There is in this person," Tchaikovsky wrote to Mrs. von Meck, "even in her handwriting, some poison that has a devastating effect on me! At the mere sight of the address written in her hand, I at once begin to feel sick, not only morally but physically as well." He claimed to have suffered such pain in his legs that he could scarcely move and all day to have felt an "unbearable depression and weakness."[44] In despair, he was driven to ask Modest, "Is it possible to conduct business with these lunatics?"[45] Clearly, he found it was not. Antonina would continue to pester him periodically. But for the fourth and, as it turned out, final time the idea of a divorce was laid to rest, this time having scarcely been broached.

Tchaikovsky spent the month of July at Brailovo and Simaki. Mrs. von Meck had gone abroad. By this time, even Tchaikovsky himself readily recognized, with some unease, how spoiled he had already become by the generosity of his benefactress and the constant assurance of his monetary well-being. Remaining largely at the margin of consciousness, his discomfort painfully surfaced at times, the more so as his continuing financial dependence on her seemed increasingly in conflict with his growing fame and recognition by even the highest society. He was no longer the struggling composer of just a few years before. But no matter how much he had, money continued to slip through his fingers and he seemed to be in perpetual need. His most difficult struggles with himself were waged over the supplementary sums of money occasionally offered him by Mrs. von Meck. However much he desired to display "civic courage," as he ironically called it, and refuse these gifts, the temptation was always too great and his resistance too weak. Only very rarely did he ask Mrs. von Meck for additional subsidies. Yet, he dreamed of them constantly, reproaching himself for his dreams even as he shared them with his brothers. "From Mme Meck I have received letters and an invitation," he wrote to Anatoly before leaving for Brailovo, "but not so much as a mention of any unusual payments, and meanwhile, I am filled with horror when I remember my debts and that until 1 October I shall not have a kopeck. Oh how spoiled I have become and how remiss in appreciating all that I owe to that wonderful woman!"[46]

The conflict in Tchaikovsky's attitude was clearly evident in his reaction to Mrs. von Meck's extravagant gift of a precious watch bearing the image of Joan of Arc on one side and that of Apollo and the Muses on the other, which she had ordered in Paris and sent to Brailovo for his arrival. So accustomed was Tchaikovsky to having Mrs. von Meck anticipate his needs and desires that he had somehow reckoned she would know instinctively that he now needed something to tide him over until autumn. But with still no word of any additional subsidy, Tchaikovsky set off for Brailovo in a state bordering on paranoia. "All the way to Brailovo I suffered from the heat and also from agitation: Will the horses come? Has not N[adezhda] F[ilaretovna] given instructions to drive me away when I appear?—and other such nonsense crept into my head," he wrote to Modest on 4 July. "I had become obsessed lately with the idea that N[adezhda] F[ilaretovna] had either changed toward me or else, on the contrary, redoubled her solicitude, and at the same time in my heart of hearts I was hoping for a little sealed box left for me with—several thousand, which I need desperately."

Awaiting him in the study, there was indeed a little sealed box. "In agitation I unseal it, open it—but instead of the thousands, there was a watch and a request to accept it as a gift. . . . The watch probably cost several thousand francs. . . . The work is most subtle, extraordinarily exquisite. Lord, how sweet is this N[adezhda] F[ilaretovna]! Yet, between ourselves," he confided frankly, "I should have preferred to receive not the watch but its value in cash."[47] After his brief resentment, however, Tchaikovsky took the watch, just as Mrs. von Meck had wished, as a genuine talisman, holding it dear and never parting with it. For some resolution of his pecuniary crisis he turned not to his benefactress but to Pyotr Jurgenson to ask for either a loan or an advance on future royalties. "She [von Meck] would have given me this money outright. She never does otherwise, and I do not want to abuse her extreme kindness and delicacy for anything in the world," he wrote his publisher. Even so, he added, "Oh, how I should have preferred to receive money in place of the watch!"[48]

Tchaikovsky was still at Brailovo when Mrs. von Meck on 10/22 July wrote from Interlaken in Switzerland telling him, among other family news, that "two days ago there came to me a young pianist from Paris who has just completed his conservatory studies, *avec le 1-r prix*. . . . I sent for him to give summer lessons to the children, to accompany Yulya [her daughter] at her singing, and to play piano duets with me. This young man plays well from the aspect of virtuosity, his technique is brilliant, but there is not the slightest expression of personal involvement in what he performs, though he has not yet lived enough for that; he says he is twenty, but he looks no more than sixteen."[49]

Only in her next letter, from the French port city of Arcachon, and then only in passing, did Mrs. von Meck mention the name of the young French pianist—"M. de Bussy." Tchaikovsky made no response to this bit of news. But in her letter of 7/19 August, Mrs. von Meck was still more enthusiastic in describing her new music teacher. "Yesterday I decided for the first time to play *our* symphony with my little Frenchman, and so today I find myself in a terribly nervous state," she wrote. "I cannot play it without a fever in every fiber of my being and cannot recover from the impression for several days. My partner performed it not well, though he played splendidly. This is his sole though still enormous merit: he reads compositions, even yours, *à livre ouvert*. His second merit, reflective so to speak, is that he is in raptures over your music." Mrs. von Meck and her young pianist, a devotee of the composer Jules Massenet, had then gone on to play one of Tchaikovsky's suites. "He was in utter ecstasy over the fugue," she reported, "expressing himself thus: 'Dans les fugues modernes je n'ai jamais rien vu de si beau. Monsieur Massenet ne pourrait jamais faire rien de pareil' [Among modern fugues I've never seen anything so beautiful. Massenet himself could never do anything like it.]." Mrs. von Meck concluded, "In general, he is a purely Parisian, plebeian, so to speak, creature. It turns out he is eighteen. . . . He composes, by the way, very nicely, but in this too he is purely French."[50]

The eighteen-year-old "little Frenchman" proved not only an exceptional musician but also a charming and undemanding guest. Virtually the whole of the sprawling von Meck tribe fell in love with his sense of humor and nicknamed him "Bussik," "Bussikov," and, on learning his actual first name, *"le bouillant* Achille." As yet the full name of the young Achille Claude Debussy conveyed little to anyone. During the summer months of 1881 and 1882 he would again form part of the von Meck entourage, in Russia as well as abroad. These three summers had considerable significance for the artistic development of Claude Debussy, most notably in the influence on the future French composer of the works of Tchaikovsky, and in particular his Fourth Symphony and *Romeo and Juliet.* For his part, Tchaikovsky thought little or nothing of Debussy's *Danse bohémienne,* which Mrs. von Meck sent for his perusal. "[It] is a very pretty piece," he wrote her after looking through her Bussik's composition, "but it is much too short. Not a single idea is expressed fully, the form is terribly shriveled, and it lacks wholeness."[51]

Returning to Kamenka on 29 July, Tchaikovsky plunged into renewed adoration of his nine-year-old nephew Bob Davydov, who, sensing this, invented ever new ways to delight his uncle. "[Bob] is embracing me and is at this moment singing in my ear in a very high, squeaking voice, 'Pitusya! Why are you teasing me, it hurts, it hurts!'" Tchaikovsky reported to Modest. "Lord, how charming he is when he does it!"[52]

The composer also found ample opportunity at Kamenka to befriend other local boys to whom he could play benefactor. Tchaikovsky's veritable obsession with patronizing and promoting young men of diverse qualities and social standing may have had, in some instances, a basis in amorous or erotic interest. Unlike Nikolay Rubinstein, for instance, Tchaikovsky never sought to promote the careers of young women at the conservatory or later. One recent object of his attentions was the Davydovs' servant boy Evstafy. But his particular protégé of this period was the fifteen-year-old Bonifatsy Sangursky, son of some local residents, whom Tchaikovsky, noting his "remarkable gifts for painting," sent to study at the School of Painting and Sculpture in Moscow. When this undertaking proved quite costly, Tchaikovsky even thought to ask his "beloved friend" to allow Bonifatsy, if possible, to live in some capacity in her own house in Moscow. Mrs. von Meck, pleading major masonry repairs and her own absence, was forced to refuse with many apologies, but in her customary generosity offered to provide a monthly stipend for his protégé's housing elsewhere. Tchaikovsky, however, eventually managed to find satisfactory lodgings for the boy at a cost he himself could afford.[53] The end result of his efforts was not unrewarding. Sangursky became a teacher of drawing, and four of his landscapes that he presented to the composer hang to this day in the house-museum at Klin.

As in all else, Modest attempted to imitate his famous brother in his patronage of promising youths. Modest's choices for potential protégés, however, were not always felicitous. The following year, searching for someone to act as servant and traveling companion, to help look after Kolya during their travels, Modest took "a great interest" in Moisey, a young shepherd boy at Kamenka. But Moisey was a disappointment, proving to be "lazy, sly, and generally a rather bad lot."[54] The attention of Modest and Tchaikovsky then turned to Grisha Sangursky, the younger brother of Bonifatsy. Tchaikovsky especially favored the choice of the younger Sangursky, and with his help, a deal with the boy's parents was made to allow Grisha to accompany Modest and his charge abroad. Shown a letter that Grisha sent to his parents from Italy, Tchaikovsky confided to Modest, "I cannot describe what a pleasant feeling it aroused in me. It somehow brought me nearer to you, . . . and Grisha himself is so sweet in this letter."[55]

Another object of the composer's philanthropy from the Kamenka neighborhood was eighteen-year-old Mikhail Klimenko (not to be confused with Tchaikovsky's friend Ivan Klimenko). Describing his newfound protégé as "very talented and clever," Tchaikovsky prevailed upon Pyotr Jurgenson to take on the youth to work at his music store in Moscow.[56] As fate would have it, however, Misha Klimenko was to bring the obliging publisher nothing but trouble, turning out to be a poor worker and of difficult character and eventually becoming involved with rather shady company. For many years Jurgenson, not knowing how to rid himself of the young man, would complain often of him to Tchaikovsky.

But certainly one of the more unsettling instances of Tchaikovsky's patronage was to unfold in the winter of 1880, the result of a most disturbing turn in an already odd epistolary acquaintance. Leonty Tkachenko, a young man of the lower class, had been quite unknown to Tchaikovsky when he had first written to him more than a year before, in October 1879. Pleading his love of music, Tkachenko had begged the composer to hire him as a manservant. Tchaikovsky politely declined, but did write a few times more with words of encouragement. Suddenly, in mid-December, Tkachenko would return all of Tchaikovsky's letters "so they might not fall into someone else's hands after his death," along with a note describing "his profound and hopeless despair and disgust for life" and announcing his decision to commit suicide.[57] All this was written so movingly and sincerely that

Tchaikovsky was stunned and wept at the realization of his inability to prevent the tragic outcome. The letter bore neither city nor date. Clearly the young man had indeed resolved to take such a step. But from the postmark on the envelope Tchaikovsky managed to make out that the letter had been sent from Voronezh in central Russia, where, it turned out, Anatoly had an acquaintance. An urgent telegram was sent to the acquaintance with the request to locate Tkachenko and prevent his suicide. A few days later, word arrived that Tkachenko had been found and was waiting for a letter from Tchaikovsky, a letter he immediately sent, enclosing fifty rubles and asking the young man to come to Moscow on 10 January to talk with him in person.

"I have no idea," he told Mrs. von Meck in a letter dated 14–17 December, "what will come of this, but I am happy that I kept him from ruin. Judging by his letters he is a strange and extravagant young man, but intelligent and very honest and good."[58]

Tkachenko's next letter reached Tchaikovsky in Kamenka, where he arrived shortly before Christmas. But, though Tchaikovsky had expected gratitude and appreciation for having come to his aid, he was mistaken. The young man insisted that it was futile to seek to persuade him of the existence of virtue or to prove that life in this world was worth living, that he did not need money, but that he would, all the same, come to Moscow as requested and listen to what Tchaikovsky had to say. Tchaikovsky shared with Mrs. von Meck his disappointment at this new turn. "The youth seemed to be perishing because he had met in no one support or compassion; now someone appears who offers him both yet in response receives trite phrases about virtue having dried up in people and, as though out of charity, an agreement to accept the helping hand so sincerely extended to him. If Mr. Tkachenko turns out to be a mere madman, I shall be very annoyed at myself. But what was there to do? How could I not attempt to save a human being from ruin?"[59]

Tchaikovsky did not discover a "mere madman" when the two finally met in Moscow in mid-January. He was quite favorably struck by the young man, and the unpleasant impression from his latest letter was "completely effaced." Tkachenko's sufferings apparently stemmed from the disparity between his ambition and hard reality. "He wants passionately to give himself to music," Tchaikovsky told Mrs. von Meck two days later. "He is a very nervous, timid, painfully shy, and, in general, morally sick and broken youth. Poverty, loneliness, and the circumstances of his life have led to a misanthropy and a hypochondriacal condition of the spirit in him. His judgments are somewhat strange, but, I repeat, he is no fool." Tkachenko's story was all too typical of the period. The pages of Turgenev and Dostoevsky are filled with similar young men, the so-called *raznochintsy*, socially displaced intellectuals with a keen sense of self-importance who had lost a taste for tradition and could find no place for themselves in their environment. Some made passionate converts and retired to monasteries. Others joined revolutionary movements. Still others, like Tkachenko, hovered precariously at the edge of madness and suicide.

"I feel extremely sorry for him and have resolved to take him into my charge," Tchaikovsky concluded to Mrs. von Meck. "Right now I have decided to place him in the conservatory for this semester and then see whether he should be kept there or turned toward another profession."[60]

Patronage was a prominent feature at all levels of the still largely paternalistic society of nineteenth-century Russia. Apart from mere social advancement, it also served to support and promote artists and to enhance culture, as it did in the case of the beneficence of Mrs. von Meck. It could be abused, as it was by Meshchersky. And it could also be a means of personal reassertion and a release of emotional or even sexual frustration through acts of generosity, as, in many instances, it was for Tchaikovsky.

CHAPTER TWENTY

Domestic Upheaval

As the autumn of 1880 approached, Tchaikovsky found himself facing a new ordeal that was to paralyze his creative life no less completely than the crisis of his marriage three years earlier. His servant Alyosha, having turned twenty-one, now became eligible for the military draft. In November, Alyosha would be required to report to Moscow for the drawing of lots in the annual levy.

When Peter the Great formed Russia's first standing national army at the beginning of the eighteenth century, military service was for life. The nobility was levied in mass to serve as officers, while the other classes were required to provide a fixed number of recruits, initially by consensus and later by lot. Over time, the period of active service was gradually reduced until, by the early 1870s, it stood at seven years, but the complicated system of recruitment, which allowed those who were drafted to send seconds in their place and even to redeem their service, inevitably led to bribery and graft. In 1874 the government of Alexander II imposed a series of much-needed military reforms. A mandatory levy for all male citizens of the middle and lower classes was introduced, with selection to be determined by an annual lottery. By 1880 active service had been shortened to just four years. But certain privileges, including a further reduction of the term of service or even exemption from service altogether, were granted according to a prospective recruit's education and profession. For this reason, Tchaikovsky exerted every effort on behalf of his beloved servant, making him pass the examinations in the local elementary school at Kamenka and writing to every acquaintance he had within military circles—all the while dreaming passionately that Alyosha might be passed up in the lottery drawing.

All these concerns Tchaikovsky even shared with Mrs. von Meck, who began conveying her personal regards to the servant of her "adored Pyotr Ilyich." Late in September, longing to see Tchaikovsky in Florence once more but knowing his wish not to leave Russia with Alyosha's fate still unresolved, she offered her advice: "I should certainly not want you to be here without Alyosha, and I happened to recall that any of his close relatives may draw the lot for him, . . . there is no need for him to be present in person, and if the lot drawn should be unlucky he will, of course, be informed. Think about this, my dear friend, . . . and bring Aleksey with you to Villa Bonchiani."[1] But Tchaikovsky wrote back that this would be impossible. Even the previous year, a year before Alyosha had become subject to the military levy, he had barely managed to obtain a foreign passport for his servant, and only then because of a personal acquaintance in the office of the provincial governor. Now, just a week before the levy, such would be entirely out of the question.[2]

On the eve of the young man's departure to Moscow for the drawing of lots, Tchaikovsky wrote again to his benefactress: "I am on tenterhooks. Aleksey leaves tomorrow or the day after, and parting with him will not be easy for me. It is difficult to lose (perhaps for a long time) someone to whom you are tied by ten years' living together. I feel sorry for myself, but mostly I pity him. He will have to go through a great deal of suffering before he becomes accustomed to his new situation. To suppress my sad feelings I have been working intensely."[3] Besides completing a third revision of *Romeo and Juliet,* Tchaikovsky buried himself in two very different compositions, the Serenade for Strings, op. 48, and the ceremonial *1812* Overture, op. 49. Firmly convinced of the merits of the serenade, describing it to Mrs. von Meck as "a heartfelt piece and so . . . not lacking in real qualities," the composer showed considerably less enthusiasm for *1812.* Commissioned to mark the consecration of the Cathedral of Christ the Savior in Moscow, which was being built in thanksgiving for the Russian victory over Napoleon, the overture had been written, as Tchaikovsky admitted, "without any warm feelings of love" and struck him as "very loud and noisy."[4]

Anxiously awaiting the outcome of the draft, Tchaikovsky several days later, on 27 October, sent a letter to Alyosha, by then in Moscow. "My dear and beloved Lyonya," he wrote in a rush of sentiment. "As if by design, I have felt unwell ever since your departure. . . . How much easier all this would be for me to bear if you were here with me! . . . Dear Lyonya, know that whatever happens, whether you go into the army or not, you will always be mine and I shall never forget you for a moment. If indeed you are fated to go into the army, then I shall count the days impatiently, waiting for your return to me. I kiss you warmly and embrace you heartily and tenderly."[5]

Tchaikovsky himself arrived in Moscow on 11 November to await word together with Alyosha. It came six days later, and that same day he sent news from Moscow of his despair. "Alyosha has been drafted," he told Modest. "I live tolerably only because I am always drinking! Were it not for continual dinners and suppers with drink, this life would literally drive me mad."[6] Then, more muted, to Mrs. von Meck, "I only know that I feel sick at heart. This is in no small part the result of the news that my Alyosha has gone into the army."[7] From this point on, Mrs. von Meck and his brother would share almost equally Tchaikovsky's confidences regarding the plight of his servant.

Production matters in both Moscow and St. Petersburg helped to divert Tchaikovsky only slightly from his worries during the succeeding weeks. On 26 November he traveled to St. Petersburg, where *The Maid of Orléans* was scheduled to be performed in February, but by 8 December he was back in Moscow for rehearsals of a new production of *Eugene Onegin* that was to open at the Bolshoy Theater shortly after the New Year. Tchaikovsky had no idea of Alyosha's precise whereabouts. "He promised to write me as soon as his situation becomes more definite," he told his benefactress, "but still I wait in vain for a letter from him."[8] Making inquiries, he finally learned that Alyosha had been stationed, as he wrote Modest on 14 December, in the Ekaterinoslavsky regiment in Moscow: "I went to the barracks to look for him, but for some reason was not admitted; I wrote him to come see me today, but he did not come. Why—I do not understand. So now I am reduced to having to search for Alyosha. How strange and unusual this all is."[9] No less strange and unusual, of course, is the image of the prominent composer going in search of his servant in the army barracks.

Two days later, on the sixteenth, master and servant met at last. Describing the meeting to Mrs. von Meck the next day, Tchaikovsky wrote of his horror at the sight of "this stifling, dirty barracks [and] the crushed and mournful appearance of Alyosha, already dressed as a soldier, deprived of freedom and forced to drill from morning to night."[10] With even more emotion and in greater detail, he recounted the same unhappy reunion to Modest. "Alyosha! How many tears I shed after visiting him in the barracks!" Tchaikovsky confessed to his brother.

"It was so dark in the barracks that I searched long before I discerned him in a crowd of other soldiers. . . . I sat with him about half an hour, surrounded by the whole crowd." He was appalled to see a sergeant clip one recruit on the back of the head, and the arduous routine of the young soldiers filled him with dismay. "They are awakened at five in the morning, drill on the square until noon, after dinner drill again, and so on," he told Modest. "Reading or writing is out of the question. And thus he will have to live for four years!"[11]

The composer's naive request that Alyosha be allowed to go with him for half an hour for some tea was flatly refused, but permission was granted for Alyosha to accompany his master to the gates. "We were both silent because we both wanted terribly to cry, and Alyosha's voice trembled so when he said good-bye to me that I could scarcely endure this agonizing moment." Arriving home, Tchaikovsky at once set about trying to pull whatever strings he could on behalf of his servant. He wrote a "desperate" letter to a relative friendly with the commander of the regiment, asking him somehow to ease the new soldier's predicament, and he also begged Rubinstein to intervene with a certain Count Shuvalov to the same purpose. "It seems to me that only now do I truly recognize the full force of my attachment to Alyosha," he continued to Modest. "But on this it is best for the time being not to elaborate, as it is a very sore spot right now in my state of morale."[12]

Tchaikovsky visited the barracks again on the nineteenth, and that same evening suffered a "terrible nervous fit such as I have never had before," the immediate cause of which, as he confided to Modest two days later, he believed to have been Alyosha, "whom I pity more than words can say."[13] That his feelings were far indeed from the simple affection of a master for his servant is brought out yet again by a curious conspiratorial postscript to this letter: "If you take it into your head to write to Alyosha, remember that the authorities read the letters."[14] Clearly, he feared that the military censors might be alert to any erotic allusions in their correspondence.

Burdened by his sorrow, Tchaikovsky decided to decline Mrs. von Meck's invitation for another stay at Simaki. "I am afraid that I shall feel too strongly there Alyosha's absence," he explained to Anatoly on 23 December. "This wound is still too fresh. At Kamenka, too, I shall suffer from this, but there I am not alone and it will be easier to bear the separation from my dear poor little soldier."[15] Mrs. von Meck, though disappointed by his turning down her invitation, responded to his grief with no little compassion. "What a sad and painful impression the present situation of your poor Alyosha has made on me!" she wrote. "For him, rather a comrade than a servant of such a master as you, matured and understanding immeasurably more than the milieu in which he now finds himself, who has seen so much and so advantageously, and who, finally, is even spoiled by material comfort, his present circumstances must be unbearable, as this is for several years. I pity him terribly; tears simply come to my eyes when I contemplate his situation."[16]

Tchaikovsky believed that he would never grow accustomed to Alyosha's absence. "Every minute I remember him and feel what an essential friend I have lost in him," he confided to Mrs. von Meck at one point, adding that "no other servant, even the most zealous, can replace him."[17] Meanwhile, service to the state was not proving easy for the young man, and the cheerless letters that he sent to his master only doubled Tchaikovsky's distress. Alyosha wrote that he was homesick and complained of the drinking and carousing of his comrades during the holidays. "Apparently, the whole barracks was turned for a time into a pub and a filthy den of all manner of iniquity," Tchaikovsky wrote Mrs. von Meck in consternation.[18]

With the start of the new year Tchaikovsky resumed his efforts, at times unprecedented, on behalf of his "little soldier." The holidays he had spent at Kamenka, but on 7 January 1881 he returned to Moscow, and by the time he wrote to Mrs. von Meck five days later, he had already managed to see Alyosha "many times." "Yesterday they allowed him to come to me for several hours," he reported, "and the poor boy was inexpressibly happy at being able to spend a considerable part of the day with me. The regiment commander has taken a liking to him and declared his express desire to grant him his protection."[19] A week later, he informed her, "I see Alyosha often. For the sake of ensuring his protection by the higher authorities, I have made the acquaintance of the regimental commander, and in accordance with his wife's wishes, I call upon them and am forced to spend entire evenings accompanying her singing and engaging in society talk. I find this a painful sacrifice. But then yesterday, thanks to this protection, he was allowed to spend nearly the whole day with me. Saying good-bye, the poor boy could not contain himself and broke into tears. It was a grievous moment for me."[20]

What is remarkable in this is not only that for the sake of his adored servant the composer of European fame was prepared to accompany the singing of the wife of a regimental commander but also that in a burst of despair he should tell of all this to his friend and benefactress, from whom he would no doubt have hidden such particulars, had he been more in control of himself. Given the social proprieties of the time, his "sacrifice" could not have been seen as other than beneath him. As during the year of his matrimonial plight, Mrs. von Meck assumed again the status of confidante. In the same letter, he said, at a high and passionate pitch, "You ask, my friend, whether it is not possible to do something to release him? I have thought much about this and consulted many. *Nothing* is *possible, nothing!* Should he fall mortally ill, with consumption for instance, then they would let him go. But I can certainly not wish that!"[21]

Tchaikovsky had returned to Moscow for the opening of *Eugene Onegin* at the Bolshoy Theater on 11 January. The production came nearly on the heels of what one Moscow paper had called the "week of Tchaikovsky." The final week of the autumn 1880 musical season had seen performances on 15 December of *The Oprichnik* at the Bolshoy and of the First Quartet, which were followed by a highly successful concert of the composer's sacred music, including the 1878 Liturgy of St. John Chrysostom, op. 41, on the eighteenth and two days later, "by popular demand," by a second performance of the *Capriccio italien*, first presented earlier that same month.

Tchaikovsky, beset by his worries about Alyosha, took little comfort in the adulation and now, arriving in Moscow three days before *Eugene Onegin*'s opening, he jotted in his notebook his present feelings about the city: "Lord! How unhappy I am living in *Moscow*, precisely in *Moscow*, which, however, I love with such painful intensity! Where is the radiant past! Or does it just seem such to me? But everything here is poisoned for me—Terrible!"[22] Without doubt, his fit of nostalgia was due in no small part to the absence of Alyosha, who had first entered his service with Tchaikovsky during the composer's early years in Moscow. The production of *Onegin* received mixed reviews, being more criticized than praised, even though the merits of the opera in communicating Pushkin's poetry in music were acknowledged.[23] Two weeks later, Tchaikovsky left Moscow for St. Petersburg, where the premiere of *The Maid of Orléans* was to be held at the Mariinsky Theater in mid-February. Before his departure he once more visited "my poor Alyosha" at the barracks, and both wept as they said their farewells.[24]

Tchaikovsky arrived in the capital in time for the theatrical debut of his brother Modest, whose comedy *The Benefactor*, written the previous year, opened at the Aleksandrinsky Theater on 9 February. Tchaikovsky himself had used his influence to help bring about the production, but the play closed after just one night. The protagonist of the play may have been drawn in part on the model of Hermann Konradi. Friction between Konradi and Modest had begun to intensify by this time, promoting Tchaikovsky on 2 January to commiserate with his brother, "Poor Modya! you are going through a very difficult time now, both as someone tied up with such a villain as Konradi and as the author of a comedy. Authorship brings the very best moments of earthly happiness—*but at the cost of great unpleasantness and much suffering.* I say this from experience. But one should never lose heart, and instead must write, write, write."[25]

The reception given *The Maid of Orléans* on 13 February proved to be even more divided than that given *Onegin*. The performance itself seems to have been a success with the public, with an ovation for the composer, but the press was unanimous in its condemnation of the opera. Especially critical was César Cui, who even during rehearsals called it "sheer banality" and later said in print that the opera was "a weak work of a fine and gifted musician, ordinary, monotonous, dull, and long (it drags on past midnight), with rare flashes of brighter, vivid music and even those are echoes from other operas."[26] Tchaikovsky himself would sense something of this a few days later when, having left the city, he confessed to Modest, "I cannot rid myself of the impression of a sort of failure I have experienced; it is simply some sort of morbid happening."[27]

The troubles with the senior Konradi had forced plans to be postponed for the brothers and Kolya to travel abroad again together, and so, the day after the premiere of *The Maid of Orléans*, Tchaikovsky left for Vienna alone. From there, he traveled to Florence, where he spent several days missing Modest and Alyosha and even Mrs. von Meck, so vividly did the city remind him of his previous stays there. Still, his longing was mixed with ecstasy. Italy was, after all, a "wonderful and blessed country." Recalling their stay there two and a half years before, his letter of 19 February/3 March to Mrs. von Meck fully reflected his nostalgic mood. "My God, how sweet are my recollections of the autumn of '78!" he wrote, then, echoing the title of one of his own early songs, "It's both painful and sweet," op. 6, no. 3, he added, "Yes! precisely: both sweet and painful. For indeed this will never return! . . . We have grown older! Yes, *both painful and sweet!* . . . I feel so fine! But also sad for some reason! I want to weep, and I do not know what sort of tears they are: humiliation and gratitude and regret are all in them. In a word—only music can express it!"[28]

But, at the Bonciani restaurant that same evening, sadness for Alyosha and "the burning realization of the irretrievability of the past"[29] so overwhelmed Tchaikovsky that he drank himself drunk, and at ten o'clock, despite his fatigue, he left for Rome. In Rome he was expected and was met the following morning at six by Nikolay Kondratyev, who was wintering in Italy, and his servant Sasha Legoshin. It was, he wrote to Modest later that evening, "very pleasant and even a downright blessing to find N[ikolay] Dm[itrievich] and dear Sasha here," and this time on arriving in the Eternal City, Tchaikovsky felt "as if I had come home." Nonetheless, he found himself reminded of Modest and Kolya at every step, especially as he was staying at the same hotel where they had all lived just the year before. Visiting a café where he and his brother used to eat, he was happy to discover that most of the waiters were the same. "I was especially pleased to see Cesare [the following word in the original is crossed out and illegible], Tito and Giovanni (the young boy with dancing eyes who began to serve at the table d'hôte at the end of our stay)," he wrote to Modest. "Amici [the young singer whom they had met during their previous stay] arrived after lunch. The poor boy has grown much thinner but is no less pretty." He mentioned also "a young druggist [who] came to see Nikolay Dmitriev- ich, a handsome youth in love (*à la lettre*) with Kondrashon [that is, Kondratyev]."[30]

Kondratyev moved much of the time within Rome's cosmopolitan homosexual milieu, and Tchaikovsky in his letters regaled his brother with stories of his friend's adventures and accounts of the endless "squabbles and spats" of Golitsyn and Masalitinov and the rest of their circle. The prince, it seemed, had managed to fall out with nearly everyone, including Kondratyev, leaving Tchaikovsky to pick his way delicately, and not always successfully, between his two feuding friends. One reason for the conflict between Kondratyev and Golitsyn was the competition between the society salons of Count Lev Bobrin- sky and of Mme Uxküll, wife of the Russian ambassador to Italy. "Yes- terday a tremendous scene took place after dinner at Golitsyn's," Tchaikovsky described to Modest in his letter of 26 February/10 March. "Both [Kondratyev and Golitsyn] were so beside themselves that I feared for them both: Golitsyn *suffoquait* in the literal sense of the word—he lost his voice in his excitement. But how comical Kon- dratyev was, both during the scene and afterward, when we were left alone and he began trying to show to me . . . that, without being con- ceited, he still cannot help recognizing his own superior development in comparison with Golitsyn's shallowness, etc., etc. But, as a result, it has now turned out that Kondrashon is already sulking because I am going today to Mme Uxküll's, and *l'entente cordiale* has seriously cracked."[31]

This assumed role of an amused observer did not prevent Tchai- kovsky from entering and even enjoying this high-society life, more reminiscent of his early days in St. Petersburg than of the reserved and self-isolated ways he usually kept to when abroad. "There was a party

at the Uxkülls' with guests, counts, princes, diplomats, and I played
[piano] a lot!!!" he wrote in a hasty postscript to one letter to Modest.
"Lord, what have I come to! . . . I am in a great rush."[32] It is not hard
to imagine that this social whirl owed something to the absence of
Alyosha, as Tchaikovsky sought distraction from his yearning for his
beloved servant.

Also in Rome at this time, visiting the Italian capital during a
cruise of the Mediterranean with two of his cousins, was the composer's august young friend Grand Duke Konstantin Konstantinovich.
Upon learning that Tchaikovsky had arrived in the city, Konstantin
had wished to see him at once, and so the very day after his arrival
Tchaikovsky found both himself and the grand duke guests at a luncheon at the home of the Russian aristocrat Count Bobrinsky. Then,
before he knew it, he found himself invited to dine the following afternoon, Sunday the twenty-second, at the Villa Sciarra, where Konstantin was staying with his cousins, the Grand Dukes Sergey and Pavel
Aleksandrovich, the two younger sons of the reigning emperor, Alexander II. Luncheon was for one o'clock.

The invitation at once caused a minor furor. Having already promised to have lunch with Prince Golitsyn that day, Tchaikovsky had first
to cancel that engagement and send the prince his regrets. It then
turned out Tchaikovsky had no tailcoat to wear. He asked to borrow
Masalitinov's, but Masalitinov's proved too tight; Kondratyev's, on the
contrary, was too large. In panic, Tchaikovsky rode all over Rome in
search of a tailcoat, but as it was Sunday, nearly all the shops were
closed. Finally, in one little store a coat was found, not the best but
tolerable, and Tchaikovsky made it to the Villa Sciarra at one o'clock
on the nose.

Konstantin and his cousins did not appear until half an hour later.
Tchaikovsky was presented to Sergey and Pavel, and they all sat down
at once to an "endlessly long luncheon." Finding all three grand dukes
"very friendly," Tchaikovsky especially liked Pavel, "whose eyes remind one of the heir apparent [the future Alexander III]." Of the three
grand dukes, the homosexuality of Sergey Aleksandrovich would become within a very few years a matter of common knowledge. There
are reasons to believe that his brother and cousin may have shared the
same orientation. All three might either have known about or guessed
at Tchaikovsky's own predilections, whether through the grapevine of
homosexual circles or, more simply, from Meshchersky, already a
prominent figure at court.

Later that same day, Tchaikovsky wrote Modest that he had been
"shown much kindness. I left Villa Sciarra at three in the afternoon

and came home on foot. . . . On Tuesday I am invited to dine at Count Bobrinsky's, where the Gr[and] Duke Konstantin Konstantinovich will also be."[33] At the dinner at Bobrinsky's in white tie and tails both the grand duke and Tchaikovsky were called upon and, though it was something Tchaikovsky always hated, consented to play. So friendly had he and the young Konstantin now grown that Tchaikovsky could call him simply by the familiar diminutive "Kostya."[34]

The three Russian imperial ships aboard which the grand dukes were traveling were anchored at Naples, and on 28 February/12 March, Tchaikovsky headed there to tour the ships and to rest from the bustle of Rome. With him went Kondratyev and Sasha Legoshin. By no means the least important factor, for Tchaikovsky, in their continuing travels together seems to have been the presence of his friend's servant. "What a delight Sasha is," he told Modest on 3/15 March. "The more I know him, the more I love him, and you know, I even find him very *poetic*. When we see each other, remind me to tell you a very touching story of Sasha's."[35] Phrases such as this one, declining to write about something and promising instead to relate it in person later, occur often in Tchaikovsky's letters to Modest and usually in relation to homosexual matters. It is interesting, moreover, that Sasha Legoshin was evidently sharing confidences with his master's friend. "With his services," Tchaikovsky wrote Anatoly on 6/18 March, "[Sasha] even partly replaces Alyosha for me. He is a very dear boy."[36] Kondratyev appears not to have been oblivious to Tchaikovsky's involvement with his servant, for in their various accounts as they traveled together Tchaikovsky found that Sasha's expenses were "for some reason divided between us."[37]

Yet, even with the comforting presence of Sasha Legoshin, Tchaikovsky's pining for Alyosha never lessened. In late February he had once again declined Mrs. von Meck's invitation to Brailovo. "Alyosha's absence spoils my life in general, and on such occasions as a visit to you it causes me the deepest distress," he wrote her. "Without him it would be the same, yet not the same."[38] He wrote frequently to Alyosha himself, telling him all about Kondratyev and Sasha, high society, and the grand dukes. But always the beloved servant remained irreplaceable and Tchaikovsky's anxiousness about him constant: "If only you knew how painful and difficult and dull it is for me without you. I think of you every minute, my dear one, and when I imagine you in the barracks or at training, I nearly weep. Please, Lyonya, write me more often. . . . I embrace you, my dear Lyonya! [signed] Your friend."[39] Given that his correspondence with Alyosha passed through the military censors and had of necessity to be restrained—as he himself had cautioned Modest just weeks before—such a shower of uncontrolled emotion is truly striking.

In Naples there was talk of having the composer accompany the grand dukes to Athens and Jerusalem. But this was not to be. From St. Petersburg on 1/13 March 1881 arrived the tragic news of the assassination of Alexander II, killed with a bomb by members of the radical group called the People's Will. These young revolutionaries had already staged several failed attempts on Alexander's life. They fanatically believed that the assassination of the tsar would unhinge the government and plunge Russia into chaos, allowing them to seize power and establish their version of "peasant socialism." The assassination of Alexander II, the liberator of the serfs and arguably the most appealing Russian monarch, was particularly tragic in that only hours before, the tsar had approved the draft of a constitution. The execution of his assassins made them martyrs in the eyes of many of the intelligentsia, and the new tsar, Alexander III, quickly canceled the proposal for a constitution and inaugurated a period of political reaction against his father's liberal reforms.

The Russian community in Italy was deeply shocked by the news of the assassination. Grand Duke Pavel suffered "a terrible fit . . . and boarded the train completely ill."[40] The grand dukes left for St. Petersburg at once. Two days later, Tchaikovsky confided to Mrs. von Meck that "this news so struck me that I nearly fell ill. In such dreadful moments of national disaster, during events that have brought such disgrace to Russia, it is painful to be in a foreign land. One wishes to fly back to Russia, learn the details, be among one's own people, take part in demonstrations of sympathy for the new sovereign, and together with others cry out for vengeance."[41]

Tchaikovsky and Kondratyev remained another week in Naples following the sudden departure of the grand dukes. The imperial ships were still at anchor in the bay, and Tchaikovsky gratefully accepted a renewed invitation to tour them. Ceremoniously received aboard all three ships, Tchaikovsky later wrote to Modest of his pleasure at seeing "these wonderful frigates and the dear faces of Russian sailors" and of his meetings with several marine officers who, as he noted pointedly to his brother, were friends of Meshchersky.[42]

It was also in Naples that Tchaikovsky received word of a most unexpected development concerning Antonina. After 1880, Antonina figured far less frequently in her husband's correspondence, and the appearances she did make were most often linked to some dramatic twist or other. Not until several weeks later did Tchaikovsky reveal to Mrs. von Meck what he had learned from his publisher shortly after his arrival in Naples. "Before last winter she [Antonina] took up with some gentleman and brought into the world a child who was given over to the Foundling Hospital," he wrote. "This whole affair in all its details Jurgenson discovered by chance, and just in case, he has very adroitly and diplomatically acquired irrefutable proof of the truth of the event. If I am not mistaken, she is now in Moscow and lives with the child's father."[43] Antonina had finally, it seems, cast all prudence and propriety to the wind. Clearly, the "diplomatic" acquisition of "irrefutable proof" was intended to silence her in the unlikely event that she might yet make some attempt at blackmail or cause other trouble.

What he did not mention to Mrs. von Meck was that the birth of the child now gave Tchaikovsky incontestable grounds for divorce. In the days following Jurgenson's revelation, Tchaikovsky had flirted with the idea of once again initiating divorce proceedings, but he soon abandoned it. Antonina had conveniently placed herself in a position that would make it relatively easy to keep her quiet and under control. Divorce not only presented the prospect of unwelcome disclosures and unsavory publicity but also entailed considerable expense, and it was the question of money that, for the moment, seems to have decided Tchaikovsky. Only recently he had learned, as he confided to his publisher, that Mrs. von Meck's affairs were "in a far from brilliant condition."[44]

This was an understatement. The tremendous fortune of the von Meck family was in serious danger of ruin. It is unclear what precisely happened to bring Mrs. von Meck's affairs to such a state of disarray. From her letters it appears that a major role was played by the very considerable debts of the late Karl von Meck, the full extent of which had only now become clear, and by obscure intrigues within the governing boards of the railroads belonging to the von Meck family. But outside observers, along with several members of the family, were certain that a sizable share of the blame for what had happened lay with the extravagant wastefulness of Mrs. von Meck's eldest son, Vladimir, who managed the estate together with his mother. This, however, was an accusation that she herself would always deny categorically.

Earlier in the year, rumors of the troubles facing the von Meck family had begun to reach Tchaikovsky, first in Moscow and later in Rome. Fearing to be indiscreet, he had not ventured to ask his benefactress about it. Then, in February, word came from Mrs. von Meck herself that she might be forced to lease Simaki and that she intended to take up permanent residence at Brailovo in an attempt to restore order to the estate and make it more profitable. Tchaikovsky's immediate response was genuine and heartfelt. He reminded her that the doors of the conservatories in both Moscow and St. Petersburg were wide open to him and that, if need be, he was fully able and willing to earn his own living. "My freedom and the materially luxurious existence that I lead are priceless blessings," he wrote. "But they would at once become a burden to me were I to know that I enjoy them to the detriment of too tactful and generous a friend!" She had already been generous beyond words. "Speaking without any exaggeration, I feel I owe you my *life*," he told her. "And so, my friend, for God's sake, do not hide the truth from me, and if indeed you are *obliged* to reduce your expenses, then let me also change my way of life and take a place again in one of the conservatories, where they will welcome me joyfully. . . . *I desire first and foremost your well-being*," he stressed. "*Any pleasure is poisoned for me if it does damage to your interests.*"[45]

No doubt, even as he wrote this Tchaikovsky knew that Mrs. von Meck would reject his offer out of hand. And indeed, at the close of her lengthy reply, in which she had attempted rather confusedly to elucidate her financial state of affairs, the idea of any change in their own arrangements was firmly brushed aside. "As concerns you, my dear beloved friend, I beg you not to worry yourself in the least about my situation and to realize that that sum about which you speak is so negligible within my million-odd ruin that it cannot be felt on either side of the scales, and for this reason I ask you, if you do not wish to distress me, not even to mention it. For my part, I promise you, my dear, to tell you myself should my situation ever become such that even this may be of significance."[46]

On the heels of the news of Mrs. von Meck's threatened bankruptcy came yet another blow. On 11/23 March, Nikolay Rubinstein, seriously ill with intestinal tuberculosis and on his way to Nice for urgent treatment, died in Paris. The last few years in the life of the "Moscow Rubinstein" had been darkened by the coarse and unjust attacks upon him by the St. Petersburg press—a persecution that had, however, helped Tchaikovsky to throw off his petty vexations and grievances and to restore his earlier feelings of sympathy for him. "How strange and obscure is the human heart," he had written to Anatoly slightly more than two years before. "I had always, or at least for a long time, believed that I did not like Rubinstein. Recently I dreamed that he had died and that I was in deep despair about it. Since then I cannot think of him without a wrenching of my heart and a most positive sensation of love."[47] This transformation was not fleeting. Two months later, on 8/20 February 1879, Tchaikovsky had again noted that "in general after all the attacks on Rubinstein . . . I am terribly *for* Rubinstein and have freed myself from the secret feeling of enmity that

I had long felt for him."[48] As for Rubinstein's attitude toward Tchaikovsky, it had never changed: he had been the first performer, propagandist, and discerning critic of his works, and to his final day, he followed his progress and rejoiced in his successes.

Jurgenson having wired from Moscow that Rubinstein lay gravely ill in Paris, Tchaikovsky had at once set out for the French capital but arrived too late to see his friend alive. A funeral service in a Russian Orthodox church was held on 14/26 March, after which the lead coffin was boarded up and put on a train to Moscow. "It was strange and terrible," Tchaikovsky wrote to Mrs. von Meck two days later, "to realize that poor Nik[olay] Grigoryevich [Rubinstein] was lying in that wooden box and was going to Moscow in the baggage car. Yes, it was indeed *painful*, but fortunately I have the rudiments of *faith*, and I find consolation in the thought that such is the *unfathomable*, but *divine*, will of God."[49] On 23 March an article about Rubinstein's last days written by Tchaikovsky would appear in the *Moscow Register*.

Profoundly shaken by Rubinstein's unexpected death and its confluence with Mrs. von Meck's troubles and jarred into seeking the comfort of faith as he had never done before, Tchaikovsky added in the same letter to his friend written 16/28 March, "As regards prayer to God, let me tell you, my dear, incomparable one, that it gives me the greatest happiness and joy to pray to God for you and to ask his blessing upon you."[50] He even reiterated, despite her flat refusal, his willingness to give up his subsidy and go back to teaching, though he confessed that he could not bring himself to do so right away, so soon after Rubinstein's death. "I should like to spend next season still at leisure," he explained, "then in a year . . . I shall either go [to the Moscow Conservatory] or else to Petersburg, where I was already invited two years ago."[51] But this show of resolve was little more than a brave face, and at heart he remained anxious about the prospect of losing her financial support. "In all probability, if not next season then the one following, I shall once again have to toil at a job somewhere," he wrote to Modest on 17/29 March, adding gloomily, "All this is quite depressing."[52]

Yet, in spite of her dramatic circumstances, Mrs. von Meck remained adamantly opposed to any talk of ceasing his subsidy. Simply to hear that Tchaikovsky was praying for her gave her, she told him, "the strength to endure all the persecutions, all the blows that rain down on me unceasingly."[53] As for his decision to return to the conservatory, she wrote, "Why put on again that heavy yoke? Your nerves and health are maybe only just beginning to settle down, to grow stronger, and now again all will be ruined and lost. You have expressed such fine religious sentiments, a faith in the mercy of God, and obedience to His will. Why do you now wish to struggle against divine providence? . . . I shall not give up my right to take care of you, nor have you the right to take it from me, until such a time as I am no longer able to enjoy it, and that boundary God will show to us both."[54] Such, clearly, was meant to be her final word on the subject.

Two weeks after Rubinstein's death, on 25 March 1881, Tchaikovsky returned to Russia and spent a month in St. Petersburg before heading for Kamenka in late April. On his way he stopped in Moscow to see Alyosha. The grief caused by his separation from his servant not only had not diminished but had become even more keen and vivid. He was dismayed to find that even a few months of barracks life had made Alyosha "coarse" both physically and, as Tchaikovsky had feared most of all, morally. The thought of what another three and a half years of service might do was almost too much to bear.

"Every evening, when I have undressed, I sit at my desk and start to grieve and to pine, remembering that you are not beside me," he wrote to Alyosha from Kamenka on 2 May. "Absurd to say, I even weep a little every time I see something that reminds me of you. . . . No one will ever replace you! . . . I embrace you heartily, my dear!"[55] Even the threat of the prying eyes of military censors did not prevent the lament from continuing unabated in another letter a week later: "When I returned home and went into your room to change, I suddenly recalled so vividly how I would rejoice, coming home, to see your face so dear to me. I recalled how you would scold me for having soiled my clothes, and I became so sad, so sad, that I began to cry like a child! Ah, dear sweet Lyonya! Know that even if you were to remain in the service one hundred years, I shall never grow out of the habit of you and shall always wait impatiently for that happy day when you return to me. I think of this hourly!"[56]

To Anatoly, transferred to Moscow the previous year, had fallen in his brother's absence the unenviable task of continuing to curry favor with Alyosha's regimental commander by visiting his wife's salon and even by singing duets with the lady. "The thought that Alyosha has a protector and intercessor in Moscow," Tchaikovsky wrote him on 13 May, "gives me much comfort in my longing for him."[57] Three days later, he confided in a letter to Modest, "Punctually every evening, that is, as night begins, I think of Alyosha, of the irretrievability of the past, and I weep. This has become a custom with me (I sleep superbly)."[58]

Most of all Tchaikovsky felt how much he needed Alyosha just now when, as he confided to Mrs. von Meck from Kamenka, "so much bitterness" from the events of the last weeks was weighing on his heart. His anxiety and emotional frustration were such that composition was impossible. "I know that his [Alyosha's] mere presence near me, the consciousness that here close at hand is a creature boundlessly devoted to me, my constant companion of many years—would give me much moral strength for overcoming the secret anguish gnawing at me and my disgust for work," he wrote to Mrs. von Meck. "I confess that I fear this anguish: I fear to lose heart and to break. . . . I need Alyosha terribly. Everything that reminds me of him brings me pain, for it reveals the whole significance of the loss I have suffered. That is why I am afraid to go to Simaki," he added, "where every minute of my life, every corner of the house will constantly rub salt in my wound." Recognizing the seeming inappropriateness of this rush of emotion, Tchaikovsky hastened to qualify his outburst. "I imagine how a stranger might laugh reading these lines," he confessed, "how surprised he would be that one could pine and *long for a lackey*. But what am I to do if this *lackey* is at the same time my friend and such a devoted and loving one besides!"[59]

Considering the great restraint always observed by Tchaikovsky in his correspondence with Mrs. von Meck when speaking of any of his male infatuations, it is clear that this letter—despite the qualifications—was the letter of an anguished lover separated from the object of his love. Mrs. von Meck neatly sidestepped the matter by focusing instead on Tchaikovsky's fears that Alyosha was being corrupted. "Let us hope, my dear friend, that this is external, temporary coarsening," she wrote, seeking to reassure him, "that the good seeds planted in good soil will not be lost, that as soon as he finds himself back under your influence, all that former good will begin to speak with renewed force, and Alyosha will turn once again into your former ward, all the excrescence of dirt cast aside together with his uniform."[60]

In time, however, Tchaikovsky's persistence in returning to the theme of his longing for Alyosha began somewhat to worry Mrs. von Meck, who contrived her own highly moral explanation for his obsession. "You are pining not only because of your separation, but are pained and burdened by the *change* that you have observed in him," she wrote. "You cannot reconcile yourself with the possibility that what you have cherished in this, so to speak, your creation, what has elevated him above others and delighted you, might be destroyed. This, truly, is so pitiful and painful that, though an outsider, my own heart contracts and tears come to my eyes when I think of it." There was, as she saw it, only one course of action: to work out a discharge for Alyosha on medical grounds, even if it meant resorting to bribery. She offered the example of her daughter Aleksandra's brother-in-law, Count Bennigsen, who had joined the Horse Guards but after a month had become "fed up with the training," and so through bribery and "without any great difficulty" obtained a certificate of "extreme nearsightedness" and was immediately discharged. "Why don't you, my dear, endeavor to arrange right now in Moscow the same thing for Alyosha?" she naively asked, disregarding the very great difference between the position of an officer of the Horse Guards and a simple soldier.[61]

Tchaikovsky had little time to puzzle over Mrs. von Meck's unrealistic proposal, for at this point joyous news arrived. Alyosha wrote that he was to be granted two months' leave. "First he will visit his mother for several days and then will come to me!" Tchaikovsky informed his benefactress on 30 June. Mrs. von Meck was slowly restoring order to her financial affairs and had recently renewed her invitation for Tchaikovsky to visit Simaki, telling him that the estate had been saved and was again at his disposal. Tchaikovsky, still pleading Alyosha's absence, had once again declined, but now, suddenly, her invitation acquired a fresh and special attractiveness. "I have been seized by a passionate desire to make use of his leave to spend September at Simaki, and want to ask your permission to do so," he wrote her. "Is this possible? Will the Simaki estate still be at your disposal? If this dream were feasible, I should be infinitely happy. It would be an immeasurable boon for me and the best possible medicine for my shattered spirits."[62] To Modest he confessed on 5 July, "I cannot without tears think that such happiness might come true." But the happiness of anticipated reunion did not quite replace the misery of present separation: "In general, Alyosha right now is my sore spot. I shall not be exaggerating in the least if I say that not a second of the day goes by that I do not think of him and suffer. Even at night I dream only of him, and recently I dreamed he was dead."[63]

All too soon the prospect of Alyosha's leave began to grow dim. Alyosha needed special permission to travel any distance, and in early July, Tchaikovsky was prepared to go to Moscow himself to petition on his behalf. Anatoly, however, offered to undertake for him the necessary appeals. Meanwhile, Tchaikovsky suffered a narrow brush with diphtheria, and although by 22 July he was able to tell Mrs. von Meck that physically he now felt somewhat better, his state of mind was dismal. "Again because of this I shed tears for Alyosha," he wrote. "Were he with me, how easily I would bear this slight indisposition."[64]

Even sadder news was still to come, and the dream of a Simaki retreat with his beloved servant gradually grew dimmer. The regimental commander whom Anatoly solicited for Alyosha's leave told him that Alexander III, visiting in Moscow, had declared that the term of military service was too short and that it would be extended to six years. "Thus, I shall have to wait another five whole years for the discharge of the person whose loss I feel ever more strongly and vividly," he lamented to Mrs. von Meck, "and five years—that is indeed an entire eternity."[65] Anatoly also brought to Kamenka other disappointing news. Alyosha himself had been in error when he thought he was to have two months' leave. In fact, he was only to have one month. "I fear that he has become different by now," his master wrote gloomily to Modest on 2 August, "and it is painful to think of that. I should like him such as he was before, with all his former virtues and defects."[66]

The atmosphere at Kamenka that summer did little to bolster Tchaikovsky's spirits. Trouble had erupted in the Davydov household. For some time his niece Tanya had been engaged to a young officer, Count Vasily Trubetskoy, but the affair had turned sour. In June, Tanya suddenly appeared in Kamenka from Moscow with tales of a drunken Trubetskoy forcing himself into her rooms and attempting to make indecent advances. The engagement was broken off, but the effect of the break on Tanya proved grievous. While still in Moscow she had turned to alcohol and, again, to morphine to soothe her distraught and high-strung nerves. At Kamenka, she grew increasingly irritable and made frequent scenes before family and servants without pretext or provocation. Tchaikovsky's feelings for his eldest niece became sharply divided. "There are moments when I love her terribly—but there are others when I almost hate her," he confessed at one point. "She pours out around herself a kind of venom that poisons everything and everyone."[67] Throughout the summer the girl made life at Kamenka ever more miserable, and in August, Tchaikovsky reported to Anatoly, "Tanya has been ill the entire day; in general, she now resumes her mad behavior. . . . Somewhere she has secretly obtained morphine and is injecting herself more than ever. On the other hand, this unfathomable girl has begun almost to take a sort of pleasure in tormenting her mother with her complaints about life . . . and has brought her to the point where poor Sasha [Aleksandra] is again no good for anything: she does not eat, sleeps badly, walks about with those eyes like tin. I simply do not know what to do: hate Tanya, or be amazed and pity her."[68]

Adding to his worries was the sudden appearance at Kamenka of Tchaikovsky's accidental protégé Leonty Tkachenko, the unstable young man who had thrust himself so dramatically into the composer's life the year before with his talk of suicide and who, supported by Tchaikovsky, had spent the past semester attending the Moscow Conservatory. One morning in early August a guard from the local railway station arrived at Kamenka to tell Tchaikovsky that a young stranger who refused to give his name was asking to see him. Bewildered, Tchaikovsky decided at first not to go, but from the guard's description of the stranger he suddenly realized that it must be Tkachenko. He rushed to the station, thinking surely the young man planned to blow his brains out the moment he appeared. He found Tkachenko in a pitiful state, exhausted, hungry, miserable, and on the verge of despair. Apparently, he had walked the distance from his sister's home in Kharkov, where he had been staying the summer. On seeing Tchaikovsky, he began sobbing hysterically. Tchaikovsky calmed him, fed him, and then sought to persuade him to return to his studies in Moscow, for the poor youth had come to give up his stipend, claiming his lack of musical abilities and will and his general worthlessness. But in the end he agreed to go back to Moscow, by way of Kharkov, promising to send Tchaikovsky from there his diary for the summer, in which he had written down everything he wanted to say to Tchaikovsky but was unable to tell him in person.

After this bizarre incident, Tchaikovsky found his sympathy and concern for the young man resurrected. At the end of the month a thick package arrived containing Tkachenko's detailed diary. Reading through it with great interest, Tchaikovsky became convinced that despite uncertain grammar, its author possessed an undoubted literary gift, and he wrote to Modest of his impressions: "Owing to the sincerity with which it is written, the bitterness permeating every line, the lack of any pretense and the unceremoniousness with which he reveals such things as even Rousseau would not have related, his strange and idiosyncratic style, with its touch of Ukrainian, Gogolian humor, and, finally, owing to the appeal of the hero of the narrative himself, sick, irritable, but at bottom unusually loving and passionate—this manuscript is something unimaginably interesting."[69]

So far as can be gleaned from Tchaikovsky's lengthy reply to Tkachenko on 31 August, the diary dealt primarily with the young man's sexual experiences. Like many of his peers, Tkachenko viewed sexuality as base and demeaning. This did not mean that his tastes were necessarily unorthodox. On the contrary, a contemptuous and fearful attitude toward sex does run throughout Russian cultural history. The nude, for instance, did not appear in Russian art until the middle of the nineteenth century. Beneath this prudish facade, of course, sexual promiscuity flourished secretly, and not so secretly, at every level of society, and this tended to generate a persistent sense of guilt. Sex could not be renounced, but submission to its demands— even in the form of sexual fantasy—was often regarded by those who indulged in it as unclean and a sign of morbidity, the more so as many young men first tasted sexuality with prostitutes. This profound dualism, a reflection of the deeper dualism of matter and spirit, was a salient theme of nineteenth-century Russian literature, from the anguish of the chastity-bound heroines of Turgenev to the torment of the lust-ridden heroes of Dostoevsky. Even within the confines of marriage, sex could be subject to stricture, as *The Kreutzer Sonata* of Tolstoy gives witness.

Tchaikovsky's response to Tkachenko after reading the diary revealed no less about Tchaikovsky than about the young man to whom he was writing. "What you in your manuscript call your 'filth' did make rather a painful impression on me, though not in the sense you suspected," he wrote. "It did not repel me from you in the slightest, but I fear that the too lavish tribute that you have paid to voluptuousness at still so tender an age has had a pernicious effect on your health. A great effort of will on your part will be needed to correct the organic damage caused by these excesses." Despite the euphemistic language, it seems likely that most of Tkachenko's confessions related to sexual fantasies, presumably heterosexual, and consequently to masturbation and perhaps to encounters with prostitutes. The name of Rousseau, whose *Confessions* contain frank passages on his own adolescent sexuality, especially his masochism, was dropped in Tchaikovsky's letter to Modest scarcely by chance. Masturbation in Tchaikovsky's time was widely regarded as a serious mental disease with degenerative physical effects, and Tchaikovsky, as we know from his early admonishments to the adolescent Modest, shared this view entirely. The letter to Tkachenko continued:

> Your entire task right now will be indeed to foster in yourself a *strength of will.* As for the moral aspect of your "excesses," in the first place, I do not have the right to cast stones at you, since I myself am not without sin, and, second, to my mind, a person finds himself in this respect fatefully dependent on his own temperament. Very often chastity is nothing other than the absence of the element of voluptuousness in one's temperament. The whole point is to know how to stand above one's carnal desires and refrain from them—and this is given by one's upbringing. In your case, this was poor or, rather, absent altogether, and for this reason I shall not call you a *debauchee.* In the true sense of the word a debauchee is one who has made bodily pleasure the aim of his life, whose soul never protests against the passions of the flesh. Yet, you have always wanted to overcome your *flesh,* but have lacked the strength, as in all

of your good intentions.... Regardless of the fact that you
punish yourself too cruelly, are exaggeratedly severe toward
yourself—take care that your mania to deny truly good feelings
in others does not have pride as its source, for indeed you seem
to be a genuine Christian even though you do not accept the
divinity of Christ! I mention this mania to you so that you may
strive to eradicate it from yourself. Just look at how much unnecessary suffering you have borne because you were unable to
believe from the first that I was motivated neither by sentimental egotism nor by calculation when I summoned you to
Moscow.... I value very much your affection (please resist the
impulse to explain these words as sentimentality), I am moved
by the sincerity and passion of your feelings, I trust them unconditionally and ask you, if not for your own sake then for
mine, to do everything deemed necessary for the healing of
your ailing soul. To begin with, conquer in yourself that which
I have called "pride."[70]

Tchaikovsky's candid admission that he himself was "not without sin"
very likely alluded, in addition to the memory of his own youth, to his
current moments of promiscuity, which he periodically regretted and
strove to overcome, regardless of the concession that such matters are
dependent on "temperament." Strikingly, however, even with this implicit comparison of the two sexual biographies, Tchaikovsky apparently gave no consideration to any differences between their respective
orientations—homosexual in his own case and presumably heterosexual in that of Tkachenko. It was masturbation as such and promiscuity
as such that he deplored and condemned, not the choice of imagined
or actual sexual object.

When Tkachenko wrote the following winter that his musical
studies had come to nothing and that music having proved not to be
his vocation, he was returning to the provinces, Tchaikovsky, solicit-
ous and looking favorably on his attempt, encouraged him to devote
himself to prose writing, for which he believed him truly gifted, and
assured him of his continuing support.[71] For another year, Tchaikovsky
sent Tkachenko twenty-five rubles a month, but then, seeing that
Tkachenko needed some more-practical occupation while developing
his talent as a writer, he suddenly proposed to the young man that he
become a village schoolteacher. After this, Tchaikovsky had no further
word from his protégé for many months until, arriving at Kamenka in
September 1883, he was surprised to find a package waiting for him.
Once again the young man was returning all the letters that Tchaikov-

sky had written to him up to then. Had the unpredictable Tkachenko again resolved to take his own life? Tchaikovsky panicked briefly, but then upon reflection decided to wait for a bit. And indeed, soon afterward, he received a letter from Tkachenko asking for money and making no mention of the package. "A pitiful, but not very likable person," Tchaikovsky, disillusioned, wrote of him to Modest.[72]

In the midst of these myriad troubles with Tanya and Tkachenko, the dream of Simaki suddenly burst, even before Alyosha was to be let out on leave. Mrs. von Meck, in the process of her financial recovery, had been forced to sell the Brailovo estate after all. Expressing his sympathy to his friend and benefactress on 24 August, Tchaikovsky did not forget his own worries. Alyosha's coming arrival, he feared, "will not only not soothe or heal the wounds of my heart but sooner will rub salt in them. To realize that he has returned to me a *different person*, and then only in order to leave me again, will be very bitter and will poison all the pleasure of the meeting."[73] But fate had prepared an even heavier blow. Having received word from Alyosha to expect him in Kamenka around 10 September, Tchaikovsky was already considering whether they ought to remain there or go somewhere else when he received a desperate letter from Alyosha saying that he was not allowed to travel beyond Moscow and its environs and therefore could not come to Kamenka. For the moment he would go to his mother's village near Moscow, but he would return on the tenth and implored his master to come to Moscow by that day.

"Of course I shall go," Tchaikovsky wrote to Mrs. von Meck on 3 September. But he added, "Alas! all my dreams are shattered. How is poor Alyosha to rest from his service when he is forced to remain in the place where he does service and where he will be constantly haunted by images of corporals, sergeant majors, company commanders, and other authorities!!!"[74]

Tchaikovsky duly arrived in Moscow on 10 September for the reunion with his beloved soldier. Alyosha was deeply distressed by the tsar's new decree, which required him, having served one year, to remain in service another five years. Moreover, he was very upset that his plans to go somewhere away from Moscow had fallen through. "I thought about going to Petersburg with him," Tchaikovsky confessed to Mrs. von Meck, "but in that case he would have to remove his soldier's uniform and go into hiding, as it were, and I should rather not have that. Thus, I shall probably remain here this whole month, though how I should like not to!" At the conclusion of this letter he noted, "Alyosha is moved beyond words and thanks you, dear friend, for your kindness and generosity."[75] Apparently, Mrs. von Meck had sent Alyosha a gift of some money.

Back in Kamenka on 5 October, Tchaikovsky plunged at once into his familiar lamentations: "Ah! if only my poor Alyosha could be here with me!"[76] The old torments resumed, as did the admonishments. "Lyonya!" he wrote on 1 November. "You just ignore me; God knows how long it has been since I have seen a letter from you! . . . How often I have thought of you lately!"[77]

Kamenka was all but deserted when Tchaikovsky returned. Lev, Aleksandra, and the children had left to spend the winter in Kiev. Meanwhile, Modest, who had visited Kamenka briefly at the end of the summer, was now abroad with Kolya. The conflict with Hermann Konradi, though still unresolved, had been at least somewhat mitigated, in part through Tchaikovsky's diplomacy. He had come to dislike the senior Konradi deeply, but in view of his brother's and his own attachment to Kolya, he had counseled patience.[78] Toward midsummer Konradi had at last relented in his opposition to his son's traveling abroad again in the company of his tutor, and by the end of September, Modest and Kolya were on their way to Italy.

Shortly after Tchaikovsky's arrival, Aleksandra sent word that the second of his nieces, Vera, then eighteen, had become engaged to a young naval officer named Nikolay Rimsky-Korsakov, no relation to the famous composer of the same name. The sight of the happy young lovers during a brief visit to Kamenka prompted from Tchaikovsky a wistful observation to Modest rare among his extant writings: "How much in love he is! Just as I used to be. He devours her with his eyes, is angry and anguished as soon as she leaves him for a moment. But one can see that this is not merely infatuation, but genuine normal love. Modya, what poor devils we are, you and I—why, we shall live out our whole lives without ever for a single second experiencing the full happiness of love."[79] Such musings were very much in contrast to the attitude normally expressed by Tchaikovsky in his letters and diaries. Amid the festive air of betrothal, Tchaikovsky felt with sudden and sharp clarity his "separateness," his inability to share in the experiences common to the majority of mankind.

Vera and Nikolay were married in Kiev in early November, and several days after the wedding, Tchaikovsky went abroad. Now, near the end of this long and eventful year, during which he had been virtually paralyzed creatively by Alyosha's absence and his own longing for him, Tchaikovsky had begun to feel stirring again the "need to compose," which he had "not felt in a long time."[80] Indeed, his only major work during the past many months had been the editing of a collection of the sacred music of the eighteenth-century Russian composer Dmitry Bortnyansky, a task thrust upon him by Jurgenson. Leaving Russia in this nascent creative mood, he arrived in Vienna on 13/25 November, spent one day there, heard Meyerbeer's *Les Huguenots* at the Court Opera the evening of the fourteenth, and then proceeded to Venice later that same night.

"Venice," he wrote to Mrs. von Meck on 16/28 November, "has made a quite special impression on me." He recollected the month he had spent in that city with Alyosha just four years before, in a similar mood of creative recovery in the wake of his disastrous marriage. "It was that time when in intense labor (I was then orchestrating our [the Fourth] symphony) and in silence I sought oblivion from the days of grief I had endured. My work, the presence of Alyosha, and, finally, your letters sweetened my solitude then and brought relief to my soul. It is both awful and pleasant to remember those days."[81] Now again, in a creative sense, the ice had begun to break, a thaw soon quickened by the happy news from Alyosha that his term of service was to be reduced to just three years, thanks to his having passed the examination for primary school on which his master had been so insistent.

From Venice, Tchaikovsky went a few days later to Florence, where Mrs. von Meck was staying at the time, but he spent barely two days there, eager to join Modest and Kolya in Rome. In vain, Mrs. von Meck tried to convince him to give up Rome for Florence to be near her. "How happy I am at your arrival, but at the same time how distressed by the thought that it is not for long," she wrote on 18/30 November.[82] But Tchaikovsky was becoming increasingly reluctant to comply with her wishes, however tactfully expressed—and no matter that this could not but leave some trace of disappointment and resentment in the heart of his benefactress.

CHAPTER TWENTY-ONE

Tanya

Before leaving Russia in November 1881, Tchaikovsky had already decided that his next work should be an opera. For a time he seemed settled on *Romeo and Juliet* for his subject, but that project never materialized, and his attention then switched to a story by Dmitry Averkiev, *Vanka the Steward*, which Tchaikovsky had seen in a dramatization during his stay in Kiev. By the time he reached Rome, his plans for *Vanka the Steward* were also dropped, owing to problems with the libretto, and Tchaikovsky soon turned for inspiration to Pushkin's historical poem *Poltava*. For several months Tchaikovsky had contemplated an opera based on this story of the Cossack leader Ivan Mazeppa, who, in a bid to free the Ukraine from Russian rule, sided with Charles XII of Sweden against Peter the Great in the Second Northern War with Sweden and who, together with Charles, was defeated at the battle of Poltava in 1709. Within two weeks of his arrival in Rome, Tchaikovsky reported to Mrs. von Meck that he had begun work on his new opera *Mazeppa*. By the end of December, however, he interrupted this project to concentrate on another composition, his Trio in A Minor, op. 50, for piano, violin, and cello, dedicated to Nikolay Rubinstein, "in memory of a great artist." Greeting the New Year in Rome with Modest and Kolya, Tchaikovsky felt well both physically and emotionally. His trio was progressing to his satisfaction, and his artistic paralysis seemed to have ended.

From Russia came news both worrisome and happy. The Davydov family had decided to spend the winter in Kiev, primarily in the hope of finding a husband for Tanya. To this end, Lev and Aleksandra had allowed their life there to become entirely dependent on the caprices and whims of their increasingly unmanageable eldest daughter. From morning to night Tanya forced her parents to behave not as they wished but as she saw fit for the purpose of finding a prospective bridegroom or merely for the sake of her own pleasure and entertainment. Her use of morphine and her consequent hysterics had become routine. Commenting plainly on the situation in Kiev in a letter to Anatoly on 12/24 January 1882, Tchaikovsky wrote, "Of course, everything going on in that household is terrible, shocking and painfully sad. Of course, Tanya's behavior is inadmissible, and she is ruining not only her own life and reputation but also her mother's and the tranquillity of the entire family. . . . Things have now gone so far that there can be no going back," he concluded pessimistically. "Tanya can neither be cured nor reformed."[1]

But there would be a wedding, though not his niece's. Anatoly, who had too long, in the opinion of his elder brother, been "playing at love like a boy of seventeen," announced his engagement to Praskovya Konshina, the daughter of a wealthy Moscow merchant. "Today I received a letter from my brother Anatoly breathing such utter happiness, such ardent love for his bride, that my heart rejoiced," Tchaikovsky told Mrs. von Meck on 8/20 February 1882. "More and more it begins to seem to me that he will indeed finally find satisfaction of those vague strivings whose nonsatisfaction always caused him such suffering and heartache. For myself, it will be the greatest of blessings if my brother Anatoly ceases to torment me with his pining and anguish: I, in vain, would always agonize morally, reproaching myself for not being able to soothe and console him. But this was impossible. Not fraternal love but only the love of a good woman's heart can slake that thirst for happiness that he has known."[2]

That same day, Tchaikovsky wrote to Anatoly to say that he was "awfully pleased that you are happy." He then added, "Though I have never experienced anything similar, still it seems to me that I understand perfectly everything you are going through. There is a certain need for tenderness and caring that only a woman can fill. I am sometimes seized by a mad longing to be caressed by a woman's hand. Sometimes I see attractive women (not young women, though), to whom I just want to go and place my head on their knees and kiss their hands. But it is difficult to express."[3] It was also a somewhat curious response to send to a bridegroom. Far from being a confession of regret at his own inability to love a woman, Tchaikovsky's outburst was both more pragmatic and more sentimental. It was a mother ("not young women, though") that Tchaikovsky sought, not a lover.

The wedding was to be held in Moscow on 4 April, still several weeks away. Tchaikovsky made plans to return to Russia in late March and meanwhile continued with his companions on their tour of Italy. The Piano Trio was completed in mid-February, after which the brothers left Rome, wandering first to Naples and Pompeii and then on to Sorrento. With them was young Grisha Sangursky, whom Tchaikovsky and Modest had hired as a companion for Kolya. Thinking him "somewhat dull" and unsociable at first, Tchaikovsky little by little found himself growing increasingly fond of the fourteen-year-old Grisha, who occupied the room adjacent to his, with Modest and Kolya on the other side. "Grisha Sangursky is a wonderful boy," he declared to Anatoly after a few weeks in Rome. "The more you know him, the more you love him." He worried about what would become of Grisha when they eventually returned him to Kamenka. "Often I think about this," Tchaikovsky confided to Anatoly.[4]

Meanwhile, Kolya, showing exceptional aptitude and intelligence, was making rapid progress. Under Modest's guidance he had begun to speak clearly and could understand what others said by reading lips. Thanks to a phenomenal memory, he had amassed a wide range of information quite rare for his age, taking a special interest in history and the natural sciences. The Tchaikovsky brothers often found themselves turning to him for information on some subject or another. Physically, however, the boy remained weak and sickly. Following the divorce of his parents, he was in constant correspondence with his mother and, when traveling with Modest, with his father, and he had now ceased to be bewildered and distressed by their not wanting to live together. But his mother, Alina, remarried and now surnamed Bryullova, always treated him with a certain coldness and never felt any real affection for her son.

On his way back to Russia in mid-March, Tchaikovsky stopped again in Florence, where Mrs. von Meck continued to hibernate, but again for a few days only. "I cannot," she wrote, in almost the same words as four months earlier, "refrain from writing how happy I am at your arrival, my incomparable friend, but at the same time, how sad it makes me that it is for so short a time."[5] In fact, never again would they dwell, with the exception of Moscow and St. Petersburg, in the same place at the same time.

On 26 March 1882, Tchaikovsky was met in Moscow by Anatoly and Jurgenson. It quickly turned out that Anatoly, though pleased and happy about his forthcoming marriage, had suddenly decided that the syphilis for which he had been treated some years before had recurred. "This morning he was in hysterics," Tchaikovsky wrote to Modest, who had remained in Italy, "and here people were arriving with congratulations! My mind tells me that this is all Tolya's morbid paranoia, but my heart is touched by his fears and I start to believe that he is infected."[6] But within a few days all suspicions were dispelled, and Anatoly began preparing for the wedding in earnest. Introduced to his brother's bride, Tchaikovsky found Praskovya gracious and unaffected and, though generally reticent, quite genuine in conversation. He noted especially her tenderness and solicitude for Anatoly.

The Davydov family arrived for the wedding from Kiev. Although they all appeared well, Tchaikovsky's observant eye did not fail to note that Tanya was perpetually nauseated, while Aleksandra would constantly withdraw and lock herself in her room for injections of morphine.[7] The wedding and banquet were held on 4 April, and immediately afterward, the newlyweds left to spend their honeymoon abroad. Tchaikovsky felt the burden of his official status as brother of the groom as he was presented to the endless stream of relatives from the bride's family and forced continually to dine in the company of people whom he did not know. To make the round of social obligations even less bearable, Tchaikovsky found he was unable to get in to see Alyosha. Because the recruits' examinations were approaching, the barracks was closed to visitors. "What *amère dérision* is there to my life here?" he complained to Modest. "The one who is so indescribably dear and beloved to me, that is, my Lyonya—for me invisible—walks and lives somewhere near me."[8]

Tchaikovsky was still in Moscow when, on 20 April, a telegram arrived from Kamenka. It read simply, "Lilies of the valley blooming. Vera."[9] The next day, Tchaikovsky was on the train to Kamenka. He stopped briefly in Kiev, where his sister had returned with Tanya, Dmitry, and Bob, there celebrating Aleksandra's name day and his own forty-second birthday, and on the twenty-sixth he arrived in Kamenka. Modest and Kolya arrived from abroad the following day, Modest having grown thin and pale, suffering from an abscess near his anus. It proved necessary to lance the abscess, during which Modest "screamed like a calf and fell into hysterics, hitherto unknown to him."[10]

With Aleksandra and three of the children still in Kiev and his nieces Anna and Natasha at school in St. Petersburg, Tchaikovsky's company in Kamenka consisted of Modest; Kolya; his brother-in-law, Lev; his niece Vera and her husband, Rimsky-Korsakov; and his youngest nephew, Yury, with his governess. Tchaikovsky was looked after by one of the Kamenka servants, a young man named Stepan, whose zeal pleased him. Feeling well, he prepared to resume work on *Mazeppa*. But on 6 May a telegram arrived with news of the sudden death of Kolya's father, Hermann Konradi. Barely recovered from his lancing,

Modest left with Kolya for Kharkov, where the body lay, and then accompanied the body to the Konradi estate at Grankino for the burial.

Neither Modest nor Tchaikovsky perceived Konradi's death as much of a catastrophe. Modest had always disliked him, and Kolya was well provided for financially. The Grankino estate, Modest knew, had been left to Kolya in his father's will, and Kolya himself had been entrusted to Modest. In addition, Modest was himself to receive ten thousand rubles. Though not mentioned in the will at all, Alina Bryullova decided nevertheless to go to Grankino in the hope that some portion of her former husband's great legacy might fall to her, or at least that she might be granted custody of her daughter, Vera, Kolya's younger sister. Her hopes proved vain, but her appearance poisoned Modest's stay at Grankino until the will was opened six weeks later.

While occupied with *Mazeppa* and the lengthy collection of sacred choral music by Dmitry Bortnyansky that he had promised Jurgenson, Tchaikovsky felt frustrated in Kamenka. "It is a strange thing," he wrote Modest on 15 May. "From morning until evening, even at night, I think about going abroad as soon as possible, and in general, I seem to yearn to leave here—but meanwhile, I feel that nowhere but in Kamenka am I *at home* in the summer, and were I to go, I should *regret* even the *boredom* that haunts me. I work conscientiously, but without enthusiasm, without even one-twentieth of the inspiration and love for my nascent creation that I have experienced previously."[11]

Much of his discontent stemmed, of course, from the situation in the Davydov household, which was becoming an increasing burden to Tchaikovsky. In late May, Aleksandra had returned from Kiev with Tanya and the two boys. Tanya's troubles were growing worse. On the pretext of continual ailments she was abusing morphine to the point that "without [it] she cannot last a single day." The composer candidly shared his anxieties with Mrs. von Meck: "It simply makes one despair to think of her. There was a time when this family was imperturbably and boundlessly happy. But ever since Tanya grew up and began first to languish *for something* and vaguely to yearn *for something*, and then to poison herself with that accursed poison, happiness has flown from them. And the illnesses of my sister are a direct result of the worries inflicted by Tanya."[12]

Both Aleksandra and her husband were utterly powerless to halt or even to slow their daughter's headlong plunge toward catastrophe. They were, as Tchaikovsky remarked in one letter to Anatoly, "like people who have been sentenced to severe punishment, know it to be inescapable, and strive merely to close their eyes to the abyss into which they are falling and to forget by any ruse possible the disaster that threatens them."[13] Tchaikovsky, equally helpless, followed a similar course, trying to ignore the girl's behavior and to spare her parents additional pain by avoiding the topic altogether. It was a pretense, and one that his sister and brother-in-law easily saw through, but for which they were no less grateful. Yet, to close his eyes completely was not possible, and in his letters Tchaikovsky would remark bitterly on Tanya's appearance, her flirting with worthless males, and her lack of decent suitors.

His niece's scandals and hysterics threatened to drive Tchaikovsky to despair. Arriving for summer vacation with his mother and sister was also his beloved nephew Bob, now aged twelve and in gymnasium, who "with every passing day becomes more enchanting and more interesting." For a time, Tchaikovsky strove to forget about Tanya and to center his attention on Bob. He wrote to Modest that "it seems to me that he will become something out of the ordinary, if not great, at least charming and infinitely appealing." His eldest nephew, Dmitry, however, continued to disappoint. "Mitya is constantly unwell," Tchaikovsky reported. "He is a representative of the sick and broken element of the family." In fact, within a few years Dmitry would begin to show symptoms of epilepsy. Traceable in various manifestations through several generations and members of the Tchaikovsky family, the condition eventually forced the boy's removal from the School of Jurisprudence and caused his uncle, little love though he had for this particular nephew, considerable concern. For the moment, however, he simply noted acidly, "I fear that he is Tanya in trousers."[14]

In early June, Tchaikovsky traveled to Grankino to be with Modest and Kolya, staying there the rest of that month and most of July. Modest had to be operated on a second time for his abscess, and not until afterward could Tchaikovsky relax somewhat and once again resume work on *Mazeppa*. Composition had proceeded sluggishly in the uncongenial atmosphere of Kamenka, causing him "painful moments of disappointment" and bringing him "near despair."[15] Yet, in the relative calm of Grankino, he began to feel a deeper involvement in the opera and soon he was making rapid progress. "I like Grankino," he wrote in one of his regular letters to his servant Alyosha. "It is very free and easy here, just as I like it: quiet, peaceful. You, I think, would not recognize Kolya—he is very much grown now and bears himself with an air of importance, as befits a wealthy landowner. Grisha Sangursky is all grown up; he is keen on hunting. The swimming is excellent here, and this is all the more pleasant in that living at foul-smelling Kamenka I was deprived of the pleasure of going for a swim. Do you remember, Lyonya, our swimming at Simaki? For me our life at Simaki is like some sweet dream! What happiness and bliss it was!"[16]

But Simaki was gone forever. Moreover, while Mrs. von Meck had ultimately managed to secure her fortune from the threat of ruin, and had recently bought a new, smaller estate at Pleshcheevo, near Moscow, the ordeals of the preceding year had not failed to leave their mark on the health of the aging and sickly woman. She began to develop sharp pains in her hand that made it impossible to write more than a few lines at a time. "No remedies help, and its condition grows ever worse and worse," she wrote on 5 July. More painful still was the prospect of losing the use of her hand, and so her pen, altogether: "The most bitter thing for me in this situation is that I will be deprived of the possibility of conversing with you, my dear, my only friend. With you I have unburdened my heart, rested, recompensed myself for much of the grief that I have had in life, and to lose this sole consolation is very painful and galling."[17]

From this time on, the pace of their correspondence noticeably slowed. Tchaikovsky perhaps justified the ever greater infrequency of his letters with the thought that he thereby spared his ailing correspondent, offering less occasion to strain her aching hand in response to each of his letters. "I beg you earnestly to limit yourself in your letters to me to just a few lines so that my joy at receiving news from you might always be absolute," he urged her.[18] Both of them were growing older, drawn more and more into a circle of routine and self-regard, responding painfully to ailments, business misfortunes, and the deaths of those close to them. Their letters, which in the beginning had been written almost every other day or even every day, gradually came to be written weekly and then once in ten days. When particularly preoccupied with rehearsals or performances, Tchaikovsky might not send word for weeks or even months. For her part, she continued to suffer from the pain in her hand, from eye ailments, and from migraines, in addition to having to withstand the whirlwind of business troubles.

One solace for Mrs. von Meck was the growing intimacy between the von Meck and Davydov families. She was delighted when, shortly after his return to Kamenka with Modest and Kolya in late July, Tchaikovsky finally made the acquaintance of her sons Nikolay and Aleksandr, who in early August visited the Davydov estate. Plans to make a match between Nikolay von Meck and Tchaikovsky's third niece, Anna, were already bearing fruit. The two, both nineteen, had first been introduced earlier that same year when Nikolay and Aleksandr visited the Davydov family in Kiev while Tchaikovsky was still in Italy. By summer the young people had fallen happily in love, and it seemed that the dream of uniting the two families through marriage might come true.

Both Nikolay and Aleksandr von Meck made an "irresistibly enchanting impression" on Tchaikovsky when he met them at Kamenka. They were apparently attractive and likable youths, and Tchaikovsky's penchant for young men must have added a particular piquancy to their meeting. "Yesterday morning your wonderful sons arrived here," he told their mother on 3 August. Noting that he generally made the acquaintance of people only with great difficulty, "even if they be youths," Tchaikovsky then admitted, "But I do not know whether it is because they are your children or just the quality of these most delightful young men, but from the very first moment I felt myself on common, familial ground with them, so that it has seemed to me as though they have become part and parcel of the household here."[19]

His letter brought "tears of gratitude" to the eyes of his benefactress. "The kindness and tenderness with which you speak of them are so precious to me that I do not even know how to express it in words," she wrote in her fervent response four days later. "In gratitude I can only ask God to grant you as often as possible such happy moments as you have granted me with your letter, my dear, precious, incomparable friend!"[20] That the meeting with the already famous composer made a strong impression on Mrs. von Meck's two sons is scarcely surprising, especially given Tchaikovsky's usual kindness and attention to young people. Thus, Nikolay wrote to his mother, and she in turn quoted in her next letter to Tchaikovsky, "Finally my cherished dream has come true—to meet Pyotr Ilyich. I must confess that what I found in reality surpassed all my expectations. I thought to find someone educated, intelligent, and kind, but such a radiant intellect, such boundless kindness, I could never have anticipated. The accumulation of such lofty qualities in one person clearly indicates the higher purpose of his nature."[21]

This early period in the relationship between the two families was filled with similar instances of mutual idealization and of that somewhat exaggerated euphoria and sentimentalism typical of the age and of these people in particular. Tchaikovsky related to Mrs. von Meck the highly favorable impression her sons made on everyone, from Modest to Kondratyev. In the coming months Nikolay von Meck, studying in St. Petersburg, became a regular visitor to Modest there, and the two soon became fast friends. As Tchaikovsky reported to Mrs. von Meck, Modest could not find words enough to "express . . . all the spiritual beauty of this boy."[22] There was, he told her, "not a single letter in which Modest does not speak with deep emotion of the amazing kindness and cordiality of your wonderful son."[23] In her turn, Mrs. von Meck wrote that her son "draws warmth from Modest Ilyich now that . . . his whole family is so far away," adding that "Kolya [Nikolay] writes me of Modest Ilyich with such gratitude, such love, that I do not know how to thank him."[24] Young Nikolay also began writing frequently to Tchaikovsky, and this correspondence, as well as that with Aleksandr, could be, generally speaking, a pleasant diversion for the composer when he was not busy and was in the right mood: "Both write me letters that require replies, and both are so nice and likable that it is impossible not to reply, but letters become sheer torment for me when I am in a hurry to finish some work."[25]

With Anna, Tchaikovsky was on good, even excellent terms, but as he confided to Modest, "we are not in harmony, there is no true friendship between us as there was earlier with Tanya and Vera. This girl behaves so irreproachably and arranges her life so energetically and with such benefit to her mental perfection; so sweet is she with the younger children and so well does she handle the governesses and servants that there is not a moment when I could be displeased with anything in her. But, at the same time, there is something that keeps me from loving her with a lively love."[26] Already he perceived in his niece's pragmatism a threat to the more tender qualities of the heart that he himself held so dear.

On 5 August, Tchaikovsky, together with Modest, left Kamenka for Moscow to attend a special concert dedicated to his work that was given three days later at the Moscow Exhibition. The program, made up of *The Tempest*, the Violin Concerto, several songs, and the *1812* Overture, was well received, and the composer had to take numerous bows, with particularly high praise going to the concerto, here performed in Russia for the first time. To Tchaikovsky's chagrin, the official nature of his visit to Moscow made impossible any attempt to remain incognito. From all sides relatives, friends, and admirers swarmed about him. In the midst of everything else, he learned that his Alyosha had been lying in the hospital for two weeks, suspected of having typhus. Tchaikovsky, very worried, managed to visit him nearly every day. Soon thoroughly exhausted both physically and emotionally, he unburdened himself in a letter to Modest, who had quit Moscow almost at once for Grankino, writing that "I suffer so much, am so deeply unhappy, that any beggar is happier than I." His "misanthropy" had resurged with a vengeance: "The whole thing is that for me life is unthinkable except in the countryside or abroad, but why this is, I swear I do not know—I am simply about to go mad. I shall probably someday pass over to the better world precisely because of this vague, poisonous, agonizing, dreadful disease, which I am unable to define but which consists in the fact that I cannot live a single day, a single hour, in the Russian capitals without fierce suffering."[27]

After several years spent for the most part either abroad or within the confined circle of those closest to him, Tchaikovsky had ceased to know the stormy whirl of celebrity life in Moscow and St. Petersburg. Introvert by nature, he erred in thinking himself unique in this respect or in elevating his anxieties to the status of mental and physical illness. But after ten days in Moscow he was more than ready to flee abroad, to Kamenka, or anywhere else. Still, while there he managed to see Anatoly and his new bride, the Kondratyevs, even Kondratyev's "unforgettable" and scandalous servant Aleksey Kiselev, and his own protégé, pressed on Jurgenson, Misha Klimenko.

Only for Mrs. von Meck's protégé Wladyslaw Pachulski, despite her specific request, did Tchaikovsky somehow fail to find time. Pachulski managed nevertheless to catch him on the very last day of his stay, even as he prepared to leave for Kamenka. "Wladyslaw Albertovich found me an hour before my departure, already in bright spirits as I anticipated the joy of flight from Moscow," Tchaikovsky wrote Mrs. von Meck. "My pleasure at seeing him was inexpressible; why, an hour before he had seen you and spoken with you. To receive news from you at the moment when freedom was returning to me anew, freedom which I owe to you, my benefactress, my best friend—in this was such a joyous, radiant feeling! No words can ever express how I revere you and how grateful I am to you!"[28] Avoiding any word about his feelings for Pachulski, Tchaikovsky very skillfully shifted the direction of his emotion back toward Mrs. von Meck. Clearly, only the thought of his benefactress enabled Tchaikovsky to tolerate the presence of this young man, whom he emphatically disliked but who by dint of circumstance was already becoming an important intermediary between himself and Mrs. von Meck, to the eventual detriment of their relations.

With Pachulski's music, things stood no better. Back in Kamenka, Tchaikovsky sent the young man a detailed and largely unfavorable critique of his most recent work. This he followed on 28 August with a note to Mrs. von Meck asking her to "tell Wladyslaw Albertovich not to be upset at my criticism," going on to explain, "Every beginning author must go through many bitter moments like that which he will experience on reading my letter."[29] But from her response it appears that Pachulski swallowed the pill with feigned good grace. "He is delighted with it [the criticism]," she wrote, "he worships you, he cannot speak of your divine kindness without enthusiasm and tears. 'How is it,' he says, 'that such a luminary, such a colossus, has not shunned such a worm as myself' (this is his exact expression)."[30] Unguessed-at by the straightforward Mrs. von Meck, Pachulski, with his exaggerated panegyric, paid Tchaikovsky in his own coin: hypocrisy for hypocrisy. The young man must have sensed the composer's dislike, however much the latter may have attempted to conceal it, and his role of sycophantic go-between can only have increased his humiliation.

At the end of August, again in passing, Mrs. von Meck mentioned that her "darling Achille Debussy" had arrived at her new estate at Pleshcheevo. "I am very happy with him," she wrote. "Now I shall listen to lots of music, and moreover, he enlivens the entire house. He is a Parisian from head to toe, a typical Parisian *gamin*, very witty, an excellent mimic, very amusingly and distinctively portraying Gounod, Ambroise Thomas, and others, always in good spirits, always content with everything, and making his whole audience laugh unbelievably, a most lovely character."[31] Tchaikovsky, busy with matters at Kamenka, had no reaction to the arrival of the young French pianist or to the news of his departure at the end of November.

Once again, worries about his eldest niece had claimed Tchaikovsky's attention. Tanya, her every whim indulged by her doting and desperate parents, had spent much of the summer in a rented apartment in Kiev. In early September the apartment was given up, the furniture sold, and Tanya moved back to Kamenka, where until then Tchaikovsky had felt almost content. His work on *Mazeppa* was exhausting, yet at least he had remained undisturbed. But with Tanya's arrival he again knew no peace, save in his room, locked away from the sight and sound of his scandalous niece. In such seclusion he managed to complete the sketches for his opera, but his mood soon blackened. To make matters worse, Tanya had become involved in an affair with a former music tutor to the Davydov children, Stanislav Blumenfeld, whom Tchaikovsky himself had recommended several years earlier and who now ran a music school and music shop in Kiev. But it was not only in the city, away from her family, that Tanya met her lover. Class prejudice and anti-Semitism were pervasive in nineteenth-century Russia, and Blumenfeld, a Jew of the lower middle class, was unthinkable as a possible suitor of a girl of Tanya's class and religious background. In his capacity as a musician, however, he was made welcome at Kamenka. It was assumed by Tchaikovsky and others that the parents were oblivious to the actual relations between Tanya and Blumenfeld, relations that were all too clear to everyone else on the estate. More likely, they willingly closed their eyes to the obvious for the sake of keeping their cherished princess happy and calm.

The situation filled Tchaikovsky with indignation and grief. On one occasion, returning with Tanya and Blumenfeld from a drive in the forest, he was shocked when he suddenly "not only felt but saw" the surreptitious play of the pair's legs beneath a rug that Tanya had spread over her own knees and those of Blumenfeld. Such flouting of accepted notions of propriety infuriated the essentially conventional Tchaikovsky. "I cannot understand the insolence with which they were doing this in my presence," he wrote to Modest on 11 September. "She probably considers me to be so innocent that she is not even afraid. . . . To fall so far as to permit oneself without embarrassment things that only prostitutes do. From birth I have always lived exclusively among women of irreproachable purity, and for that reason, this deed seemed so monstrous to me." He resolved to leave Kamenka at the first opportunity. "There is no middle," he added. "Either I am angry at her and grow annoyed or I pity terribly both her and her parents, but in either case I suffer."[32]

Yet, annoyance would fade when he saw Tanya in torment or sick. A few days later, he wrote again to Modest, "Poor Tanya has been suffering all these last days from uninterrupted nausea. Now I am no longer angry, but instead feel sorry for her. What a wretched, pitiful life!"[33] When there were no young men in the house, Tanya's behavior changed dramatically. Dropping the capriciousness and the heavy makeup, she would grow calmer and more natural, and Tchaikovsky, loving her in spite of everything, would almost relax. But the affair with Blumenfeld continued, and when the music teacher returned to Kamenka in October, Tchaikovsky was again "tormented and irritated" by the "suspicion that something nasty was going on between them."[34]

For a time he strove to curb his ill will and to put his forebodings aside. But in mid-November, when he mentioned that he was leaving for Moscow and Tanya suddenly wanted to go with him, he balked. Forced to lie to avoid this less than pleasant prospect, something he always hated doing, Tchaikovsky left Kamenka in an ambivalent humor but without regret. With guests and relations crowding in from all sides, the cosiness of his own little corner at Kamenka had ended. Increasingly, his only real link with Kamenka became his favorite nephew, Bob, more beloved with every year. "He is so tender and affectionate with me," he told Modest on 11 October 1882, "that it constantly moves me, sometimes almost to tears."[35] Tchaikovsky was beginning to feel, as he confessed to Modest, "rather a nomad." He seemed unable to settle down in Russia and feared loneliness abroad, and the thought that he had nowhere a place to call his own came more and more to weigh upon him.

With his growing desire to settle down, idyllic plans for the future began to creep into Tchaikovsky's letters to Alyosha. His longing for his beloved servant was as great as ever. "Ah, Lyonya, Lyonya," he wrote on 2 September, "when I think that there are still two years to wait, I simply want to cry."[36] But he had already begun to look beyond "these unbearable years" of Alyosha's service. "I dream that when you finish your time in the army, if I am still alive, I shall cease living in other people's homes and shall settle down in some nice little place . . . forever," he wrote in an especially tender letter. "We shall find a nice comfortable little apartment and shall live gloriously." He even added that it would be good if by that time Alyosha had married some nice girl "so that there would be someone to take care of our linen and generally perform various womanly services."

Tchaikovsky had never shown sexual jealousy of his servant, and for all his yearning for Alyosha, the young man was already growing out of that age that Tchaikovsky always found to be sexually the most attractive. Still, it is interesting that Tchaikovsky viewed this imagined bride for Alyosha as little more than a servant for the two of them, with no mention of Alyosha's personal happiness, whereas in the same letter he confessed to Alyosha, "I love you not as my servant, but as the closest of relatives, a brother or a son." Of course, he could not hint at the sexual side of this love in a letter that had to pass under the eyes of the military censors. A paternal element had, however, been present in Tchaikovsky's attitude toward his servant from the beginning, as it was, to a greater or lesser degree, in his relationships with his other young lovers and favorites. Similarly, his feelings for his young male relatives—the young Anatoly, for instance, and later Bob Davydov and his other nephews—often contained an erotic component.

"I pray to God," Tchaikovsky concluded in his letter to Alyosha, "that the two years may fly by quickly and that these dreams may come true!"[37]

But for now Tchaikovsky continued to wander. In Moscow he ran unexpectedly into Vladimir Shilovsky, whom he had not seen in the five years since their estrangement after Shilovsky's marriage. On 8 December he wrote to Modest, "Of the interesting details of my stay here let me tell you that I have made it up with Volod[ya] Shilovsky and have already gone boozing with him twice."[38] But the whirl of Moscow life, even when flattering to his ego (thus, for instance, his mornings were devoted to sitting for a portrait by the celebrated painter Vladimir Makovsky), continued to exhaust him, and with "every hour, day, and evening filled," he soon longed to tear himself away and go abroad. In the middle of December he traveled to St. Petersburg to see Modest and his friends there, but spent most of the time ill with a cold. On New Year's Eve he was already in Berlin.

"What happiness it is that I still retain the capacity to enjoy almost to the point of bliss the awareness that *I am abroad*," he wrote to Modest. Nicest of all, he told his brother, was simply being "in a city where I am not very well known. What a delight to go for a stroll without the fear of meeting any acquaintances!"[39] Tchaikovsky's dread of being recognized was often almost comical, as he himself was fully aware. Some years later, he recalled that one time while abroad he had been walking along the street lost in thought when suddenly he was stopped by a woman who cried out delightedly in Russian, "Pyotr Ilyich, what a pleasant surprise!" Tchaikovsky, without missing a beat, replied, also in Russian, "Forgive me, madam, I am not Tchaikovsky," and continued on his way.[40]

During the three days he spent in Berlin, Tchaikovsky played with the idea of visiting Kotek, who still lived there but with whom he had broken off relations at the end of 1881. The young violinist had refused, with a view to his own career, to perform Tchaikovsky's Violin Concerto, a work that had been severely criticized. In the end, Tchaikovsky decided against a meeting, dreading the explanations, the mutual reproaches, and "the false note which, alas, will always sound in my relations with him."[41]

By arrangement with Modest, Tchaikovsky was to wait for his brother in Paris, after which they planned to head to Rome for the winter—but this time without Kolya Konradi. Modest's charge was growing up. Now fourteen and the heir to a considerable fortune, he was becoming a youth with a definite character and habits of his own and with a strong urge to be independent. Modest, used to seeing in Kolya only a timid and obedient boy, was hard-pressed to adjust to the new young man before him, and relations between tutor and pupil were becoming sorely strained. In addition, after Hermann Konradi's death the question of his will and of Modest's guardianship over Kolya were long and painfully debated and disputed. All of this, aggravated by his recent ailments and operations, had come to take a heavy toll on Modest's nerves, and so a trip abroad had been proposed by Tchaikovsky "for the sake of diversion and soothing of spirits."[42] Though parting with his charge was very difficult, Modest had decided to comply.

While waiting for his brother in Paris, where he had arrived on 2/14 January 1883, Tchaikovsky spent his time working on the orchestration of *Mazeppa* and going to the theater. At a performance of *The Marriage of Figaro* at the Opéra Comique he unexpectedly met Grand Duke Konstantin Nikolaevich, who was delighted to see him and immediately invited the composer to come visit him. Fearful of being caught up in the society rush, almost inevitable if he were to appear at the residence of the grand duke, Tchaikovsky lied and said that he was leaving the next day.

But Modest still had not come. He sent telegrams, first from St. Petersburg and then from Berlin, saying that unforeseen circumstances detained him. Puzzled, Tchaikovsky began to worry. But when Modest finally arrived on 16/28 January, the riddle of his delay was explained, for he arrived not alone but with Tanya. He had, it turned out, decided some time before to make his niece accompany him to Paris in order to undergo treatment with the renowned neurologist and specialist in hypnotism, Jean Martin Charcot (who two years later would become Freud's teacher), but he had concealed these plans from his brother so as not to disturb him prematurely. Indeed, Tchaikovsky met them very coldly, annoyed and unpleasantly surprised by Tanya's unexpected appearance in Paris. But he soon realized that Modest could not have acted otherwise and that they must sacrifice the peace of their vacation for the sake of trying to save not only Tanya but also her parents, who loved her so dearly. It was clear that death or madness lay in store for the young girl if not helped soon and that this could well devastate her parents.

Even more of a shock, however, was the news, which Modest had not dared to tell his brother in St. Petersburg, that Tanya was now six-months pregnant by her lover Blumenfeld. No one else in the family knew; she had taken refuge in St. Petersburg with Modest. Now, in Paris, the brothers made every effort to keep her condition a secret from everyone except the Russian maid who served her.

Plans for Italy were abandoned. Dr. Charcot received Tanya and promised to help ease the delivery, first trying to cure her of her addiction. She was to check into Charcot's neurological clinic at the Salpê-trière Hospital for about a month. Tchaikovsky wrote to Lev Davydov explaining the situation with the clinic and assuring him that Tanya was in good hands and being "looked after most tenderly" by both Modest and himself.[43] The fact of her pregnancy was not mentioned. Treatment began with a decrease in the dosage of morphine. Tanya reacted violently, screaming and tearing her hair, falling into fainting fits, and growing delirious. The doctors, to calm her, prescribed opium and other sedatives, but these had little effect. Tchaikovsky, witnessing the agony of his niece, wrote Mrs. von Meck that he had to endure "much emotional suffering."[44]

In the midst of these worries a letter arrived from Anatoly with news that struck like lightning: Alyosha had fallen deathly ill with pneumonia. Anatoly had visited the hospital, though not the ward where Alyosha lay, because he feared carrying typhoid infection home to his now-pregnant wife. But he wrote that the illness was expected to reach its crisis within a few days, and promised to wire to Paris as soon as it was known what course the disease would take. "Between the letter and the telegram," Tchaikovsky told Mrs. von Meck afterward, "passed two very difficult days, since I was for some reason convinced that my poor servant would not survive and had prepared myself to bear this loss staunchly."[45]

Tchaikovsky had at once written to Jurgenson asking him to visit Alyosha and find out what was happening. This Jurgenson did, and when he wrote back several days later, he provided a lively and theatrical account of his mission. "Armed with nothing but the word 'Alyosha,' I went to the Pokrovsky barracks," the publisher wrote. "On the way I was tempted by a spirit of doubt: is it enough just to go up to the barracks and ask, Where is Alyosha? The voice of reason responded, Yes, it is rather foolish. But an inexhaustible reserve of goodwill and a daring thought: What? People are found without knowing at all their name or surname or their social status or their physiognomy—they are found by means of a button torn off of their trousers. And 'we' have (1) Christian name, (2) social status, (3) whereabouts, (4) condition (ill), (5) personal acquaintance with individual."

Approaching the first entrance, Jurgenson saw a "monster in a fur coat of incredible dimensions" which on closer inspection turned out to be "a sentry with a face beaming with good humor." Jurgenson reported their exchange in dialogue form, starting with the sentry:

[MONSTER]: "Who d'ya want?"

JURGENSON (*with some embarrassment*): "Tell me, how might I find a certain soldier named Alyosha here?"

[MONSTER]: "What's his family name?"

JURGENSON (*reddening*): "I don't know."

[MONSTER]: "What company?"

JURGENSON (*reddening more redly*): "I don't know."

MONSTER (*condescendingly*): "And you don't know what regiment?"

JURGENSON (*trying to be cheerful*): "I knew all that, but I've forgotten it. I only know that his name is Alyosha, that he is something like a noncommissioned officer, probably ill, and his former master is worried about him."

MONSTER (*compassionately*): "Not Sofronov?"

JURGENSON (*ecstatically*): "Precisely!"

MONSTER: "Ekaterinoslavsky regiment."
JURGENSON (*suppressing a desire to throw his arms around the watch-fur's neck*): "That's him! That's him!"

The sentry gave Jurgenson directions where to find a noncom named Rozanov. "I naively stuck my head in here and there, creating no little tumult thereby," the publisher continued. "Evidently one is not supposed to walk about the barracks on weekdays. Finally, I stuck my head in a third door, again frightened everybody, and was rather gently ousted, but was allowed to speak with the noncom outside the door. Rozanov, a fine-looking fellow and a friend of Sofronov's, told me that Alyosha was better, that he was in such-and-such section of the hospital, etc."[46]

In his letter to Mrs. von Meck, Tchaikovsky went on, "It seems that God has once again staved off the sorrow that threatened me. Two days after the letter [from Anatoly] I received word that the turning point in the illness was favorable and Alyosha is out of danger. Now I have written to Moscow to have my brother and Jurgenson petition for a year's leave for Alyosha. Severe pneumonia often leads to consumption, and since Alyosha is not of a sturdy constitution, this is something to be feared, and I should like him not to serve during the summer, but to rest and recover his strength."[47] Two weeks later, at the beginning of March, he reported that "my Alyosha . . . , thank God, has recovered."[49] Still greater relief followed, as Tchaikovsky received word that Alyosha was soon to be granted his year's leave.

The situation in Paris, however, was still grim. Tanya went from worse to better and back again. Her treatment dragged on, while money gradually dwindled. After "much agonizing hesitation" Tchaikovsky on 14/26 March decided to ask Mrs. von Meck to send the "budget sum" for June at the end of March. She agreed willingly, also at this time inviting him to be her guest at her new estate in Pleshcheevo. Again after some hesitation Tchaikovsky tentatively agreed, but he postponed the visit until some later time. Meanwhile, Mrs. von Meck, reading his descriptions of Tanya's struggles, began to have worries of another sort. The love affair between her son Nikolay and Anna Davydova continued apace—but now, though having herself engineered their acquaintance and involvement with each other, Mrs. von Meck was experiencing some legitimate fears. "I shall tell you," she wrote on 18/30 March, "another worry of mine. This *morphine* frightens me *terribly*, and I am dreadfully afraid lest Anna also be seduced by it. . . . It is very painful for me to deprive you of hope, but I confess that I am not at all confident that the doctors will cure Tatyana

Lvovna."[49] In reply, Tchaikovsky assured his friend that "none of what you fear for her [Anna] is in any way possible. . . . Moreover, Tanya's example has been for her, with her intelligence and common sense, negatively useful. . . . All in all, hers is a healthy, wholesome nature having many kindred traits with your son Kolya, and the union of these two souls will be a very gratifying thing."[50]

Tchaikovsky had made up his mind to complete at all costs the orchestration of his opera while in Paris. But repeatedly he found his progress impeded. Besides the troubles with Tanya and the scare brought on by Alyosha's illness, other projects demanded his attention. As part of the festivities surrounding the coronation of Alexander III, planned for May of that year, Tchaikovsky had received an official commission for a special arrangement of the "Glory" chorus from Glinka's *A Life for the Tsar* to be performed on Red Square in Moscow during Alexander's ceremonial entrance into the Kremlin. The work consisted of simplifying the score of the chorus—a celebration of Russian heroism and other national virtues—and composing a transition from the chorus to the national anthem, "God Save the Tsar," and was accomplished by Tchaikovsky in early February. This relatively simple task was followed by two other commissions for the festivities, one a request from the city of Moscow to write a festival march for the occasion, and the second from the coronation committee itself, which sent Tchaikovsky a text by the poet Apollon Maikov on which to compose a lengthy cantata.

Both the march and the cantata had to be completed quickly and to refuse was unthinkable, the more so as Tchaikovsky felt a personal obligation toward Alexander III. Shortly after the tsar's accession two years before, Tchaikovsky, finding himself once again in financial straits but unwilling to trouble Mrs. von Meck, who was then struggling with her own financial troubles, had ventured to request from Alexander a loan of three thousand rubles to be repaid gradually from the royalties of his works. The Russian tsar stood in a strongly paternal relation to his nobles, and to ask for such assistance in difficult circumstances was not only appropriate but even customary. Tchaikovsky was aware, moreover, that the new tsar was very well disposed toward his music. Nonetheless, he was surprised when Alexander sent him the money as a gift—a sign of great favor. Embarrassed and moved by so benevolent a reaction to his request, Tchaikovsky had even resolved to repay the debt when he was able. But he never did, and in composing the music for the coronation, he saw an occasion to express his personal gratitude to the tsar.[51]

Scarcely had Tchaikovsky completed these coronation pieces and returned to his opera when another, more irritating, interruption ensued, and he found himself obliged, at the request of Mrs. von Meck, to analyze and evaluate the most recent compositions of her protégé Pachulski. It was an occupation that soon "shattered" the composer's nerves as he sought to make sense of the "indigestible musical gibberish" of the young man.[52] In a lengthy letter to Pachulski on 10/22 April he explained in detail and with several examples the shortcomings of his work.[53] Pachulski was naturally disappointed, as acknowledged by Mrs. von Meck: "Wlad[yslaw] Alb[ertovich], although of course very upset by his unsuccessful work, is deeply grateful to you for your sympathy and attention to his labors, and I also thank you with all my heart, my kind, inimitable friend, for your unparalleled kindness to my *protégé* and for the truth that you tell him. Unfortunately, he got in Vienna a professor whom everyone extols, but whom I did not like from the very beginning because he praises everything that Pachulski brings to him and corrects nothing."[54] In his reply, Tchaikovsky assured his benefactress that "it was very painful for me to write such a lengthy censure to Wlad[yslaw] Alb[ertovich] for all his labors," and then added, "In general, the question of his future musical studies demands a detailed discussion on my part, and I shall postpone this until the summer, when there will be more leisure, and besides which an oral discussion is needed."[55] Clearly, his desire to finish his opera made Tchaikovsky particularly impatient with Mrs. von Meck's favorite, and as we have seen, when writing not to her but to his brothers, with whom no such tactfulness was required, he was quite ruthless in this regard.

Modest, feeling increasing nostalgia for Kolya, decided to return to St. Petersburg in early April. He had not wanted to leave his brother alone, but Tchaikovsky managed to persuade him to go and so Modest departed for Russia on 6/18 April. That same evening, left to his own devices, Tchaikovsky continued his nocturnal wanderings. "Having drunk two glasses of punch, I felt a desire for a stroll and went to the boulevard," he later wrote to his brother. "There I became interested in Anton [a former employee of the Hôtel Richepance, where Tchaikovsky was staying], who was walking near the Café de la Paix: I began following all his maneuvers, and this was most intriguing. Finally, having imagined myself quite secure from him, since apparently he had not recognized me, I was starting for home without due precaution when suddenly Anton, who was sitting on a bench with a Negro, recognized me and accosted me. The Negro also begged and was given one and a half francs."[56] A suspicious cut follows, eloquent in itself. Quite possibly Tchaikovsky here noted something blatant about the nature of their connection or perhaps even hinted at an ensuing sexual encounter. As the passage picks up again, it is clear that the episode took place quite late at night, for Tchaikovsky, returning to his hotel to find an "incredible mess" resulting from the things that Modest had left behind having been "heaped every which way" in his own room, tidied this up before going to bed at three in the morning.[57]

On another occasion, strolling late at night along the Champs Elysées, Tchaikovsky suddenly discovered "a club, a real club!" for those with tastes similar to his own: "Later I saw there one mysterious and dramatic incident about which you must remind me to tell you when I see you."[58] This sentence is preceded by yet another eloquent excision.

In fact, in Paris one could find not only clubs of this sort but also homosexual bordellos known as *maisons des hussards*. Medical and legal studies of the last century abound in descriptions of homosexual prostitutes in Paris, such as that found in one French law journal where the author asks, "Is it a man? The hair is parted in the middle, falling in ringlets against the cheeks like that of a young coquette, a cravat is tied carelessly about the neck . . . , the collar of the shirt lies on the shoulders, the eyes are languid, the lips a little heart, he bends to the side like a Spanish dancer, and when he is arrested, he clasps his hands together and gets such an expression on his face that one might laugh if only this did not also arouse disgust and indignation."[59] Clandestine homosexual prostitution had indeed reached vast proportions in Paris, with a growing business of blackmail and extortion on the side. That this was the milieu that had attracted Tchaikovsky's attention in the French capital is clear from his letters to Modest, in spite of the euphemistic language used both there and in his diaries with respect to this subject.

The day after Tchaikovsky's own forty-third birthday, one hour in fact after midnight on the morning of 26 April, Tanya gave birth to a boy. "Soon after I arrived," he wrote Modest, "Tanya called for me. The child (a boy) lay near her, sleeping peacefully. I was surprised by his size. Ever since yesterday I had begun to feel a kind of tenderness for this child who has caused us so much worry, a desire to be his protector. Now I felt it with tenfold force, and I told Tanya that as long as I am alive, she may rest easy on his account."[60] Tanya's social status precluded any thought of her facing the world as a single mother, even if she had been inclined to raise her son herself, nor did her lover Blumenfeld show any desire to recognize the child. Her parents, meanwhile, remained ignorant of what had happened and in fact never learned of the existence of their grandchild. Tchaikovsky made up his mind that he would himself adopt the child at a later point, and indeed he was much taken with his little grandnephew: "[He is] a splendid, well-formed child, resembling his father in the shape of his nose and having also his black hair. His hands are of striking beauty, and Tanya is especially pleased with them. Indeed, I have never yet seen any child with such beautiful fingers and nails."[61]

Quickly baptized and given the name Georges Léon, the infant was for now to be given to a wet nurse not far from Paris but was later entrusted to a French family to be brought up. Tanya displayed little sorrow at the thought of parting with her son, nor did she seem much troubled by the prospect of returning home to live in a "whirlpool of lies," much to her uncle's stupefaction. "What an unfathomable creature! On the other hand, of course, one ought to be glad that she is so calm and cheerful."[62] The official version was that Tanya had undergone an operation for an ulcer caused by her excessive use of morphine, and it was this version that Tchaikovsky related to Mrs. von Meck, pleading ignorance of the medical particulars. "I know only that it was all the result of the morphine and that special female organs were threatened," he wrote vaguely on 29 April/11 May. With Tanya's immediate problems thus off his mind, he was eager to return home. "Now I shall wait until my niece has recovered some of her strength and then shall leave. And how I long to go back to Russia! My poor Alyosha has been waiting for me a long time."[63]

Upon learning that Alyosha had been granted a year's leave for his recovery, Tchaikovsky had directed him to go first to his mother in the country and by Holy Week return to Moscow, where he himself planned to be at that time. But Holy Week had passed with Tchaikovsky still in Paris, and now Alyosha was waiting for him with great impatience. Knowing this, Tchaikovsky became especially irascible in the days preceding his departure, reacting with irritation to even minor complications. When Modest wrote that his apartment in St. Petersburg was crammed with relatives and relatives-to-be—Lev Davydov had brought Dmitry and Bob to the city to enroll them in the School of Jurisprudence and had left them in Modest's care, while Nikolay von Meck, out of a sense of duty, was a regular visitor, along with his brother—Tchaikovsky exploded. "Your letter simply drove me to despair and such depression that for two hours I sat doing nothing and thought about this terrible bustle in which you are living," he wrote to his brother. "As I see it, *anything* is better than such a life, even being locked in some dungeon. I am angry at Lev Vasilyevich, who has imposed the children upon you, and at the Mecks (oh! these new quasi-familial relations with magnificent but still alien people—this is worst of all), and at the Kondratyevs, and at that fool [Vera] Butakova [Lev's sister], who could at least have taken the children herself. All in all, this abundance of relatives and children is a terrible calamity," he concluded, adding sharply, "Take some measures. When will the boys leave? Write and tell me. I told Alyosha to come to Petersburg and wait for me there. You will have to keep him as well."[64]

His ill humor was helped little when, preparing to leave Paris on 10/22 May, Tchaikovsky realized that after paying Tanya's bills he had nearly run out of money. He feverishly sought some solution other than turning once again to the ailing Mrs. von Meck. But nothing came to mind, and though he found it "terribly, terribly painful," he reluctantly wrote asking for another advance on his allowance.

Without doubt this had been Tchaikovsky's most troubled season abroad since his postnuptial crisis of 1877–1878. Like Alyosha, Tanya remained for him a major source of distress. Writing to Anatoly on 1/13 April, he had stressed that the entire aim of his life would now be to keep as far from her as possible: "This is someone who fills me with terror and dread. I do not believe that she will ever be completely healthy—if she is weaned from morphine, she will just start drinking or otherwise poison herself."[65] And to Mrs. von Meck he continued this theme on 8/20 May: "My niece Tanya will probably be to blame for my never again being a regular inhabitant at Kamenka. I do not claim for myself the right to find her guilty of anything. Every person acts in life on the basis of his own natural qualities, upbringing, circumstances. But one thing I do know: my sole wish is to be always as far from her as possible. I can pity her—but I cannot love her. To live alongside her is torment for me, since I must force myself to hide my true feelings, to lie—and to live a lie is beyond my powers."[66]

It is telling that Tchaikovsky chose not to pass moral judgment on his niece. He knew from intimate personal experience that everyone "acts in life on the basis of his own personal qualities, upbringing, circumstances," and thus he could not condemn Tanya when he expected a similar attitude from others toward himself.

Nikolay Rubinstein, director
of the Moscow Conservatory,
c. 1878.

Alyosha Sofronov, 1876.

Kolya Konradi, Modest, Alyosha, and Tchaikovsky at San Remo, 16/28 January 1878.

Vittorio, a boy street singer in Florence, 1878.

Mrs. von Meck's trio:
Wladislaw Pachulski, Pyotr
Danilchenko, and Claude
Debussy, c. October 1880.

Tchaikovsky, c. 1884.

Tanya Davydova, the composer's niece, c. 1878.

Aleksandr Zhedrinsky, Aleksey Apukhtin, Georgy Kartsov (a distant relative of Tchaikovsky), and Tchaikovsky in St. Petersburg, 1880. The photograph, along with several others, was "touched up" by Soviet authorities.

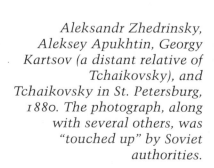

Ilya Petrovich Tchaikovsky, 1878.

Tchaikovsky playing cards.
Drawing by Jurgenson's
daughter Aleksandra.

Vladimir (Bob) Davydov, the composer's nephew, 1886. The photograph hangs in the living room at Klin.

Nikolay and Anna von Meck.

Tanya Davydova, c. 1886.

Tchaikovsky in Hamburg, 1888.

Tchaikovsky in Geneva, 1889.
Picture taken by a street
photographer.

Grand Duke Konstantin Konstantinovich.

Tsar Alexander III, by Ivan Kramskoy.

Tchaikovsky in Frolovskoe, July 1890.

*Tchaikovsky, his young friend
Vladimir Argutinsky-
Dolgorukov, and Kolya
Konradi in Tiflis, 1890.*

*Lev Davydov with his
children: from left, Natasha,
Bob, Yury, Anna, and Dmitry,
1892.*

Tchaikovsky and Bob at the spa at Vichy, France, 1892.

Alyosha Sofronov and his wife, Ekaterina.

Aleksey Apukhtin in the 1890s.

Tchaikovsky, by Nikolay Kuznetsov, 1893 (courtesy Tretyakov Gallery, Moscow). Painted during the composer's visit to Odessa.

The "Fourth Suite": Volodya Nápravník, Modest, Rudy Buchshoevden, Yury Davydov, Bob (seated at center), Vladimir Argutinsky-Dolgorukov, Kolya Konradi, Sanya Litke, and Konstantin Litke, winter 1892–1893.

Tchaikovsky in London, 1893.

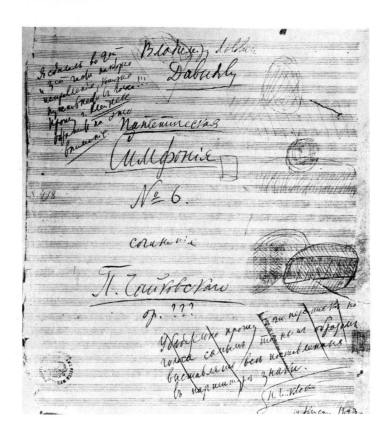

Title page from the score of the Sixth Symphony, with dedication to Bob at top.

The house at 13 Malaya Morskaya Street and the fifth-floor corner room in which the composer spent his final days.

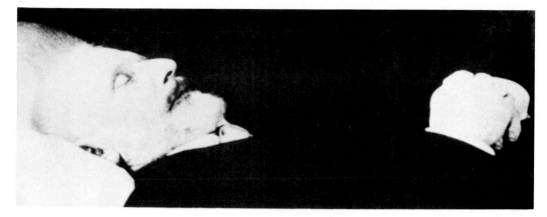

Tchaikovsky on his deathbed, 25 October 1893.

Tchaikovsky's death mask, made on 25 October 1893 by Semyon Tselinsky.

Unveiling of the monument over Tchaikovsky's grave at the Aleksandr Nevsky Monastery, St. Petersburg, 25 October 1897.

Modest Tchaikovsky in 1915.

CHAPTER TWENTY-TWO

X and Z at Kamenka

The Russian capital of St. Petersburg appeared rather emptier than usual when Tchaikovsky arrived on 15 May 1883 because of the coronation festivities then taking place in Moscow. This quite pleased him, as did the feeling of being a "participant in absentia" as the composer of the *Moscow* Cantata and the *Coronation March.* "I feel for the sovereign even greater sympathy and love in knowing from trustworthy sources that on his part he is favorably disposed toward my music," he wrote to Mrs. von Meck, "and I am very glad that it fell to my lot to write the music for the cantata. All these pleasant sensations combined with the enjoyment of a full rest, . . . all this together causes me to feel better now than I have in a long time."[1]

After two weeks in St. Petersburg, Tchaikovsky planned to visit the village of Podushkino, outside Moscow, where Anatoly was staying with his wife and their infant daughter, Tanya, born three months before. Alyosha was also there as temporary help at Anatoly's request. Arriving at his brother's country home on 31 May, Tchaikovsky was at long last reunited with his beloved servant, who, as he wrote to Modest, "is so perfectly sweet and caring toward me that I find no words to express my pleasure at sensing his nearness to me."[2] Alyosha's leave allowed him to remain with Tchaikovsky through the winter, and only in March did he have to report to his regiment and serve a few months more. The next day, Tchaikovsky wrote to Mrs. von Meck, with a reference to her invitation to visit Pleshcheevo: "I found my Alyosha completely healthy. . . . You can imagine how glad I am to have near me now this servant so dear to my heart, who is at the same time a faithful, devoted friend! To stay with him at Pleshcheevo will be delightful beyond words."[3]

But clouding Tchaikovsky's joy of reunion was a new torment that his benefactress, scarcely recovered from her financial woes, was then facing. Some months before, an incurable heart ailment was diagnosed in her youngest son, Mikhail, then twelve years old. The utter hopelessness of the condition had at first been concealed from the mother. "The news about Misha Meck is terribly sad," Tchaikovsky had written to Modest in April. "N[adezhda] F[ilaretovna], as I see from her letter, has not the slightest expectation of such an outcome, but merely waits impatiently for his recovery."[4] But as her son's condition steadily deteriorated, Mrs. von Meck feared the worst. She wrote that she had begun to hate the doctors, powerless to help her son, who "allow him to die and even contribute to that."[5] The situation had made their correspondence increasingly difficult, even tormenting, for Tchaikovsky, who felt helpless and unable to find the words to comfort his suffering friend in her agony. "You are in no mood now for letters, my dear," he wrote a week after his arrival in Podushkino, "and I feel incapable of saying anything about myself. I can only tell you that no one participates more keenly than I in your joys as also in your sorrows, for I love you, my friend, with all the force of my heart. I pray God that He may preserve you, support you in your misfortunes, if it is fated that they fall upon you, and give you the strength to live many more years for the happiness of so many people."[6]

Mikhail von Meck died on 12 June. Tchaikovsky learned of it three days later when he met with Pachulski. "It was devastating to receive this news," he told Modest. "Pachulski hinted that it was the transfer from Petersburg to Pleshcheevo that killed Misha, and it seems that this is nearly so. . . . Nadezhda Filaretovna has borne the catastrophe with incredible fortitude."[7] But the bereaved mother, however stoic in her grief, was eager for a written word from her beloved friend, and on 23 June she wrote, "My dear friend! The misfortune has occurred, but I am calm, because I myself shall die soon and the separation will not be long. I never saw my poor boy, they would not let me go to him, and they did well—two deaths at once would have been too much, and I should not have endured the sight of his death; but now I look upon his absence as a brief separation. . . . I should like very much to receive your letters, dear friend; they would be a comfort to me in my unbearable grief. . . . I do not write more because my head is empty and my heart in endless pain."[8]

Her words imply that Tchaikovsky had already fallen short of her expectations by not having written immediately upon learning the sad news. His eventual response on 27 June, for all its warmth and genuine sympathy, must also have left her with some trace of disappointment. "I did not want in the first moments after the misfortune that you have experienced to trouble you with my letters," he claimed. "In such instances, it is inappropriate to address one with words of consolation. To speak of my keenest participation in the grief of a person so dear as yourself is superfluous, for I know that you do not doubt it. This is why I preferred for a while not to write to you at all, and now, if I may, I shall resume sending you news of myself from time to time." He asked her not to worry about answering him, saying that through Pachulski and her son Nikolay he could have news of her, which, he noted, "I have been without for some time, no doubt because the mail arrives here most irregularly."[9] This was one time when Tchaikovsky's intuition, normally so acute, seems to have failed him. Mrs. von Meck indeed expected and craved his letters and words of consolation at this moment, and in assuming otherwise, he had seriously miscalculated.

From Podushkino, Tchaikovsky made frequent visits to Moscow. It had been during one such visit that he had met Pachulski and learned from him of the death of Mrs. von Meck's son. In the same letter in which he informed Modest of this tragedy, Tchaikovsky did not spare the young musician his sarcasm. Having met with him to pronounce judgment on his new symphony ("frightful rubbish"), Tchaikovsky complained, "It is a great pity that I cannot express to Pachulski frankly the utter futility of his composer's mania. When I asked Kolya [von Meck] whether he advised me to tell him the truth, he answered, 'For God's sake don't, it would upset Mama terribly!' There was no help for it; I had to discuss Pachulski's abominable scribblings seriously."[10]

Pachulski must have sensed the irritation and ill will that Tchaikovsky felt toward him, and it may well have been with this encounter and from his own wounded pride that his active hatred of the composer began to develop. But it seems that even Mrs. von Meck had by now come to realize her error of judgment regarding Pachulski's talents as a composer. "I cannot forgive myself for having pushed poor Wlad[yslaw] Alb[ertovich] into composing," she confessed. "Now he is no longer able to return to the violin and tear himself away from creative work, and he suffers such torments, poor thing, from the disparity of his needs with his means for gratifying them; his whole life is poisoned by this."[11] Tchaikovsky responded consolingly, but without softening the essence of his unfavorable verdict: "Not for a single instant can I allow the thought that you might, as you say, be somehow to blame in this. The fault is not yours, not that of Wlad[yslaw] Alb[ertovich], not mine, but simply that of circumstance and of Wlad[yslaw] Alb[ertovich]'s very nature, musically very gifted, but with no sufficiently defined inclination toward one branch of music or another."[12]

Besides meeting Pachulski and other business associates in Moscow, Tchaikovsky relaxed in the company of various acquaintances from the homosexual milieu, among them Nikolay Kondratyev and Vladimir Shilovsky. Shilovsky impressed him rather unfavorably. "Never has his stinginess been as insolently blatant as now," he wrote to Modest. "All his shortcomings have become exacerbated and stick out like disgusting sores. But certain virtues are retained still, namely, a certain agreeableness as member of a company, that is, with him, for instance, we had a very jolly time [a cut follows] at the Saratov [a Moscow restaurant]. However, I am glad all the same that I rarely see this person and I do not intend to cultivate my acquaintance with him."[13] On another occasion Tchaikovsky visited an ailing Kondratyev, but a gap in the text of this letter to Modest of 20 June conceals from us how they happened to pass the time.[14]

In July a letter arrived from the chairman of the coronation committee informing Tchaikovsky that in recognition of his contribution to the recent festivities His Majesty's cabinet was bestowing on him a gift valued at 1,500 rubles. Much in need of money, as always, Tchaikovsky promptly wrote back that he would prefer to receive the value of this gift in cash. To his great disappointment, he received instead a large diamond ring, "though a very lovely one." He did not quite dare to sell the tsar's present, but with financial obligations pressing he decided to pawn the ring for 375 rubles. Pawn ticket and money he placed in his wallet—and that same evening before bed suddenly discovered that the wallet and, with it, both ticket and money were lost. Certainly, this was one of the most wretched days of his life. Part of the money, moreover, Tchaikovsky had planned to send to Paris, where Tanya was still undergoing treatment.

There was no other solution but to appeal yet again to Mrs. von Meck, telling her the whole humiliating story. Within a few days she had sent him the thousand rubles that he needed. "I feel deeply ashamed," Tchaikovsky wrote in grateful and apologetic response, "that having been, thanks to you, so generously secured from monetary need, I still manage from time to time to make a muddle of my financial affairs. At my age such a frivolous attitude toward the material side of life is unpardonable and shameful. My only excuse is the circumstances independent of my will that force me, not for my own sake, but for the sake of others, to overstep my norm and cause confusion in my affairs."[15] When some months later Mrs. von Meck expressed a desire to redeem the ring herself and to keep it as a memento of Tchaikovsky, on condition that she might repay to him its full value, Tchaikovsky gladly and gratefully agreed.

Tanya returned to Kamenka from Paris in late July, and it was for this reason that Tchaikovsky, despite urging from Modest, resolved to remain the rest of the summer in Podushkino and not to go to Kamenka until September. His forebodings with regard to his niece proved justified. Though apparently cured of her morphine addiction, she brought new worries and grief into the Davydov household, poisoning life for everyone at Kamenka with her languishing martyr's air. Her distressed parents felt utterly helpless.

Tchaikovsky left for Kamenka on 2 September. On the train from Moscow he happened to meet Apukhtin and his lover Aleksandr Zhedrinsky, chatting with them part of the way to Kiev. He also fell to thinking about the future and about Modest and Kolya Konradi, who had been in Moscow and had seen him off, and he tended toward the conclusion that the sanest company for him was his brother and his brother's charge: with them he felt at home. His earlier misgivings about their all living together had faded now that Kolya was older. Still, he wondered, "It is interesting to know whether we shall live together when Kolya becomes independent or will he grow estranged from us. I should like us to, for indeed I love and have grown accustomed to our living together."[16]

After Podushkino the landscape at Kamenka seemed quite cheerless. Drought had destroyed the greenery, still so lush outside Moscow. The room prepared for him was cramped, and Alyosha, who had always slept close by his master since Tchaikovsky feared to sleep alone, complained loudly. To his surprise, however, Tanya proved in good spirits and treated her uncle very affectionately. Not long before, she had managed to talk her parents into allowing her to spend the coming winter in Paris. In confidence, she confessed to Tchaikovsky that she was in love with Dr. Ferré, the physician who had treated her at Charcot's clinic. Her feelings, she said, were reciprocated, and the French doctor had even made her a proposal of marriage, which she still hesitated to accept. Such a prospect pleased Tchaikovsky, not least of all the anticipation of her departure, but also, as he wrote to his brothers, he felt a rush of warmth for his niece, hoping that in this way she might finally straighten out her life. With a light heart he resumed work on his Second Suite, op. 53, begun while in Podushkino, and concluded that "the most agreeable form of life is to live in the country, the real country, far from the capitals."[17]

The atmosphere, however, was darkened by the attitude of Tchaikovsky's relatives toward Alyosha. Several years earlier, Anatoly had expressed some fleeting dislike for Alyosha, though Modest, the devoted brother who seems to have been devoted to his brother's servant as well, never did. But the real problem was with the members of the Davydov family. In a letter to Modest, Tchaikovsky shared his anger and resentment at the growing animosity shown to Alyosha by his sister's family, which had finally reached a head. "For several days running," he wrote, "from various unfinished sentences and hints and generally vague signs, I had noticed a current of hostility against Alyosha. Yesterday it exploded in a little storm." Coming upon Alyosha "haranguing" in his usual loud manner, Lev Davydov had sternly reprimanded him. The following day, Aleksandra, "in front of everyone [at dinner] and not without substantial exaggeration," told the story of this confrontation. Suddenly, "everyone in a chorus began saying that Alyosha is a boor, that he is spoiled, that he does not return other people's greetings (all of which is a lie). . . . I was sitting on burning coals. After dinner I questioned Alyosha, who both yesterday and today has been very upset about this, and now I have calmed down. The trend will pass, and the smartest thing is not to pay any attention to it."[18] Yet, the incident was a symptom of deep tensions within the Davydov family, which once had been so closely knit and so unfailingly attentive to the wishes and well-being of their famous relative.

Tchaikovsky's irritation with his sister's family was little helped by two curious bits of news that reached him in Kamenka, both related to the homosexual milieu. His publisher, Pyotr Jurgenson, told of receiving a visit at his office in Moscow from a gentleman asking for Tchaikovsky's address. "He seemed suspicious to me," Jurgenson wrote in late September. "He spoke of some package for you that he wanted to deliver himself, because to do so by mail would be cumbersome, then did not insist on the journey when I observed to him that while people may have delivered packages in person at distances of a thousand versts in the last century, nowadays it is far safer to send them by mail and insure them. In short, he spoke very enigmatically . . . [and] something seemed fishy," concluded the publisher. "Most likely, he is some passive *Urning* squeezing juice out of a lemon. . . . Perhaps he is sending you an infernal machine."[19] Jurgenson's use of the word *Urning*, coined in 1864 by the German Karl Heinrich Ulrichs to signify a homosexual, certainly suggests that the publisher was privy to Tchaikovsky's private as well as business affairs.

The second piece of news came from Modest, who informed his brother of a matter concerning Prince Meshchersky and his young lover Dmitry Zasyadko, who also happened to be Kondratyev's

nephew. Zasyadko having fallen deeply in debt, Meshchersky and Kondratyev had persuaded Modest to act as a guarantor for the young man.
Tchaikovsky was vehemently opposed to the idea. "I am quite disgusted by this fuss with Zasyadko and quite angered by him!" he wrote
to Modest, adding flatly, "I shall come to hate you if you give him so
much as a ruble."[20]

Meanwhile, matrimony was once again in the air at Kamenka. Not
unlike the previous year when his niece Vera had married, Tchaikovsky watched Nikolay von Meck's courtship of his niece Anna with a
certain wistful melancholy. The young people were by now passionately in love with each other and eagerly looking forward to being married. "I look at them with envy," he wrote Modest on 26 September,
"and keep thinking that this, surely, is true happiness and that I have
never experienced it."[21] But if this transient feeling almost of sorrow at
the happiness of others, well in keeping with Tchaikovsky's sentimental style, is something familiar to most people, regardless of sexual
orientation, a decidedly different meaning must be attached to a brief
remark in a letter to Modest on 31 October, at first glance quite similar.
Tchaikovsky wrote of a veritable outbreak of matrimony among the
Davydov servants: "All this week has consisted of an endless series of
weddings among the servants. . . . Kirila [the Kamenka coachman] got
himself married (oh, how miserable and envious I was!!!!!!)."[22] Six
exclamation points clearly indicate that Tchaikovsky may have been
erotically attracted to the coachman himself and envied Kirila's peasant bride for marrying him.

In contrast to his attitude toward the Kamenka coachman was
Tchaikovsky's dismay at realizing that he had quite captured the heart
of the Kondratyevs' French governess, Emma Genton. The year before,
when he, Modest, and the Kondratyevs had all found themselves together in Rome, Tchaikovsky had complained in a letter to Anatoly
that Emma felt for him "tender feelings more passionate than I would
have wished."[23] The situation had caused Tchaikovsky much embarrassment and unease while the Kondratyevs remained in Italy, and despite Emma's "charm," he had been relieved when they left. Yet, since
that time, the governess, who seemed to be infatuated with both the
composer and Modest, had been sending them piles of amorous letters.
"If only she were not so exceptionally devoted in her love for two
brothers," remarked Tchaikovsky in the same letter to Modest on 31
October, ". . . she might be quite pleasant. But as it is, I find it both
pitiful and tedious, for it is really too much."[24]

The year was drawing to a close. In spite of the various worries
Tanya caused him and all the rest, 1883 had been more productive for

the composer than the previous year, having seen the completion of *Mazeppa*, the *Moscow* Cantata, the *Coronation March*, the Suite no. 2, and fifteen of his *Sixteen Children's Songs*, op. 54. The creative paralysis caused by Alyosha's military service was clearly behind him. At the end of November, Tchaikovsky left for Moscow and then St. Petersburg, where he was forced to plunge briefly into the social life of the two cities. In Moscow his "sin of sweet youth," the First Symphony, was performed with much success, but the simultaneous productions of *Mazeppa* in Moscow and St. Petersburg, originally promised for the end of the year, were delayed until February.

Anna and Nikolay were married in St. Petersburg on 11 January 1884, and the dream so long cherished by Tchaikovsky and Mrs. von Meck of uniting their respective families at last came true. Mrs. von Meck, in Cannes at the time, did not attend the wedding. For all her persistence in the orchestration of this marriage, she remained true to her custom of avoiding all contact with the families of her children's spouses. Tchaikovsky, however, was present and managed to meet the rest of the von Meck clan.

Three weeks later, on 3 February, the premiere of *Mazeppa* was held at the Bolshoy Theater in Moscow, and the next day, Tchaikovsky departed abroad, upset and distraught because of the bustle preceding the production and his own recent separation from Alyosha, who, his leave ended, had had to return to military duty. Tchaikovsky declined an invitation to attend the St. Petersburg premiere of the opera at the Mariinsky Theater on 6 February, angered by a series of misunderstandings over the production. The opera was well received in Moscow, where the audience gave ovations to both composer and performers, but less well in St. Petersburg, though the tsar stayed until the very end and expressed his utter satisfaction. The critics were cool, and Tchaikovsky himself knew that he had "forced out" this work without feeling any real involvement in the subject. Abroad he would receive conflicting accounts of the St. Petersburg performance from Modest and Jurgenson, his brother claiming that it had been a success, while his publisher, to his dismay, wrote just the opposite.

Tchaikovsky arrived in Paris by way of Berlin on 9/21 February, feeling as though he had never left it. "Everything down to the trifles is just as it was last year, and even the very same characters of a certain sort [that is, homosexuals] are wandering about," he observed to Modest the next day.[25]

Tanya had not expected her uncle, but when he visited her on the day of his arrival, she seemed to him both healthy and cheerful. In fact, things were very bad with her and growing worse. Her romance with

Dr. Ferré—if indeed it was ever real and not merely a patient's fantasy—had, she claimed, been broken off some time before, and it was quickly apparent that she was far from cured of her addiction. She had begun to have pains in her uterus. She never went out. She had no wish to return to Kamenka, though living in Paris had become meaningless. Nothing interested her, even life itself. Her situation appeared tragic and very nearly hopeless, for in her ill health she had ceased even to dream of finding a husband, which appeared to be her only legitimate hope for retaining something of her social status.

Her son, Georges Léon, was in the care of a family named Auclair. Tchaikovsky visited them twice and found the nine-month-old child lively, strong, and, as he noted to Modest, "meaty and muscled as if from a Rubens painting." Only the resemblance to his father, Blumenfeld, was unnerving. Meanwhile, worries for the child's future weighed on Tchaikovsky: what surname to give him, how to bring him to Russia. "I was moved at the thought that he is *mine* and that he is in such a pitiable situation."[26] But for the moment at least there seemed no way out: it was still too early to take the infant to Russia, and Tchaikovsky decided to leave him for now with the Auclairs.

The gloom cast by Tanya's condition quickly tainted any appeal that Paris might have had for her uncle. His mood was scarcely brightened when he discovered that Golitsyn and Masalitinov were both in the city. "When I sat outdoors to drink some grog near the Café Américain," Tchaikovsky wrote to Modest, "Masalitinov accosted me out of the blue, while sitting inside the café was Golitsyn, who called me in, introduced me to some local person, and kept me about an hour."[27] The indefatigable pair was soon pestering Tchaikovsky with daily invitations to dinner and to the theater. "I dined at Masalitinov's Maison de santé at the table d'hôte," he reported to Modest. "Both he and Golitsyn were introducing me to everyone: 'Voilà notre célèbre compositeur.' How insufferable these people are, though they are very nice to me."[28] Most disturbing of all, however, was that Golitsyn and Masalitinov had somehow made the acquaintance of Tanya. "I suspect," Tchaikovsky confided to Modest, "that they know everything about her, at least I fear they do."[29]

Tchaikovsky was quickly feeling inclined to leave Paris. Indeed, he found himself increasingly haunted by thoughts of a home of his own and a steady routine. His years of wandering had left him with a profound sense of frustration and fatigue. Kamenka had for many reasons ceased to be an attractive and comfortable working retreat. "I have begun to dream of settling down in some stable and permanent home of my own," he wrote to Mrs. von Meck on 27 February/10 March. "The nomadic life is beginning to weigh heavily upon me. Whether this will be some place on the outskirts of Moscow or some place farther and more out-of-the-way, I still do not know. A thousand plans swarm in my head; but one way or another I must, finally, live in my own place."[30]

An unexpected event speeded his departure from Paris. In late February, Tchaikovsky received a letter from Eduard Nápravník telling him of a conversation the conductor had had with Alexander III. The tsar had expressed his regret that Tchaikovsky had been absent from the St. Petersburg premiere of *Mazeppa* and assured Nápravník of the high favor in which he held both the composer and his music. He had even ordered a production of *Eugene Onegin*, saying that it was his favorite opera, and had decided to confer upon Tchaikovsky the Order of St. Vladimir. Nápravník urgently advised Tchaikovsky to return to St. Petersburg at once to be presented to the tsar.

Tchaikovsky realized that if he did not go he would be torn by remorse at the thought that Alexander might find him ungrateful. He left France and was in the Russian capital by 3 March. Four days later, in "a state of indescribable agitation and anxiety," Tchaikovsky left in the early morning for Gatchina, about thirty miles from St. Petersburg and the favorite residence of Alexander III, who since the assassination of his father tended to avoid the capital for fear of terrorist attacks. Tchaikovsky was presented first to the Tsarina Maria, who, as he noted to Anatoly, "had repeatedly expressed a wish to see me," and then to the tsar himself. "Both were extremely affectionate and kind," he wrote to Anatoly. "I think that anyone who ever has the occasion to meet the sovereign *tête-à-tête* will become forever his passionate admirer, for one cannot express how wonderfully attractive are his bearing and whole manner. She is also charming."[31] Tchaikovsky appeared also before Grand Duke Konstantin Nikolaevich and later sat with him in the tsar's box through a rehearsal of a conservatory production of Gounod's *Faust*. So flattered was he by the imperial attention and benevolence that Tchaikovsky found not a thing to "grumble" about and could only "thank God, who has showered me with so many favors," as he remarked to Mrs. von Meck. "I feel a rush of energy within me and I burn with impatience to undertake some new and great labor."[32]

This burst of élan was further fueled by the happy news on 16 March that Alyosha was at last to receive his discharge. Various formalities had yet to be completed, for the duration of which Tchaikovsky moved to Moscow on the nineteenth. Alyosha "brightened immensely" his Moscow life, despite the endless invitations and visits.

Finally, on 10 April, Tchaikovsky was able to leave the city and he
proceeded at once with Alyosha to Kamenka, longing to greet there the
spring and the appearance of his beloved lilies of the valley. Kiev having grown distasteful to him because of the presence there of Blumenfeld, he traveled instead by way of Kharkov.

In Kamenka, Tchaikovsky attempted to begin a new symphony,
but found himself frustrated. Then, one day while walking in the garden, he "invented the seed," as he put it, of what was to become the
Third Suite, op. 55. In the course of a week he completed a basic sketch
of the work. He felt pleased with himself and with Kamenka. But his
peace soon ended abruptly with the arrival of his sister, Aleksandra,
who had gone to St. Petersburg to fetch Bob home from the School of
Jurisprudence, where he had been enrolled the past year. With Aleksandra's return, Tchaikovsky remarked to Modest, "the usual bustle
began, and that world which had had such a restful effect on me turned
at the very hour after her arrival into a life of turbulence and endless
irritating details." His desire for a stable existence in a home of his own
surged anew. "I begin to realize that I am already too old to be a sponger. I have reached the point where all last evening I sulked selfishly
because chicken was served for dinner and some other dish was canceled and replaced by yogurt. And there have been a thousand other
trifles besides, revealing a sponging nature in me, which can become
utterly unbearable if I do not settle down in my own place."[33]

The onset of the dry season in late April soon added to the general
unpleasantness, and the death in the main house of an elderly teacher
to the Davydov children cast gloom over the entire household. Meanwhile, Lev's sister, Vera Butakova, widowed two years before and
seeming still to harbor something of her youthful infatuation with
Tchaikovsky, appeared constantly to be luring him into embarrassing
tête-à-têtes. Her wistful recollections of the past led him to the nervous conclusion that she had not completely abandoned her former
feelings, and on at least one occasion, frightened by Vera's suggestion
that it would be nice to take a stroll, he simply fled.[34] On top of everything else, he found her to have grown "sour, dull, and slightly tiresome"—though worst of all was her terrible indignation at the daily
games of vint with which Tchaikovsky was wont to unwind in the
evenings.[35]

In the later years of his life, Tchaikovsky kept, off and on, a series
of personal diaries. Not all of these survived.[36] One of the earliest extant covers the events of his stay in Kamenka in the spring of 1884.
Inevitably the myriad inconveniences and annoyances in his sister's

household, combined with the Davydovs' dislike for Alyosha, greatly influenced the mood reflected in this diary. Evident, too, in the diary is Tchaikovsky's extreme fatigue after so many years of wandering and his longing to find a refuge where he might rest. In an entry of 24 April, on the eve of his birthday, Tchaikovsky wrote:

> Eleven o'clock. Presently I turn forty-four. How much has been lived and, in truth, without false modesty, how little done! Even in my real *work:* none of it, to be quite honest, is *perfect, exemplary.* I am still seeking, hesitating, wandering. And for the rest? I read nothing, I know nothing. Only on vint do I waste heaps of precious time. But I think my *health* will *suffer* for it. Today I was so angry, so irritated, that it seems but another instant and there would have been an ugly scene of hatred and malice. In general today I was in a very bad temper and the period of calm, undisturbed life has passed. Too much fuss, too much aggravation, too much that a maniac of my age cannot endure with equanimity. No, it is time to be living *in my own place* and *in my own way.*[37]

Throughout the Kamenka diary Tchaikovsky made reference to certain feelings he coded as X and Z and the word *sensation.* Superficial reading of the diary, often coupled with an English translation of questionable quality, has led several Tchaikovsky biographers to claim that this code relates directly to the composer's homosexuality and, moreover, that it testifies to his secret suffering from his sexual orientation. This opinion is still all too widespread. A careful scrutiny of these passages makes it quite clear that they had no connection with sexuality of any sort. In fact, Z, the principal symbol used in the diary, occurs solely in the context of cards and gambling.[38] Tchaikovsky was widely known to be an inveterate cardplayer, and he regarded a game of vint as the "most ideal pastime for someone who works a great deal."[39] Vladimir Pogozhev, the manager of the Office of Imperial Theaters, recalled that Tchaikovsky "loved to play vint" and that "he played without particular skill but heatedly and with enthusiasm, avoiding arguments and genuinely pained by his mistakes."[40] Indeed, his passion bordered on addiction, giving rise to a spectrum of negative emotions, ranging from simple envy and irritation to spite and even hatred. Such feelings—often directed at his sister, one of his regular partners in vint—were a source of great shame and repentance for Tchaikovsky, and he strove continually to overcome them, but with little success. It is perhaps not by chance that in Russian the words for "envy," *zavist*, and for "spite," *zloba*, as well as for "to be angry," *zlit-sya*, and numerous related words, all begin with the letter *z*, which may account for the use of that letter in the diary.

Reading the diary entries on this theme, one begins to see emerging distinctly this conflict between resentment directed at others and a consequent resentment directed at himself:

22 April: Vint for five: I was unlucky and grew terribly angry.
23 April: Butakova's persecution of vint. Vint in two stages. Was much *Z*. Ah, what a monstrous person I am![41]

Already it is obvious from the context that *Z* does not denote his homosexuality, but rather his unbecoming emotions as a cardplayer. Reports of the almost daily games of vint continue in the same vein.

24 April: Barely managed to finish my evening stroll . . . when I was called to supper—this is a new routine. I suffered from hunger and *lack of consideration* for me. It's petty—but why conceal that even such a trifle can anger me. Afterward, vint and fury without end.
25 April: Vint. Irritation, but less in comparison with yesterday.
26 April: I'm a sort of walking rage. Because Sasha delighted in penal-izing me, . . . I grew infuriated, the more so as out of magnanimity . . . I had been just about to yield to her. . . . What? Are these the feelings of a renowned artist? Eh! Pyotr Ilyich, for shame, old boy! . . . At supper again was somewhat angry. . . . After supper (was angry) vint for three. Oh, life!
28 April: This three-person vint irritates me so much that I begin to fear that it may have affected my health. But I've not the strength to give it up.
3 May: We sat down to vint late. . . . I was very lucky. And all the same I was irritable and found excuses to be hostile to my opponents.
6 May: No vint at all. I confess, vint is almost a necessity for me—I'm even ashamed.[42]

It is perhaps extreme to claim that card playing might affect one's health, but then, Tchaikovsky was often extreme in his sensibilities—from his "misanthropy" and his fear of crowds to his effusive senti-mentality. But no clear link exists between this and his homosexuality. Far more relevant, in fact, was the perpetual conflict between his cre-ative urge for complete concentration on his work and his tendency to succumb too easily to the various distractions and temptations pro-vided by his surroundings or by his own restless nature. It is possible, of course, to speculate on the psychological underpinnings of such extreme reactions, and Tchaikovsky himself made a tentative effort at one point to describe the feelings that he had designated X and Z:

12 May: During vint was terribly angry, though not on account of the cards, but in general, like that, for something indeterminate that can be called Z. Yes, this Z is less agonizing, and perhaps more substantial, than X, but nevertheless, it is also unpleasant.[43]

This excerpt seems to be concerned with various nuances of one and the same psychological experience, which Tchaikovsky, inclined to introspection, sought to comprehend but found difficult to express in words. In all likelihood, Z denoted a misanthropic anger at those around him, an irritation connected with card playing or exacerbated by it, though not specifically stemming from it, whereas X was quite possibly the immediate gambling fervor or the failure to resist temptation.

13 May: Played rather well, but made a lot of mistakes in the last rubber with Rom[an] Efim[ovich] [Derichenko, the family physician] and still cannot forgive myself for bidding hearts instead of spades!!!! Z especially torments me today. May the Lord forgive me such foul feelings!
14 May: Vint. I was incredibly irritated and angry, but not because of the game; rather, Z tormented me, which is all the more vexing, since in the morning it had all but subsided.
25 May: Was terribly lucky and felt terribly sorry for Sasha. Was tormented not by feeling of Z itself, but by the fact that it is in me. . . . Slept feverishly.
3 June: Vint with [Otto] Kern. Dreadfully strong feeling of Z. My God, forgive and tame me!
4 June: During whole day in general poor sister irritated me. . . . Vint. I was very unlucky. Because of this, but chiefly for a thousand other reasons constituting what I call Z, I was angry as a vicious serpent. Came home under distressing, heavy pressure of this Z.[44]

Outside the context of card playing, neither Z nor X is ever found. Still, the nature of this complex emotion, evidently spanning a spectrum of nuances, remains elusive. Tchaikovsky did not fully understand what it was that periodically came over him, and it may have been in part this very nebulousness that led him to denote it by the general symbol Z. More than once he attempted to ascribe this feeling to some physical cause. Writing to Modest from Paris a year earlier, on 14/26 April 1883, he had remarked on this peculiarity of his psyche: "My conscience continually reproaches me for poisoning the life of everyone around me, even those whom I love more than anything in the world, with my irritability and habit of forever becoming angry at *something* indefinite. My only excuse is that there is some physical cause here."[45]

Far more likely, of course, the reverse was true, and insofar as *Z* possessed any physical aspect, this was a somatic manifestation of Tchaikovsky's nervous condition. But if *Z* and *X* are more relevant to Tchaikovsky's psychological condition, the "sensation" that first appeared in the diary on 22 May evidently refers more directly to physiological troubles, at times brought on by fits of low spirits. From the following entries it is clear that the nature of this sensation was decidedly nonsexual and even mundane:

22 May: Woke during the night with a pain in my throat and nausea, and felt unwell all day.
23 May: I was very nervous, everything irritated me and not without reason: a pain, or rather a strange sensation in my throat that has not passed for some time begins to worry me, and also a slight, as it were, hemorrhoidal suffering.
25 May: Strange sensation in throat.
26 May: Woke up . . . very out of sorts and fearful about my *throat.* Refrained from eating food.
27 May: After dinner sensation began again.
29 May: It would have been very pleasant, if it were not for the sensation, which had almost begun to pass, but returned with new force.
30 May: Sensation since morning. . . . After dinner suddenly and quite unexpectedly sensation completely disappeared, but in the evening returned again.
31 May: All day the sensation.
2 June: Felt sensation a bit, but now I do not fear the enemy, for I know it; it's the same old stomach.
3 June: Sensation has passed completely.[46]

In a letter to Mrs. von Meck on 7 June, Tchaikovsky painted a less enigmatic picture of his "sensation." "I had some sort of inflammation in my throat," he wrote, "with a strong fever and such a terrible pain in my throat that during the course of one day I could not even swallow a little gulp of water."[47] In effect, then, the mysterious "sensation" turned out to be little more than a sore throat and a bout of nausea, aggravated by Tchaikovsky's habitual nervousness and his exaggerated suspiciousness. A similarly prosaic explanation lies behind a phrase from a later diary entry, written on 26 March 1887, which, like X and Z and the "sensation," has been cited by some scholars as evidence of the torment Tchaikovsky felt concerning his homosexuality: "What should I do in order to be normal?"[48] It is clear from the full entry and from the entries for the preceding several days—as well as from a letter to Yuliya Shpazhinskaya, the wife of the playwright Ippolit Shpazhinsky, also written on 26 March[49]—that Tchaikovsky was preoccupied not with his sexuality but with his recurring headaches and stomach disorders and that the phrase in question is more accurately rendered as "What should I do in order to be *regular?*"

The only hint at Tchaikovsky's homosexuality in the diaries of the spring of 1884 is an entry on 4 June: "Dreamed of M. and consequently all day was a little, and even more than a little, in love. [A cut follows.] Never mind, never mind—silence—!!!"[50] Without doubt the mysterious M. was not a lady, but a young man; otherwise, it is difficult to explain either Tchaikovsky's concealment of the name under an initial or the editors' excision of a portion of the entry. A homosexual implication is also found in a reference to the death of Masalitinov, Golitsyn's lover, of which Tchaikovsky learned in a letter from Kondratyev this same day. The news threw him into a state of "awful sadness": "I am sorry of course for him, since he could have lived some more, but how horribly Gol[itsyn] must be suffering!!!"[51] It is revealing that Tchaikovsky here immediately identified in his thoughts with Golitsyn, who had just suffered the loss of the person most beloved by him.

It was his own beloved nephew Bob who was the main source of pleasure and consolation for Tchaikovsky in Kamenka, as he confided to Modest on 2 May. "Bobik plays a large role in my life here," he wrote. "Our friendship is terrific—and for the first time he displays a strong liking toward me. Formerly he only allowed himself to be adored, while now he seems to have begun to value my adoration. And truly I do adore him, and the longer, the more powerfully. What a delightful specimen of humankind he is!"[52]

Bob was now thirteen. The intensification of Tchaikovsky's feelings for his nephew is the second striking feature of the Kamenka diary. Scarcely a day passed when Tchaikovsky failed to jot down some adoring remark about the boy's charm:

25 April: Bob all day delighted my eyes; how incomparably sweet he is in his little white suit.

26 April: Bob walked with me in the garden and stopped by to see me. Ah, what a delight this Bob is!

1 May: After supper (before that had played piano duets with my darling, incomparable, wonderful, ideal Bob, to his great joy) there was vint. . . . During entr'acte between rubbers went to my Angel Bob. He showed me his toy theater.

7 May: With Bob went looking for lilies of the valley, had tea, delighted in wonderful evening.

10 May: Lengthy competition around the [leaping] pole with Bob and Alyosha in presence of Yury. Great fun, especially because Bob enjoyed it tremendously.

11 May: Forgot to mention about strange dreams last night: wandering with Bob.

12 May: Running at pole with Alyosha and Bob (in the end he will simply drive me mad with his indescribable charm).

18 May: Sat with Bob on the roof (where will I not climb for the sake of this angel!). . . . After supper played at Bob's wish a special game—secret—a most ridiculous game.

19 May: With Bob (the sweetheart) went to the cliffs, there we joined up with a boating party and returned home with them. . . . Played children's songs for Bob. . . . Bob was infinitely amused by my playing quadrilles on themes he gave to me.

22 May: Before dinner Bob came by and I played him my songs. . . . After tea was about to start working, but Bob diverted me with his stilts. . . . Several times went out looking for Bob. As soon as I am not working and not taking a stroll (which for me is the same work)—I start longing for Bob and missing him. I do love him terribly.

31 May: After dinner was inseparable from my wonderful, incomparable Bob; first he was lolling on the balcony, on the little bench, languishing charmingly and chattering about my compositions. . . . Then he sat at my place and forced me to play.

3 June: A strange thing: I've a terrible wish not to leave here. I think it all has to do with Bob.[53]

These passages, which are but a few of the many that fill the diary, show Tchaikovsky going far out of his way to ingratiate himself with his young nephew. For all the diversity of content and tone in the entries, the emotion permeating them clearly exceeded the common attachment of a middle-aged man for a teenager. Rather, it resembled the feelings of a lover: already it was a source of anguish and longing, already it compelled the respected composer to lapse into childishness, already it absorbed no small portion of his time and energy. Even when Bob had barely entered puberty, he was already eliciting in his uncle sensations of which the erotic component can scarcely be doubted and which were increasingly to dominate Tchaikovsky's emotional life in the years to come.

Leaving Kamenka on 9 June, Tchaikovsky spent most of the summer with Modest at Grankino and with Anatoly in Skabeevka, outside Moscow. But in early September he promised Mrs. von Meck to visit her estate at Pleshcheevo. It was during this year that the role of Wladyslaw Pachulski within the von Meck household had apparently begun to increase. His name is mentioned with ever-greater frequency in the correspondence between Mrs. von Meck and Tchaikovsky, primarily in connection with his renewed efforts at composition.

Despite Tchaikovsky's negative verdict and the lengthy letters and personal conversations in which he tried tactfully to convey to Pachulski the futility of his efforts, the young man continued to seek approval from other musical quarters more sycophantic toward Mrs. von Meck than was Tchaikovsky. Thus, on 8/20 February of this year, she had written from Cannes, "Recently we listened to his [Pachulski's] compositions performed by a small orchestra. I like very much many of his ideas, but the scoring, so far as I understand it, of course leaves much to be desired. The musicians here praised him highly, and one of them, a remarkable violinist who is with Colonne and has played with Wagner in London, very much insists that Wlad[yslaw] Alb[ertovich] come this summer to Aix-les-Bains, where Colonne always goes with his orchestra and assures him . . . that Colonne will put some of his works on the program."[54] Tchaikovsky's response of 13 February had been singularly dry: "I am very very pleased at Wlad[yslaw] Alb[ertovich]'s successes."[55]

Now, in late August, Tchaikovsky sent Mrs. von Meck his last extended discourse on Pachulski, this in connection with her complaints about the lack of attention shown her protégé by Nikolay Hubert, whom Tchaikovsky had recommended as a private teacher. Knowing Mrs. von Meck to be an admirer of the philosophical materialism that was then fashionable, Tchaikovsky decided to couch his opinion in rather abstract terms of mechanics and physiology. "Instinctively I knew and was certain that he [Pachulski] must suffer repeated torment from the disparity between his strivings to compose and the degree of his achievements," Tchaikovsky wrote. "There is something morbid and abnormal in Wladyslaw Albertovich's musical organism, some hairspring is missing in the mechanism, and I have tried many times to make clear to myself what the problem is, but always without success. . . . What follows from all this? That Wladyslaw Albertovich has talent, he has desire, he has zeal, intelligence, warm feeling, but he does not have the proper balance among all these qualities, owing to, one could say, an organic, and for me enigmatic, defect of his musical nature."[56]

It was Pachulski who met Tchaikovsky when he arrived in Pleshcheevo on 3 September and showed him the house, the park, and the various landmarks. Tchaikovsky affected wonderment, but he was evidently annoyed to see him. While the words and phrases in his letters to his benefactress were familiar ones, the tone was all too clearly forced. "Although I expected the most pleasant impressions," he wrote to her, "the reality has infinitely surpassed my expectations. . . . I cannot express to you how moved I am by your thoughtfulness and unlimited kindness. One could devise nothing more marvelous and ideal for me than all that which I enjoy in Pleshcheevo."[57] In fact, Brailovo had surely been both more marvelous and more ideal. Mrs. von Meck may even have sensed the artificiality in his words, but the effusion pleased her all the same. "Although I have already written two letters today, I still want to tell you that I am immensely happy if you truly do like my little Pleshcheevo," she wrote on 13 September.[58] Yet, how little this resembled their profuse exchanges in the times of their "Florentine idyll" or of Brailovo and Simaki.

It had been arranged that Tchaikovsky's sole company at Pleshcheevo would be Alyosha. All the other servants were removed from the house, but the manager of the estate, who turned out to be Pachulski's father, stayed on. Within days of his arrival Tchaikovsky had an unpleasant run-in with the senior Pachulski. Long accustomed to having his servant nearby when he slept, and as there were only the two of them in the huge house, Tchaikovsky had moved Alyosha closer to him into what was Mrs. von Meck's boudoir. The following morning Pachulski senior, having somehow learned of this, went to Alyosha and, as Tchaikovsky told Modest, "in the rudest terms forbade him to sleep in the boudoir."[59]

Tchaikovsky was livid, the more so as he had been assured repeatedly by Mrs. von Meck in her letters that he might manage everything in Pleshcheevo as though he were master there. But he decided not to complain to Mrs. von Meck herself, fearing to upset her, and addressed himself instead to the younger Pachulski. The next day, the father came to Tchaikovsky craving an audience, but was turned away. His son's letter arrived a few days later, begging Tchaikovsky to excuse the old man and not to be angry, explaining that it had all been a misunderstanding. But Tchaikovsky remained distressed. "My stay in Pleshcheevo has been thoroughly poisoned," he wrote Modest on 7 September. "I shall endure the month somehow and then move to Moscow or I don't know where. But what a pity! Were it not for the Pole, it would be wonderful."[60]

Tchaikovsky's indignation appears out of all proportion to the relative insignificance of its cause. This attempt to separate him from Alyosha at night was perceived by Tchaikovsky as a gross invasion of his privacy. It was due to this very incident that Tchaikovsky ever afterward declined Mrs. von Meck's hospitality. Clearly, the senior Pachulski had fallen an inadvertent victim to the irritation against the son that had been accumulating in Tchaikovsky and that had finally burst out.

Having endured the month, Tchaikovsky left on 5 October for St. Petersburg, where rehearsals were getting under way for the production of *Eugene Onegin* ordered by the tsar. The production, opening on the nineteenth of the month on the stage of St. Petersburg's Bolshoy Kamenny Theater, was a tremendous success—the first true success of any of Tchaikovsky's operas. The composer was called out for a standing ovation and presented with a garland, but the agitation and emotion of the evening brought on a strong attack of nerves. Although expected, Alexander III did not show up, leaving Tchaikovsky in some bewilderment until it was explained that his attendance had been canceled for security reasons and the fear of terrorists in the capital.

While in St. Petersburg, Tchaikovsky visited the home of Mili Balakirev, where on the evening of 28 October he met Rimsky-Korsakov and made the acquaintance of the young composers Aleksandr Glazunov and Anatoly Lyadov. His attention was particularly drawn by the nineteen-year-old Glazunov, in whose work Tchaikovsky had begun to show an interest two years earlier, and their meeting quickly led to friendship.

After St. Petersburg, Tchaikovsky had intended to travel to Moscow, but his plans were changed when news came to him that Iosef Kotek lay dying of tuberculosis in Switzerland. "I go abroad, and not to Moscow," Tchaikovsky wrote to Mrs. von Meck on 28 October. His former pupil, he explained, had implored him to come see him. "I had wanted to visit him on the way to Italy, in January, but the other day I learned that he is very ill, and fearing not to find him still alive, I want to go directly there so as afterward not to be tormented by remorse for having failed to honor the wish of a dying man. Poor Kotek! . . . I want and I have to go, though it is also very painful."[61]

Kotek awaited him in the health resort at Davos, in the mountains of eastern Switzerland. When Tchaikovsky finally arrived in the town on 11/23 November, he found his young friend overjoyed to see him. Yet, despite a deceptive first impression, Tchaikovsky quickly saw that Kotek's condition was very grave indeed. "I did everything I could for him," he wrote to Modest later. "I visited his doctor secretly and asked for him to be sent to the Riviera if he should find Davos unsuitable; I gave Kotek some additional funds and in general rendered him moral and material aid." But the depressing atmosphere of Davos weighed heavily on Tchaikovsky, and after just six days he left, "knowing that I had fulfilled the duty of friendship."[62] From Switzerland he proceeded to his beloved Paris and in the City of Light sought relief from the shadow of sickness and death. He visited Tanya's son, Georges Léon, and spent time with Apukhtin's young lover Aleksandr Zhedrinsky and his brother Vladimir. But by early December, growing tired and missing both his homeland and the familiar faces of Modest, Kolya, and Bob, he returned to Russia. Stopping briefly in St. Petersburg, he arrived in Moscow on 17 December.

Kotek's condition continued to decline. Awaiting Tchaikovsky's arrival in Moscow was word from a Russian lady also living in Davos that Kotek had fallen ill with pneumonia and that it was essential that some relative come to look after him. There was little hope. Knowing that no one else could go, Tchaikovsky wondered whether he should go himself. "Perhaps I should," he wrote to Mrs. von Meck the next day, "but I feel that I simply would not have enough courage to make this long journey again in order to watch the death throes of someone, still so young, on whom everything had just begun to smile and who wants so much to live!"[63] In the end, Tchaikovsky did not dare to visit Davos a second time, and a week later he learned of the death of his friend, first from a telegram and then from a letter of 28 December from Mrs. von Meck, who wrote laconically, "You probably already know, my dear friend, that Kotek passed away: we read it here in a German newspaper."[64]

Tchaikovsky answered her on the first day of the New Year. "On the very morning of Christmas Eve, I received a telegram about Kotek's death," he told her. "Besides the shock and deep sorrow that this news brought me, there also fell to me the painful duty of notifying the unhappy parents of the loss of their most beloved eldest son, who was already becoming a source of material support as well for the poor family." He went on, "All this would have made a crushing impression on me if it had not happened that, because of pressing need and a lack of good proofreaders, I was forced to do within a few days the proofreading of my new suite myself. . . . I was angry, indignant, . . . grew utterly exhausted, but, on the other hand, had no time constantly to think and grieve about Kotek's death."[65] This oddly restrained reaction did not prevent Tchaikovsky from noting in his diary a year and a half later, "Kotek's letters. Tears."[66]

Mrs. von Meck made no further mention of Kotek's death beyond her one dry remark, and she offered no expression of condolence. Fashioning for herself an opinion of him as a flippant and philandering young man, she had driven Kotek from her retinue and deprived him of even the most meager support despite Tchaikovsky's repeated attempts at mediation. After his death, she refused Tchaikovsky's request that she help find employment for Kotek's brother-in-law, then in desperate straits. Infinitely obliging and gracious to her friend in all else, on the matter of Kotek—who had, after all, been the immediate initiator of her acquaintance with Tchaikovsky—she remained stubbornly deaf to his pleas. Her obduracy suggests even some unconscious jealousy. Out of all the persons whom she knew in Tchaikovsky's circle, only Kotek had enjoyed the composer's particular benevolence, and until his own estrangement from Kotek in 1881, Tchaikovsky had never tired of emphasizing his fondness for the young man.

At the same time, her response reflected the greater distance that now existed between her and Tchaikovsky. Perhaps she could already feel her friend growing away from her. The repeated references in the Kamenka diary to a vague but profound displeasure with himself and all around him, with his very way of life, were not accidental. Tchaikovsky was weary of dependence, on Mrs. von Meck or anyone else. He was weary of wandering.

CHAPTER TWENTY-THREE

Drama in Tiflis

"For the most part I am out of sorts here," Tchaikovsky confided irritably to Modest on 2 January 1885. In Moscow, Tchaikovsky had decided to stay with Anna and Nikolay von Meck. The arrangement was not a happy one. "The reason for this," he explained to his brother, "is that I am living with Anna, for whom I feel increasingly unkind feelings, but to express them is impossible. I bite my tongue and grow angry and wait impatiently for when I shall be able to leave their home." To make matters worse, Tanya was expected to arrive the following day, a prospect that filled Tchaikovsky with dread. "I cannot look at her without malice and loathing," he wrote.

With the marriage of Anna Davydova and Nikolay von Meck, relations between Tchaikovsky and Mrs. von Meck took on a particular ticklishness, not least of all because Mrs. von Meck, following her own eccentric principles, refused any personal acquaintance with the family of her daughter-in-law. Often Tchaikovsky found himself between two fires. The marriage proved a successful and happy one for the spouses, but from the point of view of their relatives, and especially of Tchaikovsky and Mrs. von Meck, who were chiefly responsible for the entire affair, the exaltation dissipated fairly rapidly, giving way to irritation and mutual awkwardness. Instead of strengthening their personal ties, it now became clear that, if anything, this marriage had done just the opposite.

For all her virtues, Nadezhda von Meck was not the easiest woman to get along with. It is possible that she expected from this young couple, whose happiness she had prepared so lovingly, some special show of tenderness and warm gratitude. But, if she did cherish such hopes, they were cruelly disappointed. With her customary tact, she made an effort not to touch on these painful aspects in her correspondence with Tchaikovsky. Still, in the little that can be gathered from their letters, certain things in particular disturbed her.

Nearly a match for her mother-in-law, Anna quickly turned out to be a willful young woman of a strong and even despotic character and an unusually acute sense of self-esteem. She had soon managed to dominate entirely her weak-willed husband. Moreover, landing within the wealthy von Meck family had put her very much on the defensive in regard to her own background, so that in all her behavior and conversation she strove to accentuate the importance and influence of the Davydovs, much to the irritation of Mrs. von Meck, who had been quite genuinely unaccustomed to paying attention to such matters. Anna was also becoming energetically involved in the various squabbles raging within the von Meck clan, apparently joining the faction hostile to Mrs. von Meck's eldest son, Vladimir, disliked also by her husband but defended as fanatically as ever by his mother. In his letter to Modest on 2 January, Tchaikovsky described with disgust his niece's ruinous influence over her husband. "Kolya [Nikolay] Meck," he wrote, "every day and in every way repeats that (1) Nadezhda Fil[aretovna] is at bottom a capricious and insufferable old woman; that (2) Vlad[imir] Meck is a cheat, and his wife a loose woman; (3) that Yulya [von Meck] is a malevolent fury; (4) Sasha Bennigsen [another of Mrs. von Meck's daughters] is a scandalmonger; (5) Sashok [Aleksandr von Meck] is spiteful, vindictive, callous. . . . Do you remember that nice fellow Kolya who used to be carried away by pictures of the members of his family? What Anna has made of him!"[2] In the eyes of Mrs. von Meck, Anna was very quickly relegated to the ranks of the family troublemakers.

Finally, Lev Davydov, contrary to the express opinion of Mrs. von Meck, persuaded his son-in-law Nikolay to purchase the estate of Kopylovo, for which the young man spent the greater part of the fortune that his mother had alloted to him. The estate proved to be unprofitable and Nikolay utterly incapable of managing it. This affair further strained Mrs. von Meck's relations not only with Anna herself, but with the rest of the Davydov family as well. The unhappy Tchaikovsky found himself caught squarely and awkwardly in the middle. "Oh God, how horribly wretched and unpleasant this is for me," he wrote to Mrs. von Meck when he first learned of the troubles between his benefactress and the Davydovs. "Could I ever have expected anything like this! After all, indirectly the blame for these misunderstandings falls upon me, for it was I who was the intermediary between them and you. What can be done, what undertaken, to dispel the displeasure? I know only one thing: there can be here no intentional fault on their side. They love and respect you too much to distress you consciously."[3]

But Mrs. von Meck had no intention of embroiling her adored friend in her squabbles with his relatives. Expressing her regret that he had been troubled by the reports of "certain frictions that occurred between myself and Kamenka," she begged him to dismiss the matter entirely. "All this is really so insignificant that it is not even worth thinking about," she wrote, "and I should certainly never wish to worry you with it now. My relations with the inhabitants of Kamenka are excellent, and no trace has remained of the fleeting bitterness."[4] This was far from the truth, but with time and habit the frictions became routine and ceased to arouse special irritation. The families grew used to them and to one another. Yet, for both Tchaikovsky and Mrs. von Meck, there could not but remain a bitter residue, which further distanced them from each other, just as it distanced Tchaikovsky from his relatives at Kamenka, where for some years he had known little real comfort or peace.

"I suspect some of the causes of your sadness," Tchaikovsky wrote to Mrs. von Meck some months later, "and, at the same time, I am grateful to you for not going into the details of them. I should in truth have found it devastatingly painful to read them. . . . Being powerless and incompetent to help or rectify the matter, I, of course, prefer not to see and not to know. I could tell you so very much of my own bitter disappointment, of the despair that possesses me when I think about certain of my relatives, but I do not wish to embarrass or distress you. My God! My God! Could I have ever anticipated everything that is now going on!"[5]

In St. Petersburg, on 12 January 1885, Tchaikovsky attended the first performance of his Third Suite. Conducted by Hans von Bülow at the Fifth Symphonic Meeting of the Russian Musical Society, it was a "true triumph" for the composer. "Not a single first performance of any piece of Russian symphonic music in either Petersburg or Moscow had ever been greeted with such enthusiasm," recalled Modest.[6] And Tchaikovsky, writing to Mrs. von Meck, noted, "Never before have I experienced such a triumph; I saw the whole mass of the audience stirred and grateful to me. These moments are the best adornments of an artist's life. For their sake, living and toiling are worthwhile."[7]

Yet, in the next breath, Tchaikovsky confessed that the day after the premiere he had felt "just like a sick person." The whirl of his triumph was almost more than he could bear, and the strain of being in the public eye grew worse a few days later, on 16 January, at the fifteenth performance of *Eugene Onegin*, which the tsar and his wife attended, together with other members of the imperial family. The tsar, as Tchaikovsky told Mrs. von Meck, was "extremely kind and gracious" and spoke with him personally at length, questioning him "in every detail" about his life. The tsarina also showed Tchaikovsky "very touching attention."[8] As before, Tchaikovsky was much impressed, and there is no doubt that the tsar's sympathy was reciprocated. Personal acquaintance only strengthened Tchaikovsky's deep political conservatism. These were trying times. Alexander III had abolished or curtailed many of the progressive reforms of his father, and this political reaction only exacerbated the tensions between the government and the radical intelligentsia. Russia was all too clearly in a state of profound social crisis. Nonetheless, Tchaikovsky continued to have faith in the tsar, whom he not only admired as an individual and one of the most upright of the Russian rulers but whom he also, rather surprisingly, appears to have conceived as something of a closet reformer. Mildly objecting to Mrs. von Meck's "too gloomy and despairing" view of Russian reality, he at one point observed, "Now the question is, do we have someone on whom our hopes can be set? I answer yes, and that man is the sovereign. He has made a fascinating impression on me as a person, but I am inclined quite apart from these personal impressions to see in him a fine sovereign. I like the caution with which he introduces the new and tears down the old. I like that he does not seek popularity, I like his irreproachable life and, in general, that he is an honest, kind man."[9]

Returning to Moscow the day after the performance of *Eugene Onegin*, Tchaikovsky confessed wearily in his letter to Mrs. von Meck, "I've suffered rather than taken pleasure in the awareness of my growing success. A desire to hide myself somewhere, a thirst for freedom, quiet, solitude, have prevailed over the sense of a satisfied artistic pride."[10] As never before, Tchaikovsky had now begun to feel the necessity of changing his entire way of life in order to work and create most productively. If his early years of wandering after his flight from Russia in 1877 had resulted from his ill-fated marriage and the wish to remain as far from Antonina Milyukova as possible, the years following had had as their motivation a profound inner need for solitude, or at least the company of only the few people closest to him, and a desire to devote himself to his work. But circumstances had persisted in frustrating both need and desire. Tchaikovsky now longed to stop wandering. Tired of "sponging" at Kamenka, tired of his unstable, disorganized life in the various great cities of Europe, Tchaikovsky, in February 1885, finally made up his mind to rent, for one thousand rubles a year, a neglected manor house in the village of Maidanovo, near Klin, some fifty-five miles northwest of Moscow on the bank of the river Sestra.

"My dream to settle down for the rest of my days in the Russian countryside is not a momentary caprice but a true need of my nature," he told Mrs. von Meck.[11] The turning point had come. Henceforth, however far Tchaikovsky might go and however long he might be gone, he was a nomad no more. He had a place to return to. Maidanovo, then Frolovskoe, also near Klin, Maidanovo again, and finally the quiet outskirts of Klin itself—within these boundaries Tchaikovsky would make his home for as long as he lived, invariably preserving in each successive residence the same arrangement of furniture and bric-a-brac in the rooms, the same placement on the walls of his few paintings and countless photographs.

From now on, Tchaikovsky's day was strictly ordered, and this order did not change for the rest of his life. He rose between seven and eight. After his morning tea he devoted some time either to studying English or to serious reading. This was followed by a stroll lasting no more than three quarters of an hour. From half past nine until one he worked. At one o'clock sharp he had lunch. After lunch, whatever the weather, he went for a walk. Somewhere Tchaikovsky had read that two hours of walking a day were essential to one's health, and he observed this rule religiously. Solitude during these walks was as important as when he was working, for he spent a great deal of this time composing in his head. By four o'clock he returned home for afternoon tea. At this time he would browse through the papers or chat with guests. From five until seven he worked some more. Then before supper, in summer, he took yet a third stroll, this time in the company of friends, while in autumn or winter Tchaikovsky usually played the piano alone or in duets if he had musicians visiting him. And after supper, until eleven, a game of vint, some reading, or writing letters, of which there were always many.

Tchaikovsky took the house at Maidanovo sight unseen, and when he arrived at his new home in mid-February after a brief visit to St. Petersburg, he found the house and the furnishings somewhat shabbier than he had been led to believe. Still, it was quiet and the surroundings were pleasant—and it was his own home. It is not surprising that almost immediately after settling into the house at Maidanovo, Tchaikovsky felt a creative upsurge. He was cheerful and content. "The weather continues to be amazingly wonderful," he wrote to Mrs. von Meck on 16 February. "By day, despite the frosty air, an almost spring-like sun forces the snow to melt, while the nights are moonlit, and I cannot describe to you how this Russian winter landscape enthralls me! I have begun, with feverish, flaming zeal, to work on *Vakula* [a revision of the opera, retitled *The Golden Slippers*]. . . . I am thoroughly happy."[12]

Tchaikovsky spent almost all of 1885 at Maidanovo, not as a hermit but with periodic visits to St. Petersburg or Moscow. In late March, at Modest's urging, he attended a benefit performance in St. Petersburg by the French actor Lucien Guitry (father of the future dramatist Sacha Guitry), with whom the brothers would become good friends. And on 2 April, in his capacity as newly elected director of the Moscow branch of the Russian Musical Society, Tchaikovsky joined the Grand Duke Konstantin Nikolaevich at a Moscow Conservatory production of Cherubini's *Les Deux Journées*. At much the same time, with his acceptance of the new position of director, Mrs. von Meck added to Tchaikovsky's ongoing worries with Wladyslaw Pachulski by pressing him to use his influence at the Moscow Conservatory to find a teaching position there for Pachulski's brother Henryk, who was also a musician, but Tchaikovsky's efforts were in vain.

Tchaikovsky's first work created in Maidanovo, completed between April and September 1885, was his *Manfred* Symphony, op. 58. The idea for a symphony based on the poetic drama of Byron, which tells the tale of the brooding Manfred wandering through the Alps and tormented by grief and remorse over the death of his beloved Astarte, had first been suggested to Tchaikovsky by Mili Balakirev three years before. At first unenthusiastic about the project, Tchaikovsky nonetheless, at Balakirev's repeated urging, read Byron's poem while visiting the dying Kotek in Switzerland and finally made up his mind to attempt the piece. The labor was difficult and exhausting, but he slowly found himself consumed by the new work and even ventured to suggest that it was the finest of his symphonic compositions. So engrossed did he become in his new creation and such an unexpected affinity did he find in the figure of the proud, God-abandoned sufferer that he noted with wry humor that he himself had "turned for a time into a sort of Manfred."[13] *Manfred* was followed early that autumn by two pieces written for the golden jubilee of the School of Jurisprudence, the *Jurists' March* and a song for unaccompanied chorus. Tchaikovsky chose not to attend the festivities.

In late October, Tchaikovsky visited Kamenka for a few weeks for the celebration of the Davydovs' twenty-fifth wedding anniversary. "Everything [at Kamenka] is as before when I was a constant resident here, but at the same time, I feel that I am now a stranger here and that all my inner ties to this past have been broken," he wrote Modest on 30 October, though later, in the same letter, he made this typical qualification: "Kamenka as such, the Ukrainian element, the smell of the [river] Tyasmin and of the factory, the dialect of the people, . . . Kirila the coachman, Selifan the cook—all this is pleasant to see and hear."[14] Tchaikovsky packed all his books and portraits still at Kamenka and had sent them to Maidanovo. He realized that despite his love for his relatives at Kamenka, the turmoils and tensions in that family had grown so great and his attitude toward them had changed so substantially that there could no longer be complete harmony for him there. From now on, he could be only a guest at the estate.

The last straw prompting him to this awareness was an incident involving Grisha Sangursky, back now in Kamenka after his travels abroad with Modest and Kolya. Feeling a rush of "mad joy" at seeing Grisha again, Tchaikovsky resolved to take steps in the further promotion of his young protégé, and "humbly and importunately," as he wrote to Modest on 27 November, he petitioned Nikolay von Meck, who promised to arrange a position for Grisha in the office of one of the von Meck family railroads. Both Grisha and his father were delighted, but then Tchaikovsky saw his efforts rudely quashed from an unexpected quarter. Accompanying Tchaikovsky to the train station when he left Kamenka were Grisha, Lev Davydov, Nikolay von Meck, and Tchaikovsky's niece Natasha. At the moment when Tchaikovsky began to introduce Grisha to Nikolay von Meck, Lev suddenly "came up to Grisha, who had his hat on, as did we all, . . . and, knocking Grisha's from his head, first hissed something and then shouted loudly and threateningly, 'Get out of here, you lout!' Grisha turned literally white as a sheet and left." Going after the boy to console him as best he could, Tchaikovsky returned to find Natasha "beaming with delight and spewing forth a stream of abuse and all sorts of accusations against Grisha," while her father, "hissing, was encouraging her." The entire episode must have been painfully reminiscent of the Davydovs' contemptuous treatment of his servant Alyosha. Tchaikovsky started to defend Grisha, but at that moment the train pulled in. "I departed with a terrible anger against Kamenka," he told Modest. "About how revolting all this is we shall speak at length in person. . . . I feel that I shall not soon forgive Kamenka all that I experienced there this trip, and this last impression is indelible."[15] Never before had Tchaikovsky expressed such anger and resentment against his relatives at Kamenka as in describing to his brother this truly ugly scene.

By the end of the year, Tchaikovsky was at work on a new opera. With a libretto based on a drama by Ippolit Shpazhinsky, *The Sorceress* had captivated Tchaikovsky with its story of the tragic love of the mature widow Nastasya, who is falsely accused of sorcery, for the young prince Yury. Discussing the project earlier that year with the singer Emilia Pavlovskaya, who had sung Tatyana in the recent St. Petersburg production of *Eugene Onegin* and would create the role of Nastasya in *The Sorceress*, Tchaikovsky had noted, "Seduced by *The Sorceress*, I have in no way betrayed my soul's radical need to illustrate in music what was said by Goethe: *das Ewig-Weibliche zieht uns hinan* [the Eternal Feminine draws us upward]. The fact that with Nastasya the *powerful beauty of femininity* is for so long concealed in the shape of a *loose woman* rather intensifies her theatrical appeal. Why do you love the role of *La Traviata?* Why must you love Carmen? Because in these images, beneath the rude form, beauty and power are felt."[16] The reference to Goethe's Eternal Feminine, to literary precedent rather than any personal experience with women, underscores the purely cultural and creative character of Tchaikovsky's words. Tchaikovsky, quite capable of aesthetic enjoyment of feminine beauty and charm, transformed this enjoyment into one of the constituents of his art.

That, as a homosexual, he might adore a woman, even love her with a primarily nonsexual love, is not surprising. Tchaikovsky was by no means a misogynist. Certainly, he had little patience for foolish young women at the conservatory, whom, according to one memoirist, he "persecuted outright,"[17] or for chattering with female travelers on board a steamship. Yet, in principle, he valued highly the concept of femininity and greatly respected and even delighted in it. He had a highly developed capacity for profound and intimate friendships with women, as his lifelong attachments to his cousin Anna Merkling and Vera Davydova attest. Most remarkably, of course, this was clear in his epistolary relationship with Mrs. von Meck. It is telling that by his own admission it was a matter of indifference to him what kind of love, "maternal or sexual," might play the leading role in his dramatic compositions.[18] The feminine ideal acquired in Tchaikovsky's eyes the status of an unattainable ideal and, as such, provided an emotional framework for the theme of femininity and the depiction of female characters in his music.

Overwrought and exhausted from working on *The Sorceress*, as well as the scoring of *Manfred*, Tchaikovsky arrived in St. Petersburg at the end of December to celebrate the New Year with Modest and Kolya. Within the first days of January he was lying in a state of near nervous collapse, unable at one point even to move and so frightening Modest that he called in the prominent physician Vasily Bertenson. Soon he was sufficiently recovered to subject himself during the remainder of his two-week stay to the usual round of unwelcome parties and appointments. He returned to Maidanovo on 13 January and set again to work on his new opera. Outings in the environs of Klin alternated with trips to Moscow to visit relatives and friends and to attend various musical events.

On 11 March the premiere of the *Manfred* Symphony took place in Moscow under the direction of the German conductor Max Erdmannsdörfer. The concert was a success, and the performance of the symphony was called flawless. Accompanied by Modest, who had come expressly from St. Petersburg for the concert, and by Laroche, the composer appeared on stage to receive the acclaim of the audience. On the fifteenth Tchaikovsky was again in St. Petersburg, where he attended a performance by Hans von Bülow of the First Piano Concerto. In his diary Tchaikovsky noted, "Concert. Ovations."[19] On 20 March, Tchaikovsky returned to Maidanovo, and collecting his things and deciding (despite his brother and sister-in-law's dislike of him) to take Alyosha along, set off for Tiflis (now Tbilisi), the capital of Georgia, where Anatoly was now serving as chief prosecutor.

His visit with Anatoly and his wife, Praskovya, was marked by an episode that would haunt Tchaikovsky for long afterward. It was in Tiflis that Tchaikovsky made the brief acquaintance of a young artillery officer named Ivan Verinovsky, who, as Modest wrote later, "displayed an unusual sympathy, almost adoration, toward [Tchaikovsky] and all during the latter's stay in this city was never parted from him."[20] A few days after Tchaikovsky's departure, Modest adds somewhat laconically, Verinovsky shot himself.

More material is found in Tchaikovsky's letters and diaries, but still the meaning of this brief and tragic story is elusive. The first mention of the young man comes in a letter to Modest from Tiflis written on 17 April 1886: "Of their [Anatoly and Praskovya's] immediate entourage, I especially like a certain Svinkin (assistant prosecutor, graduate of the School of Jurisprudence) and the little officer Verinovsky."[21] A few days later, on 23 April, he remarked to Modest that he had "the sensation of having known him [Verinovsky] intimately all my life."[22] Interesting is the unexpected diminutive "little officer," *ofitserik*, which may signify either Verinovsky's extreme youth, or a mixture of tenderness and condescension indicative of a budding romance, or both.

References to Verinovsky appear in nearly every entry of Tchaikovsky's diary during his visit in Tiflis, though the events relating to him are often noted in very fragmentary form. Thus, on 6 April, Tchaikovsky wrote, "Svinkin. Read. Dinner. Korganov and officer Verinovsky."

There follows a later addition in Tchaikovsky's hand: "And now he has been gone from his world more than two months already!!! 19 July 86." The original entry then concludes, "Vint. Experienced sensation . . . of special sort."[23] In this reference to a "sensation" there seems not to be the negative implication of his earlier notes on his physical indisposition or on the condition he called *Z;* rather, it is possible that in this instance his "sensation of special sort" might in fact allude to some erotic feeling.

On the surface, the life that Tchaikovsky led in Tiflis appears to have been a lighthearted round of card playing, parties, and drinking bouts. "After dinner the charming Verinovsky appeared; we played vint," Tchaikovsky noted on 8 April, while from 23 April there is this curious entry: "Dinner on balcony. Verinovsky. Dressed him in my clothes." And the next day: "At home. Dinner. Verinovsky. Exchanging clothes."[24] But behind the frivolity a disturbing drama was taking shape. An amorous and emotional triangle of sorts had formed involving the composer, the young officer, and Praskovya Tchaikovskaya, called Panya, who in Moscow before her marriage had been known for both her beauty and her coquetry. To judge from Modest's words and from certain phrases in the diary entries, as well as the devastating impression that Verinovsky's suicide was to make on Tchaikovsky, he and Verinovsky very quickly became close friends, and this friendship may well have passed into intimacy. On the other hand, it appears that the young man was infatuated, or pretended to be infatuated, with Tchaikovsky's sister-in-law, who, because of her instinctive coquetry, sought to make him fall in love with her. In so doing, she may even have given various ambiguous hints at the possible nature of the relations between the two men. This would explain not only his own fits of rage—which Tchaikovsky, not particularly jealous by nature, noted in his diary—but also the fact that in the subsequent tragedy he was to see Praskovya as partly to blame.

The exact circumstances remain far from clear, but the brief entries from Tchaikovsky's diary are disturbingly suggestive:

14 April: Again an exaggerated manifestation of love on the part of I[van, that is, Verinovsky].
15 April: Verinovsky, whom I invited for vint, and Panya's caprices. . . . Verinovsky's attractiveness.
16 April: Worked for a bit and at 11 A.M. headed for rendezvous with Verinovsky. . . . With me Kolya [Nikolay Peresleni, a nephew of Lev Davydov], Verin[ovsky], Svinkin. Dancing in circle. Panya hostess. Vint. . . . Heavy drinking with Svinkin and Kolya. Panya in cotillion with Verin[ovsky].

19 April: Upon rising, worked for a while, but soon went as arranged to Svinkin's, where besides Kolya there was later Verinovsky. Breakfast with him at the London. Caroused pleasantly. . . . With Panya. Her disgraceful behavior concerning Verinovsky. . . . Tolya. Verinovsky.
26 April: At breakfast quarrel with Panya over Verinovsky.
27 April: Met Verinovsky. . . . Dinner at the Sakharshveli. Merriment and endless fun, interrupted by disgraceful stunt of Praskovya Vladimirovna. . . . Drinking bout. Cards. Supper. Am infinitely sorry for Verinovsky and angry at the wretched woman.
28 April: Arose with painful memory of yesterday.[25]

This, essentially, is all. Whether Verinovsky was enamored of Tchaikovsky and his flirting with Praskovya was feigned; whether he was enamored of Praskovya and his infatuation with Tchaikovsky, encouraged by the latter, was only subconscious; or whether, in fact, he was amorously infatuated with both on a conscious level is impossible to ascertain, as is whether the repeatedly mentioned Svinkin was in any way related to these events.

Tchaikovsky left Tiflis at the end of April. He and Alyosha boarded a steamer at the Black Sea port of Batum bound for Marseilles, from there to travel to Paris, where, among other things, Tchaikovsky intended to make arrangements to bring Georges Léon to Russia. An agreement had been made with Tchaikovsky's elder brother, Nikolay, and his wife, Olga, that they would secretly adopt Tanya's three-year-old son, and Olga was to meet him in Paris for this reason. Anatoly and Praskovya accompanied him to the ship. Tensions among them at this point clearly ran high. Before the departure there was even what Tchaikovsky later called a "terrible scene" between Anatoly and Alyosha, who very nearly came to blows. "Tolya (most kindhearted Tolya!!!) makes an ugly scene with Alyosha over a mere trifle," Tchaikovsky recorded in his diary for 30 April. "To tell the truth, despite all Alyosha's tactless inability to deal with people, Tolya is entirely to blame. . . . Embarrassment. . . . Painful feelings. Alyosha. Explanations and his tears."[26]

A few days later, Ivan Verinovsky committed suicide. It was not until some weeks later in Paris that Tchaikovsky, happening upon a letter to Alyosha from one of Anatoly's servants, learned of the young officer's death. Shocked and distressed, he wrote to Praskovya ten days later, "I await with feverish impatience details about Verinovsky. I have wept much over this event, and even now, in spite of all the bother and bustle of traveling, I think of him constantly, every hour, and I keep feeling that had I only stayed another week in Tiflis, this would never have happened."[27] But to Modest he wrote on 4 July,

"Panya writes me almost nothing, and I know why: her conscience is not clear. . . . She is very much to blame in this incident."[28]

He went so far as to share his grief with Sasha Legoshin, and when on 14 July he finally learned the details of Verinovsky's death from Praskovya's letter (unfortunately lost), he noted in his diary that he "could not work" and that he "wept so hard, sobbing almost hysterically, that I was not up to eating at all."[29] He responded to his sister-in-law on 18 July with a sort of litany, confessing how he had hoped against hope that the news might not be true. "Worst of all is that his death has drawn a veil over my radiant memories of Tiflis. Now I think back to that place with a wrenching of my heart, with dread and deep sorrow."[30]

Obsessively, he returned to the episode the same day in another letter to Modest, reiterating his earlier accusations against his sister-in-law. "Panya's conscience is not clear in this affair," he wrote. "Without cause she hated and offended him, and there was one incident not long before my departure after which I even quarreled with Panya over Verinovsky. . . . He was young, extremely likable, cheerful, healthy, loved by all and suddenly he up and shot himself. I am quite unable to get used to this idea and have thought of him persistently and without letup for nearly two months now."[31] Here Tchaikovsky perhaps came closest to revealing his own interpretation of the events and of the actions and motivations of everyone involved. His claim that Praskovya tormented Verinovsky because of an unfounded hatred was, of course, misguided. No one hates without cause. Either Praskovya behaved in this way because she was jealous, or she simply decided to play a coquette. In any event, in her émigré years in Paris decades later, Praskovya confessed that she "stole a lover" from her famous composer brother-in-law.[32] This suggests that she was well aware of Tchaikovsky's attraction to the young officer.

Still unsatisfied with Praskovya's account of events, Tchaikovsky later made further inquiries of his own, requesting information on Verinovsky's death from the Tiflis music critic and composer Mikhail Ippolitov-Ivanov. "The reason for his death still remains a mystery to us," replied Ippolitov-Ivanov, who went on to write that in a note that Verinovsky had left addressed to his senior officer he explained nothing, but that the common assumption was that the motive was his failure at his military school examinations. "It is said that he could not go on living as he had lived—he had few means and did not get along with his relatives—his only way out of this situation was to enter the academy and leave Tiflis," wrote Ippolitov-Ivanov, "but with his failure at the examination this path to the salvation of his incredible pride was cut off as well—and so he killed himself."[33]

Ippolitov-Ivanov's letter contained precious little to reconcile Tchaikovsky to his young friend's untimely death. Still, he professed himself grateful to learn that there was at least some external pretext for suicide, however improbable. "Otherwise," he told Ippolitov-Ivanov in his response, "one would simply have to get used to the sad thought that he perished for want of the compassion that his kind and gentle nature needed and that he did not find where he went looking for it. The death of any fine young person affects me deeply: even more so when the death is a suicide. . . . Oh my God, my God, how I pity him!"[34]

A few days later, he wrote to Anatoly, "I finally have from various quarters the details of Verinovsky's death. . . . I still weep quite often when I think of him." He remained tormented by the thought that somehow he had failed the young officer in his hour of need, that perhaps he might have done something to save him if only he had known of his anguish. "Sometimes I grow angry at him and hurl reproaches: why did he not write to me? why did he not look for support and moral succor in my friendship? In short, it has been a long time since anyone's death has made so strong an impression upon me as this one."[35] Indeed, by 2 October he still had not recovered, writing in his diary, "Wept endlessly over Vanya Verinovsky."[36] This was the second time that a young man to whom Tchaikovsky had been clearly attracted had taken his own life (the first having been Eduard Zak). The story was to have a startling postscript when some two and half years later another Tiflis acquaintance mentioned several times in Tchaikovsky's diary, Nikolay Svinkin, followed Verinovsky's example. "I remember clearly now, in reference to Verinovsky, Svinkin wrote to me that suicide is folly," a stunned Tchaikovsky would tell Praskovya on 1 December 1888. "And here he himself has done the same thing! Why, they have gone mad, all of them!"[37]

Tchaikovsky arrived in Paris on 16/28 March. On the voyage from Batum the ship had stopped briefly in Trebizond, where Tchaikovsky found the people "very attractive. . . . I do not know about the women, but the men and especially the boys are most beautiful."[38] Arriving in Marseilles, Tchaikovsky had also made this telling note in his diary, familiar from his amorous quests in other cities: "Wandered about the city. . . . Searching, without success."[39] Shortly after their arrival in the French capital, Alyosha was sent back to Russia. Meeting his sister-in-law Olga, Tchaikovsky began the necessary adoption procedures that would enable Georges Léon to be taken out of France. Neither Lev nor Aleksandra would ever know the truth about the child.

Apart from these arrangements and meetings with various French musicians, Tchaikovsky spent a great deal of time in the company of a young cellist, Anatoly Brandukov. Given Tchaikovsky's habitual sentimentality, it is not always possible to determine the degree to which his emotional involvement with a particular young man may have had an erotic coloring. But there can be no doubt of the depth and sincerity of Tchaikovsky's attachment to young Brandukov, who must, in some respects, have taken the place for him of Kotek. "Brandukov is almost inseparable from me," Tchaikovsky wrote to Modest on 1/13 June, "and is of much benefit and comfort to me."[40] With Brandukov, Tchaikovsky visited the celebrated singer Pauline Viardot, who, though married, had maintained a liaison with the Russian novelist Turgenev until his death in 1883. The two also spent time with Prince Golitsyn in the company, as Tchaikovsky put it, of his "minions." These visits to Golitsyn—and in particular Tchaikovsky's characterization of the prince's companions as "minions," a term often used at that time to denote homosexual favorites—suggest that the young cellist was not altogether a stranger to homosexual circles. During the month that Tchaikovsky spent in Paris they continually dined and supped and breakfasted together, often in the company of a boy named Ovsyannikov, "a lover of music and quite a pleasant youth, though . . . a liar."[41] Soon, as Tchaikovsky noted in his diary, he and Brandukov were *na ty*, or addressing one another by the familiar "thou."[42]

The death of Masalitinov had by no means put an end to Tchaikovsky's relations with Golitsyn, and they met many times while Tchaikovsky was in Paris—generally, to judge by allusions in Tchaikovsky's diary, in a homosexual milieu. Thus, on 2/14 June he wrote, "Having risen and performed the usual ceremonies, went . . . to Golitsyn's. Found him getting ready for church. He had no idea that I was here. A young friend of his with him." It is interesting to note that on this occasion Tchaikovsky, despite his earlier tendency to avoid Golitsyn, clearly went to see him on his own initiative; Golitsyn, meanwhile, would pay Tchaikovsky a return visit a month later at Maidanovo. The entry continues, "Breakfasted at the Café d'Orléans. . . . Brandukov. With him [back] to Golitsyn's. There yet another handsome (weak-chested) youth, an elegant gentleman, and a doctor. Injections of morphine. [It is unclear who was receiving the injections.] All to the Maire for dinner. It was delicious and cheerful." On 6/18 June, Tchaikovsky wrote, "At six o'clock drove in rain to Golitsyn's. Two nice young men, especially the little dark one." On 8/20 June he noted, "After dinner with Golitsyn all three to café on foot. Grog. Saw old acquaintance." And also, from 5/17 June, "Nearby there was a kind German (the handsome friend of the late Masalitinov)."[43]

On his own Tchaikovsky roamed the streets of the city, frequenting the areas around the *cafés chantants* and the notorious clubs he had mentioned to Modest on earlier visits. He struck up an "unexpected" acquaintance with "two very bold Frenchmen," falling into conversation with one of them.[44] "Strange and bold phenomena" continued over the course of several days.[45] "Curious incident near Alcazar," he wrote in his diary. "Somebody's impudence and boldness."[46] And to Modest he wrote, "Remind me, when we see each other, to tell you about what goes on near the *cafés chantants* and what amusing episodes occur there."[47] The vocabulary of the diary entries here is worth noting. Certainly its specifics—"strange," "bold," "impudence"—tend to reflect the ambivalence of Tchaikovsky's attitude to the homosexual subculture and his perpetual sense of being torn between desire and a rather prim notion of social propriety. Interesting in this light is a comment to Mrs. von Meck on the death of the homosexual King Ludwig II of Bavaria, who, declared insane, drowned in Lake Starnberg while wrestling with his physician on 13/25 June of this year. Tchaikovsky wrote: "The poor king of Bavaria!. What a tragic end, and what an outrage this whole story is!!!"[48]

On 16 June, together with his sister-in-law Olga and Georges Léon, Tchaikovsky arrived in St. Petersburg. By the eighteenth he was back in Maidanovo. Four days later, barely resettled, he had a rude surprise. "A mass of letters," he noted in his diary. "One from Ant[onina] Iv[anov]na that worried me, but not very much." Yet, in less than a week, a second letter appeared. Even nine years after their rupture Tchaikovsky was reduced to hysterics. "Could eat nothing," he wrote in his diary on 28 June after the second letter, "and all day was not myself. Only toward evening felt better. What's to be done with this madwoman???" On the next day, he wrote, "I am all out of sorts. Ant[onina] Iv[anovna]'s letter is the cause. Hemorrhoidal pains. At times during the day it seemed I was dying. Wrote my will." And the day after that, "All morning and the whole time from tea until evening I was writing drafts of a letter to Ant[onina] Iv[anovna]. Could write absolutely nothing. Intense moral torments. Both hatred and pity. . . . Ah, such agonies Ant[onina] Iv[anovna] causes me! This will be the death of me in the end." On 1 July he "finally wrote a letter to Ant[onina] Iv[anovna] (oh! how difficult not to offend and at the same time not to indulge)."[49]

That same day, Tchaikovsky referred obliquely to his troubles in a letter to Yuliya Shpazhinskaya, where, apologizing for his silence, he wrote that he had "had a great misfortune and all week literally could not take pen in hand."[50] Though neither of Antonina's latest letters is extant, the essence of their content is made clear in a letter that Tchaikovsky wrote to Pyotr Jurgenson, also on 1 July. "Ant[onina] Iv[anovna] is bombarding me with letters," he told his publisher. "She has thought up a new trick: declaring her mad love for me, asking to meet, and at the same time telling me that she has a lover who worships her passionately, but since he has an irritable disposition, she has again fallen in love with me and is prepared to offer me incredible amorous pleasures. She is, I think, quite mad."[51]

Two days after this, Tchaikovsky noted in his diary that the "incident with Ant[onina] Iv[anovna] begins to sink into the past," and then he added, "My conscience is clear—but still, despite everything, even the fact that she's the most worthless creature in all the world, I pity her. She has not been lucky, poor thing."[52] Hoping to pay her off, he offered her six hundred rubles, promising to increase this if she left him alone. From this point on, Tchaikovsky empowered Jurgenson to resolve any and all subsequent requests from Antonina at his own discretion, without consulting him. Jurgenson was to be a constant intermediary between them and to forward no more letters from her. Such an agreement reached, Tchaikovsky with some relief wrote Modest on 18 July, "I am through with Ant[onina] Iv[anovna] for the time being. She has accepted the money and is quite content. Pyotr Iv[anovich] [Jurgenson] saw her: she has aged much, but tries to make herself look young. . . . She has become so enmeshed in contradictions and false reports about herself that it is absolutely impossible to figure out with whom, where, and how she has been living recently."[53]

But Tchaikovsky was not quite done with her. He noted in his diary for 23 July, "In the morning mail there was . . . a strange and wild letter from Ant[onina] Iv[anovna], in which she asks me to dedicate something to her and also that I take her children to be brought up."[54] Antonina wrote that she now had three children, all of them in an orphanage, one of whom she had named Pyotr—in honor, it seemed, of Tchaikovsky—and she proposed that he take all or one of them to bring up. She also sent an embroidered shirt. "A complete utter madwoman," Tchaikovsky wrote to Modest several days later. "But behaves like a lamb. Thank God, she left after taking a substantial sum from Jurgenson."[55] It was Antonina's last desperate attempt to work a miracle and win back her idiosyncratic husband.

CHAPTER TWENTY-FOUR

Gentlemanly Games

On his return to Maidanovo in June 1886, Tchaikovsky found waiting for him not only Alyosha but also the Kondratyevs, who had rented for the summer a country house not far from Tchaikovsky, and with them were both Sasha Legoshin and Emma Genton.

Of the Kondratyevs' young governess Tchaikovsky remarked to Anatoly on 30 July that apart from her many virtues Emma had "only . . . one flaw: that she is in love with me, with Modest, or with both of us."[1] Clearly, Emma did not understand that Tchaikovsky, despite his kindness and his easy friendship with women, preferred young men. Her woefully misguided attempts at flirtation aroused in Tchaikovsky a mixture of sympathy, pity, and irritation. "Agonized over my cruelty to Emma," he wrote in his diary on 9 July, adding, "But what am I to do? Emma becomes simply unbearable. And the more compassion she deserves, the less of it she inspires in me." She sent him "secret letters" and showered him with "compliments and artificial playfulness," all of which served only to exasperate the composer. "Emma irritates me more than ever," he noted on 23 July. "Poor Emma."[2]

At the end of July the Kondratyevs returned to St. Petersburg, and the young governess with them. With relief Tchaikovsky wrote to Modest on 31 July, "Emma had become so persistent and affected lately that I yearned for her to be gone, yet at the same time felt ashamed of my unkind feelings toward her. But I must confess that I am *very pleased at her absence*."[2] Yet, it was not the last of Mlle Genton. Pass-

463

ing through Klin a week later, she left for the composer a book and a letter "with the usual sugary-sweetnesses." In his diary Tchaikovsky berated himself for his annoyance at her gesture. "Truly it's shameful to respond thus to so fine a feeling," he wrote. "But I can't help it. I am angry."[4] Two months later, in early October, Emma was again passing through Klin, and Tchaikovsky reluctantly met her at the station briefly. "Was terribly annoyed at the interruption," he grumbled in his diary. "But was gracious to her. Transferred her to the mail train."[5]

None of the ambivalence and irritation found in the comments about Emma Genton appeared in the references from the same period in Tchaikovsky's diary to Sasha Legoshin, whose name is rarely met without the epithet "dear" and who takes up nearly more space than his master, Kondratyev. Tchaikovsky even indulged in the following striking apostrophe, in a diary entry of 23 June of this year: "Legoshin. Jam. What a pleasure to have Legoshin around so often; he is such a wonderful person. Lord! and there are people who stick up their noses at a lackey just because he's a lackey. But I do not know anyone whose spirit is nobler and purer than this Legoshin. And he is a lackey! The sense of people's equality relative to their position in society has never made itself felt so decisively as in this instance."[6] Cited by Soviet authors as evidence of Tchaikovsky's progressive social views, this passage is, in fact, no less revealing of his sexual tastes than of his social sentiments. Whether or not Legoshin was actually engaged in physical relations with his master or with his master's famous friend, there can be no doubt as to the intensity of Tchaikovsky's emotional attachment to the young man. At times, it seems often no less adoring than his attitude toward his own servant Alyosha, whose name is also among the most frequently found in that summer's diary, where he and his master by turns console one another, quarrel over trifles and later make up, and discuss their future plans, including Alyosha's getting married.[7]

And there were other young men besides Alyosha whom Tchaikovsky from time to time took into temporary service. One of these was Modest's servant Nazar Litrov, who is mentioned in the diary from late August and who on 5 September appeared to Tchaikovsky in a patently erotic dream. "I slept fitfully," Tchaikovsky recalled, "and had strange dreams (flying with Nazar in the nude, needing and at the same time being unable to do something with the help of Sasha, the deacon's son, etc.)."[8]

While Tchaikovsky may have professed (in theory if not always in practice) the universal equality of man, there remained in late-nineteenth-century Russia a clear distinction in both status and conduct between, say, the landlord Kondratyev and his servant Legoshin. Patterns of behavior ingrained by centuries of serfdom could not simply be eradicated by a few decades of emancipation. This was especially so for the lowest classes of the populace, not only in the countryside but also in the cities, where, in fact, the lower classes were made up largely of former serfs. Education of workers and peasants remained the exception rather than the rule, leaving the Russian masses but little touched by the liberal ideas spreading among the aristocracy and the intelligentsia. As history has so paradoxically shown, it is often more difficult for the oppressed to be persuaded of the egalitarian ideal than for the oppressors.

Thus, for the poor and uneducated in Russia, both before the abolition of serfdom in 1861 and after, the rich, the nobles, and the intellectuals remained the "masters," who traditionally demanded total and unquestioning obedience to their orders, desires, and caprices. The situation led inevitably to exploitation, and in particular sexual exploitation, of servant by master, which extended, not surprisingly, to homosexual involvements. Modern social historians have yet to tackle to any significant degree the question of homosexuality and the homosexual world in Russia during this period. Despite certain similarities with the situation in western Europe at the same time, a number of specifics remained peculiar to Russia, as the scattered accounts of contemporary authorities attest. One of the first experts in the field, the physician Ivan Merzheevsky, asserted unequivocally about Russian homosexuals from "the educated and even the highest classes of society" that "the persons with whom they satisfy their passion are ordinarily recruited by them from the lowest strata of the population."[9] The theme was elaborated by the jurist Venyamin Tarnovsky: "The common uneducated people in St. Petersburg, according to what all the homosexuals I have known inform me, appear to be extremely indulgent to indecent solicitations—'gentlemanly games'—as they call them. These simple people do not consider such solicitations at all insulting, and whether they accept or decline, they never dream of their own initiative to denounce them or complain to the authorities."[10]

Characterizing the homosexual mores of the time, Tarnovsky pointed out that male prostitutes in the Russian capital were recruited almost entirely from among "young droshky drivers, house porters, [and] apprentices of different trades who have not been long in employment."[11] He offered the example of one "active homosexual who for many years used to seduce young doorkeepers who at night sleep on the doormats. His advances were certainly often repulsed, sometimes in very rough fashion, but not one of them had ever threatened him with lodging a complaint." Another gentleman, meanwhile, "exploited more particularly young droshky drivers, used to converse with them during the drive, make closer acquaintance, visited their quarters, and was never subject to any unpleasantness. His proposals were either accepted or refused, but always in a good-humored manner."[12]

One young man engaged in homosexual activities with his master explained frankly to Tarnovsky, "I came to Petersburg a short time ago from a village, and not knowing what might be the customs of this place, I did not complain, because I thought that here all the masters did the same."[13] Even many years after emancipation, the presumed will of the "masters" continued to hold sway. But there were no complaints, no reproaches: sex between men was simply a "gentlemanly game." Nor was there any difference between the sexes in this sort of behavior. Vasily Rozanov, the essayist and cultural philosopher, recalled, "One droshky driver told me of his village, . . . in response to my remark that a village girl or woman would easily give herself for around three rubles, 'Why girls? Married women! In my village any woman would give herself for three rubles. Even my own wife, if anyone would have her.' I was frightened. It was so simple. He was handsome, with a small moustache. Slender. Young. Around twenty-seven."[14]

It was in fact with a young droshky driver or cabman named Vanya (although it was customary in nineteenth-century Russia to call all cabmen by this diminutive of the common name Ivan) that Tchaikovsky was clearly involved in sexual relations for several months through the summer and autumn of 1886. Owing largely to personal inclination, but also in accordance with the style of the period, Tchaikovsky tended to be reluctant to enter into sexual relations with people of his own social circle. He was far more willingly attracted by members of the lower classes, whose simple manners and artless beauty together served as the cause of his amorous democratism and the source of his erotic pleasure. It was evidently the young cabman of whom Tchaikovsky wrote Modest on 18 September, "I could say something more about this stay in Moscow, but better when I see you. In a word, in my old age I have fallen rather heavily into Cupid's net."[15] Although the fragmentary entries from Tchaikovsky's diary provide scant details and conjectures at times must be made, in general outline the course of events is clear enough.

Vanya was, to all appearances, a coachman who used to drive Tchaikovsky from Klin to Moscow, as well as around Moscow itself. He seems first to be mentioned in Tchaikovsky's diary only in passing at the beginning of the year, but from July, after Tchaikovsky's return from Paris, his name began to appear with regularity.[16] By early autumn the composer was infatuated, and on 2 September he wrote, "Unexpectedly Ivan. Glad. Park. Long walk in woods. . . . In love with V[anyush]a [Ivan]. Wavering. Virtue triumphs." Several days later, on 14 September, he noted, "My Vanya. Endless visits to pubs. Stinking [drunk]." The following day saw a confusion of emotions: "Misunderstanding with Vanya. I find him at the entrance on my return. Very pleasant and happy moment of my life. But then a sleepless night, while the torment and anguish I felt in the morning—this I cannot even express." And the next day, "Sensation of anguish. Searching for Vanya near the hotel. . . . Decrease in amorous feelings. A strange phenomenon, as one would think the reverse."

The affair lasted through the autumn. There are indications of material recompense by Tchaikovsky, as when he noted on 5 October, "Home with Vanya. . . . Vanya received money yesterday and today." On 28 November he wrote, "On the way conversations with Vanya. Surge [of love]. . . . Conversations with Vanya. He is especially talkative today." Several times one finds only the barest of hints, as on 2 December: "Vanyusha. Hands." Virtually identical entries (one with "hand," the other with "hands") follow a week later on 9 and 10 December. Tchaikovsky, of course, had a special obsession with hands in general, and with those of young men and boys in particular—but it is also possible that these entries allude to something less innocent. By the middle of December the relations were apparently beginning to deteriorate. On 11 December, Tchaikovsky noted tersely, "Drunken Vanka," while the next day he added, "Yesterday Vanya made me angry. Today I melted." Three months later, on 21 March, after a long interval with no mention whatsoever, he wrote, "Coolness toward Vanya. Desire to get rid of him."[17] But the last entry, half a year later, on 24 September 1887, was kindly in tone: "Met Vanka—the cabman. Glad."[18]

Strikingly different in their psychology and behavior from the genuine members of the lower classes, such as the cabman Vanya, were those young men of higher social origin who had sunk below their station and become part of the emerging homosexual subculture. The nineteenth-century social historian Vladimir Mikhnevich provides a sharply disapproving but still enlightening description of one group of young men of basically middle-class extraction whose activities landed them in court. "They are all almost boys, barely out of adolescence," wrote Mikhnevich. "The oldest among them is twenty. They have been accused of having systematically, as a group, engaged in what one of them has termed a 'lucrative profession' consisting of homosexuality, which, in addition, they quite often exploited for outright black-mail. . . . After every successful catch, the young men, having put in their honest day's work, would hire a swank cab and ride carelessly to aristocratic restaurants . . . where they would conclude their adventures with a merry luxurious supper with champagne." The rest of their leisure and earnings, noted Mikhnevich, the young men expended on equally extravagant amusements and pleasures. "But who are these sybarites with such aristocratic tastes?" asked the historian. "One of them is a corporal's son, another is a petit bourgeois, a third is the son of a collegiate secretary [a low civil service rank], and the remaining two are 'citizens of Riga.' At their trial it was revealed that they all had received no education whatsoever, had neither occupation nor a penny to their name, and were, so to speak, products of the Petersburg streets, representatives of the dregs of society."[19]

On the basis of similar cases, Ivan Merzheevsky, studying the problem in some depth, arrived at a conclusion that was no less gloomy. "If, as it appears, we do not have a fully organized society of homosexuals similar to that in Paris, nevertheless one finds more than a few separate individuals who have made homosexuality a special trade for wringing money out of people who have carelessly fallen into their hands," wrote the physician. "The insolence of such individuals extends to the point where, having laid the trap for their victim and surrounded themselves with bribed companion-witnesses, they will, in the event the sum that they demand is not paid, appear themselves before the court as accusing guardians of public morality. These people can work things out so adroitly that only in exceptional cases is it possible for the prosecutor's office to put them also in the dock as accomplices to the crime."[20]

The same author described the organized homosexual corruption of the bathhouses, which, together with certain restaurants, were the main locations of homosexual activities and where various social and behavioral currents mingled. One bathhouse attendant, a young peasant of between seventeen and twenty, testified:

> I began to engage in buggery [*muzhelozhstvo*] . . . with the visitors to the bathhouse from the day I started working at the baths. I was taught this by some former attendants at the baths, Aleksey and Ivan. . . . They themselves were also engaged in this. . . . It happens this way: when someone comes who wants to do it, he asks for an attendant, me or anyone else, since everyone who works as an attendant in the bathhouses does this, and orders me to wash him, but meanwhile I already

see that it is not washing he wants, and he starts embracing and kissing me, and will ask my name, and then will do with me either as with a woman, or, depending on what he wishes, will sit while I stand before him, or will lie with me as with a woman, or will order me to do with him as with a woman, only in the anus, or bending forward and lying on his stomach, with me over him, all of which I would do. . . . I never allowed myself to be taken in the anus, because it is painful, that is to say, because I believe that it must be painful. I would receive payment for this from the people who came through, whatever they would give, a ruble or more, while those who gave less we would curse, because why sin for the sake of a trifle? All the money we got for this we would set aside together and then on Sundays would divide it.[21]

The same young man reported that the manager of the bathhouse knew of these goings-on and appropriated half their earnings from these activities as a sort of commission. He also noted that these same activities flourished in all the bathhouses of the Russian capital.

Particular areas in the large cities also became known as places for homosexual encounters. In St. Petersburg such an area had traditionally been (and remains to this day) Nevsky Prospect, the city's main thoroughfare, and in particular the Ekaterininsky and the Aleksandrovsky gardens. Apart from his taste, developed in his early years, for strolling along Nevsky for hours on end, Tchaikovsky's diaries also contain fragmentary allusions to encounters, often anonymous, in certain bathhouses and restaurants, especially in Moscow, where restaurants such as the Hermitage, the Bolshoy Moskovsky, and in particular the Bruce served as homosexual meeting places. The Bruce is mentioned in a notation from 27 July 1886: "Bruce, even though it's Sunday. Pleasure and remorse."[22] (To engage in sexual relations on the Sabbath was considered profane by the Orthodox church.) It was at the Bruce and the other restaurants that Tchaikovsky would frequently meet with a certain Andrey, possibly a waiter, and other nebulous figures.[23] Now and then there are also elliptical references to the bathhouses, as in an entry from 16 May 1887 during a visit to St. Petersburg: "Znamenskie [baths]. Timofey."[24] The bathhouse attendant Timofey appears also in two entries from 1886, the first from 16 June: "With Timosha [Timofey]. Somehow wasn't any fun. It's not the same anymore."[25] Despite the note of disappointment, on 18 July, Tchaikovsky wrote, "Letters, about which Alyosha mustn't know (to Tim[ofey] . . .)."[26] However meager such information may be, it sheds some glimmer of light on the shadowy underground dimension of Tchaikovsky's life during these years.

At the same time, Tchaikovsky's erotic urges found a more innocent, sublimated, and even touching outlet in his relationship with the peasant children in the area about Klin. The memoirists speak with one accord of his extraordinary fondness for these children, although for the children themselves these relations tended to be parasitic. Exploiting Tchaikovsky's weakness for them, they were merciless in their demands for presents and handouts. Modest recalled that during his first years living in Maidanovo his brother "managed to poison the pleasure of his walks" with his habit of handing out "tips" to the local children. "At first this amused him," noted Modest, "but it soon turned into a true calamity." As the children's demands became more and more importunate and Tchaikovsky as a result began to avoid them, they would shadow his walks and pop out to accost him where he least expected them. "Little by little the children infected adolescents and grown men and women with the pleasure of receiving the fifteen-kopeck and twenty-kopeck pieces, and Pyotr Ilyich could not stir a step without meeting a beggar. Actual chases began to be organized, hunts for the generous master. He became quite adroit in coming up with ways to avoid his pursuers—and they in ways to catch him and ruin his cunning schemes. All the pleasure of walking was spoiled, and for a time Pyotr Ilyich had to confine himself to the park at Maidanovo for his obligatory two-hour constitutional."[27]

The diary entries support this picture, but with one distinction: Tchaikovsky's chief interest was not in "children" in general, but specifically in adolescent boys. Of these, his particular favor was bestowed on a young fellow named Egor Tabachok, whom Tchaikovsky met on 7 August 1886 and almost immediately began spoiling with tips and presents. Suddenly the nearby village of Praslovo, which he had earlier avoided to escape being pestered, became considerably more appealing. "After dinner walked to town through Praslovo, hoping to see an individual of interest to me," Tchaikovsky wrote in his diary for 8 August. The "individual of interest" was young Tabachok, whom he saw the next day: "Saw Egor, he asked [for money] and received double." On 16 August he noted, "After dinner walked to the grove and returned through Praslovo. Did not see Egor, though I looked for him." A week later, remarking that "something keeps drawing me to Praslovo," he wrote that he had passed twice through the little village, where he "saw Egor Tabachok flying a kite."

A month later, Tchaikovsky himself was flying the kite with his young friend. As with his nephews at Kamenka, the composer felt completely at ease with Egor and his companions, and their clamors for handouts did not irritate him the way those of the other local children did. He bought them presents, and on 11 October he wrote, "Despite the divinely marvelous weather, I walked with great effort and in the foulest temper. I would not even have gone, but I promised Egor to buy him a hat. . . . Sweets for him and his comrade. . . . Boys and money." A week later, he made note of "a promise of skates, etc." for Egor. The promise was not forgotten, and the skates, like the hat before, were bought and duly delivered. Further entries in this vein are found nearly every other day throughout the diary of 1886. Names of other boys—Osip, Ignat, Sasha—also appear, but obviously it was Egor who dominated the scene. At one point, Tchaikovsky wrote, "After dinner walked as ever toward Praslovo, and in the end, Egor, unfortunately not alone, ran out to meet me." Mentions of Egor continued into late September of the following year before breaking off.[28] But the attraction lasted much longer, and three years later, Tchaikovsky wrote to Modest, "Today from behind the bushes suddenly appears the mysterious Tabachok 3d, having quite grown up and become very handsome."[29] This amusing "flirtation" between the celebrated composer and a village boy embraced many elements, from the sentimental commitment to children rooted in Tchaikovsky's own family background, his delight in play, and the infantile side of his character, to his compassion for the less privileged.

In marked contrast to his involvements with peasant and servant youths, Tchaikovsky's passion for various young men among his relatives tended to be sublimated into lofty and poignant spiritualized emotion. Mentioned frequently in Tchaikovsky's diary during the course of this year are two young nephews of Lev Davydov, Nikolay (nicknamed Kokodes) and Vadim Peresleni. Nikolay was living in Tiflis at the time of Tchaikovsky's visit there, and his name appears in nearly every diary entry of the Tiflis stay. Almost certainly, Nikolay shared Tchaikovsky's sexual tastes. He was intimate with Aleksey Kiselev, Kondratyev's scandalous lover, while in one entry of the Tiflis diary Tchaikovsky wrote of a visit to the theater and, "during the entr'-acte, a scene that Kolya [Nikolay] and I were following."[30] This was a typical case of the coded language that Tchaikovsky used in his diary to refer to homosexuality. It is likely that he and Nikolay were watching the unfolded drama of certain homosexual advances within the audience, from which it follows that the young man shared his interest and was aware of his inclinations.

Tchaikovsky's attitude toward Nikolay Peresleni had changed and visibly improved over the years. In 1878 he had complained to Modest that Nikolay "has grown uncommonly disagreeable" and that he "wears incredibly wide modish trousers and exaggeratedly large collars, babbles all sorts of trivial nonsense without stop and in general gives the impression of being a good-for-nothing booby."[31] But by the time of the events at Tiflis eight years later, Tchaikovsky would come to like and appreciate the young man, offering him "subsidies," sleeping in the same room with him at one point, and writing in his diary, "What a precious person Kolya Peresleni is!"[32]

A similar pattern marked his relationship with Nikolay's brother, Vadim, who, however, appears to have been a more decadent and morally dubious character. In the same letter of 1878 to Modest, he wrote that Vadim "also makes one wonder sadly," and then went on to refer to a confession that Vadim, "without any shame," had made to him in the presence of Anatoly. Unfortunately, the lines immediately following are struck out in the original, making it impossible to know the nature of this shocking confession. "His cynicism knows no bounds," Tchaikovsky had then added, "and all the same I cannot help almost liking this disgraceful boy."[33] From later diary entries, we learn that Tchaikovsky on occasion gave Vadim "subsidies," as he did to his brother, but at times continued to find his presence annoying. "At home had just started to feel complacent and happy," he noted on 18 June 1886, ". . . when a guest arrived, Vadim Peresleni. There was no end or limit to my anger. Was completely upset and said so."[34]

But the young man persevered and on 30 July turned up again: "In the morning, after a night that passed wonderfully, I learned that Dima [Vadim] had arrived. Little by little, in the course of the day, I gave into his affectionate manner. . . . After dinner went with Dima to Klin. . . . Returned through Praslovo. Tea, conversation. Dima left. An incomprehensible sadness and thirst for human company came over me."[35] Many times later that year, Tchaikovsky would visit Vadim in Moscow or receive him at his country home, and as his diary shows, harmony and affection were established between the two. They had breakfast and dinner together and went for walks, and at one point Tchaikovsky even referred to the younger man, rather surprisingly, as a "dear little rat."[36]

But it was, of course, Bob Davydov who most occupied Tchaikovsky's thoughts. Traveling to St. Petersburg in late October, Tchaikovsky was struck by how tall and good-looking his favorite nephew was becoming, and he wrote to his sister-in-law Praskovya on 10 November, "Bob has grown so amazingly fast that you would be surprised if you saw him. He is already taller than Modest and the same height as myself—and he is only fifteen. Wherever will it end!"[37] The "incom-

prehensible, wonderful, ideal, infinitely divine" Bob was beginning to take on an ever-greater importance in Tchaikovsky's life, and during the few weeks Tchaikovsky spent in St. Petersburg, his name is found in nearly every entry of his uncle's diary. He wrote of taking Bob's photograph (this photograph, which later hung in Tchaikovsky's living room at Klin, has survived and shows an adolescent with bold but somewhat sad eyes and a head held proudly), of worry when Bob ("my joy!") felt indisposed, of anger and jealousy when Bob did not show up as expected, of jealousy even of Bob's attachment to his sister Tanya, who was by this time living in St. Petersburg. Or he made more brooding observations, such as this on 8 November: "When everyone had left, I chatted a long time with Bob. . . . I have a strange sensation when I'm with Bob. I feel that he not only does not love me but simply feels something like antipathy for me. Am I mistaken or not?"[38]

In this ambivalent mood Tchaikovsky left the capital. By 10 November he was back in Maidanovo, and there, the following month, he celebrated the holidays in the company of both Modest and his old friend Hermann Laroche. Given to drunkenness and philandering, Laroche was at this time in constant need of money, had no roof of his own over his head, and would stay with various friends by turns. Tchaikovsky found his presence more agreeable than not, as he wrote to Praskovya: "[Laroche] has gone to pieces in an intellectual sense. He eats, drinks, sleeps, with effort walks, again eats, drinks, and sleeps and about thirty times a day repeats, 'Ah, Petya, how I love women.' But still at mealtimes he does have fits of merriment and wit. We play many piano duets together."[39]

On 19 January 1887, Tchaikovsky himself conducted the first performance of *The Golden Slippers*, his reworked version of *Vakula the Smith*, at the Bolshoy Theater in Moscow. It was Tchaikovsky's first experience as a conductor, and despite his terror at the prospect of so public an ordeal, the performance was a great success. On 5 March he was to be equally successful conducting a concert of his works at the Philharmonic Society in St. Petersburg. Of these first efforts as a conductor, he would write to Mrs. von Meck that "enjoyment of this sort was unknown to me until recently; it is so powerful and so extraordinary that it is impossible to express it in words; and if my attempts at conducting have cost me an enormous painful struggle with myself, if they have taken several years off my life—still I do not regret it. I experienced moments of perfect happiness and bliss."[40]

But the relief of surviving unscathed his first experience on the podium was quickly followed by sorrow. Just after the premiere of *The Golden Slippers* Tchaikovsky received word of the sudden death of his

niece Tanya in St. Petersburg. She had been attending a masked ball at the Assembly of Nobles and collapsed, apparently suffering heart failure. Death was instantaneous. Tchaikovsky knew well that after moving to St. Petersburg, Tanya had resumed her frivolous and reckless way of life. He had also been informed that she had occasionally been to see her son, Georges Léon, at the home of Nikolay and Olga, and he could also guess that the morphine doses were increasing. It had occurred more than once to Tchaikovsky that death might indeed be the best and only solution to the unfortunate young woman's predicament. Still, the news shook him deeply. He decided not to travel to St. Petersburg for the funeral. He had committed himself to conducting two more performances of *The Golden Slippers*, and after these he returned to Maidanovo. But a "heavy feeling" of loss did not leave him, and on 21 January he wrote in his diary, "A strange state. Tanya's death, like something that has burst tragically into my life, has haunted me."[41] Sometime later, he and his nephew Yury, then at the Cadet Academy, visited Tanya's grave at the Aleksandr Nevsky Monastery. "Above the grave hung an icon in a marble frame, and I learned for the first time from Pyotr Ilyich that this was a copy of the famous Murillo Madonna," Yury recalled.[42]

Tanya's death was a severe blow to the entire Davydov family, but Tchaikovsky worried most of all about its effect on Bob. "My brother Modest," he wrote to Mrs. von Meck on 22 January, "telegraphs me that our nephew Volodya [Bob], for whom I was very much afraid, since he is morbidly impressionable and nervous, is, thank God, well."[43] A few weeks later, he wrote, this time from St. Petersburg, "My favorite Volodya has still, however, not recovered from the impression made on him by my niece Tanya's death. My ardent love for this wonderful boy keeps growing. It is difficult to articulate what a wonderful, refined, richly attractive nature he has. But he is so unlike other boys of his age, he is so morbidly impressionable, that sometimes I fear for him."[44]

At the beginning of April the adored nephew visited Maidanovo. "Bob arrived!!!" Tchaikovsky wrote in his diary. "Had tea together. Walked along the embankment to the Cathedral in Klin. . . . Bob's inexpressibly sweet chatter. . . . Looking through drawings with Bob and talking until 11:30."[45] Three days later, the boy had to return to St. Petersburg, and Tchaikovsky wrote an emotional account of the brief visit: "Bob left this morning. . . . I cannot even express how pleasant and delightful his stay was for me and how I adore him. We behaved like children: building aqueducts, making canals from the melting water, and constantly chattering like magpies. Unfortunately, our *tête-à-tête* was interrupted on the second day of his visit by the unexpected

arrival of two guests, though not unpleasant ones, Albrecht and Kashkin. But Bob has now learned to imitate Albrecht perfectly. Today I feel sad without Bob, whom I accompanied in the morning to the mail train."[46]

Within a month, Tchaikovsky himself was once again in St. Petersburg. For some time Tchaikovsky had been aware that the health of his friend Nikolay Kondratyev, who had been suffering for several years from poorly treated syphilis and dropsy, was failing rapidly and irrevocably. After meeting with Kondratyev on 10 May, the day after his arrival in the capital, Tchaikovsky wrote in his diary, "Terrible impression. He has changed beyond recognition."[47] Every day for a week, he visited Kondratyev's apartment. There was no hope of survival, he learned, but his friend's final struggle might last an uncertain time, and so, on 16 May, Tchaikovsky left the capital to head for Tiflis, where his brother and sister-in-law were expecting him. He stopped in Moscow, joined Alyosha there, and devoted a few days to various business appointments at the conservatory and the Musical Society, and then, with his servant, proceeded by train to Nizhny Novgorod. Here, on 21 May, the travelers switched from train to steamship and began a journey down the Volga River.

For Tchaikovsky, accustomed to traveling mostly abroad, the river journey was an unusual and enjoyable experience. He reveled in the magnificent Russian landscapes, less so in some of his fellow passengers. Tchaikovsky never liked to be recognized as the composer and would try to disappear when he saw a familiar face. Among the ship's passengers he especially disliked two "not very pleasant young ladies, of whom one sings abominably (although she has a good repertoire), while the other pipes [sic] at the piano."[48] But Tchaikovsky did quickly single out one "very amusing" young man, Mikhail Shelemyatyev, about whom he wrote in his diary that "my friendship with an unusually attractive schoolboy is going along at a crescendo." At one point, Tchaikovsky became so engrossed in conversation with Shelemyatyev that he did not even notice Alyosha moving all their baggage from second class to first class and, another time, almost missed the ship while saying good-bye to Shelemyatyev at the young man's stop.[49] On 28 May, Tchaikovsky and Alyosha arrived in Baku, where they boarded the train, and two days later, they were met in Tiflis by Anatoly, Praskovya, and Nikolay Peresleni.

In June, Tchaikovsky journeyed with his brother's family to the famous spa of Borzhom in the Caucasus. On doctors' recommendations, Tchaikovsky began drinking mineral waters and taking the baths to improve his physical condition, of which he was so fond of complaining. At the end of the month a telegram in French arrived from the dying Kondratyev: "Beg you to come, your arrival can revive me."[50] Kondratyev was by this time himself at the German spa of Aachen in hopes of some betterment in his condition. Despite distress and panic, his fear and hatred of death, Tchaikovsky made up his mind to go to Aachen, and as it turned out, he spent more than a month there—a tribute to friendship reminiscent of his earlier attempts to comfort the dying Bochechkarov and Kotek. He set off for Aachen on 11 July, leaving his servant behind. "Anguish to the point of tears," he wrote in his diary. "My departure. It was terrible to part with Alyosha."[51] Even anticipation of the company of Sasha Legoshin in Germany was on this occasion little consolation.

Kondratyev's dying was long and painful. He wept with joy to see his friend, who arrived in Aachen on 15/27 July. Five days later, Tchaikovsky confessed to Mrs. von Meck that "the awareness of having fulfilled the duty of friendship reconciles me with the sad aspects of my stay here."[52] But these sad aspects were soon becoming more unpleasant and intolerable by the day.

The diary entries made at Aachen reflect with particular clarity the ambivalence of Tchaikovsky's feelings about this friendship, especially when compared with the unending flow of praise for Legoshin. While part of him felt deep compassion for the sufferer, another part felt only loathing for the physical details of both the illness and its treatment. Various trifles he might find amusing, but others drove him to despair. The idea of death filled him with panic and fear, and he longed to run away. He wept over the patient's condition and at the same time grew annoyed at his behavior and character. Indeed, these entries reveal not only Tchaikovsky's concrete attitudes toward this particular friendship but also nuances of his own personality, his inherent capacity for merciless self-analysis, and the emotional contradictions that could tear him apart. One of the most telling entries from those few weeks is dated 16/28 August 1887:

> Cannot describe the scenes that took place, but I shall never forget them. Unimaginable nervous distress. . . . Agonizing hours. Strange thing!—I was entirely under the pressure of *horror* and *anguish* but *not of compassion!!!* Perhaps it is because N[ikolay] D[mitrievich] [Kondratyev] displays fear and faint-heartedness in the face of death, and though I myself am perhaps just as cowardly in regard to death, still when he begins to wail with despair like a child or a woman, I feel more terror than pity. But, meanwhile, God how he suffers!!! And why I am so embittered—I don't understand. No! I know that I am

neither wicked nor heartless. This is merely my nerves and egoism, which whispers ever more loudly in my ear, "Leave, don't torture yourself, spare yourself!" . . . But I don't dare even think of departure yet.[53]

Not surprisingly, this was the time of Tchaikovsky's closest intimacy with Sasha Legoshin. The day after his arrival in Aachen, Tchaikovsky wrote to Modest, "Sasha and I went to have supper, with dear Sasha expressing to me most movingly his joy and gratitude for my having come. It was obvious that he had been frightened and terrified alone and that my arrival brought him great relief from his worries and fears."[54] And in a later letter, he wrote, "I appreciate Sasha more and more. I might wish anyone to show me among the gentry a purer, worthier, more radiant soul."[55] They naturally saw each other every day, and soon got into the habit of going out for a stroll and some beer in the evenings after Kondratyev had gone to bed. Tchaikovsky's sympathy and concern for the young man became so great that at one point, in an apparent loss of perspective, he grew passionately indignant when the dying Kondratyev showed himself indifferent to the stomach indisposition of his servant. "Sasha worries me," Tchaikovsky noted in his diary on 17/29 August. "He is deathly sad; it is clear that he suffers terribly. What if he falls ill—that would be a most terrible tragedy!!!"[56] And three days later, he noted that "Sasha's face that day, especially in that moment, was so terribly pale that I trembled at the thought that he might fall ill."[57]

Three days later still, Kondratyev's nephew Dmitry Zasyadko arrived in Aachen to take Tchaikovsky's place at his uncle's deathbed. Tchaikovsky left the following day. "Parting without particular tears," he noted in his diary.[58] He arrived back in St. Petersburg on 28 August, and the following day, he went to Peterhof, outside the city, to comfort Kondratyev's wife, Mary. His gloomy spirits were helped little when he learned from Mary that Modest was also in St. Petersburg, though he had believed him to be still in Kamenka. "I argued with Zasyadko to the point of tears that you would not give a single extra day to Petersburg," he complained irritably in a note to Modest written that day.[59] By 30 August a weary Tchaikovsky was back in Maidanovo. In his diary he noted, "Klin. Alyosha. Bad weather. But all the same it was terribly pleasant to see my Alyosha's mug. . . . Unexpected rush of tenderness toward Alyosha."[60]

Tchaikovsky did not see Kondratyev again. Three weeks later, on 22 September, he made a final laconic entry: "News of the death of N[ikolay] Dm[itrievich] Kond[ratyev], which happened yesterday."[61]

Commenting later on his brother's five-week stay in Aachen, Modest observed that Tchaikovsky "miscalculated the commensurateness of the enterprise with his own personal strength," adding, "In the abstract, no one sympathized with his neighbor more keenly than he; in fact, no one could do less." His ardent compassion, combined with an utter inability to do anything at all to ease the suffering of his friend, had made Tchaikovsky's useless stay in Aachen even more agonizing. "He suffered," wrote Modest, "both for the patient and for himself. . . . And in the end, having done 'too much' for friendship, he did 'too little' for the patient, in comparison to the colossal outlay of strength demanded of him by the generous act."[62] It is possible to add one further aspect, of which neither Tchaikovsky nor his biographer-brother was likely to have been fully aware: his ambivalent attitude toward the personality of Kondratyev, an attitude that on some very deep level corresponded to the ambiguity he often felt in regard to the social aspects of the homosexual world.

Tchaikovsky's experience at Aachen served to accentuate his most private religious thoughts. The day before his friend's death, Tchaikovsky wrote in his diary, "My religion has revealed itself infinitely more clearly. I have thought a great deal about God, about life and death, all this while, and especially in Aachen the fateful questions—why? how? what for?—were often on my mind, nagging at me. . . . But life with its vanity rushes by, and I don't know whether I shall have time to express that creed which has lately been generated in me."[63] Death is always intricately related to both love and creativity. What he witnessed at Kondratyev's deathbed left Tchaikovsky acutely aware of the ephemeral nature of human life, sharpening his sense of the conflict between the spiritual and the earthly and endowing his further work with a new poignancy.

The end of September found Tchaikovsky once again in St. Petersburg, this time for rehearsals of *The Sorceress*, which had its premiere on 20 October. Tchaikovsky conducted the first four performances of his opera, yet despite the ovations on opening night *The Sorceress* was not a real success. Critical response was decidedly less than favorable. One St. Petersburg paper noted Tchaikovsky's "inexhaustible inventiveness" in the symphonic elaboration of the music, but spoke also of his "inability to convey in music the dramatic situation."[64] César Cui concurred, writing in the *Musical Review* that "Tchaikovsky is primarily a lyric poet who is gentle, feminine, most often melancholy, though sincere and attractive, . . . his music has little passion, force, or energy, and it was easy to guess that the dramatic scenes in his new opera would not be satisfactory . . . in terms of the music."[65] The criticism stung Tchaikovsky sharply, and two weeks later, he arrived in

Moscow exhausted and depressed. "Forgive me, for God's sake, that I write you so rarely!" he wrote to Mrs. von Meck on 13 November. "I am going through a very turbulent period in my life and find myself continually in such an excited state that I have no opportunity to converse as I should like, even with you." He was still shaken and baffled by the lashing that the St. Petersburg press had given his opera. "On no other opera," he explained, "have I ever labored so or exerted such effort, and at the same time never before have I been the object of such persecution on the part of the press."[66]

A week later, he wrote Mrs. von Meck almost wistfully: "I have missed you. Circumstances have fallen out in such a way that for some time now I've written you very infrequently, the contact between us has been not so constant, and at times it seems to me that I have become almost a stranger to you. Meanwhile, never before have I thought of you so often and so much as in these last few days."[67]

Caught up in his own affairs and spoiled by habit as he was, Tchaikovsky had indeed been somewhat neglecting his benefactress. With the growth of his fame, the demands on his time increased considerably: the tours abroad, with their intensive schedules; the administrative commitments; the necessity of frequent appearances in society and at court. His decision to begin conducting only exacerbated the situation, consuming what little time and energy might remain. Over the past year he had responded with little more than token sympathy to Mrs. von Meck's growing concern for Pachulski, who had been suffering from a nervous disorder. In the summer of 1886 she had mentioned that Pachulski's "nerves, poor thing, are now so shattered that his musical studies are completely ruined," going on to explain, "Nowadays people's nerves are the curse of the times, the disease of the age, and now he, poor thing, is made a victim of this cruel fate, is immersed in hypochondria and hides himself from people, and in such a condition, any persistent study is of course impossible. I cannot even convey to him your dear, kind concern, because as it is, he suffers constantly that he does nothing."[68]

To be sure, Pachulski's status within the von Meck family was hardly an enviable one. For many years he had been forced to cater to the whims of an admiring but by no means even-tempered benefactress, constantly dissembling and looking for new ways to please her, able to indulge in his favorite occupation, music, only occasionally, and even then having continually to heed her advice and respect her protection, listening with a grateful smile to devastating criticism of his work from the greatest of Russian composers and having, moreover, to serve as constant intermediary between this man and their mutual benefactress and to sing his praises to her unremittingly, while envy and even hatred festered in his heart. Pachulski must have felt painfully that he was neither one thing nor the other: a member of the family and not a member, an employee and not an employee, a musician and not a musician.

Mrs. von Meck, somewhat naively, confided to Tchaikovsky her view that Pachulski's illness "had long been threatening, for fate, in spite of his inborn nervousness, pushed him to music, and this art is devastating on the nerves." A year later, Pachulski's condition had deteriorated still further. "He is constantly fearful," Mrs. von Meck wrote in July 1887, "and thinking that everyone conspires against him and that he will be arrested; he is indifferent and apathetic to everything, quiet, taciturn, in a word, unrecognizable, and it breaks my heart to look at him. . . . How cruel is fate to me; not only has it taken from me a man who looked after me and took care of me like my own son, but now I must take care of him, and to look at him is terrible."[69] Tchaikovsky, burdened at the time with his own worries over Kondratyev, had mustered only a faint show of concern for Pachulski. Remarking on "what a multitude of unpleasant moments" Mrs. von Meck must now be suffering, he had added, "I hope that if the cause of the illness is nerves alone, sooner or later he may completely recover. Please be so kind as to convey to him my keenest sympathy."[70]

Yet, if Mrs. von Meck felt any sorrow or irritation at her friend's growing distance, she did not show it in her letters. Indeed, when Tchaikovsky wrote from Moscow of his fear that he had become a stranger to her of late, she answered staunchly and with her usual passion, "How could you think, my dear, that you might have become more a stranger to me than you were earlier? On the contrary, the more time passes, the more disappointments and grief I experience, the closer and dearer you are to me. In your unfailing friendship and in your unfailingly divine music I have the one pleasure and comfort of my life. Everything that comes from you always gives me only happiness and joy."[71] She knew, perhaps, that he neglected his letters to her only when he was truly overburdened or when he knew that she was unwell and did not wish to disturb her. Exceptions were rare, and while he might at times through absentmindedness forget to send her greetings on her name day or the New Year (she herself never forgot), the habitual terms of endearment—"dear," "beloved," "priceless," "incomparable friend"—continued unabated.

The day after a parting concert in St. Petersburg on 14 December 1887, Tchaikovsky left for his first concert tour abroad. In the course of the winter he visited Leipzig, Hamburg, Berlin, Prague, Paris, and

London, in each city conducting programs of his own works. He did not have time to include Vienna and Copenhagen in the tour, although he had been urged to come. Everywhere he was met with passionate response from the audience, warm welcome from the musicians, and mixed but generally favorable reviews from the critics. New Year's Eve found Tchaikovsky alone in a hotel room in Lübeck. It was at this time that Tchaikovsky developed a habit of traveling without Alyosha. For all his devotion to his servant, he had gradually been forced to concede that Alyosha was more of a burden abroad than an asset, in part because of the unnecessary complications brought on by Alyosha's ignorance of foreign languages but also, and more important, because Tchaikovsky knew from experience that Alyosha all too quickly began to suffer from homesickness whenever they moved about without stopping in one place for any length of time.

On 2/14 January 1888 an official telegram reached the composer in Germany from Ivan Vsevolozhsky, director of the imperial theaters: Tchaikovsky had been granted by Alexander III a lifetime pension of three thousand rubles annually. Moved even more than he was gladdened, Tchaikovsky wrote the same day to Mrs. von Meck that "in truth, one cannot help being infinitely grateful to a tsar who attaches significance not only to military and bureaucratic but also to artistic activities."[72] She shared his enthusiasm entirely, writing on 19/31 January, "With all my heart I congratulate you, my dear, on the monarch's favor and warmly rejoice that you have such a patron and admirer; may the Lord grant him health for his ability to appreciate and reward talents."[73]

The tsar's action was indeed of great significance. The granting of the pension bound Alexander to Tchaikovsky in a manner not unlike that in which the subsidy of the *Citizen* had forever fixed the tsar's relationship with Prince Meshchersky. In both cases, the official support set on the recipients the monarch's personal stamp of approval, making it all but impossible later to disavow those so favored. Any excess or scandal associated with them would, if not suppressed, unavoidably compromise the tsar himself. This fact had already played a crucial role in the troubled life and career of Meshchersky, who more than once might have been ruined were it not for the personal intervention of the tsar. The Russian capital was still buzzing about one such incident that had occurred just months before. Meshchersky had come by this time to exercise a very substantial influence on Alexander III, although the journalist and the tsar preferred to correspond rather than meet regularly. Their correspondence, however, was intensive. It was during these years that Meshchersky began to write for the tsar's consumption his weekly political diary, with its uncannily shrewd analysis of domestic and international events.

The incident in question occurred in July 1887. Infatuated with the beauty of a young bugler in the Imperial Guards battalion, Meshchersky recommended him to the tsar, persuading him to enlist the young man in the court music choir. Alexander ordered Count Fyodor Keller, the battalion commander, to transfer the bugler to the Ministry of the Court. But Keller, surmising the true reasons behind the transfer, not only failed to carry out the order but also succeeded in catching Meshchersky and his bugler at their rendezvous, and then brought the matter to the public prosecutor. The prosecutor did not dare to initiate legal proceedings without the permission of the minister of justice, who in his turn forbade it. At this point, Meshchersky complained to the tsar about the count's actions, and as a result, Keller was discharged. But the former battalion commander turned out to have numerous connections, many of them powerful, and his dismissal caused an uproar in society circles.

One of the most influential officials in the empire, the reactionary chief procurator of the Holy Synod, Konstantin Pobedonostsev, was appointed to investigate the matter. In time, the truth was established, and Count Keller was rehabilitated and soon afterward made director of the Page Corps. But the story of Meshchersky and the young bugler spread throughout St. Petersburg and had resounding consequences for the prince: he was publicly repudiated by his relatives and anathematized by Pobedonostsev, who attempted also to set the court against him.[74] But Meshchersky defended himself fiercely and eventually succeeded in winning back the tsar's support. Not only was the scandal suppressed with no lasting effect for the culprit, but what is more, as one later scholar wrote, "it is an extraordinary circumstance that at the height of his scandals Meshchersky should also have reached the height of his power, that at this moment of all others he became the trusted counselor of one of the most personally virtuous rulers who ever sat on the throne of Russia."[75] Thus could the foreign minister, Nikolay Ghirs, two years later remark on the striking similarity between official speeches by the tsar and the editorials published by Meshchersky in the *Citizen*.[76]

Certainly, Tchaikovsky must have derived a lesson from this scandal—that in amorous activities of this kind one must take as many precautions as possible. At the same time, even at the height of the uproar surrounding his former schoolmate, Tchaikovsky never stopped meeting Meshchersky. Moreover, he saw too that the storm would eventually be weathered, and with the help of the tsar himself. Indeed, evidence exists that Alexander III was by and large tolerant of these unorthodox tastes. Besides Prince Meshchersky, the tsar's own brother, Grand Duke Sergey Aleksandrovich, was widely known for his uninhibited homosexuality. The grand duke had even established in St. Petersburg an exclusive male club whose members were young homosexual men drawn from the ranks of the Imperial Guards and the aristocracy. Only some time after a series of extravagant scandals in 1889 involving the Guards, actors from the Aleksandrinsky Theater, the grand dukes, and Meshchersky was the tsar forced to take measures, however mild. He removed his brother from the capital, appointing him governor-general of Moscow in 1891, while twenty officers of the Guards were dismissed from their posts without trial, which "did not prevent them . . . from going on to make more or less successful careers."[77] A quip about the grand duke's new appointment became popular in the capital: "Until now Moscow stood on seven hills, but now she must stand on one hillock." In this play on words, the Russian for "hillock," *bugor*, puns with *bugr*, a distorted form of French *bougre*, cognate to English *bugger.*[78]

The news of the favor bestowed on Tchaikovsky by the Russian emperor no doubt further boosted the success of the concert tour. Everywhere he went, the composer was flooded with new experiences and new acquaintances. At the start, as always abroad, Tchaikovsky suffered from "unbearable, deathly anguish," but in Leipzig he found in the families of the violinist Adolph Brodsky and of the young, handsome, and gifted pianist Aleksandr Siloti "such likely, kindred sympathy and love that it gave me much strength and good spirits."[79]

Tchaikovsky's friendship with young Siloti seems to have been strikingly free of any overt homoerotic element. The references to Siloti in Tchaikovsky's diaries and in his letters to Siloti and others are extremely friendly in tone but in no way amorous. Contrary to his habit, for instance, Tchaikovsky while addressing the young man in the familiar *ty* almost never closed his letters to him with his usual "I kiss you." To be sure, Siloti was married, and Tchaikovsky both liked and respected his wife, Vera. In any event, he felt a rush of gratitude to Siloti for the young man's practical and emotional support, particularly in his habitual moments of frustration and hypochondria. "With me all the time was dearest Siloti," Tchaikovsky wrote to Modest on 10 February, "who looked after me like a nanny and many times saved me from utter exhaustion."[80] He was grateful, too, for Siloti's "energetic propagation of my music in Leipzig" and for the "noble, sublime, passionate feeling [that] lies at the root of all his endless exertions on my behalf."[81]

Only once during his stay in Germany did Tchaikovsky's gratitude burst into something more emotional and a tone familiar from his correspondence with the young cellist Brandukov, for instance, appear in a letter to the young pianist. After an attempt to intervene on Siloti's behalf with his own concert agent in Berlin, Tchaikovsky wrote on 27 December, "I think of you incessantly and miss having your dear face nearby. I embrace you!!! . . . Once again, I kiss you warmly."[82] But since the negotiations with the agent had had no tangible success, one suspects that the special tenderness of this letter may have been designed specifically to soften the impact.

Tchaikovsky's relations with another young musician who accompanied him on the tour, the pianist Vasily Sapelnikov, developed in a noticeably more passionate key. On 12 January he wrote to Modest that "Sapelnikov created a true sensation in Hamburg. . . . He is indeed a great talent. And in his heart he is a charming, most kind youth."[83] The praise continued in subsequent letters. "I have grown terribly fond of him," Tchaikovsky confessed on 20 January. "It is difficult to imagine a more likable, kinder boy."[84] Three days later, he wrote, "I have been inseparable from him for almost three weeks now and have grown so fond of him, and he has become so close and dear to me, that he is just like the closest of relatives. Since the time of Kotek I have never loved anyone so warmly as him. You cannot imagine a more attractive, gentle, sweet, delicate, noble individual. . . . I consider him (and not I alone) a future piano genius."[85]

So great was his enthusiasm that it shows through in less confidential letters to Jurgenson as well. Tchaikovsky even boasted a bit to his servant Alyosha, remarking that "a great consolation to me is the fact I have traveling with me now one Russian musician who loves me dearly and takes great care of me."[86] In the diary entries of the time Sapelnikov also figured prominently. "Sapelnikov, poor fellow, came for money," Tchaikovsky wrote on 8 January. "A kind, splendid boy!" On 17 January he wrote that "many found out today that he is a genius and I myself am of the same opinion," while a few days later, he noted, "Chatted with Vasya [Sapelnikov]. What a lovely person! . . . What a consolation Vasya is to me!" Then, on 21 January, he wrote, "Seeing off my dear Vasya."[87] Another letter to Modest the following day mentioned "the departure of Vasya (whom I absolutely adore)."[88]

As in the case of Brandukov, it seems very likely that an erotic element was present in Tchaikovsky's friendship with Sapelnikov and that he recognized it as such. Both men were quite young and good-looking. Almost certainly, however, their relations remained chaste, of a sentimental and aesthetic character, though the emotional attachments were clearly mutual. Of course, the young men may, and indeed must, have been aware that their sentimental friendship with the great and famous composer could be beneficial to them in a material as well as an emotional sense. They could confidently expect from him powerful and influential support that might substantially further their own musical careers.

During his stay in Paris, Tchaikovsky met Golitsyn accompanied by "a blond lyceum pupil, a comrade of Sasha [Aleksandr] Zhedrinsky [Apukhtin's lover],"[89] and went drinking with Brandukov in the company of a female prostitute, after which Tchaikovsky, as he noted in his diary, returned to his hotel while Brandukov, it appears, went with the prostitute.[90] In Leipzig he met Johannes Brahms, who impressed him as "a potbellied boozer," and immediately became friends with Edvard Grieg, "an extraordinarily charming man."[91] In Berlin he ran by chance into Désirée Artôt, with whom he had not spoken in nearly twenty years. They met and chatted like old friends, "without touching on the past with a single word."[92] From Germany he traveled to Prague, where he found an unprecedented celebration of his achievements and ten days of uninterrupted musical festivities. His presence, moreover, was by no means merely a convenient pretext for the Czech people, chafing under Austro-Hungarian domination, to indulge in a display of Pan-Slavic feeling. In the work of the Russian composer they were able better to comprehend their own affinities to the best in Russian culture.

But behind the brilliant successes remained a gnawing anguish. From time to time it would surface in a diary entry or in a brief confession to an intimate correspondent. To be sure, any upheaval in his now settled way of life was bound to upset the psychological balance of so introverted a creative artist as Tchaikovsky. The long separation from his beloved homeland, the irritating social life, the meaningless meetings, the formal conversations, the diplomatic courtesies and endless banquet ceremonies, not to mention the strain of conducting itself—all this was an unremitting assault on his nerves and on his psyche. It had always been so. From now on, however, there would be less and less possibility of hiding.

By 12 March, Tchaikovsky was on his way to Vienna. From there, he proceeded to Taganrog, on the Black Sea, to visit his brother Ippolit, and then finally, on 26 March 1888, he arrived in Tiflis to stay with Anatoly and Praskovya. Here at last he was able to relax and collect his thoughts. The ordeal of Aachen at the bed of his dying friend and the renewed confidence in himself as a composer born of the success of this first concert tour abroad persistently called for new artistic endeavors. In May he began writing a new symphony.

Part Six

FAME
1888–1893

CHAPTER TWENTY-FIVE

A Second Wind

At the end of March 1888, Alyosha informed his master that he had been able to rent a small estate in the village of Frolovskoe, not far from Klin. While quite comfortable at Maidanovo, Tchaikovsky had been plagued by the crowds of summer vacationers who constantly distracted him from his work and disturbed his solitary walks. After a month in Tiflis and a brief stay in Moscow, Tchaikovsky arrived at his new home. He liked the house and especially the garden, which bordered directly on the woods. There were few people about, as the house stood rather apart from frequented routes. In this seclusion, Tchaikovsky was about to enter what was arguably the most creative period of his life.

The household that Tchaikovsky found on his arrival in Frolovskoe already resembled the idyllic vision of the future that he had described to Alyosha while the young man was still in the army. In his master's absence Alyosha had finally married. He had, in fact, very nearly married a year before. Plans had been made and a date set. Tchaikovsky, at his servant's request, had even left for Moscow that day in order to give the couple and their guests complete freedom at Maidanovo. But in a tragicomic twist on Tchaikovsky's own matrimonial fiasco, the bride at the very last moment had changed her mind and left the poor bridegroom virtually standing at the altar. His second try, however, had fared rather better, and Tchaikovsky, on meeting Alyosha's wife, Fyokla, when he arrived in Frolovskoe, found her "pretty and pleasant."

Tchaikovsky scarcely had time to settle into his new home before he was off again. On 28 April, without having really rested, he was obliged to travel to St. Petersburg to appear before Alexander III and thank him for the official pension that had been granted him. Though somewhat rushed, the tsar received him with his usual graciousness and courtesy. While in the capital Tchaikovsky also met his sister, whom he had not seen in two years. He was shocked to see how Aleksandra had aged. Her hair had turned gray and she was ill during the whole time of his visit. She suffered from stones in her liver that caused her such agony that she would cry out in pain for days on end. Aleksandra was also by now a desperate morphine addict, and as a result of her addiction, she had developed two large ulcers, for which she had had to have surgery. "This meeting has brought me nothing but grief," Tchaikovsky wrote to Yuliya Shpazhinskaya on 9 May. "This woman had, and still has even now, all the conditions for happiness, but meanwhile, nothing can be imagined more terrible than her life."[1]

Further distressing news came from Tchaikovsky's niece Vera, who had traveled to Paris to be treated for tuberculosis. The chances of her recovery, it seemed, were slim. Even his beloved nephew Bob was a disappointment this time, for he had grown abnormally overweight and looked awful. Only Modest, looking forward to summer, was cheerful. Tchaikovsky told his brother of a new friend he had recently made in Tiflis, the fourteen-year-old Prince Vladimir Argutinsky-Dolgorukov, and such was his enthusiasm for the boy that Modest was inspired to pay a visit to Anatoly himself so as to see this new favorite. Jokingly Tchaikovsky noted to Praskovya that "Modest and Kolya will come to Borzhom only if Argutinsky is also there; otherwise, they will stay [at the Konradis' country house] in Peterhof."[2]

While still in Tiflis, Tchaikovsky had set down the first drafts for his Symphony no. 5 in E Minor, op. 64. Dating from 15 April, the earliest notebook sketches include a "program" of the new work that offers a general indication of the contents rather than a detailed scenario: "Intr[oduction]. Complete submission before Fate, or, which is the same, before the inscrut[able] predestination of Providence. Allegro. (1) Murmur of doubt, complaints, reproaches to XXX. (2) To leap into the embrace of *Faith*!!! A wonderful program, if only it can be carried out." Beside the sketch of a theme not incorporated into the symphony Tchaikovsky wrote, "*Consolation*. A ray of light," and below the sketch stand the words "No, no hope!"[3]

These notes show the emotional context of the symphony, reflecting the soul of a man in a time of deep crisis. There is every reason to believe that the crisis sparking the creation of the Fifth Symphony was that which Tchaikovsky had experienced in Aachen eight months earlier as a witness to Kondratyev's deathbed struggle. At that time he had written to Modest, describing his friend's sheer panic in the face of death: "His despair is expressed quite childishly somehow. Can it be that we are all so afraid when we die?!"[4] During the days that followed, he had repeatedly described in his diary his own torment. "At times, he [Kondratyev] complained and wept," he noted on 21 August 1887. "Painful, terrible hours! Oh, never will I forget all that I have suffered here." Two days later, he wrote, "All today has felt like a nightmare. Violent egoism has tormented me. My one thought: to leave!!! No more patience. . . . Lord! will the time ever come when I shall no longer suffer such torments?"[5]

Tchaikovsky confessed to Mrs. von Meck soon after his departure from Aachen that this had been "one of the darkest periods" of his life. "I have aged much and grown thin during this time," he told her. "I feel a sort of weariness with life, a sort of sad apathy, the feeling that I myself must die soon, and because of this nearness everything that I had held to be important and essential in my life now appears to me trivial, insignificant, and utterly pointless."[6] Tchaikovsky's attitude toward Kondratyev during the course of their long acquaintance was never stable and often depended on his own mood or on outward circumstances. Perhaps the clearest formulation of this ambivalence is found in a diary entry of 11 July 1886: "What an enigma this man is. A kind person, but at the same time he takes pleasure *in vexing* others."[7] After his friend's death, however, the positive emotions triumphed and words of praise become frequent in his letters.

Even before the Tiflis programmatic outline Tchaikovsky had made some rough sketches of the future symphony. These jottings date from August 1887 when Tchaikovsky was still in Aachen.[8] Yet, several months were needed for the shattering experience in Aachen to be absorbed and expressed in music. Tchaikovsky began the symphony in earnest in the middle of May 1888. He thought constantly of Kondratyev. Of a visit to the park at Maidanovo, he wrote that "everything there seemed to me somehow melancholy and sad, and nowhere else have I experienced so vividly the grief of N[ikolay] D[mitrievich] Kondratyev's departure from this world as there, especially along his little path. In Maidanovo, in general I painfully regretted the past, and it was awful to realize the precipitateness and irreversibility of the past."[9] The themes of fate and death, of unalterably triumphing forces, and of man's desperately proud resistance to them constitute, for the composer, the work's principal motifs.

Through most of the summer Tchaikovsky worked on his sym-

phony. It was slow going, and Tchaikovsky grew depressed, repeatedly
took chill, and felt generally unwell. He even found himself suffering
from loneliness and longing for company and diversion. But he was not
totally forsaken. Sasha Legoshin visited Frolovskoe, having by this
time followed Alyosha's example and gotten married, but also having
lost his job because of Kondratyev's death. Tchaikovsky allowed him
to stay on for a while at Frolovskoe and to bring his wife and infant
daughter there. At the same time, Tchaikovsky felt obliged to do what
he could for another of Kondratyev's former servants, young Vasily Fi-
latov, and asked both Jurgenson and Anatoly to hire him. Both refused,
in part because the young man would be eligible for military service
in another year.

Living with Alyosha and his wife began to have its disadvantages.
More than once Tchaikovsky traveled to Moscow or St. Petersburg for
no other reason than that Alyosha and Fyokla had to visit their own
village on some matter, and in their absence he was unable to take care
of either the house or himself. Thus, in early July he found himself in
the capital. He had little money, and there was much work still to be
done on the symphony, but Alyosha had needed to visit relatives for a
church holiday. The stay, however, turned out to be pleasant. The first
day Tchaikovsky had called on Kondratyev's nephew (and Meshchersky's lover) Dmitry Zasyadko, but finding him not in, he spent the day
"sauntering about alone," as he wrote Modest, then in the Caucasus,
on 7 July: "I have already wandered quite a bit along Nevsky. I had lots
of encounters; I'll tell you about them in person. In certain respects,
Petersburg is indeed a curious city."[10] A few days later, he reported to
his brother from Frolovskoe that he had spent "a most pleasant time"
in St. Petersburg. "Zasyadko and I saw each other continually, caroused
a fair amount, and traveled here together."[11]

At the beginning of August his old friend Hermann Laroche, still
beset by financial troubles, again took refuge with Tchaikovsky, this
time accompanied by his wife. Kolya Konradi stopped briefly in Frolovskoe on his way back to St. Petersburg from the Caucasus, followed
a few days later by Modest. In Tiflis they had met Tchaikovsky's young
favorite Prince Vladimir Argutinsky-Dolgorukov, and Kolya brought
from the boy a drawing done expressly for Tchaikovsky. Writing to
thank him, Tchaikovsky noted the great impression he had made on
Kolya Konradi, who spoke of him incessantly, and avowed that he himself therefore loved him now "twice as much."[12]

The scoring of the Fifth Symphony was completed by the middle
of August. Already Tchaikovsky was at work on his *Hamlet* Overture,
op. 67, but he interrupted his work in late August to visit Kamenka,

where he had not been in a long while. Before his departure he wrote a letter to Mrs. von Meck in which, bewailing his own "incomprehensible wastefulness and childish inability to manage affairs," he had to ask for another advance on his subsidy, that is, the remaining two-thirds of the allowance for the following year, or four thousand rubles (since he had already requested and received an advance of the first third for 1889 some time before).[13] The money was waiting for him on his arrival from Kamenka to Moscow at the beginning of September. On 3 September he was back in Frolovskoe.

A few weeks later, word arrived of what was, for Tchaikovsky at least, a quite unexpected change in the status of Wladyslaw Pachulski within the von Meck family. "My circumstances are in general disarray," wrote Mrs. von Meck on 22 September. Her daughter Yuliya had announced her intention to marry Pachulski, with whom she had been carrying on an affair for the past seven years. "I had hoped that this cup might not touch my lips in my lifetime," confided Mrs. von Meck, "but it has turned out otherwise, and this, then, is one of the main causes of my nervous disorder." She viewed the coming marriage as "a great grief," though not, as she hastened to add, because she had anything against Pachulski, but rather because of "the enormous and irreplaceable loss" that she now faced. "I am losing my daughter, who is *essential* to me and without whom my existence is impossible," she explained. "Of course, she desires and begs me to let her stay with me, but it will not be the same, not the same at all—and she herself will perhaps find it too difficult to have two persons in her care."[14]

Mrs. von Meck's letter leaves a number of things unclear. Certainly, it is difficult to correlate her claim that this affair had lasted for seven years with her usual moral strictness. It was, after all, on moral grounds that she dismissed Kotek, an earlier favorite. The explanation may lie in the degree of influence that Yuliya and, at a later stage, Pachulski had upon her. Yuliya had always been Mrs. von Meck's favorite daughter and, what is more important, her only confidante within the family. It is possible that for a time she had even reconciled herself to the thought that her fate was indeed to remain forever an old maid at her mother's side. Pachulski, meanwhile, had also managed in time to make himself indispensable in Mrs. von Meck's eyes. In her letter to Tchaikovsky, Mrs. von Meck mentioned that the affair had endured "various peripeteias," and it is conceivable that chief among these was Mrs. von Meck's own resistance to the match. But whatever compromises the three had made over the years, they clearly could not continue indefinitely. Quite possibly, the couple finally gave her an ultimatum, appealing to the young man's state of health.

Tchaikovsky, faced with the accomplished fact, responded affectionately to his friend's news. "Your daughter Yuliya Karlovna is marrying a man who has lived near you continually now for more than ten years, they will both remain with you, and nevertheless you grieve and give way almost to despair," he wrote on 24 September. "The fact is that both these people, so needed and familiar, once they are joined in matrimony, will become different; your attitude toward them will acquire a different meaning. The light, the circumstances are different, and this is enough for you, who have lived so long in a confined domestic situation, to feel pain and dread."[15]

Having won Yuliya von Meck, who at thirty-five was admittedly somewhat past her prime, Pachulski must have felt a sense of genuine triumph: condescendingly tolerated by his social superiors, he had broken into the ranks of a family of millionaires. Still, he never abandoned his dream of composing music, as various remarks from Tchaikovsky's letters to Mrs. von Meck bear witness. "If Wlad[yslaw] Alb[ertovich] would like to send me anything of his to look over, I should be very glad," he wrote on 27 March 1890,[16] while on 30 June 1890 he promised that "in a day or so I shall write a detailed letter to Wlad[yslaw] Alb[ertovich] about his scores."[17] These were now clearly intended as gestures of benevolence toward his friend's new son-in-law, and so toward Mrs. von Meck herself. For their part, the newlyweds, it would seem, returned the gesture. Mrs. von Meck regularly conveyed their greetings and salutations: "Yulya and Wlad[ylsaw] Alb[ertovich] send you their deepest regards. Wlad[yslaw] Alb[ertovich] is delighted with his correspondence with you."[18] To what extent all these well-wishing gestures were sincere is, of course, debatable. If Pachulski was indeed the opportunistic sycophant he appears to have been, he must have gained no little satisfaction from this boost in family and social status and the new relation in which he now stood to the composer, who had earlier treated him, courteously but unmistakably, as a near nonentity and had never seen in him anything more than Mrs. von Meck's factotum. His feelings for Yuliya aside, Pachulski, as a full-fledged member of the von Meck clan, was now undeniably in an excellent position to wreak some small revenge for the slights he had suffered over the years by perhaps stirring in the hearts of Mrs. von Meck's family some resentment toward her "beloved friend."

In late September, Tchaikovsky's old conservatory friend Nikolay Hubert died, bringing Tchaikovsky to Moscow for several days to attend his funeral. Through the month of October he was busy correcting proofs of the Fifth Symphony and scoring his *Hamlet* Overture. The symphony was first performed, with Tchaikovsky conducting, in a concert of his own works at the St. Petersburg Philharmonic Society on 5 November. The *Musical Review* wrote that the concert was accompanied by loud ovations from audience and orchestra alike, and the composer was elected an honorary member of the society. Some critics, however, remained dissatisfied. The melodious polyphony of the symphony's finale was perceived as showing a certain incompleteness, and it was undoubtedly the unusual ending that led to widely disparate opinions in the attempt to assess the symphony's design and content. Immediate critical response was for the most part sharply unfavorable. Tchaikovsky's old opponent César Cui found the work to be unoriginal and to show a lack of ideals and a predominance of "sound" over "music." Many were outraged by the replacement of the usual scherzo with a waltz, one reviewer even mockingly calling it, with reference also to the waltz episodes in the first and second movements, "the symphony with three waltzes." Tchaikovsky, as he so often did, came eventually to agree with these negative comments about his latest symphony, telling Mrs. von Meck that "there is something repulsive in it, a kind of excessive diversity of color and insincere artificiality. And the public recognizes it instinctively."[19]

On 13 November, Tchaikovsky traveled to Prague, in the company of his young pianist friend Vasily Sapelnikov, to attend the premiere there of *Eugene Onegin* and to conduct a concert of the Fifth Symphony and the Piano Concerto no. 2 in G Major, op. 44, written in 1879. Both events were tremendous successes, but all was soon clouded for Tchaikovsky by the news, received in Vienna on the way home, of his niece Vera's death from tuberculosis in Nice and of the suicide in Tiflis of his acquaintance Svinkin. Back in St. Petersburg in mid-December, Tchaikovsky conducted his fantasy *The Tempest* at the Fourth Russian Symphonic Concert, and celebrated Christmas with his relatives. The next day, he returned to Frolovskoe where he plunged at once into a new ballet, *The Sleeping Beauty*, op. 66.

When Ivan Vsevolozhsky, the director of the imperial theaters in St. Petersburg, first proposed a ballet based on Charles Perrault's *La Belle au bois dormant* in May 1888, the idea quickly took hold of Tchaikovsky. By autumn he had received from the choreographer Marius Petipa an intricately detailed scenario, with precise suggestions for the dances and even the music. It was Tchaikovsky's first collaboration with the brilliant Frenchman who reigned supreme as ballet master at St. Petersburg's renowned Mariinsky Theater, where he was in the process of all but single-handedly bringing classical dance in Russia to an unrivaled zenith. The fairy-tale subject and Petipa's meticulous plot combined to stir Tchaikovsky's creativity. The furious surge of composition helped to throw off the gloom that had followed in the wake of the recent deaths of Hubert, Vera, and Svinkin, and so engrossed did Tchaikovsky become in the ballet that, as he wrote Modest on 9 January 1889, "there is no time left for letters."[20]

He did, nevertheless, interrupt his work to visit Moscow for a day to meet with his old friend Ivan Klimenko, and on 19 January he traveled again to St. Petersburg, where he spent four days. While in the capital, he saw several friends, but most of all, he wished to see Bob, who had gone to Moscow to visit his sister Anna for the New Year holiday but was due back in the capital by this time. On 23 January, Tchaikovsky noted in his diary, with no trace of his disappointment of the previous spring, "Tea with Bob (who is a hundredfold divine)."[21]

From St. Petersburg, Tchaikovsky left on his second foreign concert tour, which this time was to include Cologne, Frankfurt, Dresden, Berlin, Leipzig, Geneva, Hamburg, Paris, and London, and would last until mid-April. At the start, as always when alone abroad, Tchaikovsky experienced bouts of homesickness. "All last night," he complained in a letter to Modest from Cologne on 30 January/11 February, "I dreamed of Bob, under most poetic circumstances, and today I've been thinking about him without stop."[22] To Bob himself he wrote nostalgically on 20 February/4 March from Geneva, where he had visited the Davydov family in the winter of 1875:

> I recalled so vividly Tanya and Vera with hands red from running to school in the cold and all of you, and yourself with your small little nose and not that tower that you now have instead of a nose, and myself not so gray, a full thirteen years younger!!! I grew terribly sad! However, do not think that it is your *tower* that makes me sad . . . —no, but in general
>
> > Nessun dolor maggiore [sic]
> > Che ricordarsi del tempo felice
> > Nella miseria!
> >   (Dante, L'Inferno, V)
>
> [Francesca da Rimini's lament: No greater grief than to remember happy times in the midst of misery.] Although my tour, on the one hand, is by no means *miseria,* since I have had great success everywhere, . . . still I feel such longing and homesickness that there are no words to express it. Especially terrible is that I am never alone here. Forever visiting, and forever receiving visitors. And how much longer still I will have to put up with this![23]

In Hamburg, Tchaikovsky conducted a performance of his Fifth Symphony. To his surprise, Johannes Brahms remained in Hamburg an extra day to hear the symphony in rehearsal. Afterward, the two composers had lunch together and "got quite drunk." In a letter to Modest of 28 February/12 March, Tchaikovsky wrote that he found Brahms "very charming and I like his straightforwardness and simplicity."[24] Yet, while he admired and respected the man himself, Brahms's music remained alien to Tchaikovsky. He felt that it was "not warmed by genuine emotion," that it lacked "poetry" but had "great pretensions to profundity." Brahms "never expresses anything," Tchaikovsky once wrote, "or, when he does, he fails to express it fully. His music is made up of fragments of some indefinable *something* skillfully welded together."[25]

Tchaikovsky spent three weeks in Paris, mainly to relax and to wait for Sapelnikov, who had promised to join him for the London engagement. Again he enjoyed the company of Brandukov, who now made his permanent home in Paris, and he spent long hours wandering about the streets and boulevards of the city, lingering about familiar cafés. On 22 March/3 April he noted in his diary, "In the Café with [the following is cut] and in [Café de la] Paix [another cut]. Back home alone. A Negro. They came to my place."[26] In another curious entry a few days later he wrote, "Together with Brand[ukov] in the Café de Paris. *They* pay no attention."[27] The word "they" written in italics very likely signified the homosexuals who gathered at this café. With Sapelnikov's arrival the twosome became a threesome, breakfasting, dining, and supping together regularly.

In the midst of this Parisian idyll Tchaikovsky quite unexpectedly received a letter from Antonina. Since 1886, Tchaikovsky had been paying her, through Jurgenson, a pension of fifty rubles a month, doubled at her request to one hundred rubles a month the previous year. Now she was asking for it to be doubled again. Tchaikovsky was almost of a mind to grant her request, if only to be rid of her, but he worried that in another year she would be back demanding four hundred. "A woman so stupid, so worthless, capable of giving up several children to the foundling hospital and not worrying about them in the least, does not deserve the slightest compassion," he wrote to Jurgenson on 21 March/2 April, "and I cannot believe that she is in need, since one can live quite decently on a hundred rubles. But, on the other hand, the more conscious I am of making her happy, the better it is for me and the easier I feel. Indeed, there are months when I pity this foolish woman. Is it her fault that she is silly, pathetic, lacking in any pride, any decency?"[28]

Still wavering, but inclined to grant the request "by way of en-

couragement," Tchaikovsky asked Jurgenson to have a talk with Antonina. Yet, when he received several days later Jurgenson's account of
his interview with Antonina, Tchaikovsky, while authorizing his publisher at his own discretion to supply her with money for medical
treatment, decided to refuse any increase in her monthly pension.

"It is impossible to persuade her of anything," he wrote, indulging
once more in a castigation of her character, "for once she has taken
some foolishness into her head, she accepts it as fact and refuses to
hear differently. . . . With her, one cannot discuss but only pontificate.
However, I do not grudge giving her more money than she deserves,
and I leave it to you, should she ask for any emergency funds, to give
her as much as you see fit."²⁹ But, "on second thought," Tchaikovsky
soon changed his mind and later that same day wrote Jurgenson instructing him to raise Antonina's pension to one hundred and fifty rubles a month, explaining his decision thus: "The fact is that in the first
place, Ant[onina] Iv[anovna]'s letters literally make me ill, so unpleasant to me is any reminder of that person, and in the second, owing to
my weakness of character, I will always grant her request in the end.
So it has turned out in this case. . . . Open all her letters, read them,
decide for yourself and tell me nothing about her until I myself ask
you to give me news of her."³⁰

Tchaikovsky arrived in London on 28 March/9 April. His concert
was held two days later in St. James's Hall, the program including the
First Suite and, with Sapelnikov at the piano, the First Piano Concerto.
The success was considerable for both the composer and his young
pianist. But the fog and damp weather of the British capital depressed
Tchaikovsky. Leaving London on 31 March/12 April, he longed to see
Florence again, but he had already promised Anatoly, recently promoted to the position of deputy governor of the district, to visit him
in Tiflis, and so he headed for the Caucasus, deciding to make the journey by sea by way of Marseilles, Constantinople, and Batum. Before
his departure he "kissed Vasya [Sapelnikov] as he slept."³¹

On board ship Tchaikovsky made a chance acquaintance that was
to leave a deep trace in his memory. He wrote of it to Modest on 8/20
April from Constantinople: "Two Russians traveled with me: a fourteen-year-old boy, Sklifosovsky (son of the surgeon [Nikolay Sklifosov-
sky]), and his companion Germanovich, a student at Mosc[ow] University. Both are charming types, with whom I became great friends."³²
Volodya Sklifosovsky, whose well-known father's name is still borne
by a hospital in Moscow, was phenomenally charismatic and gifted.³³
He was also terminally ill. "An attractive youth Sklifosovsky and a
student," jotted Tchaikovsky in his diary on 1/13 April, and during the

next week the three were inseparable. At each port of call they all went ashore together, and back on the ship Tchaikovsky delighted in "Volodya's chatter in the quiet of the night." On 8 April he wrote, "Champagne. Saying good-bye to my dear friends." The next day, he felt "both well and somewhat sad," and added, "It's a pity to hear no more Volodya's chatter, his merry laughter."[34]

However laconic the entries, the experience was sufficient to give rise to a short-lived but tender friendship that Tchaikovsky never forgot. The boy passed away less than a year later, on 25 January 1890. Modest, writing of his brother's parting with Sklifosovsky in Constantinople, remarks that Tchaikovsky seemed to have a presentiment that he was not fated to meet the boy again. "Pyotr Ilyich, after bidding him farewell, returned to the ship and there wept for a long while. Learning of his death, he grieved as for a relative."[35] Later, in 1893, Tchaikovsky dedicated his "Elegiac Song," one of the Eighteen Pieces, op. 72, for piano, to the memory of young Sklifosovsky, met by chance on that ship four years before.

In Tiflis, where he arrived on 12 April, Tchaikovsky had little opportunity to work on his ballet. With his arrival, Anatoly's home was thronged with visitors and invitations streamed in daily from all sides. A comfort amid all the turmoil was seeing again his adolescent friend "darling Volodya Argutinsky," who, as he told Modest on 26 April, "visits me often. Yesterday he presented me with a bouquet (!) and a drawing."[36] The boy's name is mentioned several times in Tchaikovsky's diary during his stay. As on previous occasions, he also saw much of Lev Davydov's rather frivolous nephew Nikolay Peresleni, mostly over drinks.

Several letters awaited or arrived for Tchaikovsky in Tiflis. Modest was in a terrible state because the Ministry of Education had refused to grant permission for Kolya Konradi, despite his handicaps, to take an external examination for his high school diploma. Alyosha wrote that he had been very upset and had even wept when he found out that Tchaikovsky planned to visit Anatoly instead of coming home directly and that everything there had been made ready for his return. Mrs. von Meck reported that Yuliya had finally married Pachulski in Paris on 16 April. And from Ivan Vsevolozhsky, meanwhile, came word that the premiere of *The Sleeping Beauty* had been set for December: Tchaikovsky would have to hurry if the ballet was to be completed in time. The composer was in Moscow by 7 May, but traveled to St. Petersburg a week later to meet briefly with Vsevolozhsky and Marius Petipa to discuss the impending production. He also managed in the few days he spent in the capital to see Modest and Kolya in their new apartment on the Fontanka River, to visit the Kondratyev family and his cousin Anna Merkling, and even, while dining out, to run across his old friend Shilovsky, who quite predictably made a drunken public scene.

Tchaikovsky spent all summer at home in Frolovskoe. He was soon absorbed again in *The Sleeping Beauty,* completing the composition in late May and setting to work at once on the orchestration. Despite the quiet at Frolovskoe, there were distractions. He had scarcely returned home than he found himself besieged by a nervous youth named Lukyan Kalganov, brother of the nursemaid to Anatoly's daughter, who begged Tchaikovsky "with tears in his eyes" to help him find employment. Moved by the request, Tchaikovsky briefly considered giving the boy some money, but on reflection he decided that "money received for nothing only corrupts a man"—a revealing conclusion, given his own financial relations with Mrs. von Meck. Instead, he furnished the boy with a letter of recommendation to relatives of Praskovya in Moscow and let him stay with him for a few days.[37]

There were other visitors as well that summer, some unexpected and inopportune, others more welcome. Modest stayed for several days, which the two brothers spent in long walks and conversations, playing Anton Rubinstein's Fifth Symphony in a four-hand version, and discussing Modest's latest play. A visit by Bob was made even more pleasant by a new show of musical abilities in the favorite nephew. Seeing him off, his uncle, as he noted jokingly in his diary, "stood with a white flag as the train pulled past."[38] Also, Sasha Legoshin arrived from Moscow bringing with him, to Tchaikovsky's delight, his little daughter Klerochka, whom he left for a time with Alyosha and Fyokla.

Tchaikovsky had gradually grown used to the idea that his servant had married. Though her health was weak, Fyokla had become their laundress. Periodically, however, mutual misunderstandings, quarrels, and even accusations erupted between master and servant. As a rule, Tchaikovsky, indignant at first, would soon be the one to yield. But several diary entries testify to his fits of irritation. One from earlier in the year, apparently concerning a missing sum of money and an obscure suspicion on Tchaikovsky's part, was written in English, evidentally so as to forestall his servant's snooping in his master's journal: "I am not satisfayed [*sic*] with my domestic. I think he is not very honest (900)!!!"[39] Another entry was in a macaronic mixture of four languages, comical in itself: *"Posle uzhina une querelle avec der Diener* [After supper a quarrel with the servant]. He is not delicat [*sic*]."[40] Occasionally Alyosha got drunk and made problems with the locals. But while their daily life had its definite downs as well as its ups, the attachment between Tchaikovsky and his servant endured.

The scoring of *The Sleeping Beauty* was completed by 16 August.

Tchaikovsky then left immediately for two weeks' rest in Kamenka, where Bob was spending the last days of his summer vacation. "Living with Bob," he wrote Modest on 31 August, "brought me indescribable pleasure. Alas! It has lasted too short a time. Seeing how Bob's significance in my life continues to grow, I have finally decided to take up residence in Petersburg beginning next year. To see him, to hear him, and to feel him near to me will soon, it seems, become the paramount condition for my well-being."[41] As it turned out, Tchaikovsky never did resettle in St. Petersburg. To do so, given the social life of the capital and his enormous number of acquaintances there, would have meant abandoning his creative work altogether. It is nonetheless telling that he even considered it.

From the middle of September straight through to early January of the following year, Tchaikovsky's life was saturated with musical activities. In Moscow on 18 September, *Eugene Onegin* was revived at the Bolshoy Theater with Tchaikovsky conducting, while in St. Petersburg rehearsals for *The Sleeping Beauty* were already getting under way. For October a series of symphonic concerts had been scheduled in connection with Anton Rubinstein's fifty years of artistic activity, at which Tchaikovsky had agreed to conduct. In addition, there were plans for another foreign tour. At the beginning of October, Tchaikovsky even moved temporarily from Frolovskoe to Moscow, renting there for convenience' sake a small apartment.

Later that month, in one of his regular letters from Grand Duke Konstantin, Tchaikovsky received a poem that the grand duke had dedicated to him, "O people, you often wounded me so painfully." Reading it, Tchaikovsky felt a feeling "of proud consciousness that a splendid poem . . . had been created in part as a result of my letters of last year."[42] The correspondence between Tchaikovsky and the grand duke had, as Tchaikovsky confided to Mrs. von Meck at one point, grown "very lively." It was distinguished not only by a genuine amicability but also by an intellectual level rarely matched in Tchaikovsky's letters, apart from those written to select musical colleagues and to Mrs. von Meck. His letters to the grand duke contain numerous comments on his own work and the creative process and, in the several letters addressed to K.R. the poet, interesting opinions about versification, verse forms, and poetic genres. Tchaikovsky's name appears frequently in the personal diary that Konstantin kept regularly from the age of nine. Though the diary, preserved in Soviet archives, has unfortunately never been published, a Soviet commentator remarks that the grand duke's notes are primarily of a private and intimate nature and include aspects "which it is customary not to mention."[43]

In late 1887, Tchaikovsky wrote his Six Songs, op. 63, to verses by the grand duke. Konstantin often sent his poems to Tchaikovsky for his opinion of them. Of one such poem, entitled "St. Sebastian," Tchaikovsky wrote to Mrs. von Meck that he had "praised it on the whole, but frankly criticized certain particulars."[44] The homoerotic aura of the pictorial image of St. Sebastian is beyond doubt, and it is curious to note Tchaikovsky's "criticisms" of his august friend's poem, reflecting as they do a very particular bent of Tchaikovsky's mind. "I must confess," he had told the grand duke, "that at a first reading my full artistic enjoyment was somewhat hampered by the fact that the very vivid image of your Sebastian could not coincide at all in my imagination with the Sebastian of Guido Reni. In this wonderful painting he is depicted as very young; when one reads in your poem about 'years that had flown by like an arrow,' about 'the victorious laurels of a chief,' etc., one imagines a young but mature man, whereas memory presents an image, long ago stamped upon it, of a youth or even an adolescent, as the Italian painter presented him."[45]

In his letter of October 1889, Konstantin wrote also that the tsar continued to take an interest in his work and had in fact recently asked Konstantin whether he could play any new works by the composer. "The news that His Majesty has deigned to inquire about me pleases me deeply!!!" responded Tchaikovsky with enthusiasm on 29 October. "How to interpret His Majesty's question about small *pièces?* If it is an indirect encouragement for me to compose such pieces, then I shall devote myself to them at the first opportunity." But he had in mind also a far more ambitious project, worthy of an increasingly loyal subject. "I should like terribly to write some grandiose symphony, which would be, as it were, the crowning of my entire creative career, and to dedicate it to His Majesty," he told the grand duke. "A vague plan for such a symphony has been floating around in my head for a long time, but a confluence of many favorable circumstances is needed for my design to be carried out. I hope not to die without having fulfilled this intention."[46]

During the jubilee celebrations for Anton Rubinstein that autumn, in a minor episode that was nonetheless indicative of the tsar's attitude toward Tchaikovsky, the Grand Duchess Aleksandra Iosifovna, Konstantin's mother, made an attempt to intercede with the tsar on Rubinstein's behalf. In a note delivered through her son, she argued that the pension of three thousand rubles a year granted to Rubinstein was clearly insufficient, since Tchaikovsky, his pupil, was receiving the same. The tsar, according to the Deputy Foreign Minister Vladimir Lambsdorf, who recorded the incident in his diary, responded angrily, "First, Tchaikovsky is not Rubinstein's pupil; second, I consider him superior to Rubinstein; and third, I do not wish to add anything to the established pension." And with that, noted Lambsdorf, Alexander "tore the paper to shreds."[47]

Tchaikovsky conducted two Rubinstein programs for the maestro's jubilee, one of which, a performance of Rubinstein's 1870 oratorio *The Tower of Babel* with seven hundred singers, he described to Mrs. von Meck as a "martyrdom."[48] The whirl of concerts and rehearsals of the last weeks of 1889 left Tchaikovsky in a state of physical and emotional collapse, and he had little time or energy to worry deeply about news of further financial difficulties confronting the von Meck family that autumn. The minister of public transportation had lately begun to put pressure on all private railroads in Russia, in consequence of which Mrs. von Meck, whose wealth lay chiefly in shares of the Ryazan Railroad, stood in fear of losing her revenues and thus her fortune. "For me this is the more terrible in that my children are being deprived of their livelihood," she wrote in November, "and I cannot come to their aid, since I lose mine as well, while at my age and with my health it is too painful to suffer privations. And it is this expectation, this situation, which depresses me to the point of exhaustion and despair."[49]

Tchaikovsky's response, though sympathetic, seemed almost perfunctorily optimistic. "I understand how difficult it will be for you if your means should diminish," he told his friend. "You need wealth, and you are virtually the only wealthy person I know who deserves it, to whom it is essential, for whom fate would be too unjust were it to take it away from you. I shall console myself with the hope that your affairs are not so hopeless as they appear to you at this moment."[50] Notable in his letter is the absence of any suggestion that she cease her subsidy to him for the time being, though he had been quick to make this gesture before. Of course, Mrs. von Meck had already advanced Tchaikovsky, at his request, the budget sum through July 1890, so that to make such a gesture now would make little sense, while to offer to return the money would have looked ridiculous. Moreover, all previous experience must have shown Tchaikovsky that any such offer on his part would be unfailingly and even indignantly rejected by Mrs. von Meck. Whatever his reasons, Tchaikovsky's optimism proved justified: the von Mecks coped with this financial storm as they had with others in the past. But victory took a serious toll on Mrs. von Meck's already poor health, and for a long while Tchaikovsky would receive news of her only through Pachulski. Their personal correspondence did not resume until late March of the following year.

During rehearsals for *The Sleeping Beauty*, which had at first been scheduled for mid-December but then had been postponed until early January, Tchaikovsky and Ivan Vsevolozhsky began discussing prospects for staging a new opera by the composer in St. Petersburg for the coming season. Tchaikovsky, however, had no new project for an opera in mind, until the possibility arose of setting to music an unused libretto that Modest had written for the composer and conductor Nikolay Klenovsky based on Pushkin's *The Queen of Spades*. Klenovsky had recently abandoned the work, and soon Tchaikovsky was aflame with enthusiasm for this haunting tale of the sinister countess and the young officer whose gambling fever brings about his tragic downfall. Before a note was written, the major roles were assigned, and Tchaikovsky was confronted with the difficult but exciting task of plunging immediately and entirely into his new work. After some consideration, he resolved to cancel all conducting engagements for the winter and spring and to go abroad, preferably to Italy, in order to find the necessary creative solitude.

His departure was precipitated by another abrupt and highly unpleasant reemergence of Antonina. Insulted by Jurgenson's refusal to provide her with a ticket to a concert by Rubinstein in early January, she wrote her husband a long letter, dated 15 December, in which, not content merely to rail against the publisher, she dredged up yet again the whole story of their ill-fated marriage, accusing Tchaikovsky of various intrigues and even alluding obliquely to his sexual orientation. Tchaikovsky was enraged, though in a letter to Mrs. von Meck of 26 December he tried still to exercise some restraint. "I have had a great unpleasantness," he wrote, "and the perpetrator of this unpleasantness was the lady whom I used to call in my letters to you 'the certain individual.' I shall not elaborate on this, for it is all too disgusting. To leave as soon as possible, to go anywhere! To see no one, to know nothing, to work, work, work. . . . This is what my soul thirsts for."[51] Once again, Tchaikovsky's first reaction to the critical situation was to escape abroad, repeating the pattern that eventually resolved the crisis of 1877.

Writing to his publisher, Tchaikovsky was far less restrained, even savage: "I have decided against seeing A[ntonina] I[vanovna]. I swear I have not the strength. I fear that she may say something to make me lose my temper, and in the heat of the hatred that her letter has fanned anew—I should strangle her. Truly it is possible. She is far too repulsive to me. Please read the letter I am sending her, and if you have nothing against it, then send it together with a ticket to Rubinstein's concert. . . . I enclose for this *three rubles*."[52]

It was not, of course, the petty matter of a three-ruble ticket that had driven Tchaikovsky to the verge of abandoning all self-control but Antonina's implicit reference to his homosexuality. To underscore her own magnanimity, she mentioned in her letter her family's connections, more than ten years before, with the police department. Her mother, she wrote, was a close friend of the sister of Nikolay Mezentsov, the Moscow chief of police killed by terrorists in 1878. "He knew about you and suggested frankly that I should write an official complaint that would have empowered him to act against you. . . . If I so wished, even now I could do you harm. But that will never happen."[53] She did not add that to do so would have run distinctly counter to her own interests. In any event, it is doubtful whether Antonina truly comprehended the obstacles facing an accusation of homosexuality. Indeed, for Russian jurists of the late nineteenth century the procedural difficulties, often insurmountable, in establishing the fact, nature, and scope of the crime of sodomy, or *muzhelozhstvo*, served as one of the principal arguments in favor of repealing antihomosexual legislation. One disapproving contemporary of Tchaikovsky noted, "The shameful vice was indulged in by many well-known men in Petersburg: actors, writers, musicians, grand dukes. Their names were on everyone's lips, many made a show of their way of life. The scandals accompanying the discovery of this person or that in adventures of this sort continued without interruption, but as a rule the filthy affairs never made it to court."[54] Tchaikovsky had little to worry about. Even scandal was not a serious possibility, given his position and Antonina's own excesses. He needed only time to calm down after her wild letter.

The end of December found Tchaikovsky back in St. Petersburg, where he celebrated the New Year with Modest. Two days later, on 2 January 1890, the final dress rehearsal of *The Sleeping Beauty* was held in the presence of the tsar. The production was lavishly staged, boasting elaborate sets and magnificent costumes, the finest dancers, and, of course, Tchaikovsky's brilliant and exquisite melodies. The only disappointment was the reaction of the tsar, who remarked merely that it was "very nice." Having expected somewhat more, Tchaikovsky noted in his diary, "His Majesty treated me very condescendingly. So be it!"[55] But the ballet's premiere the following day was an unprecedented success, and was recognized as such by all the St. Petersburg papers. The composer himself unhesitatingly ranked *The Sleeping Beauty* among his best works, seeing the ballet as a sort of "dancing symphony" centered on the combat of Fate with the forces of Life.

Exhausted by the whirl of the past several weeks and concerned with his new opera commission, Tchaikovsky returned the next day to Moscow to prepare for his trip abroad. He left Russia a week later, passing through Berlin, and arrived on 18 January in Florence—chosen, very likely, because of memories of his happy and fruitful stay there in the winter of 1878 when he was completing his First Suite and beginning *The Maid of Orléans*. But this time he was indifferent to the city's countless beauties. He stayed at the Hotel Washington, where he had at his disposal four small rooms, an entire floor of the narrow building. From his windows overlooking the Arno River he would listen to the singing of a young street singer named Ferdinando, performing below. Tchaikovsky's working schedule in Florence differed little from his routine at home: he rose around eight, worked in two shifts separated by lunch and a stroll, had dinner at seven, and then relaxed by reading, going to the theater, writing letters, or, as sometimes happened, simply feeling bored. "Sometimes I compose very easily," he wrote Modest on 6/18 February, "sometimes not without effort. But it doesn't matter. The effort is perhaps the result of wanting to write as well as possible and not being satisfied with the first thought that comes."[56]

Alyosha was not with his master. His wife, Fyokla, had tuberculosis and was even now but weeks from death. News of her death would reach Tchaikovsky in Florence in late February, upsetting him deeply for many days. Accompanying and looking after Tchaikovsky in Alyosha's place, and certainly more than willing to follow the temporary master abroad, was Modest's young servant Nazar Litrov. Tchaikovsky seems to have been pleased with the boy. Together they strolled about the city, and when Nazar at one point badly injured his foot and could not walk, Tchaikovsky nursed him. His diary records few instances of annoyance with his brother's servant, though in one amusing entry from 3 February he wrote, in French: "Je crois que Nazar qui est un excellent garçon—est très curieux et qu'il s'amuse à déchiffrer ce que son maître provisoire écrit sur ces feuilles. Dorénavant j'écrirai an français. [I believe that Nazar, who is an excellent boy, is very curious and that he enjoys deciphering what his temporary master writes in these pages. From now on I'll write in French.]"[57] This intention to write henceforth in French was, however, not maintained.

While abroad, Nazar, no doubt following the master's example, began himself to keep a diary. It is unfortunate that this diary has not yet been published in full. Written by a semiliterate but very observant young man, the portions that are available provide an uncanny reflection of the atmosphere in which *The Queen of Spades* was created, as in the entry for 29 January/10 February:

> P[yotr] I[lyich] is in a good mood today. Yesterday he started a new scene, and as I see, it goes well. . . . Every time before the end of his work, I go into the room and say that it is time for

dinner or for supper. I do not know, maybe I disturb him thereby, but he seems to show no displeasure. If I had noticed, of course I would not go in. . . . P[yotr] I[lyich] maybe thinks I come in out of boredom, that I see he has free time, and he pretends to be affectionate and good-natured. But no, so far I have not felt bored at all. I go in to give him a break, and if I did not do this, then, maybe, he would even think that I was upset with him, but anyway, for now everything is fine, and thank God. At seven o'clock I went in. P[yotr] I[lyich] had not finished yet. I said, "Time to finish." He answered, but continues to make his little notations. "Yes," I say, "it's almost seven." "Just a minute," he says, and made one more notation, struck the piano keyboard with his hand. I stand there. He took out his watch, opens it. "It is still twenty to, I can work ten minutes yet." I said something. And he: "But only ten minutes." I left. Ten minutes later he comes up to me. "Well, I finished"—and he started to inquire what I was doing (I was writing; as soon as he came in, I closed the notebook), and went to his room. P[yotr] I[lyich] began walking to and fro about the room, while I stand at the table. We talked of Feklusha [Fyokla], Aleksey, etc. For the first time I heard P[yotr] I[lyich] speak flatteringly about his future work. "This opera, God willing, will turn out so well that you will burst into tears, Nazar." I said, "God grant that it go well," and to myself I thought, "and God grant you good health."[58]

Tchaikovsky's "good mood" was short-lived. The next day, 30 January/11 February, he received a letter from Jurgenson informing him that the indefatigable Antonina had now written an eight-page letter to Anton Rubinstein, asking him to grant her a position at the St. Petersburg Conservatory, as he had to the widow of Nikolay Hubert. The news at once plunged Tchaikovsky into depression. All day after reading Jurgenson's letter he raged "like a madman," unable to work, to read, even to eat. "For God's sake, never write to me about Ant[onina] Iv[anovna] without exceptional need," he begged his publisher. "Any news about her, about some new trick of hers of no benefit to anyone at all, irritates and kills me!" He confessed that there was "a certain morbid exaggeration" in his reaction. "So what if the madwoman has done another crazy thing? But here the abnormal, hysterical part of my nature plays a role. Something must be done to make that madwoman stop her scandalous demands. . . . I have written her a letter and I am sending it to you. If you think it necessary, send it."[59]

A draft of the letter to Antonina has been preserved. In it, almost

brutally, Tchaikovsky informed his wife that because of "a whole series of childishly thoughtless actions," he was "forced to punish" her
as children are punished, that is, by deprivation of some material benefit. "I am depriving you of one-third of your pension," he wrote. "From
now on, and until there is some change, you will receive one hundred
rubles." He then went on to list all the examples of her misbehavior:
refusing a divorce, entering into a union with a man unknown to him,
and, in spite of possessing sufficient means, placing her own children
in the foundling hospital. Yet, he wrote, regardless of the fact that such
conduct ought to have led to his refusal of any financial support, he
had consented to pay her fifty rubles a month, and when his means
had increased, thanks to the tsar's benevolence, he had doubled this
pension. And a year later, at her request, he had increased it again. But
now, with her pestering his friends and colleagues, among them Rubinstein, all that was at an end.[60]

It was a cruel letter but had an undercurrent of pity, an ambivalence that almost always, even in his bitterest moments, showed
through in Tchaikovsky's attitude toward his wife. The letter, which
appears to have been the last attempt at direct communication between the spouses, was never sent to the addressee. In the end, Jurgenson simply decreased Antonina's pension to one hundred rubles.

Inevitably, as was seen in his letter to Jurgenson, all this had an
effect on Tchaikovsky's emotional state. That same day, he wrote in
his diary that the letter from Jurgenson "upset me horribly. Was like a
crazy man all day. Slept badly. Did not work."[61] His distress quite naturally also conveyed itself in his other correspondence of that day,
among which was a letter to the composer Aleksandr Glazunov. Often
cited—out of context—as an illustration of Tchaikovsky's alleged pessimism and despair toward the end of his life, this letter to Glazunov
in fact reflected no more than a depression of the moment, brought on
by this reminder of Antonina. "I am going through a very enigmatic
stage on the path to the grave," he told Glazunov. "Something is happening inside me, something I myself do not understand, a sort of
weariness with life, a disappointment, at times a mad anxiety, but not
the kind in whose depths is foreseen a new rush of love for life, but
something hopeless, final, and even, as is the way with finales, banal.
But, at the same time, I have a frightful desire to write. The devil only
knows what the matter is: on the one hand, I seem to feel that my song
has been already sung, while on the other, I have an irresistible desire
to strike up the same, or better yet, a new song."[62]

But by the next day Tchaikovsky could already note in his diary,
"Worked better; in the evening was visited by genuine inspiration."[63]

And three months later, in a letter, Tchaikovsky would claim, "I am now in a period of particular love for life. I am filled with the consciousness of a great labor successfully completed."[64] As so many times before, creative stirrings had drawn him over the unpleasant stretches of life.

Work on *The Queen of Spades* lasted forty-four days. On the next to the last day, 2/14 March, Tchaikovsky wrote in his diary, "Wept terribly when Hermann [the opera's protagonist] breathed his last. The result of exhaustion, or maybe because it is truly good."[65] In his disingenuous way Nazar elaborated in his own journal:

> While he washed, Pyotr Ilyich was telling me how he finished his opera. Lately Pyotr Ilyich shares everything with me—granted except myself there is no one else for this. "Well, Nazar," he addressed me and began telling me how he had finished Hermann's last words and how Hermann had taken his own life. Pyotr Ilyich said that he had been weeping all evening, his eyes at this time were still red, and he was completely exhausted. Tired, and despite this tiredness, he still, it seems, wanted to weep. . . . I love these tears, and so, I think, does everyone who has experienced this. And with Pyotr Ilyich it is the same. He pities poor Hermann, and for this he felt rather sad. When P[yotr] Ilyich played through the death of Hermann that he had composed, he shed again the tears that had filled his soul during the composition. . . . I want to note P[yotr] Ilyich's tears. If, God willing, P[yotr] I[lyich] finishes as well, and this opera comes to be seen and heard on the stage, then probably, following P[yotr] Ilyich's example, many will shed tears.[66]

His opera completed, Tchaikovsky spent most of March in poor health. He caught cold and felt weak and depressed. Upsetting news concerning two of his young protégés added to the gloom. For a time, Tchaikovsky had been making great efforts to procure for Anatoly Brandukov a professorship at the Moscow Conservatory. In February it became clear that these efforts were in vain, owing chiefly to the opposition of the new director of the conservatory, Vasily Safonov. In a gesture of protest, Tchaikovsky resigned his own directorship of the Musical Society and furthermore canceled six conducting engagements for the coming year, citing the dread and nervousness that he always experienced when having to conduct.[67] Jurgenson, meanwhile, had written telling of new complications with the troublesome Misha Klimenko, whom to his lasting regret he had let Tchaikovsky talk him into hiring. Seeing in every order from his employer a desire to belittle him and exhibiting an increasingly ill temper, Klimenko had finally left the printing house and now, in great want and misery, was dying of consumption. The news of his illness caused in Tchaikovsky a rush of compassion, and he wrote Jurgenson from Florence, "Klimenko is indeed ungrateful, but now, when he is dying, he can be forgiven much. Here is a man of great abilities and great ambitions who has not been lucky. Hence the awful bitterness. But at our last meeting he so movingly asked my forgiveness that I forgot everything."[68]

With every passing day, Florence grew more tiresome to Tchaikovsky, until finally he decided to move on to Rome, where he arrived on 27 March/8 April. No sooner did he step out into the street and smell the familiar Roman air and see the once so familiar places than he decided he had been foolish in not having settled in Rome from the start. "But," he wrote to Modest later that day, "I shall not scold poor, blameless Florence, whom I had come to hate without knowing why myself, when I ought to be grateful to her for being able to write *The Queen of Spades* without hindrance."[69] Yet, the pleasure he felt in finding himself once again in the Eternal City was mixed with a melancholy awareness of the years that had passed into oblivion, of his old friend Kondratyev, now gone, and even of Masalitinov, gone as well. For the sake of the famous statue of Antinoüs, the lover of the Roman emperor Hadrian, Tchaikovsky visited the Vatican without much desire to see anything else in the museums. Within several days an indispensable fixture of the Roman landscape, Prince Golitsyn, appeared, and this time, as Tchaikovsky confessed in a letter to Modest, he found himself "very pleased to see him."[70] Still unwell on his arrival from Florence, Tchaikovsky rapidly recovered, and during the three weeks he spent in Rome, he saw no one, aside from Golitsyn and a couple whom he had met in Florence, the Count and Countess Palen.

Mrs. von Meck's health, meanwhile, had by this time also improved, so that at the end of March, after a nearly four-month interval, they resumed their correspondence—he from Rome, she from Nice. Everything seemed as it had always been. Tchaikovsky had no inkling of the shock that he was about to receive.

CHAPTER TWENTY-SIX

Mrs. von Meck's Last Letter

Tchaikovsky's fiftieth birthday, on 25 April, 1890, found him back in St. Petersburg, where he celebrated quietly in the company of Modest and a few close friends. By early May he had returned to Frolovskoe, having again rented the house there after the previous autumn's hectic stay in Moscow. To his dismay, he found Alyosha thinner and much changed in the wake of Fyokla's death. And although the house had been prepared and done up according to his tastes, he was horrified to discover that the woods where he had loved to go walking had been sold and entirely cut down by the new owner. The thought of the felled forest unsettled him for a long time, haunting him like a nightmare.

On 1 July a servant from Mrs. von Meck arrived in Frolovskoe to deliver in person a letter from his mistress with six thousand rubles enclosed—his allowance for an entire year in advance. Made without Tchaikovsky's request, the delivery was a marked irregularity in the established manner of their business relations. He thanked Mrs. von Meck in a short letter and immediately felt obliged to respond to Pachulski who not long before had sent some of his compositions for Tchaikovsky to look over. As always, Tchaikovsky was sharply critical of their dilettantism and a technique "that still suffers from a certain immaturity and lack of purity," and advised him "to study guileless symphonic forms in the spirit of classicism" before beginning "to write things steeped in modernity."[1] Such advice, like sending a graduate student back to the first grade, could not have made the ambitious addressee at all happy. Nonetheless, in reply, Pachulski asked for permission to visit Frolovskoe to discuss his music. He arrived on 14 July, accompanied by a photographer commissioned by Mrs. von Meck to take several shots of the estate and Tchaikovsky himself. A short while later, she sent Tchaikovsky an album with the photographs.

It is uncertain whether Tchaikovsky met Pachulski a second time, as he had planned, in Podolsk, on his circuitous way toward Tiflis during the last three weeks of August. His route took him first to Grankino, where Modest, Kolya, and Bob were staying, after which the four planned to go to Kamenka, with a visit also to Nikolay and Anna von Meck at their estate of Kopylovo. While spending an enjoyable time at Grankino, Tchaikovsky was soon appalled by the worsening state of affairs he found at Kamenka. His sister was continuously ill and had begun to suffer seizures resembling epilepsy as a result of her increasing morphine abuse; and on top of everything else she had also developed an addiction to alcohol. Misha Klimenko, meanwhile, had returned to his parents' home in Kamenka to die, and Tchaikovsky, during his stay, was obliged to visit his former protégé several times a day. In early September, leaving Bob with his mother in Kamenka, Modest returned to St. Petersburg, while Tchaikovsky, breathing a sigh of relief as he left the gloom of Kamenka, headed for Tiflis with Kolya Konradi.

Tiflis, as always, disposed Tchaikovsky more to rest and relaxation than to work. He found his young favorite Volodya Argutinsky-Dolgorukov—by now inseparable friends with Kolya Konradi, though more at Volodya's initiative than Kolya's—"still charming" but "grown terribly coarse and having lost his good looks."[2] Meanwhile, in the company of Nikolay Peresleni, his inevitable Tiflisian guide, his stay passed swiftly in a round of reunions, restaurants, and cards.

In Tiflis, Tchaikovsky received two letters from Mrs. von Meck. The first, dated 13 September 1890, in no way differed in tone from any of her previous letters. It opened with the usual salutation, "My dear beloved friend!" and concluded no less affectionately, "Take care, my dear, incomparable friend, rest well, and do not forget your infinitely loving Nadezhda von Meck." A postscript assumed that the correspondence naturally would continue: "Please address me in Moscow."[3]

The letter dealt with a persistent sore spot—how her children were squandering their hereditary fortune. Most of the reproaches were directed toward her son Nikolay, in connection with his ill-advised purchase of Kopylovo and his inability to manage the estate. It was Lev Davydov who had urged his son-in-law to buy Kopylovo in the first place, in disregard of Mrs. von Meck's own opposition to the idea, and it was Lev, unsurprisingly, who became a target of her anger in this letter. "I cannot blame Kolya for this," she wrote, "because he was very young and completely inexperienced, but I am amazed that Lev Vasilyevich cared so little for the welfare of his own daughter that he could push a young and inexperienced boy onto so slippery a path as the worries of an estate."[4]

Usually in her letters Mrs. von Meck tried to spare Tchaikovsky's relatives, and the fact that in this case she gave free rein to her bitterness suggests that her nerves were being stretched to the limit. Indeed, at times the letter sounds as though it was written on the very verge of hysteria. "My God, my God, how terrible it all is!" Mrs. von Meck exclaimed at one point. "You spend your entire life, all your strength and abilities, to provide your children with a secure, good life, and you achieve this, only to see, very soon, the whole edifice that you have erected with such toil and effort fall apart like a house of cards. How cruel this is, how ruthless!"[5] The fixation with Nikolay and Kopylovo no doubt arose from the fact that it was from there that Tchaikovsky had written his previous letter to her on 4 September, in which, among other things, he remarked, "I am confident, dear friend, that you, too, will be pleasantly impressed by a visit to Kopylovo."[6] But Mrs. von Meck, while she was never to set foot on the property, was herself far from confident that any favorable impression awaited her there—and she was too experienced a businesswoman to misjudge.

Her other children fared little better. Her son Aleksandr, she wrote, had already lost half of his fortune in meat exports and now risked losing the rest. "Here is another ruin, and you cannot imagine, my dear friend, in what a depressed and miserable state I am." Then there was the principal thorn in her side, Prince Shirinsky-Shikhmatov, the husband of her youngest daughter, Lyudmila. "Their fortune continues to diminish, the prince, now as before, acts like a raving lunatic, while she is madly in love with him and, like a child, understands nothing and signs everything that he puts in front of her, and does not see that she is headed toward ruin." It is not surprising that her nerves were on the verge of collapse. "I cannot mend anything anywhere," she wrote, "and I fear only lest I myself should go mad from constant worry and my constantly aching heart. But forgive me, my dear, for bothering you with my complaints; they are not much fun for anyone to have to hear."[7]

However poignant in its expression of pain for her children, this letter contained not the slightest hint that the circumstances it related might in any way affect her friendship with Tchaikovsky. Neither in content nor in tone was it in any way unusual. More than once, Mrs. von Meck had shared her financial and other concerns with her "only friend," and he, insofar as he was able, would try to offer moral support. But, as it turned out, this letter is the last of Mrs. von Meck's letters to Tchaikovsky that we possess. A second letter from her, which he received in Tiflis on 22 September and which informed him of her bankruptcy and the cessation of her subsidy to him, is no longer extant. The break in their relationship, coming without warning, is the most mysterious incident in Tchaikovsky's life.

What little can be gleaned of Mrs. von Meck's last letter to Tchaikovsky comes from his own response, written from Tiflis later that same day:

> My dear beloved friend! The news that you convey in your letter, which I have just received, has grieved me deeply, yet not for my own sake but for yours. These are by no means empty words. Of course, I should be lying were I to say that such a radical cut in my budget will have no effect at all on my material situation. But it will have far less of an effect than you probably think. . . . The point is that you, with your habits and your grand way of life, are faced with suffering privations! This is terribly painful and upsetting. I feel a need to dump the blame onto someone for all that has happened (since, of course, you yourself are not to be blamed), and at the same time, I do not know who is truly to blame. But this anger is useless and futile, and I do not consider myself as having the right to seek to pry into the area of your purely family affairs. I'd better ask Wladyslaw Albertovich to write me, when he has the chance, as to what arrangements you intend to make, where you will live, to what extent you have to subject yourself to privations. I cannot express how greatly I pity and fear for you. I cannot imagine you without wealth! . . . The last words of your letter hurt me somewhat, but I think that you cannot seriously believe what you wrote. Can you really consider me capable of remembering you only while I enjoy your money! Could I ever forget for even a single moment what you have done for me and how much I owe to you? I will say without exaggeration that you saved me and that I should probably have gone mad and perished if you had not come to my aid and supported, with .your friendship, compassion, and material assistance (then it was an anchor of my salvation), my utterly extinguished energy and struggle to follow my path upward! No, my dear friend, rest assured that I will remember this until my last breath, and will bless you. I am glad that precisely now, when

you can no more share your means with me, I can express with all my might my boundless, ardent, altogether ineffable gratitude. You probably yourself do not suspect the full immensity of your good deed! Otherwise it would never have occurred to you that now that you are poor, I shall recollect you sometimes!!!! Without any exaggeration I can say that I have never forgotten you and never will forget you for even a single minute, for my thoughts, whenever I think of myself, always and invariably encounter you. I warmly kiss your hands and beg you to know once and for all that no one sympathizes and shares in all your afflictions more than I.[8]

It was Tchaikovsky's last letter to his benefactress, though his words give no indication that he saw the cessation of his subsidy as the mark of a formal break. From his reply it is clear that Mrs. von Meck explained the termination of the subsidy by her family's financial collapse. It is also clear that her letter contained a phrase approximately reconstructable thus: "Do not forget me and remember me sometimes."[9]

Perhaps the most striking feature of the break was its apparent suddenness. After all, barely a week passed between Mrs. von Meck's intimate, confessional, and loving letter of 13 September and her announcement that she was ceasing his subsidy. The impression of a sudden decision by Mrs. von Meck is, however, misleading. That the break must take place sooner or later she had to have known from at least the previous July, when, with no prompting from Tchaikovsky, she sent one of her personal servants to Frolovskoe with the "budget sum" for an entire year in advance.[10] The only logical explanation for such an irregularity in their business dealings is that Mrs. von Meck wanted to secure her friend for a year in advance because she feared that she would not be able to send him regular payments in the future. It is obvious that she would not have done this if she had intended to break with Tchaikovsky for moral considerations. This action, together with her plea that he think of her sometimes, refutes any notion that Mrs. von Meck waxed indignant in the face of some sudden and irrefutable proof of Tchaikovsky's homosexuality and that acting in accordance with her strict views on sexual morality, she cut him off. It is this conception that underlies, explicitly or implicitly, most attempts over the years to explain what happened. Many years before, Mrs. von Meck had, it is true, written Tchaikovsky that she would support him as long as their relationship remained on a level that suited her. Yet, when one breaks off relations with a person in a fit of righteous indignation at moral perversity, one does not ask that person "not to forget and to remember sometimes." Rather, Mrs. von Meck's adjuration implies her own discomfort, even guilt, at terminating Tchaikovsky's allowance.

It is, in fact, likely that Mrs. von Meck had known about the inevitability of a break even earlier and that she had been preparing for it from the middle of 1889. From time to time, when his chronic wastefulness landed him in straitened circumstances, Tchaikovsky would ask Mrs. von Meck for the "budget sum" several months in advance. Yet, no advances had ever before been paid on her own initiative. The very first such initiative on her part took place on 24 July 1889. "I want to ask you," she wrote then, "whether you might allow me to send you now a check for the budget sum from 1 October 1889 until 1 July 1890, . . . as it would be more convenient for me to change the date for sending it to you to 1 July, since at that time I am usually in Russia. If you permit this, would it be possible for you, when you are in Moscow, to stop by my house and get from Ivan Vasilyev [one of her servants] a packet with the check that I shall have left with him to give you? If this is possible, please let me know, my dear friend."[11]

This proposal was made in a letter that spoke of Tchaikovsky and his art with undiminished ardor. "Listening to [your music]," she wrote, "I bless you each time for the good that you bring to mankind, for the solace that you bring to life—to mine, for example, so barren of joys and happiness."[12]

Her suggestion was accepted with enthusiasm. "Your proposal to give me now a check for the budget sum until 1 July 1890 I accept with deepest gratitude," responded Tchaikovsky on 25 July 1889. "This is especially nice for me in that I must very shortly start to furnish my Moscow apartment and shall be in great need of money. Then, too, in general I am always in somewhat of a financial crisis by the end of the summer, and for this reason, your proposal is surprisingly timely for me. Thank you, my dear, kind, beloved friend! . . . Thank you again and again!"[13]

Tchaikovsky, then, was content and in no way worried. But why did Mrs. von Meck, a woman of established habits who always followed a fixed routine in her affairs, suddenly decide to change that routine by such a precedent?

To judge from her letter, one of her chief concerns in the transfer not only of the budget sum from October 1889 to July 1890, but also of the next installment, was that she herself be in Russia, not abroad. Dozens of times before, she had simply sent the check, and even money itself, by mail. Now, suddenly, not only did she wish to avoid the post, but the whole operation was to be carried out not through some member of the family but through a trusted servant, Ivan Vasilyev, for whom Tchaikovsky himself had warm feelings. By this time, Mrs. von Meck was already very ill and quite probably could not control her correspondence personally. By refusing to use the post, she evidently meant to conceal this transaction altogether, or at least not to draw it to the attention of those around her. Significantly, she chose not to involve Pachulski, who had long been their intermediary and frequently acted as her factotum. She did not trust even him, then, in this role.

Even more suggestive was her conduct a year later. "My dear, I have a favor to ask you," she wrote in her letter of 28 May 1890. "The date for sending the budget sum is 1 July, but I shall not arrive in Moscow until 1 July, so would you permit me to be a few days late in sending the check, since I do not want to entrust this to anyone in Moscow and prefer to do it myself when I return? Be so kind, my dear friend, as to let me know your response, and [if] my request should cause you even the slightest difficulty, I implore you not to be in the least embarrassed to tell me so and I shall then order it to be sent from Moscow at once."[14] For all her customary refined delicacy, one cannot fail to notice a certain imperative air: Mrs. von Meck wanted very much for him to agree to her request. The letter concluded, "With all my heart, forever affectionately and devotedly yours."

Tchaikovsky, professing himself "moved to tears by your solicitude and thoughtfulness for me," hastened to assure her that whatever way was best and most convenient for her, "so be it."[15] To all appearances, however, he had not expected to receive his allowance for an entire year in advance this time, and he was surprised but grateful when Ivan Vasilyev made a special trip from Moscow to Frolovskoe to deliver to him the full sum through to the following July. "There are no words with which I can express how grateful I am to you, how moved by your attention and solicitude," he wrote her the day after receiving the money. Once again, Mrs. von Meck had chosen to use the services neither of the post nor of anyone other than her trusted servant. What is more, though the letter that Mrs. von Meck sent with the final allowance check is not extant, in his reply Tchaikovsky makes reference to her advice to place the bulk of the sum in the bank. In other words, Mrs. von Meck betrayed again her fears about the future. Should she be forced to discontinue the subsidy, money that had been placed in the bank would last longer. Tchaikovsky, in his ignorance, suspected nothing. "I have firmly made up my mind," he promised, "that beginning this year I shall start setting aside part of the money I receive and with time acquire, after all, some piece of property, very possibly Frolovskoe, which, despite the cutting down of the forest, I like very much."[16]

Clearly, Mrs. von Meck, from the middle of 1889, found herself beset by circumstances forcing her toward a break with Tchaikovsky. At first glance, such circumstances might have been financial: fearing possible ruin, she was sending large sums of money in advance in order to fulfill in some fashion the obligation that she had taken upon herself and to secure Tchaikovsky, at least to some extent, against the event of her bankruptcy. This explanation, however, is far from sufficient. Mrs. von Meck had observed several years before that given the size of the family capital, even in the event of bankruptcy the sum she paid to Tchaikovsky was virtually negligible. Yet, even if this were no longer true, such fears do not account for the mania of secrecy in her financial dealings with Tchaikovsky that took possession of Mrs. von Meck from the middle of 1889. On the contrary, Mrs. von Meck, with her unrelenting frankness and honesty, would be expected to warn Tchaikovsky well in advance of such a threat to his subsidy so that he not be caught by surprise.

If, as the evidence strongly suggests, Mrs. von Meck foresaw the impending rupture and could not have wanted it, yet nevertheless allowed it to happen, there can be only one conclusion: she did not herself desire the break but was forced to make it. And if, as her failure to warn Tchaikovsky earlier implies, it was not financial circumstances that for more than a year propelled her toward the break, some other external force was at work. This force, in all likelihood, was pressure from her own family.

There were numerous reasons for Mrs. von Meck's children to resent the relationship between their mother and Tchaikovsky. They were ashamed of the intensity of her infatuation with the composer. In society there was already talk about Tchaikovsky and "la Meck." Increasingly the situation smacked of something scandalous, or at least might be construed as such in the eyes of hostile relatives. Moreover, it galled them to watch Tchaikovsky continue to take her money freely even after he had been granted a generous pension by the tsar. As their own financial situations fell into ever-deeper disarray, they can only have grown more resolute in their determination to put an end to the arrangement between the composer and his benefactress.[17] Mrs. von Meck, in her turn, appears to have displayed a capacity for resistance verging on the heroic. Subjected to powerful pressure from her rebellious children, this aging and very ill woman stubbornly delayed while she could, at the same time securing Tchaikovsky financially for as far into the future as possible, in case something were to happen to her because of her worsening nervous condition. This hypothesis can explain both the secrecy of her monetary arrangements and her unrequested advances on Tchaikovsky's allowance. Whether Mrs. von Meck ever actually admitted to herself the possibility of ultimate capitulation or whether in fact she relied on the tenacity of her character to rescue her now as it had before, she could not allow Tchaikovsky to guess anything and could not warn him about the possible loss of his subsidy.

The situation evidently became heated by the middle of the summer of 1890, when Mrs. von Meck sent the last of the budget sums. In the course of that June and July she was visited by almost all of her elder children, with the notable exception of Nikolay and his wife, Anna, who, as Tchaikovsky's relatives, very likely remained uninformed of the events. The break, however, occurred only in September, and it must have been caused by some concrete event that paralyzed Mrs. von Meck's will to resist.

The first to point to Pachulski as a possible cause of what happened was Alyosha Sofronov, in a letter to his master on 13 October 1890. "But you know, my dear benefactor, I think N[adezhda] F[ilaretovna] has not been so ruined as she writes; rather, I think this is the work of your Pole Pachulski, since shares of the Ryazan Railroad are standing much higher than last year," Alyosha wrote. "Because of this, I think that Pachulski has played the main role here. In the summer he was quite envious of you and how well you live when I went about with him taking the photographs."[18] Yury Davydov also believed in Pachulski's guilt.[19] Far more important, however, an allusion to that guilt comes also from the opposite camp, that is, from the von Meck family. Olga Bennigsen, who was Mrs. von Meck's granddaughter by her daughter Aleksandra and, as such, was bound to be privy to the most probable versions of the affair, later ridiculed the alleged motive of material envy ascribed to Pachulski in Alyosha's letter. But she followed this with the enigmatic remark that "though the motives attributed to him were wrong, Alexis [Alyosha] may have manifested a measure of perspicacity when he indicted Pakhulski [sic] as the culprit."[20]

Until new archival material is made available, one can only conjecture about the nature of Pachulski's guilt. From the hints of Olga Bennigsen and the others, it would seem likely that Pachulski was a leader and perhaps even the chief instigator of a family campaign to persuade Mrs. von Meck to sever her ties with Tchaikovsky. It would seem likely, too, that sometime between 13 and 20 September her family presented Mrs. von Meck with some sort of ultimatum. What Pachulski and her children told Mrs. von Meck that pushed her finally to make the break may never be known with any certainty. The idea of a sudden discovery of Tchaikovsky's homosexuality is untenable. Mrs. von Meck had very probably either known or surmised the truth for many years. More plausible is the theory that Pachulski and her children ultimately threatened to make a public disclosure of Tchaikovsky's homosexuality should she not comply. Tchaikovsky, of course, knew that he had little to fear from the threat of scandal. Mrs. von Meck very likely did not and might well have broken with her "incomparable friend" to save from scandal his reputation and emotional health. From her one phrase "do not forget and remember sometimes" it is possible, under such circumstances, to infer the measure of suffering brought upon her by compliance with some sort of family ultimatum for the sake of saving one whom she so loved. In any case, this is the only scenario that takes into account all the known facts, from the ironclad silence of Mrs. von Meck, who would ultimately escape bankruptcy yet again, to the slippery evasions of Pachulski's subsequent letters.

To Mrs. von Meck's letter informing him of the cessation of the subsidy, Tchaikovsky responded emotionally but judiciously. The same cannot be said of his reaction to what happened as revealed in his letters to Modest and, especially, to Jurgenson. Tchaikovsky put off telling Modest and Jurgenson the news for several days while he waited and hoped for a response to his letter of 22 September. But no response came. His incomprehension is not surprising. The absence of any explanation or tangible cause must have maddened him and deeply wounded his self-esteem. In the letters to Modest and Jurgenson this wounded self-esteem was given free rein, and sad though it may be, his initial reaction would concentrate for the most part on the financial aspect and the loss of his subsidy.

"I bore this blow philosophically, but nevertheless was unpleasantly struck and surprised," he wrote to Jurgenson on 28 September. "She had written me so many times that I was secure in receiving this subsidy until my last breath that I had come to believe this and thought that to this end she had somehow contrived things so that, come what may, I would not be deprived of my principal and, as I thought, most certain income. I was to be disappointed." Most of all, Tchaikovsky felt that he had been treated unceremoniously. He was pained by the abruptness of Mrs. von Meck's action and by the inadequacy of her explanation. "I am very, very, very *offended*, actually *offended*," he told Jurgenson. "My relations with N[adezhda] F[ilaretovna] von Meck were such that I never felt her generous dole as a burden. Now I am burdened in retrospect; my pride has been insulted, my trust in her infinite readiness to support me materially and to make any sacrifice for my sake has been betrayed. Now I should wish her to go utterly bankrupt so that she might need my help. But I know perfectly well that from our point of view she is still awfully rich; in a word, a banal, stupid game has been exposed that makes me feel sick and ashamed."[21] Nowhere in this passage is there even a trace of the sympathy so plentiful in the letter to the beloved friend herself.

Professing himself "shocked beyond words" by the news, in his reply Jurgenson recalled the period of Mrs. von Meck's earlier financial difficulties in 1881, when she had firmly maintained that Tchaikovsky's subsidy could in no way suffer. "I do not know what has happened to [the von Mecks], a true crash or a fit of insanity, but I've been very, very pained for you. Tears somehow sit in my throat, and I want to sob, but cannot. I cannot make proper sense of anything."[22]

For several days Tchaikovsky was in a state of depression. His mood was reflected in a letter to Bob of 4 October. "You cannot imagine, Bob, how lazy I have grown about letters," he wrote. "I have almost stopped writing them altogether. . . . This letter I address to you, but please give it to Modya to read as well, for I don't feel like writing him separately. Tell Modya that in view of the altered material conditions of my existence I no longer wish to rent a separate apartment in Petersburg, but shall simply put up in a more or less comfortable room in the former Znamenskaya Hotel. So let Modya stop his search for a luxurious apartment."[23] Only a week later, on 10 October, did he write to Modest himself, telling him, more briefly than in the letter to Jurgenson, about the sudden change in his financial situation and adding that they would speak orally about the feelings aroused in him by Mrs. von Meck's action.[24] Modest quickly responded with the same intonation of distress as Jurgenson. "The news of your new material situation contributed not a little to my melancholy," he told his brother. "Of course, it is not the six thousand rubles that I regret (in my opinion, that trouble is not great, since you have only to cancel subsidies like mine and you will be almost in your former position). It is the blow to your pride that is heavy."[25]

The wound did not heal. Tchaikovsky seems never once to have conceived that Mrs. von Meck might have been forced to act as she had by circumstances beyond her control and might even have done so in his own interests. No formal break had occurred. There is no evidence that Mrs. von Meck ever expressed any wish that their correspondence or their relationship be severed altogether. Nor would there have been any reason for such a rupture if the sole issue had been her financial crisis and the suspension of his subsidy. Tchaikovsky was simply blocked from any further direct communication with her—a point that gives further weight to the supposition that Mrs. von Meck was pressured by her children to cut off not only his allowance but also all relations with him, though in such a manner as not to cause socially damaging repercussions for the von Meck family. Receiving no response from Mrs. von Meck to his last letter, Tchaikovsky once again turned to Pachulski. In the past when gravely ill, Mrs. von Meck would stop writing temporarily and Pachulski would take over. The same thing happened now. In his replies Pachulski conveyed Mrs. von Meck's regards and reported news about her health and her family.[26] Most of Tchaikovsky's letters to Pachulski from this period are lost. Those of Pachulski to Tchaikovsky have not yet been published in full and are known only in brief fragments and adaptations from Soviet commentaries, making any judgment about their general character difficult.

At the end of October, Pachulski informed Tchaikovsky that Mrs. von Meck's illness had resurged. He wrote of her bronchitis without mentioning the serious condition of her nerves, but observed, "Our whole life is extremely uneasy."[27] The best physicians were summoned, and a week later, on 3 November, Pachulski wrote that "Yuliya Karlovna has just commissioned me to tell you from Nadezhda Filaretovna that she feels very ill and that her morale is very poor."[28] The following day, he added that "Nadezhda Filaretovna has instructed me to convey to you her warmest regards and deep gratitude for your attention."[29]

Through the end of the year and the beginning of the next, Tchaikovsky lived under the weight of the break. In his letters to almost everyone a sense of emotional exhaustion became evident, a disappointment with people and with life. With Kolya Konradi he visited his elder brother, Ippolit, in Taganrog in late October and by 1 November was back in Frolovskoe. Within a few weeks he left for St. Petersburg for the rehearsals of *The Queen of Spades*, which had its premiere on 7 December. Now deservedly considered one of Tchaikovsky's finest creations, the opera met in its first production with a mixed response. Despite audience acclaim for the work, many critics, perceiving an extreme unevenness in the music, praised the effectiveness of the orchestration but lamented the antipathetic character of Hermann and the insignificance of Modest's libretto, which simplified and vulgarized Pushkin's original story. Three days later, Tchaikovsky was already in Kiev for rehearsals of the same opera, which opened in that city on 19 December to a far better reception. After the Kiev premiere

Tchaikovsky left to spend the holidays at Kamenka, where Bob was also visiting. He left Kamenka the day after New Year's and, back in Frolovskoe, took up work at once on incidental music for a benefit production of *Hamlet* to be given by the French actor Lucien Guitry at the Mikhailovsky Theater in February.

On 3 January 1891, Pachulski, replying to a letter, now lost, from Tchaikovsky, wrote asking the composer to forgive him "for having led you with my blundering and inaccuracy to an assumption that is completely opposite to what is felt for you by all who have the happiness to be close to you. . . . I myself am to blame for everything—myself and, in that respect, the circumstances of life, which confuse and unsettle me." The entire von Meck family, he told Tchaikovsky, "loves Pyotr Ilyich, and marvels at and admires the greatest Russian composer." He added that "the success of *The Queen of Spades* makes us all infinitely happy, and although in our opinion it is also something quite natural, since it is only the tribute proper to your genius, still it is pleasant to see that the audience is growing to an understanding of your works." As for Mrs. von Meck and her feelings for Tchaikovsky, Pachulski made a special effort to persuade the composer that nothing was wrong: "Nadezhda Filaretovna, to whom I gave your letter to read, has told me to convey to you 'that it is an impossibility that she could ever be angry at you and that her attitude toward you is unchanged.'"[30]

Yet, Tchaikovsky never received a single line to the same effect written by Mrs. von Meck herself. In fact, some years later, Anna von Meck would unwittingly give evidence that, contrary to Pachulski's claim, Mrs. von Meck was never allowed to see another letter from her beloved friend after her own last letter to him. Naively and somewhat romantically, Anna von Meck attributed the break between her mother-in-law and her uncle to Mrs. von Meck's failing health, coupled with her grief over the illness of her eldest son, Vladimir, who was dying of tuberculosis.[31] This version fails, of course, to account for the obsessive secretiveness of Mrs. von Meck's last financial transactions involving Tchaikovsky. Had her health declined so radically or even had she found herself overwhelmed by spiritual and emotional anguish, she would have told Tchaikovsky about this directly and the break would not have been a break — and certainly not a termination of material support — but merely a suspension of personal communication. But then, Anna was hardly one of her mother-in-law's favorite relatives, despite her attempts to suggest the opposite in her later recollections. Of all who surrounded Mrs. von Meck, Anna and her husband were least likely to be entrusted with the secret of Mrs. von Meck's motives. Nor is it likely that Tchaikovsky's niece would have been made aware of the full intensity of the ill will felt for him by Mrs. von Meck's other children or of their efforts to sever the friendship between them.

However dubious her theory about the cause of the break, Anna's brief reminiscence is noteworthy for its account of a conversation she had with her mother-in-law some time after the rupture. "It was then that I understood for the first time how keenly she felt the break with my uncle," Anna recalled. "Her feeling of ecstatic worship for my uncle had not changed. 'I knew that I was no longer necessary to him and could give him nothing more, and I did not want our correspondence to become a burden for him, while for me it had always been a joy. . . . If he did not understand me and if I was necessary to him, why did he never write me again? He promised! True, I denied him material aid, but can that really have been so important?' That is what she told me."[32]

If Anna's account can be credited (and certainly she would have had little to gain by inventing a complaint that was essentially damning to her famous uncle), it betrays the outright lie of Pachulski's claim that he was showing Mrs. von Meck the composer's letters, which, though formally addressed to him, were necessarily concerned with her and, as during her previous illnesses, essentially directed to her. By continuing to send Tchaikovsky "greetings" and "regards" allegedly from Mrs. von Meck while preventing any direct communication between the two Pachulski apparently expected the situation gradually and quietly to pass. For a time, it seemed that it would. Tchaikovsky wrote to Pachulski less and less often, seeking instead the solace of work.

On 15 January 1891, Tchaikovsky received an invitation, arranged by his Berlin concert agent, Hermann Wolff, to make a conducting tour to the United States in April. He accepted, agreeing also to conduct Edouard Colonne's orchestra in a concert of his own works on 24 March/5 April in Paris. All other offers and invitations he declined, citing a painful right arm and having in mind other creative plans. From the directorate of imperial theaters had recently come a commission to write both a one-act opera, *King René's Daughter* (later called *Iolanta*), and a ballet, *The Nutcracker*. The ballet and the opera were planned as two halves of a double bill.

Meanwhile, in St. Petersburg, *The Queen of Spades*, despite playing to packed houses, was removed from the program when the immensely popular tenor Nikolay Figner, who sang the role of Hermann to his wife, Medea's, Liza, refused to perform in the opera without his wife, who had become pregnant and so could not sing. Tchaikovsky, however, decided that the real reason the opera had been withdrawn was that the tsar had not liked it—and indeed, Alexander had not attended the premiere or any subsequent performances after having attended the dress rehearsal. He wrote an annoyed letter on the subject to the director of theaters, Ivan Vsevolozhsky, who wrote back assuring him that the tsar had indeed liked *The Queen of Spades* very much at the dress rehearsal. The minister of the court, Count Vorontsov-Dashkov, on reading Tchaikovsky's sharp letter to Vsevolozhsky, told him to assure Tchaikovsky that the tsar "values him enormously" and that he often spoke of *The Queen of Spades* with great praise and "every Sunday" commanded his orchestra to play tunes from *The Sleeping Beauty*.[33]

In February, Tchaikovsky traveled to St. Petersburg to attend Lucien Guitry's successful benefit performance of *Hamlet*, with Tchaikovsky's incidental music (op. 67a). Returning to Frolovskoe, he found himself heading back to the capital several days later, this time at Alyosha's urging. His servant was getting married a second time and had asked his master to absent himself for the occasion. Remarkably, the master had complied. By an irony of fate, the marriage took place on 19 February, a year to the day from the death of Alyosha's first wife, Fyokla. A requiem mass was held in the morning and the wedding that same evening.

The new Mrs. Sofronova, Ekaterina, turned out to be "very pretty and piquante, awfully in Laroche's taste," as Tchaikovsky described her to Modest a few days later. But his own feelings about his servant's remarriage were more than a little mixed. "I grow angry at her every time I enter Aleksey's room when they are having tea and I see this man so terribly in love with his wife," he confided to his brother. "I remember poor kindest Feklusha [Fyokla], rotting a few meters away from us. It must be because I often recall Feklusha that I have felt sad here these last days, and I think of my departure with pleasure." But then, noting that Alyosha had been very upset when he found out that Tchaikovsky was leaving soon for America, he conceded, "How glad I am that he is married and in love with his wife. Otherwise, it would have been agonizing to leave."[34]

On 6/18 March, Tchaikovsky left Russia for Berlin, stayed there a few days, and then went to Paris to conduct the Colonne Orchestra before his departure to America. But he continued to be tormented by thoughts of the break with Mrs. von Meck. Pachulski in a letter of 16/28 March informed him that his mother-in-law had been taken to Nice and "thank God, goes out of doors and little by little seems to be recovering."[35] Tchaikovsky's reply, written on 26 March/6 April, is the first of his letters to Pachulski from this period to survive and may give some idea of the general style of their correspondence until then. It is concerned chiefly with Tchaikovsky's own musical affairs but also speaks warmly of Mrs. von Meck. "I rejoice that Nadezhda Filaretovna has borne her journey so well," Tchaikovsky wrote, "and hope that the wonders of Nice's climate will soon restore her health completely." At the close of the letter "greetings and salutations" were sent both to her and to Pachulski's wife, Yuliya.[36]

But Tchaikovsky's sense of hurt and outrage had not left him. On 6 June, after the American tour, exasperated by eight months of suspense and delay and entirely in the dark as to what was going on, Tchaikovsky finally exploded in a long, bitter, and emotional response to a letter, since lost, from Pachulski:

> I have just received your letter. I quite believe that Nadezhda Filaretovna is ill, weak, nervously distressed, and still cannot write to me. Nor would I wish her to suffer because of me for anything in the world. I am pained, disturbed, and, to speak frankly, deeply offended, not by the fact that she does not write to me, but by the fact that she has altogether ceased to take any interest in me. If she had wanted me to conduct a regular correspondence with her as before, would this not have been perfectly feasible, since you and Yuliya Karlovna might have been continuous intermediaries between us? But not once has she commissioned either of you to ask me to inform her about how I live and what is going on with me. I have made attempts through you to establish regular written relations with N[a-dezhda] F[ilaretovna], but your every letter has been merely a polite response to preserve, at least to some extent, the shadow of the past. You of course are aware that in September of last year N[adezhda] F[ilaretovna] informed me that, being ruined, she could no longer offer me her material support. Of my reply to her you are probably also aware. I *wanted*, I *needed* that my relations with N[adezhda] F[ilaretovna] not be changed in the slightest as a result of my having ceased to receive money from her. Unfortunately, this proved impossible, owing to N[adezhda] F[ilaretovna]'s quite obvious cooling toward me. As a result, it happened that *I* stopped writing N[adezhda] F[ilaretovna], ceased virtually all relations with her, *after having been deprived of her money.* Such a situation humiliates me in my own eyes, makes intolerable for me the recollection of my having accepted her subsidies, constantly torments and pains me beyond measure. In the autumn, in the country, I re-

read N[adezhda] F[ilaretovna]'s previous letters. Neither her illness nor misfortunes nor material difficulties could, it would
have seemed, change the feelings expressed in those letters.
Yet, they have changed. Perhaps precisely because I never *personally* knew N[adezhda] F[ilaretovna], she appeared to me an
ideal person; I could not imagine inconstancy in such a demi-
goddess; it seemed to me that the globe of the world might
crumble to bits before N[adezhda] F[ilaretovna] ever became
different toward me. But the latter occurred, and it turns upside
down all my views of people, my faith in the best of them; it
disturbs my peace of mind, poisons that share of happiness
which fate has allotted me. Without, of course, wishing to,
N[adezhda] F[ilaretovna] has treated me very cruelly. Never
have I felt so humiliated, so wounded in my pride, as now. And
most painful of all is the fact that in view of N[adezhda]
F[ilaretovna]'s so terribly weakened health, I cannot, for fear of
grieving or upsetting her, tell her of all that torments me. I am
unable to speak out—and this alone might have brought me
relief. But enough of this. Perhaps I shall regret that I have written what I have, but I was obeying a need to vent something at
least of the bitterness that has accumulated in my heart. Of
course, not a word of this to N[adezhda] F[ilaretovna].[37]

In a postscript Tchaikovsky added an injunction: "Do not answer this
letter." But Pachulski disregarded this, and in his reply he assured
Tchaikovsky that he misunderstood Mrs. von Meck and was "entirely
mistaken" on her account. "You have no need to express anything at
all to Nadezhda Filaretovna," Pachulski wrote, "and if you were to
write to her, as before, about yourself and to ask her about herself, I
guarantee that she then would respond with all her heart, and then you
will see that her attitude toward you has not changed in the least; but
you must not ask why she has changed, because she has not."[38] Yet,
Tchaikovsky, despite his remark that it was he who stopped writing
first, had in fact waited in vain more than eight months for a response
to his last letter to Mrs. von Meck, as Pachulski well knew. Quite apart
from this, Pachulski only a few lines earlier in his letter claimed, as he
had been claiming since the break, that the ailing Mrs. von Meck was
still "unable to write herself." His proposal that Tchaikovsky resume
direct correspondence with Mrs. von Meck was therefore patently absurd.

Moreover, Pachulski, who in the months since the break had styled
himself both intermediary and peacemaker, continuing to send greetings purportedly commissioned by Mrs. von Meck, now suddenly in-

formed Tchaikovsky that his own relationship with Mrs. von Meck had "also changed greatly, and for this reason, it is no wonder that she has no wish to make me an intermediary between herself and you." If there was perhaps a reflection of the truth in this claim, it would seem to go back well before the break and before the past eight months of seeming mediation—back, in fact, to the previous summer, when Mrs. von Meck, relieving her ailing son Vladimir of the management of her affairs, handed them over to the inexperienced Nikolay and not, significantly, to the far more experienced Pachulski, even though he was by now a son-in-law and a member of the family. In any event, by making reference only now to their worsening relationship, Pachulski conveniently allowed himself a smooth exit from the difficult situation. The alternative suggestion of Yuliya as an intermediary was simply ignored.

Tchaikovsky's frustration was absolute. Pachulski, claiming that he had "no right to keep it with me," returned Tchaikovsky's letter of 6 June to the composer, with no other apparent purpose than to prevent the letter being seen by those around Mrs. von Meck, who might have been more amicably disposed toward Tchaikovsky. Anna von Meck later insisted in her recollections that Tchaikovsky "wrote for some reason of his resentment, his pain, to Pachulski, whom he knew perfectly and who, he could be sure, would not show us the letter once my uncle asked him not to."[39] Evidently, she was speaking of the same letter of 6 June. But in that letter Tchaikovsky only wrote, "Not a word of this to N[adezhda] F[ilaretovna]." He in no way forbade the showing of the letter to anyone else, least of all to his relatives, to Anna and Nikolay.

This was the last exchange between Tchaikovsky and Pachulski. The correspondence between the two men was broken off, and with it, the last thread connecting the composer and Mrs. von Meck. In the three years that passed between their estrangement and his death, Tchaikovsky never overcame the bitterness and pain caused him by Mrs. von Meck's enigmatic "betrayal." The periodic financial strains brought on by his habitual extravagance, no longer relieved by her generosity, only deepened his feelings of resentment, especially when a few years later it became clear that Mrs. von Meck had in fact once again escaped ruin.

"O Nadezhda Filaretovna, why, perfidious old woman, did you betray me?!!" he exclaimed in a perhaps only half-joking postscript to a letter to Jurgenson written three months before his death. "I was recently rereading the letters of Nadezhda Filaretovna von Meck and was amazed at the fickleness of female infatuations. One might think, reading these letters, that fire would sooner turn to water than her subsidy stop, and one might also wonder that I should have been satisfied with such a paltry sum when she was ready to give me almost anything. And suddenly—good-bye! Above all, I really almost believed that she had been ruined. But it turns out it was nothing of the sort. Simply female inconstancy."[40] Least of all could Nadezhda von Meck be accused of inconstancy. But Tchaikovsky, angry and hurt, failed to see this. Ultimately, he failed to understand the woman with whom he conducted for thirteen years so intimate a correspondence and who had been his partner in arguably one of the most extraordinary unions between a man and a woman known to modern history.

CHAPTER TWENTY-SEVEN

The "Fourth Suite"

The concert hall in Paris was filled to overflowing when Tchaikovsky conducted the Colonne Orchestra in a program of his works on 24 March/5 April 1891. The concert was a resounding success. His young friend Sapelnikov received loud praise for his performance of the Second Piano Concerto, and Tchaikovsky himself was called back repeatedly and was presented with a laurel wreath. The reviews in the papers, almost without exception, were full of glowing words. In less than two weeks Tchaikovsky was due to set sail for New York and his American tour. His international fame was ascending by leaps and bounds.

All the acclaim, however, did little to raise Tchaikovsky's spirits. He was worried about the coming transatlantic voyage and about his pressing commitments to both a new opera and a new ballet. In addition, there was the customary annoyance at what he saw as senseless social visits and dinners. Even the presence of Modest, in Paris for the past month, and of Sapelnikov and another friend, Sophie Menter, a pianist and composer, helped little. Most of all, he wanted to go off by himself somewhere and begin composing. To this end, he decided to travel alone to Rouen for several days and there attempt to work until his departure for America. Modest remained in Paris, and it was there, on the morning of 29 March/10 April, that he received a telegram reporting the death of their sister, Aleksandra. He went to Rouen that same day, but decided against telling his brother the sad news, fearing lest it aggravate his already low spirits and perhaps jeopardize the en-

tire American trip. Instead, he told Tchaikovsky that, feeling homesick, he was returning to Russia and postponing his planned journey
to Italy for another time. The announcement quite pleased Tchaikovsky, who had never much liked his brother's evident lack of homesickness when abroad, a feeling so pronounced in himself.

After Modest's departure Tchaikovsky's anguish over his futile efforts to make progress on *Iolanta* and *The Nutcracker* turned to despair. He realized that he would never manage to complete the works
successfully before the start of the 1891–1892 season. The prospect of
having to live in constant tension on the way to America and afterward
came to seem like some "threatening murderous specter," and when to
this was added his own growing homesickness, which by this time
always accompanied him on his foreign tours without Alyosha, Tchaikovsky began to feel his situation utterly unbearable.[1] Finally, after
painful consideration, he made up his mind to write to Vsevolozhsky
in St. Petersburg and request that the production of both opera and
ballet be postponed to the following season. With this weight removed
from his shoulders, Tchaikovsky quickly shook off the tension that
had plagued him in Paris and had so worried his brother.[2] He left Rouen
and returned to Paris for the remaining few days before his departure.
In Paris, on his way to visit Sapelnikov and Sophie Menter, Tchaikovsky happened to stop in at a reading room where he often looked
through the latest papers and journals. There, on the last page of an
issue of the Russian newspaper *New Times*, he came suddenly upon
an announcement of the death of his sister.

Tchaikovsky fled the reading room "as if stung."[3] He thought at
once of canceling the American tour, but then realized that he could
not, having already received a large sum of money in advance, which
would then have to be returned. He wrote to Modest on 4/16 April, "I
suffer very much emotionally. I am terribly afraid for Bob, although I
know from experience that at that age such sorrows are borne with
relative ease."[4] But even Tchaikovsky, in the end, bore with relative
ease the ordeal of his sister's death. Worry about Bob and the upcoming
American tour seem to have outweighed his own feelings of grief. The
circumstances of the last years of Aleksandra's life, her morphine addiction and alcoholism, had substantially distanced brother and sister.
By this time, Aleksandra had become for him, in Modest's words, more
"a sacred relic of his childhood, youth, and the Kamenka period of his
life" than a living human being. Several days after learning the news,
Tchaikovsky noted to his brother that "Sasha's death and all the torment linked to my thoughts of it appear as though recollections from

a very remote past that I try without particular effort to drive away, and I try to think anew of the interests of that *not-I* that goes in me to America."[5]

The next day, 5/17 April, Tchaikovsky set sail at Le Havre aboard the steamship *La Bretagne*. He mourned, and in his thoughts he was with Modest and Bob back in St. Petersburg, yet gradually during the ten days of the sea voyage he grew composed and resigned, made acquaintances among the other passengers, and waited patiently for his arrival in America.

He reached New York on 14/26 April. Back on dry land and alone finally in his room at the Normandie Hotel at Broadway and Thirty-eighth Street, he gave vent to his tension in a flood of tears. Thus easing his grief, he set out to explore the city. He recorded his impressions and experiences in his diary, to show later to friends and relatives. He was awestruck by Broadway, with its one-story and two-story buildings alternating with others of seven and even nine stories—a sight he had never before seen in Europe. And he was charmed by the people he met. "Amazing people, these Americans," he wrote admiringly. "After Paris, where in every courtesy from a stranger one senses an attempt at exploitation, the straightforwardness here, the sincerity, generosity, cordiality without ulterior motive, willingness to be of service and pamper one—are simply staggering, and touching at the same time. This, and in general American ways, American customs and mores, I find very attractive—but I enjoy all this like a man sitting at a table laden with gastronomical wonders but having no appetite. Only the prospect of return to Russia can whet the appetite in me."[6] Crammed with meetings and rehearsals, the days flew by. "I am petted, honored, and entertained here in every way possible," he wrote to Bob on 18/30 April. "It turns out that in America I am ten times more renowned than in Europe. At first when they told me this, I thought it was an exaggerated courtesy. Now I see that it is true. . . . Here I am much more of a *bigwig* than in Russia. Isn't that curious?!! At the rehearsal the musicians . . . received me ecstatically."[7]

Tchaikovsky was finding American life much to his liking. Dazzled by its grandiosity, its colossal scale in comparison with Europe, he was also greatly impressed by the fact that despite their commitment to material interests, the Americans put a strong emphasis on the arts. This, he felt, was evidenced by the construction of Carnegie Hall, the inauguration ceremonies of which he had been invited to take part in later that month. The comforts of his hotel delighted him as well, with its novelties and luxuries virtually unknown as yet in Europe, not to mention Russia: electric lighting, a lavatory with basin and bath, and a device for speaking with the hotel's main desk. He was introduced to Andrew Carnegie himself, whom he took to at once and whom he especially liked for the fact that the famous millionaire "adores Moscow, which he visited two years ago."[8] Several days later, Tchaikovsky had dinner at Carnegie's home. "This vastly rich man lives, in fact, no more luxuriously than other people," he noted in his diary. "Carnegie, this amazing original, who over the years grew from a telegraph boy into one of the richest men in America and yet has remained a simple, modest, and in no way arrogant man, inspires an extraordinary liking in me — perhaps because he too is filled with liking for me." Tchaikovsky marveled in amusement at Carnegie's effusive displays of affection. "He grasped my hands, crying that I am the uncrowned but veritable king of music, embraced me (without kissing: here men never kiss) and, exclaiming about my greatness, raised himself on tiptoe and held his arms high and finally delighted the entire company by imitating how I conduct. He did this so seriously, so well, so like me—that I myself was carried away."[9]

Tchaikovsky's first performance in New York took place on 23 April/5 May at the ceremonies inaugurating Carnegie Hall, at which he conducted his *Coronation March* of 1883. He was, as always, very anxious, but everything went well. The *New York Herald* wrote the following day that "Tchaikovsky is a tall, gray, well-built, interesting man, well on sixty. He seems a trifle embarrassed, and responds to the applause by a succession of brusque and jerky bows. But as soon as he grasps the baton his self-confidence returns. There is no sign of nervousness about him as he taps for silence. He conducts with the authoritative strength of a master and the band obeys his lead as one man."[10]

Tchaikovsky was taken aback by the habit of the American press to comment not only on his music or his conducting but also on himself as a person and was especially shocked by the mention of his embarrassment and "brusque and jerky bows" before the start of the concert. Some papers also reported that he had arrived with his "young and pretty wife," this being in fact the daughter of Morris Reno, the president of the New York Music Hall Company, who had met Tchaikovsky on his arrival in New York.

The reported conjecture that Tchaikovsky was "well on sixty" made yet another unpleasant impression, coming as it did on the eve of his fifty-first birthday. Moreover, when he mentioned this to Carnegie, the latter was also very much surprised, he, too, having thought Tchaikovsky to be much older. After such conversations, the impressionable Tchaikovsky found himself plagued by terrible nightmares in which he was sliding inexorably down a gigantic rock face toward the sea, trying desperately to grasp the narrow edge of some crag. "All this seems to be an echo of the evening talk about my old age," he noted in his diary.[11] Still, all the American papers unanimously praised not only his music but also his skill as a conductor, to the point where Tchaikovsky, who held a low opinion of his conducting abilities, began to wonder whether he might not in fact be much better at it than he had thought.

He gave three more concerts in New York, one on his birthday, 25 April/7 May, at which he conducted his Third Suite. The next evening, two of his choral songs were sung, "The Lord's Prayer" and an arrangement of his "Legend," op. 54, no. 5. At Tchaikovsky's final concert at Carnegie Hall on 27 April/9 May, the First Piano Concerto was performed, conducted by the composer with the young German pianist Adele Aus der Ohe as soloist. Tchaikovsky wrote in his diary, "My concerto went splendidly. . . . The enthusiasm was such as I have never managed to arouse even in Russia. They called me out endlessly, shouting 'upwards' [*sic*] and waving their handkerchiefs—in short, it was clear that I had truly pleased the Americans. But especially dear to me was the enthusiasm of the orchestra."[12] After the last concert in New York, Tchaikovsky visited Niagara Falls and then traveled to Baltimore, where on 3/15 May a concert including the Serenade for Strings and the First Piano Concerto, again with Aus der Ohe as soloist, met with great success. On 4/16 May he left for Washington, where his Piano Trio was performed at a reception at the Russian embassy, and on 6/18 May he was in Philadelphia, where he conducted the same program as in Baltimore, to an equally warm response. On his return to New York on 8/20 May, the Piano Trio was performed once more, together with the Third String Quartet, at a concert for the Composer's Club at the Metropolitan Opera House. The next day, Tchaikovsky noted in his diary, "I sat in the first row. . . . The program was too long. Midway through the evening Mr. Smyth [*sic*] made a speech addressed to me. I replied briefly in French. Of course, an ovation. One lady tossed a splendid bouquet of roses straight into my face."[13]

On 9/21 May, Tchaikovsky left America for Hamburg aboard the *Prince Bismarck*, casting one final glance, early in the morning, at the Statue of Liberty. Tired, worn out, but deeply content, he dreamed now of the moment when he would again see his beloved Bob. He had written to him, indeed with passion, a few days before, "[Our meeting] seems to me an unattainable, fabulous happiness; I try to think of it as little as possible, so as to be able to endure a few more days of torment." But, he added, he would always remember America with love.[14]

Arriving in Hamburg on 17/29 May, Tchaikovsky proceeded from there to Berlin and finally to St. Petersburg. He spent a week in the capital in the company of his nephew and then returned home, this time to the former house at Maidanovo, where Alyosha had managed to move their things in his absence. He had been forced to give up the house in Frolovskoe, which had been put up for sale by the owners at a price he could not afford. The house at Maidanovo was in poor shape and the park around it teemed with vacationers. Almost immediately Tchaikovsky began looking for another place to rent.

At Maidanovo he was shortly visited again by Bob, together with Modest and Aleksandr Litke, their young first cousin once removed, who was beginning at this time to play a noticeable role in Tchaikovsky's life. But it was with Bob that Tchaikovsky throughout this whole year was growing more and more obsessed. Never before had his desire for Bob's constant presence, his desire to caress and indulge him, been so pronounced as during these months. In March, writing from Berlin on his way to Paris, he had told Bob of the "terrible, inexpressible, maddeningly agonizing homesickness" that had come upon him almost as soon as he found himself abroad. "Most of all," he wrote, "I thought, of course, of you and so longed to see you, to hear your voice, and this appeared to me such unbelievable bliss, that, it seems, I would have given up ten years of my life (and, as you know, I value my life very much) to have you appear even for a second. . . . Bob! I adore you. Do you remember, I told you that even greater than my joy at beholding you with my own eyes is my suffering when I am without you!"[15] Later, in July, he wrote, "Like a youth having received a letter from the girl he loves, I kissed over and over again, mercilessly, the traces of your wretched, abominable hand. My dear, wonderful fellow, I adore you!"[16] The same analogy to someone in love was also at the heart of a musical joke that Tchaikovsky composed and addressed to Bob a year later. The stylized folk ditty, in which the composer identified himself with a young girl pining for her beloved, began:

> No news from my darling,
> I can't take it anymore,
> If only he would write me
> Just an itty-bitty note.[17]

At twenty, Bob was now nearly past the age that Tchaikovsky normally found erotic. Yet, his hold on his uncle's heart never slipped, and in the last years of Tchaikovsky's life Bob reigned supreme in his emotional world. Tchaikovsky increasingly felt not merely erotic attraction but the same blend of fondness and responsibility toward his nephew that he had earlier felt toward Anatoly and Modest, and the pleasure of shaping this young mind in accord with his own design. The path of his adoration was not always smooth. After one of Bob's earlier visits to Maidanovo, Tchaikovsky had been disappointed to learn in a letter from the Davydov children's governess that Bob could have stayed with him some three days more, though his nephew had assured him that he could not. "From which I conclude," Tchaikovsky told Modest, "that his visit to me was a sacrifice, though not a burdensome one. I only take note of this fact, but in no way feel offended, for I know by my own experience that one can love a person but not especially love to spend more than a certain amount of time with that person."[18] The mature composer was undergoing a hard schooling. A letter to Bob after that visit showed the blend of passion, didacticism, ironic self-awareness, and banter that was characteristic of Tchaikovsky's correspondence with his nephew. "Were you an interesting and intelligent boy, one might have killed time somehow," he wrote. "But having taken into consideration your dreadful denseness and silliness, I am filled with horror at what I would have experienced in the course of three [more] days."[19]

Despite his joking disparagements, Tchaikovsky continued to perceive in the object of his affections a multitude of merits. "You are definitely climbing a most respectable distance above the ranks of common mortals," he wrote Bob on 11 July. "I am inclined to think that you will be either a writer-artist or a writer-philosopher. I have long since noticed that you are given to serious theorizing."[20] And on 22 July, in response to Bob's complaint that he felt like a mere "container" with no real content of his own, he wrote, "You are by no means a 'container.' You have a great deal of content, only everything contained in the container is still heaped about in disorder. . . . In fact, . . . everything will work out on its own. Enjoy your youth and learn to value time. My dear, good, darling beloved! My adorable little container!"[21]

By the end of the year, Tchaikovsky was telling Bob that he was "constantly in my thoughts, for at every sensation of grief, of anguish, at every darkening of my mental horizon, like a ray of light the thought appears that you exist and that I . . . shall see you."[22] Some months later still, he wrote about an "enormous favor" he had to ask his nephew. "There is a group portrait of your family, taken in Kiev, probably in 1881," he told him. "You are divinely enchanting in this photograph and recall to me one of the most delectable seasons (???) of your bloom. Thus, I want a big print, enlarged twenty times, of you. . . . This is my *idée fixe*."[23]

But there were, besides Bob, a number of other adolescent boys and young men, relatives and others, who gravitated around the composer. Among them was twelve-year-old Aleksandr Litke, nicknamed Sanya, who became very close to both Tchaikovsky brothers and their nephew. The second son of Tchaikovsky's first cousin Countess Amaliya Litke, née Shobert, Sanya Litke was much sought after as an amateur actor in household theatricals. He spoke fluent French and the title of count opened all doors for him, and for this reason, his circle of acquaintances was unusually wide. Yury Davydov recalled that Sanya "knew absolutely everyone" and that his uncle would therefore use Sanya "for various commissions within society, primarily for polite refusals to invitations. 'Sanechka, dear fellow, run round to X and tell him that I have already died or some such thing, just so he is not offended by my not going to dine with him.' And Sanechka, infinitely devoted to Pyotr Ilyich, would rush off to carry out this not always pleasant mission."[24] Young Sanya Litke was often mentioned in Tchaikovsky's correspondence, sometimes with details suggesting a great familiarity between the two. "Modest and Sanya and I went to . . . the Uspensky Cathedral for the night service," he wrote Bob from Moscow in June 1891. "The service was so beautiful that even the heretic Sanya was moved to tears. We dined with old Konshin [Anatoly's father-in-law]. Sanya was angry that Konshin was calling him 'young man' and not 'count.'"[25]

In early July, Tchaikovsky was again in St. Petersburg, where, as he later wrote Bob from Maidanovo, he "visited the Zoological Garden almost every day and in general behaved like a merchant on a spree after receiving an inheritance. Sanya Litke delighted me with his dear company. Lately he has also advanced tremendously in my service. Now he is already a *général de suite*. Which is not far from adjutant generalship."[26] This mention of the rank of *général de suite*, apart from its expression of Tchaikovsky's particular liking for the boy, referred specifically to the punning sobriquet for his entourage of young male relatives and their friends during his stays in the Russian capital. Tchaikovsky composed three orchestral suites during his lifetime (the *Mozartiana*, op. 61, written in 1887 and based on four pieces by Mozart, was not included among his numbered suites until after his death). This group of young men and boys had come to be known among themselves as his "Fourth Suite."

A favorite spot for Tchaikovsky and his young friends was the St.

Petersburg Zoological Garden. Stretching in a wide sweep behind the Peter and Paul Fortress, the garden was the city's main amusement quarter and by the 1890s and early 1900s was widely considered an area of somewhat ill repute. "Upon entering there you will immediately find yourself in a chaos of petty pimps and cheap courtesans," wrote one St. Petersburg paper of the garden around the turn of the century. "A small percentage of the ordinary public gaze wildly at everything and conduct themselves cautiously. The habitués are various loud Germans, merry shop assistants and quiet apothecary boys behaving very pharmaceutically. A rich bouquet of petty hooliganish humor." Everything blazed and glowed in the anemic light of the white nights of summer. On the stages of the garden appeared magicians, bicyclists, and acrobats. "Lazy, greedy, frivolous, wretchedly poor, immeasurably rich, miserly, generous, and slow-witted—here is Petersburg amusing itself—a Petersburg of champagne and the cancan, embroidered, bejeweled and jolly—with that special Petersburg boredom that a certain decadent, crazed with his own genius, once called 'green.'"[27] Such were the surroundings in which Tchaikovsky might be found when in St. Petersburg "almost every day" with his young friends in these years. And not surprisingly so, perhaps, after his wanderings through the *cafés chantants* and music halls of Paris and elsewhere, for something always drew him to this tasteless, libidinous, and jubilant world.

During his July visit to St. Petersburg, Tchaikovsky made through Sanya Litke the acquaintance at the garden of an attractive Italian youth named Emilio Colombo, a temporary recruit to the Fourth Suite. The sixteen-year-old Emilio played the mandolin in a Neapolitan orchestra then appearing at one of the summer theaters in the park. The two became close, to the point that Tchaikovsky subsequently helped to arrange an appearance for the orchestra in Moscow, singling out in particular the talent of young Emilio. Hoping to see him in Moscow, Tchaikovsky wrote to him in Italy a year later, in a mixture of French and hesitant Italian, "Sanya Litke . . . is bored in Petersburg and will be very glad to see you. . . . How is your health? Are you still as thin as you were in Petersburg?"[28] A photograph of Emilio Colombo from that period shows a pleasant, mischievous-looking youth, casually self-confident with one hand in his pocket and in the other a walking stick on which is propped an elegant top hat. For Emilio the encounter with the famous Russian composer proved pivotal: his father allowed him to study music seriously, and Colombo would go on to achieve celebrity as a violinist.

Back in Maidanovo in late July, Tchaikovsky was still, in his thoughts, with his St. Petersburg companions. To Sanya Litke he sent a "musical joke," the text of which referred to three "darling" letters received from Bob and recalled also how "we found pleasure in visits to the Zoological Garden."[29]

That summer the composer began work in earnest on his one-act opera *Iolanta,* op. 69. With a libretto by Modest based on the Danish writer Heinrik Hertz's play *King René's Daughter,* which Hertz had drawn from a story by Hans Christian Andersen, *Iolanta* told the tale of King René of Anjou and his blind daughter Iolanta who, falling in love with the voice of the young Count Vaudémont, eventually regains her sight. Though Tchaikovsky was soon so immersed in the composition that he even neglected his correspondence, the work went sluggishly, driving Tchaikovsky at times to doubt his abilities. *The Nutcracker,* op. 71, which Vsevolozhsky planned to include in a double bill with *Iolanta,* also disappointed him at first, an opinion that changed only gradually as he completed the sketch for the ballet in June and began to work on its orchestration. In mid-August he interrupted his labors for a visit to his brother Nikolay's estate of Ukolovo, in the Kursk district north of the Ukraine, and to Kamenka. Returning home by early September, he soon managed to finish the one-act opera and set to work on scoring it.

In the midst of all this, an unpleasant event occurred that stirred in Tchaikovsky bitter recollections of Mrs. von Meck and their past. The beautiful watch decorated with the image of Joan of Arc that she had presented to him several years before was stolen from his bedroom desk while the window was open. Nothing else was taken. The police apprehended a local youth who was, it turned out, the valet of the neighboring landowner Novikov, one of whose properties Tchaikovsky himself was renting. The young man was scared and confused. One day he confessed to the robbery, and the next day denied it. In either event, it could not be got out of him where the watch might be hidden—or more precisely, a new story was got out of him every other day. Eventually Tchaikovsky was asked to meet with the suspect in the hope that he might then be moved to tell the whole truth. He noted at once the valet's "uncommonly likable" face and was so struck by the young man's smile that he found it difficult to believe that he could be a villain and a thief. Tchaikovsky tried to reason with him. He reproved him for his actions and asked him where the watch was. The youth tried to tell him that it was in the possession of his master, Novikov. Then he promised to tell the truth, but only in private. They were left alone. At once the fellow was on his knees, sobbing and begging forgiveness. Tchaikovsky quickly forgave him and asked him again where he had hidden the watch. But the valet jumped up, suddenly calm, and announced that he had never stolen it.

Tchaikovsky's dismay at the loss of the watch was worsened by the police's handling of the suspect. To force a truthful confession, the interrogators variously deprived the suspect of food, fed him salt herring but deprived him of water to drink, made him drunk, arranged with a plainclothes detective a sham escape attempt, and whipped the youth—all to no avail. The valet's story simply became more and more muddled. Meanwhile, the whole of Klin followed these developments avidly. Most were convinced that the Novikovs themselves had either participated in the theft or assisted in it, a turn of events that distressed Tchaikovsky. The whole affair seemed to drag on endlessly, financed perforce by Tchaikovsky, who had initiated proceedings, but the watch was never found.

The presence of Laroche, who came to visit during one of his regular periods of unproductivity and financial straits, contributed little to the improvement of Tchaikovsky's mood. Nor did the arrival at this time of a telegram from America inviting Tchaikovsky to make a second concert tour to the United States. The fee proposed this time was little more than a third of what he had received for his earlier visit. Taking offense, Tchaikovsky declined. Still, money, or the lack of it, was beginning to worry him. In the year since the cancellation of his subsidy from Mrs. von Meck, he had continued to live, almost by inertia, as extravagantly as before. He hated to think about money, but now had begun to feel palpably the loss of six thousand rubles a year. Indeed, his changed material situation and, on top of this, the theft of the watch, which he had already bequeathed to his nephew Bob, moved Tchaikovsky to consider drawing up a new will. Further inducement came with new regulations allowing him to bequeath to his heirs future royalties from his works, and on 30 September he signed the revised document, in which he strove to mention all those dear to him whom he wished to benefit after his death.

Uneasy financial arrangements were also the reason behind a brewing conflict between Modest and Kolya Konradi, already a young man of twenty-three. Modest's former pupil—who since the death of his father had become very wealthy—had begun to display a marked tendency toward penny-pinching. Kolya's former tutor, meanwhile, in no way differed in his handling of money from the prodigality of his famous brother. With time Modest had grown accustomed—on grounds of friendship and as his due—to dispose of the Konradi money as though it were his own. The young man's resentment at this intensified and was abetted by his mother. There was little love lost between Alina Bryullova and her son's tutor, and Kolya, despite his mother's scant show of affection for him during his childhood, had not forgotten what he felt to be Modest's insults directed at her in the past. "I have constant quarrels with Modest because of tips," Kolya complained to Tchaikovsky at one point. "Not for nothing do I hate them so terribly, they are at the root of the dwindling of Modya's money."[30] On the Tchaikovsky brothers, both of whom were used to living grandly, Kolya's practicality began to grate noticeably. By the autumn of 1891 the situation had become acute, and Tchaikovsky felt compelled to write of it candidly in a letter to his brother. Two versions of the letter have survived—a lengthy rough draft of 22 October and the shorter letter actually sent, written five days later.

In the draft, Tchaikovsky recalled a striking episode of some two years earlier in which Kolya, as if "driven by some sudden misfortune to complete and boundless despair," had broken down in his presence. So unexpected and strange was the confession that followed, "so cynically heartless and without conscience," that Tchaikovsky had been stupefied. In essence, Kolya had claimed that Modest was a burden to him and that he did not know how to be rid of him, that in fact he did not need him but meanwhile was paying him money, and that Modest was wrong to think that Kolya was attached to him. A stunned Tchaikovsky could think of nothing to say except some advice to tell all this to Modest as soon as possible and have done with it. But even though Kolya had then given hints to Modest along these lines, Modest, out of compassion for Kolya, had resolved to stay with him, much to his brother's displeasure. "I remember," he continued in the draft, "that I cast Kolya utterly from my heart, where he had occupied a very high place. But he went off to the Caucasus, I did not see him for a long while, and when I saw you both in Petersburg, there seemed to be the brightest, most untroubled unity between you." Time had passed, and little by little the episode was forgotten. Tchaikovsky began to treat Kolya exactly as before, "diligently driving from myself the loathsome memory."

But now, this summer, learning that Kolya had again begun to complain to anyone who would listen that Modest was a burden to him, he insisted that his brother part from his former charge forever. "Can you really not see, not understand, that he is unable to recognize what you have done for him and how much he owes to you?" Tchaikovsky asked in the draft. "He regards you as a hired man who at one time received money and full room and board for a certain job. Now there is no job; consequently, all that you have had from him you no longer deserve." Kolya would never recognize that Modest had given him the best years of his life and that no amount of money could ever pay back the sacrifice Modest had made for him, "the paternal and maternal affection of which he would have been deprived had it not been for you, the element of light and warmth that, for all your shortcomings and errors, you brought to his childhood, adolescence, and youth." In Tchaikovsky's view, Modest's relations with his former charge would only be entirely correct, and might even remain friendly, when he had ceased to enjoy any and all material benefits from Kolya. Yet, Modest must try to part without quarreling with Kolya. "He is not to blame for seeing things otherwise than he ought," wrote Tchaikovsky, "that is his nature. . . . We all made the mistake of thinking of him as *our own blood.* No, he is, or course, fond of us all in his way—but his *blood* draws him toward Vasilyevsky Island [that is, toward his mother], toward a world, in essence, foreign to us, however close the external relations may seem."[31]

In some respects, the antagonism between tutor and pupil recalled another, earlier such antagonism—between Tchaikovsky and his student Vladimir Shilovsky, where financial dependence had again played, if not the principal role, then at least an important one. The letter finally sent to Modest on 27 October presented only briefly the detailed argument of the draft. Still, it continued to stress his brother's belief that he would be "a thousand times more comfortable and freer living in your own little furnished room than among Tiflis carpets and the luxury surrounding the son of Alina Ivanovna."[32] Despite his advice, it would be nearly another two years before the long cohabitation so deplored by Tchaikovsky finally came to an end, when Modest and Bob (who was living with Modest at the Konradi home) in August 1893 decided to take an apartment separately from Kolya Konradi.

For the next few months, Tchaikovsky's life became again busy and hectic. He spent three weeks in late October and early November in Moscow, meeting with the visiting conductor Edouard Colonne and rehearsing *The Queen of Spades* at the Bolshoy, where the opera had a highly successful premiere on 4 November. He also conducted the first performance of his Mickiewicz-based symphonic ballad *The Voyevode*, op. 78, begun in September 1890 but completed only recently. Even before the performance, however, he had made up his mind that it was a mediocre work at best, and after the concert he became so intensely disenchanted with it that he actually destroyed the score, though the work was later reconstructed from the orchestral parts.

Spending two weeks in Maidanovo and completing there the scoring of *Iolanta*, Tchaikovsky next left for St. Petersburg to take part in a concert to benefit the hungry, scheduled for 1 December. His brother Anatoly, meanwhile, had been appointed deputy governor of Revel (now Tallinn), and so, Tchaikovsky proceeded from St. Petersburg to Estonia to visit his brother briefly before returning back through the capital to Maidanovo, where he set about working on a revision of his string sextet, *Souvenir de Florence*, op. 70. At the end of December he conducted a concert of his works in Kiev, then spent Christmas at Kamenka, and from there traveled to Warsaw for another concert engagement on the second day of 1892. The concert was, as Tchaikovsky himself noted to Modest the following day, "brilliant in all respects," while "the orchestra (which grew very fond of me) played beautifully."[33] While in Warsaw he met with a former pupil, the violinist Barcewicz, and heard for the first time Mascagni's *Cavalleria Rusticana*, which he especially liked for its "wonderfully happy choice of subject."[34]

By 4/16 January, Tchaikovsky was already in Berlin on his way to Hamburg for the premiere there three days later of *Eugene Onegin*. The production was well received, albeit, as Tchaikovsky noted, in restrained German fashion. Still, the composer had curtain calls and was applauded after each scene, and Tchaikovsky attributed this success to the young conductor Gustav Mahler, whom he described as "not some average sort, but simply a *genius* burning with a desire to conduct."[35] The next day, 8/20 January, Tchaikovsky departed for Paris, where he wanted to relax somewhat before concerts scheduled later that month in Amsterdam and The Hague. He stayed at his usual hotel, and to his pleasant surprise he discovered his young pianist friend Aleksandr Siloti and his wife also staying there. His ten days in Paris were filled with visits to the theater and to the Folies-Bergère, and with reading Zola's *La Bête humaine*. But he found the theaters dull and the novel, with its pointed naturalism, annoying, and when suddenly he learned that the concerts in Holland had been canceled, he rejoiced and left for Russia at once. He spent a week in St. Petersburg visiting with Modest, Kolya, and Bob and then, on 28 January, returned to Maidanovo to start work on the orchestration of *The Nutcracker*.

He returned home not alone but in the company of Eduard Nápravník's son Vladimir. Tchaikovsky and young Nápravník, who was now twenty-three, had been corresponding for several years, and Tchaikovsky at this time appeared to the youth "a sort of idol," as Vladimir later recalled. "Despite the fact that he was of the same age as my father, he took me 'seriously,' acquainted me with his brother Modest Ilyich, . . . and introduced me also to the company of his nephews and their friends."[36] Vladimir had asked for permission to spend some time at the composer's home in Maidanovo while preparing for his university examinations. He later wrote that Tchaikovsky "answered that he would be glad to see me, but that he feared I might grow bored buried in the countryside, in the winter, 'in the company of a gray-haired, grumbling old man with a silly habit of spending his time scribbling music.'"[37]

But Vladimir was undeterred, and during the month he stayed at Maidanovo, Tchaikovsky found him to be "a very agreeable room-mate," as he noted to Anatoly. "He is seriously preparing for his examination and is busy even more hours during the day than I, while his musical talent is great pleasure for me, as in the evenings I delight in playing piano duets with him or sometimes simply have him play me my favorite pieces."[38] To Modest he exclaimed simply, "An inestimable companion!"[39] The young guest later recalled that his father, "receiving most enthusiastic letters from me, wrote to Tchaikovsky that he and my mother sent Pyotr Ilyich a thousand thanks for the hearty welcome, hospitality, cordial attention, and affection shown to their son."[40] Tchaikovsky's own letter to the elder Nápravník confirmed this. "I am extremely pleased that Volodya [Vladimir] is enjoying his stay with me," he wrote, "but believe me that I am probably enjoying our unfortunately temporary cohabitation even more than he. One could not imagine a more pleasant, agreeable, even-tempered, likable roommate. . . . It is simply moving to see how industriously he works, not losing a single minute of the day."[41]

With such diligence, he felt, his young friend had well earned the right to amuse himself, and in the middle of February the two made a five-day excursion to Moscow during which, as Tchaikovsky wrote Modest afterward, they "caroused terribly."[42] A few days later, both Tchaikovsky and Vladimir left Maidanovo for St. Petersburg, where, on 3 March, Tchaikovsky conducted the student orchestra of the School of Jurisprudence in a performance of the waltz from *The Sleeping Beauty* and his "Song Without Words." Then on 7 March, at an assembly of the St. Petersburg branch of the Musical Society, he conducted his *Romeo and Juliet* and, for the first time, a suite from *The Nutcracker*, which was not scheduled to have its premiere until late that same year.

"I am in ecstasy over the Russian spring!" Tchaikovsky exclaimed in a letter to Siloti soon after his return to Maidanovo two days later.[43] Again he did not arrive alone, this time bringing Sanya Litke with him. "Sanya and I are enjoying our life immensely," he wrote Modest on the seventeenth. "My work is in full swing, . . . and by Holy Week, I hope to finish the scoring [of *The Nutcracker*]. Every morning we wait in vain for Bob."[44] Bob finally appeared the next day, and both young men began preparing for their examinations. Meanwhile, Tchaikovsky, at

Alyosha's urging, made up his mind to move to a new and larger house he had found in nearby Klin. It was a beautiful house, comfortable, with a garden and no neighbors whatsoever. As before, Alyosha promised to handle the move in his master's absence, and on 27 March, Tchaikovsky, accompanied by Bob and Sanya, left Maidanovo, traveling first to St. Petersburg, where he attended a memorial service for Aleksandra, and then to Moscow, where he stayed nearly the whole of April, conducting Gounod's *Faust*, Anton Rubinstein's *The Demon* and his own *Eugene Onegin* for the private Pryannishnikov Opera.

On 13 April the Moscow paper *News of the Day* published an interview with Tchaikovsky. Describing the composer as "European [that is, Westernized] to the tips of his fingernails," the reporter noted also that he was "enchantingly courteous, pleasant, and spoke willingly of his favorite subject, music." In particular, Tchaikovsky revealed in the interview that he was "now thinking about a new symphony."[45] In a letter to Siloti a week earlier Tchaikovsky had also spoken of his latest idea. "I am already considering a new large composition," he wrote, "that is, a symphony with a *secret* program."[46] The project in question, the forerunner of his great *Pathétique* Symphony, was an abortive symphony in E-flat major, a work that was to cause him such frustration that he would eventually abandon most of what he had written.

Life in Moscow revolved as usual around rehearsals and burdensome social obligations, with a few pleasant distractions. Modest's play *Symphony* proved a success at the Maly Theater, and for his fifty-second birthday Tchaikovsky was delighted to receive from his friend and former student Sergey Taneev a musical joke entitled *The Composer's Birthday: A Ballet*. Taneev had not only concocted his composition on themes from works by Tchaikovsky but had also worked out an elaborate scenario in which appeared various characters from Tchaikovsky's operas and which concluded with a children's galop and a whirl of cranes.

Tchaikovsky could not yet go to Klin, even for a day. Although the house was now ready and Alyosha and his wife had moved in, Alyosha asked his master not to arrive until his wife, now in the last stages of pregnancy, was delivered of her child. Finally, on 23 April, a boy was born, Georgy, nicknamed Egorka, and on his way to St. Petersburg a week later, Tchaikovsky stopped in Klin for the baptism and to see, at last, his new home after the move. He found everything very much to his liking and, without lingering in the capital, soon returned and became occupied with proofs for the piano arrangement of *The Nutcracker* and for his early Festival Overture on the Danish National Anthem, op. 15, which was being published now for the first time.

After the end of examinations at the School of Jurisprudence in late

May, Tchaikovsky and Bob made plans to travel to the French resort town of Vichy to try the waters. They had wanted also to take Sanya Litke with them, but Sanya's mother would not let him go. "I regret it very much," Tchaikovsky confessed to Kolya Konradi at the time, "even though Sanya's trip would have been a great strain on my budget."[47] But what had promised to be a pleasant vacation alone with Bob turned out to be an unexpected ordeal when Anatoly's wife, Praskovya, who was then visiting the capital with her husband, suddenly decided to join them. "I am very displeased at this, Bob is nearly in despair," Tchaikovsky wrote bitterly to Modest in Grankino from St. Petersburg on 31 May. "And indeed, this both inconveniences us and in all respects has poisoned what trifling pleasure Bob and I had felt at the forthcoming journey. She will constrain us dreadfully in all respects."[48]

To Tchaikovsky's disgust and Bob's extreme discomfort, Praskovya, still an inveterate coquette, had begun flirting shamelessly with Bob. Though Anatoly had lately been in depressed spirits, she left him and their daughter, Tanya, in Russia to meet Tchaikovsky and Bob in Paris on 10/22 June. "Bob is very much distressed," Tchaikovsky wrote Modest the next day. "I also feel extremely hostile toward her. We go to Vichy today by the evening train. I fear that Panya's being with us (if we do not make peace with her) will wipe out the whole benefit of the waters. . . . (She is unbearable to Bob, owing to special circumstances about which it is awkward to write.)"[49] These "special circumstances" clearly involved Praskovya's infatuation with Bob. From Vichy, Tchaikovsky reported that "proper relations have been established with Panya," but that the situation was still far from comfortable. "She is undoubtedly in love with Bob and has come here for that reason alone. It is not particularly pleasant for him. Meanwhile, I feel vexed for his sake and cannot forgive her for having abandoned Anatoly and Tanya at a time when she should by no means have done so."[50]

More disturbing than Praskovya's behavior, however, was the state of Bob's health. "The doctor finds that Bob is *seriously* unwell, that his liver is in an abominable condition, and that independently of Vichy he must always lead a strictly hygienic life," Tchaikovsky wrote Modest from Vichy. "Otherwise all kinds of ailments threaten him—but most of all *obesity* and *diabetes.* Bob is not the least bit hypochondriacal and was barely disturbed by the doctor's threats. On the whole, it seems, absolutely everything is all one to Bob, nothing fascinates him and nothing frightens him. . . . But it cannot be said that Bob particularly pines or feels melancholy. Just like myself, some moments he is very merry, but for the most part just so-so, and we both think only of departure."[51] With Anatoly he shared concerns of a different sort:

"Bob worries me very much. If possible, I seem during this trip to have come to love him even more than before, but at the same time, I begin to think about his future with alarm and anxiety. He has a very morbid, unbalanced, abnormal nature, in many respects resembling Tanya's."[52]

Bob and Tchaikovsky returned to Russia in early July and were met in St. Petersburg by Sanya Litke and Baron Rudolph Buchshoevden, a classmate and friend of Bob's. Staying at the Konradi apartment, Tchaikovsky spent that day and the next in the company of his young relatives and their friends. "[Yesterday] evening we went to the Zoological Garden and the Aquarium [a summer theater in the garden]," he wrote to the absent Kolya on 9 July, two days after their return. "Now Bob has gone to Oranienbaum [outside St. Petersburg]. Tomorrow he departs for Kamenka, while I shall stay another three days on business. Both Bob and I are very glad to be back in Russia. In the Aquarium I was unexpectedly given an ovation."[53]

If the charming Sanya Litke and his brother Konstantin were favorite young companions of Tchaikovsky, reckoning with some of Bob's own intimate friends was not always so easy. Tchaikovsky was particularly dismayed by his nephew's acquaintance with Aleksey Apukhtin. When Bob wrote to his uncle of his meetings with the flamboyant poet in St. Petersburg, Tchaikovsky responded with swift displeasure. He beseeched Bob to stay away from Apukhtin. "I do not wish to tell you my reasons, since I should have to spell out an opinion about Apukhtin that I established long ago in the depths of my heart, but never express, as it is not in keeping with my seemingly friendly relations with him," he told his nephew. "Apukhtin is someone who is very pleasant in a group, and you may enjoy his wit as much as you like within a numerous company. But, for God's sake, do not enter into a friendship with him or frequent *tête-à-têtes*. . . . If during my stay in Petersburg you should see him often, it will utterly poison my life there."[54] Clearly, Tchaikovsky was concerned about the possibility of a seduction of the beloved nephew by an old and cunning friend.

But his nephew's principal and most ardent attachment was to the young Baron Rudolph Buchshoevden. This Rudy, as he was called, was openly disapproved of by Tchaikovsky, who often spoke of him in his letters with irritation and displeasure. "In order for me to decide to come to Kamenka," he wrote Bob on 11 July 1891, "it would be necessary for you to wish this very much. But you do not especially wish this at all; provided your disagreeable Rudy comes, nothing else matters to you."[55] Later, Bob would take evident offense at his uncle for having called his favorite friend "stupid." Tchaikovsky was quick to retreat, but not without qualifications. "If I did in fact say that Rudy is stupid, then I take that word back," he wrote. "No, it is not that he is stupid, but he is not very interesting, he lacks personality. Take, for example, Sanya Litke. . . . In all likelihood, they are equals in terms of intelligence, but Sanya has so much originality, zest, refinement—in short, he is quite often able to manifest a certain individual charm all his own." But, in Tchaikovsky's apparently jealous eyes, the young Buchshoevden possessed no charm whatsoever. "He is simply a kind, elegant, delicate, and pretty (but not handsome) fellow. But on my honor, I am very fond of Rudy; I just do not understand all your fuss over him."[56]

Bob did, however, have at least one other interest besides Buchshoevden. "It turns out that Bob has taken a great interest in his own grooming and will engage in this lovingly," Tchaikovsky noted at one point. "I am very pleased by this and try to add fuel to the fire."[57]

Back in Klin, Tchaikovsky was soon involved in the pressing job of proofreading the scores for *Iolanta* and *The Nutcracker*. By early September, in need of a break and hoping to see there his young friends Sapelnikov and Siloti, he was happy to head for Vienna, where he had agreed to conduct at the International Musical and Theatrical Exhibition. On his arrival, however, Tchaikovsky was dismayed to discover that the promised "luxurious hall" proved to be, in his words, "a hovel," while the orchestra, though very conscientious, was "shabby."[58] Angered, he left after two rehearsals on a pretext of illness and went to Itter in the Tyrol, where he joined Sapelnikov and Sophie Menter at her castle. He spent two weeks there, leaving for Prague at the end of the month to attend the highly successful Czech production of *The Queen of Spades*.

By 3 October, Tchaikovsky had returned to St. Petersburg, spending several days there with Modest and Bob before proceeding to Klin to work on the new E-flat symphony and continue correcting proofs. But three weeks later, he was back in the capital, this time to supervise rehearsals of both *Iolanta* and *The Nutcracker*, which were to be presented together on the same program at the Mariinsky Theater. He decided not to stay at the Konradi apartment where, Modest and Kolya having returned, tension continued to increase, but took up residence instead at the Grand Hotel, a few blocks from St. Isaac's Square. It was during this visit that the painter and art critic Igor Grabar, then a young man, vividly recalls discussing music with Tchaikovsky one moonlit night as the two walked slowly along the banks of the Neva River toward the hotel on Malaya Morskaya Street.[59] Tchaikovsky was still in St. Petersburg when, in November, he received word from France of what he rightly saw as a singular honor and a sign of his worldwide recognition: by a majority of votes he had been elected a corresponding member of the prestigious Académie des Beaux Arts. Until that time, only one other Russian, the sculptor Mark Antokolsky, had been so honored. Later that same month Tchaikovsky attended the premiere of Modest's latest play, *A Day in Petersburg.* The production closed after one performance, and the play was never staged again.

Finally, on 5 December, the dress rehearsal of *Iolanta* and *The Nutcracker* took place in the presence of the tsar. "His Majesty was delighted, summoning me to his box and heaping compliments on me," Tchaikovsky wrote to Anatoly the following day. "The staging of both the one and the other was magnificent, and that of the ballet even too magnificent—the splendor tires the eyes."[60] Neither the press nor the musical community, however, thought much of either of Tchaikovsky's "latest creations." In terms of its composer's "melodic inspiration," the opera was judged to be "far from his usual high level," and "no creativity whatsoever" was found in the ballet.[61] Rimsky-Korsakov thought *Iolanta* the weakest of Tchaikovsky's compositions. "Everything in this opera is unfortunate," he would write later, "from the shameless borrowings [from Anton Rubinstein] . . . to the orchestration, which this time Tchaikovsky did haphazardly."[62] Rimsky-Korsakov had a particular reason for finding fault with Tchaikovsky: his own recent opera-ballet *Mlada* had been temporarily removed from the repertory of the Mariinsky to make room for *Iolanta,* and as if to add insult to injury, Tchaikovsky's opera had been favored not only by the presence of the tsar, who had not attended Rimsky's, but also by the participation of the popular tenor Nikolay Figner and his equally popular wife, the soprano Medea Mei-Figner.

By this time, Tchaikovsky had grown almost accustomed to such initially hostile attacks on his theatrical works. "I am quite indifferent to it," he told Anatoly, "for it is not the first time, and I know that in the end I shall prevail."[63] Still, a sense of emptiness plagued him in the weeks after the premiere. His young friends rallied to distract him by various means from his melancholy mood. In propagating their cult of the composer, the members of the Fourth Suite often arranged new meetings for him with artistically promising and presumably physically attractive young men. So it was that several days after the double premiere the future conductor and musician Aleksandr Khessin was brought to Tchaikovsky. Khessin was a student of law at St. Petersburg University when his classmates Vladimir Nápravník and Sanya Litke discovered that Khessin in fact spent much of his time studying music theory in secret. Learning that he was a passionate admirer of Tchaikovsky, they shortly presented him with a surprise that took his breath away.

"Pyotr Ilyich Tchaikovsky will meet with you on 12 December 1892 at the Grand Hotel, in his room, at eleven o'clock in the morning!" Vladimir Nápravník informed Khessin solemnly one day.

"This news positively overwhelmed me, and I almost fainted from the unexpected joy," Khessin later recalled, "but coming to my senses I grew terribly somber, wondering with what could I possibly present myself before Pyotr Ilyich?" After much deliberation the young man decided on several of his own musical works to show Tchaikovsky. The day arrived, "the memorable day that decided my fate," as Khessin later called it. He arrived at the Grand Hotel, where he was met by Nápravník, and Litke. "I could not get a word out for nervous tension," writes Khessin. "We greeted each other silently and went to Pyotr Ilyich's room. Pyotr Ilyich appeared to be in a good mood. Movingly kissing Volodya and Sanya, he warmly and cordially held out his hand to me." In his embarrassment Khessin was struck dumb. An awkward silence fell. Then "Pyotr Ilyich smiled, and the extraordinarily kind smile lit up his face. Taking me gently by the hand, he had us sit down at the table.... Our conversation became easy and spontaneous, helped not a little by the presence of my comrades, Litke and Nápravník, who felt quite at home with their 'Uncle Petya.'"

After listening to his visitor's compositions, Tchaikovsky gave his estimation of the young man's creative prospects. "Your musical gifts, general culture, excellent performing abilities, and fine taste give reason to think that you will amount to something," he told Khessin. "I do not presume to predict just what gift you will pursue, whether that of a pianist, a conductor, or a composer, but gifted young men like yourself, so devoted to music, must dedicate themselves wholly to this art. Quietly pass your civil examinations at the university and enter the conservatory, the composition class."

Khessin never forgot "how Pyotr Ilyich, bidding us farewell, embraced me affectionately, and warmly kissed all three of us. That kiss left an indelible impression on my memory.... Winged with the most rainbowlike hopes, I flew from the Grand Hotel and raced home." It was an encounter, indeed, that shaped Khessin's entire later life and career.[64]

That same winter, after Tchaikovsky had left the capital, the core of his young St. Petersburg entourage gathered for a group photograph. In it were Bob and Yury Davydov, Sanya and Konstantin Litke, Vladimir Nápravník, Kolya Konradi, Rudy Buchshoevden, and Volodya Argutinsky-Dolgorukov, along with Modest. Modest sent a copy of the group portrait to his brother with the comment, "Why write a Fourth Suite when you already have a Fourth Suite?"[65] Throughout the last years of his life this lively and attractive young entourage exercised a consistently beneficial influence on Tchaikovsky. In their company, his creative frustrations and the petty irritations of daily routine melted away. Most likely there existed no sexual ties between the composer and his adored and adoring young men, but their relations produced a romantic atmosphere of playful eroticism and intimate tenderness, and Tchaikovsky, despite his customary inclination to melancholy, found life with his beloved Fourth Suite filled with warmth and joy.

CHAPTER TWENTY-EIGHT

"Let Them Guess"

"I literally cannot live without working," Tchaikovsky once wrote to Grand Duke Konstantin, "for no sooner has some labor been completed and I begin to think about resting than instead of rest, instead of the pleasure of a tired laborer who has earned the right to the tempting *dolce far niente*, there comes anguish, melancholy, thoughts of the vanity of everything earthly, fear for the future, fruitless regret for the irrevocable past, agonizing questions about the meaning of earthly existence, in a word, all that poisons the life of a man not engrossed in labor and at the same time inclined to hypochondria—and as a result, there appears a desire to begin at once some new labor." It stood to reason, the composer told the grand duke, "that under such circumstances this new labor is not always provoked by true creative necessity."[1] It was precisely the absence of "true creative necessity" or of an inner urging that doomed the unfinished symphony in E-flat major.

In early December 1892, Tchaikovsky received an inquiry from the vice-chancellor of Cambridge University asking if he would be agreeable to traveling to England to accept an honorary doctorate of music from the university on the occasion of the fiftieth anniversary of its Academic Musical Society in June of the coming year. Tchaikovsky accepted the invitation, although not without, by this time, growing reservations about traveling any further than Moscow or St. Petersburg. That winter he was expected in Hamburg, Schwerin, Brussels, and Odessa. But it had been a long while since Tchaikovsky's tours abroad had inspired in him anything but displeasure, having become a routine, and an exhausting one at that. Not having yet left St. Peters-burg, he suddenly decided to cancel his visits to both Hamburg and Schwerin for productions of *Iolanta* and to go instead to Paris, "which alone can quiet to some degree any anguish" gnawing at him.[2]

Despite his brave front, the composer had not been altogether un-affected by the beating that the press had given to *Iolanta* and *The Nutcracker.* But there was more than wounded pride in his desire to escape the demands of public appearances. From Berlin he confided to Bob his dissatisfaction with his work-in-progress, the E-flat major sym-phony with, as he had written earlier, its "secret program" and which was by this time nearly completed. "The past few days, I have given myself up to important meditations fraught with consequences," he wrote in a letter on 16/28 December. "I carefully glanced through and, so to speak, objectively concerned myself with my new symphony, which fortunately I had not had time to orchestrate and publish. My impression of it was most unflattering; that is, the symphony has been written simply in order to write something—there is nothing particu-larly interesting or symphonic in it. I decided to throw it away and forget about it. This is an irreversible decision, and it is wonderful that I made it." But he had begun to brood over whether the failure of the symphony meant that he was "played out, dried up," as he put it. "It is about this that I have been thinking these past three days," he told his nephew. "Perhaps *a plot* can still inspire me, but I ought no longer to write pure music, that is, symphonic or chamber music. Meanwhile, to live without occupation, without some work to absorb one's time, thoughts, and energy, is very tedious. But what should I do? Throw up my hands and forget about composing? It is very difficult to make any decision. And so I think and think, and know not what to do."[3]

The failure of the E-flat major symphony had left Tchaikovsky in a state of virtual creative paralysis. But Bob's response to the news that the symphony was being abandoned surprised his uncle. "I feel sorry of course," the nephew wrote on 19 December, "for the symphony that you have cast down from the cliff as they used to do with children in Sparta, because it seemed to you deformed, whereas it is probably as much a work of genius as the first five."[4] Impressed by such a rebuke from Bob, Tchaikovsky decided not to destroy his creation completely and later incorporated some sketches for the first movement of the E-flat major symphony into his Piano Concerto no. 3 in E-flat Major, op. 75. More important, he did not abandon altogether the idea of a pro-gram symphony. In many ways the original E-flat major project was to influence the conception shortly thereafter of his Sixth Symphony, known popularly as the *Pathétique.*[5]

The day after he wrote his letter to Bob, Tchaikovsky left Berlin and traveled to Basel, Switzerland, where at her home in the nearby town of Montbeliard he planned to visit his childhood governess, Fanny Dürbach. The two had not met in over four decades, but earlier in the year Tchaikovsky had received a letter from Fanny, who asked to see him. From Basel he wrote to Modest on 19/31 December in much the same melancholy vein as in the letter to his nephew. "I have no desire to write anything except tearful effusions," he confessed. "It is truly amazing that I do not go mad or fall ill from phenomenal, monstrous anguish." He found Basel "filthy and depressing," and he looked forward to the "whirlwind of vanity" awaiting him in Paris and Brussels. There at least he would have no time to feel depressed. But never again, he vowed, would he go abroad alone for even the shortest period. "This psychopathic phenomenon recurs with every trip I make abroad," he told Modest of his morbid depression, "and with ever-greater force."[6]

Perhaps most striking was Tchaikovsky's dread of the visit to Montbeliard. He looked forward to the meeting with Fanny Dürbach, now seventy, "almost with terror, as though [I go] to the realm of death and of people long since vanished from the world stage."[7] But the journey into the long-dead past proved anything but terrifying. Being with his former governess was "powerful, strange, magical: just as though for two days I was carried back to the 1840s."[8] From Paris he wrote to Modest of these two days that "Fanny made no scenes on my arrival, she did not weep, or marvel at the change in me—it was simply as though we had parted only a year ago. But both days, going through old memories and rereading letters, we were both continually holding back our tears. . . . Fanny is awfully young-looking, as like to her former self as two drops of water, and since she positively lives only in her memories of Votkinsk, . . . this came to life in my own memory with startling vividness."[9]

He caught his breath in Paris, taking a "certain pleasure" in its theaters, restaurants, and boulevards.[10] But he continued to feel sad and nostalgic, and one thought remained uppermost in his mind: to go home as soon as possible. In addition to his official appointments and engagements, he met with Emma Genton, who had left the Kondratyev family and taken a job in Paris. He was glad to see that she looked happy and seemed, at least, to have lost her amorous interest in him. In late December he went to Brussels for rehearsals and, having celebrated the New Year alone, on 2/14 January 1893 conducted a brilliant concert of his works. After another week in Paris, Tchaikovsky headed finally for Russia, first to Odessa.

Members of the Odessa branch of the Russian Musical Society met Tchaikovsky at the railroad station on 12 January. Among the crush of unfamiliar faces cheering the arrival of the celebrated composer, he was happy to make out those of Vasily Sapelnikov and Sophie Menter. During the course of the next two weeks Tchaikovsky was lionized so fervently by the Odessa residents that even the star reception that he had enjoyed four years earlier in Prague paled in comparison. "Never yet have I experienced anything like what is going on now," he wrote to his cousin Anna Merkling. "I am honored here like some great man, almost like a savior of the fatherland, and pulled in all directions to the point where I have no opportunity to breathe freely. It is almost two weeks now that I have been here, and during this time, I have already managed to conduct five concerts, to lead innumerable rehearsals, to eat a mass of dinners and suppers given in my honor. All this tires me out terribly, but it would be ridiculous to complain, for in the end, it will be pleasant for me to recall these unprecedented ovations and raves."[11]

Every move the composer made was covered in the almost daily accounts in the city's papers. The details of his life were outlined, his person was described, every gala dinner in his honor was reported. There were ecstatic reviews of his concerts and of the current production of *The Queen of Spades*, seen there for the first time. Tchaikovsky's mood predictably improved, even though it was the kind of life he always found particularly tiresome. One eyewitness recalled a theatrical performance at which, when "the audience learned that Tchaikovsky was sitting in one of the boxes, the theater exploded in loud and prolonged applause. The composer, who had been hiding behind the backs of those with him, was forced to lean out from the box and take a bow. The impresario of the theater, Ivan Grekov, begged in vain for Pyotr Ilyich to appear [on stage] before the audience."[12]

A steady stream of people passed through Tchaikovsky's hotel room on various pretexts—from asking for his autograph to begging him to listen to their child prodigies play. Tchaikovsky heard them out patiently, though often the parents of the adolescent musicians were not satisfied with oral assurances of their children's abilities and demanded written attestations. One such would-be prodigy was a fifteen-year-old pianist, the daughter of an old acquaintance of Ippolit Tchaikovsky, who chanced also to be in Odessa at the time and asked his elder brother to listen to the girl. As it happened, that same day and at almost the same time a young boy, Konstantin Dumchev, was also scheduled to play the violin for Tchaikovsky. Just thirteen, Konstantin had already begun to give concerts and wanted to devote himself seriously to music. Charmed by the daughter of his friend, Ippolit was irritated by the boy and thought him spoiled by his early success. But in actual performance the girl failed to distinguish herself, playing Liszt without expression and unable to perform anything from memory. The embarrassed father took her away at once. But even Ippolit was forced to admit that Konstantin played brilliantly, and watching his brother, he noted that his "face showed satisfaction."[13] In fact, irrespective of musical acumen, the "boy in a velvet suit" must immediately have captured Tchaikovsky's attention in much the same degree as the "pretty girl" had caught the eye of his brother. Konstantin Dumchev later recalled that "Pyotr Ilyich treated me with charming affability and cordiality and made me promise to visit him every day and take morning tea with him. And so, every morning toward nine o'clock, I visited him at the Northern Hotel and delighted in conversation with him."[14]

It was during these hectic days in Odessa that by all accounts the best, and the only surviving, painted portrait of the composer was executed. In hurried sittings sandwiched between rehearsals, social engagements, and performances, the artist Nikolay Kuznetsov succeeded in capturing with his brush the emotional and intellectual intensity of Tchaikovsky the creator. Now hanging in the Tretyakov Gallery in Moscow, the portrait preserves an image of the composer as he was in the last years of his life, at the zenith of his powers.

Odessa was a turning point. Returning to Klin in early February with a renewed feeling of confidence and inspiration, Tchaikovsky embarked at once on what was destined to be his last and crowning creation, the Symphony no. 6 in B Minor, op. 74. He worked so furiously and with such heat that in less than four days after his arrival the first part of the symphony was already complete and the rest was clearly outlined in his head. "You cannot imagine what bliss I feel," he wrote excitedly to Bob on 11 February 1893, "assured that my time has not yet passed and that I can still work."[15]

In those notes, passages, and pronouncements which unmistakably refer to his work on the Sixth Symphony, Tchaikovsky made it quite clear that he was composing with an explicit program in mind. It was during his traveling, he told Bob in his letter of 11 February, that there had come to him the idea for another symphony, "this time with a program, but with such a program that will remain a mystery to everyone—let them guess." The new work, he told his nephew, would simply be called "Program Symphony (no. 6)." Even to Bob he would reveal only that "the program itself, whatever it may be, is imbued with subjectivity, and quite often during my wanderings, composing it in my mind, I wept terribly."[16]

In 1907 the Czech musicologist Rudolph Batka inquired of Modest the actual meaning of his brother's last masterpiece. He received this answer: "You would like to know the program of the Sixth Symphony, but unfortunately I cannot tell you anything, since my brother kept it secret in his thoughts. He carried this secret with him to the grave."[17] The riddle of the symphony's program has remained a source of lasting controversy. There are essentially two schools of thought on the subject. The first seeks to interpret the work in a narrow autobiographical sense, often reducing its meaning to an artistic expression of the homoerotic torment allegedly suffered by the composer. The other takes a reverse approach, often seeing in the symphony so broad a meditation on the issues of life and death that the entire notion of a "program" becomes meaningless. Both views would seem to be extreme and, in the final analysis, trivializing. The former limits the symphony's significance to private idiosyncrasy, while the latter underestimates the plain fact that life and death are the ultimate and inevitable subjects of any work of art. In his letter to Bob, after all, the content of the work is characterized as "imbued with subjectivity"; the original impetus must, it follows, have been distinctly personal.

Some years before, in a letter to Mrs. von Meck on 5/17 December 1878, Tchaikovsky had defined his understanding of program music. The inspiration of a symphonic composer, he told her, could be either subjective or objective. "In the first instance, he uses his music to express his own feelings, joys, sufferings; in short, like a lyric poet he pours out, so to speak, his own soul," he wrote. "In this instance, a program is not only not necessary but even impossible. But it is another matter when a musician, reading a poetic work or struck by a scene in nature, wishes to express in musical form that subject that has kindled his inspiration. Here a program is essential. . . . In any event, to my mind both sorts possess completely identical *raisons d'être*." Furthermore, "it goes without saying that not every subject is fit for a symphony, just as not every subject is fit for an opera—but still program music can and must exist, just as it is impossible to demand that literature make do without the epic element and limit itself to lyricism alone."[18]

The new composition was genetically linked to the uncompleted E-flat major symphony. A few written notes have survived that shed some light on the complex dynamics of the composer's creative spirit. They seem to have referred to the original idea for the E-flat major symphony, but may also have been reflected, implicitly and however indirectly, in his later and final artistic endeavor. On 10/22 May 1891, during his return voyage to Europe from America, Tchaikovsky recorded in his diary, "At eight o'clock breakfast. . . . Then I stroll about the lower deck, work, read. By 'work' I mean sketches for future symphony."[19] As scholars have established, these sketches were made in a notebook with materials for *The Nutcracker*, but Tchaikovsky later tore them out because they were unrelated to the ballet.[20] One note reads, "Following is essence of plan for a symphony *Life!* First movement—all impulse, confidence, thirst for activity. Must be short. (Finale *death*—result of collapse.) Second movement love; third disappointment; fourth ends with a dying away (also short)." On another, separate sheet written at the same time, a musical sketch for the symphony is found. A heading reads "Life. (I) Youth." On the reverse side the composer wrote, "(II) Obstacles!" Then, above the following bar, "Nonsense!" and on the second line, "Coda. Forward, forward!"[21] Probably slightly earlier, in the context of other sketches, Tchaikovsky wrote in his notebook, "A motif: for what? for what? why? The beginning and the main idea of the whole symphony."[22] During his ocean voyage he also made one more musical sketch, in E minor, "creating an image filled with estrangement and a sort of sublime suffering."[23]

Tchaikovsky had always sought to interpret through music the most fundamental questions of existence—the meaning of life, death, love, beauty. The desire to characterize musically the main stages of human life was too strong in him merely to be cast aside after his work on the E-flat major symphony was abandoned in September 1892. This idea, in conjunction with that of a secret program, took hold of him and continued to grow, gradually acquiring a very different shape. The major thrust in this evolution likely involved the painful transition from a theme of human life in general to that of his own life specifically, a transition that led eventually to the concept of the new symphony, with the earlier, somewhat abstract philosophical concerns now enriched and articulated through the immediate experience of his personal life-drama. For this, the intervening year became crucial. His meeting with Fanny Dürbach provided a powerful added stimulus, helping to resurrect in him the whole intimate world of his childhood and youth.

But it is to Bob Davydov that the Sixth Symphony is dedicated. Arguably, it was only now that the aging composer recognized the full extent of his longing for Bob, even as he faced the unlikelihood of its physical fulfillment. Tchaikovsky's letters and diaries leave no doubt that not only did he adore Bob but he also felt for him a homoerotic passion as strong as any of which he was capable. In the Sixth Symphony, dedicated to Bob, Tchaikovsky embodied the anguish of unrequited love, a conflict between platonic passion and the desires of the flesh, held forcibly in check so as not to profane the sublimity of passion. Here was the perennial spiritual dilemma reformulated by the Romantics and taken by them out of the realm of religion and into the realm of aesthetics, the secret and proud struggle with one's own sensual appetites for the sake of the beautiful and the good.

That the Sixth Symphony was intentionally conceived by its author as autobiographical is borne out by the recollections of the singer Aleksandra Panaeva-Kartsova[24] and is confirmed outright by Yury Davydov, with reference to the accounts of both Modest and Bob, who were convinced that this was so.[25] Modest himself offers the same autobiographical interpretation in his letter to Rudolph Batka. For Tchaikovsky there evidently arose an irresistible desire to retell in music the story of his life and his soul and to dedicate it to Bob so that his beloved nephew might be able to share and appreciate all that he himself had gone through. But, if the Sixth Symphony was indeed intended to be somehow autobiographical, why then was it so pervasively tragic in tone? All available evidence leaves no doubt that—beyond the untimely deaths of certain relatives and friends—no truly catastrophic events accompanied Tchaikovsky's final years. He was at the peak of his creative powers, famous, and loved by those whom he loved. Tchaikovsky himself had little desire to turn back the clock, even as the years advanced, a sentiment stressed in a letter to Anna Merkling some years before on his forty-fourth birthday. He would never agree, he told his cousin, to be made young again and relive his life. "Once is enough," he claimed. "Of course, one regrets the past. . . . [But] each age has its charm and its good sides, and the important thing is not to remain young forever but to have as little physical and moral suffering as possible. I do not know what sort of old man I shall be, but for the time being, I cannot help recognizing that the sum of the blessings I now enjoy is far greater than that granted me in my youth."[26]

Tchaikovsky possessed an ultimately tragic creativity. Some element of tragedy is present in the very nature of art, in man's contemplation of mortality and the insignificance of his earthly lot, in the constant struggle of good and evil, in man's precarious relations with God, the world, society, and himself. Such a view of human destiny is fully consonant with Tchaikovsky's outlook on life as expressed in his letters and as recorded by others. The wide gamut of emotion in his music, while certainly far more difficult to gauge and conceptualize, clearly ranges from the innocent simplicity of *The Nutcracker* to the necessarily tragic force of *Romeo and Juliet*, the Piano Trio, and the Sixth Symphony. Only occasionally, however, does the tragic in art re-late directly to the artist's own outward or even inward perturbations. The fundamental conflict of spirit and body necessarily left a tragic imprint on the somber mood of the Sixth Symphony's final movement.

For Tchaikovsky, despite his sincere and deep religious strivings, death was a constant concern in living. That the fear of death haunted him throughout his life is well documented. In his letter to Anna Mer-kling on his forty-fourth birthday he wrote, "I have not the slightest wish to die and even hope to reach a ripe old age. . . . What I need is not to fear death. In this particular matter I can make no boast. I am not sufficiently imbued with religion to see in death the beginning of a new life, nor am I a philospher that I might reconcile myself to that abyss of nonbeing into which we must sink. I envy no one more than truly religious people."[27]

Hermann Laroche recalled that Tchaikovsky "enjoyed excellent health, but was exceptionally fearful of death, and even of anything that only hinted at death; in his presence one could not use the words 'coffin,' 'grave,' 'funeral,' etc.; one of his greatest griefs in Moscow lay in the fact that the entrance to his apartment [in the 1860s] . . . was located next door to a funeral parlor."[28] Laroche did go on to note that Tchaikovsky later grew far more relaxed about the subject, not only allowing others to speak of it in front of him but even himself man-aging, for example, to relate in detail how Kondratyev had died almost in his arms. But even in these later years his fear of death did not leave him entirely. In 1890 he could still write, in reference to the untimely death of a young acquaintance, that death, "this snub-nosed reptile, is revoltingly base in general, but when she strikes someone in his prime, I especially hate her."[29] The young cellist Yulian Poplavsky, who would see Tchaikovsky shortly before the composer's death, recalled that on that occasion Tchaikovsky was unwilling to talk about the subject.[30]

Obsessed by his fear of death, Tchaikovsky felt especially drawn to youth. In his young nephew Bob he wished to see the resurrection of his own youthful self. Here was the source of the emphatic theme of death in both the first and last movements of the Sixth Symphony with their allusions to a requiem, as Tchaikovsky himself would later ob-serve in a letter to Grand Duke Konstantin. The composer felt inca-pable of overcoming his metaphysical angst in the face of eternal noth-ingness, a nothingness where everything he loved, everything he had all his life thought to be eternal, was inexorably threatened with dis-solution. In the symphony's finale, an unexpectedly mild adagio, the pathos of muted sobbings and wild outcries gradually dissolves into a silence that signifies nothingness. It is a poignantly subjective artistic moment, charged with deep emotional force. The title that seems originally to have been in Tchaikovsky's mind, *Life*, might well have been, after all, better suited than the essentially accidental *Pathétique*.

In mid-February, work on the symphony was interrupted when Tchaikovsky had to visit Moscow. "I am now full of a new composition (a symphony)," he wrote to Anatoly some days before his departure, "and find it very difficult to tear myself away from this labor. It seems that what is taking shape is the best of all my works."[31]

In Moscow, Tchaikovsky met with his former student Vladimir Shilovsky, now fallen on misfortune. Just weeks before, rumor had reached Modest that Shilovsky was gravely ill with dropsy. He visited him and found him slowly dying. "He himself told me that he was condemned," Modest later recalled. "I wrote of this to Pyotr Ilyich."[32] In reply to this letter from his brother, Tchaikovsky had written on 5 February, "Next week I must visit Volodya Shilovsky. This worries and frightens me. Tell me, has he changed terribly? How is his dropsy manifest? I fear tears and generally dread this meeting. Is there really no hope at all?"[33]

Through an odd twist of fate, the former close friends found themselves reconciled in the last months of their lives. Tchaikovsky was deeply moved by his former pupil's outpouring of joy at their meeting and still more by the majestic calm with which he regarded his hopeless situation. It was music that again united the old friends. In spite of his condition, Shilovsky had decided to set about the unusual task of writing waltzes for Moscow's Saratov tavern, with the object of bettering the tavern-goers' aesthetic sensibilities. To play through the finished waltzes for him and arrange them for mechanical organ, Tchaikovsky recommended to his friend young Yulian Poplavsky, whom he favored at the time. They also resumed their correspondence. "My dear Volodya!" wrote Tchaikovsky on 2 March. "I am displeased that you do not recover as rapidly as you should, but I have no doubt at all that somehow or other you will soon be quite well. . . . Poplavsky is a wonderful and likable young fellow, but if he is terribly bad at the piano, please do not hesitate to say so; I shall find you someone else. I thought it might be pleasant for you to see often not only a good musician but also a nice fellow."[34] A week later, he reported that he had listened to the new waltzes with Poplavsky. "There are many very striking and interesting parts," he noted, "but generally the music is somewhat heavy for patrons of a tavern."[35]

Whether or not former teacher and student were at one time lovers, the attachment between them was clearly deep and strong. Even now, when Tchaikovsky had long since lost faith in Shilovsky's artistic future and, in terms of interests and way of life, they no longer had much in common, gratitude for their earlier love maintained Tchaikovsky's good relations with Shilovsky until the younger man's death later that summer.

On 11 March, Tchaikovsky arrived in Kharkov by express train for a scheduled concert appearance there. At the station a great crowd had gathered to greet the famous composer, and its loud applause accompanied Tchaikovsky to his waiting carriage. The response to the concert itself three days later, at which Tchaikovsky conducted his Second Symphony, *The Tempest*, and the *1812* Overture, surpassed all expectations. The hurrahs and bravos seemed to go on forever, and afterward an ecstatic throng waited at the exit of the hall. As soon as Tchaikovsky appeared in the doorway he was lifted up and carried to his coach, to which students of Kharkov University proceeded to harness themselves in place of the horses and lead the composer in triumphal procession to his hotel.

Ivan Klimenko, his old friend from the early 1870s, traveled down to Kharkov from Poltava, where he now lived with his wife, specifically for the purpose of seeing Tchaikovsky. He happened upon the composer at the opera, "in the company," as Klimenko later recalled ingenuously, "of a lady (!!), which I would never have expected."[36] By this time, few in Russian social circles would have expected to see Tchaikovsky escorting a lady. World fame brought with it increasing gossip, all the worse for one so retiring and phobic as Tchaikovsky. He had to resign himself to the fact that he was now talked about and discussed in salons and musical circles from the capital to the farthest provinces of the empire and that inevitably his personal life was being touched upon as well. The ambiguous situation of a supposedly married man who never saw nor was seen with his wife certainly provided rich matter for conjecture and rumor.

It would not be an exaggeration to say that by this time most of society was aware of the composer's homosexuality. The Russian painter Mstislav Dobuzhinsky, a young student in 1893, later recalled visits to his mother's home in the provinces when the two would often play music. Though his mother adored Beethoven, Schumann, and Liszt, she disliked Tchaikovsky. The young man found this strange, until one day his mother confessed that she found his music "extremely lachrymose" and "overly sentimental," but that, most important, she considered Tchaikovsky himself a "sick person." By this, Dobuzhinsky explained, she had in mind Tchaikovsky's "well-known unnatural tastes, . . . which people at the time whispered about with a kind of horror."[37] Even as Tchaikovsky was being borne through the streets of Kharkov in triumph, Aleksey Suvorin, the well-informed and influential editor of the *New Times*, noted in his diary for 14 March that "Maslov said that Tchaikovsky and Apukhtin used to live together like husband and wife in the same apartment [most likely in late 1865, before Tchaikovsky left St. Petersburg for Moscow]. Apukhtin would be lying in bed. Tchaikovsky would go over to him and say that he was going to bed and Apukhtin would kiss his hand and say, 'Go, my dear, I shall join you in a moment.'"[38] Quite probably Suvorin's informant, mentioned only by last name, was none other than Fyodor Maslov, the classmate with whom Tchaikovsky had been so intimate at the School of Jurisprudence and with whom he had quarreled on account of Apukhtin. By the time of Suvorin's diary entry, Fyodor Maslov was chairman of the Moscow Appellate Board, and the two might easily have crossed paths in Moscow society circles.

Tchaikovsky returned from Kharkov on the evening of 18 March and, the next day, was back at work on his symphony, hoping to make up for more than a month's lost time. He finished the finale first and took up the second movement last, and within five days had completed a full sketch of the entire work. At once he left for St. Petersburg to relax for several days in the company of his adored Fourth Suite. By 5 April he was back again in Klin, where he began work on Eighteen Pieces, op. 72, for piano, commissioned by Jurgenson. Demanding little imaginative involvement, the morceaux were hardly more than a creative respite, and while skillfully crafted, most of the pieces give the impression that the composer was deliberately abstracting himself from his symphony, distancing himself in order to go back to it with a fresh and more stringently self-critical eye. Of his work on these pieces, he wrote to Bob that "every day I *give birth* to another musical *offspring*. These *offspring* are terribly premature and imperfect: I have no great desire to create them and I do so for the money. I endeavor only to have them turn out not too badly."[39]

Tchaikovsky's spiritual and physical forces at this time were, as Vasily Sapelnikov, who had seen Tchaikovsky in Odessa, recollected, in full bloom. The composer "burned with the thirst for creation and labor," recalled Sapelnikov, who added that "within his imagination sounds and melodies were already floating about which were to have found their expression in new symphonies and operas that he was planning to write." Even though the entire world considered him a great composer, Tchaikovsky simply would not acknowledge his past merits and still dreamt of writing "a really good opera."[40] Hermann Laroche speaks eloquently of Tchaikovsky's creative enthusiasm in 1893 in particular. Several opera projects and ideas dating specifically from this year are known. One was Shakespeare's *Merchant of Venice,* a subject suggested to him by Kolya Konradi, but which the composer rejected because he wanted "something original and profoundly moving."[41] Nor did he care for Modest's proposal of the translation by the poet Vasily Zhukovsky of the legend of Nal and Damayanti from the *Mahabharata.* "It is too far removed from life; I need a subject like *Cavalleria Rusticana,*" he wrote to his brother.[42] He was more intrigued by the possibility of creating a work based on George Eliot's tale, "Mr. Gilfil's Love-story." According to Laroche, Eliot's short story "particularly enthralled him by the pathos of its subject matter."[43]

On completing the morceaux for piano, Tchaikovsky spent several days in Moscow, where he attended performances at the conservatory, had dinner with Nikolay Kashkin and with his young cellist friend Poplavsky, and began composing the Six Songs, op. 73, on verses by Daniil Rathaus, a young poet from Kiev who had written Tchaikovsky several letters in the past year and sent some of his poems. He traveled to see Anatoly, now deputy governor of Nizhny Novgorod, then returned by way of Moscow to Klin, where he completed the set of songs, and on the evening of 5 May departed for St. Petersburg.

During his visits to the capital in these later years Tchaikovsky's meetings with Nikolay Rimsky-Korsakov and with younger composers of that circle, such as Aleksandr Glazunov and Anatoly Lyadov, had grown more frequent. Glazunov and Lyadov had succumbed readily to Tchaikovsky's charm and were very friendly with him. With Rimsky-Korsakov the situation was more complex. In addition to the old frictions between Tchaikovsky and the Mighty Five stemming from their differences concerning the relative importance of Russian nationalism in music, an element of jealousy suffused the attitude of Rimsky-Korsakov, who observed not without annoyance Tchaikovsky's increasing popularity among his own disciples. "At this time," notes Rimsky in his later memoirs, "there had begun to be noticeable a considerable cooling-off and even a somewhat inimical attitude toward the memory of the Five in the time of Balakirev. On the contrary, a worship of Tchaikovsky and a tendency toward eclecticism were growing stronger. Nor could one help noticing the predilection (which sprang up in our circle) for Italian and French music of the era of the wig and the farthingale [that is, the eighteenth century], music introduced by Tchaikovsky in his *Queen of Spades* and *Iolanta.*"[44]

Rimsky also recalls that in their late-night gatherings with Lyadov, Glazunov, and others, Tchaikovsky showed a remarkable ability to "drink a great deal of wine and yet retain his full powers." Few, remarks Rimsky somewhat drily, could keep up with him in this respect. Indeed, his stay in St. Petersburg in the spring of 1893 on the eve of his departure for England found Tchaikovsky in a particularly jocular and cheerful mood, regaling his friends and acquaintances with stories of amusing episodes from the past. It may well have been on this occasion that he told them of an incident involving the importunate baritone Bogomir Korsov, whose unexpected visit on one occasion Tchaikovsky had sought to avoid by slipping full-length under the sofa in his study. Korsov, meanwhile, settled himself comfortably on the same sofa to await the composer's return, intending, as Tchaikovsky well knew, to pressure him into composing an additional aria for him in *The Oprichnik*. According to the story, Korsov waited some three hours before finally leaving, during which time Tchaikovsky remained stretched out under the sofa unable to move. When at last the singer left, Tchaikovsky, released from captivity, immediately produced the expected aria.[45]

Tchaikovsky spent a week in St. Petersburg and on 13 May set off for England to receive his honorary degree from Cambridge. He was barely out of Russia before he was overwhelmed by feelings of homesickness and especially of longing for Bob, who was now preparing for his final examinations at the School of Jurisprudence. So fixedly did his thoughts now center on his nephew that this time he experienced their separation with particular pain. From Berlin, on 15/27 May, he poured out his anguish in a letter to him. "This time, probably because I have been remembering too often our journey last year, I have pined and suffered and wept more than ever," he wrote. "It is simply some kind of psychopathy. . . . It is absolutely essential that I know in London, without fail: are you going to Grankino, and do you wish me to come? . . . I should like very badly to spend some time together with you in Grankino."[46]

His torments reached the point where he could neither sleep nor eat, and only the embarrassment of coming home empty-handed stopped him from turning right around and racing back to Russia. Arriving in London two days later, he at once wrote Bob again. "I write to you with a sort of voluptuousness," he confided. "The thought that this bit of paper will be in your hands, at home, fills me with joy and makes me weep. Is it not curious, in fact, that I voluntarily subject myself to these tortures? . . . I suffer not only from an anguish that cannot be expressed in words (in my new symphony there is a passage that seems to express it well) but also from a hatred of strange people, from some vague dread and devil knows what else. Physically this condition manifests itself in a pain in the lower part of my stomach and an aching and weakness in my legs."[47]

Tchaikovsky was once again put off by London, complaining bitterly that he could find nothing in the "wretched city," from public restrooms to a hat that would fit him. His schedule was exhausting. Only with the appearance of his old friend Saint-Saëns, arriving for the same honor, did Tchaikovsky's spirits somewhat revive. The two composers were feted at the Westminster Club and took part together in a concert of the New Philharmonic Society. Of the performance of Tchaikovsky's Fourth Symphony in the first part of the program, the *Daily Telegraph* reported that with the exception of one movement the symphony was "striking in its Slavic element" and "produced a great impression, and judging by the long and persistent applause—delight."[48] Following this enormous success, the French composer met with a noticeably more muted response to his own Second Piano Concerto and *Le Rouet d'Omphale* in the latter half of the joint concert.

Gradually Tchaikovsky's impression of London improved, so much so that his beloved Paris began to seem "positively a village" in comparison. "During a drive along Regent Street or through Hyde Park there are so many carriages, such a luxuriance and beauty of harness, that one is just dazzled," he wrote to Modest on 22 May/3 June. But still he was pained by the constant whirl of social engagements. "I have just been with the ambassador's wife for afternoon tea. . . . In general, what a lot of people I see here! And how exhausting it all is! In the mornings I suffer dreadfully in morale, then find myself in a sort of daze, but I have only one thought: may all this be over soon!!"[49]

In Cambridge, where he arrived on 31 May/12 June, Tchaikovsky stayed with the eminent legal historian and professor of law Frederic William Maitland, who had invited him to be his guest at the West Lodge of Downing College. Ill at ease at first, he soon found the professor and his wife, Florence, to be "charming and delightful people— and Russophiles to boot."[50] Florence and her sister Adeline both played for Tchaikovsky. The festivities lasted two days. On the afternoon of his arrival Tchaikovsky directed the first performance in England of *Francesca da Rimini* at a concert in Cambridge's Guildhall and then attended a "gala dinner and still more gala reception."[51] The next day, the ceremony awarding him the honorary doctorate took place. Before he left the Maitlands' house, Florence and Adeline pinned a rose in Tchaikovsky's buttonhole and took his photograph. The ceremony included an official luncheon and reception given by the wife of the university vice-chancellor. Doctor of Music degrees *honoris causa* were conferred not only on Tchaikovsky and Saint-Saëns but on composers from three other countries, Max Bruch of Germany, Arrigo Boito of Italy, and Edvard Grieg of Norway, although Grieg, for reasons of ill health, was not present at the ceremony.

Later that same day, Tchaikovsky returned to London and, the next morning, left for Paris, where finally he could relax from his three weeks of tension and exhaustion. After the bustling traffic of London the streets of Paris seemed almost deserted. The *cafés chantants* and all the rest had by now begun to lose the charm of novelty, but still he took pleasure in roaming about the city's boulevards and avenues. Out of "the whole notorious Fourth Suite," as Tchaikovsky put it, only Vladimir Nápravník had written him in London, and he now replied with a detailed account of the Cambridge festivities. A few days later, he traveled to the Tyrol to spend a week with Vasily Sapelnikov and Sophie Menter, and by 18 June he was back in Russia, at Grankino. "Strangely enough," he wrote Anatoly from the Konradi estate, "the beauties of the Tyrol among which I lived at Menter's did not afford me even half the pleasure I felt at the sight of the endless steppe through which I rode here yesterday from the railway station. No, decidedly, the Russian countryside is infinitely dearer to my heart than all the much-vaunted beauties of Europe."[52] At Grankino he found Bob, Bob's friend Rudy Buchshoevden, and Kolya Konradi. Modest at this time was staying at the Optino Monastery in Kaluga province, where he was working on a new play. Tchaikovsky wrote to him from Grankino that "all three youths have gotten very suntanned and look healthy and jolly. Of course, Bob sometimes falls into a fit of spleen, but unfortunately that follows him everywhere. It is, however, an exception; in general, he, too, is in fine spirits."[53]

After resting a few weeks in Grankino, and after a brief visit to his brother Nikolay near Kursk, Tchaikovsky returned to Klin in the latter part of July and set to work at once on scoring the Sixth Symphony. "Only at home can I work properly," he wrote to Modest on 22 July. "I am now immersed up to my neck in my symphony. The farther along the scoring goes, the more difficult I find it. Twenty years ago I used to plow ahead without thinking, and it would turn out well. Now I have become cowardly, unsure of myself. Today I sat the entire day over two pages—and still it doesn't come out as I should like it. But the work progresses all the same, and nowhere else would I have done as much as I do at home."[54]

Undaunted by the slowness of the work, Tchaikovsky was growing increasingly confident about the symphony itself. He told Bob in early August, "I am very pleased with its contents—although I am not satisfied, or rather, not completely satisfied, with the orchestration. . . . I shall find it quite usual and not surprising if this symphony is torn to pieces or little appreciated, for it will not be the first. But I absolutely believe it to be the best and in particular the 'most sincere' of all my works. I love it as I have *never* loved a single one of my other musical creations."[55] By mid-August the score was finally completed, and Tchaikovsky began giving the work its final polish.

But, meanwhile, a flood of sad news kept coming from Moscow and St. Petersburg. While Tchaikovsky had been abroad, his old friends Karl Albrecht and Konstantin Shilovsky had both passed away. In late June, Vladimir Shilovsky had also died. All summer, disquieting reports had been coming from St. Petersburg about the failing health of Aleksey Apukhtin, incurably ill with dropsy. During the last years Tchaikovsky, owing in part to his own feverish professional schedule, had rarely seen his old friend, but the two friends had not grown distant. In letters to Bob, Kolya Konradi, and others in the capital, Tchaikovsky asked insistently after the health of the aging poet, who, suffering from obesity, had not been well for some years. The Russian jurist Anatoly Koni later recalled the last time he ever saw Apukhtin, about a year before his death. Visiting him on a hot and stifling summer day in his city apartment, he found Apukhtin seated "on an enormous ottoman, in a light silk Chinese robe cut widely out around his plump neck—looking as he sat there like the traditional figure of Buddha. But in his face there was none of the contemplative Buddhist tranquillity. It was pale, his eyes looked mournful. From all the furnishings emanated a frost of loneliness, and it seemed that death had already brushed with the tip of its wing the soul of the pensive poet."[56]

On learning that Tchaikovsky had been awarded an honorary doctorate by Cambridge University and was to go to England for the ceremony, Apukhtin had written a poem dedicated to his former schoolmate. It summed up, as it were, the long years of their friendship:

> For a musician-friend's departure
> My verse adopts a minor key,
> And the fugue of our old friendship,
> Ever evolving, grows.
> . . . .
> We believed in our talents,
> Shared a multitude of feelings and ideas—
> And you were like the dominant
> In the chords of my youth.[57]

Apukhtin died on 17 August 1893. The news of the death of his oldest
friend seemed to touch Tchaikovsky less deeply than might have been
expected, especially coming as it did in the wake of the almost simultaneous deaths of several other close friends. Modest later observed
that "one felt that now he would not go, as he had before, . . . several
thousand versts to see a friend before their eternal separation." Perhaps
his sensitivity had hardened with the years and with experience, suggested Modest, or else "the moral ordeals that he endured during the
last years had taught him at times to see in death a deliverance."[58]
What seems likely is that Tchaikovsky, wholly absorbed at the time in
his new symphony and anxious about its performance, was temporarily unable to see the rest of the world as much more than a distant
backdrop to his own pressing concerns. Still, his grief, though outwardly less frantic, was profound. "Even as I write this," he wrote in a
letter to Bob three days after the poet's death, "they are reading the
burial service for Lyolya Apukhtin!!! Although his death was not unexpected, still it is awful and painful. He was once my closest friend."[59]

When Grand Duke Konstantin some weeks later suggested that
Tchaikovsky compose a "requiem" to Apukhtin's poem of that name,
Tchaikovsky declined. "I am somewhat concerned that my latest symphony, just written and scheduled to be performed on 16 October (I
should like *terribly* for Your Highness to hear it), is imbued with a
mood very close to that which also fills [Apukhtin's poem]
'Requiem,'" he told the grand duke. "I believe my symphony to have
turned out a success, and I fear to repeat myself by undertaking at once
a composition akin in spirit and character to its predecessor."[60] More
than this, Tchaikovsky had no wish to write any requiem whatsoever,
whether for Apukhtin or, as is often suggested in the case of the Sixth
Symphony, for himself. "There is another reason why I am little inclined to compose music for any sort of requiem, but I am afraid to
touch indelicately upon your religious feelings," he wrote in his following (and last) letter to the grand duke, in which he decisively rejected
the grand duke's proposal. "In the requiem a great deal is said about
God the Judge, God the Chastiser, God the Avenger (!!!). Forgive me,
Your Highness, but I shall dare to hint that I do not believe in such a
God, or at least that such a God cannot rouse in me those tears, that
ecstasy, that awe before the creator and source of every good which
might inspire me."[61]

On the day of Apukhtin's funeral Tchaikovsky traveled to St. Petersburg. There he stayed with Laroche, who, having come into some
money, was then living along the fashionable English Embankment.

Modest and Bob had finally moved out of the Konradi apartment on the Fontanka River and were now spending the summer at Kamenka. The growing tension in Modest's relations with Kolya had come to a head at last. Modest's plays brought him very little income, and the subsidy from his brother had decreased sharply with the cessation of Tchaikovsky's own allowance from Mrs. von Meck. But Modest, an even greater spendthrift than his brother, had failed to retrench significantly and live his life on a correspondingly lesser scale. Now Kolya, whose money Modest was running through as though it were his own, had had enough, and citing a poor harvest at his estate, he made it unequivocally clear to his former tutor that he could no longer support him.

Tchaikovsky was incensed. In his letters Modest tried to smooth over the impression made by Kolya's behavior toward him, claiming extenuating circumstances for the young man's conduct. But his brother remained implacable. "As for Kolya," he wrote on 20 August, "no matter what you write me, I still consider him a great swine, but I shall try as far as possible not to show him my feelings. The question of your arrangements very much worries me. Everything is fine, but what about money, money!!! As if on purpose, I have now very little."[62] His anger was still evident in a letter to Anna Merkling written in late September. "The more I think about the base and swinish behavior of Kolya Konradi, the more indignant and outraged I become," he told his cousin. "But, my God, to tell the truth, only such people as Kolya Konradi . . . live happily on this earth. A callous heart, a mediocre mind incapable of penetrating the essence of things—these are the prerequisites for a successful vegetative life in this world."[63]

In late August, Tchaikovsky visited Hamburg briefly to attend a production there of *Iolanta* conducted by Gustav Mahler. Back in Russia, he traveled to the Nizhny Novgorod district to visit Anatoly and his family at their country home, but by 17 September he was in Moscow—exiled again from Klin as Alyosha's wife, expecting another child, neared her time. Tchaikovsky put up at a hotel and waited patiently. While in the city, he attended the Moscow premiere of Modest's comedy *Prejudices* at the Maly Theater. He quite liked the production, but the critics thought otherwise and the play was not a success. Modest wrote from St. Petersburg to announce that he and Bob had found themselves an apartment on the corner of Malaya Morskaya and Gorokhovaya streets and that they hoped to move in by 1 October. With the composer's mediation Modest borrowed a necessary thousand rubles from Fyodor Mülbach, the owner of a piano factory in the capital, which Tchaikovsky promised to repay shortly. And at last, Alyosha sent word from Klin that his wife had given birth to a daughter.

Tchaikovsky had barely returned home when news reached Klin of the death of another old acquaintance, the conservatory professor Nikolay Zverev. Word arrived too late, however, for Tchaikovsky to be able to attend the funeral for his former colleague. On 3 October he finished scoring his Third Piano Concerto. Two days later, he sent a telegram to his young cellist friend Anatoly Brandukov, then living in Moscow, saying that he was expecting him the following day in Klin with both Yulian Poplavsky and the cello concerto by Saint-Saëns that Brandukov had promised to play.

Met at the station by a "sprightly, curly-haired coachman," as Poplavsky later recalled, the young men were brought to Tchaikovsky's "two-storied wooden home with a glass-roofed balcony, the last house along the Moscow highway."[64] Their host was delighted to see them, and together the three spent the rest of that day studying the Saint-Saëns concerto and bantering cheerfully. Tchaikovsky told many stories of his foreign tours and acquaintances, interspersing his accounts with droll asides to his guests. Time passed imperceptibly, and suddenly it was eleven o'clock. Before going to bed, Tchaikovsky personally inspected the rooms prepared for them and brought them extra blankets lest they take a chill during the night.

At half past eight the next morning, Poplavsky found the composer already having his tea and glancing through the newspapers. All morning they talked about music and, before lunch, headed out for a walk around Klin, Tchaikovsky delighting in showing his young guests the beauties of the local landscape. But a strong wind blew up, and chilled through, they turned back somewhat earlier than was their host's habit. Alyosha met them "with a displeased face" and announced that dinner was not yet ready. To fill the time, Tchaikovsky suggested that they look over Laroche's *Karmozina* Overture, which he was planning to conduct in St. Petersburg.[65]

During dinner Tchaikovsky told them something about his symphony, scheduled to be performed for the first time in St. Petersburg on the sixteenth of the month, and of his plans to write a new opera, for which he was still seeking a subject. After dinner they visited the grocer's in Klin, and Tchaikovsky showed Brandukov and Poplavsky around his simple house and garden. By five they were collecting their things and making ready for their return trip to Moscow. Tchaikovsky was to accompany them. "The contents of [Tchaikovsky's] two . . . bags," recollected Poplavsky, "were gone through and supplemented by

Aleksey [Alyosha]. Egorka appeared, Aleksey's two-year-old son and our host's godson. Taking leave of them, Pyotr Ilyich exchanged kisses with both son and father. Aleksey, handing his master sixty rubles, bade him buy in Moscow cloth for a coat and some other wardrobe articles. We hopped in the cab and twenty minutes later were cheerfully boarding a car on the evening train."[66]

The following morning, 8 October, Tchaikovsky attended a requiem mass for Zverev and met with Sergey Taneev. The next day he visited the Moscow Conservatory, where students from one of the classes performed for Tchaikovsky his vocal quartet *Night*, a transcription for four voices based on the music of Mozart's Piano Fantasia in C Minor (K. 475). Sitting next to Kashkin, Tchaikovsky was so deeply moved by the performance that he nearly wept. He told Kashkin that the beauty of Mozart's music was "a mystery to him and that he himself could not explain the irresistible charm of the simple melody of that quartet."[67]

That same evening, Tchaikovsky left for St. Petersburg.

CHAPTER TWENTY-NINE

The Fortuitous Tragedy

In the early morning of 10 October, Tchaikovsky was met at the Nikolaevsky Railroad Station in St. Petersburg by Modest and Bob. He was in high spirits and liked the new apartment rented by his brother. His fine mood stayed with him, especially during the first few days of his visit, while his arrival was not yet known in the city and he could still dispose of his time freely.

The man now visiting the Russian capital was very different from the young conservatory student who had once promenaded along Nevsky Prospect happy and insouciant, responding to the greetings of countless acquaintances. The former civil servant had succeeded in becoming a universal celebrity, while the number of his acquaintances seemed to have diminished tenfold. Hermann Laroche, his friend from conservatory days, recalled strolling again with Tchaikovsky along Nevsky in the 1890s, when "it could happen that we would not meet a single acquaintance." He had grown elegant and scrupulous in his attire, but he had long since ceased to be a man about town, and only rarely would he attend the aristocratic salons in his capacity as a "star."[1] Numerous photographs and recollections by contemporaries preserve an image of Tchaikovsky at this time. As Andrew Carnegie and others had remarked in New York, he looked older than his fifty-three years. His sparse hair had gone completely white, his face was lined, his teeth yellowed. He spoke in a somewhat hoarse voice. But his figure was fine and still vigorous, and his pure, clear, trusting eyes and his warm smile and ready laugh prompted immediate sympathy.

His days in St. Petersburg were occupied with preparations for the concert at which his new symphony was to be performed with himself conducting. Even before his arrival in the capital, musical circles were talking of his new creation and, in particular, its schematically original finale, which, as Tchaikovsky had noted to Bob, was "not a loud allegro, but, on the contrary, the most leisurely adagio."² There were four rehearsals, at which the musicians, to Tchaikovsky's dismay, were little impressed with the work.³ Their indifferent response constrained him and made him nervous, and he tended to get the rehearsals over with as quickly as possible in order to release the musicians from so boring an occupation.⁴ After the rehearsals he relaxed in the company of his nephews and the rest of the Fourth Suite. The composer and his young friends would visit the theater and then end their evenings at the restaurant of either the Grand Hôtel or the Hôtel de France. "It began with what Pyotr Ilyich used to call a binge," recalled Yury Davydov of one typical gathering. "We drank the health of him who had gathered us together and of all those present, and the party grew very lively. Pyotr Ilyich was somewhat excited, very merry and impish as never before, and his jokes poured forth as from a horn of plenty."⁵

It was during these days that the twenty-year-old actor Yury Yuryev visited Modest's apartment. Yuryev had recently graduated from the Theatrical School in Moscow and had joined the company of the Aleksandrinsky Theater just a month earlier. Of his first visit to the Tchaikovsky apartment Yuryev later recalled that nervous and embarrassed, he had barely finished excusing himself from Modest's invitation to stay for dinner "when the door opened and the so easily recognizable figure of Pyotr Ilyich appeared on the threshold, accompanied by a young man in military uniform." The young man was Bob Davydov, who, after graduating from the School of Jurisprudence, had decided to join the army for a few years. The three were introduced and Bob exclaimed mischievously, "But Uncle Petya and I have been eavesdropping on you! My uncle got down on his knees and was looking through the keyhole."

Both brothers proceeded to beg the young actor to stay for dinner. "I stubbornly declined because of my timidity," recalled Yuryev. "But their irresistible hospitality ultimately won, and I was compelled to acquiesce." Sitting across from Tchaikovsky at dinner, the young man marveled that the famous composer, who "always appeared to me an extraordinary, inaccessible being, different from other mortals," was in reality "so modest and spoke of such ordinary things and—strangest of all—addressed me often."⁶ But Tchaikovsky's interest in the actor, as well as their mutual sympathy at this first encounter described by Yuryev with subtly erotic overtones, was perhaps not strange at all. By this time the Aleksandrinsky Theater had acquired a decided homosexual notoriety. Two of its leading actors, Konstantin Varlamov and Vladimir Davydov (no relation to the Kamenka Davydovs), were involved in the public scandal of 1889 that had also involved Prince Meshchersky.[7] Though the affair was hushed up, the theater's scandalous fame had continued to grow. Yuryev's own homosexuality later became a matter of common knowledge, something that did little to affect his popularity even under the Soviet regime, which granted him many awards and honorific titles.

Spending his days in the amiable company of his young favorites and admirers, Tchaikovsky was in good spirits. There is little indication at this time of any particular preoccupation with death. To the cholera epidemic that was then raging in the capital, as happened every so often, he seems to have given little thought.

Asiatic cholera first entered the eastern part of Russia in 1823. The disease reappeared in 1830, this time spreading rapidly through the entire empire. It reached Moscow in September of that year and St. Petersburg the following June, and from there passed westward across Europe. Panic and so-called cholera riots erupted in the wake of the epidemic, and a terrified populace even accused physicians of mass poisoning. Subsequent epidemics occurred at intervals of roughly ten years. One of the most severe reached St. Petersburg in the summer of 1892. In that year, more than a quarter of a million people died from cholera in Russia as a whole.[8] During the winter months the disease abated, but with the return of warm weather it surged anew. Unlike the previous year, however, the outbreak of cholera in 1893 began in St. Petersburg not in the summer but in the early autumn. Though a few cases were registered toward the end of August, the disease did not spread widely until well into September. The newspapers expressed bewilderment: "It would seem that everything is now conducive to throttling the epidemic. The winter cold has all but arrived. . . . There is no reason why the infection should develop. Meanwhile, both the number of those taken ill and the death rate from cholera increase."[9] By 12 September there were 292 infected persons in the hospitals.[10] Throughout the autumn the epidemic waxed and waned. By early October it seemed to be already in decline, only to rise again toward the end of November. By December the number of victims was increasing daily and the mortality rate in the capital alone was higher than in many entire provinces. Even in October, when the disease was believed to be generally on the wane, there were occasional brief fluctuations.[11]

According to Modest, of all sicknesses Tchaikovsky feared cholera the least, even though it was cholera that had caused the death of his mother. By the 1890s cholera had ceased to be regarded as necessarily fatal, as it had been previously. Everyone knew that the majority of the victims belonged to the lower classes, among whom hygiene was poor at best. The typical cholera victim was "a docker, a manual laborer, a plasterer, a scavenger, a cabman."[12] In February 1884 the German bacteriologist Robert Koch isolated the microscopic bacillus known as *Vibrio cholerae*, the causative agent in the disease, which enters the human body through the mouth. It was rightly conjectured that human excrement was the chief source of contagion and that contaminated water was the most common means of dissemination.[13] Proper sanitation, drinking only boiled water, and avoiding uncooked foods were known to be effective precautions against the disease, thus fostering a belief among the wealthy and educated classes that the tragedy of the epidemics had little to do directly with them. But in September 1893 even privileged Russians were growing uneasy and asking, "Can anyone be confident that the infection will not spread further and penetrate the more prosperous strata of society?"[14] This is precisely what began to happen when on 30 September the special "Bulletin on the Movement of Cholera Patients in St. Petersburg Hospitals," published daily in the major newspapers of the capital, included for the first time the heading IN PRIVATE APARTMENTS and informed a nervous readership of two such deaths that had occurred before the victims could be cared for.[15] By 24 October six people had died under similar circumstances in private residences.[16] The epidemic had reached the upper classes, though life for them continued socially and culturally much the same.

The Sixth Symphony was performed for the first time on 16 October at the Russian Musical Society's first symphonic concert of the season. "All St. Petersburg" turned out for its favorite artist. A standing ovation greeted the composer's appearance on stage. The response to the music itself, however, was ambivalent. Despite the coolness of the musicians at the rehearsals, Tchaikovsky had continued to maintain that he had never written and never would write anything better than this symphony.[17] Yet, he failed to make either the performers or the public agree on this occasion. The audience, noted Yury Davydov, "was somewhat perplexed and did not know what to think about this new pearl of Pyotr Ilyich's creation."[18] The young composer Anatoly Lyadov recalled that when the concert ended, he visited the dressing room and found there one of the directors of the Russian Musical Society attempting, in polite conversation with Tchaikovsky, to disguise the fact that he had not liked the symphony. Tchaikovsky addressed Lyadov immediately with the suggestion that he must have liked the symphony. "He well perceived," remarked Lyadov, "that despite their applause the public remained cool to his new composition. But I could express my genuine opinion, since I had been greatly impressed by the Sixth Symphony."[19] Leaving the concert with Aleksandr Glazunov, Tchaikovsky "complained bitterly" that the symphony "had not been much of a success and that the musicians seemed to dislike it." Glazunov noted that Tchaikovsky "always tended to be disappointed after the first performance of his works, but this time he was pleased with his offspring."[20] Two days later, Tchaikovsky wrote to Jurgenson, telling him that "something strange is going on with this symphony! It is not that it wasn't liked, but it has caused some bewilderment."[21]

Rimsky-Korsakov was also at the concert, and he later recollected that during the intermission, after the symphony had been performed, he asked Tchaikovsky whether he had any program for the composition. "He said that of course he had, but that he did not intend to reveal it," Rimsky recalled. "It was only at this concert that I saw him during this, his last visit."[22]

On rising the next morning, Modest found his brother already long since awake. He sat at the dining table, the score of his symphony lying before him. It had to be sent to Jurgenson in Moscow, as Tchaikovsky had promised, but he wanted first to think up some title for it. He did not wish to write simply "Sixth," and by now he had changed his mind about his earlier intention to call it the *Program Symphony*. "What kind of program symphony is it when I don't want to give away the program?" he told Modest. Modest's first suggestion to call the symphony *Tragic* sparked little enthusiasm in his brother. Then he proposed the title *Pathétique*—which in the Russian borrowing, as in the original French, means not "pathetic" in its common sense so much as "emotive, passional, full of pathos." This Tchaikovsky decided to accept, and in Modest's presence he inscribed on the first page of the score the title that, as Modest later wrote, "remained forever."[23]

Yet, there remains some confusion. Modest himself asserts that "having sent the score to Moscow with the new title, Pyotr Ilyich, however, had second thoughts and decided to abandon it, which is clear from his following last letter to Jurgenson of 18 October: 'Please, my dear, inscribe the following on the frontispiece: "To Vladimir Lvovich Davydov (#6). Op. ??? by P. Tch." I hope it is not too late.'"[24] Thus, according to Modest, the final title omitted the epithet *Pathétique*. It is, then, uncertain whether the title *Pathétique*, suggested by Modest and reflecting, in fact, little of Tchaikovsky's original idea, was ultimately confirmed by Tchaikovsky himself. As a matter of fact, *Pathétique*, declared by Modest to be missing from the letter to Jurgenson, appears in the title only in Soviet publications of the letter, which raises the question of whether this is the genuine title of the symphony or a later imposition by Soviet editors.[25] The original of the letter remains, of course, locked in Soviet archives. The matter is not trivial, since some biographers have used this title in conjunction with the dedication to Bob Davydov as specious evidence for their speculation that the composer committed suicide as a result of a desperate and tragic homosexual love affair.

The next morning, Monday, 18 October, Tchaikovsky went to the Imperial Public Library. He had decided to look through the library copy of his *Oprichnik* with the object of reworking the early opera and thus retrieving the royalty rights that he had granted to the firm of Vasily Bessel in 1874.[26] Tchaikovsky discussed his plans that same day with Bessel's representative, Avgust Gerke, a lawyer and an old friend of Tchaikovsky's from their days together at the School of Jurisprudence. Bessel, knowing of the composer's strong dislike of him, had chosen Gerke as an intermediary in these negotiations. The two agreed that Bessel would draw up a new contract the following day that would return the rights to the opera to Tchaikovsky.

After looking through the four large volumes of the score, Tchaikovsky decided to take the first part of the opera home and there work quietly on the necessary alterations.[27] That afternoon he was present at rehearsals of *Eugene Onegin* by the Kononov private opera company.[28] He was pleased with the production and talked briefly with the conductor of the opera. Their conversation soon turned to *The Oprichnik*, which the Kononov company was planning to put on in the near future. Tchaikovsky promised that his revisions would not take long and personally handed him the score.[29]

Early that evening, Tchaikovsky was a guest at a dinner given in honor of one of the participants in the concert of two days before, the German pianist Adele Aus der Ohe, with whom he had first become acquainted during his American tour.[30] Later the same evening, he attended a different performance of *Onegin*, at the Mariinsky.[31] It seems that on this occasion he discussed certain changes in the second part of *The Maid of Orléans* with Vladimir Pogozhev, the manager of the Office of Imperial Theaters.[32] The tenor Nikolay Figner later recalled that on that evening Tchaikovsky "was cheerful as usual and talked of the last symphony concert and of our projected tour to Paris (Pyotr Ilyich planned to go there with my wife and myself for a series of concerts)."[33]

On Tuesday morning Tchaikovsky wrote a letter to the Dutch composer and conductor Willem Kes, agreeing to come to Amsterdam

for a concert appearance in early March of the following year.³⁴ That
evening found him again at the Kononov Opera, where he saw a production of *The Maccabees*, by Anton Rubinstein.³⁵ It seems likely that
by this time Tchaikovsky had already changed his original intention
of returning to Klin two days later, on the twenty-first.³⁶ Instead, he
yielded to Modest's insistence and agreed to delay his departure so as
to be present at the St. Petersburg premiere of *Prejudices*, scheduled
for 26 October, after its unsuccessful Moscow premiere the previous
month. Having resolved to stay longer in the capital, he spent the time
relaxing socially instead of busying himself with hasty preparations for
leaving.

On the morning of Wednesday the twentieth, Tchaikovsky met
with Avgust Gerke to go over the new contract with Bessel for *The
Oprichnik*.³⁷ Later in the day, he took a stroll with Sanya Litke, sharing
with him stories of his old friend Bochechkarov, whom, he confessed,
he missed almost as badly now as just after his death in 1876. He dined
that day with Vera Butakova, and at half past seven that evening he
had a box at the Aleksandrinsky Theater, where Aleksandr Ostrovsky's
play *The Ardent Heart* was being performed.³⁸ Surrounded by his
Fourth Suite, he appeared to Yury Yuryev, who saw him at the performance, to be in good health and a cheerful mood.³⁹ During the intermission, Tchaikovsky visited the dressing room of Konstantin Varlamov and chatted with him lightheartedly about various matters,
including the current fashion for spiritualism. From the theater Tchaikovsky proceeded to Leiner's restaurant, together with Bob Davydov,
Sanya and Konstantin Litke, and Rudy Buchshoevden.⁴⁰ At the restaurant they were joined by Aleksandr Glazunov and Fyodor Mülbach,
both of whom were invited by Tchaikovsky to visit him the following
day. Modest, who was the only one of those present to provide a description of the supper at Leiner's, arrived about an hour later, when
he found his brother "eating macaroni and washing it down, as usual,
with white wine and mineral water." The supper lasted only a short
time, and soon after one o'clock, Tchaikovsky and Modest returned
home on foot. The composer, his brother later noted, "was quite
healthy and calm."⁴¹

They arrived home around 2:00 A.M. The next morning, Thursday
the twenty-first, Modest came out of his bedroom to find that his
brother was not in the sitting room taking tea as usual, but was in his
own room and that he complained of having spent a bad night because
of a stomach upset.⁴² Despite the growing discomfort, Tchaikovsky attempted to follow his day's schedule. Modest did suggest that they
send for a doctor, but Tchaikovsky refused. "I did not insist," Modest

later admitted, "knowing that he was accustomed to illnesses of this sort and that he always managed to get over them without anyone's help. Usually castor oil would bring him relief in these cases. Convinced that he would resort to it this time as well and knowing that anyway it could do him no harm, I was quite unworried about his condition and, going about my own affairs, did not see him again until one in the afternoon." His brother had indeed suffered from such stomach disorders, partly nervous in origin, all his life: his letters and diaries provide abundant evidence of this fact.

Around eleven Tchaikovsky decided to visit Eduard Nápravník, but no sooner had he set out than he began to feel much worse and returned home by cab almost immediately in great distress from a sharp stomach attack. Back at his brother's apartment, Tchaikovsky tried to appear cheerful, even joking with the doorman, telling him of his absentmindedness in always misplacing his galoshes.[43] Yet, his desperate search for medication quite frightened Sanya Litke, who would later recall that he seemed "very upset by something else."[44] Feeling some relief from a dose of castor oil, his habitual remedy, Tchaikovsky sent a note to Nápravník's wife: "Dear Olga Eduardovna, I shall not depart today, but I kiss your hands."[45] In addition, he composed letters to Kolya Konradi (in which he again attempted to mediate between his brother and his former charge) and to the impresario of the Odessa Opera Theater, Ivan Grekov. This latter is almost certainly the last of Tchaikovsky's letters that we possess. In it, he spoke of his various plans for the coming months and stressed his busy schedule. Nevertheless, he agreed to come to Odessa between 15 December and 5 January and requested Grekov to take care of the necessary accommodations.[46]

Modest's return at lunchtime coincided with the visit of Fyodor Mülbach, who had come on business. Tchaikovsky sat with them but did not eat, drinking only mineral water. By the end of lunch he had started to feel nauseated and left the room to lie down for a while with a hot compress on his stomach. For the second time Modest proposed sending for a doctor, but received the same firm refusal. He did not insist. "Neither he [Tchaikovsky] himself nor those of us around him were at all anxious," Modest noted later. "All this had often happened before. Although his indisposition grew worse, we attributed this to the action of the mineral water." Moreover, a little while later, Tchaikovsky improved and asked to be allowed to sleep. Following this, Modest left again for the Aleksandrinsky Theater, where dress rehearsals for his new play were under way.

During his brother's absence Tchaikovsky's condition grew sharply worse. The only person at home was Modest's servant Nazar Litrov, who began to employ all the home remedies known to him, though all without success. Precious time for diagnosis and treatment was slipping away. When Aleksandr Glazunov, invited the day before, showed up late that afternoon he found Tchaikovsky in a poor state. He felt very ill and asked to be left alone, even remarking lightly that perhaps he had contracted cholera. Though he then confessed that he thought it unlikely, since he had experienced similar attacks many times, this is the first indication that Tchaikovsky was at all mindful of the epidemic then plaguing the city and that the possibility of cholera had been both entertained and rejected by him.[47]

Toward five o'clock Modest returned, and seeing that the illness was much worse, he ignored his brother's renewed protests and sent a note to Tchaikovsky's "favorite doctor," Vasily Bertenson: "Petya does not feel well. He has continuous nausea and diarrhea. For God's sake, come see what this means."[48] Then, placing another hot compress on his brother's stomach, Modest left again around six o'clock.

After his departure the situation deteriorated still further. The vomiting and diarrhea became increasingly severe, though Tchaikovsky was still strong enough to get up every time he needed to. Nazar managed to transfer Tchaikovsky from his bedroom into the drawing room, which was closer to the toilet.

Dr. Bertenson, it turned out, was not at home. Sometime between six and eight o'clock Nazar gave up waiting for Bertenson and sent for the first doctor who could be found. Still no one was thinking seriously about cholera.

It is not known whether the physician sent for by Nazar ever appeared. Vasily Bertenson did not arrive until a quarter past eight. Because none of Tchaikovsky's excretions had been preserved, the doctor could not at once make a firm diagnosis. But Bertenson was convinced at once of the extreme seriousness and gravity of the illness, realizing that Tchaikovsky did not have an acute catarrh of the stomach, as the composer and the other members of the household had assumed, but something worse. Up to this time Vasily Bertenson, as he himself later admitted, "had not had occasion to witness an actual case of cholera." Even so, he was left with little doubt that Tchaikovsky did indeed have a "classic case" of the disease.[49] Nazar was sent to fetch Modest, who was "discovered in the theater."[50] Prescribing what was later termed "all that was necessary," Vasily Bertenson remained reluctant to undertake to treat such an illness alone and decided to call in his famous brother, the court physician Lev Bertenson.

Tchaikovsky's condition was growing more alarming. He was now too weak even to move. His vomiting became more agonizing, and while vomiting and for several moments afterward, he would become frenzied and cry out at the top of his voice, complaining of the unbearable pain in his chest. At one point he turned to his brother and said, "I think I'm dying. Farewell!" He later repeated the words several times. After every movement he sank back on the bed exhausted. It was already after ten when Lev Bertenson finally arrived. He at last made a firm diagnosis of cholera. Moreover, he found the disease already in its second and most dangerous phase, the so-called algid stage, or stage of collapse. "The picture of the illness was indisputably characteristic, and I had immediately to recognize a very severe case of cholera," he later recalled.[51] According to Nikolay Figner, Lev Bertenson made it clear "that he had had no prior occasion to confront this particular form" of cholera.[52] From the appearance of the first acute symptoms in the early hours of Thursday morning until the establishment of the diagnosis late Thursday night, nearly a full day had elapsed.

It is impossible to know precisely when and how Tchaikovsky became infected. Unboiled water was naturally assumed to be the source of the contagion. One widely popular version, first offered in newspaper accounts by confused relatives of the composer, alleged that Tchaikovsky recklessly drank a glass of unboiled water during the late supper at Leiner's restaurant Wednesday evening.[53] But Modest, who does not mention this story at all and who judiciously decided not to accuse any specific establishment of carelessness in his brother's illness, later seized upon a glass of unboiled water that he claimed Tchaikovsky drank during lunch on Thursday. "It seems to me that that lunch has a fateful significance," he insisted, "since it was right in the middle of our conversation about the medication he had taken that he poured a glass of water and took a sip from it. The water was unboiled. We were all frightened: he alone was indifferent to it and told us not to worry." This proposition no doubt had a beneficial effect on Modest's conscience, since it would make forgivable any negligence about his brother's health earlier that day and could imply that precious hours for an appropriate diagnosis had not been lost. Neither story, however, makes sense from a medical point of view. The incubation period for cholera is from one to three days.[54] Since Tchaikovsky began to experience difficulties early Thursday morning, he could not have been infected later than Wednesday morning—certainly far earlier than lunchtime on Thursday and even earlier than supper the night before.

But even though both versions are medically unsound, there remains Modest's suggestion that his brother had little fear of catching cholera. If he did not hesitate to drink unboiled water at lunch on Thursday, when he was already feeling indisposed, then nothing would have prevented him from drinking unboiled water at any time during the three-day incubation period from early Monday to early Wednesday. Tchaikovsky was in the habit of drinking cold water at meals. Indeed, in July of that year, while visiting his brother Nikolay at his home near Kursk, Tchaikovsky was forced to delay his departure when he "became terribly ill . . . from the abuse of cold water at dinner and supper," as he wrote to Bob afterward.[55] He might also have caught the infection even less wittingly. Just weeks after Tchaikovsky came down with the disease, the cholera bacillus was discovered not only in the water of the Neva River but even in the water supply of the Winter Palace itself. A special sanitary commission further established that in certain restaurants, in order to make the water cooler, boiled water was being mixed with unboiled tap water before being offered to patrons.[56] In addition, there was the risk of catching the infection from uncooked foods, especially salads, and any food that had been left uncovered and exposed to flies, important carriers of the disease. Another factor may have been a glass of the alkaline mineral water Huniadi-Janos that Tchaikovsky, already feeling unwell, was said to have drunk on Thursday morning and that might actually have stimulated the growth of the cholera bacillus by neutralizing the stomach acids.[57]

Besides the Bertensons, Modest, and Modest's servant Nazar, Bob Davydov and the two Litke brothers remained with the patient. Immediately after establishing the diagnosis, Lev Bertenson summoned a medical attendant and ordered everyone to put on white aprons as a hygienic measure. About midnight Tchaikovsky began to experience spasms that became so violent that he cried aloud. Soon after the appearance of the first spasms, he asked his brother, "It's not cholera, is it?" Modest tried to conceal the truth from him, but when Tchaikovsky overheard the doctor warn the family about the basic precautionary measures against infection, he exclaimed, "So it is cholera!" As the spasms continued, the doctors and the others directed their efforts to massaging now this part of his body, now that. Tchaikovsky's head and bodily extremities began to turn very blue and became completely cold. After one o'clock the spasms lessened and the bouts of diarrhea and vomiting became less severe. Issuing instructions to Vasily and the attendant, Lev Bertenson departed, leaving his brother with the patient.

Treatment of cholera at the end of the nineteenth century remained largely the treatment of symptoms. The rapid and severe depletion of body fluids and salts was still inadequately addressed, and no satisfactory means of replacing fluid yet existed.[58] Even with early correct diagnosis Russian physicians for the most part could do little more than attempt to purge the infection through the use of laxatives, while at the same time employing massage, warm baths, and doses of camphor, musk, and other stimulants in an effort to counteract the deadly decline of the patient's vital signs. Great hopes were placed in the hot bath as means of restoring the patient's failing circulation and pulse rate. Most people at the time firmly believed that in cholera cases, especially in the dangerous algid phase, warming the body was essential, and the appearance of sweat was regarded as success in that treatment, indicating that the bodily fluids were beginning to flow again.[59] Yet, for some reason, Lev Bertenson chose not to prescribe the bath treatment that night, nor did he on Friday. Bertenson would later note that the death of Tchaikovsky's mother under similar circumstances had instilled in the composer "and in his relatives a superstitious fear of the bath." Nor did Modest contradict this when he recalled that he and his elder brother Nikolay, who by Saturday had arrived at Modest's apartment, "involuntarily regarded this necessary measure with superstitious fear." He further reported that when Bertenson on Saturday finally asked Tchaikovsky whether he wished to have the bath, the composer replied, "I'm very glad to wash, only I shall probably die like my mother when you put me into the bath." It appears to have been precisely the emotional or superstitious resistance of the Tchaikovsky brothers, coupled with the fears of Tchaikovsky himself, that proved decisive in Lev Bertenson's long delay in ordering the bath.

After Lev Bertenson left, the spasms returned, and the next few hours became one uninterrupted struggle with Tchaikovsky's cramps and his numbness, which yielded less and less to the energetic rubbing and artificial warming of his body. At times, it seemed that death had come, and toward dawn the action of his heart became so weak that Vasily Bertenson administered injections of musk and camphor to revive him. Throughout the attacks, Tchaikovsky apologized repeatedly for the trouble he was causing, telling everyone to go to bed and thanking them for the slightest service. He was distressed by the anxiety of those around him and feared that the outward aspects of his illness would disgust them. Sometimes he tried to joke. "I'm afraid you'll lose all your respect for me after all these unpleasant things," he told Bob at one point. By five o'clock the worst of the spasms were over, and Tchaikovsky became relatively calm, complaining only of a depressed condition. The vomiting and diarrhea, though less severe, continued, and the spasms returned whenever Tchaikovsky tried to move. He grew thirsty, but whenever he was given a sip of something to drink, he turned away in revulsion. Early in the morning, Vasily Bertenson sent Modest to tell the police what had happened, in accordance with official regulations concerning cholera epidemics.

At nine o'clock on the morning of Friday, 22 October, Vasily Bertenson was replaced by Dr. Mamonov, his brother's medical assistant.[60] Vasily Bertenson apparently did not return to the apartment, but instead relied on his eminent brother to take charge and direct further treatment. Lev Bertenson himself arrived that morning at eleven, the time of the first apparent improvement in the patient's condition. The lividity had gone, but there remained black spots on his face. Then these also disappeared, and by midday the lingering spasms had ceased. Bertenson was convinced that the attacks that during the night had threatened the life of his patient had passed. Modest noted that the composer's "general state was so much better that he considered himself saved." When Bertenson asked him how he felt, Tchaikovsky replied, "Vastly improved. Thank you. You have snatched me from the jaws of death. I feel immeasurably better than during the first night."

Mamonov was replaced at three that afternoon by another medical assistant, Aleksandr Zander. Everyone thought that the disease was gradually yielding to the treatment. For the moment, Tchaikovsky was only suffering from an insatiable thirst. The sharp decline in circulatory activity in the early stages of the illness had led to failure of the renal artery and complete blocking of urine. Though the urine was still blocked, there were as yet no signs of uremia, that is, poisoning of the blood from an excess of urea. Nor was there evidence of the so-called typhoid stage, an acute and exhausting fever sometimes occurring in the last phase of cholera. Indeed, Tchaikovsky's condition had improved to such an extent that Mamonov, on returning, insisted that those present go to bed since no new dangerous symptoms were expected during the night.

By the morning of Saturday the twenty-third, Tchaikovsky seemed to have passed safely into the third stage of the disease, the stage of reaction. The risk of a relapse or further complications still loomed, but with the most dangerous phase of the illness over, the spirits of Tchaikovsky's physicians and family rose in hope of a full recovery. Tchaikovsky had passed the stage of acute infection, so that after the room and patient were disinfected, it became possible to allow his friends and relatives into the room. They came and shook his hand, and he, smiling, responded with a feeble handshake. As they left, more as a formality than out of any real fear of infection, the physicians had the visitors wash their hands in a solution of mercuric chloride.[61]

The disturbing news began to spread through the city that the famous composer had been taken "dangerously ill," as Eduard Nápravník noted in his diary on Friday.[62] There was some confusion about the nature of the illness, apparently stemming from rumors about the possible onset of the typhoid stage. "The entire musical world is worried by the news of the serious illness of P. I. Tchaikovsky," reported one newspaper on Saturday, adding that "fortunately, according to the latest information, the illness (allegedly typhus) is taking a favorable course."[63] Crowds of friends and admirers hastened to Modest's apartment on Malaya Morskaya Street. Most, despite the protests of the doorman, mounted the stairs to the fifth-floor apartment and rang at the door, disturbing those within. All that day, people were told that "the situation was still very dangerous but that the patient was now better."[64] Vasily Yastrebtsev recorded in his diary a meeting he had with Rimsky-Korsakov on Saturday evening. "When I asked him whether it was true that Tchaikovsky was so dangerously ill," wrote Yastrebtsev, "he informed me that today he himself had visited Pyotr Ilyich . . . at home and had learned that the rumors are correct; that last Wednesday (20 October) Tchaikovsky had been at the Chamber Society and afterward went to Leiner's, where, having eaten spaghetti, he drank a glass of unboiled water; that the same night, he had developed all the symptoms of Asiatic cholera, with convulsions and spasms; that at present there is a turning point, but the doctors (Bertenson and the others) fear that the cholera will reach the kidneys—and if so, everything will be over." However, added the diarist, "according to the doctors, there is little prospect that typhus will develop, and if so, he could survive, with God's help—but who really knows?"[65]

In response to the steady stream of people inquiring about Tchaikovsky's health, the doctors decided to issue bulletins on the progress of the illness, instructing the doorman to show these to all those seeking information but to allow no one access to the apartment bell.[66]

For Tchaikovsky, Saturday passed tolerably, yet the lack of urine and the growing threat of uremia began to worry the physicians. All possible means were employed to galvanize the kidneys, but to no avail. By evening, the signs of uremic poisoning became evident, and Lev Bertenson, despite the superstition of the Tchaikovsky brothers, made up his mind to resort to the use of a hot bath in hopes of restoring the blood circulation and thus supporting the kidneys. But the idea of the bath was abandoned when the diarrhea suddenly worsened and became uncontrollable, indicating the paralytic condition of the intestines. The renewed diarrhea had a very dispiriting effect on the already weak Tchaikovsky, who turned to Bertenson with the words "Let me go, don't torment yourself. It's all the same to me if I don't recover."

Lev Bertenson left after two o'clock in the morning, "dissatisfied with the state of affairs."

That night passed relatively well, but by the next day, Sunday the twenty-fourth, Tchaikovsky's condition was far worse. He seemed less alert than on previous days, and he was even unable for some time to recognize Alyosha, who had arrived that morning from Klin. To all inquiries about his condition he simply replied, "Terrible!" At times, he grew slightly delirious, angrily repeating the words "hope" and "accursed."[67] The Russian for "hope" is *nadezhda*, leading Modest to assume that his brother in his incoherent delirium was reproaching Nadezhda von Meck for her "betrayal." In fact, the epithet "accursed" almost certainly pertained to the approach of the "accursed snub-nosed creature," as Tchaikovsky once referred to death, while the word "hope" more likely signified hope for recovery in the face of the "accursed creature."

The doctors' anxiety over the inactivity of the kidneys increased. Lev Bertenson arrived toward one o'clock that Sunday afternoon and immediately decided on the urgency of a bath. While it was being prepared, the physician had time to dash off a few lines describing Tchaikovsky's condition for the crowd gathered in front of the house eagerly awaiting news of the beloved composer. At half past two the first medical bulletin was sent down to the doorman: "The dangerous fits continue and are not responding to treatment; complete retention of the urine, together with drowsiness and a marked general weakness; the diarrhea is not as strong as before, but still continues."[68] The bath was ready at two o'clock. The various preparations, however, took nearly an hour. During this time, Tchaikovsky was in a semiconscious state. It was nearly three when he was finally placed in the bath.[69] "It appears that he did not quite clearly grasp at first what they wanted to do with him," Modest recalled, "but then he consented to the bath, and when he was lowered into it, he was fully aware of what was happening." After a while Tchaikovsky, complaining of weakness, began asking to be lifted out. "The bath," as Modest noted later, "did not have the anticipated effect." A few days later, other relatives of the composer would admit to reporters that "it was already too late by the time Pyotr Ilyich was placed in the hot bath, and after it he lost the last of his strength."[70] As a consequence of the bath, the patient's weakness became so great that the doctors again attempted an injection of musk to restore his strength. It was for the moment successful, and despite the perspiration, the patient's pulse rose and he grew calm.

Lev Bertenson left at this point, and it is not surprising that his impression was that "the immediate effect of the bath was beneficial:

a warm sweat appeared, and with it a hope that the uremic poisoning might diminish and the functioning of the kidneys be restored." His assistant Mamonov confirmed this when he noted that "until 8:00 P.M. it seemed to us that his condition was improving." At eight o'clock Mamonov was again replaced by Zander, who later recalled that by this time Tchaikovsky "had grown completely quiet, drawing into himself and scarcely speaking. He no longer showed any interest in those around him."[71] According to Modest, around a quarter past eight Zander noticed a sudden weakening of the pulse and grew worried. Consequently, he administered yet another injection of musk and sent for Lev Bertenson. Tchaikovsky was becoming comatose. Modest was advised not to leave him alone for a minute. Tchaikovsky's head was hot, and his breathing was labored and accompanied by moans. Shortly after ten o'clock Zander noted the onset of edema of the lungs.

Lev Bertenson and Mamonov returned to find the patient's condition, which before eight had seemed to be improving, drastically worsened. His heartbeat had sharply weakened, and he lay in a semicomatose state, from which he could only manage to be brought out for the very shortest time. When asked if he wanted to drink, he would become momentarily conscious and answer "Yes" or "Of course," and then afterward would say, "That's enough." By half past ten, according to Bertenson, "all hopes for a possible favorable turn in the course of the illness completely vanished." Tchaikovsky's drowsiness became ever deeper, and his pulse remained undetectable, despite frequent injections of stimulants. An oxygen mask was applied every five minutes. After midnight he was all but unconscious. Despite the brief rally earlier in the evening, the general picture was one of irreversible deterioration, as reflected in the language of a second bulletin posted at half past ten that evening: "Urinary function has not been restored and signs of blood poisoning from the constituents of the urine are extremely pronounced. Since three o'clock this afternoon there has been a rapidly growing decline in the action of the heart and fading consciousness. Since ten o'clock this evening the pulse has been almost imperceptible and there is edema of the lungs."[72]

It was this second bulletin that prompted Nápravník to note in his diary that day, "The state of P. I. Tchaikovsky's health is hopeless!!"[73]

A priest was sent for from the nearby St. Isaac's Cathedral, but arriving and finding Tchaikovsky too weak to receive the Holy Sacraments, he prayed by his bed in loud tones, which Tchaikovsky showed no signs of hearing. Soon after this the patient's fingers moved slightly, as though he had an itch in various parts of his body.

Lev Bertenson decided that there were too many people in the rather small room. The tenor Nikolay Figner and the young violinist Dmitry Bzul, who had slipped in earlier, now departed. The window was opened.

At half past one in the morning a third bulletin was issued: "The patient's condition has so worsened that a sanitary inspector and police officials have arrived at the house."[74]

Around two o'clock, having recognized that the patient's condition was hopeless, Bertenson and Zander left the apartment. They commissioned Mamonov to stay with him until the very end. Lev Bertenson's son Sergey later wrote in his memoirs, "I shall never forget the look on my father's face when he returned home and said, 'It's all over,' and broke into sobs."[75]

Tchaikovsky's breathing grew more and more shallow. He could still be brought to consciousness by asking him whether he wanted a drink, but he no longer responded with words, only with affirmative or negative signs. In these last moments of his life, Tchaikovsky was surrounded by those whom he loved: his brothers Modest and Nikolay, his adored nephew Bob, Sanya and Konstantin Litke, and his irreplaceable Alyosha. In addition to Mamonov and a medical assistant, Rudy Buchshoevden and Modest's servant Nazar Litrov and his wife were also present.

The clock showed a little after three in the morning.

Not ten minutes before his death the dying man opened his eyes. His expression was one of full consciousness, and it seemed to Modest that "even at this moment he was not thinking about himself but only appeared to be begging our forgiveness for causing us such terrible grief."[76]

Tchaikovsky's gaze rested on his brother and his nephew. Infinite love and anguished farewell were said to have been expressed in that look.[77]

CHAPTER THIRTY

Death in St. Petersburg

"The cruel epidemics have not spared even our famous composer P. I. Tchaikovsky." On Monday morning, 25 October, all the St. Petersburg newspapers published their first brief announcements of Tchaikovsky's death. "He fell ill during the day on Thursday," continued the report in the *News and Exchange Gazette*, "and immediately the illness acquired a dangerous character. . . . At 3 A.M. P. I. Tchaikovsky was no more. P. I. Tchaikovsky was treated by several doctors, led by the court physician L. B. Bertenson."[1] The *New Times* wrote, "The renowned composer P. I. Tchaikovsky fell ill from cholera on Thursday. [Yesterday] at 3 P.M. the decline in cardiac activity rapidly increased, his consciousness dimmed. . . . Between the third and fourth hour after midnight Pyotr Ilyich died."[2]

Later that day, Lev Bertenson sent Modest his personal condolences. "My very dear Modest Ilyich," he wrote, "I should like to embrace you warmly and tell you how deeply shocked I am by our horrible common misfortune, but I am unable to do so because I can hardly walk and cannot go out. The dreadful disease that took the life of your unforgettable brother has struck me down along with him, with you and with all those to whom he was dear. I cannot recover from this terrible tragedy that I have had to witness, and I am quite unable to express to you all the agonies I am going through now. I can tell you only one thing: *that I feel what you feel*."[3] A telegram also came from Vasily Bertenson: "There are no words to express my sorrow; may God grant you strength to bear such a terrible loss."[4]

That morning, Modest sent a telegram to Grand Duke Konstantin informing him of the composer's death. "Pyotr Ilyich died at three o'clock this morning," Konstantin wrote in his diary moments after receiving the telegram. "My heart bleeds. . . . I shall miss him."[5]

On the morning of his death Tchaikovsky's body lay at first in a small room on the ottoman on which he had died. Routine measures against the spread of cholera were taken by a special sanitary commission. Most press accounts paid scant attention to the customary procedures, the *Son of the Fatherland*, for example, stating simply that "the entire apartment has been thoroughly disinfected."[6] From early morning, the street doors remained open as a steady stream of students, colleagues, and admirers of the composer made their way to Modest's apartment. No one could believe the terrible news. A reporter from the *New Times* who managed to see the body that morning noted that "the deceased lies . . . as if alive and appears, as it were, to have fallen asleep."[7]

The first requiem was scheduled for two o'clock that afternoon. The apartment was quickly choked with those who had come to see the great composer one last time. By one o'clock so many people had gathered that it was impossible to push past the entrance hall and gradually the line of those waiting anxiously to get in stretched along all four flights of the stairway leading up from the street. A host of figures from society and the musical world, literati, and artists were present in the crowd. In an attempt to accommodate the great number of mourners, relatives of the composer went to the Holy Synod later that day seeking permission to move the deceased to the nearby St. Isaac's Cathedral, but it was decided that it was already too late to make any changes. At two o'clock the doors were opened to a corner reception room where the composer's body, already dressed in a black suit, had been transferred and now lay on a low catafalque draped in white satin. A transparent shroud covered the body up to the neck. "His face, completely exposed, no longer reflects the suffering of the painful illness," wrote the *Petersburg Gazette*. "It is of a parchmentlike yellow, but tranquil, impassive—the face of an exhausted man sleeping peacefully, and only the presence near the head of someone continually touching the lips and the nostrils of the deceased with a bit of light-colored material soaked in carbolic solution reminds one of the terrible illness that struck down the deceased."[8]

At the sight of the body, sobs were heard here and there, which turned into loud weeping. Several ladies grew faint. Modest was so struck by grief that he could not be present at the service, but remained in a neighboring room in the company of a few devoted persons.[9]

Tchaikovsky's body had been placed with his head toward a corner of the room where a wax candle flickered before a crucifix. Unlit tapers stood around the body on tall candlesticks trimmed with black crepe. No other furniture was in the room. The walls of the low room, with its five windows, were hung with engravings and several paintings of biblical subjects. A portrait of the late composer had been placed there as well. It showed him deep in thought.

The requiem service began, sung from an adjoining room by the male chorus of the Imperial Russian Opera. People continued to arrive. The room was stifling, but the atmosphere was solemn and reverential, disturbed only as someone from the sanitary commission passed through with a hissing atomizer or as someone in charge was heard giving loud instructions. Among the musicians and composers attending the service were Laroche, Lyadov, Nápravník, and Rimsky-Korsakov.[10] Ten years later, Rimsky-Korsakov remarked in his memoirs that he had found it "odd that although death was the result of cholera, there was free access to the requiems. I remember that [Aleksandr] Verzhbilovich [a cellist and professor at the St. Petersburg Conservatory], totally drunk after some sort of binge, kissed the corpse on the face and head."[11] In fact, there was nothing odd about it at all. Despite lingering prejudice and fear concerning the disease, the prevailing medical opinion of the time held that cholera was less contagious than was previously supposed. Although earlier government policy had strongly discouraged crowded funerals and funeral banquets for victims of cholera, and in particular those of the lower classes, a special resolution of the Central Medical Council in the spring of 1893 specifically allowed public services and rituals in connection with the funerals of cholera victims.[12] Even the decision to have an open casket was in no way improper.[13] "In view of the fact that Pyotr Ilyich died not from cholera (the cholera had been arrested on Friday) but from an infection of the blood and that there can therefore be no question of contagion, his coffin remained open for a time," noted the *Petersburg Gazette*.[14] With the added precaution of the constant disinfection of the lips and nostrils of the body, even the drunken cellist Verzhbilovich had little cause for worry.

Tchaikovsky had been photographed before the first service, and after the service his death mask was taken.[15] The second and final service on Monday lasted from seven o'clock until after eight, after which special prayers were offered, and at nine o'clock, Tchaikovsky was placed in the coffin in the presence of a few intimate friends. All the prescribed measures against the spread of cholera were taken. The body was wrapped in a sheet soaked in a solution of mercuric chloride. The inner coffin, made of metal, was soldered, and the outer, made of varnished oak with a carved wooden cross on its lid, was screwed shut. As was required in the case of a cholera victim, all this was done in the presence of the police.[16] Nikolay Kashkin, who arrived for Tchaikovsky's funeral with a delegation from the Moscow Conservatory the next day, recalled that he found the coffin both sealed and shut.[17]

On Tuesday the twenty-sixth all the morning papers published on their front pages the official announcement of the composer's death, together with their obituaries. On the same day, four services took place. Two of these were special services, one at the request of the School of Jurisprudence and attended by former and present students of the school, and the other at the request of the Imperial Russian Opera. The remaining two services were public, with the participation of the private Arkhangelsky and Sheremetyev choruses. The lines of carriages and coaches along Malaya Morskaya blocked the entire street. Droshkies pulled up in endless procession to let out dignitaries and ladies, students and artists—representatives of every stratum of St. Petersburg society. Two countercurrents of people flowed unceasingly along the staircase, which was lined on both sides with hothouse plants. The room in which the coffin lay was a solid mass of flowers. Garlands were hung about the walls, and the coffin itself was covered and crowded all about with wreaths. Among these, one was from the Directorate of the Imperial Theaters, another from the French conductor Colonne and his orchestra with the inscription "Ami, nous te pleurons tous" (Friend, we all mourn you), and one also from Mrs. von Meck.

On the coffin lay a black velvet pillow with the Order of St. Vladimir. Candles and a chandelier shone brightly across the flowery carpet. The crush of people filled the corridor and the three small rooms. Everything, wrote the New Times, "from a mirror turned to face the wall to a piano with its keyboard locked, reminds one of the sad event. The ottoman on which the deceased passed away stands in the same spot, but nobody sits upon it and the edge on which one would sit is protected with pillows."[18] Beneath the low ceilings the chanting of the priests sounded dully.

On Wednesday the flood of people bidding farewell to the composer continued. The visitors stood like a wall at the entrance, along the staircase and into the apartment. All the rooms were jammed with people. It was scarcely possible even to move. The final requiem was distinguished by a particular solemnity. Public attendance was enormous. Not until ten that evening was the apartment successfully cleared out. It was only on this day that Anatoly finally arrived from Nizhny Novgorod.

A debate had begun over just where the composer was to be buried. The Muscovites, led by Anatoly Brandukov and Sergey Taneev, demanded that he be buried at either Moscow or Klin, claiming that such had been Tchaikovsky's final wish. But his relatives were disposed otherwise, deciding that he should be buried in St. Petersburg. "In Petersburg my brother's best years were spent," Modest told reporters later. "He received his education here, first at the School of Jurisprudence, then at the conservatory; here his operas and symphonies enjoyed their first success, here he had so many artistic attachments! But Pyotr Ilyich always held Petersburg dear for other reasons as well. Here in Petersburg our parents died and are buried, and as late as last year, our sister also was laid to rest in the Aleksandrovskoe Cemetery."[19]

Alexander III, on receiving word of Tchaikovsky's death, decided to bear himself the costs of the composer's burial and charged the Directorate of the Imperial Theaters with organizing the funeral. The imperial beneficence testified clearly to the exceptional regard in which Tchaikovsky had been held by his sovereign. Only twice before had a Russian monarch shown such a degree of favor to an artistic or scholarly figure at his death. In both instances, the monarch had been Nicholas I, who wrote a letter to the dying Pushkin after the poet's fatal duel and who came personally to pay his last respects to the historian Nikolay Karamzin on the eve of his burial. Special tickets were distributed for participation in the funeral procession, for entrance to the Kazan Cathedral, where the funeral service was to take place, and for access to the cemetery of the Aleksandr Nevsky Monastery. But the numbers of those who wished such tickets were too great and could not be satisfied. Kazan Cathedral holds six thousand, but sixty thousand applied.

The funeral for the great man so devotedly cherished by his nation took place on Thursday, 28 October. Early in the morning an elaborate wreath composed of white roses arrived, sent by Alexander III himself. It seemed that all the inhabitants of St. Petersburg had come out on to the streets to pay their last respects. The whole of Nevsky Prospect was packed with people. After a short liturgy the coffin was placed on a hearse and the funeral procession set out in the direction of the Kazan Cathedral, following a special route that took it past the Mariinsky Theater. Grand Duke Konstantin and other members of the imperial family arrived at the cathedral in time for the main religious service. The honor guard was made up of students from the School of Jurisprudence. Nikander, the bishop of Narva, performed the service. The chorus of the Russian Opera, conducted by Fyodor Bekker, sang, among other pieces, two hymns written by the composer, the Orthodox Credo and the Te Deum. In addition, the military orchestra played a funeral march—the first time that this had been allowed at a funeral for a civilian.

The ecclesiastical portion having concluded, the procession set out for the monastery. "That was truly a grandiose picture!" the actor Yury Yuryev recalled. "Petersburgers could not remember such a concourse of people, and in the past it would hardly have been allowed."[20] Behind whole rows of wreaths and before the hearse, to which were harnessed three pairs of horses, marched the clergy in their white cassocks. Tchaikovsky's relatives and friends followed the coffin, and following them, in order of importance, were the representatives of various institutions. The procession reached the monastery at four o'clock. Tchaikovsky's grave was located near those of Borodin and Mussorgsky. The coffin was placed in the ground, and the priest threw in a handful of earth.

The farewell speeches were delivered. Vladimir Gerard, Tchaikovsky's former classmate from the School of Jurisprudence and now a prominent public figure, was one of the most eloquent speakers. "Everyone in Russia who is capable of thought, and especially of feeling, is deeply shaken," Gerard told the gathering. "We who grew up with him, shared the joys and anxieties of his childhood, knew what a human being he was. I do not believe that any perceptive expert in the human heart would be able to define his character so well as his comrades at boarding school could; and we all loved him because there was among us no one more charming, more cordial, more kind and sympathetic than Petya Tchaikovsky. These were the distinctive features of his character that attracted everyone who became close to him; these are also the distinctive features that shine brightly in his creative works." Thus invoking the years of their youth and schoolboy camaraderie, Gerard movingly closed his oration, "Within the great Russian family there is a numerically tiny but cordially and strongly united family of Tchaikovsky's comrades from the School of Jurisprudence. This family has suffered an even greater loss: it is now burying a beloved comrade. . . . Farewell, our dear one! The earth will be light on you, I do not doubt. It is always light for one who leaves of himself an eternal and dear memory."[21]

The funeral ended by five o'clock. Detailed accounts were published in all the major papers the next day.[22]

A curious epilogue concluded the day of the funeral, for it was that

evening that the St. Petersburg premiere of Modest's comedy *Prejudices* was finally held. It had been in anticipation of this event that
Tchaikovsky had decided to delay his return to Klin. Originally scheduled for that Tuesday, the opening had naturally been postponed because of the composer's death and was rescheduled for Thursday,
which then happened to be the day of the funeral. But Modest decided
against a second postponement, presumably feeling the need for some
distraction. A reviewer for the *St. Petersburg Register* wrote of the production, "On Thursday, the day of P. I. Tchaikovsky's burial, a comedy
by the composer's brother, M. I. Tchaikovsky, was buried at the Aleksandrinsky Theater. By this we do not mean that the play was very bad
or that it was very poorly acted. Neither the one nor the other is true.
But it is a comedy with a rottenness at its source, and the closer we
come to the denouement, the clearer it becomes that this is a dying
play, that there is no life in it, but only the final throes of death."[23]
Other critics agreed with this view, remarking that despite fine performances from the actors, the theme of the play was never clearly expressed, nor were the characters fully drawn, and that the author failed
to provide answers to the questions posed. Nevertheless, this did not
prevent the play from lasting for several more performances with varying success.

In the following days the papers continued to comment on so sudden an end to the life of the great man. "Tchaikovsky died. . . . These
two words formulate our mood during the last days," wrote the *News
and Exchange Gazette* on 30 October. "To be Tchaikovsky—and to die
from cholera! This trick of chance is too cruel. . . . The years will pass
and this cholera will be remembered. It will be called the epidemic that
stole Tchaikovsky from Russian art."[24]

Throughout the capital the initial response to the sudden news had
been one of shock and disbelief. "Even yesterday, even last evening no
one wanted to imagine that *he* would be no more," the *News and Exchange Gazette* had remarked in an article written the Monday he died
and printed the following day. "From lips to lips the anxious news was
carried, but there was no recognition of the dreadful closeness of the
fatal outcome. . . . Everyone still hoped!" And the paper added bitterly,
"Only eight persons fell ill with cholera in Petersburg last week, and
P. I. Tchaikovsky was the eighth. From among the million people in
the capital the merciless epidemic took no care to find a more deserving victim!"[25]

Much of the public response to Tchaikovsky's death was colored
and even dominated by the fact that cholera, while in fact touching all
levels of society, was largely considered a disease of the poor and thus

vulgar and socially demeaning. That the world-famous composer might die of cholera seemed to degrade his reputation in the eyes of the upper classes and struck many as inconceivable. People began speculating on the actual nature of the illness. For some days neither the public nor the press knew virtually any detail beyond the brief medical bulletins. Questions began to be asked and conjectures made. "How could Tchaikovsky, having just arrived in Petersburg and living in excellent hygienic conditions, have contracted the infection?" asked the *Petersburg Gazette* quite reasonably,[26] while *Russian Life* noted that "everyone is astounded by the uncommon occurrence of the lightning-fast infection with Asiatic cholera of a man so very temperate, modest, and austere in his daily habits."[27] The *Son of the Fatherland* went furthest of all in its comments. "We find it extremely strange that a good restaurant could have *served* unboiled water during an epidemic," the paper wrote, referring to the rumor that Tchaikovsky had been infected by drinking a glass of unboiled water during the supper at Leiner's restaurant. "There exists, as far as we can recollect, a binding decree that commercial establishments, eating houses, restaurants, etc., should have boiled water."[28]

The newspapers sought to respond to the questions with a variety of possible explanations for what had happened: contamination of the water of the Neva, negligence on the part of restaurant employees, the effect of Huniadi-Janos mineral water on Tchaikovsky's stomach. Despite some ambiguous statements, however, not a single major metropolitan paper indulged in any blatant insinuations about the possible cause of Tchaikovsky's death. The *News and Exchange Gazette*, without dealing in specific conjecture itself, simply informed its readership that "concerning the causes of Tchaikovsky's illness as well as his death, the most contradictory rumors are circulating in the city."[29] Still, some of the leading St. Petersburg papers could not resist the temptation of pretending to know more than the others about the circumstances surrounding the composer's death. One of the more flagrant examples of this appeared in the *Petersburg Gazette*, which on 26 October printed a lengthy piece on the course of the illness. Along with various inaccuracies about when Tchaikovsky had fallen ill and when the doctors had first arrived, more or less understandable at this stage, the paper actually invented various "opinions of Dr. Bertenson" about the treatment, with an abundance of intimate details, and described Tchaikovsky's last hours in melodramatic tones as "the fatal denouement."[30]

That same day, in fact, the *News and Exchange Gazette* provided the first eyewitness accounts of Tchaikovsky's final days with its publication of interviews with Bertenson's medical assistant Dr. Mamonov, the tenor Nikolay Figner, and an unnamed relative of the composer.[31] While these accounts, quite naturally, differed somewhat in emphasis and detail, they painted a fairly accurate picture of what happened in those last days. But it was the piece in the *Petersburg Gazette*, caught up by several smaller papers, that prompted Lev Bertenson on 27 October to make a special refutation, which was published in the *New Times* the following day. "Certain papers have in connection with the illness of P. I. Tchaikovsky ascribed to me opinions and comments in such distorted form that I am compelled to deny them," Bertenson wrote, "especially as I have seen no members of the press except a reporter from the *New Times*, and therefore cannot have spoken with any of them."[32]

To the reporter from the *New Times*, Bertenson had in fact given, on 26 October, his only interview, which appeared in the paper the next day.[33] Occasioned, in part, by the contradictions in the various reports printed in the papers on Tuesday, Bertenson's brief and essentially accurate account of his treatment of the composer's illness did little, however, to calm the growing public concern. Bertenson's statement appeared, in particular, to conflate the chronology of events, giving the impression that the bath, for example, had been administered on Saturday rather than on Sunday and that Tchaikovsky had died early Sunday morning rather than Monday. Whether this was done purposely by Bertenson to slide over the troubling issue of the belated bath or, as seems more likely, a day was simply lost in the interview process or perhaps omitted inadvertently by the reporter who wrote up the interview, the slip went unmentioned by the press at the time.[34] Nor was this surprising, since the correct chronology of events, including the belated bath, had by this time been established by other newspaper accounts. Even so, it no doubt muddled matters still further for the readership of the *New Times*. As confusion mounted and rumor spread, Modest was finally forced to step forward himself. On 1 November both the *New Times* and the *News and Exchange Gazette* published Modest's detailed account of his brother's illness.[35] At the head of this description of the composer's last days Modest wrote pointedly that "in addition to the short but thoroughly accurate account by Lev Bertenson of the last days of my brother's life, I feel it necessary, in order to dispel all conflicting rumors, to offer you for publication as full an account as possible of everything I witnessed."[36]

It is likely that Modest, in writing his description of his brother's illness, relied to some degree on the advice or even the written notes of Lev Bertenson—a natural procedure, given that Modest was not a doctor by profession and was, no doubt, still deeply shaken by the events of the preceding week.[37] The publication of this day-by-day account, abounding in medical details, seemed to satisfy the public and dispel confusion as to the nature of the composer's illness. Lev Tolstoy not only accepted the truth of Modest's account of his brother's death but, in a letter to the critic and essayist Nikolay Strakhov two days later, even made it the basis for a sweeping Tolstoyan lesson on the place of death in life. "Today I read Tchaikovsky's description of the illness and death of his celebrated brother," wrote Tolstoy from Yasnaya Polyana. "Here is a reading helpful to us: sufferings, cruel physical sufferings, fear: can it be death? doubts, hopes, an inner conviction that it is death, and still, all the while, unceasing suffering and exhaustion, a dulling of the senses, and almost a resignation and oblivion, and, just before the end, a kind of inner vision, an elucidation of everything—'So that's it'—and . . . the end. Here is for us a necessary, a good reading. Not that we should think only of this and not live, but rather we must live and work, yet constantly with one eye seeing and remembering this source of everything steadfast, true, and good."[38]

The wild speculations on the nature of Tchaikovsky's death subsided after Modest's article appeared, but in various quarters the resentment over the fact that the doctors had not managed to save his life did not. Many people, still reeling from the shock of unexpected death, began to ask themselves whether Tchaikovsky's passing had been truly unavoidable or simply the result of poor treatment. As one contemporary cautiously phrased it, "the weight of the loss was increased by a consciousness of its fortuitous nature and the certainty that it might easily have been averted."[39] Aroused public opinion demanded an answer, and the doctors became convenient scapegoats. Less than two weeks after Tchaikovsky's death, all the thunder of the St. Petersburg salons came crashing down upon Lev Bertenson.

In the midst of the ensuing controversy, there were some who conceded that "contemporary medicine has no effective or specific treatment for cholera, and so recommends exclusively preventive measures" and, further, that "if you summon a hundred physicians to the bedside of a cholera victim, the chances of recovery will still depend on the strength of the infection and on the degree of the patient's predisposition to this kind of illness."[40] Still, even though today there is little evidence that the hot bath ever did more than give the patient something of a shock, the bath was still widely viewed in late-nineteenth-century Russia as the most effective treatment in cholera cases. In the growing debate over Tchaikovsky's treatment, attention was very quickly focused on the question of the bath and the delay in prescribing it. It was the episode of the belated bath that was picked up by, among others, the influential editor of the *New Times*, Aleksey Suvorin, who became Lev Bertenson's chief persecutor. In Berlin at the time of Tchaikovsky's death and evidently misinformed about the date of the funeral, among other particulars, Suvorin, on 27 October, wrote in his personal diary, "Tchaikovsky buried yesterday. Dreadfully sorry for him. He was treated by the Bertensons, two brothers, and they did not give him a bath. To my mind these Bertensons are not at all deserving of their reputation."[41] After his return to Russia at the end of October, Suvorin set out to intensify the defamation campaign against Lev Bertenson, charging him and his colleagues with professional incompetence. On 3 November, nine days after Tchaikovsky's death, an article by Suvorin appeared in his "Little Letters" column in the *New Times*. "I returned to Petersburg," he began, "when we had grown fewer by one great man, one resounding and splendid talent. . . . And to have died of cholera! . . . It is a dreadful shame." He then plunged into his scathing attack on the court physician:

> Not only am I indignant at this death, I am also displeased with Mr. Bertenson, who treated Tchaikovsky. I know that it is easy to blame any doctor and that they are often blamed unjustly and even senselessly. . . . I am displeased with Mr. Bertenson, not because he did not cure Tchaikovsky, but because he left the patient, handing him over to his brother and his "assistant." . . . Mr. Bertenson did not do everything necessary, and there seems to me to be grounds for asking him: why did he not hold a consultation? Because he trusted his own authority or because he believed in the patient's recovery? Whether he trusted in the one or the other, he was, in any event, mistaken, and the words of the dying man, who obtained some relief at first, "you have snatched me from the jaws of death," ring now with cruel and just irony for Mr. Bertenson. And this irony is not eliminated by the letter of Mr. M. Tchaikovsky, who records *en toutes lettres* the names and patronymics of the two Bertenson brothers and testifies to their unremitting concern for the patient. Everything, he says, was done, but death is inexorable. No, everything was not done. . . . Bertenson stresses the fact that Tchaikovsky's mother had died of cholera when she was placed in the bath and that this is why he delayed so long in proposing this remedy to him. Mr. Bertenson evidently sees in this act of his a particular delicacy toward that patient. But what we have here is simply an utter failure

to understand that patient and a lack of genuine delicacy on the part of the doctor. Who can prove that Tchaikovsky would have been opposed to a consultation if it had been held without having asked him? Who can say positively that the doctors gathered for a consultation would not have persuaded him against this prejudice about the bath and perhaps have inspired him with moral energy as well? And can Mr. Bertenson not affirm that Tchaikovsky believed in him as in God and that this faith was never once shaken in him? And if this was so, then Mr. Bertenson did not do everything that he ought to have done, having in his charge a patient dear to all Russia. . . . My lines may strike Mr. Bertenson as cruel, especially as they are altogether useless to him who has died, but I write them for the living in general and for physicians in particular, who can draw from this event a certain lesson for themselves.[42]

Following the *New Times*, the *Petersburg Gazette* the next day also criticized Bertenson. "We have received a number of letters from which it is clear that many people are very dissatisfied with Dr. Bertenson," the paper announced. "The doctor apparently did not take all the measures that, had he resorted to them, might have made it possible to prevent the fatal outcome of the illness. Mr. Bertenson would perhaps be acting in his own best interest by at once referring this entire incident, so regrettable for his professional prestige, to a court of arbitration for consideration." The paper went on to accuse Bertenson of "excessive self-conceit" in not consulting with specialists in cholera cases and of a "lack of attention to the patient" and errors in treatment, such as the belated bath, and it even questioned whether Bertenson did in fact have a medical diploma.[43]

The campaign against Bertenson grew. On 5 November the *New Times* called for a full public inquiry "to determine whether and how conscientiously scientific methods were applied" in attempting to save Tchaikovsky. "Only the corporate spirit has kept physicians from expressing censure of their colleague in print and in scholarly meetings," the article in the *New Times* continued. "The corporate spirit must not, however, hinder a clarification of the truth and determination of blame, if someone was to blame in this. By all indications, someone was, be it only for the reason that no consultation was called." Lev Bertenson, it was pointed out, was "in all probability little familiar with the treatment of Asiatic cholera," whereas such treatment "is familiar to clinical physicians and in particular to physicians of the large city hospitals." Since symptoms of cholera were diagnosed in Tchaikovsky, Dr. Bertenson was obliged, the paper noted, to call in immediately the doctors of one of the city hospitals. "From these doctors he would have learned that in the hospitals the majority of cholera cases, if treatment is begun before the onset of spasms, do end happily."[44] Also on 5 November the *Petersburg Gazette* published an article entitled "Who Should Have Treated P. I. Tchaikovsky?" in which the paper once again condemned in harsh terms the Bertenson brothers' treatment of Tchaikovsky.[45]

Although placing the blame for Tchaikovsky's death on Lev Bertenson may have helped to ease the public sense of frustration or outrage, the accusations of Suvorin and the other journalists were ultimately unfounded. Neither a more timely bath nor a consultation with leading specialists could have done much to turn things around. By the time an accurate diagnosis was made, Tchaikovsky's illness had progressed to the most acute and dangerous stage of the disease, at which point, even today, no known cure avails. If Tchaikovsky had been taken to the hospital and placed in the charge of doctors more experienced in treating cholera, his chances for recovery would still not have improved. Given the medical knowledge and methods of treatment available at the end of the nineteenth century, there is little doubt that Lev Bertenson did everything possible to save his patient.[46]

Sergey Bertenson later recalled that in these days of hardship for his father the family received a visit from Modest Tchaikovsky, who came "to express sympathy to my father on behalf of the entire Tchaikovsky family" concerning the recent appearance of Suvorin's article in the *New Times* and the veritable persecution of Bertenson that had followed. Modest "put an end to this by printing in all the Petersburg papers an open letter on behalf of the Tchaikovsky family, expressing profound gratitude to my father and his assistants for the exceptional care shown to the deceased."[47] This letter by Modest was published on 7 November 1893. "On behalf of all those who were constantly with my late brother during the final days of his life," wrote Modest, "I ask you to put in print . . . that we consider any reproaches whatsoever directed against the treatment of Pyotr Ilyich's fatal illness to be absolutely unjust. Despite the fact that we sense the bitterness of this loss more strongly than anyone, none of us feels for L. B. Bertenson, his brother V. B., and assistants N. N. Mamonov and Zander anything other than a sense of gratitude for their sincere and irreproachably thorough treatment of the deceased's illness."[48]

Clearly, all this controversy was a source of great anguish for Modest. Aleksandr Siloti expressed his sympathy in a letter of 19 November in which he wrote, "I can imagine how upsetting for you all this business between Suvorin and Bertenson must be."[49] Modest's refutation, however, made its mark. Thus, the *News and Exchange Gazette*, also on 7 November, turned from an attack of Lev Bertenson to his justification. The practice of blaming a physician for the death of his patient was, the paper noted, nothing new. "The mob disorders during last year's cholera epidemics occurred primarily because savage and ignorant people had been spreading rumors that the doctors were poisoning the cholera victims," the article went on. "The savage and ignorant masses may yet be forgiven such views. But a man believing himself to be educated and humane should not search blindly for a scapegoat to feed his grief, however deep and sacred."[50]

Both the *New Times* and the *Petersburg Gazette*, however, retained their condemnatory tone in commenting on the statement by Modest on 8 November. "Of what significance can such a statement be?" the *New Times* asked. "In our opinion, almost none at all. It is of almost no significance, because in the present case a certain portion of the responsibility falls on Mr. [Modest] Tchaikovsky, who delayed in summoning the doctor and did not see to it that a consultation was called and also because the doctors whom Mr. Tchaikovsky defends are obliged to answer not only to the relatives of the late composer but also to Russian society."[51] Yet, in time, even Suvorin came to understand that he had been intemperate in his accusations against Lev Bertenson, and a few years later at a large dinner of the Literary Fund, the editor made a public apology to the court physician for his unjust claims.[52]

A memorial concert was held on Saturday, 6 November. Performed under the direction of Eduard Nápravník, Tchaikovsky's Sixth Symphony, which just eight days before his death had met with so lukewarm and bewildered a response, now created a tremendous impression. It was an overwhelmingly somber impression, however, made even more so by the atmosphere of the hall itself, draped in mourning and decorated with tropical plants and a huge bust of the composer rendered by the sculptor Semyon Tselinsky on the model of the death mask he had made earlier. Another reason for the feeling of gloom was seen in the symphony itself, and in its unusual sequence of movements, which began and ended with an adagio. "It is indeed a sort of swan song, a presentiment of imminent death, and from this comes its tragic impression. . . . The symphony ends as with a weeping, a sobbing," wrote the *Russian Musical Gazette*.[53]

One must acknowledge the perspicacity of Rimsky-Korsakov when he later wrote, in refutation of the widespread opinion about the symphony's unsatisfactory first performance under Tchaikovsky's direction, "I imagine that the composer's sudden death (which gave rise to all sorts of rumors), as well as stories of his presentiment of approaching death (to which mankind is so prone) and, further, the propensity to seek a connection between the gloomy mood of the symphony's final movement and such a presentiment—all these now focused the public's attention and sympathies on this work, and the splendid composition soon became famous and even fashionable."[54]

It was around this time that the popular though erroneous view of Tchaikovsky as a tragic soul tormented by his homosexuality, a view that is still all too much alive today, began to take shape. A need emerged in the public imagination to resolve the perceived paradox of the famed composer's homosexuality, to reconcile the stereotypical image of homosexuality as a vice or a sickness with the universal adoration that surrounded Tchaikovsky during his life. Providing this resolution, and ultimately enhancing his stature as a tragic figure, was the premise that Tchaikovsky had been the lifelong victim of a painful and tragic crisis arising from his unorthodox, and thereby compromising, sexual orientation. He was thus worthy of compassion, not condemnation. He began to acquire the romantic halo of a doomed sufferer, and from this was born, in time, the rumors of Tchaikovsky's supposed suicide.

The death of a great man marks the minds of his contemporaries. There are instances when the most clear-cut circumstances of a tragic end generate rumor and legend. The poet Mikhail Lermontov was whispered to have fallen, not to his opponent Martynov's bullet, but to that of an assassin hiding near the site of the duel and sent by Nicholas I himself. To this very day the death of Mozart is attributed by many to Antonio Salieri. Some ends, of course, are so impressive in and of themselves as to have no need of any romantic transfiguration— Byron's death during the struggle for the liberation of Greece, for example, or the dramatic flight of Lev Tolstoy from Yasnaya Polyana. Others are less neatly transcendent. Even when notables depart from this world with the limelight of public attention focused on them day by day and hour by hour, surrounded by relatives, friends, and admirers, our imagining and our secret yearning for sensation is not easily held in check. This is all the more true when the lives of the deceased are less cut-and-dried than the circumstances of their deaths. That Nikolay Gogol died in the clear light of day, his death attested by proper medical examination, did little to prevent the spread of the wild rumor that he had been mistakenly buried alive. Such a notion was congenial to the image of the author of "Vii" or "A Terrible Vengeance," tales concerned, as they are, with living corpses. In Tchaikovsky's life there was one important component that many found incomprehensible and that was less than ordinary by the standards of the time—namely, his homosexuality.

An open secret in certain circles, Tchaikovsky's homosexuality and the secretiveness it involved nonetheless fostered misunderstanding and fed rumor and gossip. "His private life was always surrounded by a kind of haze and mysterious mist," recalled one contemporary about Tchaikovsky.[55] The same sense of an enigma surrounding Tchaikovsky was expressed, somewhat confusedly, by Tolstoy in a letter to his wife written on 26 or 27 October 1893, immediately after the composer's death. "I feel very sorry about Tchaikovsky," Tolstoy wrote, "sorry, because it seemed to me that we had something in common. . . . Sorry about him as a man with whom something was not quite clear, even more than as a musician. It was so quick, and so simple and natural and unnatural, and [it strikes] so close to home."[56] His final symphony, with its secret program, inevitably contributed still further to the mystery enveloping Tchaikovsky's personality. And since some had already heard that the symphony had been dedicated to the composer's nephew Bob, certain conclusions arose of their own accord.

The rumors about Tchaikovsky's supposed suicide have been a part of popular mythology for nearly a century. They almost certainly originated within the musical circles of St. Petersburg and Moscow—circles which, on the one hand, were in the best position to know the details about Tchaikovsky's private life, but which, on the other hand, tended, like most artistic milieus, to indulge freely in idle gossip and groundless speculation. The earliest record of the suicide rumor seems to be found in the as yet unpublished memoirs of R. A. Mooser, a Swiss writer on music who arrived in St. Petersburg in 1896 and spent almost thirteen years employed as a church organist and as a critic for the *Journal de St-Pétersbourg*.[57] Despite his prolonged stay, Mooser had little influence on the history of Russian culture and was never regarded by his Russian colleagues as one of their own. Perhaps for this reason, Mooser in his memoirs appears to make an effort to portray himself as privy to their secrets. It is worth noting, however, that virtually all of Mooser's informants were themselves foreigners.

Mooser recalls that he first learned about Tchaikovsky's homosexuality from an unnamed critic at the *St. Petersburger Zeitung*. Then, sometime later, Riccardo Drigo, ballet conductor at the Mariinsky Theater, confided to him the story of the composer's alleged suicide. According to Drigo's story, Tchaikovsky seduced the son of the caretaker of Modest's apartment house. The boy's father complained, and his allegations eventually reached the tsar—in itself a highly improbable development. The tsar then decreed—in an equally improbable twist, given Alexander III's suppression of the far graver scandal involving Meshchersky—that the culprit must immediately disappear. Hearing the pronouncement and realizing that his career was at an end, Tchaikovsky, according to the story, poisoned himself. In refuting the official version of Tchaikovsky's death, Drigo cited the open casket at the funeral service of the Kazan Cathedral (though by this time, of course, the coffin was in fact already sealed). This open casket was clear evidence, he contended, that Tchaikovsky had died not of cholera but of poison. His view shows, of course, the same outmoded conceptions witnessed in Rimsky-Korsakov's observation on the supposed strangeness of open access to the earliest requiems in Modest's apartment. It was this lack of knowledge about proper precautions against cholera—and the sight of mourners apparently acting against their own safety—that contributed, as much as anything, to the general confusion and fueled speculation that Tchaikovsky's relatives had somehow neglected the prescribed sanitary regulations and that accordingly there had been something unnatural about the composer's death.[58]

The final point in Mooser's account is his recollection of a conversation that he had with Aleksandr Glazunov on the subject of Tchaikovsky's alleged suicide. According to Mooser, Glazunov became distressed but confirmed the details of the story told by Drigo. This report is plagued, however, by logical and psychological inconsistencies. Mooser himself praises very highly Glazunov's personal integrity and moral probity. Given this, Glazunov could not have confirmed the suicide story unless he was absolutely certain of its truth. But he could only have been absolutely certain of its truth if he had heard it from someone in Tchaikovsky's most intimate circle, that is, someone who had been present at his deathbed. It was, however, precisely the members of this inner circle who were alleged by Drigo to have gone so far in their efforts to conceal the "truth" that they had demanded false testimonies from authorities, physicians, and priests alike. Only by swearing him to strictest secrecy could anyone from this circle have dared to reveal the "truth" to Glazunov. That he would then turn around and share this information with Mooser, whom he scarcely knew, is virtually inconceivable: it would have compromised him utterly.

Clearly, if Mooser's account of this conversation is to be credited at all, it must be assumed that Glazunov confirmed (and, no doubt, lamented) the existence of the rumors themselves—but nothing beyond that. Glazunov's own memoirs, published in Russia in 1924, at a time when censorship was negligible, refer only to Tchaikovsky's "fa-

tal illness" and make no allusion to his supposed suicide. Nor did Glazunov mention it in private communications with Tchaikovsky's biographer Nina Berberova when she met with him in Paris in the early
1930s.[59]

Over the years, as truthful information about Tchaikovsky's private life was more and more suppressed, first by the composer's relatives and later by the Soviet authorities, new waves of even more bizarre speculations about his final days spread through Russia. Various
versions have surfaced, all sharing an emphasis on the alleged irregularity of the open casket and requiems open to the public, but often
little else. One story, which Nicolas Slonimsky heard—and promptly
dismissed—during a visit to the Soviet Union in 1962, contends that
Tchaikovsky had a homosexual affair with a member of the imperial
family and that, when ordered by the tsar to choose between being
tried for sodomy and exiled to Siberia and taking poison, he chose the
latter.[60] Another popular version, which managed to win over George
Balanchine, holds that the composer had been undergoing some profound personal crisis that led him to play a sort of Russian roulette by
deliberately drinking unboiled water in spite of the cholera epidemic
then raging in the city.[61] Most recently, considerable notice has been
given in the West to the claim that Tchaikovsky was the victim of a
clandestine "court of honor" made up of his former classmates from
the School of Jurisprudence, who, learning of an impending scandal
concerning the composer's affair with a young nobleman, forced the
"treasure of Russian music" to take poison so as not to sully the honor
of their alma mater.[62] That this latest story does not square in any way
with the earliest story, reported by Mooser, is in itself enough to cast
immediate doubt on the pretensions to truth of all such rumors.

As early as 1912, Vasily Bertenson found himself compelled in his
memoirs to repudiate the spreading gossip. "Despite the fact that all
thoughtful Russians, and not only Russians but also Europeans,
stricken by such a loss, read with intense interest all the details of
Tchaikovsky's [last] days . . . ," wrote Bertenson, "despite the presence
at the patient's bedside of four physicians, there were people even then,
as there are now, who declared confidently that Tchaikovsky did not
die from cholera at all but perished from poison taken with the intention of committing suicide! . . . Is it worth even speaking about such
insinuations, particularly in light of the nasty innuendos about the reason that provoked the suicide?!"[63]

Tchaikovsky's close relatives and friends consistently denied the
suicide stories. Moreover, not a single shred of concrete evidence exists
to support these stories. Nonetheless, the "insinuations" and "nasty

innuendos" have survived, satisfying an ever-present need for myth-making and sensationalism. They have found their way into the memoirs of various writers who, though never having belonged to Tchaikovsky's intimate circle, felt qualified to embroider their notion of the composer's suicidal personality—and of whom the most influential, certainly, was Nikolay Kashkin. In time, the rumors of poison and suicide became fixed in Soviet folklore, a reflection less and less of historical reality and more and more of wishful thinking. Myth, in the end, became the mediator introduced to relieve an emotional tension perceived to be inherent in Tchaikovsky's personality and behavior.

Rarely do we encounter a genius in art who fully lived a genuinely interesting life parallel to his creativity, yet historically significant and engaging in itself. Tchaikovsky is one of these. What matters most is certainly Tchaikovsky's enduring artistic achievement as one of the great composers of all time. Scholarly accounts of his music abound. To tell his life story, to ascertain the truth within the abundantly extant record of diaries, letters, and memoirs and to communicate that truth in its profoundly rich variety has been a less easy task. Fiction, in such matters, is not always adequate to fact. Fact is often more richly intriguing and satisfying.

Out of a love for art may spring a desire for fact, and often the desire, all too human, is merely meretricious. Seldom can art be explained by fact and seldom can fact lead to art. Life for art's sake can be a well-recognized sacrifice. Still, the impulse to balance one's life and one's art is commoner and perhaps nobler. Tchaikovsky once confided to Mrs. von Meck that having lived to a mature age, he had found nothing, neither religion nor philosophy, to ease his troubled soul, but that he would "go mad were it not for *music*." Music, he told her, was heaven's best gift to humanity. "It alone clarifies, reconciles, and consoles. But it is not a straw just barely clutched at. It is a faithful friend, protector, and comforter, and for its sake alone, life in this world is worth living. Who knows, perhaps in heaven there will be no music. So let us live on the earth while we still have life!"[64]

There is nothing to add. Whatever Tchaikovsky's sins and confusions, however great his music, the life he led in itself is a generous achievement worth telling for its own sake.

Epilogue

After his death Tchaikovsky, increasingly venerated, rose swiftly toward immortality. A special committee was formed by the Russian government immediately following the funeral and charged with the creation of a Tchaikovsky Fund. The main sources for the fund were royalties from memorial concerts and private donations. Part of the money thus raised, along with further contributions by the composer's relatives, was used to erect a monument over the grave. The project was sponsored by the Directorate of Imperial Theaters, and the director himself, Ivan Vsevolozhsky, sketched the design for the monument, in which a bust of the composer set on a granite pedestal is surrounded by a weeping Muse and by an angel with outstretched wings bearing a huge cross. Executed by the theatrical sculptor Pavel Kamensky, the monument was unveiled at a solemn ceremony held on 25 October 1897, the fourth anniversary of Tchaikovsky's death.

Disappointment was the first reaction to the memorial. "The Muse sobbing over a sheet of music and the angel hovering over the bronze bust—all this is really rather commonplace," complained the architectural periodical *Builder's Week*,[1] while the *Petersburg Gazette* wrote that "unfortunately there are no particular artistic merits in the monument."[2] The actual bust of Tchaikovsky drew the most criticism, owing to the dry, academic manner of its design. For many years there were plans to raise a second memorial to the composer elsewhere in the capital, but these were finally quashed by the outbreak of World War I.

A more effective and fitting tribute to the composer's memory came nine years after his death when interest accruing from the fund was used to establish a scholarship in his name for students of both the Moscow and St. Petersburg conservatories.

But while Tchaikovsky, who in his later years had become more and more private, was being immortalized as an institution, the lives of his family and friends went on following their own diverging courses and disparate fates. Tchaikovsky's will, signed on 30 September 1891, named Jurgenson and his son Boris executors of his estate, a duty for some reason declined by the elder Jurgenson. The bulk of the capital was left to the ten-year-old Georges Léon Tchaikovsky, Tanya's illegitimate son, adopted by the composer's brother Nikolay, with the proviso that one-seventh of the capital was to go to Alyosha Sofronov. Moreover, Georges Léon (who died in 1940) was also to receive twelve hundred rubles annually from the composer's royalties, and Alyosha six hundred rubles, while to Modest was to go one-fifth of the royalties from *The Queen of Spades* and *Iolanta* (the operas for which Modest had served as librettist) but not less than eighteen hundred rubles annually. Legal possession of the royalties themselves went to Bob, to whom were assigned all copyrights as well as the duty to divide the royalties among his relatives. In the event of Bob's death, the copyrights were to pass to Georges Léon on the same conditions. In addition, a special provision granted an annual pension of twelve hundred rubles to Antonina Milyukova. All movable property was willed to Alyosha.

It was in the first days following his brother's death that Modest conceived the idea of making the house at Klin into a museum and archive, but he soon found himself hampered in his efforts by Alyosha. The former servant began by demanding the exorbitant sum of five thousand rubles for the furniture left to him by his late master. When Modest had paid this price, he was stunned to learn that Alyosha had in the meantime managed to purchase for eighty-three hundred rubles the house itself, which Tchaikovsky, of course, had only rented, being unable actually to buy it. The new owner allowed Modest to live in the house, but demanded a rent of fifty rubles a month. Only three years later, in 1897, did Modest succeed in ransoming the house and grounds from the enterprising servant, using money given to him for this purpose by Bob. Bob, who had been serving in the Preobrazhensky regiment, resigned from the army that same year and, with Modest, moved into the house at Klin, to which they added several rooms.

But the great hopes that Tchaikovsky had once had for his favorite nephew were never fulfilled. Bob never developed into the outstanding personality that his uncle saw in him, and while endowed with certain musical and artistic gifts, he never became more than a dilettante. His presence at the deathbed agony of his beloved uncle seems to have severely traumatized his own psyche, and he soon lost all interest not only in success in life but even in life itself. There have been rumors of morphine addiction, not at all surprising given the fate of his mother and his elder sister, with whom he had become particularly close in the last years of her life. Continuous awareness of his role in his uncle's life and of the fact that he must inevitably live in his uncle's shadow may have further contributed to his deterioration. Throughout his life Bob suffered agonizing headaches that drove him to despair—and, according to his brother Yury, to suicide. While such an explanation is obviously shaky, until new documentary evidence is brought to light we shall not know the direct cause and circumstances of Bob Davydov's death. In 1906, at the age of thirty-four, Bob shot himself in an apparent fit of depression. The house in Klin he left in his will to Modest.

Less than three years after her husband's death, Antonina Tchaikovskaya was confined to a mental asylum on the outskirts of St. Petersburg and there spent the last twenty years of her life. Modest visited her regularly until his own death in 1916, and she died a year later.

Nadezhda von Meck did not attend Tchaikovsky's funeral, although she sent an expensive funeral wreath. By this time, she was already very ill and moved with great difficulty. Anna Davydova-von Meck was later asked how her mother-in-law endured Tchaikovsky's death. "She did not endure it," Anna replied simply. Mrs. von Meck soon felt much worse, and she died three months after him, on 13 January 1894 in Nice.[3]

Anna lived into World War II and died during the German occupation in 1942. Her husband, Nikolay von Meck, had perished tragically some years before: a victim of the first wave of the Stalinist Terror, he was executed in 1929 in connection with the so-called Shakhty affair, when a false charge of sabotage brought about the destruction of a group of prominent engineers.

Kolya Konradi married soon after his break with Modest. Some years later, he and Modest were reconciled. Kolya prospered until the time of the Bolshevik Revolution and died in 1922. Three years later, Alyosha Sofronov quietly passed away in Klin. In accordance with his will, his son donated to the museum at Klin numerous scores of his master's music that Alyosha had earlier concealed from Modest.

In 1895, after vain attempts to press the project on Hermann Laroche, Modest himself had set to work on a detailed biography of his brother. Four years later, his *Life of Pyotr Ilyich Tchaikovsky* began appearing in separate installments eagerly awaited by the public, and between 1900 and 1902 the entire work was published, by Jurgenson, in three sizable volumes. It was a beautifully executed effort, despite all the cunning strategy used by its author to suppress and distort every single fact related to the composer's homosexuality. Modest's biography possesses substantial literary merit far superior to that of his fiction or plays. Quite apart from being a monument of brotherly love, it constitutes his one lasting contribution to Russian literature.

During his last years, suffering from cancer, Modest continued to write plays and worked on several translations, among them the sonnets of Shakespeare. But his chief occupation was building up the museum at Klin and arranging his brother's archives. A photograph from these years shows Modest in his study at Klin surrounded by piles of papers and with Greek statuettes standing in the background.

Prince Sergey Volkonsky, a former director of the imperial theaters, used to meet Modest in Rome. While they had known each other for some time in St. Petersburg, Volkonsky recalled, it was only in Rome, which Modest had loved ever since his stays there with his brother and Kolya Konradi years before, that they became friends. There they saw each other often over the course of several winters. Modest rented an apartment on the Piazza di Spagna, which he shared with Bob until his suicide. "The concert life of Rome was close to Modest Tchaikovsky," noted Prince Volkonsky. "Most of the students in the symphony orchestra were his acquaintances, and the first violin [Zuccharini, the son of a restaurateur] and the first cello [Margalloti, who came from a very poor and numerous family] were, one could say, his fledglings. . . . And how many such musical careers were started and continued thanks to Modest Ilyich's aid! To one he would give an instrument, to another a tailcoat for his first concert, to yet another the money for lessons."[4]

Emulating his famous brother, Modest, to the end of his life, attempted to promote gifted young men and to help them find their vocations or launch their careers. One of these was the remarkable poet and novelist Sergey Klychkov, a young man of peasant origin, who in 1940 fell victim to the Stalinist Terror and whose work is only now beginning to be appreciated both within the Soviet Union and abroad. Klychkov acknowledged that he owed to Modest Tchaikovsky his literary commitment and cherished his memory as "something sacred."[5] Helping the young peasant boy to complete his studies at secondary school and assisting with his first publications, Modest, in 1908, took the nineteen-year-old Klychkov and Sanya Litke to Italy, where he in-

troduced Klychkov to Maksim Gorky and Anatoly Lunacharsky, subsequently People's Commissar of Culture under the Bolshevik regime.[6]

Modest outlived by less than a year his twin brother. Anatoly had
reached the distinguished rank of senator by the time of his death in
1915; his widow, Praskovya, eventually emigrated to the West, where
she died in Paris in 1956. Modest Tchaikovsky died in Moscow on 2
January 1916. Prince Volkonsky received a telegram announcing his
death from the only person who had been by his side at the end, a
young violinist from Klin whom he had helped enter the conservatory
and who had been his companion in his final days. The house at Klin
was left in his will to the Russian Musical Society, and in 1921 it was
turned by the Soviet authorities into a state museum.

Tchaikovsky's other relatives did not relinquish their claim of expertise in the composer's life and work. The eldest brother, Nikolay,
died in 1910, but Ippolit Tchaikovsky, the last surviving member of
the immediate family, worked at the Klin Museum from 1919 until his
own death in 1927 and published an edition of the composer's diaries
in 1921. Though trained as an agronomist, the youngest member of the
Davydov clan, Yury, was invited to become chief curator of the museum in 1945. Three years before his death in 1965, he produced his
own memoir of his celebrated uncle, most of it a retelling of material
already known. To the present day, Soviet authorities have kept strict
watch over the correspondence and papers of the composer and his
brothers, and shielded them from virtually all outside eyes.

Universal recognition of Tchaikovsky's musical genius and continued closeting of his archive: such gross irony can of course easily be
resolved by the Soviet government. His artistic creations have been
continuously and widely honored in his native land by publication of
his *Complete Works* (although "complete" is quite inaccurate), by the
famous Tchaikovsky Competition, and by countless performances of
his music. It is long since time that the truth of his life as he lived it
be acknowledged by the opening, without stint, of all sources and documents. Only in that way can proper justice be done to the enduring
legacy of Pyotr Ilyich Tchaikovsky.

Notes

Works Frequently Cited, with Abbreviations

DC   P. I. Chaikovskii, *Dnevniki (1873–1891)* (Diaries), ed. I. I. Chaikovskii (Moscow-Petrograd, 1923).

PJ   P. I. Chaikovskii, *Perepiska s P. I. Iurgensonom (1877–1893)* (Correspondence with P. I. Jurgenson), ed. Vladimir Zhdanov and Nikolai Zhegin, 2 vols. (Moscow, 1938–1952).

PM   P. I. Chaikovskii, *Perepiska s N. F. fon Mekk (1876–1890)* (Correspondence with N. F. von Meck), ed. Vladimir Zhdanov and Nikolai Zhegin, 3 vols. (Moscow-Leningrad, 1934–1936).

PR   P. I. Chaikovskii, *Pis'ma k rodnym (1840–1879)* (Letters to relatives), ed. Vladimir Zhdanov (Moscow, 1940).

PSS   P. I. Chaikovskii, *Polnoe sobranie sochinenii: Literaturnye proizvedeniia i perepiska* (Complete collected works: Literary works and correspondence), 17 vols. to date (Moscow, 1953–).

VC   *Vospominaniia o P. I. Chaikovskom* (Reminiscences of Tchaikovsky) (Moscow, 1962; 4th ed., Moscow-Leningrad, 1980).

ZC   M. I. Chaikovskii, *Zhizn' Petra Il'icha Chaikovskogo* (Life of Pyotr Ilyich Tchaikovsky), 3 vols. (Moscow-Leipzig, 1900–1902).

Preface

1. Leon Edel, "Biography and the Sexual Revolution—Why Curiosity Is No Longer Vulgar," *New York Times Book Review*, 24 Nov. 1985, 13.
2. Tchaikovsky to Mrs. von Meck, 9–18 Aug. 1880, *PM*, 2:398; *PSS*, 9:234.
3. Tchaikovsky to Sergey Taneev, 14 Jan. 1891, *PSS*, 16a:29.
4. The sensational story of Tchaikovsky's suicide as the result of a "court of honor" set up by his former schoolfellows was brought to the West ten years ago by the Soviet émigré writer on music Alexandra Orlova and was first outlined by Joel Spiegelman in "The Trial, Condemnation, and Death of Tchaikovsky," *High Fidelity* 31 (February 1981): 49–51; then presented by Orlova in her own article "Tchaikovsky: The Last Chapter," *Music &* *Letters* 62 (1981): 125–45, as well as in her book *Tchaikovsky: A Self-*

portrait (New York, 1990), 406–414. Orlova's hopelessly confused theory was first refuted by three distinguished Slavic scholars, Nina Berberova, Malcolm H. Brown, and Simon Karlinsky, in "Tchaikovsky's 'Suicide' Reconsidered: A Rebuttal," *High Fidelity* 31 (August 1981): 49, 85; later by the Dutch specialist Elisabeth Riethof-van Heulen in "Zijn de onthullingen van Orlova wel voldoende onderzocht?" (Have Orlova's revelations been explored sufficiently?), *Mens & Melodie* 42 (1987): 307–317; and, finally, by the present author in a detailed article, "Tchaikovsky's Suicide: Myth and Reality," *19th Century Music* 11 (1988): 199–220.

5. *Baker's Biographical Dictionary of Musicians*, 7th ed., rev. Nicolas Slonimsky (New York, 1984), xxviii.
6. *The Diaries of Tchaikovsky*, translated from Russian with notes by Wladimir Lakond (New York, 1945).
7. Galley proofs of the second volume of *Letters to Relatives* have been preserved in the Tchaikovsky Museum at Klin.
8. P. I. Chaikovskii, *Pis'ma k blizkim: Izbrannoe* (Moscow, 1955).
9. Piotr Ilyich Tchaikovsky, *Letters to his Family: An Autobiography*, trans. Galina von Meck (New York, 1981).
10. *Dni i gody P. I. Chaikovskogo: Letopis' zhizni i tvorchestva* (Moscow-Leningrad, 1940); or Orlova's compilation of various selections from Tchaikovsky's letters in *Tchaikovsky: A Self-portrait*.
11. *DC*, 213–14.
12. Nina Berberova, *Chaikovskii: Istoriia odinokoi zhizni* (Berlin, [1936]); see also her new preface to the French edition of her book, *Tchaïkovski: Biographie* ([Arles], 1987).
13. Herbert Weinstock, *Tchaikovsky* (New York, 1943).
14. Vladimir Volkoff, *Tchaikovsky: A Self-portrait* (Boston-London, 1975); see also his French edition, *Tchaïkovski* (Paris, 1983).
15. David Brown, *Tchaikovsky: A Biographical and Critical Study*, vol. 1, *The Early Years (1840–1874)*, vol. 2, *The Crisis Years (1874–1878)*, vol. 3, *The Years of Wandering (1878–1885)*, vol. 4 (forthcoming) (New York, 1978–).
16. David Brown, "Tchaikovsky," *The New Grove Dictionary of Music and Musicians*, ed. Stanley Sadie (London, 1980); also in *The New Grove Russian Masters 1* (New York-London, 1986).

Chapter 1. Early Anguish

1. *ZC*, 1:14–15.
2. Polina Vaidman, "Nachalo: Novye materialy iz arkhiva P. I. Chaikovskogo," *Nashe nasledie*, 1990, no. 2:19.
3. Ibid., 20.
4. *PR*, 665.
5. *ZC*, 1:15
6. Ibid., 21
7. Ibid., 305–6.
8. *PR*, 702.
9. *ZC*, 1:12.
10. Ibid., 17.
11. Ibid., 25.
12. Ibid., 29.
13. Ibid.
14. *PM*, 1:92; *PSS*, 6:253.
15. *ZC*, 1:25.
16. Ibid., 25–26.
17. Ibid., 27.
18. Ibid., 39.

19. Ibid., 27.
20. Ibid., 44.
21. Ibid.
22. Ibid., 43.
23. *PSS*, 5:5.
24. *ZC*, 1:47.
25. Ibid., 48.
26. Ibid., 54.
27. Ibid., 58n.
28. *PSS*, 5:7–8.
29. *ZC*, 1:23.
30. *PSS*, 5:10.
31. Ibid., 11.
32. Ibid., 10.
33. Ibid., 37.
34. L. Shestakova, "Moi vechera," *Ezhegodnik Imperatorskikh teatrov*, 1895, no. 2:121.
35. *PSS*, 5:13.
36. Ibid., 14.
37. *ZC*, 1:61.
38. Ibid., 60–61.
39. *PR*, 659.
40. *ZC*, 1:61.
41. *PR*, 13, 30, 33, 43, 46; *PSS*, 5:16, 33, 37, 50, 52.
42. *ZC*, 1:74.
43. Ibid., 60.
44. *PR*, 12; *PSS*, 5:13.
45. *ZC*, 1:63.
46. *PR*, 25; *PSS*, 5:27.
47. *PR*, 18; *PSS*, 5:21.
48. *PR*, 19; *PSS*, 5:22.
49. *PR*, 42; *PSS*, 5:48.
50. *ZC*, 1:78.
51. Ibid.
52. *PM*, 2:239; *PSS*, 8:402.
53. *PM*, 2:140; *PSS*, 8:255.
54. *PSS*, 5:58.
55. Ibid.
56. *PM*, 1:92; *PSS*, 6:252.

Chapter 2. In the School of Jurisprudence
1. For a more detailed account of the founding of the School of Jurisprudence, see Allen A. Sinel, "The Socialization of the Russian Bureaucratic Elite, 1811–1917: Life at the Tsarskoe Selo Lyceum and the School of Jurisprudence," *Russian History* 3 (1976):1–31.
2. About the school's curriculum, see Richard S. Wortman, *The Development of Russian Legal Consciousness* (Chicago, 1976), 198–223.
3. V. I. Taneev, *Detstvo, iunost', mysli o budushchem* (Moscow, 1959), 152.
4. V. I. Sobolevskii, *Imperatorskoe uchilishche pravovedeniia v 1885–1910 godakh* (St. Petersburg, 1910), 38.
5. V. V. Stasov, "Uchilishche pravovedeniia sorok let nazad," in his *Izbrannye sochineniia*, 3 vols. (Moscow, 1952), 2:305.
6. K. K. Arsen'ev, "Vospominaniia ob Uchilishche pravovedeniia, 1849–1855," *Russkaia starina* 50 (1886):200.
7. Stasov, "Uchilishche pravovedeniia," 2:324–25.

8. Taneev, *Detstvo*, 156.
9. Ibid.
10. See Jonathan Gathorne-Hardy, *The Public School Phenomenon, 596–1977* (London, 1977), 108–12, and Ian Gibson, *English Vice: Beating, Sex and Shame in Victorian England and After* (London, 1978), 64–79, 99–119; about flogging in German schools, see Gibson, *English Vice*, 44 n. 40.
11. *ZC*, 1:87.
12. Taneev, *Detstvo*, 259.
13. Ippolit Chaikovskii, "Epizody iz moei zhizni," *Istoricheskii vestnik*, 1913, no. 1:83.
14. *ZC*, 1:97.
15. Ibid., 89.
16. Taneev, *Detstvo*, 193.
17. Arsen'ev, "Vospominaniia ob Uchilishche pravovedeniia," 200.
18. Taneev, *Detstvo*, 166.
19. Ibid., 135.
20. Ibid., 330.
21. Ibid., 362.
22. Ibid., 300.
23. *DC*, 36.
24. Arsen'ev, "Vospominaniia ob Uchilishche pravovedeniia," 201.
25. Taneev, *Detstvo*, 383–84.
26. Ibid., 298–99.
27. *DC*, 211.
28. G. Siuzor, *Ko dniu 75-letnego iubeleia Imperatorskogo Uchilishcha pra-vovedeniia* (St. Petersburg, 1910), 223.
29. *PM*, 2:262; *PSS*, 8:434.
30. *ZC*, 1:123; cf. *VC* (1980), 27.
31. *VC* (1980), 29.
32. Siuzor, *Ko dniu*, 225.
33. Taneev, *Detstvo*, 321.
34. *PR*, 621.
35. *PSS*, 14:147.
36. *PM*, 3:381; *PSS*, 13:160.
37. *PM*, 3:386; *PSS*, 13:181.
38. *PSS*, 13:187.
39. Siuzor, *Ko dniu*, 76.
40. *PSS*, 13:206.
41. P. Chaikovskii, *Pis'ma k blizkim*, 604.
42. *VC* (1980), 108.
43. P. Popov, "Poslanie A. N. Apukhtina P. I. Chaikovskomu," *Golos minuv-shego*, 1919, nos. 1–4:100.
44. Siuzor, *Ko dniu*, 78.

Chapter 3. Special Friendships

1. *VC* (1980), 29.
2. Ibid., 27.
3. *ZC*, 1:97; Taneev, *Detstvo*, 345.
4. A. V. Mikhailov, "Iz proshlogo: Vospominaniia pravoveda," *Russkaia shkola*, 1900, no. 1:30.
5. *PM*, 1:50.
6. Taneev, *Detstvo*, 148.
7. Ibid., 376–77.
8. See, for example, Lionel Tiger, *Men in Groups* (New York, 1969).

9. See Stasov, "Uchilishche pravovedeniia," 2:343.
10. Taneev, *Detstvo*, 241.
11. Steven Marcus, *The Other Victorians: A Study of Sexuality and Pornography in Mid-Nineteenth-Century England* (New York, 1966), 259–61; Gibson, *English Vice*, 44.
12. "Confession sexuelle d'un Russe . . . ," in Havelock Ellis, *Études de psychologie sexuelle*, 6 vols. (Paris, 1926), 6:157–58.
13. *The Memoirs of John Addington Symonds*, ed. Phyllis Grosskurth (New York, 1984), 94.
14. F. F. Vigel', *Zapiski*, 7 vols. (Moscow, 1891–1893), 5:156.
15. *Eros russe: Russkii Erot ne dlia dam* ([Geneva], 1879), 19–58.
16. Ibid., 10, 12–14; William H. Hopkins, "Lermontov's Hussar Poems," *Russian Literature Triquarterly* 14 (1977):36–47, 416–29.
17. A. N. Vul'f, *Dnevnik: Liubovnyi byt pushkinskoi epokhi* (Moscow, 1929), 133.
18. *Eros russe*, 67. In a similar instance of the relatively tolerant attitude toward homosexuality even among teachers and school officials, the author of "Adventures of a Page," Aleksandr Shenin, was forced to give up his position as inspector of classes at the Pavlovsky Cadet Corps only when, in 1846, he became involved in a public scandal, and even then his subsequent public career was unaffected.
19. Stasov, "Uchilishche pravovedeniia," 2:370.
20. Taneev, *Detstvo*, 399.
21. *Eros russe*, 68; partially in Wortman, *Development of Russian Legal Consciousness*, 313.
22. Volkoff, *Tchaikovsky*, 205n.
23. Glenn V. Ramsey, "The Sexual Development of Boys," *American Journal of Psychology* 56 (1943):217–33.
24. A. I. Herzen, *Sochineniia*, 9 vols. (Moscow, 1956), 4:82.
25. Taneev, *Detstvo*, 344–45.
26. Ibid., 346.
27. *VC* (1980), 29.
28. *ZC*, 100.
29. Ibid.
30. Ibid., 103.
31. Ibid., 93.
32. *Dni i gody*, 623.
33. Orlova, "Tchaikovsky: The Last Chapter," 125–26; also idem, *Tchaikovsky*, x–xi.
34. *VC* (1980), 27–28.
35. *ZC*, 108.
36. Ibid., 109.
37. V. V. Iakovlev, "Chaikovskii i Apukhtin," in his *Izbrannye trudy o muzyke*, 2 vols. (Moscow, 1964), 1:373–78; for references to an unpublished article by F. N. Malinin, "Apukhtin i Chaikovskii," kept in Soviet archives, see *PSS*, 9:144.
38. A. N. Apukhtin, *Sochineniia* (St. Petersburg, 1900), vii–x.
39. *VC* (1980), 29.
40. *ZC*, 1:101.
41. [K. Raich], "K biografii A. N. Apukhtina," *Istoricheskii vestnik* 107 (1880):580.
42. *VC* (1980):33.
43. *ZC*, 1:101; Apukhtin, *Sochineniia* (1900), xi.
44. *Novosti i birzhevaia gazeta*, 27 Oct. 1893.

45. A. N. Apukhtin, *Stikhotvoreniia* (Leningrad, 1961), 300.
46. Ibid., 252–53.
47. Ibid., 172–73.
48. *PR*, 339; *PSS*, 6:321–22.
49. *ZC*, 1:102.
50. Ibid.
51. A. N. Apukhtin, *Sochineniia* (St. Petersburg, 1895), 278.
52. Taneev, *Detstvo*, 209.
53. Siuzor, *Ko dniu*, 225.
54. F. N. Malinin, "Zametki o poeticheskom nasledii P. I. Chaikovskogo," *Novyi mir*, 1940, no. 7:210.
55. Apukhtin, *Stikhotvoreniia*, 250.
56. V. S. Solov'ev, *Stikhotvoreniia i shutochnye p'esy* (Leningrad, 1974), 148, 315.
57. *PSS*, 5:62; cf. *ZC*, 1:135, where Meshchersky is coded as *M*; entire passage absent in *PR*, 62.
58. *PR*, 672.
59. *Dni i gody*, 623.
60. *ZC*, 1:128.
61. *PR*, 148; *PSS*, 5:209.
62. *PSS*, 5:62.
63. Ibid.
64. *Sovetskaia muzyka*, 1940, nos. 5–6. The thirteen dots are also reproduced quite clearly in *Piotr Il'ich Chaikovskii*, ed. E. M. Orlova (Moscow-Leipzig, 1978), 31.
65. *PR*, 101–2; *PSS*, 5:127–28.
66. N. Pashennyi, *Imperatorskoe Uchilishche pravovedeniia v gody mira, voiny i smyty* ([Madrid], 1967), 135.

Chapter 4. Man About Town

1. *VC* (1980), 366; E. Gershovskii, "Chaikovskii v Departamente Iustitsii," *Sovetskaia muzyka*, 1959, no. 1:83–88.
2. "Confession sexuelle d'un Russe," 6:183.
3. Vasilii Rozanov, *Izbrannoe* (Munich, 1970), 483.
4. *ZC*, 1:112.
5. *PSS*, 17:97.
6. *PR*, 375; *PSS*, 7:115.
7. *VC* (1962), 28–29.
8. *PR*, 56; *PSS*, 5:70.
9. *PSS*, 5:62.
10. *ZC*, 1:115.
11. [Raich], "K biografii A. N. Apukhtina," 581.
12. A. V. Zhirkevich, "Poet milostiu bozhiei," *Istoricheskii vestnik* 106, no. 11 (1906):474.
13. *PSS*, 5:61–62.
14. *ZC*, 1:119.
15. Ibid., 118.
16. Konstantin de Lazari, "Vospominaniia o Petre Il'iche Chaikovskom," *Rossiia*, 31 May 1900.
17. *VC* (1962), 400; omitted in *VC* (1980), 34.
18. *VC* (1980), 34–35.
19. M. Sabinina, "Larosh i Chaikovskii," *Sovetskaia muzyka*, 1954, no. 10:72.
20. I. A. Klimenko, *Moi vospominaniia o Petre Il'iche Chaikovskom* (Ryazan, 1908), 9.
21. *VC* (1962), 29.

22. *PR*, 94; *PSS*, 5:116.
23. *ZC*, 1:133.
24. Ibid., 280.
25. Ibid., 281.
26. Klimenko, *Moi vospominaniia*, 6.
27. *PR*, 50; *PSS*, 5:64.
28. *PR*, 49; *PSS*, 5:63.
29. *PR*, 54; *PSS*, 5:68–69.
30. *PR*, 57; *PSS*, 5:71.
31. *PR*, 59–60; *PSS*, 5:73–74.
32. *ZC*, 1:149.
33. *PR*, 60; *PSS*, 5:74.
34. *ZC*, 1:126.
35. Ibid., 127.
36. *New York Herald*, 27 Apr. 1891.
37. *PR*, 48; *PSS*, 5:61.
38. N. D. Kashkin, *Vospominaniia o P. I. Chaikovskom* (Moscow, 1954), 11.
39. *VC* (1980), 35–36.
40. *ZC*, 1:164.
41. Ibid.
42. *PSS*, 16b:104.
43. Klimenko, *Moi vospominaniia*, 5.
44. Ibid., 30.
45. *ZC*, 1:185.
46. *DC*, 65.
47. Apukhtin, *Stikhotvoreniia*, 95–97, 333.
48. *ZC*, 1:190–91.
49. *PR*, 64; *PSS*, 5:80.
50. *PSS*, 5:81.

Chapter 5. His Brothers' Keeper

1. *VC* (1980), 371.
2. Ibid., 371–72.
3. *PR*, 65; *PSS*, 5:82.
4. *VC* (1980), 33.
5. *ZC*, 1:137–38.
6. Ibid., 138–39.
7. *PR*, 61; *PSS*, 5:75.
8. *PM*, 1:93; *PSS*, 6:253.
9. *PR*, 218; *PSS*, 5:398.
10. Iu. Iur'ev, *Zapiski*, 2 vols. (Moscow-Leningrad, 1939–1945), 2:79.
11. *PR*, 150; *PSS*, 5:212.
12. *PR*, 122; *PSS*, 5:154–55.
13. *PR*, 115; *PSS*, 5:146.
14. *PR*, 83; passage omitted in *PSS*, 5:102.
15. *VC* (1980), 33.
16. *PR*, 144; passage omitted in *PSS*, 5:202. According to Vladimir Zhdanov, the missing words were deleted from the original letter by someone else, most likely Modest himself.
17. *PSS*, 5:86–87. Through one of the unpredictable paradoxes of Soviet censorship, this letter was not included in *PR*.
18. In *PR* the name Lenin is persistently transcribed as Lepin; cf. *Pamiatnaia knizhka Imperatorskogo Uchilishcha pravovedeniia na uchebnyi 1864–1865 god* (St. Petersburg, 1864), 7.
19. *PR*, 122; *PSS*, 5:155.

20. *PR*, 147; *PSS*, 5:207.
21. Iu. L. Davydov, *Zapiski o P. I. Chaikovskom* (Moscow, 1962), 49.
22. *PR*, 93; *PSS*, 5:114.
23. *PR*, 94; *PSS*, 5:115.
24. *PR*, 80; *PSS*, 5:100.
25. *PR*, 68; *PSS*, 5:85.
26. Gosudarstvennyi Dom-muzei P. I. Chaikovskogo, Klin, f. A[4], No. 4630; *PR*, 665.
27. *PR*, 69; *PSS*, 5:86.
28. *ZC*, 1:181.
29. *Sankt-Peterburgskie vedomosti*, 24 Mar. 1865.
30. *PR*, 75; *PSS*, 5:93.

Chapter 6. The Lovable Misanthrope

1. V. A., "Iz vospominanii o N. G. Rubinshteine i Moskovskoi konservatorii," *Russkii arkhiv*, 1897, no. 11:445.
2. Ibid., 449–50.
3. Ibid., 448.
4. *PR*, 77; *PSS*, 5:97.
5. *PR*, 213; *PSS*, 5:389–90.
6. Kashkin, *Vospominaniia*, 53.
7. *PM*, 1:172; *PSS*, 7:64.
8. *PR*, 75; *PSS*, 5:95.
9. Gosudarstvennyi Dom-muzei P. I. Chaikovskogo, Klin, f. A[4], No. 4631; P. Chaikovskii, *Pis'ma k blizkim*, 555–56.
10. *PR*, 88; *PSS*, 5:108–9.
11. *ZC*, 1:248.
12. V. B. Bertenson, *Za tridtsat' let: Listki iz vospominanii* (St. Petersburg, 1914), 92.
13. *PR*, 294; passage omitted in *PSS*, 6:173.
14. *PR*, 87; *PSS*, 5:107.
15. *PR*, 670 (partial); *ZC*, 1:241–43.
16. *PR*, 79; *PSS*, 5:98.
17. *PR*, 688.
18. Ibid., 99; *PSS*, 5:122.
19. *Rossiia*, 25 May 1900.
20. Ibid.
21. Klimenko, *Moi vospominaniia*, 35.
22. *Rossiia*, 25 May 1900.
23. E. Balabanovich, *Chekhov i Chaikovskii* (Moscow, 1978), 51.
24. K. F. Val'ts, *Shest'desiat piat' let v teatre* (Leningrad, 1928), 38–39.
25. *ZC*, 1:258–59.
26. *PSS*, 5:124.
27. V. A., "Iz vospominanii o Rubinshteine," 451.
28. *VC* (1980), 62–63.
29. *PR*, 83; *PSS*, 5:102–3.
30. *PR*, 669.
31. Ibid., 84; *PSS*, 5:103.
32. *PR*, 87; *PSS*, 5:108.
33. *ZC*, 1:242.
34. *PR*, 92; *PSS*, 5:113.
35. *ZC*, 1:246–47.
36. *Rossiia*, 18 July 1900.
37. *PM*, 2:268; *PSS*, 8:445.

38. *PR*, 96; *PSS*, 5:117.
39. *ZC*, 1:271.
40. *PR*, 96–97; *PSS*, 5:119–20.
41. V. Bertenson, *Za tridtsat' let*, 91–92.
42. *PM*, 2:234; *PSS*, 8:393.
43. *PSS*, 5:205.
44. *PR*, 242; *PSS*, 6:54.
45. *PR*, 412; *PSS*, 7:266.
46. *PR*, 69; *PSS*, 5:86.
47. *PR*, 97; *PSS*, 5:120.
48. *PR*, 100; *PSS*, 5:125.
49. *PR*, 107; *PSS*, 5:136–37.
50. *PR*, 111–12; *PSS*, 5:141–42.
51. *Rossiia*, 25 May 1900.
52. *ZC*, 1:275.
53. *Rossiia*, 25 May 1900.
54. Klimenko, *Moi vospominaniia*, 26–27.
55. *VC* (1980), 40.

Chapter 7. Desires and Flames

1. *PR*, 108; *PSS*, 5:137–38.
2. Ibid.
3. *Rossiia*, 25 May 1900.
4. *PR*, 108; *PSS*, 5:138.
5. *Rossiia*, 12 June 1900.
6. *PR*, 109; *PSS*, 5:139.
7. *ZC*, 1:301.
8. Ibid., 300.
9. *Rossiia*, 31 May 1900.
10. *PR*, 110; *PSS*, 5:139.
11. *PR*, 114; *PSS*, 5:144.
12. *PR*, 115; *PSS*, 5:145.
13. *PR*, 115–16; *PSS*, 5:146.
14. *Rossiia*, 31 May 1900.
15. "Dnevnik V. F. Odoevskogo," *Literaturnoe nasledstvo* 22–24 (1935):248.
16. *PR*, 677.
17. Ibid., 116–17; *PSS*, 5:147.
18. *PR*, 118; *PSS*, 149–50.
19. *PR*, 678; *ZC*, 1:305–8.
20. *PR*, 677.
21. Ibid., 676.
22. *Rossiia*, 31 May 1900; *PR*, 677–78.
23. *PR*, 120; *PSS*, 5:153.
24. *Rossiia*, 12 June 1900; *PR*, 679–80.
25. *PR*, 122; *PSS*, 5:155.
26. *PR*, 680–81.
27. Ibid., 134; *PSS*, 5:179.
28. *PR*, 683.
29. Ibid., 136; *PSS*, 5:182.
30. Kashkin, *Vospominaniia*, 92.
31. Ibid., 92–93.
32. *PR*, 224; *PSS*, 5:424.
33. Kashkin, *Vospominaniia*, 72; Klimenko, *Moi vospominaniia*, 77.
34. *PR*, 123; *PSS*, 5:156.

35. *Sankt-Peterburgskie vedomosti*, 9 May 1870.
36. A. Sokolova, "Komicheskii sluchai s P. I. Chaikovskim," *Istoricheskii vestnik* 119 (1910):557–71. Soviet editors, evidently nervous about undesirable allusions, did not include the story in the standard edition of *VC*.
37. *VC* (1980), 81–82.
38. *PR*, 147; *PSS*, 5:208.
39. V. V. Iastrebtsev, *N. A. Rimskii-Korsakov: Vospominaniia*, 2 vols. (Leningrad, 1959–1960), 1:52.
40. *ZC*, 1:334.
41. *PSS*, 5:262.
42. Ibid., 5:319.
43. Ibid., 325.
44. P. E. Vaidman, *Tvorcheskii arkhiv P. I. Chaikovskogo* (Moscow, 1988), 68.
45. *PSS*, 5:333.
46. Ibid.
47. *DC*, 176–77.
48. Ibid.
49. *Sankt-Peterburgskie vedomosti*, 29 Jan. 1876.
50. Orlova, "Tchaikovsky: The Last Chapter," 125–26.
51. *ZC*, 1:334.
52. *PR*, 143; *PSS*, 5:201.
53. Ibid.
54. *PR*, 100; *PSS*, 5:123.
55. *PR*, 681.
56. Ibid., 109; *PSS*, 5:139.
57. *PR*, 111; *PSS*, 5:140–41.
58. V. Bertenson, *Za tridtsat' let*, 83.
59. *Epigramma i satira; Iz istorii literaturnoi bor'by deviatnadtsatogo veka, 1840–1880* (Moscow-Leningrad, 1932), 424.
60. V. Bertenson, *Za tridtsat' let*, 87–88.
61. Apukhtin, *Stikhotvoreniia*, 337–38.
62. *PR*, 161; *PSS*, 5:232.
63. Apukhtin, *Stikhotvoreniia*, 345.
64. Ibid., 324.
65. *PSS*, 2:163.
66. M. A. Protopopov, "Pisatel'-diletant," *Russkoe bogatstvo*, 1896, no. 2:58.
67. *PR*, 129; *PSS*, 5:168.
68. *PR*, 151–52; *PSS*, 5:219.
69. *PR*, 160; *PSS*, 5:229–30.
70. *PR*, 135; *PSS*, 5:182.
71. Ibid.
72. *PR*, 138; *PSS*, 5:188.
73. *PR*, 140; *PSS*, 5:193.
74. *PR*, 165; *PSS*, 5:240.
75. *PR*, 130; passage omitted in *PSS*, 5:170.
76. *PR*, 134–35; *PSS*, 5:179.
77. *PR*, 139; *PSS*, 5:190.
78. *PR*, 161; *PSS*, 5:231.
79. *PR*, 162; *PSS*, 5:234.
80. *PR*, 185; *PSS*, 5:288.
81. *PSS*, 5:214.
82. *PR*, 127; *PSS*, 5:166.
83. *PR*, 128; *PSS*, 5:168.
84. *PR*, 132; *PSS*, 5:172.

85. *PR*, 149; *PSS*, 5:209.
86. *PR*, 151; *PSS*, 5:213.
87. *PR*, 152; *PSS*, 5:219.
88. *PR*, 156; *PSS*, 5:226.
89. *PR*, 161; *PSS*, 5:239.
90. *Dni i gody*, 75.

Chapter 8. The Petrolina Letters

1. N. D. Kashkin, "Iz vospominanii o P. I. Chaikovskom," in *Proshloe russkoi muzyki: Materialy i issledovaniia*, vol. 1, *P. I. Chaikovskii* (Petrograd, 1920), 104.
2. Ibid., 105.
3. *PR*, 188; *PSS*, 5:294 (partial).
4. *PR*, 222; cf. *DC*, 135.
5. *PR*, 204; *PSS*, 5:353.
6. *PSS*, 5:406.
7. Ibid., 6:44; cf. ibid., 52.
8. *PM*, 2:634.
9. *PR*, 327; passage omitted in *PSS*, 6:285.
10. *PR*, 501; *PSS*, 8:15.
11. *DC*, 61.
12. *PR*, 254; passage omitted in *PSS*, 6:69.
13. *ZC*, 1:356.
14. Ibid., 357.
15. Ibid., 358.
16. Ibid., 359.
17. Ibid.
18. Ibid.
19. Ibid., 360
20. L. N. Tolstoi, *Polnoe sobranie sochinenii*, 90 vols. (Moscow, 1929–1964), 18:185.
21. Cf. the poet Mikhail Kuzmin's autobiographical essay, "Histoire édifiante de mes commencements," in *Mikhail Kuzmin i russkaia kultura dvadtsatogo veka* (Leningrad, 1990), 147–55.
22. Klimenko, *Moi vospominaniia*, 60; *PSS*, 5:238 (partial).
23. Klimenko, *Moi vospominaniia*, 61–62, 71.
24. Ibid., 60–61; *PSS*, 5:261 (inset).
25. Klimenko, *Moi vospominaniia*, 62.
26. *PR*, 184–85; *PSS*, 5:287–88.
27. *PR*, 188; *PSS*, 5:294 (partial).
28. *ZC*, 1:394.
29. *PR*, 198; *PSS*, 5:335.
30. *ZC*, 1:421.
31. *PR*, 208, 209; *PSS*, 5:372, 380.
32. *PR*, 222; *PSS*, 5:414.
33. Ibid.
34. *PR*, 340; *PSS*, 8:326.
35. *PR*, 542; *PSS*, 8:126.
36. *ZC*, 1:353.
37. Ibid., 354.
38. Ibid.
39. Ibid., 354–55.
40. Ibid., 356.
41. *PSS*, 14:88.

42. "Confession sexuelle d'un Russe," 6:161.
43. *PR*, 173; *PSS*, 5:258.
44. *PR*, 199; *PSS*, 5:335.
45. *PR*, 183; *PSS*, 5:287.
46. *PR*, 199; *PSS*, 5:335.
47. *PR*, 201; *PSS*, 5:341 (partial). In fact, the word Tchaikovsky used here was most probably "pederast." In Russia as elsewhere in Europe during this period, "pederasty" (*pederastiia*) was the most commonly accepted general term for male sexual relations, without being necessarily restricted to relations between men and boys. "Homosexuality"—while coined in 1869 and thus by no means anachronistic in the 1870s—did not come into widespread use until the end of the century. However, to avoid the modern-day pedophilic connotations of "pederast" and "pederasty," the more neutral terms "homosexual" and "homosexuality" have been employed throughout this book.
48. *PR*, 208; *PSS*, 5:372.
49. *PR*, 218; *PSS*, 5:399.
50. *PR*, 230; *PSS*, 6:21 (partial).
51. *PR*, 236; *PSS*, 6:38.
52. *Chaikovskii na moskovskoi stsene* (Moscow-Leningrad, 1940), 305.
53. *PR*, 238; *PSS*, 6:41.
54. *PSS*, 9:229.
55. Ibid., 11:184.
56. *DC*, 203.
57. *PR*, 199; *PSS*, 5:335.
58. *PM*, 1:427; *PSS*, 7:383.

Chapter 9. Becoming the Composer

1. *PR*, 174; *PSS*, 5:265.
2. *VC* (1980), 63.
3. Klimenko, *Moi vospominaniia*, 25–26.
4. Davydov, *Zapiski*, 28.
5. *PR*, 175; *PSS*, 5:266.
6. *PR*, 174; *PSS*, 5:265.
7. *PR*, 177; *PSS*, 5:271.
8. *PR*, 180; *PSS*, 5:273.
9. *Sankt-Peterburgskie vedomosti*, 9 Feb. 1872.
10. *PR*, 182; *PSS*, 5:283–84; cf. *ZC*, 1:380.
11. Klimenko, *Moi vospominaniia*, 66; *PSS*, 5:289.
12. *PR*, 184; *PSS*, 5:287.
13. *PR*, 192; *PSS*, 5:303.
14. *Moskovskie vedomosti*, 1 Feb. 1873.
15. *PR*, 191; *PSS*, 5:301.
16. *PR*, 192; *PSS*, 5:303.
17. *PR*, 197; *PSS*, 5:326.
18. *PM*, 1:307–8; *PSS*, 7:232.
19. Kashkin, *Vospominaniia*, 98.
20. *PSS*, 5:343.
21. *Russkie vedomosti*, 12 Mar. 1874.
22. V. Bessel', "Moi vospominaniia o P. I. Chaikovskom," *Ezhegodnik Imperatorskikh teatrov, 1896/1897*, app. 1, 35.
23. *Sankt-Peterburgskie vedomosti*, 23 Apr. 1874.
24. *PSS*, 5:353.
25. *PR*, 204; *PSS*, 5:353–54.

26. *PR*, 202; *PSS*, 5:347–48.
27. *PR*, 206; *PSS*, 5:359.
28. *PR*, 220; *PSS*, 5:403.
29. *PM*, 1:173–74; *PSS*, 7:64–65.
30. *PR*, 213–14; *PSS*, 5:389–90 (partial).
31. *PR*, 217; *PSS*, 5:397.
32. *PR*, 219; *PSS*, 5:403.
33. *PSS*, 5:420.
34. *ZC*, 1:473.
35. Ibid.
36. Ibid., 474.
37. *PSS*, 17:219.
38. *PR*, 225; *PSS*, 5:427.
39. *PM*, 1:137–38; *PSS*, 6:330–31.
40. *PR*, 226; *PSS*, 6:15.
41. *PR*, 223; *PSS*, 5:424.
42. *PR*, 225; *PSS*, 5:427.
43. *PR*, 166; *PSS*, 5:243.
44. *PR*, 138, 141, 169, 174; *PSS*, 5:188, 194, 253, 266.
45. *PR*, 178; *PSS*, 5:274.
46. *PR*, 160; *PSS*, 5:230.
47. *PSS*, 17:212.
48. *PR*, 172; *PSS*, 5:254.
49. *PR*, 227; *PSS*, 6:16.
50. Ibid.
51. Ibid.
52. *PR*, 228; *PSS*, 6:18.

Chapter 10. Tensions, Temptations, Melancholy

1. *PR*, 230; *PSS*, 6:20.
2. *PR*, 229; *PSS*, 6:20.
3. *Dni i gody*, 124.
4. Ibid.
5. *PR*, 231; *PSS*, 6:24.
6. *PSS*, 5:412.
7. *PR*, 230; *PSS*, 6:20.
8. *PR*, 230; *PSS*, 6:24.
9. *PR*, 230–31; *PSS*, 6:20–21, 24.
10. *PR*, 232; *PSS*, 6:28 (partial).
11. *PR*, 357; *PSS*, 7:53.
12. *PR*, 443; *PSS*, 7:381.
13. *PSS*, 6:34.
14. *PR*, 234; *PSS*, 6:33.
15. *PR*, 235; *PSS*, 6:33.
16. *PR*, 234; *PSS*, 6:33.
17. *DC*, 198.
18. *VC* (1980), 63.
19. Ibid., 69–70.
20. *ZC*, 2:1.
21. *PR*, 272; *PSS*, 6:107.
22. *PJ*, 1:322, n. 5 to letter 25.
23. *PR*, 355; *PSS*, 7:51 (partial).
24. Kashkin, "Iz vospominanii," 131.
25. *PR*, 239; *PSS*, 6:43.

26. *PSS*, 6:50.

27. *PR*, 229; *PSS*, 6:20.

28. *PR*, 243; *PSS*, 6:53 (partial).

29. G. V. Kuznetsova, "Modest Il'ich Chaikovskii kak surdopedagog," *Uchenye zapiski Moskovskogo pedagogicheskogo instituta imeni V. I. Lenina* 16 (1964):200–1.

30. *PM*, 2:285–86; *PSS*, 8:479.

31. *PR*, 243; *PSS*, 6:53.

32. *ZC*, 1:488.

33. *PR*, 252; *PSS*, 6:66.

34. *PR*, 254; *PSS*, 6:69 (partial).

35. *PR*, 256; *PSS*, 6:72.

36. *PR*, 249; *PSS*, 6:61–62 (partial).

37. *PR*, 252; *PSS*, 6:65.

38. *PR*, 250; *PSS*, 6:64.

39. *PR*, 251; *PSS*, 6:65.

40. *PR*, 255; *PSS*, 6:70.

41. *PR*, 253; *PSS*, 6:66 (most of passage omitted).

42. *PR*, 253–54; *PSS*, 6:69 (most of passage omitted).

43. *PR*, 255–56; *PSS*, 6:71.

44. *PR*, 257; *PSS*, 6:72–73 (partial).

45. *PR*, 701.

46. Ibid., 261; *PSS*, 6:78.

47. Ibid.

48. *PM*, 1:26; *PSS*, 6:145.

49. *PR*, 259–60; *PSS*, 6:76 (most of passage omitted).

50. *PR*, 259; passage omitted in *PSS*, 6:76.

51. *PM*, 1:94; *PSS*, 6:254.

52. *PR*, 185; *PSS*, 5:290–91.

53. *PR*, 259; passage omitted in *PSS*, 6:76.

54. *PM*, 2:398; *PSS*, 9:233.

55. *PJ*, 1:76–77; *PSS*, 8:55 (partial).

56. Kashkin, "Iz vospominanii," 105.

57. *PR*, 145; *PSS*, 5:203.

58. *PR*, 264; *PSS*, 6:85.

59. *PR*, 284; *PSS*, 6:144.

60. *PR*, 281; *PSS*, 6:138.

61. *PSS*, 8:211–14.

62. *PR*, 257; *PSS*, 6:73.

63. *PR*, 262; *PSS*, 6:80.

64. *PR*, 263; *PSS*, 6:81.

65. *PSS*, 6:88–89.

66. *Sankt-Peterburgskie vedomosti*, 30 Nov. 1876.

67. *DC*, 210–11.

68. *ZC*, 1:520–21. For a detailed account of the relations between Tchaikovsky and Tolstoy, see S. L. Tolstoi, "Tolstoi i Chaikovskii: Ikh znakomstvo i vzaimootnosheniia," in *Istoriia russkoi muzyki v issledovaniiakh i materialakh* (Moscow, 1924), 1:114–24; also Edward Garden, "Tchaikovsky and Tolstoy," *Music and Letters* 55 (1974):307–16.

69. *PM*, 1:3.

70. Ibid.; *PSS*, 6:97.

Chapter 11. Two Women

1. *PR*, 281; *PSS*, 6:139.

2. *ZC*, 2:7.

3. Ibid.
4. *PM*, 3:197.
5. Ibid., 1:291.
6. Ibid., 211.
7. Ibid., 104.
8. Ibid., 5.
9. Ibid., 3:122.
10. Ibid., 1:6.
11. Ibid., 14; *PSS*, 6:125. This reaction, as well as many further signs in his letters of embarrassment in regard to financial matters, speak against a widespread insinuation apparently emanating from those close to the von Meck family (though not from Nadezhda herself, who was utterly estranged from the environment of her children). According to this version, Tchaikovsky consciously and hypocritically exploited the abnormal attachment to him of his wealthy patroness, getting money out of her and caring little for her as a person or for her concerns. This view is reflected, for instance, in an article by Mrs. von Meck's granddaughter Olga Bennigsen, "A Bizarre Friendship: Tchaikovsky and Mme von Meck," *Musical Quarterly* 22 (1936):420–29; also idem, "More Tchaikovsky–von Meck Correspondence," ibid. 24 (1938):129–38.
12. *PM*, 1:14; *PSS*, 6:125.
13. *PM*, 1:15; *PSS*, 6:125.
14. *PM*, 1:17.
15. Ibid., 4.
16. Ibid., 6.
17. Ibid., 8; *PSS*, 6:115.
18. *PM*, 1:7.
19. Ibid., 9; *PSS*, 6:116.
20. *PM*, 1:10.
21. Ibid., 250.
22. *PR*, 281; *PSS*, 6:138.
23. *PSS*, 6:131.
24. *Chaikovskii na moskovskoi stsene*, 306.
25. *PM*, 1:25; *PSS*, 6:144–45.
26. Antonina Chaikovskaia, "Iz vospominanii vdovy P. I. Chaikovskogo," *Petersburgskaia gazeta*, 3 Apr. 1894; idem, "Vospominaniia vdovy P. I. Chaikovskogo," *Russkaia muzykal'naia gazeta* 42 (1913):915–27.
27. Kashkin, "Iz vospominanii," 130. Modest's strategy was successful: subsequent authors have dismissed out of hand Milyukova's recollections as either the product of a mental patient or a forgery—the latter claim never supported by any argument.
28. *PM*, 1:26; *PSS*, 6:145–46.
29. A. Chaikovskaia, "Vospominaniia vdovy," 918.
30. Cf. Tchaikovsky's letter to A. Ia. Aleksandrova-Levenson, 13 July 1877, *PSS*, 6:154.
31. Kashkin, "Iz vospominanii," 109.
32. *PM*, 1:569.
33. Ibid., 569–70.
34. Klimenko, *Moi vospominaniia*, 70–71; *PSS*, 6:132.
35. *PR*, 278; *PSS*, 6:135. As recent researchers have suggested, Tchaikovsky composed the libretto for *Eugene Onegin* himself, despite the early involvement of Konstantin Shilovsky. See Vaidman, *Tvorcheskii arkhiv*, 71.
36. Kashkin, "Iz vospominanii," 119–20.
37. *PSS*, 7:21.
38. Kashkin, "Iz vospominanii," 120.

39. *PM*, 1:25; *PSS*, 6:145.
40. See *Dni i gody*,
41. A. Chaikovskaia, "Vospominaniia vdovy," 918.
42. *PM*, 1:25–26; *PSS*, 6:145.
43. A. Chaikovskaia, "Vospominaniia vdovy," 918–19.
44. Kashkin, "Iz vospominanii," 120–21.
45. *PM*, 1:26; *PSS*, 6:145.

Chapter 12. Marriage

1. A. Chaikovskaia, "Vospominaniia vdovy," 919.
2. *PR*, 281–82; *PSS*, 6:141.
3. *PSS*, 6:159.
4. *PR*, 281; *PSS*, 6:139.
5. *PR*, 282; *PSS*, 6:141.
6. *PR*, 282; *PSS*, 6:142.
7. *PR*, 283; *PSS*, 6:143.
8. *PR*, 702.
9. Ibid., 285; *PSS*, 6:148.
10. *PR*, 702.
11. Ibid., 285; *PSS*, 6:150.
12. *PR*, 284; *PSS*, 6:143–44.
13. *PM*, 1:27; *PSS*, 6:146–47.
14. A. Chaikovskaia, "Vospominaniia vdovy," 920–21.
15. *PSS*, 6:150–51.
16. Kashkin, "Iz vospominanii," 123.
17. *PR*, 286–87; *PSS*, 6:151–52 (partial).
18. *PR*, 287; passage omitted in *PSS*, 6:152.
19. *PR*, 287; *PSS*, 6:152.
20. *PR*, 287; passage omitted in *PSS*, 6:152.
21. *PR*, 290; letter omitted in *PSS*.
22. *PR*, 287; passage omitted in *PSS*, 6:152.
23. *PR*, 287–88; passage omitted in *PSS*, 6:152.
24. *PR*, 288; *PSS*, 6:153.
25. *PR*, 289–90; letter omitted in *PSS*.
26. *PR*, 289; *PSS*, 6:154.
27. *PR*, 290; letter omitted in *PSS*.
28. *PSS*, 6:155; letter omitted in *PR*.
29. *PR*, 290–91; *PSS*, 6:158.
30. *PM*, 1:28–29.
31. Ibid., 30; *PSS*, 6:156–47.
32. *PM*, 1:30–31.
33. Ibid., 32; *PSS*, 6:160.
34. *PR*, 290–91; *PSS*, 6:158.
35. *PM*, 1:33; *PSS*, 6:162.
36. *PM*, 1:33; *PSS*, 6:163.
37. *PSS*, 6:160.
38. *PM*, 1:33; *PSS*, 6:163.
39. *PSS*, 6:161; letter omitted in *PJ*.
40. Kashkin, "Iz vospominanii," 108.
41. *PM*, 1:32–34; *PSS*, 6:161–63.
42. *PM*, 1:382.
43. Ibid., 34; *PSS*, 6:163.

Chapter 13. Escape Abroad

1. *PR*, 293; *PSS*, 6:172.
2. *PR*, 296; *PSS*, 6:176–77.

3. Kashkin, "Iz vospominanii," 110.
4. Ibid., 111.
5. A. Chaikovskaia, "Vospominaniia vdovy," 924.
6. *PM*, 1:45–46; *PSS*, 6:175.
7. Kashkin, *Vospominaniia*, 128–29; idem, "Iz vospominanii," 124–25.
8. *PSS*, 6:194.
9. Ibid.
10. It is amusing to note the embarrassment of the Soviet editors of *PSS* with regard to the epithet "reptile" as applied to Antonina: having let it pass uncensored in the earlier volumes, they took a new tack in the later volumes, where the word in this particular context is fastidiously expunged.
11. *PR*, 302; *PSS*, 6:190 (partial).
12. *PR*, 297; *PSS*, 6:180.
13. *PR*, 299; *PSS*, 6:183.
14. *PR*, 302; *PSS*, 6:190.
15. Kashkin, "Iz vospominanii," 111–12.
16. Ibid., 125.
17. *ZC*, 2:30.
18. Kashkin, "Iz vospominanii," 112.
19. *PR*, 296–97; *PSS*, 6:179–80.
20. Ibid.
21. Kashkin, "Iz vospominanii," 112–13.
22. A. Chaikovskaia, "Vospominaniia vdovy," 924–25.
23. Ibid., 924.
24. *PM*, 1:48–49; *PSS*, 6:184–85 (final sentence omitted).
25. *PM*, 1:55–58; *PSS*, 6:196–99.
26. *PR*, 305; *PSS*, 6:207 (partial).
27. *PM*, 1:58–59; *PSS*, 6:199–200.
28. *PR*, 326–27; *PSS*, 6:285.
29. *PR*, 365; passage omitted in *PSS*, 7:91.
30. *PR*, 367; passage omitted in *PSS*, 7:99.
31. *PSS*, 13:385.
32. *PM*, 1:50; *PSS*, 6:186.
33. *PM*, 1:47.
34. Ibid., 53; *PSS*, 6:191.
35. *PM*, 1:51–52.
36. *PR*, 305; *PSS*, 6:208.
37. *PM*, 1:54–55; *PSS*, 6:196.
38. *PM*, 1:51.
39. Ibid., 76.
40. Ibid., 158.

Chapter 14. Consequences

1. *PM*, 1:95; *PSS*, 6:255–56.
2. Ibid.
3. *PR*, 302; *PSS*, 6:202.
4. *PR*, 310; *PSS*, 6:227–28.
5. *PR*, 307; *PSS*, 6:215.
6. *PR*, 313; *PSS*, 6:236 (partial).
7. *PR*, 312; *PSS*, 6:232.
8. *PM*, 1:97; *PSS*, 6:257.
9. *PM*, 1:102; *PSS*, 6:267.
10. *PR*, 495; *PSS*, 7:568. Cf. *PR*, 492, 494; *PSS*, 560, 562 (partial).
11. Cf. *PR*, 351; passage omitted in *PR*, 7:32.
12. Ibid.
13. *PSS*, 6:264; passage omitted in *PR*, 316.

14. *PR*, 345; *PSS*, 7:18.
15. *PR*, 318; *PSS*, 7:269 (partial).
16. *PR*, 705.
17. Ibid., 318–20; *PSS*, 6:272–73 (partial).
18. *PR*, 339; passage omitted in *PSS*, 6:321.
19. *PR*, 343; *PSS*, 6:337.
20. *PR*, 401; passage omitted in *PSS*, 7:237.
21. *PR*, 377; *PSS*, 7:118.
22. *PR*, 297; *PSS*, 6:180 (partial).
23. *PR*, 301; passage omitted in *PSS*, 6:190.
24. *PSS*, 6:188.
25. *PR*, 319; *PSS*, 6:273.
26. *PM*, 1:98; *PSS*, 6:261.
27. *PR*, 297; *PSS*, 6:181.
28. *PR*, 299; *PSS*, 6:183.
29. *PR*, 302; *PSS*, 6:190–91.
30. *PR*, 704.
31. Ibid., 308; *PSS*, 6:219–20.
32. *PR*, 312; *PSS*, 6:232–33.
33. *PR*, 316; *PSS*, 6:263–64.
34. *PM*, 1:114–15; *PSS*, 6:291.
35. *PR*, 329; *PSS*, 6:296.
36. *PR*, 324–25; *PSS*, 6:282.
37. *PM*, 1:109–10; *PSS*, 6:279–80.
38. *PM*, 1:140; *PSS*, 6:334.
39. *PM*, 1:94; *PSS*, 6:254–55.
40. *PM*, 1:583.
41. Ibid.
42. *PSS*, 6:230.
43. *Istoriia russkoi muzyki*, 172; *PSS*, 7:15 (partial).
44. *Istoriia russkoi muzyki*, 162.
45. *PR*, 706.
46. *PM*, 1:83.
47. Ibid., 111; *PSS*, 6:288.
48. *PR*, 343; *PSS*, 6:336–37 (partial).
49. *PM*, 1:141; *PSS*, 6:339.
50. *PR*, 350; passage omitted in *PSS*, 6:25–26.
51. *PR*, 345; passage omitted in *PSS*, 7:18.
52. *PR*, 380; *PSS*, 7:138.
53. *PR*, 368; *PSS*, 7:99
54. *PR*, 390; *PSS*, 7:172.
55. *PM*, 1:140; *PSS*, 6:334.
56. *PM*, 1:154; *PSS*, 7:38.
57. *PM*, 1:124–25; *PSS*, 6:309–10.
58. *PR*, 376; *PSS*, 7:117.
59. *PR*, 378; passage omitted in *PSS*, 7:129.
60. *PR*, 379 (partial); *PSS*, 7:133–34 (partial).
61. *PR*, 379–80; *PSS*, 7:134.
62. *PM*, 1:222; *PSS*, 7:132–33.
63. *PSS*, 6:325.
64. *PR*, 367–68; passage omitted in *PSS*, 7:99.
65. *PR*, 365; passage omitted in *PSS*, 7:91.
66. *PM*, 1:428; *PSS*, 7:384.
67. *PJ*, 1:30; *PSS*, 7:57–58 (partial).
68. *PR*, 367; *PSS*, 7:98.

69. *PM*, 1:213.
70. *Peterburgskaia gazeta*, 29 Nov. 1879.
71. *Golos*, 7 Dec. 1879.
72. *PM*, 1:216–19; *PSS*, 7:124–27.
73. *PM*, 1:220; *PSS*, 7:128.
74. *PM*, 2:220; *PSS*, 8:371.
75. *PM*, 1:228.
76. *PR*, 374; *PSS*, 7:115 (partial).

Chapter 15. Elective Affinities

1. *PM*, 1:70; *PSS*, 6:224.
2. *PR*, 351; *PSS*, 7:32.
3. *PSS*, 7:82; passage omitted in *PR*, 363.
4. *PR*, 481–82; *PSS*, 7:540.
5. *PM*, 1:212.
6. Ibid., 226–27; *PSS*, 7:141.
7. *PR*, 385; *PSS*, 7:145.
8. *PM*, 1:175; *PSS*, 7:67.
9. *PM*, 1:226; *PSS*, 7:140.
10. *PM*, 1:223; *PSS*, 7:136.
11. *PR*, 331; *PSS*, 6:297.
12. *PSS*, 7:45–46.
13. *PM*, 1:27.
14. Ibid., 158.
15. Ibid., 250.
16. Ibid., 423; *PSS*, 7:378.
17. *PM*, 1:417.
18. Ibid., 425.
19. Ibid., 190.
20. Ibid., 210–11.
21. Ibid., 212.
22. Ibid., 213.
23. Ibid., 204–5; *PSS*, 7:105–6.
24. *PM*, 1:259–60; *PSS*, 7:174.
25. *PM*, 1:282.
26. Ibid., 322.
27. Ibid., 323–24; *PSS*, 7:250.
28. *PM*, 2:239; *PSS*, 8:402.
29. *PM*, 1:43.
30. *PM*, 1:460; *PSS*, 7:430.
31. *PM*, 1:428; *PSS*, 7:377.
32. *PM*, 2:387.
33. *PM*, 1:405; *PSS*, 7:356.
34. *PM*, 1:103–4.
35. Ibid., 112; *PSS*, 6:289.
36. *PM*, 3:170–71.
37. Ibid., 173; *PSS*, 12:123–24.
38. *PM*, 1:147.
39. Ibid., 3:491.
40. Ibid., 480.
41. Ibid., 2:331.
42. Ibid., 1:255.
43. Ibid., *PSS*, 7:171.
44. *PM*, 1:544.

Chapter 16. Freedom to Create

1. *PR*, 708.
2. *PM*, 1:197; *PSS*, 7:95.
3. *PR*, 366; passage omitted in *PSS*, 7:91.
4. *PM*, 1:197; *PSS*, 7:95–96.
5. *PM*, 1:209–10.
6. Ibid., 226; *PSS*, 7:140–41.
7. *PR*, 390; *PSS*, 7:167.
8. *PR*, 391; *PSS*, 7:176.
9. *PSS*, 7:166; passage omitted in *PR*, 390.
10. *PR*, 392; *PSS*, 7:176 (partial).
11. *PR*, 471; *PSS*, 7:511–12.
12. *PR*, 387–88; *PSS*, 7:157–58.
13. *PR*, 389; *PSS*, 7:158.
14. *PJ*, 1:43; *PSS*, 7:325.
15. *PM*, 1:296; *PSS*, 7:220.
16. *PM*, 1:297; *PSS*, 7:221.
17. Davydov, *Zapiski*, 31.
18. *PM*, 1:301; *PSS*, 7:226.
19. *PR*, 402; *PSS*, 7:242 (partial).
20. *PR*, 713–14; *PSS*, 7:243–44.
21. *PM*, 1:323; *PSS*, 7:249.
22. *PM*, 1:590–91.
23. Ibid., 338; *PSS*, 7:271.
24. *PR*, 363; *PSS*, 7:82.
25. *PR*, 417; *PSS*, 7:285.
26. *PM*, 1:84.
27. *PR*, 406; *PSS*, 7:259.
28. *PR*, 412; *PSS*, 7:266–67.
29. *PR*, 429; *PSS*, 7:344.
30. *PR*, 395; *PSS*, 7:191.
31. *PR*, 409; *PSS*, 7:264.
32. *PR*, 411; *PSS*, 7:265.
33. *PR*, 412; *PSS*, 7:266.
34. *PM*, 1:357; *PSS*, 7:296.
35. *PM*, 1:355–56; *PSS*, 7:294–95.
36. *PM*, 1:356; *PSS*, 7:295.
37. *PM*, 1:357; *PSS*, 7:295.
38. *PR*, 422; *PSS*, 7:298.
39. *PM*, 1:364–65; *PSS*, 7:304–5.
40. *PR*, 426–27; *PSS*, 7:327–28.
41. *PM*, 1:379; *PSS*, 7:322.
42. *PM*, 1:385–86; *PSS*, 7:329–30.
43. *PR*, 420–21; *PSS*, 7:296–97.
44. *PR*, 421; *PSS*, 7:297.
45. *PR*, 424; *PSS*, 7:311.
46. *PM*, 1:411; *PSS*, 7:366.
47. *PR*, 442–43; *PSS*, 7:380–81.
48. Ibid.
49. Ibid.
50. *PM*, 1:427; *PSS*, 7:382–83.
51. *Novoe vremia*, 26 Aug. 1878.
52. *PM*, 1:428–29; *PSS*, 7:384.
53. *PM*, 1:431; *PSS*, 7:386.

54. *PR*, 444; *PSS*, 7:390 (partial).
55. *ZC*, 1:17.
56. *PR*, 184; *PSS*, 5:287.
57. *DC*, 46.
58. *PR*, 445; *PSS*, 7:390.
59. *PR*, 447–48; *PSS*, 7:399–400.
60. *PM*, 1:440.
61. Ibid., 447; *PSS*, 7:411.
62. *PM*, 1:446; *PSS*, 7:409.

Chapter 17. Invisibility Presumed

1. *PM*, 1:242.
2. Ibid., 253–54; *PSS*, 7:170.
3. *PM*, 1:271.
4. Ibid., 463.
5. Ibid., 466; *PSS*, 7:439.
6. *PM*, 1:468.
7. Ibid., 474; *PSS*, 7:443–44.
8. *PR*, 459; *PSS*, 7:458.
9. *PR*, 461; *PSS*, 7:464.
10. *PR*, 466; *PSS*, 7:484.
11. *PR*, 467; *PSS*, 7:492–93.
12. *Birzhevye vedomosti*, 3 Dec. 1878; cf. *Sankt-Peterburgskie vedomosti*, 9 Dec. 1878.
13. *PR*, 472–73; *PSS*, 7:516.
14. *PM*, 1:485–86; *PSS*, 7:468–69.
15. *PM*, 1:487.
16. Ibid., 490–91; *PSS*, 7:470–71.
17. *PM*, 1:493.
18. Ibid., 511.
19. Ibid., 516.
20. Ibid., 2:19.
21. *PSS*, 7:465–66; omitted in *PR*, 463.
22. *PSS*, 7:484; omitted in *PR*, 466.
23. *PM*, 1:533.
24. *PR*, 473–74; *PSS*, 7:519.
25. *PM*, 1:533–34; *PSS*, 7:517.
26. *PR*, 483; *PSS*, 7:541.
27. *PM*, 2:407.
28. *PR*, 475; *PSS*, 7:523.
29. *PR*, 490–91; *PSS*, 7:559.
30. *PR*, 493–94; *PSS*, 7:562 (partial).
31. *PR*, 494, 496; *PSS*, 7:563, 567.
32. *PR*, 461; *PSS*, 7:464.
33. *PR*, 468; *PSS*, 7:496.
34. *PR*, 460; *PSS*, 7:461.
35. *PR*, 487; *PSS*, 7:548.
36. *PM*, 1:553; *PSS*, 7:558.
37. *PR*, 480–81; *PSS*, 7:534.
38. *PM*, 1:553; *PSS*, 7:558.
39. *PR*, 488; *PSS*, 7:551.
40. *PM*, 1:552–53; *PSS*, 7:556.
41. *PR*, 488–89; *PSS*, 7:555 (partial).
42. *PR*, 490–91; *PSS*, 7:559–60.

43. *PR*, 493; *PSS*, 7:562 (partial).
44. *PR*, 366; passage omitted in *PSS*, 7:91.
45. *PR*, 493; *PSS*, 7:562.
46. *PR*, 496; passage omitted in *PSS*, 7:567.
47. *PR*, 555; *PSS*, 8:176.
48. *PM*, 2:25; *PSS*, 8:41.
49. *PR*, 495; *PSS*, 7:568.
50. *PM*, 1:560; *PSS*, 7:566.
51. *PR*, 518; *PSS*, 8:63.
52. *PR*, 529; *PSS*, 8:90.
53. *PR*, 502, 518, 524; *PSS*, 8:17, 62 (passage omitted), 74 (partial).
54. *PSS*, 8:17; omitted in *PR*, 502.
55. *PM*, 2:41.
56. Ibid., 45.
57. Ibid., 47; *PSS*, 8:95.
58. *PJ*, 1:78; *PSS*, 8:76.
59. *PM*, 2:48; *PSS*, 8:95.
60. *PR*, 534; *PSS*, 8:102.
61. *PM*, 2:41.
62. Ibid., 46.
63. *PR*, 542; *PSS*, 8:129.
64. *PM*, 2:86–87; *PSS*, 8:159–60.
65. *PM*, 2:608.
66. *PR*, 551–52; *PSS*, 8:168.
67. *PM*, 2:91; *PSS*, 8:166–67.
68. *PR*, 554; *PSS*, 8:176.
69. *PR*, 555; *PSS*, 8:176–77.
70. *PM*, 2:105–6; *PSS*, 8:191.
71. *PM*, 2:109.
72. *PR*, 559, 723; *PSS*, 8:192.
73. *PR*, 560; *PSS*, 8:196.
74. *PM*, 3:99.
75. *PR*, 545; *PSS*, 8:128.
76. Davydov, *Zapiski*, 23.
77. *PR*, 558; *PSS*, 8:189.
78. *PM*, 2:157; *PSS*, 8:291.
79. *PM*, 2:104; *PSS*, 8:190.
80. Davydov, *Zapiski*, 28.
81. *DC*, 26.
82. *ZC*, 3:15–16.
83. *PM*, 2:105; *PSS*, 8:191.
84. *PR*, 261; *PSS*, 6:79.
85. *PR*, 545; *PSS*, 8:128.
86. *PR*, 558; *PSS*, 8:189.
87. *PM*, 2:105; *PSS*, 8:190–91.
88. *PM*, 2:349; *PSS*, 9:121.
89. *PSS*, 9:142.
90. *PR*, 478; *PSS*, 7:531.

Chapter 18. Fireworks at Simaki

1. *PR*, 482; *PSS*, 7:541.
2. *PR*, 561; *PSS*, 8:200.
3. *PM*, 1:166; *PSS*, 7:50.
4. *PR*, 484–85; *PSS*, 7:542–43.

5. *PR*, 500; *PSS*, 7:576.
6. *PM*, 1:564; *PSS*, 7:578–79.
7. *PM*, 2:17.
8. *PM*, 2:134; *PSS*, 8:241.
9. *PM*, 2:109–10.
10. *PR*, 564; *PSS*, 8:210–11.
11. *PSS*, 8:309.
12. *PM*, 2:113; *PSS*, 8:203–4.
13. *PM*, 2:119.
14. Ibid., 122–23; *PSS*, 8:221–22.
15. *PM*, 2:127.
16. *PR*, 581; *PSS*, 8:249.
17. *PM*, 2:135–36; *PSS*, 8:242–43.
18. *PM*, 2:137.
19. Ibid., 2:140; *PSS*, 8:255.
20. *PR*, 587; *PSS*, 8:260 (partial).
21. *PR*, 601; *PSS*, 8:285.
22. *PR*, 612; *PSS*, 8:321–22.
23. *PR*, 605; *PSS*, 8:299.
24. *PR*, 608; *PSS*, 8:305.
25. *PM*, 2:150; *PSS*, 8:279.
26. *PM*, 2:166; *PSS*, 8:306.
27. *PR*, 609; *PSS*, 8:308.
28. *PM*, 2:170.
29. *PR*, 609; *PSS*, 8:308.
30. *PM*, 2:202; *PSS*, 8:348.
31. *PR*, 613; *PSS*, 8:320.
32. *PM*, 2:174; *PSS*, 8:318.
33. *PM*, 2:175–76.
34. *PR*, 617; *PSS*, 8:340.
35. *PM*, 2:193–94; *PSS*, 8:338.
36. *PM*, 2:192; *PSS*, 8:337.
37. *PM*, 2:195.
38. Ibid., 212–13.
39. Ibid., 220; *PSS*, 8:371.
40. *PM*, 2:197; *PSS*, 8:344.
41. *PM*, 2:215.
42. Ibid., 196; *PSS*, 8:344.
43. *PM*, 2:209; *PSS*, 8:361.
44. *PM*, 2:270; *PSS*, 8:447.
45. *PR*, 632; *PSS*, 8:397.
46. *PR*, 633; *PSS*, 8:411.
47. *PR*, 634; *PSS*, 8:412.
48. *PM*, 2:246.
49. Ibid.; *PSS*, 8:413.
50. *PR*, 641; *PSS*, 8:437.
51. *PR*, 635; *PSS*, 8:416.

Chapter 19. Patrons, Friends, and Protégés

1. *PR*, 545; *PSS*, 8:133.
2. *PR*, 647; *PSS*, 8:452.
3. *PR*, 649; *PSS*, 8:461.
4. *PR*, 650; *PSS*, 8:464.
5. *PR*, 653; *PSS*, 8:483.

6. *PR*, 654; *PSS*, 8:484.
7. *PR*, 652; *PSS*, 8:472.
8. *PR*, 653; *PSS*, 8:483.
9. *PR*, 655; *PSS*, 8:489.
10. *PSS*, 9:27.
11. Ibid., 42.
12. *PM*, 2:287; *PSS*, 8:486.
13. *PSS*, 9:32
14. *PM*, 2:303; *PSS*, 9:33
15. *PM*, 2:225; *PSS*, 8:383.
16. *PM*, 2:296; *PSS*, 9:26.
17. *Revue et gazette musicale de Paris*, 1 Feb. 1880.
18. *PM*, 2:306; *PSS*, 9:35.
19. *PSS*, 9:58.
20. Ibid., 64–65.
21. Ibid., 68.
22. Ibid., 63.
23. Ibid., 67.
24. R. F. Krafft-Ebing, *Psychopathia Sexualis: A Medico-forensic Study* (New York, [1965]), 401; V. O. Merzheevskii, *Sudebnaia ginekologiia*, (St. Petersburg, 1878), 205.
25. *PSS*, 9:69–70.
26. Ibid., 70.
27. Ibid., 74–75.
28. Ibid., 75.
29. *PM*, 2:315; *PSS*, 9:53.
30. *PSS*, 9:75.
31. E. M. Feoktistov, *Vospominaniia* (Leningrad, 1929), 244–45.
32. S. Iu. Witte, *Vospominaniia*, 2 vols. (Berlin, 1922), 2:526.
33. V. S. Frank, "Iz neizdannoi perepiski imp. Aleksandra III i Nikolaia II s kniazem V. P. Meshcherskim," *Sovremennye zapiski* 70 (1940):168.
34. Ibid., 169.
35. Ibid., 183.
36. *PSS*, 9:82.
37. *PM*, 2:330; *PSS*, 9:89.
38. *PSS*, 9:90.
39. Ibid., 101.
40. *PM*, 3:245, 1:417.
41. Ibid., 2:353; *PSS*, 9:134.
42. *PM*, 2:624.
43. Ibid.
44. Ibid., 377; *PSS*, 9:187.
45. *PSS*, 9:192.
46. Ibid., 147.
47. Ibid., 173–74.
48. *PJ*, 1:157; *PSS*, 9:172.
49. *PM*, 2:374.
50. Ibid., 394.
51. Ibid., 429; *PSS*, 9:295.
52. *PSS*, 9:165.
53. *PM*, 2:410, 418.
54. *PSS*, 10:135, 150.
55. Ibid., 197, 211, 213, 223–24, 244.
56. *PJ*, 1:209; *PSS*, 10:239.

57. *PSS*, 9:336.
58. *PM*, 2:458; *PSS*, 9:334.
59. *PM*, 2:463; *PSS*, 9:347–48.
60. *PM*, 2:466–67; *PSS*, 10:17.

Chapter 20. Domestic Upheaval

1. *PM*, 2:418.
2. Ibid., 422–23; *PSS*, 9:286.
3. *PM*, 2:431; *PSS*, 9:298.
4. *PM*, 2:429; *PSS*, 9:294.
5. *PSS*, 9:308.
6. Ibid., 317.
7. *PM*, 2:448; *PSS*, 9:316.
8. *PM*, 2:455; *PSS*, 9:326.
9. *PSS*, 9:332.
10. *PM*, 2:458.
11. *PSS*, 9:336–37.
12. Ibid.
13. Ibid., 339.
14. Ibid., 340.
15. Ibid., 340–41.
16. *PM*, 2:460.
17. Ibid., 462–63; *PSS*, 9:347.
18. *PM*, 2:464; *PSS*, 9:348.
19. *PM*, 2:467; *PSS*, 9:17.
20. *PM*, 2:468; *PSS*, 9:19.
21. Ibid.
22. *Dni i gody*, 248.
23. *Moskovskie vedomosti*, 15 Jan. 1881; *Novoe vremia*, 17 Jan. 1881.
24. *PM*, 2:471; *PSS*, 10:23.
25. *PSS*, 10:14.
26. *Golos*, 19 Feb. 1818.
27. *PSS*, 10:37–38.
28. *PM*, 2:480; *PSS*, 10:39.
29. *PSS*, 10:40.
30. Ibid.
31. Ibid., 51.
32. Ibid., 52.
33. Ibid., 47.
34. Ibid., 48.
35. Ibid., 57.
36. Ibid., 59.
37. Ibid., 56.
38. *PM*, 2:483; *PSS*, 10:45–46.
39. *PSS*, 10:50–51.
40. Ibid., 58.
41. *PM*, 2:484; *PSS*, 10:54.
42. *PSS*, 10:61–62.
43. *PM*, 2:515; *PSS*, 10:116–17.
44. *PJ*, 1:185; *PSS*, 10:53.
45. *PM*, 2:482–83; *PSS*, 10:45–46.
46. *PM*, 2:487.
47. *PR*, 472; *PSS*, 7:515.
48. *PR*, 533; *PSS*, 8:99.

49. *PM*, 2:493; *PSS*, 10:71.
50. Ibid.
51. *PM*, 2:493; *PSS*, 10:75.
52. *PSS*, 10:73–74.
53. *PM*, 2:494.
54. Ibid., 496–97.
55. *PSS*, 10:94–95.
56. Ibid., 102–3.
57. Ibid., 108.
58. Ibid., 109.
59. *PM*, 2:506–7; *PSS*, 10:90–91.
60. *PM*, 2:508.
61. Ibid., 524–25.
62. Ibid., 528; *PSS*, 10:158.
63. *PSS*, 10:164–65.
64. *PM*, 2:535; *PSS*, 10:175.
65. *PM*, 2:537; *PSS*, 10:179.
66. *PSS*, 10:182.
67. Ibid., 14.
68. Ibid., 212.
69. Ibid., 210.
70. Ibid., 215–16.
71. Ibid., 273–74.
72. Ibid., 12:237.
73. *PM*, 2:546; *PSS*, 10:207.
74. *PM*, 2:551–52; *PSS*, 10:221.
75. *PM*, 2:533–34; *PSS*, 10:226–27.
76. *PM*, 2:560; *PSS*, 235.
77. *PSS*, 10:259.
78. Ibid., 91, 98.
79. Ibid., 244.
80. *PM*, 2:570; *PSS*, 10:264.
81. *PM*, 2:572; *PSS*, 10:268.
82. *PM*, 2:573.

Chapter 21. Tanya

1. *PSS*, 11:23.
2. *PM*, 3:27; *PSS*, 11:54–55.
3. *PSS*, 11:55–56.
4. Ibid., 289.
5. *PM*, 3:43.
6. *PSS*, 11:95.
7. Ibid., 100.
8. Ibid., 102.
9. Ibid., 107.
10. Ibid., 111.
11. Ibid., 120.
12. *PM*, 3:58; *PSS*, 11:125.
13. *PSS*, 11:23.
14. Ibid., 126.
15. *PM*, 3:70–71; *PSS*, 11:158–59.
16. *PSS*, 11:159.
17. *PM*, 3:71.
18. Ibid., 75–76; *PSS*, 11:170.

19. *PM*, 3:81; *PSS*, 11:178–79.
20. *PM*, 3:82–83.
21. Ibid., 87.
22. Ibid., 124; *PSS*, 11:288.
23. *PM*, 3:127; *PSS*, 11:293.
24. *PM*, 3:125.
25. *PSS*, 11:275.
26. Ibid., 199.
27. Ibid., 184.
28. *PM*, 3:90; *PSS*, 11:186–87.
29. *PM*, 3:96; *PSS*, 11:197.
30. *PM*, 3:99
31. Ibid., 94.
32. *PSS*, 11:212.
33. Ibid., 213.
34. Ibid., 262.
35. Ibid., 247.
36. Ibid., 205.
37. Ibid., 219.
38. Ibid., 291.
39. Ibid., 303.
40. *VC* (1980), 86.
41. *PJ*, 1:272; *PSS*, 12:16.
42. *PSS*, 12:29.
43. Ibid., 49.
44. Ibid., 51.
45. *PM*, 3:153; *PSS*, 12:63–64.
46. *PJ*, 1:283.
47. *PM*, 3:153–54; *PSS*, 12:64.
48. *PM*, 3:157; *PSS*, 12:77.
49. *PM*, 3:164.
50. Ibid., 166; *PSS*, 12:92.
51. *PSS*, 10:113–15.
52. Ibid., 12:110.
53. Ibid., 111–16.
54. *PM*, 3:172.
55. Ibid., 173; *PSS*, 12:124.
56. *PSS*, 12:108.
57. Ibid.
58. Ibid., 134.
59. Merzheevskii, *Sudebnaia ginekologiia*, 206.
60. *PSS*, 12:139–40.
61. Ibid., 143.
62. Ibid.
63. *PM*, 3:176; *PSS*, 12:147.
64. *PSS*, 12:152.
65. Ibid., 100.
66. *PM*, 3:183; *PSS*, 12:161.

Chapter 22. X and Z at Kamenka

1. *PM*, 3:185; *PSS*, 12:166.
2. *PSS*, 12:186.
3. *PM*, 3:190; *PSS*, 12:171.
4. *PSS*, 12:125.

5. *PM*, 3:152.
6. Ibid., 191; *PSS*, 12:171.
7. *PSS*, 12:179.
8. *PM*, 3:193.
9. Ibid., 193–94; *PSS*, 12:181.
10. *PSS*, 12:179.
11. *PM*, 3:198.
12. Ibid., 201; *PSS*, 12:194.
13. *PSS*, 12:172.
14. Ibid., 179.
15. *PM*, 3:205; *PSS*, 12:203.
16. *PSS*, 12:220.
17. Ibid., 236.
18. Ibid.
19. *PJ*, 1:308. Most likely, Jurgenson's mysterious visitor was Aleksey Kiselev, Kondratyev's servant and lover. Tchaikovsky never completely broke ties with Kiselev and, in fact, corresponded with him even when Kiselev was in prison, in 1890; see Kiselev's letter to Tchaikovsky, Gosudarstvennyi Dom-muzei P. I. Chaikovskogo, Klin, f. Aa⁴, N. 1447.
20. *PSS*, 12:244.
21. Ibid., 243.
22. Ibid., 270.
23. Ibid., 11:37.
24. Ibid., 12:270.
25. Ibid., 315.
26. Ibid., 318.
27. Ibid., 315.
28. Ibid., 327.
29. Ibid., 317.
30. *PM*, 3:261; *PSS*, 12:330–31.
31. *PSS*, 12:335.
32. *PM*, 3:265; *PSS*, 12:336.
33. *PSS*, 12:361.
34. *DC*, 15.
35. *PSS*, 12:361; *DC*, 14.
36. Tchaikovsky's diaries are extant for the years 1873 (a very brief record of his vacation in Europe), 1884, and 1886–1891.
37. *DC*, 14–15.
38. First noted by Igor Glebov (Boris Asaf'ev) in *P. I. Chaikovskii: Vospominaniia i pis'ma* (Leningrad, 1924); also in *VC* (1980), 166n.
39. *PSS*, 12:32.
40. *VC* (1980), 166.
41. *DC*, 14.
42. Ibid., 15–19.
43. Ibid., 21.
44. Ibid., 21–28.
45. *PSS*, 12:119.
46. *DC*, 24–28.
47. *PM*, 3:283; *PSS*, 12:387.
48. *DC*, 135.
49. *PSS*, 14:74.
50. *DC*, 28. The last phrase is the refrain from Nikolay Gogol's story "A Madman's Diary," also quoted by Masha in Chekhov's play *Three Sisters*.
51. Ibid.

52. *PSS*, 12:365.
53. *DC*, 15–28.
54. *PM*, 3:257.
55. Ibid., 258; *PSS*, 12:316.
56. *PM*, 3:303; *PSS*, 12:423–24.
57. *PM*, 3:308–9; *PSS*, 12:429.
58. *PM*, 3:312.
59. *PSS*, 12:433.
60. Ibid.
61. *PM*, 3:320–21; *PSS*, 12:468–69.
62. *PSS*, 12:493–94.
63. *PM*, 3:328–29; *PSS*, 12:511.
64. *PM*, 3:330.
65. Ibid., 331; *PSS*, 13:13.
66. *DC*, 82.

Chapter 23. Drama in Tiflis

1. *PSS*, 13:16.
2. Ibid.
3. *PM*, 3:332; *PSS*, 12:474.
4. *PM*, 3:323.
5. Ibid., 354; *PSS*, 13:68–69.
6. *ZC*, 3:20.
7. *PM*, 3:337; *PSS*, 13:25.
8. Ibid.
9. *PM*, 3:347; *PSS*, 13:45.
10. *PM*, 3:337; *PSS*, 13:25.
11. *PM*, 3:343; *PSS*, 13:35.
12. Ibid.
13. *PM*, 3:373; *PSS*, 13:122.
14. *PSS*, 13:185.
15. Ibid., 207–8.
16. Ibid., 64.
17. *PR*, 687.
18. *PSS*, 6:118.
19. *DC*, 44.
20. *ZC*, 3:121.
21. *PSS*, 13:322.
22. Ibid., 327.
23. *DC*, 49.
24. Ibid., 49, 53.
25. Ibid., 51–54.
26. Ibid., 55.
27. *PSS*, 13:369.
28. Ibid., 389.
29. *DC*, 79.
30. *PSS*, 13:403.
31. Ibid., 405–6.
32. Berberova, *Tchaïkovski*, 11.
33. M. M. Ippolitov-Ivanov, *Pis'ma, stat'i, vospominaniia* (Moscow, 1986), 41.
34. *PSS*, 13:411.
35. Ibid., 420.
36. *DC*, 100.
37. *PSS*, 14:599.

38. Ibid., 13:332.
39. *DC*, 59.
40. *PSS*, 13:358.
41. Ibid., 355; *DC*, 63.
42. *DC*, 70.
43. Ibid., 65–69.
44. Ibid., 60.
45. Ibid., 61.
46. Ibid., 63.
47. *PSS*, 13:358.
48. *PM*, 3:423; *PSS*, 13:363.
49. *DC*, 72–75.
50. *PSS*, 13:385.
51. Ibid., 387; passage omitted in *PJ*, 2:44.
52. *DC*, 75.
53. *PSS*, 13:405.
54. *DC*, 81.
55. *PSS*, 13:429.

Chapter 24. Gentlemanly Games

1. *PSS*, 13:421.
2. *DC*, 77–81.
3. *PSS*, 13:424.
4. *DC*, 86.
5. Ibid., 100.
6. Ibid., 72–73.
7. Ibid., 80, 81, 85, 86, 102, 111.
8. Ibid., 93.
9. Merzheevskii, *Sudebnaia ginekologiia*, 204.
10. B. Tarnowsky, *The Sexual Instinct and Its Morbid Manifestation from the Double Standpoint of Jurisprudence and Psychiatry*, trans. W. C. Costello and Alfred Allinson (Paris, 1898), 146.
11. Ibid.
12. Ibid., 146–47.
13. Ibid., 147.
14. Rozanov, *Izbrannoe*, 348.
15. *PSS*, 13:455.
16. *DC*, 36.
17. Ibid., 79–133.
18. Ibid., 181.
19. V. Mikhievich, *Iazvy Peterburga* (St. Petersburg, 1886), 13.
20. Merzheevskii, *Sudebnaia ginekologiia*, 208.
21. Ibid., 238–39.
22. *DC*, 82.
23. Ibid., 42, 72, 115, 124, 123.
24. Ibid., 144.
25. Ibid., 71.
26. Ibid., 80.
27. *ZC*, 3:66.
28. *DC*, 86–106.
29. *PSS*, 15b:145.
30. *PR*, 437; *PSS*, 7:364, 13:327; *DC*, 48.
31. *PR*, 425; *PSS*, 7:312.
32. *DC*, 55.

33. *PR*, 425; *PSS*, 7:312 (partial).
34. *DC*, 71.
35. Ibid., 83.
36. Ibid., 96.
37. *PSS*, 13:495.
38. *DC*, 110.
39. *PSS*, 13:379.
40. *PM*, 3:467; *PSS*, 14:58.
41. *DC*, 123.
42. Davydov, *Zapiski*, 61.
43. *PM*, 3:461; *PSS*, 14:24.
44. *PM*, 3:468; *PSS*, 14:58–59.
45. *DC*, 136.
46. *PSS*, 14:84.
47. *DC*, 143.
48. Ibid., 146.
49. Ibid., 146–47.
50. *PSS*, 14:141.
51. *DC*, 160.
52. *PM*, 3:492; *PSS*, 14:154.
53. *DC*, 170.
54. *PSS*, 14:148.
55. Ibid., 177.
56. *DC*, 170.
57. Ibid., 172.
58. Ibid., 173.
59. *PSS*, 14:200; cf. *DC*, 174.
60. *DC*, 174.
61. Ibid., 181.
62. *ZC*, 3:180.
63. *DC*, 213.
64. *Peterburgskii listok*, 22 Oct. 1887.
65. *Muzykal'noe obozrenie*, 5 Nov. 1887.
66. *PM*, 3:503; *PSS*, 14:255.
67. *PM*, 3:505; *PSS*, 14:273.
68. *PM*, 3:429.
69. Ibid., 490.
70. Ibid., 494; *PSS*, 14:171.
71. *PM*, 3:508.
72. Ibid., 513; *PSS*, 14:324.
73. *PM*, 3:514.
74. Prince S. D. U[rusov], *Gospoda Romanovy i tainy russkogo dvora* ([London], 1909), 148–49; Witte, *Vospominaniia*, 515; P. A. Zaionchkovskii, *Rossiiskoe samoderzhavie v kontse 19-ogo veka* (Moscow, 1970), 78.
75. Igor Vinogradoff, "Some Russian Imperial Letters to Prince V. P. Meshchersky (1839–1914)," *Oxford Slavonic Papers* 10 (1962):122.
76. V. N. Lambsdorf, *Dnevnik, 1886–1890* (Moscow-Leningrad, 1926), 223.
77. [V. P. Obninskii], *Poslednii samoderzhets* [Berlin, 1912], 34.
78. V. N. Lambsdorf, *Dnevnik, 1891–1892* (Moscow-Leningrad, 1934), 106.
79. *PSS*, 14:318.
80. Ibid., 365.
81. Ibid., 321.
82. Ibid., 301.
83. Ibid., 337.

84. Ibid., 345.
85. Ibid., 354.
86. Ibid., 353.
87. *DC*, 191–95.
88. *PSS*, 14:359.
89. *DC*, 201.
90. Ibid., 203.
91. *PSS*, 14:295.
92. Ibid., 354.

Chapter 25. A Second Wind

1. *PSS*, 14:426.
2. Ibid., 425. Later a noted art expert, Argutinsky-Dolgorukov was made curator of the Hermitage Museum in 1917 and then in 1920 emigrated to France, where he became closely associated with Sergey Diaghilev and his circle.
3. *Muzykal'noe nasledie Chaikovskogo* (Moscow, 1958), 239.
4. *PSS*, 14:195.
5. *DC*, 172.
6. *PM*, 3:494; *PSS*, 14:203.
7. *DC*, 78.
8. Vaidman, *Tvorcheskii arkhiv*, 125.
9. *PSS*, 14:464.
10. Ibid., 478.
11. Ibid., 484.
12. Ibid., 502.
13. *PM*, 3:549–50; *PSS*, 14:510.
14. *PM*, 3:552–53.
15. Ibid., 553–54; *PSS*, 14:545.
16. *PM*, 3:592; *PSS*, 15b:116.
17. *PM*, 3:598; *PSS*, 15b:193.
18. *PM*, 3:593.
19. Ibid., 559; *PSS*, 14:600.
20. *PSS*, 15a:24.
21. *DC*, 222.
22. *PSS*, 15a:38.
23. Ibid., 61.
24. Ibid., 68.
25. Ibid., 2:343.
26. *DC*, 231.
27. Ibid., 232.
28. *PSS*, 15a:78; passage omitted in *PJ*, 2:118.
29. *PSS*, 15a:82–83; passage omitted in *PJ*, 2:119–20.
30. *PSS*, 15a:84; passage omitted in *PJ*, 2:120.
31. *DC*, 232.
32. *PSS*, 15a:93.
33. *ZC*, 3:15.
34. *DC*, 233–34.
35. *ZC*, 3:15.
36. *PSS*, 15a:102.
37. Ibid., 116.
38. *DC*, 242.
39. Ibid., 219.
40. Ibid., 221.

41. *PSS*, 15a:174.
42. Ibid., 204.
43. Zaionchkovskii, *Rossiiskoe samoderzhavie*, 22.
44. *PM*, 3:539; *PSS*, 14:467.
45. Ibid., 14:437
46. Ibid., 15a:205.
47. Lambsdorf, *Dnevnik, 1886–1890*, 223.
48. *PM*, 3:587; *PSS*, 15a:212.
49. *PM*, 3:587.
50. Ibid., 587–88; *PSS*, 15a:212.
51. *PM*, 3:590; *PSS*, 15a:220.
52. *PSS*, 15a:221.
53. *PM*, 3:649.
54. [Obninskii], *Poslednii samoderzhets*, 34.
55. *DC*, 249.
56. *PSS*, 15b:43.
57. *DC*, 253.
58. P. Chaikovskii, *Pis'ma k blizkim*, 614.
59. *PSS*, 15b:35; passage omitted in *PJ*, 2:135.
60. *PM*, 3:648–49; *PSS*, 15b:32–34.
61. *DC*, 253.
62. *PSS*, 15b:30.
63. *DC*, 253.
64. *PSS*, 15b:143.
65. *DC*, 258.
66. P. Chaikovskii, *Pis'ma k blizkim*, 617.
67. *PSS*, 15b:53–56.
68. Ibid., 57.
69. Ibid., 118.
70. Ibid., 132.

Chapter 26. Mrs. von Meck's Last Letter

1. *PSS*, 15b:201.
2. Ibid., 260.
3. *PM*, 3:604.
4. Ibid.
5. Ibid.
6. Ibid, 602; *PSS*, 15b:254.
7. *PM*, 3:604.
8. Ibid., 605–6; *PSS*, 15b:263–65.
9. *PM*, 3:609.
10. Cf. ibid., 613.
11. *PM*, 3:579–80.
12. Ibid., 579.
13. Ibid., 580; *PSS*, 15a:160.
14. *PM*, 3:596.
15. Ibid., 596; *PSS*, 15b:166.
16. *PM*, 3:599; *PSS*, 15b:195.
17. See *PM*, 3:613.
18. Ibid., 610.
19. Davydov, *Zapiski*, 75.
20. Bennigsen, "More Tchaikovsky–von Meck Correspondence," 137.
21. *PJ*, 2:183; *PSS*, 15b:268.
22. *PJ*, 2:183.

23. *PSS*, 15b:271.
24. Ibid., 274.
25. *PM*, 3:610.
26. Ibid., 611.
27. Ibid.
28. Ibid.
29. Ibid.
30. Ibid.
31. *VC* (1980), 230. This version acquired the authority of family tradition; cf. Catherine Drinker Bowen and Barbara von Meck, *Beloved Friend: The Story of Tchaikovsky and Nadejda von Meck* (New York, 1937), 437.
32. *VC* (1980), 231.
33. *ZC*, 3:429.
34. *PSS*, 16a:64.
35. *PM*, 3:611.
36. *PSS*, 16a:71.
37. *PM*, 3:611–12; *PSS*, 16a:131–32.
38. *PM*, 3:612–13.
39. *VC* (1980), 231.
40. *PSS*, 17:158; entire letter omtited in *PJ*.

Chapter 27. The "Fourth Suite"

1. *PSS*, 16a:87.
2. *ZC*, 3:431.
3. *PSS*, 16a:88.
4. Ibid.
5. Ibid., 93.
6. *DC*, 265.
7. *PSS*, 16a:99.
8. *DC*, 264.
9. Ibid., 279.
10. *New York Herald*, 6 May 1891.
11. *DC*, 276.
12. Ibid., 277.
13. Ibid., 290.
14. *PSS*, 16a:112. For a more detailed account of the composer's visit to America, see the compilation of Tchaikovsky's letters and diaries by Elkhonon Yoffe, *Tchaikovsky in America* (New York, 1986).
15. *PSS*, 16a:66.
16. Ibid., 173–74.
17. *Dni i gody*, 483.
18. *PSS*, 15b:179.
19. Ibid., 173.
20. Ibid., 16a:178.
21. Ibid., 180.
22. Ibid., 300.
23. Ibid., 16b:15.
24. Davydov, *Zapiski*, 53–54.
25. *PSS*, 16a:133.
26. Ibid., 174.
27. *Stolitsa Rossii (nechto, vrode monografii)* (St. Petersburg, 1913), 52–55.
28. *PSS*, 16b:124–25; also *Novyi zhurnal* 85 (1966):273.
29. *PSS*, 16a:182.
30. P. I. Chaikovskii and S. I. Taneev, *Pis'ma*, ed. V. Zhdanov (Moscow, 1951), 257.

31. Ibid., 257–58 (partial); *PSS*, 16a:244–48.
32. *PSS*, 16a:254.
33. Ibid., 16b:13.
34. Ibid., 16a:304.
35. Ibid., 16b:16.
36. *VC* (1980), 217.
37. Ibid., 219.
38. *PSS*, 16b:37.
39. Ibid., 43.
40. *VC* (1980), 222.
41. *PSS*, 16b:41–42.
42. Ibid., 44.
43. Ibid., 58.
44. Ibid., 60.
45. *Novosti dnia*, 13 Apr. 1892.
46. *PSS*, 16b:70.
47. Ibid., 96.
48. Ibid., 108.
49. Ibid., 110–11.
50. Ibid., 115.
51. Ibid.
52. Ibid., 134.
53. Ibid., 127.
54. Ibid., 15b:271–72.
55. Ibid., 16a:178.
56. Ibid., 17:194–95.
57. Ibid., 16b:115.
58. Ibid., 181.
59. I. E. Grabar, *Moia zhizn': Avtobiografiia* (Moscow-Leningrad, 1937), 82–84.
60. *PSS*, 17:201.
61. *Novoe vremia*, 14 Dec. 1892; *Birzhevye vedomosti*, 13 Dec. 1892.
62. N. A. Rimskii-Korsakov, *Polnoe sobranie sochinenii: Literaturnye proizvedeniia i perepiska* (Moscow, 1955), 1:184.
63. *PSS*, 16b:202.
64. *VC* (1980), 281–87.
65. P. Chaikovskii, *Pis'ma k blizkim*, 626; *ZC*, 3:628n.

Chapter 28. "Let Them Guess"

1. *PSS*, 14:552.
2. Ibid., 16b:207.
3. Ibid., 208.
4. Ibid., 17:43.
5. In 1951–1955 the E-flat major symphony was reconstructed from existing score parts and the piano concerto version by the Soviet musicologist Semyon Bogatyrev and even performed in public in February 1957, and later recorded, as the Symphony no. 7 in E-flat Major. See P. I. Chaikovskii, *Simfoniia mi-bemol' mazhor: Partitura* (Moscow, 1961).
6. *PSS*, 16b:211–12.
7. Ibid., 211.
8. Ibid., 215.
9. Ibid.
10. Ibid., 214.
11. Ibid., 17:24–25.
12. *VC* (1980), 418.

13. Ibid., 304–5.
14. Ibid., 417.
15. *PSS*, 17:43.
16. Ibid., 42.
17. Franz Zagiba, *Tschaikowsky* (Vienna, 1953), 328.
18. *PM*, 1:531–32; *PSS*, 17:513–14.
19. *DC*, 292.
20. N. V. Tumanina, *Chaikovskii: Velikii master (1878–1893)* (Moscow, 1968), 405.
21. *Dni i gody*, 517, 519, 621.
22. Tumanina, *Chaikovskii*, 404.
23. Ibid., 406.
24. *VC* (1980), 136.
25. Iu. L. Davydov, *Klinskie gody tvorchesta Chaikovskogo* (Moscow, 1965), 96; cf. Iastrebtsev, *Rimskii-Korsakov*, 2:69.
26. *PSS*, 12:362.
27. Ibid., 362–63.
28. *VC* (1962), 29.
29. *PSS*, 15b:141.
30. *VC* (1980), 323.
31. *PSS*, 17:42.
32. *ZC*, 3:601.
33. *PSS*, 17:35.
34. *PSS*, 17:54.
35. Ibid., 61.
36. Klimenko, *Moi vospominaniia*, 41.
37. M. V. Dobuzhinskii, *Vospominaniia*, 2 vols. (New York, 1976), 1:180–81.
38. A. S. Suvorin, *Dnevnik* (Moscow-Petrograd, 1923), 29.
39. *PSS*, 17:79.
40. *VC* (1980), 423.
41. *PSS*, 17:35.
42. Ibid., 79.
43. *VC* (1980), 352.
44. Rimskii-Korsakov, *Polnoe sobranie sochinenii*, 1:175.
45. Iastrebtsev, *Rimskii-Korsakov*, 2:208.
46. *PSS*, 17:93–94.
47. Ibid., 97.
48. Ibid., 102 n. 4.
49. Ibid., 102–3.
50. Ibid., 108.
51. Ibid., 109.
52. Ibid., 119.
53. Ibid., 122.
54. Ibid., 142.
55. Ibid., 155.
56. Iakovlev, "Chaikovskii i Apukhtin," 377.
57. Apukhtin, *Stikhotvoreniia*, 273–74.
58. *ZC*, 3:626.
59. *PSS*, 17:169.
60. Ibid., 186.
61. Ibid., 194.
62. Ibid., 172.
63. Ibid., 197.
64. *VC* (1980), 318.

65. Ibid., 323.
66. Ibid., 324. Yulian Poplavsky later abandoned the study of music and went on to enjoy a successful career at the Moscow Stock Exchange. He was the father of the Russian émigré poet Boris Poplavsky, much admired by Vladimir Nabokov.
67. Ibid., 362.

Chapter 29. The Fortuitous Tragedy

1. VC (1962), 29–30.
2. PSS, 17:43.
3. Davydov, Zapiski, 78.
4. ZC, 3:642.
5. VC (1980), 330.
6. Ibid., 278; Iur'ev, Zapiski, 2:75–76.
7. Suvorin, Dnevnik, 246.
8. B. V. Vladykin, Materialy k istorii kholernoi epidemii 1892–95 gg. v predelakh Evropeiskoi Rossii (St. Petersburg, 1899); Entsiklopedicheskii slovar' F. A. Brokgauza i I. A. Efrona, 41 vols. in 82 (St. Petersburg, 1890–1907), s.v. "kholera"; Encyclopedia Britannica, 10th ed. (1910), s.v. "cholera."
9. Novosti i birzhevaia gazeta, 6 Sept. 1893.
10. Ibid., 12 Sept. 1893.
11. Ibid., 30 Sept.–24 Oct. 1893.
12. Ibid., 10 Sept. 1893.
13. Entsiklopedicheskii slovar', s.v. "kholera"; Encyclopedia Britannica, s.v. "cholera"; for a more detailed discussion of the transmission of cholera, see Richard J. Evans, Death in Hamburg: Society and Politics in the Cholera Years, 1830–1910 (New York, 1987), 227–28.
14. Novosti i birzhevaia gazeta, 12 Sept. 1893.
15. Ibid., 30 Sept. 1893; Novoe vremia, 30 Sept. 1893.
16. Novosti i birzhevaia gazeta, 24 Oct. 1893; Novoe vremia, 24 Oct. 1893.
17. ZC, 3:643.
18. VC (1980), 328.
19. Ibid., 397.
20. Ibid., 209.
21. PSS, 17:205.
22. Rimskii-Korsakov, Polnoe sobranie sochinenii, 1:193.
23. ZC, 3:644.
24. Ibid., 645–46.
25. PSS, 17:205.
26. V. V. Bessel', "Neskol'ko slov po povodu vozobnovleniia 'Oprichnika' P. Chaikovskogo na stsene Mariinskogo teatra," Russkaia muzykal'naia gazeta, 1897, no. 12:1720.
27. Ibid.; ZC, 3:646.
28. Peterburgskii listok, 26 Oct. 1893.
29. Bessel', "Neskol'ko slov," 1720.
30. Peterburgskii listok, 26 Oct. 1893.
31. Novosti i birzhevaia gazeta, 26 Oct. 1893; Novoe vremia, 26 Oct. 1893.
32. VC (1980), 196–97.
33. Novosti i birzhevaia gazeta, 26 Oct. 1893.
34. PSS, 17:206.
35. ZC, 3:647; Novoe vremia, 26 Oct. 1893.
36. PSS, 17:205 n. 2, 207 n. 1; VC (1980), 330; Novosti i birzhevaia gazeta, 26 Oct. 1893.

37. Bessel', "Neskol'ko slov," 1720.
38. *ZC*, 3:647; *Novoe vremia*, 26 Oct. 1893.
39. *VC* (1980), 279–80.
40. According to Modest, neither Yury Yuryev nor Yury Davydov was present at Leiner's restaurant, despite their contrary claims in their memoirs.
41. *ZC*, 3:647.
42. A detailed account of Tchaikovsky's illness by Modest was published as "Poslednie dni zhizni P. I. Chaikovskogo (Pis'mo v redaktsiiu)," in *Novosti i birzhevaia gazeta*, 1 Nov. 1893; also as "Bolezn' P. I. Chaikovskogo," in *Novoe vremia*, 1 Nov. 1893; and in *ZC*, 3:648–54. Hereafter cited in the text without further notes.
43. *Peterburgskii listok*, 26 Oct. 1893.
44. Pyotr Ilyich Tchaikovsky, *Letters to His Family: An Autobiography*, trans. Galina von Meck (New York, 1981), 555.
45. *PSS*, 17:206.
46. *Odesskii listok*, 27 Oct. 1893; *PSS*, 17:207.
47. *VC* (1980), 209–10.
48. V. Bertenson, *Za tridtsat' let*, 97.
49. Ibid., 98.
50. *VC* (1980), 119.
51. Lev Bertenson's brief interview on the course of Tchaikovsky's illness was published as "Bolezn' P. I. Chaikovskogo," in *Novoe vremia*, 27 Oct. 1893; also in *VC* (1980), 425–26. Hereafter cited in the text without further notes.
52. "Bolezn' i poslednie minuty P. I. Chaikovskogo: U N. N. Fignera," *Novosti i birzhevaia gazeta*, 26 Oct. 1893.
53. *Novoe vremia*, 26 Oct. 1893; cf. Iastrebtsev, *Rimskii-Korsakov*, 1:125.
54. *The Merck Manual of Diagnosis and Therapy*, ed. Robert Berkow, 15th ed. (New York, 1987); *Entsiklopedicheskii slovar'*, s.v. "kholera."
55. *PSS*, 17:131.
56. *Syn otechestva*, 6 Nov. 1893.
57. *Novoe vremia*, 26 Oct. 1893; *Novosti i birzhevaia gazeta*, 26 Oct. 1893; *ZC*, 3:648.
58. Despite the fact that as early as 1830, the year cholera first invaded Europe, Moscow physicians Jaenichen and Hermann had already grasped the fundamental principle that governs cholera treatment today—rehydration by intravenous infusion—it was many years before developments in bacteriology and physiology made possible the successful application of this principle. See Norman Howard-Jones, "Cholera Therapy in the Nineteenth Century," *Journal of the History of Medicine and Allied Sciences* 27 (1972):385–93.
59. I. M. Dogel', *Aziatskaia kholera, preduprezhdenie i lechenie eia* (Kazan, 1905); Evans, *Death in Hamburg*, 337–39.
60. Dr. Nikolay Mamonov's short interview on Tchaikovsky's illness was published as "Bolezn' P. I. Chaikovskogo: U doktora N. N. Mamonova," in *Novosti i birzhevaia gazeta*, 26 Oct. 1893. Hereafter cited in the text without further notes.
61. *Peterburgskaia gazeta*, 26 Oct. 1893.
62. E. F. Napravnik, "Pamiatnaia kniga," no. 2, Institut teatra, muzyki i kinematografii, Leningrad, f. 21, op. 1; cf. *Journal de St.-Pétersbourg*, 25 Oct. 1893.
63. *Novosti i birzhevaia gazeta*, 24 Oct. 1893.
64. *Russkaia zhizn'*, 25 Oct. 1893.
65. Iastrebtsev, *Rimskii-Korsakov*, 1:125.

66. *Peterburgskaia gazeta*, 25 Oct. 1893.
67. *ZC*, 3:652; *PM*, 3:614.
68. *Peterburgskaia gazeta*, 25 Oct. 1893; *Novosti i birzhevaia gazeta*, 25 Oct. 1893.
69. *Novosti i birzhevaia gazeta*, 26 Oct. 1893; *Peterburgskaia gazeta*, 25 Oct. 1893; *Sviet*, 26 Oct. 1893.
70. *Sviet*, 26 Oct. 1893.
71. B. V. Asaf'ev, "Klinskaia tetrad'," Tsentral'nyi gosudarstvennyi arkhiv literatury i iskusstva, Moscow, f. 2658, op. 1, no. 450, l. 30.
72. *Peterburgskaia gazeta*, 25 Oct. 1893; *Novosti i birzhevaia gazeta*, 26 Oct. 1893.
73. Napravnik, "Pamiatnaia kniga," 24 Oct. 1893.
74. *Peterburgskaia gazeta*, 26 Oct. 1893; *St.-Petersburger Zeitung*, 26 Oct. 1893.
75. Sergei Bertenson, *Vokrug iskusstva (1885–1962)* (Hollywood, Calif., 1957), 20.
76. Modest to Ivan Klimenko, 9 Nov. 1893; quoted in Klimenko, *Moi vospominaniia*, 75.
77. *Novosti i birzhevaia gazeta*, 26 Oct. 1893.

Chapter 30. Death in St. Petersburg
1. *Novosti i birzhevaia gazeta*, 25 Oct. 1893.
2. *Novoe vremia*, 25 Oct. 1893; see also reports on the same date in *Syn otechestva*, *Peterburgskaia gazeta*, and *Peterburgskii listok*.
3. Gosudarstvennyi Dom-muzei P. I. Chaikovskogo, Klin, f. B, B^{10}, no. 493.
4. Ibid., A12, no. 40^2.
5. Tsentral'nyi gosudarstvennyi arkhiv Oktiabr'skoi Revoliutsii, Moscow, f. 660, op. 1, d. 40, l. 137.
6. *Syn otechestva*, 27 Oct. 1893.
7. *Novoe vremia*, 26 Oct. 1893.
8. *Peterburgskaia gazeta*, 26 Oct. 1893; cf. *Birzhevye vedomosti*, 27 Oct. 1893.
9. *Novosti i birzhevaia gazeta*, 26 Oct. 1893.
10. Ibid.; cf. Napravnik, "Pamiatnaia kniga," 25 Oct. 1893.
11. Rimskii-Korsakov, *Polnoe sobranie sochinenii*, 1:193.
12. *Pravitel'stvennyi vestnik*, 25 Mar. 1893.
13. *Trudy Dvienadtsatago (Ekstrennogo) Gubernskago s'ezda vrachei Moskovskago zemstva: Mart 1893 goda: Zhurnaly i doklady* (Moscow, 1894), 138–44.
14. *Peterburgskaia gazeta*, 26 Oct. 1893. By this time it was known that the cholera bacillus succumbed readily to disinfectant, and literature of the period emphasized that with proper precautionary measures the victim was not contagious. See M. Galanin, *O kholere* (St. Petersburg, 1893); *Meropriiatiia protiv kholery* (St. Petersburg, 1892); G. Zakharin, "Ne nuzhno slishkom boiat'sya kholery," *Klinicheskie lektsii*, *vypusk 1* (Moscow, 1894).
15. *Novoe vremia*, 26 Oct. 1893; *Novosti i birzhevaia gazeta*, 26 Oct. 1893; *Sviet*, 26 Oct. 1893; *Birzhevye vedomosti*, 27 Oct. 1893.
16. *Novosti i birzhevaia gazeta*, 26 Oct. 1893; *Peterburgskaia gazeta*, 26 Oct. 1893; *Novoe vremia*, 27 Oct. 1893; *Russkie vedomosti*, 27 Oct. 1893; *Moskovskii listok*, 28 Oct. 1893.
17. Kashkin, *Vospominaniia*, 183; cf. *Peterburgskii listok*, 27 Oct. 1893; *Novoe vremia*, 27 Oct. 1893. The only account that places the sealing of the coffin after 25 October belongs to the pen of the utterly incompetent re-

porter of the *Moscow Register,* who even speaks of two of Tchaikovsky's children (*Moskovskie vedomosti,* 28 Oct. 1893).

18. *Novoe vremia,* 27 Oct. 1893.
19. *Novosti i birzhevaia gazeta,* 2 Nov. 1893.
20. Iur'ev, *Zapiski,* 2:85; cf. Napravnik, "Pamiatnaia kniga," 28 Oct. 1893.
21. *Novoe vremia,* 29 Oct. 1893; cf. *Novosti i birzhevaia gazeta,* 29 Oct. 1893.
22. Ibid.
23. *Sankt-Peterburgskie vedomosti,* 30 Oct. 1893.
24. *Novosti i birzhevaia gazeta,* 30 Oct. 1893.
25. Ibid., 26 Oct. 1893.
26. *Peterburgskaia gazeta,* 26 Oct. 1893.
27. *Russkaia zhizn',* 28 Oct. 1893.
28. *Syn otechestva,* 26 Oct. 1893.
29. *Novosti i birzhevaia gazeta,* 26 Oct. 1893.
30. *Peterburgskaia gazeta,* 26 Oct. 1893.
31. *Novosti i birzhevaia gazeta,* 26 Oct. 1893.
32. *Novoe vremia,* 28 Oct. 1893.
33. Ibid., 27 Oct. 1893.
34. The text of Lev Bertenson's account is clearly divided into three sections. Ellipses at the end of the first and second sections indicate that the three parts very probably represent separate responses to three questions posed by the reporter from the *New Times.* In these questions, which were edited out of the printed version of the interview, the reporter would appear to have asked Bertenson to describe how Tchaikovsky became ill, the course of the illness, and Tchaikovsky's last day. It may never have been the reporter's intention to get a full day-by-day account, and it may well have been the reporter, not Bertenson, who jumped ahead to the events of Sunday, interrupting Bertenson before he could explain that despite his desire to administer the hot bath on Saturday, it was postponed to Sunday because of the patient's condition.
35. See n. 42 for Chapter 29.
36. *Novoe vremia,* 1 Nov. 1893.
37. It is also quite possible that Modest relied on various newspaper accounts; cf. *Peterburgskii listok,* 26 Oct. 1893.
38. L. Tolstoi, *Polnoe sobranie sochinenii,* 66:419.
39. *VC* (1980), 345.
40. *Novosti i birzhevaia gazeta,* 7 Nov. 1893.
41. Suvorin, *Dnevnik,* 73.
42. *Novoe vremia,* 3 Nov. 1893.
43. *Peterburgskaia gazeta,* 4 Nov. 1893.
44. *Novoe vremia,* 5 Nov. 1893.
45. *Peterburgskaia gazeta,* 5 Nov. 1893.
46. The powerlessness of nineteenth-century physicians in the face of cholera and the tragic results of attempts to treat it are discussed in full in Howard-Jones, "Cholera Therapy in the Nineteenth Century," 373–95; and in Michael Durey, *The Return of the Plague: British Society and the Cholera, 1831–32* (Dublin, 1979).
47. S. Bertenson, *Vokrug iskusstva,* 21.
48. *Novoe vremia,* 7 Nov. 1893.
49. A. I. Ziloti, *Vospominaniia i pis'ma* (Leningrad, 1963), 179.
50. *Novosti i birzhevaia gazeta,* 7 Nov. 1893. On the impact of the cholera crisis of 1892–1893 on physicians in Russia, see Nancy M. Frieden, "The Russian Cholera Epidemic, 1892–93, and Medical Professionalization," *Journal of Social History* 10 (1977):538–59.

51. *Novoe vremia*, 8 Nov. 1893.

52. S. Bertenson, *Vokrug iskusstva*, 21.

53. *Russkaia muzykal'naia gazeta*, 1894, no. 1:17–18.

54. Rimskii-Korsakov, *Polnoe sobranie sochinenii*, 1:194.

55. *VC* (1980), 345.

56. L. Tolstoi, *Polnoe sobranie sochinenii*, 84:200–1.

57. R. A. Mooser's unpublished memoirs were made available to me by their translator, Professor Mary S. Woodside, of the University of Guelph, Canada, to whom I extend my very deep gratitude. Professor Woodside's summary of Mooser's account of the rumors about Tchaikovsky's death also appeared in *19th Century Music* 13 (1990):273–74.

58. Mary Woodside, "Comments and Chronicle," *19th Century Music* 13 (1990):274.

59. *VC* (1980); Berberova, Brown, and Karlinsky, "Tchaikovsky's Suicide Reconsidered," 49.

60. *Baker's Biographical Dictionary of Music and Musicians*, xxviii.

61. Ibid., 2283; Solomon Volkov, *Balanchine's Tchaikovsky* (New York, 1985), 219–26.

62. Orlova, *Tchaikovsky*, 411–12.

63. V. Bertenson, *Za tridtsat' let*, 99; *VC* (1980), 343 (partial).

64. *PM*, 1:92; *PSS*, 6:252.

Epilogue

1. *Nedelia stroitelia*, 2 Dec. 1897.

2. *Peterburgskaia gazeta*, 28 Dec. 1898.

3. *VC* (1980), 232.

4. S. M. Volkonskii, *Moi vospominaniia*, 2 vols. ([Munich, 1923]), 1:41.

5. Sergei Klychkov, *Seryi barin* (Kharkov, 1926), 17.

6. Michel Niqueux, "Ital'ianskoe pis'mo Sergeia Klychkova M. I. Chaikovskomu," *Russkaia mysl'*, 5 June 1987 (Literaturnoe prilozhenie, no. 3/4, xii).

Index